Doll Values

ANTIQUE TO MODERN

SIXTH EDITION

OUR #1 BESTSELLING DOLL BOOK!

PATSY MOYER

COLLECTOR BOOKS

A Division of Schroeder Publishing Co., Inc.

On the Cover:

Right:
18" hard plastic Madame Alexander Glamour Girl, "Madame Alexander//All Rights Reserved//New York, U.S.A." on dress tag, wig in original set, blue sleep eyes, real lashes, painted lower lashes, multi-stroke brows, closed mouth, hard plastic jointed body, walking mechanism, original pink taffeta dress, black velvet bodice, hoop slip, net stockings, black strap shoes, black hat trimmed with flowers and tulle ties, flower bouquet at waist, hat box, circa 1953, $1,900.00. Courtesy McMasters Doll Auctions.

Left top:
20" hard plastic Madame Alexander Cissy, blue sleep eyes, closed mouth, pierced ears, blond synthetic wig, jointed vinyl arms, yellow dress and matching coat, black lace scarf, diamond ring, circa 1956, $325.00. Courtesy Mary Sakraida.

Left center:
16" vinyl Robert Tonner Tyler Wentworth, long brown rooted hair, plastic eyes, closed mouth, hard plastic body, dressed in TW 1101 "The Look of Luxe," limited edition of 2000, cashmere sweater of a mocha and cream mixture over a woven cashmere skirt, an overcoat of a custom-made synthetic created to mimic shearling, matching hat and pumps, circa 2001, $124.99. Courtesy Robert Tonner Doll Company.

Left lower:
20" bisque Jumeau Tete Jumeau marked "Depose//Tete Jumeau//Bte S.G.D.G.//9" on back of head, "Jumeau//Medaille d'Or//Paris" on back, "9//Paris//(bee)//Depose" on shoes, human hair wig, blue paperweight eyes, painted lashes, heavy feathered brows, closed mouth, pierced ears, jointed wood and composition body with jointed wrists, nicely re-dressed in beige and red sailor-type dress, antique underclothing, socks, shoes, beige and red striped bow in hair, circa 1885+, $4,300.00. Courtesy McMasters Doll Auctions.

Cover by Beth Summers
Book design by Holly C. Long

Collector Books
P.O. Box 3009
Paducah, KY 42002-3009

www.collectorbooks.com

The current values in this book should be used only as a guide. They are not intended to set prices, which vary from one section of the country to another. Auction prices, as well as dealer prices, vary greatly and are affected by availability, condition, and demand. Neither the author nor the publisher assumes responsibility for any losses that might be incurred as a result of consulting this guide.

Credits

My special thanks to a great group of collectors who show their love of collecting by sharing their dolls with others.

June Allgeier, Barbara Andersen, Ashton-Drake Galleries, Susana Auza-Smith, Deborah Baron, Sandy Johnson Barts, Lee Ann Beaumont, Dorothy Bohlin, Ruth Brown, Travis Cannon, Patricia Christlieb, Judie Conroy, Martha Cramer, Marilyn Cross, Debbie Crume, Debby L.Davis, Jane Darin, Sally DeSmet, Cathy DeWolfe, Judy Domm, Elizabeth Fielding, Allyson Flagg-Miller, Yvonne Flipse, Darlene Foote, Cornelia Ford Betty Fronefield, Sondra Gast, Angie Gonzales, Pat Graff, Isobel Grover, Irene Grundvig, Donna Hadley, Adrienne & Don Hagey, Debbie Hamilton, Emilie Hance, Robert V.Hardy, Sharon Harrington, Janet Hill, Barbara Hull, Patrice Hunker, Barbara Jones, Iva Mae Jones, Jeff Jones, Glenda Koenigsberg, Sharon Kolibaba, Nancy Lazenby, Anita Ladensack, Jackie Litchfield, Marguerite Long, Connie Lee Martin, Rita Mauze, Karen McCarthy, Shari McMasters of McMasters Doll Auctions, Shirley Meade, Pidd Miller, Peggy Millhouse, Bev Mitchell, Art Mock, Pat Moulton, Chad Moyer, Michele Newby, Dorisanne Osborne, Kathy S. Patton, Bernard P. Perzyk, Ginger Pennington, Jeanne M. Perkins, Rose Pitzer, Joan Radke, Marilyn Ramsey, Pat Rather, Penny Reeve-Griffith, Ginger Reid, Joan Rice, Catherine Ritter, Robert Tonner of the Robert Tonner Doll Company, Debra Ruberto, Jill Sanders, Mary Alice Scheflow, Jennifer Scott, Nelda Shelton, Joan Sickler, Gay Smedes, Kathy & Roy Smith, Harlene Soucy, Michae Stitt, Betty Strong, Elizabeth Surber, Ellen Sturgess, Linda Lee Sutton, Nancie Swanberg, Martha Sweeney, Leslie Tannenbaum, Geri Teeter, Stephanie Thompson, JoAnn Threadgill, Odessa Tiefel, Maria Traver, Sandra Tripp, Atelier Bets Van Boxel, Carol Van Verst-Rugg, Diane Vigne, Linda Smith of Vogue Doll Company, Kay Walimaa, Susan Ware, Betty Warder, Thelma Williams, Patricia Wright.

How to Use this Book

Welcome to the world of doll collecting. For as long as there have been little girls who played with dolls, there have been people who so treasured those playthings they wanted to keep them forever. In this book, we present an overview of doll collecting, the doll market, and resources associated with dolls. You are encouraged to seek more knowledge to help you understand more about dolls so you can make wise decisions as you acquire your collection.

This book is divided into two sections, ANTIQUE and MODERN as general ways to separate dolls made of older materials like bisque, wax, cloth, and wood, and dolls made of newer materials such as composition, hard plastic, and vinyl. This immediately becomes confusing to the novice, because some of the composition modern dolls are as old as the bisque dolls in the antique section. We do this only to help the reader who can save time looking for older dolls in the front antique section and newer dolls in the back modern section. A new classification is emerging that refers to dolls made in the last 30 years as "collectible." In this book, collectible dolls are grouped with modern.

Appendixes are included at the back of the book. There are several. First a Bibliography lists many of the doll book references I find helpful. Next, the Collector's Network lists special interest groups and individuals. Then there are four Indexes to help you identify the marks often found on the back of the head or torso of your doll. The first is the Symbol Index with text describing the symbol and then the company who uses that symbol. Next is a Letter Index that lists letters that may help you discover the company that made the doll. Next is the Mold Mark Index listing mold numbers and then the page number in this book with an example and the name of the companies that used those mold numbers. Finally there is the Name Index which lists the names of the dolls and the names of the doll companies.

Many published references have been used for descriptions and marks. Every effort was made to check early advertising, where possible, but the main references are Johanna Anderton; John Axe; Dorothy, Jane, and Ann Coleman; Jurgen and Marianne Cieslik; Jan Foulke; Judith Izen; Pam and Polly Judd; Ursula Mertz; and Patricia N. Schoonmaker. My thanks to these respected authorities and others who have contributed so much in research to collectors.

The dolls in each section are listed alphabetically by manufacturer or type, including a brief history, marks, description, and prices. Dolls are identified by the type of material used on the head — for example; if the head is hard plastic, the doll is referred to as hard plastic, even though the body may be of another material. They may be further classified as a category, such as Oriental, black, or souvenir dolls. Most black and brown dolls are grouped in the category Black. Souvenir dolls are from special occasions, functions, or events that all who attend receive. We have tried to use the general categories set forth in prior issues of this book, but have taken the liberty to add new categories or delete some of them. Your suggestions will be considered if enough data is available to research. We will continue to refine categories, descriptions, and data.

In addition to separating dolls generally into antique and modern sections, we have also **grouped them by manufacturer or type**. Modern manufacturers might be Alexander, Mattel, and Remco. Types are another way dolls can be grouped. Although Barbie is a Mattel doll, she has such a following that she has her own category. Another modern category is artist dolls; this category is for dolls of any medium created for sale to the public, whether they are one-of-a-kind works of art or numbered limited editions. They reflect dolls that are not mass produced, but may be produced in numbers.

Where practical, we have also **classified dolls by material,** such as bisque, cloth, composition, hard plastic, porcelain, and vinyl. Look for all-cloth dolls except Lenci, Käthe Kruse, and Steiff under the category Cloth. For the novice collector, decide what material the head of your doll is, remembering that antique dolls are generally made of bisque, china, cloth, papier-mâché, wax, or wood. Modern dolls may be made of composition, porcelain, hard plastic, vinyl, or some other material. Look for little known manufacturers in broad categories such as bisque, German, hard plastic, or vinyl.

Some of the things to consider in evaluating a doll are **quality, condition, rarity, originality, and desirability**. These can vary considerably as any two collectors may rate one or more of these attributes differently or two identical dolls can differ greatly with those same factors. All of these things are desirable factors to keep in mind. Since doll collectors mostly have limited budgets, it is smart buyers who familiarize themselves with as much about the subject as is available. This guide is a good starting place and is written with the novice as well as the more experienced collector in mind.

All dolls were not born equal. Dolls from the same mold can vary because of the conditions at the time of their manufacture. Successful production techniques developed over time; some of which arose only with the passage of time. Bisque dolls could be made with different grades of porcelain giving a range from fine to poor quality. Humidity and temperature could affect the production techniques of composition made up of various formulas of glue, wood pulp, sawdust, and other ingredients, causing their finish to later crack or peel. The formula used for some rubber and early plastic dolls caused them to turn darker colors or become sticky. The durability of the material did not show up immediately — only after the passage of time.

It is important for the collector to become aware of the many different factors that influence the manufacture, durability, popularity, and availability of a doll. Many influences can affect your decision to choose a particular doll to add to your collection. It takes time and effort before you can know the particular subtle differences in the exact same model of one doll, much less the endless variations and levels of differences that can exist in a particular era, category, or type of doll. This guide will serve as the starting point for your search for knowledge in the areas you choose to pursue.

Quality is an important consideration when purchasing a doll. Buy the best doll you can afford. Look at enough dolls so that you can tell the difference in a poorly finished or painted doll and one that has been artistically done. The head is the most important part of the doll. Signs of quality include good coloring; original clothing, wig, and body; and a pleasing appearance.

The condition of the doll is a very important factor in pricing a doll. A beautiful doll re-dressed, dirty, and missing a wig should not be priced as high as a beautiful doll with original clothing, a well-done wig, and clean and unrepaired body. Only consider composition dolls that have cracks, peeling paint, or lifting of paint *if* they have added incentives, such as wonderful coloring, original clothes, boxes, and tags. Look for a smooth finish with rosy cheek color on the face as well as bright crisp clothing.

Originality is also important. Original clothing is an advantage on any dolls, but especially if the clothing is in good condition. It is becoming more difficult to find a completely original doll, so dolls found with original clothing may double or triple in price.

Also important is the correct body with the correct head and original wig on the doll. Patricia Schoonmaker once told me that we are only caretakers of our dolls for awhile — they then are passed on to someone else to care for. As some older dolls come on the market, they may be found on different bodies as they were acquired before the importance of originality became known and the ability to identify the correct body became available.

Rarity is another consideration in dolls. Many dolls were made by the thousands. Some dolls were not made in such quantity. If a doll was a quality, beautiful doll and not many were made, it may be more desirable and higher priced. Age can play a factor in pricing dolls, but not age alone. Modern dolls such as Shirley Temple dolls or Barbie dolls can out price some older antique dolls.

Desirability is another factor in choosing a doll. Some dolls may be rare in original clothing, and still just not appeal to others. Beauty can be in the eye of the beholder; but some dolls are just not as appealing as others because they were poorly made or unattractive from the start. A well-made doll of quality is generally the one sought after, even in dirty, not original condition. A poorly made doll of inferior quality will always be a poorly made doll whether it is in top condition or cracked and damaged.

The pricing in this book is based on a number of factors including information from informed collectors, doll shows and sales, auctions, and doll-related publications. These factors have led us to build a database of actual sales. The pricing in this book is based on 12,000 to 16,000 dolls. You will see what actually is happening in the auction marketplace. Although any one auction's prices may vary widely; tracking the results over a period of time does reveal some consistency. The rarity and desirability of the same doll will fluctuate from area to area and with time. When a limited number of a certain doll is in the database, I have added the notation, "Too few in database for reliable range." I have arbitrarily set this figure at less than five dolls and the figure may change.

Demand sets the price. If a buyer has just won the lottery or has their own gold mine, the average buyer cannot compete with them. The good news is that these buyers usually cannot cover every collector, shop, or show that may have dolls for sale. The limited few that do have big bucks, cannot be everywhere at once. So the prudent may wish to back off, when the "high rollers" appear. Persons who have the ready cash have the right to spend it wherever they wish. If they want a particular doll and have the means to acquire it, more power to them. Many of these collectors share their dolls via museums, lectures, and exhibits, and that is wonderful. Extraordinary dolls may command higher prices because of all of the above factors.

So what price is too much to pay for a doll? That is a personal decision left entirely up to you and your bank account. The one great thing about collecting is that you are free to make your own choices of what you can afford and what you want to spend. You owe no explanation to others. You may, however, wish to arm yourself with knowledge if your funds are limited, so you can get the most for your money. Perhaps the greatest influence on doll collecting today is the Internet. Auction sites, like eBay have opened up the field of collecting worldwide and brought forth a rapidly changing market place, making the doll market extremely volatile. Items you may have hunted for years are now at your fingertips. Sellers and buyers may have varying degrees of expertise, and it is necessary to constantly do research to be sure what you are getting is what you are seeking.

Doll collecting need not be a short term intense pursuit. More often it becomes a long-term hobby of gathering things to love around you and good values as well. And after some years of loving enjoyment, one might look around and, in the process of collecting dolls, realize they have accumulated a solid investment as well — much as collecting fine art. Wise collectors will document their collection so their estate will show the gains from their endeavors.

This guide makes no attempt to set price standards and should not be considered the final authority. It is simply meant to report prices realized in areas that can be tracked and reported. Every effort has been made to present an unbiased and impartial viewpoint to the collector of the results found in the areas researched. But remember, this is a compilation of data, and can only represent input from the various sources used. The goals are to bring together information from many sources to give collectors an additional viewpoint so that they can make their own personal choice. Collectors have the final decision in buying or selling a doll; it is their decision alone.

The number of categories is immense and no one can be familiar with all of the changing and different areas. For this reason, I have consulted with a broad group of collectors who keep up to date with the market in their particular fields. Some of these collectors have agreed to provide their names and addresses as references in certain areas. These can be found in the Collectors' Network section at the back of the book. If you would like to become part of this network and are willing to share your knowledge with others in your particular field, please send your name, address, field of specialty, and references to: P.O. Box 311, Deming, NM 88031. Please also include your e-mail or website address, if you have one.

The more collectors share, the more we all gain from the experience. If you have questions, you may write the individual collector listed. It is common courtesy to send a self-addressed stamped envelope if you wish to receive a reply to your question. If you would like to see other categories added to this guide, please drop us a line and tell us your areas of interest. If possible, we will add categories when there is enough interest and data is available. We would like to hear from you.

The collector needs to be well informed to make proper judgment when spending his/her hard earned money buying a doll. The more information accumulated, the better the judgment. Collectors can turn to a national organization whose goals are education, research, preservation, and enjoyment of dolls. The United Federation of Doll Clubs can tell you if a doll club in your area is accepting members or tell you how to become a member-at-large. You may write for more information at:

United Federation of Doll Clubs, Inc.
10920 North Ambassador Drive, Suite 130
Kansas City, MO 64153
UFDC has a website: http://www.ufdc.org

There are also many smaller groups that focus on particular dolls or on some aspect of doll collecting. A list of some of those groups and their interests is located in the Collectors' Network at the back of the book. You gain more knowledge, and the collecting experience is more enjoyable when you participate with others.

Happy collecting!

Antique and Older Dolls

20" bisque Jules Steiner Le Parisien, "A. 13 (incised)//Le Parisien//Bte. S.G.D.G.//A. 13" stamped on back of head, "Le Petit Parisien//Bebe Steiner//Medaille d'Or//Paris 1889" on front of left hip, "France" stamped in red on upper back, human hair wig, paperweight eyes, heavy feathered brows, painted lashes, closed mouth, pierced ears, jointed compositionSteiner body, re-dressed in new blue silk lace-trimmed dress, old socks, shoes, circa 1889, $2,700.00. Courtesy McMasters Doll Auctions.

14" bisque Francois Gaultier socket head, large blue paperweight eyes, feathered brows, painted upper and lower lashes, accented nostrils, open/closed mouth with molded tongue, pierced ears, replaced mohair wig, jointed wood and composition body with straight wrists, re-dressed, F.G. scroll mark, minor touch up to fingers, circa 1887 – 1900, $2,200.00. Courtesy McMasters Doll Auctions.

26" bisque Tete Jumeau socket head, marked "Depose//Tete//Jumeau//2" with partial red Jumeau stamp on body, large blue paperweight eyes, heavily feathered brows, painted upper and lower lashes, accented nostrils, closed mouth with accented lips, pierced ears, human hair wig, nicely dressed, minor hairline, circa 1885 – 1900, $2,100.00. Courtesy McMasters Doll Auctions.

Alexandre, Henri

1888 – 1892, Paris. Bisque head, paperweight eyes, closed mouth with a white space between the lips, fat cheeks, and early French bodies with straight wrists.

First price indicates doll in good condition, but with flaws or nude; second price indicates doll in excellent condition, in original clothes, or appropriately dressed.

17"	$4,350.00	$5,800.00
19"	$4,950.00	$6,500.00
21"	$5,300.00	$7,100.00

Bébé Phénix, 1889 – 1900+

Phénix trademark first used by Alexandre, then Bébé Phénix in 1895 was used by Mme. Lafosse and then Jules Mettais, both worked for Jules Steiner. Bisque head, closed mouth, paperweight eyes, pierced ears, composition body.

Child, closed mouth

10"	$1,375.00	$1,800.00
14"	$2,175.00	$2,900.00
17"	$2,925.00	$3,900.00
18"	$3,375.00	$4,500.00
20"	$3,900.00	$5,200.00
22"	$4,125.00	$5,500.00
24"	$4,275.00	$5,700.00

Child, open mouth

17"	$1,500.00	$2,000.00
19"	$1,650.00	$2,200.00
22"	$1,800.00	$2,400.00
25"	$2,000.00	$2,700.00

All-Bisque, French

1880+. Jointed neck, shoulders, hips; more delicate body with slender arms and legs, glass eyes, molded shoes or boots and stockings. Many all-bisque once thought to be of French manufacture are now believed to have been made in Germany expressly for the French market.

First price indicates doll in good condition, with some flaws, undressed; second price is for doll in excellent condition, with original or appropriate clothing. Allow more for original clothes and tags, less for chips or repairs.

Glass eyes, swivel head, molded shoes or boots

2½"	$525.00	$725.00
5"	$2,175.00	$1,000.00
7"	$2,925.00	$1,750.00

Child, closed mouth

5"	$1,575.00	$2,100.00
6"	$1,875.00	$2,500.00
7"	$2,175.00	$2,900.00

Too few in database for reliable range.

All-Bisque, French

Five-strap boots, glass eyes, swivel neck

6"	$1,500.00	$2,100.00

Painted eyes

2½"	$170.00	$225.00
4"	$425.00	$550.00

Circa 1910 – 1920, glass eyes, molded socks, boots

5"	$300.00	$400.00
7"	$400.00	$550.00

Too few in database for reliable range.

Marked E.D., F.G., or similar French makers

7"	$1,875.00	$2,500.00+

Marked S.F.B.J., Unis, or similar French makers

6"	$475.00	$625.00

5" unmarked girl, swivel neck, blonde wig, blue glass eyes, jointed neck, shoulders, hips, delicate body with slender arms and legs, bare feet, blue dress trimmed with lace, matching hat, circa 1880+, $1,250.00. Courtesy Kathy S. Patton.

All-Bisque, German

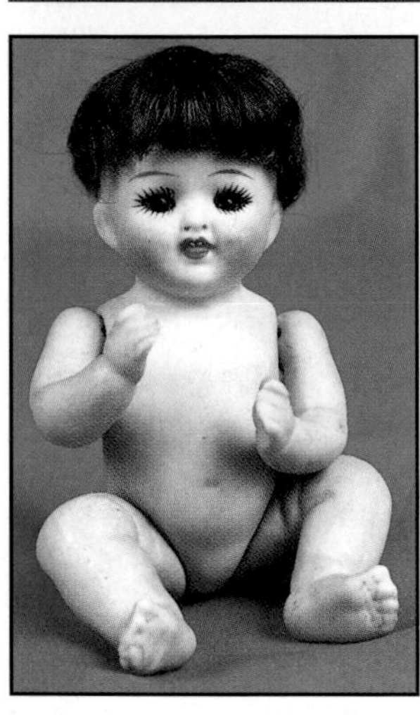

5" Baby, marked "833//3" on back of head, "Germany" on back, "830//3" on upper arms and legs, original mohair wig, stiff neck, brown sleep eyes, single stroke brows, painted upper and lower lashes, open/closed mouth with two upper teeth, bent-limb baby body, yellow knit outfit with matching hat and booties, undressed in photo, circa 1900+, $160.00. Courtesy McMasters Doll Auctions.

Many German firms made all-bisque dolls in smaller sizes from 1860 until 1930. Some were made by well-known firms such as Amberg; Alt, Beck & Gottschalck; Bähr & Pröschild; Hertel Schwab & Co.; Kämmer & Reinhart; J.D. Kestner; Kling; Limbach; Bruno Schmidt; and Simon & Halbig, and may have corresponding mold marks. Some are only marked "Made in Germany" and/or may have a paper label. They are often marked inside the arms and legs with matching mold numbers.

First price indicates doll in good condition, with some flaws or nude; second price is for doll in excellent condition, original clothes, or well dressed. More for labels, less for chips and repairs.

For All-Bisque, Black or Brown, see Black or Brown Section.

Babies, ca. 1900+

Rigid neck (molded to torso), jointed shoulders and hips only, bent limbs, painted hair

Glass eyes

3"	$200.00	$250.00
5"	$250.00	$350.00

Painted eyes

6"	$150.00	$200.00
8"	$200.00	$275.00

Swivel necks (socket neck), jointed shoulders and hips, wigs or painted hair

Glass eyes

4"	$175.00	$300.00
6"	$300.00	$475.00
8"	$450.00	$600.00

Painted eyes

3"	$145.00	$195.00
5"	$245.00	$325.00
7"	$175.00	$350.00

Babies with Character Face, ca. 1910+

Jointed shoulders and hips, molded hair

Glass eyes

5"	$325.00	$450.00
7"	$400.00	$525.00

Painted eyes

5"	$165.00	$225.00
7"	$225.00	$300.00

Swivel neck, glass eyes

5"	$375.00	$500.00
9"	$750.00	$1,000.00

Swivel neck, painted eyes

5"	$250.00	$325.00
7"	$375.00	$500.00

Mold 391, 830, 833, and others

7"	$375.00	$500.00
9"	$750.00	$1,000.00

Baby Bo Kaye, mold 1394

Designed by Kallus, distributed by Borgfeldt

5"	$850.00	$1,125.00
7"	$1,050.00	$1,425.00

Baby Bud, glass eyes, wig

6 – 7"	$975.00	$1,300.00

Baby Darling, mold 497, Kestner, 178

One-piece body, painted eyes

6"	$500.00	$600.00
8"	$600.00	$700.00
10"	$635.00	$825.00

Swivel neck, glass eyes, more for toddler body

6"	$450.00	$600.00
8"	$625.00	$825.00

Baby Peggy Montgomery

Made by Louis Amberg, paper label, pink bisque with molded hair, painted brown eyes, closed mouth, jointed at shoulder and hips, molded and painted shoes/socks

3½"	$225.00	$400.00
5½"	$450.00	$600.00

Bonnie Babe, 1926+, designed by Georgene Averill

Glass eyes, swivel neck, wig, jointed arms and legs

4½"	$500.00	$650.00
7"	$600.00	$800.00
8"	$750.00	$1,000.00

4½" Averill "Bonnie Babe" with sleep eyes, molded hair, open/closed mouth, in molded painted pink one strap shoes and white socks, appropriately dressed in pink silk and old lace, circa 1926+ $1,200.00. Courtesy Connie Lee Martin.

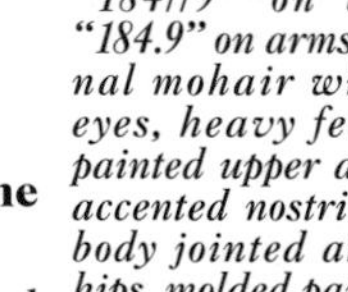

6½" Kestner mold 184, marked "184//9" on back of head, "184.9" on arms, stiff neck, original mohair wig, brown sleep eyes, heavy feathered brows, painted upper and lower lashes, accented nostrils, closed mouth, body jointed at shoulders and hips, molded painted white socks with blue garters, yellow boots with black side gussets, toes, and heels, probably original ecru wool dress with blue ribbon trim, wool slip, circa 1880+, $435.00. Courtesy McMasters Doll Auctions.

5" Alt, Beck & Gottschalck girl, marked "83/35" on back of head, "Made in Germany//Blonde-Blue//No. 83/00/35" on end of original box, stiff neck, blue sleep eyes, painted lashes, open/closed mouth, blonde wig with hair bow, jointed at shoulders and hips, molded painted white socks and black one-strap shoes, original cardboard box with tissue paper at bottom, circa 1890+, $350.00. Courtesy McMasters Doll Auctions.

Molded-on clothes, dome head, swivel neck, jointed arms and legs

5"	$400.00	$600.00
6"	$600.00	$775.00

Immobiles, one-piece, in various poses

3"	$175.00	$350.00

Mildred (The Prize Baby), mold 880, ca. 1914+

Made for Borgfeldt; molded, short painted hair; glass eyes; closed mouth; jointed at neck, shoulders, and hips; round paper label on chest; molded and painted footwear

5"	$950.00	$1,250.00
7"	$900.00	$1,800.00

Tynie Baby, made for E.I. Horsman

Glass eyes

5"	$525.00	$725.00
8"	$950.00	$1,250.00

Painted eyes

5"	$350.00	$475.00

Pink Bisque Candy Baby, ca. 1920+

May be German or Japanese, lesser quality paint finish, given away with purchase of candy

3½"	$25.00	$35.00
6"	$35.00	$45.00

Mold 231 (A.M.), toddler, swivel neck, with glass eyes

9"	$1,025.00	$1,400.00

Mold 369, 372

7"	$545.00	$725.00
9"	$875.00	$1,100.00
11"	$1,050.00	$1,400.00+

Children

All-Bisque Child, Rigid Neck, Glass Eyes, 1890+

Head molded to torso, sometimes legs also, excellent bisque, open/closed mouth, sleep or set eyes, good wig, nicely dressed, molded one-strap shoes. Allow more for unusual footwear such as yellow multi-strap boots.

3"	$165.00	$275.00
5"	$165.00	$285.00
7"	$250.00	$400.00
9"	$550.00	$700.00

Bent knees

6"	$145.00	$285.00

Mold 100, 125, 150, 225 (preceded by 83/)

Rigid neck, fat tummy, jointed shoulders and hips, glass sleep eyes, open/closed mouth, molded black one-strap shoes with tan soles, white molded stockings with blue band. Similarly molded dolls, imported in 1950s by Kimport, have synthetic hair, lesser quality bisque. Add more for original clothing.

Mold number appears as a fraction, with the following size numbers under 83; Mold "83/100," "83/125," "83/150," or "83/225." One marked "83/100" has a green label on torso reading, "Princess//Made in Germany."

100	5¾"	$225.00	$325.00
125	6¾"	$275.00	$350.00
150	7½"	$325.00	$425.00
225	8¼"	$350.00	$475.00

Mold 130, 150, 168, 184, 257, 602, 790, 791, 792 (Bonn or Kestner)

Painted blue or pink stockings, one-strap black shoes

4"	$150.00	$295.00
6"	$200.00	$385.00
7"	$215.00	$425.00
8"	$250.00	$500.00
9"	$300.00	$675.00
10"	$375.00	$750.00
11"	$450.00	$900.00

4½" and 5" with molded hair, painted eyes, in original Danish costume, circa 1900 – 1920, $225.00 each. Courtesy Jill Sanders.

Mold 155, 156 (smile)

6"	$225.00	$450.00

Swivel neck

5½"	$300.00	$600.00
7"	$165.00	$325.00

All-Bisque Child, Glass Eyes, Swivel Neck, ca. 1880+

Pegged or wired joints, open or closed mouth, molded-on shoes or boots and stockings. Allow more for unusual footwear such as yellow or multi-strap boots.

3"	$175.00	$300.00
4"	$200.00	$350.00
5½"	$350.00	$525.00
7"	$375.00	$675.00
8"	$600.00	$800.00
9"	$675.00	$900.00
10"	$975.00	$1,300.00

Mold 130, 150, 160, 208, 602 (Kestner)

4"	$250.00	$500.00
6"	$300.00	$600.00
8"	$450.00	$900.00
10"	$650.00	$1,300.00

Mold 184 (Kestner)

4 – 5"	$350.00	$700.00
8"	$800.00	$1,600.00

Simon & Halbig or Kestner types

Closed mouth, excellent quality

5"	$400.00	$775.00
6"	$600.00	$1,150.00
8"	$975.00	$1,900.00

7½" child marked "1" on back of head, arms and legs at joints, original mohair wig, stiff neck, blue sleep eyes, painted lashes, feathered brows, open smiling mouth, four upper teeth, jointed at shoulders and hips, molded painted socks and black one-strap shoes, antique white dress with lace inserts, slip, old straw bonnet, circa 1900+, $450.00. Courtesy McMasters Doll Auctions.

7" Kestner, marked "208/5" with molded shoes and stockings, glass sleep eyes, closed mouth, circa 1910+, $700.00. *Courtesy Jill Sanders.*

Jointed knees

6"	$1,500.00	$3,000.00

Original factory box with clothes/accessories

5"	$1,750.00	$3,500.00

Bare feet

5"	$1,350.00	$1,800.00
7½"	$1,950.00	$2,600.00

Early round face

6"	$525.00	$900.00
8"	$900.00	$1,300.00

Mold 881, 886, 890 (Simon & Halbig)

Painted high-top boots with four or five straps

4½"	$600.00	$800.00
7½"	$1,200.00	$1,600.00
9½"	$1,500.00	$2,100.00

Long stockings, above knees

4½"	$325.00	$650.00
6"	$450.00	$900.00

Mold 102, Wrestler (so called)

Fat thighs, arm bent at elbow, open mouth (can have two rows of teeth) or closed mouth, stocky body, glass eyes, socket head, individual fingers or molded fist

6"	$900.00	$1,250.00
8"	$1,250.00	$1,650.00
9"	$1,600.00	$2,150.00

All-Bisque Child with Painted Eyes, ca. 1880+

Head molded to torso, molded hair or wig, open or closed mouth, painted-on shoes and socks, dressed or undressed, all in good condition. Allow more for unusual footwear such as yellow boots.

2"	$45.00	$85.00
4½"	$105.00	$190.00
6½"	$125.00	$250.00
8"	$175.00	$350.00

Black stockings, tan slippers

6"	$275.00	$400.00

Ribbed hose

4½"	$150.00	$200.00
6"	$275.00	$375.00
8"	$425.00	$575.00

Molded hair

4½"	$90.00	$175.00
6"	$175.00	$350.00

Early very round face

7"	$1,200.00	$2,300.00

6" child, painted eyes, closed mouth, in fur garments with hood, circa 1890 – 1900, $200.00. *Courtesy Emilie Hance.*

All-Bisque Child Characters, ca. 1910+

Campbells Kids, molded clothes, Dutch bob

5"	$125.00	$245.00

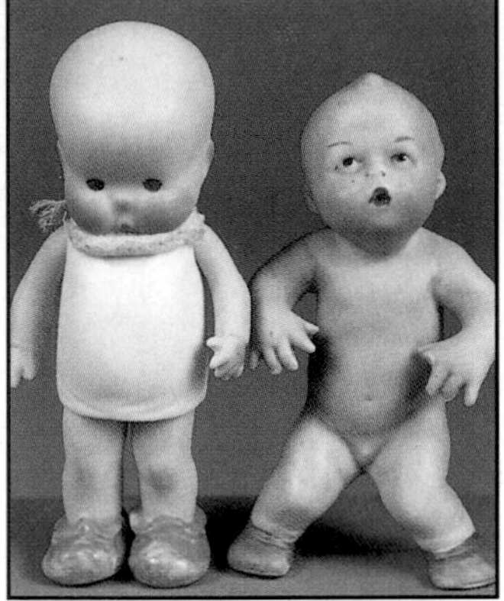

Left, 4" Sheebee $265.00; right, 4" baby figurine, painted molded shoes, $225.00. Courtesy McMasters Doll Auctions.

Chin-chin, Gebruder Heubach, ca. 1919, jointed arms only, triangular label on chest

4" $225.00 $300.00

Happifats, designed by Kate Jordan for Borgfeldt, ca. 1913 – 1921

4" $200.00 $275.00

Jeanne Orsini, ca. 1919+, designed by Orsini for Borgfelt, produced by Alt, Beck & Gottschalck; Chi Chi, Didi, Fifi, Mimi, Vivi

Glass eyes

5" $2,300.00*

Painted eyes

5" $675.00 $925.00

Max, Moritz, Kestner, ca. 1914, jointed at the neck, shoulders, and hips, many companies produced these characters from the Wilhelm Busch children's story

4½" $2,300.00*

Mibs, Amberg, ca. 1921, molded blond hair, molded/painted socks and shoes, pink bisque, jointed at shoulders, legs molded to body, marked "C.//L.A.&S.192//GERMANY"

3" $200.00 $275.00

5" $375.00 $425.00

Our Fairy, mold 222, ca. 1914 (see Googly under Hertel & Schwab)

Peterkin, ca. 1912, one-piece baby, side-glancing googly eyes, molded painted hair, molded blue pajamas on chubby torso, arms molded to body with hands clasping stomach

6" $1,485.00*

September Morn, ca. 1913, jointed at shoulders and hips, Grace Drayton design, George Borgfeldt

5" $2,775.00 $3,700.00

7" $4,400.00*

All-Bisque Child with Molded Clothes, ca. 1890+

Jointed at shoulders only or at shoulders and hips, painted eyes, molded hair, molded shoes or bare feet, excellent workmanship, no breaks, chips, or rubs

3½" $85.00 $115.00

5" $200.00 $275.00

Lesser quality

3" $45.00 $85.00

4" $50.00 $100.00

6" $70.00 $140.00

Molded on hat or bonnet

In perfect condition

5 – 6½" $190.00 $365.00+

8 – 9" $250.00 $500.00+

4" Little Annie Rooney, with jointed arms, molded clothing, yarn braid, $250.00. Courtesy Catherine Ritter.

* at auction

Stone (porous) Bisque

4 – 5"	$70.00	$135.00
6 – 7"	$85.00	$165.00

All-Bisque with Slender Bodies, ca. 1900+

Slender dolls with head molded to torso, usual wire or peg-jointed shoulders and hips. Allow much more for original clothes. May be in regional costumes. Add more for unusual color boots, such as gold, yellow, or orange, all in good condition.

Glass eyes, open or closed mouth

3"	$145.00	$200.00
5 – 6"	$250.00	$350.00

Swivel neck, closed mouth

4"	$225.00	$300.00
5 – 6"	$350.00	$500.00
8½"	$600.00	$900.00
10"	$900.00	$1,300.00

Bent at knees

6"	$100.00	$200.00

Jointed knees and/or elbows with swivel waist

6"	$1,000.00	$1,950.00
8"	$1,600.00	$3,200.00

Swivel waist only

6"	$1,000.00	$2,000.00

Painted eyes, swivel neck, open or closed mouth, painted one-strap shoes

4"	$100.00	$200.00
6"	$175.00	$350.00
8"	$250.00	$475.00
10"	$350.00	$675.00

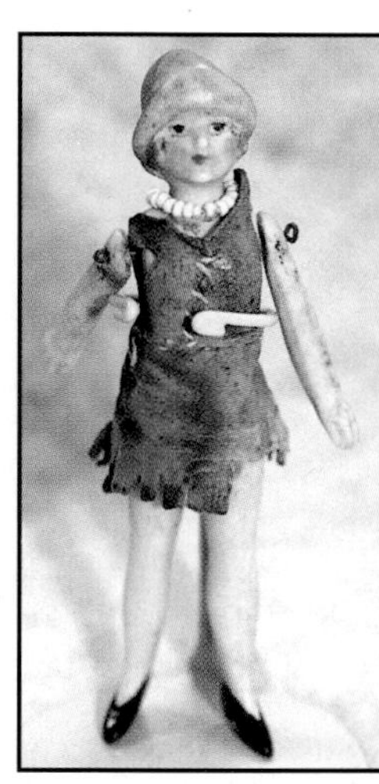

3¼" bonnet head flapper, molded painted blue cloche hat, wire jointed, stiff neck, painted black high heels, tan leather dress, circa 1920s, $75.00. *Courtesy Dorothy Bohlin.*

All-Bisque Child with Flapper Body, ca. 1920+

One-piece body and head with thin limbs, fired-in fine bisque, wig, painted eyes, painted-on long stockings, one-strap painted shoes

5"	$225.00	$300.00
7"	$325.00	$450.00

Molded hair

6"	$250.00	$350.00
8"	$325.00	$450.00

All-Pink Bisque Child

Wire joints, molded hair, painted eyes

4"	$40.00	$75.00

Molded hat

4"	$185.00	$250.00

Aviatrix

5"	$175.00	$250.00

Swivel waist

4½"	$300.00	$400.00

Molded cap with rabbit ears

4½"	$275.00	$400.00

All-Bisque Immobiles, figures with no joints

Child		
3"	$25.00	$50.00
Adults		
5"	$75.00	$165.00
Santa		
4"	$70.00	$140.00
Child with animal on string		
4"	$75.00	$165.00

All-Bisque Nodders, ca. 1920

When their heads are touched, they "nod," molded clothes, made both in Germany and Japan, decoration not fired in so wears off easily, all in good condition.

Animals, cat, dog, rabbit		
3 – 5"	$45.00	$100.00
Child/Adult, made in Germany		
4 – 6"	$35.00	$150.00
Child/Adult with molded-on clothes		
4"	$65.00	$135.00
Child/Adult comic characters		
3 – 5"	$65.00	$250.00
Child/Adult, sitting position		
5"	$70.00	$140.00
Santa Claus or Indian		
6"	$150.00	$190.00
Teddy Bear		
5"	$125.00	$200.00
Japan/Nippon		
3½"	$10.00	$25.00
4½"	$20.00	$45.00

All-Bisque Figures, Painted

Top layer of paint not fired on and the color can be washed off, usually one-piece figurines with molded hair, painted features, including clothes, shoes, and socks. Some have molded hats.

First price indicates with paint chips, second price is good condition with no paint chips, can be German or Japanese.

Baby, German		
3½"	$35.00	$50.00
5"	$40.00	$60.00
Baby, Japanese		
3"	$9.00	$15.00
5"	$15.00	$25.00
Child, German		
3"	$20.00	$30.00
5"	$45.00	$65.00
Child, Japanese		
3"	$7.50	$15.00
5"	$15.00	$25.00

4" Betty Boop type, large eyes painted to side, molded, painted hair, bobbed hair style, with wardrobe and trunk, circa 1920s, $125.00. Courtesy Nancie Swanberg.

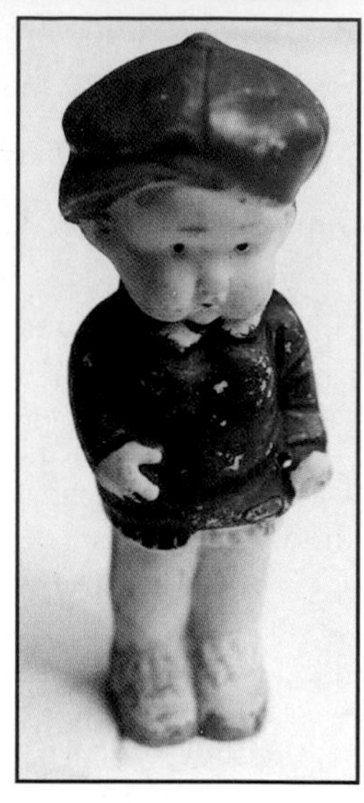

3½" painted Jackie Coogan unmarked, stiff joints, some paint flaking, $45.00. Courtesy Marguerite Long.

Made by various Japanese companies. Quality varies greatly. They are jointed at shoulders and may also be jointed at hips. Good quality bisque is well painted with no chips or breaks.

The first price indicates poorer quality, flaking paint, flaws; second price indicates good quality, nicely finished.

5" boy with side-glancing painted eyes, painted blonde hair, open/closed mouth, molded on blue swimsuit, jointed arms only, stiff legs, marked "Nippon," $175.00. Private collection.

Baby, with Bent Limbs

May or may not be jointed at hips and shoulders, very nice quality

3"	$20.00	$30.00
5"	$35.00	$70.00

Bye-Lo Baby-type, fine quality

3½"	$45.00	$85.00
5"	$70.00	$140.00

Children

Child with molded clothes

4½"	$23.00	$35.00
6"	$35.00	$50.00

Child, ca. 1920s – 1930s

Pink or painted bisque with painted features, jointed at shoulders and hips, has molded hair or wig, excellent condition

3"	$7.50	$15.00
4"	$15.00	$35.00

Betty Boop

Bobbed hair style, large eyes painted to side, head molded to torso

4"	$20.00	$40.00
6"	$35.00	$60.00

Bride & Groom, all original costume

4"	$75.00	$100.00

Indian

5"	$15.00	$25.00

Skippy

6"	$55.00	$135.00

Snow White

5"	$55.00	$110.00

Boxed with Dwarfs

	$325.00	$650.00

Three Bears/Goldlilocks, boxed set

	$165.00	$325.00+

Nippon mark

5"	$40.00	$75.00

Occupied Japan mark

4"	$13.00	$35.00
7"	$25.00	$55.00

Alt, Beck & Gottschalck

Established as a porcelain factory in 1854 at Nauendorf, Thuringia, Germany, the Ciesliks report the company exported doll heads to the USA by 1882. They made heads in both china and bisque for other companies such as Bergmann, using Wagner and Zetzsche kid bodies. The Colemans report mold numbers from 639 to 1288.

First price indicates doll in good condition, with some flaws, or nude; second price is for doll in excellent condition, original clothes or appropriately dressed.

Mark:

Babies, ca. 1920+

Open mouth, some have pierced nostrils, bent-leg baby body, wigs, more for toddler body or flirty eyes

11"	$275.00	$365.00
15"	$350.00	$475.00
20"	$575.00	$775.00
24"	$850.00	$1,150.00

Character Baby, ca. 1910+

Socket head on jointed composition body, glass or painted eyes, open mouth, nicely dressed with good wig or molded hair

Mold 1322, 1342, 1346, 1352, 1361

12"	$325.00	$425.00
16"	$425.00	$600.00
19"	$500.00	$675.00
24"	$700.00	$950.00

Child, All-Bisque: See All-Bisque Section.

Child, Bisque

Mold 630, glass eyes, closed mouth, ca. 1880

22"	$1,650.00	$2,200.00

Open mouth

9"	$575.00	$775.00

Mold 911, 916, swivel head, closed mouth, ca. 1890+; **Mold 915,** shoulder head, closed mouth, ca. 1890

22"	$1,975.00	$2,650.00

Mold 938, closed mouth

20"	$4,500.00*	

25" bisque mold 1361 Character Baby marked "ABG(entwined)//1361//62//Made in Germany//18," human hair wig, blue flirty sleep eyes, painted lashes, pierced nostrils, open mouth/two upper teeth, wobble tongue, composition baby body, white baby dress, bonnet, circa 1910+, $375.00; 12" cloth plush mohair Yes/No Bear, glass eyes, floss nose/mouth, applied ears, jointed at shoulders and hips, felt pads on paws, yes/no mechanism in head, circa early 1900s, $625.00. Courtesy McMasters Doll Auctions.

19" bisque mold 974, marked "974 # 6" on bottom of shoulder plate, molded painted blonde hair falls on shoulders, exposed ears, painted blue eyes with red accent line, single stroke brows, closed pouty mouth, cloth body with crude bisque lower arms, rivet joints at hips and knees, white dotted Swiss blouse, blue print skirt, underclothing, new socks and shoes, circa 1880+, $625.00. Courtesy McMasters Doll Auctions.

Character Child, ca. 1910+

Mold 1357, ca. 1912, solid dome or wigged, painted eyes, open mouth; **Mold 1358, ca. 1910,** molded hair, ribbon, flowers, painted eyes, open mouth

15"	$750.00	$975.00
20"	$1,250.00	$1,700.00

Mold 1322, 1342, 1352, 1361, glass eyes

12"	$325.00	$425.00
14"	$375.00	$500.00
18"	$500.00	$650.00

Mold 1362, ca. 1912, Sweet Nell, more for flapper body

14"	$335.00	$450.00
20"	$400.00	$525.00
26"	$600.00	$800.00

Mold 1367, 1368, ca. 1914

15"	$355.00	$475.00

Shoulder Heads, Bisque, Ca. 1880+

Mark:
1000 # 10

Mold 639, 698, 784, 870, 890, 911, 912, 916, 990, 1000, 1008, 1028, 1032, 1044, 1046, 1064, 1123, 1127, 1142, 1210, 1234, 1235, 1254, 1304, cloth or kid body, bisque lower limbs, molded hair or wig, no damage and nicely dressed. Allow more for molded hat or fancy hairdo.

Glass eyes, closed mouth

11"	$400.00	$550.00
15"	$500.00	$750.00
18"	$750.00	$1,000.00
21"	$925.00	$1,250.00

Painted eyes, closed mouth

14"	$300.00	$385.00
21"	$485.00	$650.00

Turned Bisque Shoulder Heads, 1885+

Bald head or plaster pate, kid body, bisque lower arms, all in good condition, nicely dressed. Dolls marked "DEP" or "Germany" after 1888. Some have Wagner & Zetzsche marked on head, paper label inside top of body. Allow more for molded bonnet or elaborate hairdo.

* at auction

Closed mouth, glass eyes

18"	$600.00	$800.00
21"	$775.00	$1,050.00

Open mouth

15"	$300.00	$400.00
18"	$375.00	$500.00
22"	$490.00	$650.00

Shoulder Heads, China, ca. 1880+

Mold 639, 698, 784, 870, 890, 912, 974, 990, 1000, 1008, 1028, 1032, 1044, 1046, 1064, 1112, 1123, 1127, 1142, 1210, 1222, 1234, 1235, 1254, 1304, cloth or kid body, bisque lower limbs, molded hair or wig, no damage and nicely dressed. Allow more for molded hat or fancy hairdo.

15"	$275.00	$365.00
19"	$318.00	$425.00
23"	$395.00	$525.00
28"	$475.00	$625.00

Amberg, Louis & Sons

Ca. 1878 – 1930, Cincinnati, Ohio; from 1898 on, New York City. Used other name before 1907. Imported dolls made by other firms. First company to manufacture all American-made dolls of composition.

Baby Peggy Mark:
"19 ©. 24//LA & S NY// GERMANY"

Newborn Babe Marks:
"L.A.&S. 1914/G45520 GERMANY, L. AMBERG AND SON/7886" or "COPYRIGHT By LOUIS AMBERG"

Body Twist Tag attached to clothes reads:
"AN AMBERG DOLL/ BODY TWIST/PAT. PEND. #32018."

Bisque

Baby Peggy, ca. 1924

Bisque socket head, sleep eyes, closed mouth, original wig with bangs, dimples, composition or kid body with bisque lower arms

Mold 972, solemn socket head; Mold 973, smiling socket head

17"	$1,725.00	$2,300.00
22"	$1,995.00	$2,650.00

Mold 982, solemn shoulder head; Mold 983, smiling shoulder head

17"	$1,800.00	$2,400.00
22"	$2,100.00	$2,800.00

Baby Peggy, All-Bisque, see All-Bisque section.

Mibs, All-Bisque, 1921, see All-Bisque section.

Newborn Babe, ca. 1914, reissued 1924

Bisque head with cloth body; either celluloid, composition, or rubber hands; lightly painted hair; sleep eyes; closed mouth with protruding upper lip

8"	$275.00	$365.00
11"	$325.00	$425.00
14"	$400.00	$550.00
18"	$655.00	$825.00

Open mouth, marked *"L.A.& S. 371"*

10"	$300.00	$400.00
15"	$340.00	$450.00

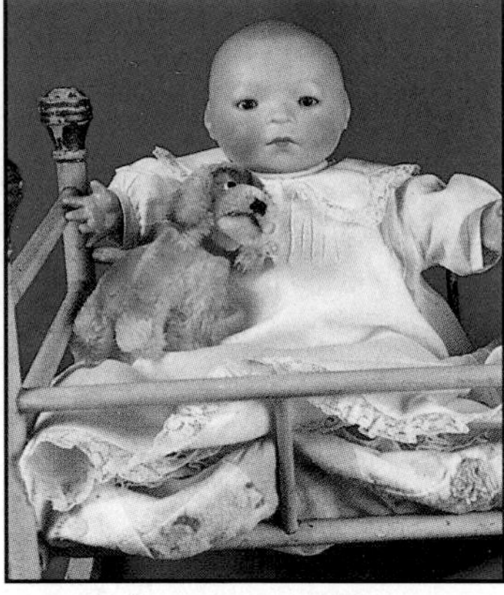

Left: 12" bisque Newborn Babe, marked "©L. Amberg & Son//Germany//886/3" on head, brown sleep eyes, closed mouth, painted hair, cloth body, non-working crier, celluloid hands, white baby dress, diaper, booties, circa 1914, reissued in 1924, $290.00. Courtesy McMasters Doll Auctions.

Vanta Baby, ca. 1927 – 1930

Bisque head, sleep eyes, crier, bent-limb body, in sizes from 10" to 25", distributed by Sears with advertising promotion for Vanta baby garments

Glass eyes, open mouth		
18"	$825.00	$1,100.00
21"	$950.00	$1,275.00
Closed mouth		
18"	$1,050.00	$1,400.00
24"	$1,500.00	$2,000.00

Composition

First price is for doll in good condition, but with flaws, crazing, or nude; second price is for doll in excellent condition, may have light crazing, original or appropriate clothing.

Baby Peggy, ca. 1923

Portrait doll of child actress, Peggy Jean Montgomery; composition head, arms, and legs; cloth body; molded brown bobbed hair; painted eyes with molded lower eyelids; closed mouth. More for boxed, mint.

15"	$85.00	$365.00
18"	$125.00	$500.00
20"	$200.00	$775.00

Body Twists (Teenie Weenies, Tiny Tots), ca. 1929

All-composition with swivel waist made with ball attached to torso, boy or girl with molded hair and painted features

7½ – 8½"	$50.00	$200.00

Charlie Chaplin, ca. 1915

Composition portrait head, painted features, composition hands, cloth body and legs

14"	$175.00	$650.00

Edwina (Sue or It), ca. 1928

All-composition with painted features, molded hair with side part and swirl bang across forehead, body twist (waist swivels on ball attached to torso)

14"	$125.00	$475.00

Happinus, 1918+

Coquette-type, all-composition with head and body molded in one-piece, jointed shoulders and hips, painted molded brown hair, molded ribbon, closed mouth, painted features, unmarked, well modeled torso, original clothes

10"	$75.00	$300.00

Charlie Chaplin Mark: Black suit, white suit, cloth label on sleeve or inside seam of coat that reads: CHARLIE CHAPLIN DOLL// World's Greatest Comedian// Made exclusively by Louis Amberg//&Son, NY//by Special Arrangement with//Essamay Film Co.

Edwina Sue Mark: AMBERG PAT. PEN. L.A. & S.

Mibs Mark: Original dress has ribbon label that reads: "L.A.&S.//Amberg Dolls//The World Standard//Created by//Hazel Drukker//Please Love Me/I'm MIBS."

Sunny Orange Maid Mark on head: "A.//L.A. & S.//1924." Label on dress reads: "SUNNY ORANGE MAID."

Mibs, ca. 1921

Composition turned shoulder head designed by Hazel Drukker, painted molded hair, painted eyes, closed mouth. Two different body styles: cork-stuffed cloth, composition arms and legs with molded shoes, painted socks; and a barefoot, swing-leg, mama-type cloth body with crier.

16"	$225.00	$900.00

Sunny Orange Maid, 1924

For a photo of Sunny Orange Maid, see 1997 edition.

Composition shoulder plate, cloth body, composition arms and legs, molded orange cap

14½"	$400.00	$1,200.00

Vanta Baby, ca. 1927 – 1930

Composition head, sleep eyes, crier, bent-limb body, in sizes from 10" to 25", distributed by Sears with advertising promotion for Vanta baby garments

18"	$75.00	$275.00
23"	$100.00	$400.00

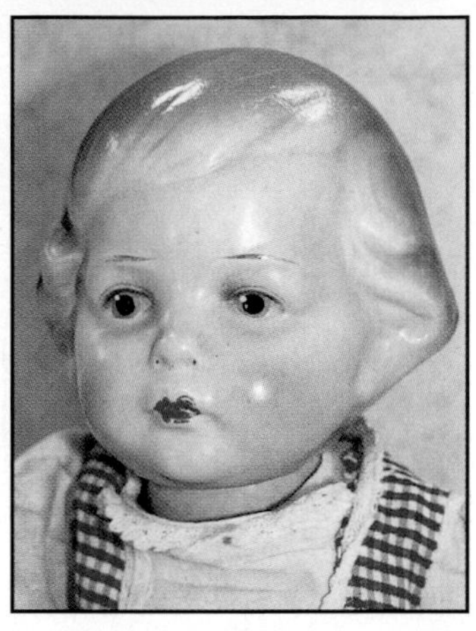

14" composition Edwina marked "Amberg//Pat.Pend.//LA&S © 1928," painted molded hair with side part and swirl bangs across forehead, painted brown eyes, swivel waist, red and white checked skirt and vest over white top, circa 1928, $450.00. *Courtesy Sharon Kolibaba.*

Arnold, Max Oscar

Ca. 1878 – 1925, Neustadt, Thuringia. Made jointed dressed dolls and mechanical dolls including phonograph dolls.

Mark:

Baby, Bisque Head

12"	$125.00	$165.00
16"	$215.00	$285.00
19"	$375.00	$500.00

Child, Mold 150, 200, 201, 250, or "M.O.A."

Excellent bisque

12"	$190.00	$250.00
15"	$265.00	$350.00
21"	$450.00	$600.00
32"	$1,150.00*	

Poor to medium quality bisque

15"	$125.00	$165.00
20"	$200.00	$300.00
24"	$340.00	$450.00

30" bisque girl child, dolly face, open mouth, glass eyes, mohair wig, wood and composition body, circa 1920, $1,000.00. *Private collection.*

Various manufacturers used many different mediums including bisque, wood, wax, cloth, and others to make dolls that performed some action. More complicated models performing more or complex actions bring higher prices. The unusual one-of-a-kind dolls in this category make it difficult to provide a good range. *All these auction prices are for mechanicals in good working order.

Left: 12" unmarked china shoulder head, molded painted hair, exposed ears, painted eyes, closed smiling mouth, kid body, tiny waist, gussets at hips, replaced cloth arms, kid hands, white wool jacket, black pants, circa 1840+, $650.00; Right: 10" untinted bisque, "Patented July 15th, 1862; also in Europe 20 Dec. 1862" on wooden base, molded painted hair, painted eyes, carton body, clock work walking mechanism, metal feet, leather arms, circa 1862, $800.00. Courtesy McMasters Doll Auctions.

Autoperipatetikos, circa 1860 – 1870s

Bisque by American Enoch Rice Morrison, key wound mechanism

12" $1,000.00*

Ballerina

Bisque Simon & Halbig mold 1159 key, rotates, head and arms lower, leg extends, keywound, Leopold Lambert, ca. 1900

23" $4,250.00*

Bébé Automate Respirant

Bisque Bru Jne R sockethead, fully jointed body, keywound mechanism in torso, eyelids open and close, bellows allow to breathe, by Paul Girard for Maison Bru, ca. 1892

20" $9,000.00*

Bébé Cage

Bisque Jumeau Mold 203, keywound, turns head, hand gives berry to bird, bird flies, one tune, Leopold Lambert, ca. 1890

19" $13,500.00*

Bébé Eventail

Bisque Tete Jumeau, keywound, moves head, lifts flower and fan, plays "La Mascotte," blue silk costume, Leopold Lambert, ca. 1890

19" $12,500.00*

Bébé Piano

Bisque Jumeau, socket head, carton body, plays piano with four tunes, keywound, Leopold Lambert, ca. 1886

20" $31,000.00*

Bébé with Fan and Flowers

Bisque Tete Jumeau, keywound, moves hand, fans herself, sniffs flower, plays "Le Petit Bleu," Leopold Lambert, ca. 1892

19" $16,500.00*

* at auction

Garden Tea Party

Three bisque children, painted eyes, move head and arms at tea table on 9" x 9" base

12" $3,050.00*

Laughing Girl with Kitten

Bisque laughing Jumeau socket head, carton torso, keywound mechanism, turns head, smells flower, kitten pulls ribbon, Leopold Lambert, ca. 1890

20" $10,000.00*

Little Girl with Marionette Theater

French bisque socket head, keywound, head moves, lifts curtain, stage rotates, shows five different players, Renou, ca. 1900

16½" $16,500.00*

Waltzing Lady with Mandolin

Bisque socket head, carton body, rotates, turns head, strums mandolin, keywound, Alexandre Theroude, ca. 1865

15" $8,000.00*

Averill, Georgene

Ca. 1915+ New York City, New York. Georgene Averill made composition and cloth dolls operating as Madame Georgene Dolls, Averill Mfg. Co., Georgene Novelties, and Madame Hendren. The first line included dressed felt dolls, Lyf-Lyk, the patented Mama Doll in 1918, and the Wonder line. She designed dolls for Borgfeldt, including Bonnie Babe.

First price indicates doll in good condition, some flaws; second price doll in excellent condition, original clothes, or appropriately dressed.

Tag on original outfit reads: "BONNIE BABE COPYRIGHTED BY GEORGENE AVERILL MADE BY K AND K TOY CO."

Mark:
COPR GEORGENE AVERILL
1005/3652 GERMANY

Original tag reads: "I WHISTLE WHEN YOU DANCE ME ON ONE FOOT AND THEN THE OTHER//PATENTED FEB. 1926//GENUINE MADAME HENDREN DOLL."

***13" bisque mold 1005 Bonnie Babe, marked "Copr. By//Georgene Averill//1005//3652//Germany" on back of solid dome flange head, 9½" circumference, painted hair, blue sleep eyes, softly blushed brows, painted upper and lower lashes, open mouth, two lower teeth, molded tongue, cloth body, rubber hands, antique lace-trimmed baby dress, matching slip, undershirt, diaper, long socks, and booties, circa 1926 – 1930+, $575.00.** Courtesy McMasters Doll Auctions.*

Bisque

Bonnie Babe, ca. 1926 – 1930+

Designed by Georgene Averill, distributed by Borgfeldt. Bisque head, open mouth, two lower teeth, composition arms (sometimes celluloid) and legs on cloth body

Mold 1005, 1368, 1402

12"	$865.00	$1,150.00
14 – 15"	$1,075.00	$1,450.00

* at auction

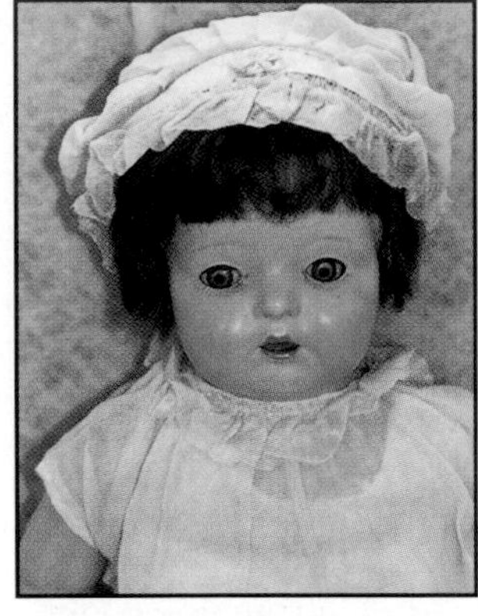

19" composition Madame Hendren "Mama Doll," marked "Genuine//Madame Hendren//Doll//1720//Made in USA," shoulder plate, blue sleep eyes, auburn wig, open mouth with teeth, cloth body, swing legs, composition arms and legs, crier, pink dress and matching bonnet, circa 1922+, $225.00. *Courtesy Robert V. Hardy.*

Celluloid head

10"	$300.00	$500.00
16"	$350.00	$675.00

All-Bisque Bonnie Babe, see All-Bisque section.

Cloth Dolls, 1930+

Mask face with painted features, yarn hair, cloth body

12"	$40.00	$125.00
15"	$70.00	$150.00
22"	$85.00	$295.00
24"	$115.00	$335.00

Characters designed by Maud Tousey Fangel, ca. 1938, Peggy-Ann, Snooks, and Sweets

13"	$350.00	$675.00
17"	$450.00	$875.00
22"	$900.00	$1,150.00

Animals, ca. 1930s

B'rer Rabbit, Fuzzy Wuzzy, Nurse Jane, Uncle Wiggly, etc.

18"	$175.00	$650.00+

Krazy Kat, 1916, felt, not jointed

14"	$90.00	$350.00
18"	$125.00	$500.00

Brownies and Girl Scouts

14"	$85.00	$275.00

Comic Characters

Alvin, Little Lulu, Nancy, Sluggo, Tubby Tom, 1944 – 1961, with mask and painted features

13 – 14"	$500.00+

Little Lulu, in cowgirl outfit

16½"	$585.00

Becassine, 1950s, French cartoon character

13"	$500.00	$750.00

Dolly Dingle, 1923+, designed by Grace Drayton

12 – 14"	$115.00	$450.00

Tear Drop Baby, one tear painted on cheek

16"	$60.00	$335.00

Composition

First price is for doll in good condition but with flaws; second price is for doll in excellent condition with original clothes or appropriately dressed. Add more for boxed with tags or exceptional dolls.

Patsy-type, 1928+

All-composition, with jointed arms and legs, molded or wigged hair, painted or sleep eyes, open or closed mouth, all in good condition, original clothing

14"	$250.00	$300.00
17"	$325.00	$350.00

Baby Georgene or Baby Hendren

Composition head, arms, and lower legs; cloth body with crier; and marked with name on head

16"	$85.00	$275.00
20"	$95.00	$335.00
26"	$200.00	$600.00

Character or Ethnic

Composition head, cloth or composition body, character face, painted features, composition arms and legs. Whistlers, such as Whistling Dan, Sailor, Indian, Dutch Boy had bellows inside body. When pushed down on feet bellows created a whistling sound. Clothes often felt.

12"	$40.00	$150.00
16"	$75.00	$300.00

Black

14"	$125.00	$450.00

Dolly Reckord, 1922 – 1928

Composition head, arms, and legs; human hair wig; sleep eyes; open mouth and teeth; record player in torso

26"	$250.00	$650.00

Mama Doll, 1918+

Composition shoulder head and arms, cloth torso with crier, composition swing legs, molded hair or mohair wig, painted or sleep eyes, good condition, original clothes

15 – 18"	$200.00	$300.00
20 – 22"	$400.00	$500.00

Snookums, 1927

Child star of Universal-Stern Bros. movie comedies, has laughing mouth, two rows of teeth, pants attached to shirt with safety pin

14"	$100.00	$375.00

Bähr & Pröschild

Ca. 1871 – 1930+, Ohrdruf, Thuringia, Germany. This porcelain factory made china, bisque, and celluloid dolls, as well as doll parts and Snow Babies. They made dolls for Kley & Hahn, Bruno Schmidt, Wiesenthal, Schindel & Kallenberg.

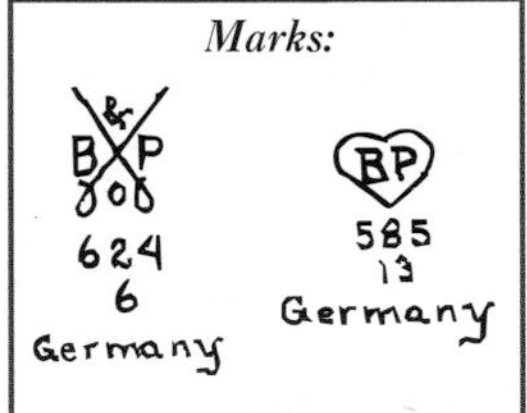

Baby, Character Face, 1909+

Bisque socket head, solid dome or wigged, bent leg, sleep eyes, open mouth

Mold 585, 586, 587, 602, 604, 619, 620, 624, 630, 641, 678

13"	$355.00	$475.00
17"	$500.00	$675.00
22"	$650.00	$875.00

Toddler body

18"	$750.00	$1,000.00
20"	$1,200.00	$1,600.00

16" bisque mold 585 character toddler marked "B & P 0 (in crossed lines)//585//8//Germany" on back of head, antique human hair wig, brown sleep eyes, painted lashes, feathered brows, open mouth, two upper teeth, five-piece composition toddler body with diagonal hip joints, antique black and white clown dress, slip, and hat, panties, old cotton socks, new black shoes, circa 1909+, $350.00. Courtesy McMasters Doll Auctions.

Mold 526, other series 500, and 2023, 2072, or marked BP baby body, open closed mouth

14"	$2,100.00	$2,800.00
18"	$2,625.00	$3,500.00

Child

Belton-type or Dome head

Mold 200 series, with small holes, socket head or shoulder plate, composition or kid body

12"	$1,300.00	$1,750.00
16"	$1,550.00	$1,900.00
24"	$2,350.00	$3,100.00

Child, open or closed mouth

Mold 200 and 300 series, full cheeks, jointed composition German body, French-type, or kid body

Mold Numbers 204, 224, 239, 246, 252, 273, 274, 275, 277, 286, 289, 293, 297, 309, 325, 332, 340, 379, 394

9"	$1,450.00* Mold 204	
14"	$510.00	$675.00
17"	$600.00	$800.00
23"	$825.00	$1,100.00

Mold 224, open mouth, dimpled cheeks

15"	$715.00	$950.00
23"	$1,050.00	$1,400.00

Child, kid body, open mouth

16"	$300.00	$400.00
24"	$510.00	$675.00

Mold 642, character, open mouth

17" $2,700.00*

Mold 520, character, closed mouth

13" $2,500.00*

Mold 247, character, open/closed mouth

26" $2,100.00*

Barrois, E.

Ca. 1844 – 1877, Paris, France. Dolls marked "E.B." are attributed to this early manufacturing firm that used bisque and china heads with that mark. It is not known who made the heads for them. Bisque shoulder head with glass or painted eyes, closed mouth, kid body, may have wooden and bisque arms, good condition. China head has painted eyes and painted, molded hair. Exceptional dolls may be more.

12"	$1,500.00	$2,000.00
13"	$2,500.00	$3,000.00

Marks:
E 3 B
E. 8 DEPOSE **B.**

Fashion Type

Pressed bisque head, glass eyes, cloth or kid body

15"	$2,500.00	$3,300.00
15"	$10,000.00* with trousseau	
21"	$3,500.00	$4,600.00

* at auction

3¾" all-bisque, marked "Bavaria (stamped in black)//2739 B (incised)" on bottom, 5" long unjointed figure has finely painted pale blue eyes with red accent lines, single stroke brows, open/closed mouth with white space between lips, original wig and turban, unjointed bisque body in sitting position, playing a banjo, lavender high heel shoes molded on feet, circa 1920s, $625.00. Courtesy McMasters Doll Auctions.

Bathing Beauties, ca. 1920. All-bisque figures, usually one piece, in various poses, were made by most porcelain factories in Germany and the U.S. in the 1920s. Beautifully detailed features, undressed or molded-on clothing or dressed in bathing costumes. All in excellent condition, no chips or damage.

Painted eyes		
3"	$100.00	$250.00
6"	$300.00	$400.00
Glass eyes		
5"	$300.00	$400.00
6"	$490.00	$650.00
Swivel neck		
5"	$510.00	$675.00
6"	$545.00	$725.00
Elderly woman in suit with legs crossed		
5¼"	$2,200.00*	
With animal		
5½"	$1,125.00	$1,500.00
Two modeled together		
4½ – 5½"	$1,600.00+	
Action figures		
5"	$340.00	$450.00+
7½"	$490.00	$650.00
Wigged action figure		
7"	$450.00	$600.00
Marked Japan		
3"	$50.00	$75.00
5 – 6"	$65.00	$100.00
9"	$125.00	$175.00

Belton Type

Ca. 1870+. No dolls marked "Belton" found; only mold numbers. Belton-type refers to small holes found in tops of solid bisque head dolls; holes were used for stringing. Used by various German firms such as Bähr & Pröschild, Limbach, and Simon & Halbig. Socket head, paperweight eyes, wood and composi-

* at auction

15½" bisque, marked "137//8" on back of head, bisque socket head with flat top, two stringing holes, mohair wig, set brown paperweight eyes, painted upper and lower lashes, feathered brows, closed mouth, pierced ears, jointed wood and composition body, straight wrists, pale blue satin French-style dress, straw bonnet, underclothing, new socks and shoes, circa 1880+, $2,500.00. Courtesy McMasters Doll Auctions.

Marks: None, or may have Mold 100, 116, 117, 120, 125, 127, 137, 154, 183, 185, 190, or others.

tion jointed French type body with straight wrists, appropriately dressed in good condition.

Bru-type face		
14"	$1,800.00	$2,400.00
18"	$2,200.00	$2,925.00
French-type face, Mold 137, 183		
9"	$900.00	$1,200.00
12"	$1,500.00	$2,000.00
16"	$1,775.00	$2,350.00
20"	$2,250.00	$3,050.00
24"	$2,800.00	$3,700.00
German-type face		
9"	$800.00	$1,100.00
12"	$900.00	$1,250.00
18"	$1,450.00	$1,950.00
23"	$2,050.00	$2,750.00
25"	$2,250.00	$3,000.00

Bergmann, C.M.

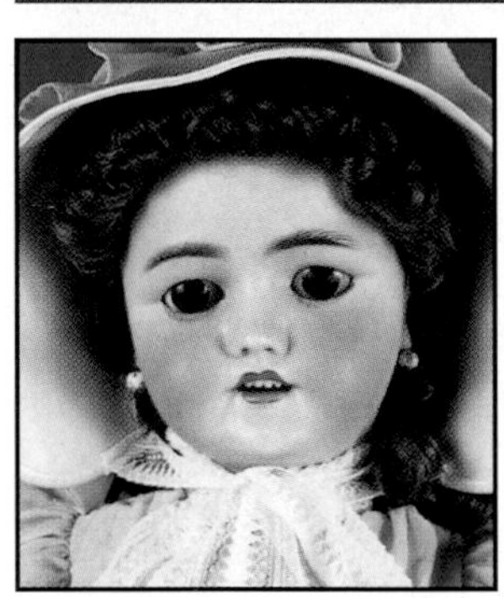

30" bisque girl, marked "C.M. Bergmann//Simon & Halbig//13½," synthetic wig, brown sleep eyes, molded feathered brows, open mouth, four upper teeth, pierced ears, jointed wood and composition body, re-dressed in pale blue antique style dress, large bonnet framing her face, new underclothing, socks, and shoes, circa 1900+, $450.00. Courtesy McMasters Doll Auctions.

Ca. 1889 – 1930+, Thuringia, Germany. Made dolls, but also used heads made by Alt, Beck & Gottschalck, Armand Marseille, and Simon & Halbig.

Mark:

C.M.B
SIMON & HALBIG
Eleonore

Baby

Mold 612, open/closed mouth

14"	$1,150.00	$1,600.00
15"	$2,200.00*	

Character Baby, open mouth, socket head, five-piece bent-leg body

14"	$245.00	$325.00
18"	$435.00	$575.00
21"	$525.00	$700.00

Child

Head by A.M., or unknown maker, open mouth, wig, jointed composition body

10"	$275.00	$375.00
15"	$300.00	$400.00
20"	$335.00	$450.00

* at auction

23"	$425.00	$535.00
30"	$900.00*	
34"	$1,000.00	$1,400.00
42"	$1,575.00	$2,100.00

Mold 1916 and other heads by Simon & Halbig

14"	$300.00	$400.00
19"	$375.00	$500.00
23"	$475.00	$650.00
28"	$675.00	$900.00
33"	$900.00	$1,200.00

Eleonore

18"	$490.00	$650.00
25"	$640.00	$850.00

Lady, flapper-style body with thin arms and legs

12"	$470.00	$625.00
16"	$1,125.00	$1,500.00

Bisque, Unknown or Little Known Maker

English

Diamond Tile Co. Ltd., 1933 – 1943, Stoke-on-Trent, Staffordshire, England

12"	$200.00

Too few in database for reliable range.

French

Ca. 1870+. A number of French doll makers produced unmarked dolls with only a size number, Paris or France. Many are also being attributed to German makers who produced for the French trade. Also included here are little known companies that produced wonderful rarely seen dolls. Unmarked, pressed bisque socket head, closed or open/closed mouth, paperweight eyes, pierced ears, excellent quality bisque and finely painted features, on French wood and composition body with straight wrists. No damage, appropriately dressed.

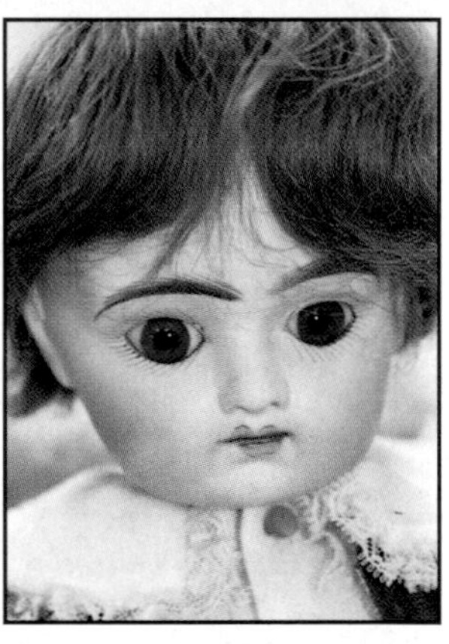

17" possibly Henri Pintel & Ernest Godchaux child, marked "PB 7 G//Depose," blue glass eyes, painted upper and lower lashes, closed mouth, red human hair wig, dressed in rust colored Little Lord Fauntleroy outfit, white shirt with collar and cuffs trimmed in lace, circa 1890+, $2,000.00+. Courtesy Ginger Pennington.

Unknown Maker

Early desirable very French-style face. Marks such as *"J.D."* (possible J. DuSerre) *"J.M. Paris,"* and *"H. G."* (possibly Henri & Granfe-Guimonneau).

17"	$12,750.00	$17,000.00+
21"	$15,750.00	$21,000.00+
27"	$20,250.00	$27,000.00+

Jumeau or Bru style face, may be marked *"W. D."* or *"R. R."*

14"	$1,900.00	$2,650.00
19"	$2,400.00	$3,175.00
24"	$3,775.00	$5,050.00
27"	$4,000.00	$5,350.00

Marks:
E. (Size number)
D. on head.
Eiffel Tower
"PARIS BEBE"
on body; shoes with
"PARIS BEBE"
in star.

11" J. Verlingue Gibson Girl, marked "Lutin//France//J (anchor) V//3/0" on head, mohair wig in Gibson Girl style, brown painted eyes, black lash line, single stroke brows, closed mouth, kid body with bisque lower arms, gussets at hips and knees, rose silk outfit, matching hat, possibly original underclothing, replaced socks and shoes, circa 1915 – 1920s, $400.00. Courtesy McMasters Doll Auctions.

Closed mouth, Marks: *"F.1," "F.2," "J," "137," "136,"* or others

Excellent quality, unusual face

10"	$1,250.00	$1,700.00
15"	$3,000.00	$4,000.00
18"	$3,600.00	$4,750.00
23"	$4,500.00	$6,000.00
27"	$5,250.00	$7,000.00

Standard quality, excellent bisque

13"	$1,825.00	$2,450.00
18"	$2,600.00	$3,450.00
23"	$3,375.00	$4,500.00

Lesser quality, may have poor painting and/or blotches on cheeks

15"	$900.00	$1,200.00
21"	$1,350.00	$1,800.00
26"	$1,725.00	$2,300.00

Open mouth

Excellent quality, ca. 1890+, French body

15"	$1,125.00	$1,500.00
18"	$1,725.00	$2,300.00
21"	$1,800.00	$2,400.00
24"	$2,325.00	$3,100.00

High cheek color, ca. 1920s, may have five-piece papier-mâché body

15"	$475.00	$625.00
19"	$600.00	$800.00
23"	$725.00	$950.00

Known Makers

CSFJ, Chambre Syndicale des Fabricants de Jouets et Jeux et Engrins Sportif, 1886 – 1928+, Paris, France. Trade organization composed of French toy makers. Numbers refer to numbered list of manufacturers. First price is for doll in good condition, but with flaws; second price indicates doll in excellent condition with original or appropriate clothing.

Child, closed mouth, excellent quality bisque

12"	$700.00	$925.00
16"	$975.00	$1,300.00

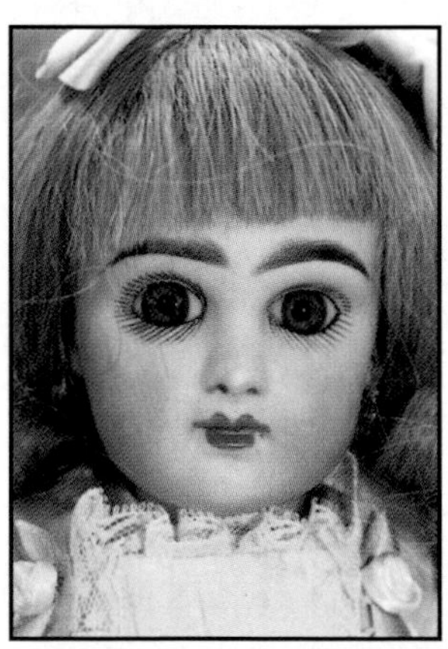

13" French, possibly Jumeau, marked "DX" in red low on back of head, blue glass eyes, painted lashes, closed mouth, red human hair wig, peach dress, circa 1880 – 1890, $2,700.00. Courtesy Ginger Pennington.

Danel & Cie, 1889 – 1895, Paris. Danel, once director of Jumeau factory, was sued by Jumeau for copying Bébés Jumeau.

Paris Bébé

Bisque socket head, appropriate wig, pierced ears, paperweight eyes, closed mouth, nicely dressed in good condition

First price is for doll in good condition, but with flaws; second price indicates doll in excellent condition with original or appropriate clothing.

19"	$4,500.00	$6,000.00
21"	$4,725.00	$6,500.00
29"	$16,500.00*	

Delcrois, Henri, ca. 1865 – 1867

Bisque socket head, closed mouth, pierced ears, paperweight eyes, wig, marked *"PAN"* with size mark that varies with size of doll, wood and composition jointed French body

13"	$2,100.00	$3,000.00*

Too few in database for reliable range.

Halopeau, A, ca. 1880

Marked *"H,"* pressed bisque, open/closed or closed mouth, glass paperweight eyes, pierced ears, cork pate, French wood/composition body with straight wrists

21½"	$36,340.00*
22½"	$52,693.00*

Too few in database for reliable range.

24" Pansy II, marked "Pansy//II//Germany" on back of head, replaced human hair wig, blue sleep eyes, real lashes, painted lashes, feathered brows, open mouth, four upper teeth, jointed wood and composition body, nicely re-dressed in peach taffeta dress, antique white pinafore, new underclothing, socks, and shoes, circa 1900+, $525.00. Courtesy McMasters Doll Auctions.

J.M. marked Bébé, ca. 1880+

Socket head, closed mouth, pressed ears, French composition and wood body

13" $5,000.00 – 7,000.00

Mascotte, 1882 – 1901

Trademark of May Freres Cie, using sizes similar to Bébés Jumeau. Became part of Jules Steiner in 1898. Bisque socket head, wig over cork pate, closed mouth, paperweight eyes, pierced ears, jointed composition French style body.

18"	$2,800.00	$3,750.00

Too few in database for reliable range.

Marks:
On head:
MASCOTTE
On body:
Bébé Mascotte
Paris
Child marked:
Mascotte on head

Mothereau, ca. 1880 – 1895

Bébé Mothereau was made by Alexandre C. T. Mothereau patented a joint for doll bodies. Upper arms and legs of wood, lower arms and legs have rounded joint and metal bracket for stringing. Pressed bisque socket head, glass eyes, closed mouth, pierced ears, cork pate, jointed composition body, *marked B.M.*

Bébé17½" $23,000.00*

Too few in database for reliable range.

Pannier, ca. 1875

Marked *"C 8 P,"* pressed bisque head, closed mouth, glass paperweight eyes

20" $57,986.00*

P.D., Frederic Petit & Andre Dumontier, 1878 – 1890, Paris

Made dolls with bisque heads from Francois Gaultier factory. Pressed bisque socket head, rounded face, glass eyes, closed mouth, pierced ears, wig over cork pate, French composition and wood jointed body

19"	$10,000.00	$13,000.00
25"	$11,450.00	$15,250.00

Mark:
P 3 D

* at auction

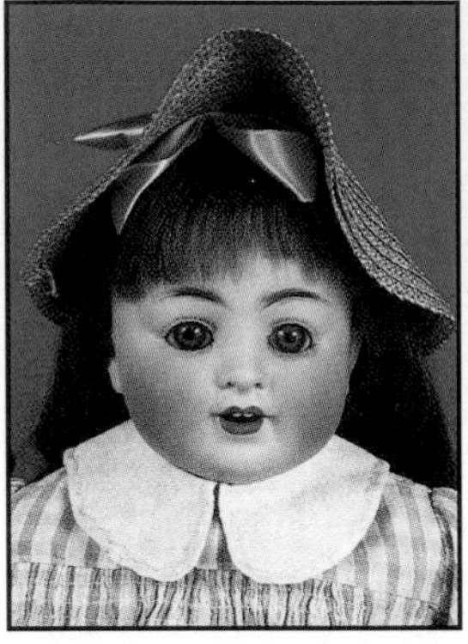

19" K & K Mama Doll, marked "42" on head, "K & K//56//Made in Germany" on shoulder plate, replaced wig, blue sleep eyes, feathered brows, painted upper and lower lashes, open mouth, two upper teeth, cloth body with non-working crier, composition lower arms, oilcloth legs, old blue/white dress with smocked bodice, white romper underwear, replaced socks and leather shoes, blue straw bonnet, circa 1924, $345.00. Courtesy McMasters Doll Auctions.

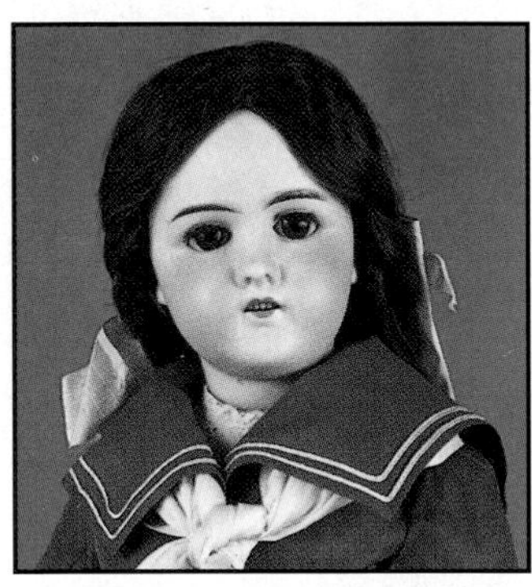

24½" German doll marked "Made in Germany//H.W.//300-3" on back of socket head, antique human hair wig, blue sleep eyes, real and painted lashes, feathered brows, open mouth, five upper teeth, jointed wood and composition body, antique brown sailor dress, antique underclothing and socks, replaced brown shoes, circa 1890+, $375.00. Courtesy McMasters Doll Auctions.

Radiguet & Cordonnier, ca. 1880

Marked *"R C Depose"* on breast plate, bisque head, shoulder plate with molded bosom, closed mouth, glass eyes, bent bisque arm, molded shoes

17" $9,993.00*

Too few in database for reliable range.

Rochard, Antoine Edmond, ca. 1868

Pressed bisque swivel head, open mouth to hold kaleidoscope, glass eyes, used Stanhope lenses, multicolored with scenes as jewel decor

Head only

6¾" $24,530.00*

Too few in database for reliable range.

Rostal, Henri, 1914, Paris

Made a bisque socket head, open mouth, glass eyes, wood and composition jointed body. *Mark: "Mon Tresor"*

35" $2,500.00*

German, Ca. 1860+

Unknown or little-known German factories

Marks: May be unmarked or only a mold or size number or Germany.

Baby – Newborn, ca. 1924+

Cloth body

Bisque head, molded/painted hair, composition or celluloid hands, glass eyes, good condition, appropriately dressed

11"	$225.00	$300.00
14"	$345.00	$450.00
17"	$450.00	$600.00

Baby

Composition body

Solid dome or wigged, five-piece baby body, open mouth, good condition, appropriately dressed

Glass eyes

10"	$200.00	$275.00
15"	$400.00	$550.00
20"	$525.00	$700.00

Painted eyes

11"	$150.00	$200.00
16"	$210.00	$315.00
18"	$340.00	$450.00

Allow more for closed, or open/closed mouth, unusual face, or toddler body.

Child

Character face, 1910+

Glass eyes, closed or open/closed mouth. Unidentified, may have wig or solid dome, excellent quality bisque, good condition, appropriately dressed

15"	$2,800.00	$3,800.00
19"	$3,400.00	$4,600.00

* at auction

Mold 111, glass eyes

22"	$16,500.00	$22,000.00+

Too few in database for reliable range.

Mold 128

18"	$6,250.00	$8,950.00+

Too few in database for reliable range.

Mold 163, painted eyes, closed mouth

16"	$900.00	$1,200.00

Too few in database for realiable range.

Child, closed mouth

Excellent bisque, appropriately dressed, jointed composition body

13"	$575.00	$765.00
16"	$800.00	$1,075.00
20"	$1,115.00	$1,350.00
24"	$1,450.00	$1,950.00

Kid, or cloth body, may have turned head, bisque lower arms

13"	$475.00	$625.00
15"	$650.00	$850.00
19"	$875.00	$1,150.00
23"	$1,000.00	$1,350.00

Child, open mouth, ca. 1880+

Dolly face, excellent pale bisque, glass eyes, jointed composition body

12"	$140.00	$190.00
15"	$220.00	$290.00
20"	$345.00	$455.00
25"	$440.00	$580.00
28"	$480.00	$630.00

Kid body

12"	$110.00	$145.00
15"	$135.00	$180.00
18"	$165.00	$215.00
22"	$200.00	$265.00

Molded hair doll, ca. 1880+

Bisque shoulder head with well modeled hair, often blond, painted or glass eyes, closed mouth with kid or cloth body, bisque lower arms, good condition, appropriately dressed. Mold 890, 1000, 1008, 1028, 1064, 1142, 1256, 1288 may be made by Alt, Beck & Gottschalck.

American Schoolboy, 1880+

Side-parted painted hair swept across forehead, glass eyes, closed mouth

Jointed composition body

11"	$950.00* original	
15"	$485.00	$650.00

Kid or cloth body

13"	$375.00	$500.00
15"	$400.00	$575.00
20"	$525.00	$700.00

6½" bisque shoulder head, unmarked, set blue eyes, multi-stroke brows, painted upper and lower lashes, closed mouth, pierced-in ears, heavily molded and painted blond hair with sausage curls and blue ribbon decoration, circa 1870s+, $675.00. Courtesy McMasters Doll Auctions.

* at auction

Child or lady, molded hair or wigged, closed mouth

Glass eyes		
8"	$145.00	$195.00
15"	$375.00	$500.00
19"	$650.00	$875.00
23"	$1,075.00	$1,450.00
Painted eyes		
8"	$85.00	$115.00
15"	$245.00	$325.00
19"	$350.00	$475.00
23"	$575.00	$775.00

Decorated shoulder plate, fancy hairdo

Glass eyes		
20"	$2,075.00	$2,750.00+
Painted eyes		
22"	$1,800.00*	

Smaller unmarked doll

Head of good quality bisque, glass eyes, on five-piece papier-mâché or composition body, good condition, appropriately dressed

Open mouth		
6"	$140.00	$185.00
8"	$165.00	$225.00
10"	$235.00	$325.00
Jointed body		
6"	$170.00	$225.00
8"	$250.00	$335.00
10"	$345.00	$460.00
Poorly painted		
6"	$65.00	$85.00
9"	$95.00	$125.00
12"	$135.00	$175.00
Closed mouth		
Jointed body		
6"	$245.00	$325.00
8"	$300.00	$400.00
11"	$425.00	$575.00
Five-piece body		
6"	$170.00	$235.00
9"	$245.00	$335.00
12"	$300.00	$415.00

JAPANESE, CA. 1914 – 1921+

Various Japanese firms such as Morimura and Yamato (marked *"Nippon"* or *"J.W."* from 1914 – 1921, after that were marked *"Japan"*) made dolls for export when supplies were cut off from Germany during World War I. Quality varies greatly.

First price indicates doll in good condition, but with flaws; second price is for doll in excellent condition, appropriately dressed or original clothes. Add more for boxed, tagged, or labeled.

* at auction

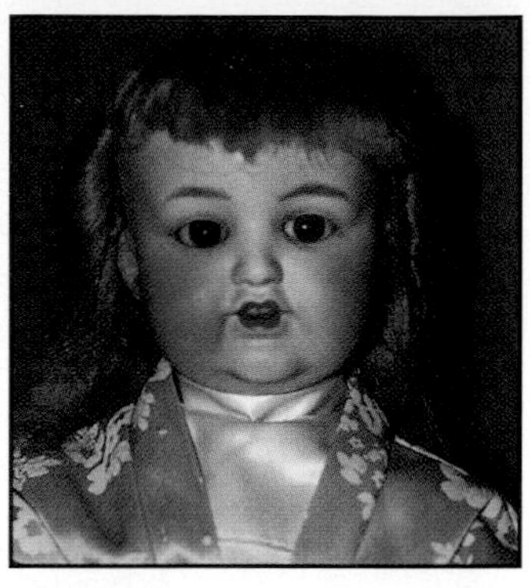

20" Nippon socket head, mold #70018, with glass eyes, red/brown feathered eyebrows and lashes, open mouth with upper teeth, red wig, composition body, circa 1930s – 1940s, $575.00. Courtesy Angie Gonzales.

Baby, character face, ca. 1910+

Good to excellent quality bisque, well painted, nice body and appropriately dressed

9"	$120.00	$155.00
11"	$160.00	$215.00
15"	$225.00	$300.00
19"	$400.00	$525.00
23"	$575.00	$765.00

Poor quality bisque

11"	$85.00	$115.00
15"	$125.00	$165.00
19"	$185.00	$250.00
23"	$300.00	$400.00

Gold Medal, marked Nippon

12"	$175.00	$250.00

Hilda-type

Excellent quality, glass eyes, open mouth with two upper teeth

14"	$525.00	$700.00
17"	$635.00	$850.00

Poor quality bisque

14"	$85.00	$115.00
18"	$160.00	$215.00

Mold 600, marked *"Fy"*

13"	$285.00	$395.00
17"	$400.00	$535.00

Mark:

Russian

Juravlev & Kocheshkova, before the Revolution, ca. 1915+. Bisque socket head, sleep eyes, wig, jointed wood and composition body

26" $400.00* with repair to head

Too few in database for reliable range.

Black or Brown Dolls

Black or brown dolls can have fired-in color or be painted bisque, composition, cloth, papier-mâché, or other materials. The color can be from very black to a light tan. They can have the typical open mouth dolly faces or ethnic features. The quality of this group of dolls varies greatly and the prices will fluctuate with the quality.

13" bisque Ernst Heubach mold 399 baby, marked "Heubach-Kosslesdorf//399 - 5/0 D.R.G.M//Germany" on head, solid dome socket head, painted black hair, dark sleep eyes without pupils, molded indicated brows, painted lashes, closed mouth, pierced ears, brown composition baby body, dressed in old red felt skirt and jacket with number 13 embroidered on it, white lace front only, slip, circa 1930, $275.00. Courtesy McMasters Doll Auctions.

* at auction

16½" brown bisque Heinrich Handwerck child, marked "Germany//Heinrich//Handwerck//Simon & Halbig//0½" on head, black mohair wig, brown sleep eyes, feathered brows, painted lashes, open mouth, four upper teeth, brown wood and composition body, nicely redressed in ecru French-style dress, matching bonnet, stockings, shoes, circa 1890+, $800.00; six umarked brown glass Russian Christmas ornaments, $55.00. Courtesy McMasters Doll Auctions.

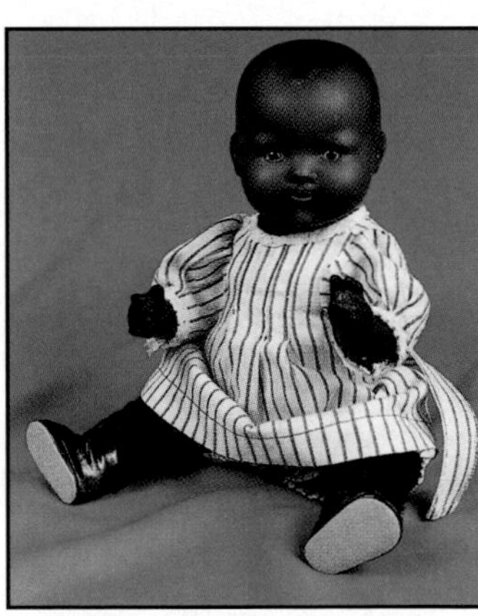

13" brown bisque Armand Marseille mold 351 My Dream Baby, marked "A.M.//Germany//351//3K" on head, molded painted hair, dark brown sleep eyes, soft brows indicated, painted upper and lower lashes, open mouth, two lower teeth, dark brown composition baby body, antique gray-white striped dress and matching pants, new black socks and shoes, circa 1926, $275.00. Courtesy McMasters Doll Auctions.

The first price indicates doll in good condition, but with flaws, perhaps nude; the second price indicates doll in excellent condition with original clothes or appropriately dressed. Add more for boxed, labeled, tagged, or exceptional quality.

ALL-BISQUE

Glass eyes, head molded to torso

4 – 5"	$200.00	$385.00+

Swivel neck

5 – 6"	$300.00	$500.00+

Painted eyes, head molded to torso

5"	$125.00	$245.00

Swivel head

5"	$250.00	$500.00

French-type

4"	$300.00	$500.00

All-bisque, marked by known maker such as J.D. Kestner or Simon & Halbig

6 – 7"	$975.00	$1,300.00

Automaton

Bisque standing man, key-wound, smoker

29"	$3,630.00*

Belton-type

Closed mouth

12"	$1,350.00	$1,800.00
15"	$2,025.00	$2,700.00

BISQUE, FRENCH

Bru (circle dot or Breveté)

13"	$6,000.00*
19"	$50,000.00*

Too few in database for reliable range.

Bru-Jne

23"	$26,250.00	$35,000.00+

Too few in database for reliable range.

E.D., open mouth

16"	$1,725.00	$2,300.00
22"	$1,950.00	$2,600.00

Fashion-type unmarked

Bisque shoulder head, kid body, glass eyes

14"	$1,500.00	$2,000.00+

Swivel neck, articulated body, original

16"	$9,750.00	$12,750.00

Shoulder head, original

16"	$4,500.00	$6,000.00

F.G., open/closed mouth

Kid body, swivel neck

14"	$1,800.00	$2,400.00
17"	$2,800.00	$3,800.00

* at auction

29" brown bisque Kestner mold 171, marked "M made in Germany 16//171//6¼" on back of head, replaced black wig, brown sleep eyes, real lashes, feathered brows, painted upper and lower lashes, open mouth, six upper teeth, painted brown wood and composition body, gold silk bead trimmed dress, pale yellow underclothing, wonderful antique socks and brown leather shoes, circa 1900, $450.00. Courtesy McMasters Doll Auctions.

French, unmarked or marked DEP		
Closed mouth		
11 – 12"	$1,350.00	$1,800.00+
15"	$2,250.00	$3,000.00
20"	$3,150.00	$4,200.00
Open mouth		
10"	$450.00	$600.00
15"	$825.00	$1,100.00
22"	$1,650.00	$2,200.00
Jumeau-type		
Closed mouth		
12"	$1,950.00	$2,600.00
15"	$2,700.00	$3,600.00
19"	$3,600.00	$4,800.00
Open mouth		
12"	$825.00	$1,100.00
15"	$1,575.00	$2,100.00
19"	$2,400.00	$3,200.00
Painted bisque		
Closed mouth		
15"	$735.00	$975.00
20"	$800.00	$1,200.00
Open mouth		
15"	$375.00	$500.00
20"	$750.00	$1,000.00
With ethnic features		
18"	$3,450.00	$4,600.00+
Jumeau		
Tête Jumeau, closed mouth		
15"	$3,525.00	$4,700.00
18"	$3,825.00	$5,100.00
23"	$4,575.00	$6,100.00
Open mouth		
10"	$1,650.00	$2,200.00
15"	$2,025.00	$2,700.00
18"	$2,250.00	$3,000.00
23"	$2,625.00	$3,500.00
E. J., closed mouth		
15"	$6,200.00	$8,200.00+
17"	$7,000.00	$9,300.00+
19"	$31,000.00*	
Paris Bébé		
16"	$3,450.00	$4,600.00
19"	$4,125.00	$5,500.00
S.F.B.J.		
Mold 226		
16"	$2,175.00	$2,900.00
Mold 235, open/closed mouth		
15"	$1,950.00	$2,600.00
17"	$2,212.50	$2,950.00

* at auction

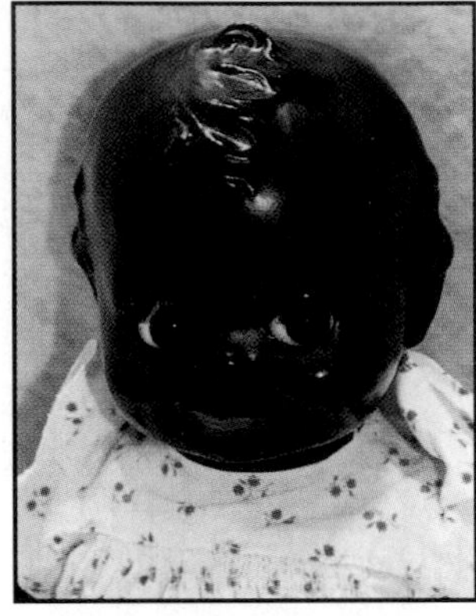

16" composition unmarked girl, molded hair in tufts on top and sides, black side-glancing sleep eyes, real lashes, closed smiling mouth with red painted lips, jointed composition body, original white dress with flower print, circa 1920s – 1930s, $700.00. Courtesy Anita Ladensack.

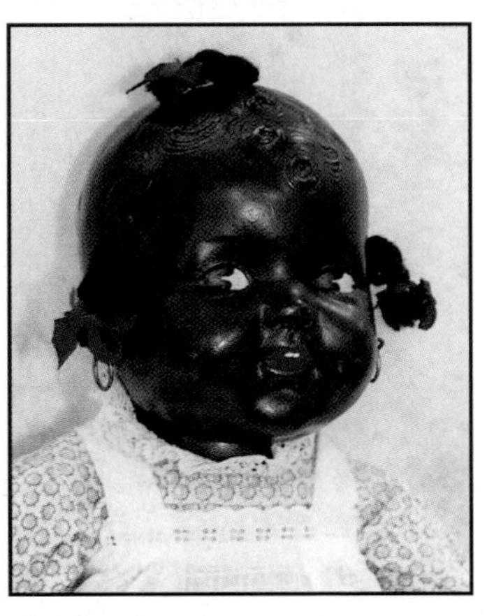

17" composition unmarked, molded brown hair with three braided tufts, one on top and two above ears, painted side-glancing eyes, closed mouth, hoop earrings, composition baby body, pink print dress with white apron, circa 1920s – 1930s, $350.00. Courtesy Sharon Kolibaba.

S & Q (Schuetzmeister & Quendt)

Mold 251

9"	$450.00	$600.00
15"	$1,500.00	$2,000.00

Mold 252, baby

20"	$1,250.00	$1,650.00

Child

20"	$1,350.00	$1,800.00

Jules Steiner

A series, closed mouth

18"	$4,425.00	$5,900.00
22"	$4,875.00	$6,500.00

Open mouth

13"	$3,225.00	$4,300.00
16"	$3,600.00	$4,800.00
21"	$5,750.00*	

C series

18"	$4,000.00	$6,000.00
21"	$4,650.00	$6,200.00

Unis France

Mold 301 or 60, open mouth

14"	$340.00	$450.00
17"	$600.00	$800.00

BISQUE, GERMAN

Unmarked

Closed mouth

10 – 11"	$225.00	$300.00
14"	$300.00	$400.00
17"	$395.00	$525.00
21"	$600.00	$800.00

Open mouth

10"	$375.00	$500.00
13"	$490.00	$650.00
15"	$640.00	$850.00

Painted bisque

Closed mouth

16"	$265.00	$350.00
19"	$375.00	$500.00

Open mouth

14"	$225.00	$300.00
18"	$375.00	$500.00

Ethnic features

15"	$2,250.00	$3,000.00
18"	$2,850.00	$3,800.00

Bähr & Pröschild, open mouth, mold 277, ca. 1891

10"	$525.00	$750.00
12"	$1,050.00*	

* at auction

Bye-Lo Baby

16"	$2,250.00	$3,000.00

Cameo Doll Company

Kewpie (Hottentot) bisque

4"	$400.00
5"	$565.00
9"	$985.00

Composition

12"	$400.00
15"	$725.00

Papier-mâché

8"	$265.00

Scootles, composition, original outfit

13"	$750.00
13"	$1,050.00*

Handwerck, Heinrich, mold 79, 119

Open mouth

12"	$600.00	$800.00
18"	$1,200.00	$1,600.00
22"	$1,425.00	$1,900.00
29"	$1,950.00	$2,600.00

Heubach, Ernst (Koppelsdorf)

Mold 271, 1914, shoulder head, painted eyes, closed mouth

10"	$300.00	$475.00

Mold 320, 339, 350

10"	$325.00	$425.00
13"	$400.00	$535.00
18"	$525.00	$700.00

Mold 399, allow more for toddler

10"	$300.00	$400.00
14"	$415.00	$550.00
17"	$525.00	$700.00

Mold 414

9"	$340.00	$450.00
14"	$1,100.00*	
17"	$715.00	$950.00

Mold 418 (grin)

9"	$510.00	$675.00
14"	$650.00	$900.00

Mold 444, 451

9"	$300.00	$400.00
14"	$525.00	$700.00

Mold 452, brown

7½"	$285.00	$375.00
10"	$360.00	$475.00
15"	$510.00	$675.00

Mold 458

10"	$350.00	$465.00
15"	$525.00	$700.00

13" composition Cameo Scootles, molded painted brown hair, painted brown eyes, closed mouth, dimples, fully jointed composition head and body, original peach striped romper and blue shirt, circa 1930s, $975.00. Courtesy Sharon Kolibaba.

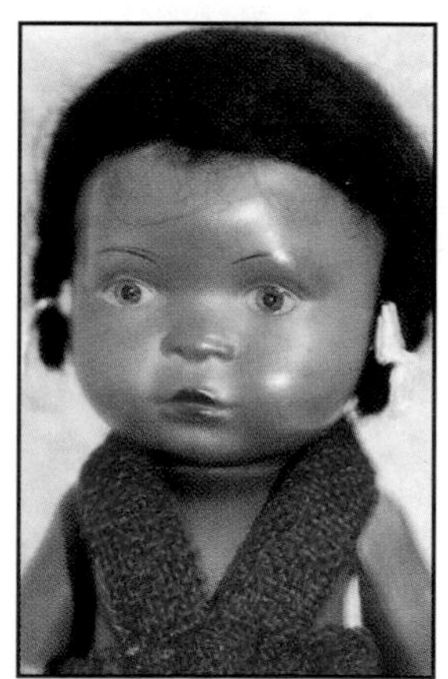

12" celluloid Rheinsche Gummi und Celluloid Fabrik Co. child, marked with "Turtlemark (in diamond)//32 34" on head, black mohair wig, brown glass eyes, closed mouth, jointed celluloid body, red knit dress, circa 1930+, $350.00. Courtesy Betty Strong.

* at auction

9" cloth American Black Sambo, black yarn hair, painted features, cloth body, red shirt with big white buttons, blue shorts, felt shoes, carrying green umbrella, original owner, circa 1948 – 1950, $50.00 to $100.00. Courtesy Stephanie Thomson.

19" vinyl Royal Emma Sue, unmarked, rooted black saran hair, brown sleep eyes, real lashes, painted lower lashes, closed mouth, fully jointed brown hard plastic walker body, long white dotted Swiss gown with pink ribbon and rose at waist, circa 1950s, $55.00. Courtesy Pat Graff.

Mold 463

12"	$475.00	$625.00
16"	$715.00	$950.00

Mold 1900

14"	$375.00	$500.00
17"	$450.00	$600.00

Heubach, Gebruder, Sunburst mark

Boy, eyes to side, open/closed mouth

12"	$1,875.00	$2,500.00

Mold 7657, 7658, 7668, 7671

9"	$950.00	$1,250.00
13"	$1,300.00	$1,800.00

Mold 7661, 7686

10"	$900.00	$1,200.00
14"	$1,950.00	$2,600.00
17"	$2,850.00	$3,800.00

Kammer & Reinhardt (K * R)

Child, no mold number

7½"	$340.00	$450.00
14"	$515.00	$675.00
17"	$660.00	$875.00
19"	$2,000.00*	

Mold 100

10"	$525.00	$700.00
14"	$825.00	$1,100.00
17"	$1,200.00	$1,600.00
20"	$1,785.00*	

Mold 101, painted eyes

15"	$3,300.00*	

Mold 101, glass eyes

17"	$3,700.75	$4,925.00

Mold 114

13"	$3,150.00	$4,200.00

Mold 116, 116a

15"	$2,250.00	$3,000.00
19"	$2,800.00	$3,725.00

Mold 122, 126, baby body

12"	$565.00	$750.00
18"	$845.00	$1,125.00

Mold 126, toddler

18"	$1,200.00	$1,600.00

Kestner, J. D.

Baby, no mold number, open mouth, teeth

10"	$1,500.00*	

Hilda, mold 245

12"	$2,100.00	$2,800.00
14"	$4,125.00	$5,500.00

* at auction

Child, no mold number		
Closed mouth		
14"	$475.00	$625.00
17"	$715.00	$950.00
Open mouth		
12"	$340.00	$450.00
16"	$490.00	$650.00
Five-piece body		
9"	$215.00	$285.00
12"	$265.00	$350.00
Konig & Wernicke (KW/G)		
14"	$900.00*	
18"	$565.00	$750.00
Ethnic features		
17"	$750.00	$1,000.00
Kuhnlenz, Gebruder		
Closed mouth		
15"	$675.00	$900.00
18"	$1,350.00	$1,800.00
Open mouth, mold 34.14, 34.16, 34.24, etc.		
3"	$725.00* boxed	
3½"	$450.00*	
6"	$700.00*	
12"	$415.00	$550.00
Ethnic features		
16"	$3,000.00	$4,000.00
Marseille, Armand		
No mold number, ebony		
11"	$850.00*	
Mold 341, 351, 352, 362		
10"	$300.00	$400.00
16"	$545.00	$825.00
20"	$925.00	$1,200.00
Mold 390, 390n		
16"	$415.00	$550.00
19"	$585.00	$775.00
23"	$675.00	$895.00
25"	$2,200.00*	
28"	$825.00	$1,100.00
Mold 451, 458 (Indians)		
9"	$265.00	$350.00
12"	$375.00	$500.00
Mold 966, 970, 971, 992, 995 (some in compo)		
9"	$200.00	$265.00
14"	$415.00	$550.00
18"	$660.00	$875.00
Mold 1894, 1897, 1912, 1914		
12"	$400.00	$525.00
14"	$550.00	$750.00
18"	$635.00	$850.00

* at auction

19" composition unmarked Mama Doll, replaced human hair wig, tin sleep eyes, real lashes, open mouth, four teeth, composition arms and swing legs, cloth body, old red and white dress with matching bloomers, white socks, possibly original black shoes, circa 1920s, $400.00. Courtesy Pat Graff.

Recknagel, marked "R.A.," mold 126, 138

16"	$545.00	$725.00
22"	$1,075.00	$1,430.00

Schoenau Hoffmeister (S PB H)

Hanna

8"	$285.00	$375.00
10 – 12"	$415.00	$550.00
15"	$525.00	$700.00
18"	$640.00	$850.00

Mold 1909

16"	$400.00	$525.00
19"	$525.00	$700.00

Simon & Halbig

Mold 639

14"	$5,100.00	$6,800.00
18"	$7,500.00	$10,000.00

Mold 739, open mouth

16"	$1,300.00	$1,800.00
22"	$2,250.00	$3,000.00

Closed mouth

13"	$1,500.00*	
17"	$1,950.00	$2,600.00

Mold 939, closed mouth

18"	$2,475.00	$3,300.00
21"	$3,375.00	$4,500.00

Open mouth

13"	$2,300.00* original outfit	

Mold 949, closed mouth

18"	$2,550.00	$3,400.00
21"	$3,000.00	$3,950.00

Open mouth, fat cheeks

15"	$2,250.00	$3,000.00

Too few in database for reliable range.

Mold 1009, 1039, 1079, open mouth

11"	$1,600.00* mold 1009	
12"	$950.00	$1,250.00
16"	$1,250.00	$1,700.00
18"	$1,500.00	$2,000.00

Pull-string sleep eyes

19"	$1,725.00	$2,300.00

Mold 1248, open mouth

15"	$1,125.00	$1,500.00
16"	$4,100.00*	
18"	$1,350.00	$1,800.00

Mold 1272

20"	$1,600.00	$2,000.00

Mold 1302, closed mouth, glass eyes, black character face

18"	$5,250.00	$7,000.00

Indian, sad expression, brown face

18"	$5,500.00	$7,400.00

* at auction

Mold 1303, Indian, thin face, man or woman

16"	$4,574.00	$6,100.00
21"	$6,000.00	$8,000.00

Mold 1339, 1368

16"	$4,450.00	$5,900.00

Mold 1358, ca. 1910

23"	$1,900.00*	

Celluloid

The first price indicates doll in good condition, but with flaws, perhaps nude; the second price indicates doll in excellent condition with original clothes or appropriately dressed.

All-celluloid

10"	$150.00	$200.00
15"	$265.00	$350.00
18"	$400.00	$600.00

Celluloid shoulder head, kid body, add more for glass eyes

17"	$265.00	$350.00
21"	$340.00	$450.00

French-type, marked "SNF"

14"	$265.00	$350.00
18"	$400.00	$600.00

Kammer & Reinhardt, mold 775, 778

11"	$150.00	$200.00
18"	$350.00	$475.00

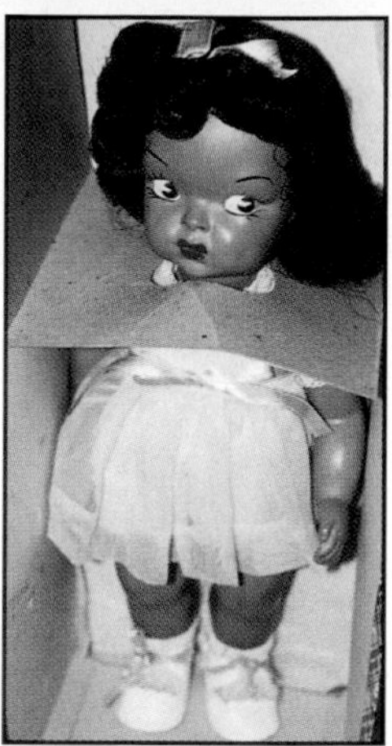

16" composition Terri Lee Bonnie Lou, chestnut brunette hair evenly curled around head, mannequin wig style, black single stroke brows, brown eyes/white highlights, five painted lashes above, three painted lashes below, red accent dots in nose, all original, mint in pink outfit, satin bows, red and white plaid Terri Lee Toddler box with porthole lid. Circa 1947, before Jackie Ormes' Patty Jo faces, $3,800.00. Courtesy Pat Rather.

Cloth

The first price indicates doll in good condition, but with flaws, perhaps nude; the second price indicates doll in excellent condition with original clothes or appropriately dressed.

Alabama, see Cloth dolls.

Bruckner, see Cloth dolls.

1930s Mammy-type

14"	$85.00	$125.00
18"	$125.00	$275.00

Golliwog, 1895 to present

Character from 1895 book, *"The Adventures of Two Dutch Dolls and a Golliwogg,"* all cloth, various English makers. See also Cloth, Deans Rag.

1895 – 1920

13"	$375.00	$750.00

1930 – 1950

11"	$150.00	$300.00
15"	$250.00	$400.00

1950 – 1970s

13"	$150.00	$250.00
18"	$200.00	$400.00

33½" plush cloth possibly Robertson's Golliwog, tagged "Made in Korea," felt features, all plush, red pants, blue jacket, yellow vest, and white shirt all make up body, circa 1950s, $125.00. Courtesy Ginger Reid.

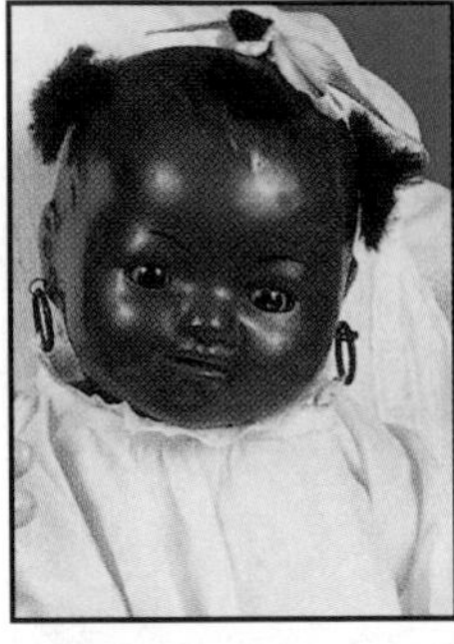

11" painted bisque-type composition baby, illegible mark on head, molded painted black hair, three short tufts of hair from holes in head, sleep eyes, open mouth, teeth, composition baby body, white baby dress, circa 1900+, $195.00. Courtesy McMasters Doll Auctions.

Stockinette, oil-painted features, excellent condition

16"	$1,800.00	$2,400.00
22"	$2,475.00	$3,300.00

COMPOSITION

The first price indicates doll with heavy crazing, perhaps nude; the second price indicates doll in excellent condition, may have very fine crazing, with original clothes. More for boxed, labeled, or exceptional quality.

Unmarked, or unknown company

16"	$200.00	$600.00

Borgfeldt, Geo

Tony Sarg Mammy with baby

18"	$150.00	$600.00

Effanbee

Baby Grumpy

10"	$75.00	$300.00
16"	$115.00	$475.00

Bubbles

Light crazing, original clothing, very good condition

17"	$110.00	$450.00
22"	$165.00	$700.00

Candy Kid

With original shorts, robe, and gloves

12"	$75.00	$300.00

Skippy, with original outfit

14"	$900.00*	

Horsman

12"	$475.00*	

Ideal

Marama, Shirley Temple body, from the movie, *Hurricane*

13"	$800.00*	

CHINA

Frozen Charlie/Charlotte

3"	$100.00	$135.00
6"	$190.00	$250.00
8 – 9"	$265.00	$350.00

Jointed at shoulder

3"	$150.00	$200.00
6"	$265.00	$350.00

HARD PLASTIC

Terri Lee, Patty-Jo

16"	$450.00	$600.00
16"	$1,904.00*	

PAPIER-MÂCHÉ

Leo Moss, late 1880s – early 1900s

Papier-mâché or composition head and lower limbs, molded hair or wig, inset glass eyes, closed mouth, ethnic features with full lips, excelsior filled brown twill body, more with tear on cheek

17"	$3,700.00	$5,500.00

* at auction

Papier-mâché with ethnic features

8"	$210.00	$275.00
17"	$625.00	$825.00

Bonnet Head

1860 – 1940+. Heads of various materials with painted molded bonnets, hats, or headgear.

All bisque

German, one-piece body and head, painted or glass eyes

5"	$135.00	$175.00
7"	$175.00	$235.00
8"	$215.00	$285.00
10"	$285.00	$375.00

Bisque

Painted eyes, bisque head, hat or bonnet

Five-piece papier-mâché, kid, or cloth body

7"	$75.00	$100.00
12"	$95.00	$125.00
20"	$225.00	$275.00

Glass eyss, bisque arms, jointed composition, kid or cloth body

7"	$150.00	$200.00
9"	$265.00	$350.00
12"	$365.00	$485.00
15"	$545.00	$725.00

Alt, Beck & Gottschalck

Glass eyes

18"	$2,907.00*

Painted eyes

18"	$1,430.00*

Handwerck, Max, WWI military figure, painted eyes, marked *"Elite"*

12"	$2,200.00*

Heubach, Gebruder, Baby Stuart, mold 7977

10"	$825.00	$1,100.00
15"	$1,125.00	$1,500.00

Japanese

8 – 9"	$55.00	$85.00
12"	$95.00	$135.00

Molded shirt or top

15"	$625.00	$825.00
21"	$1,015.00	$1,350.00

Recknagel, painted eyes

8"	$300.00	$450.00

* at auction

20" bisque, marked "Germany" with fancy gold bonnet with white ruffle, blue bow tie, blue bow on top, pale yellow hair, creamy pale flesh-tone face and shoulder plate, painted blue eyes, blushed cheeks, original leather body, stitched fingers, bisque legs with decorated shoes, circa 1860s+, $225.00. Courtesy Travis Cannon.

20" untinted bisque, marked "Germany," fancy golden color bonnet with white ruffles, blue bow tie, blue bow on top, pale yellow hair, creamy pale flesh-toned face and shoulder plate, painted blue eyes, blushed cheeks, original body, leather arms with stitched fingers, bisque legs with decorated shoes, circa 1860+, $225.00. Courtesy Travis Cannon.

Bonnet Head

Stone bisque

8 – 9"	$125.00	$165.00
12"	$170.00	$225.00
15"	$290.00	$385.00

Googly, see that section.

Borgfeldt & Co., George

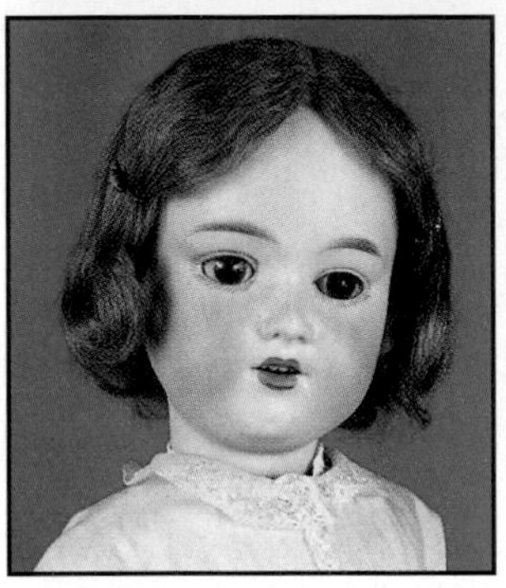

24" bisque girl, marked "Germany//G.B." on back of socket head, original mohair wig, brown sleep eyes, real and painted lashes, feathered brows, open mouth, four upper teeth, jointed wood and composition body, antique dropped waist dress, underclothing, replaced socks and old shoes, circa 1890+, $265.00. Courtesy McMasters Doll Auctions.

Ca. 1881 – 1930+, New York. Assembled and distributed dolls. Used dolls from many companies and employed designers such as Rose O'Neill, Grace Corry, Grace Storey Putnam, Joseph L. Kallus, Georgene Averill, and others. Konig & Wernicke made dolls for Borgfeldt.

Bisque Baby, 1910+

Five-piece bent-leg baby body, open mouth

10"	$225.00	$300.00
17"	$425.00	$575.00
27"	$675.00	$900.00+

Mold 251, 1915+

Made by Armand Marseille, character baby, closed mouth

17"	$3,100.00*

Baby BoKaye

Designed by Joseph Kallus, made by Alt, Beck & Gottschalk for Borgfelt, bisque molded hair, open mouth, glass eyes, cloth body, composition limbs, Mold 1394

11"	$1,700.00*	
15"	$1,725.00	$2,300.00
18"	$2,025.00	$2,700.00

Babykins, 1931

Made for Borgfeldt by Grace Storey Putnam, round face, glass eyes, pursed lips

14"	$735.00	$980.00
17"	$900.00	$1,190.00+

251
G.B.
Germany
A 1 M
DRMR 2498

Bisque Child, Mold 325, 327, 328, 329, or marked *"G.B.," "My Girlie," "Pansy"*

1910 – 1922, bisque head, fully jointed composition body, open mouth, good condition, and appropriately dressed

11"	$175.00	$250.00
14"	$200.00	$275.00
16"	$250.00	$375.00
19"	$350.00	$500.00
21"	$500.00	$650.00
24"	$425.00	$550.00

Composition

Hug Me, closed mouth, googly eyes

9"	$750.00*

* at auction

Boudoir Dolls

20" cloth unmarked doll, brunette human hair wig, felt face, painted features, blue side-glancing painted eyes, jointed arms and legs, black pantsuit with yellow trim and blouse, matching turban, circa 1920s – 1930s, $140.00. Courtesy Judy Domm.

Ca. 1915 – 1940. Bed dolls, originally used as decorations to sit on the bed, usually French, with extra long arms and legs, heads of cloth, composition, ceramics, wax, and suede, mohair or silk floss wigs, painted features, some with real lashes, cloth or composition bodies, dressed in fancy period costumes. Other manufacturers were Italian, British, or American.

First price is for doll in good condition, but with minor flaws; second price indicates doll in excellent condition, original clothes. Add more for boxed, labeled, or exceptional quality. Less for nude, flaking, cracked.

Standard quality, dressed		
16"	$95.00	$125.00
28"	$135.00	$175.00
32"	$175.00	$235.00
Excellent quality, with glass eyes		
15"	$225.00	$300.00
28"	$365.00	$475.00
32"	$75.00	$500.00
Lenci		
18 – 26"	$1,500.00	$2,250.00+
Smoker, cloth		
16"	$215.00	$285.00
25"	$375.00	$525.00
Composition		
25"	$185.00	$245.00
28"	$285.00	$375.00
Black		
	$450.00	$600.00+

Bru

Bru Jne. & Cie, ca. 1867 – 1899. Paris and Montreuil-sous-Bous French factories, eventually succeeded by Société Francaise de Fabrication de Bébé & Jouets (S.F.B.J.) 1899 – 1953. Bébés Bru with kid bodies are one of the most collectible dolls, highly sought after because of the fine quality of bisque, delicate coloring, and fine workmanship.

Identifying characteristics: Brus are made of pressed bisque and have a metal spring stringing mechanism in the neck. Add more for original clothes and rare body styles.

Bébé Breveté, ca. 1879 – 1880

Pressed bisque swivel head, shoulder plate, mohair or human hair wig, cork pate, paperweight eyes, multi-stroke eyebrows, closed mouth with space between lips, full cheeks, pierced ears, kid or wooden articulated bodies.

Bébé Breveté Marks:
"Bébé Breveté"
Head marked with size number only; kid body may have paper Bébé Breveté label.

* at auction

24" bisque, marked "Bru Jne//9" on back of head, "No. 10" on right shoulder, "Bru Jne" on left shoulder, replaced wig, large brown paperweight eyes, heavy feathered brows, painted upper/lower lashes, closed mouth with accented lips and molded tongue, pierced ears, kid body, bisque lower arms, wooden lower legs, new French-style plum and black outfit, black fur cape, hat, and muff, circa 1880 – 1891, $4,000.00. Courtesy McMasters Doll Auctions.

First price is for doll in good condition, but with some flaws; second price is for doll in excellent condition, appropriately dressed, add more for original clothes and marked shoes.

14"	$10,000.00	$13,750.00
19"	$14,500.00	$18,500.00
20"	$20,000.00* original dress, labeled body	

Bru Jne, 1880 – 1891

Pressed bisque swivel head, deep shoulder molded breastplate, mohair or human hair wig, cork pate, paperweight eyes, multi-stroke eyebrows, open/closed mouth with painted molded teeth, pierced ears, bisque lower arms, good condition, nicely dressed. Add more for original clothes and marked shoes.

12"	$8,750.00	$11,500.00
14"	$10,500.00	$14,000.00
17"	$12,750.00	$17,000.00
21"	$17,500.00*	
23"	$23,500.00*	
27"	$19,250.00	$25,500.00

Bru Jne R, 1891 – 1899

Pressed bisque swivel head, mohair or human hair wig, cork pate, paperweight eyes, multi-stroke eyebrows, open mouth with four or six upper teeth or closed mouth, pierced ears, articulated wood and composition body, good condition, nicely dressed. Add more for original clothes.

Bru Jne Marks: "BRE JNE," with size number on head, kid over wood body marked with rectangular paper label.

Bre Jne R. Marks: "BRU. JNE R." with size number on head, body stamped in red, "Bébé Bru," and size number.

Circle Dot Bébé Mark: Head marked dot within a circle or half circle.

Closed mouth

11"	$1,900.00	$2,500.00
14"	$2,900.00	$3,800.00
17"	$3,800.00	$5,000.00
19"	$4,300.00	$5,750.00
21"	$4,875.00	$6,500.00

Open mouth

12"	$1,100.00	$1,400.00
14"	$1,100.00	$1,500.00
16"	$1,600.00	$2,100.00
20"	$2,250.00	$3,000.00

Circle Dot Bébé, 1879 – 1883

Pressed bisque swivel head, deep shoulder molded breastplate, mohair or human hair wig, cork pate, paperweight eyes, multi-stroke eyebrows, open/closed mouth with painted molded teeth, pierced ears, gusseted kid body, bisque lower arms, good condition, nicely dressed. Add more for original clothes.

11"	$8,500.00	$11,500.00
14"	$10,500.00	$13,750.00
16"	$14,500.00*	
18"	$13,000.00	$18,000.00
23"	$16,500.00	$22,000.00
26"	$18,750.00	$25,000.00

* at auction

Fashion-type (poupee), 1867 – 1877+

Fashion-Type Mark: Marked "A" through "M," "11" to "28," indicating size numbers only

Swivel head of pressed bisque, bisque shoulder plate, metal spring stringing mechanism in neck, kid body, painted or glass eyes, pierced ears, cork pate, mohair wig. Add more for original clothes.

12"	$2,300.00	$3,050.00
15"	$2,500.00	$3,300.00

Fashion-type (poupee), Smiler 1873+

Pressed bisque swivel head, shoulder plate, articulated wood with metal spring stringing mechanism in neck, wood and kid or kid gusseted lady body, cork pate, mohair or human hair wig, glass paperweight eyes, pierced ears, closed smiling mouth, nicely dressed. Add more for original clothes.

Kid body, kid or bisque arms, allow more for wooden arms

13"	$2,250.00	$3,000.00
15"	$3,500.00*	
21"	$4,200.00	$5,600.00

Wood body

16"	$4,500.00	$6,000.00
18"	$5,500.00*	

Variants

Bébé Automate (breather, talker), 1892+

With key or lever in torso, activates talking and breathing mechanism

19"	$4,600.00*
24"	$17,000.00

Bébé Baiser (kiss thrower), 1892

With a simple pull-string mechanism, which allows doll's arm to raise and appear to throw kisses

11"	$4,100.00*

Bébé Gourmand (eater), 1880

Open mouth with tongue to take food, which fell into throat and out through bottom of feet, had shoes with specially designed hinged soles to take out food. Legs bisque from knees; used Breveté version

16"	$25,000.00+

Too few in database for reliable range.

Bébé Marchant (walker), 1892

Clockwork walking mechanism which allows head to move and talk, has articulated body with key in torso

17"	$6,800.00
21"	$7,400.00
25"	$9,500.00*

Bébé Modele, 1880+

Carved wooden body

19"	$19,000.00+

Too few in database for reliable range.

Bébé Têteur (nursing), 1879

Open mouth to insert bottle, usually with screw type key on back of head to allow the doll to drink

14"	$7,000.00
17"	$9,200.00
20"	$9,600.00

* at auction

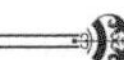

Bru

Accessories

Bru shoes (marked) $500.00 – 800.00+

Bye-Lo Baby

1922 – 1952. Designed by Grace Storey Putnam to represent a three-day-old baby, manufactured by various firms, such as Kestner; Alt, Beck & Gottschalck; Hertel & Schwab; and others; body made by K&K, a subsidiary of George Borgfeldt & Co., New York, the sole licensee. Composition Bye-Lo Babies made by Cameo Doll Company, and came in sizes 10", 12", 14", and 16½".

First price is for doll in good condition with some flaws; second price is for doll in excellent condition, nicely dressed, add more for tagged original clothes, labels, and pin-back button.

Mark:

© 1923 by
Grace S. Putnam
MADE IN GERMANY
7372 145

4" all-bisque, marked "Bye-Lo Baby//©//Germany//G.S. Putnam" on round label on chest, "20 – 10" on back and arms, "16 – 10" on legs, lightly blushed hair, stiff neck, painted blue eyes, softly blushed brows, closed mouth, all-bisque baby body jointed at shoulders and hips, dressed in diaper only, comes with wicker cradle and celluloid rattle, circa 1923, $350.00. Courtesy McMasters Doll Auctions.

All-Bisque

All-bisque versions made by J.D. Kestner were 4" to 8" and marked "G.S. Putnam" on back, with dark green sticker on chest that read "Bye-Lo Baby."

Painted eye		
4"	$300.00	$400.00
Glass eye		
5"	$400.00	$600.00

Bisque Head

Bisque head, painted molded hair, blue sleep eyes, closed mouth, flange neck, cloth baby-shaped ("frog") body, some stamped "Bye-Lo Baby," celluloid hands

Head circumference		
8"	$350.00	$475.00
10"	$375.00	$500.00
12"	$400.00	$525.00
15"	$525.00	$650.00
17"	$975.00	$1,200.00

Composition Head

Painted molded hair, sleep or painted eyes, closed mouth, cloth body. First price indicates doll with crazing, flaws; second price is for doll in excellent condition, with good color and original clothes, or appropriately dressed.

12"	$95.00	$375.00
16"	$150.00	$575.00

Celluloid

All-celluloid		
4"	$45.00	$165.00
6"	$100.00	$200.00
Celluloid head, cloth body		
12"	$175.00	$350.00
15"	$245.00	$465.00

Wax

Poured, sold NY boutique, 1925

14½" $2,100.00*

* at auction

VARIATIONS

Fly-Lo Baby, 1926 – 1930+

Ceramic, bisque, or composition head, glass or metal sleep eyes, painted molded hair, flange type neck, cloth body. Marked *"Copr. by//Grace S. Putnam."* Cloth bodies with celluloid hands, satin wings, in green, gold, or pink.

Bisque, less for ceramic

11"	$2,100.00*	
13"	$3,750.00	$5,000.00

Composition

14"	$300.00	$900.00

VINYL, CA. 1950S

Vinyl head, cloth stuffed limbs, marked *"Grace Storey Putnam"* on head.

16"	$65.00	$225.00

Two 20" bisque Grace S. Putnam Bye-Lo Babies, 17" circumference, marked "Copr by//Grace S. Putnam" on back of heads, "Bye-Lo Baby//Pat. Appl'd For//Copy by//Grace//Storey//Putnam" stamped on body," solid dome, lightly molded painted hair, sleep eyes, painted lashes, closed mouths, cloth body, "frog" legs, celluloid hands, white baby dresses, bonnets, booties, circa 1923, left has original button, $600.00; right, $400.00. Courtesy McMasters Doll Auctions.

Catterfelder Puppenfabrik

1894 – 1930+, Catterfeld, Thüringia, Germany. Made dolls using Kestner bisque head on composition bodies.

Mark:

1100

Catterfelder Puppenfabrik

2

BABY

1909 and after, wigged, or painted molded hair, bent-leg body, glass or painted eyes. Add more for toddler body

Mold 200 (similar to K*R #100), domed head, painted eyes, open/closed mouth, also black version

15"	$400.00	$500.00

Mold 201, domed head, painted eyes, closed mouth, more for toddler body

13"	$500.00	$750.00

Mold 207, character head, painted eyes, closed mouth

Mold 208, character baby or toddler with domed head or wigged, sleep eyes, open mouth, two teeth, movable tongue

Mold 209, character baby, movable tongue

Mold 218, character baby, domed head, sleep eyes, open mouth, movable tongue

Mold 262, character baby, sleep eyes, open mouth, movable tongue, only marked with mold number

Mold 263, character baby

14"	$485.00	$550.00

14" bisque girl, marked "3½//Catterfelder//Puppenfabrik//2/0" on head, blue glass eyes, open mouth with teeth, pierced ears, red human hair wig, blue dress with white trim, circa 1916, $500.00. Courtesy Elizabeth Surber.

* at auction

Catterfelder Puppenfabrik

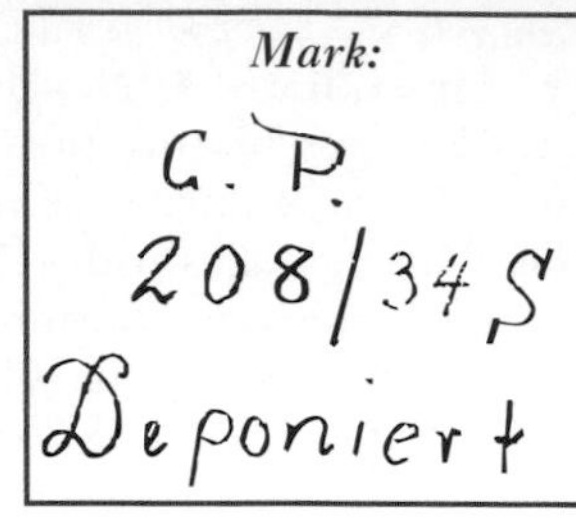

CHILD, DOLLY FACE

Open mouth, sleep eyes

18" $550.00 $750.00

CHILD, CHARACTER FACE

Composition body, open or open/closed mouth

Mold 210, painted eyes, closed mouth

14" $5,000.00*

Mold 212, wide open/closed laughing mouth, painted teeth and eyes

Mold 215, 219, character face, wig, painted eyes

215 15" $3,570.00*

Mold 220, character doll, sleeping eyes, open/closed mouth with two molded teeth

17" $7,300.00

Mold 264, character face, socket head, sleep eyes, open mouth

27" $550.00*

34" $1,100.00*

Mold 270, character face, socket head, open mouth, sleep eyes

Molds 1100, 1200, and 1357 were used for ball-jointed dolls

Celluloid

1869+, celluloid became more durable after 1905 and in 1910, when better production methods were found. Dolls were made in England, France, Japan, Germany, Poland, and the United States. When short hair became faddish, the demand for celluloid hair ornaments decreased and companies produced more dolls.

American manufacturers:

Averill, Bo-Peep (H. J. Brown), Du Pont Viscoloid Co., Horsman, Irwin, Marks Bros., Parsons-Jackson Co. (stork mark), Celluloid Novelty Co.

English manufacturers:

Wilson Doll Co. and Cascelloid Ltd. (Palitoy)

French manufacturers:

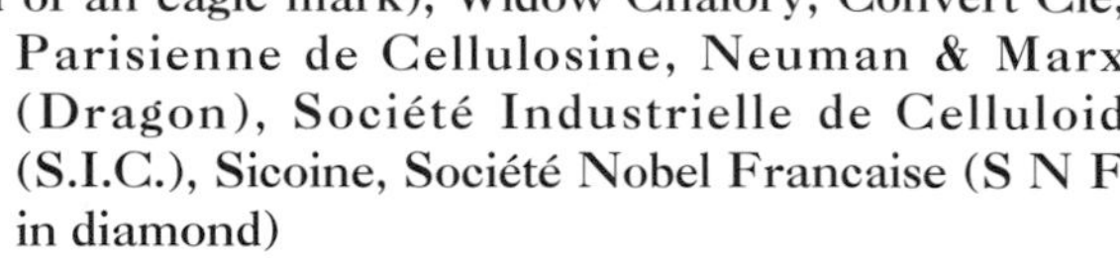

Peticolin (profile head of an eagle mark), Widow Chalory, Convert Cie, Parisienne de Cellulosine, Neuman & Marx (Dragon), Société Industrielle de Celluloid (S.I.C.), Sicoine, Société Nobel Francaise (S N F in diamond)

German manufacturers:

Bähr & Pröschild, Buschow & Beck (helmet), Minerva, Catterfelder Puppenfabrik Co., Cuno & Otto Dressel, E. Maar & Sohn (3 M), Emasco, Kämmer & Reinhardt, Kestner, König & Wernicke, A. Hagedorn & Co., Hermsdorfer Cellu-

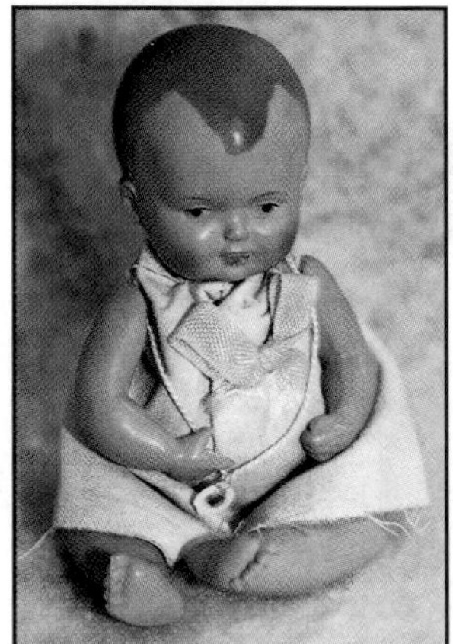

5" Rheinsche Gummi und Celluloid Fabrik Co. baby with turtle mark (in diamond), painted hair and eyes, jointed bent-leg baby body, baby dress, part of set — other in green jacket, matching hat, white pajama bottoms, in wooden crib with red wheels, circa 1926+, $300.00 for pair in baby bed. Courtesy Marilyn Cross.

loidwarenfabrik (lady bug), Dr. Paul Hunaeus, Kohn & Wengenroth, Rheinsche Gummi und Celluloid Fabrik Co. later known as Schildkrote (turtle mark), Max Rudolph, Bruno Schmidt, Franz Schmidt & Co., Schoberl & Becker (mermaid) who used *Cellba* for a tradename, Karl Standfuss, Albert Wacker

Japanese manufacturers:

Various firms may be marked Japan

Polish manufacturers:

Zast ("A.S.K." in triangle)

First price is for doll with some flaws or nude; second price is for doll in excellent condition. More for boxed set, labeled, or tagged.

All Celluloid

Baby

Painted eyes

4"	$15.00	$60.00
8"	$20.00	$80.00
12"	$45.00	$125.00
15"	$50.00	$180.00
19"	$70.00	$285.00

Glass eyes

13"	$45.00	$185.00
15"	$60.00	$250.00
19"	$100.00	$400.00

Child

Painted eyes, jointed shoulders, hips

5"	$10.00	$40.00
7"	$15.00	$60.00
11"	$30.00	$115.00
14"	$45.00	$185.00
19"	$100.00	$400.00

Jointed shoulders only

6"	$7.50	$30.00
8"	$13.00	$50.00
11"	$25.00	$95.00

Glass eyes

10"	$45.00	$125.00
14"	$60.00	$210.00
17"	$100.00	$400.00

21" Rheinsche Gummi und Celluloid Fabrik Co. boy, and 19" girl, boy marked with turtlemark in diamond "50/56" on head, turtlemark on back; girl marked with turtlemark in diamond "350/49" on head, turtlemark "49" on back, both with closed mouths, five-piece celluloid bodies, boy has molded painted hair, set blue eyes, girl has blond wig, blue sleep eyes, both in original clothing and celluloid shoes, circa 1950s, $140.00. Courtesy McMasters Doll Auctions.

16" toddler, marked "Schutz Marke//(heart)//42/ /Germany," molded painted hair, painted eyes, open/closed mouth, two teeth, fully jointed toddler body, diagonal hip joints, two-piece boys suit, argyle socks, imitation leather shoes, circa 1940s – 1950s, $295.00; 14" cloth Woolnough Winnie the Pooh, marked "Woolnough//.The-Pooh" on foot, gold mohair swivel head, glass eyes, black floss nose/mouth, applied ears, long curved arms, circa 1940s – 1950s, $645.00. Courtesy McMasters Doll Auctions.

* at auction

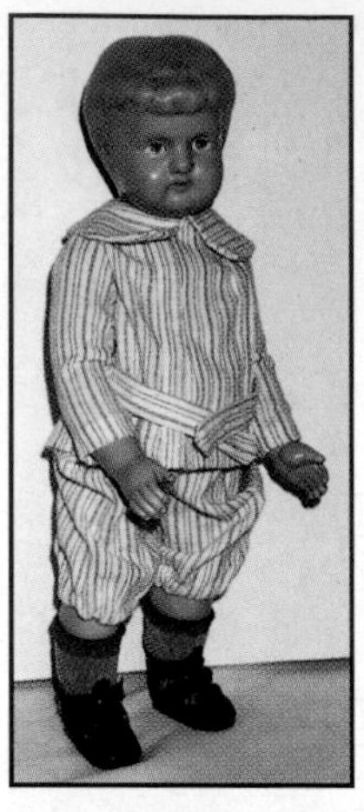

12½" Parsons-Jackson Co. toddler, marked "Parsons-Jackson Co.//Cleveland, Ohio," lower back marked "K K K," molded painted hair, painted blue eyes, spring-jointed celluloid body, re-dressed, circa 1913, $200.00. Courtesy Pat Graff.

14" mechanical child, marked "Made in Japan," molded painted hair, painted blue eyes, closed mouth, red metal shoes, keywind mechanism, legs and arms move, red and white print skirt and matching hat, white blouse, circa 1930s, $125.00. Courtesy Adrienne & Don Hagey.

Marked "France"

7"	$30.00	$130.00
9"	$45.00	$180.00
15"	$70.00	$280.00
18"	$140.00	$525.00

Molded-on clothes, jointed shoulders only

3"	$10.00	$40.00
5"	$15.00	$60.00
8"	$30.00	$110.00

Immobiles, no joints

3"	$4.00	$15.00
6"	$10.00	$45.00

Black, all-celluloid: see Black Dolls section.

Carnival Dolls

May have feathers glued to body/head, some have top hats

8"	$10.00	$40.00
12"	$20.00	$80.00
17"	$45.00	$175.00+

Shoulder head, 1900+

Germany, molded hair or wigged, open or closed mouth, kid or cloth bodies, may have arms of other materials

Painted eyes

13"	$85.00	$165.00
16"	$110.00	$215.00
18"	$180.00	$365.00

Glass eyes

15"	$110.00	$215.00
17"	$185.00	$375.00
20"	$240.00	$475.00

Averill, 1925

Bonnie Babe, cloth body, composition limbs

18" $1,300.00*

Bye-Lo Baby: see that section.

Celluloid/Plush, 1910+

Teddy bear body, can have half or full celluloid body with hood half head.

12"	$325.00	$650.00
14"	$400.00	$785.00
17"	$475.00	$925.00

Hitler youth group

8"	$90.00	$175.00

Hermsdorfer Celluloidwarenfabrik, 1923 – 1926, ladybug mark

17" $90.00* with neck repair

Heubach Köppelsdorf, Mold 399

11"	$18.00	$70.00

Jumeau, marked on head, jointed body

13"	$245.00	$485.00
16"	$295.00	$585.00

* at auction

Kämmer & Reinhardt (K*R) shoulder head

Mold 225, 255, ca. 1920

14"	$185.00	$370.00
17"	$250.00	$485.00

Kämmer & Reinhardt (K*R) socket head

Mold 406, ca. 1910, glass eyes, open mouth

Mold 700, child or baby, ca. 1910, painted eyes, open/closed mouth

14"	$250.00	$400.00

Mold 701, ca. 1910, character, painted eyes, closed mouth

14"	$500.00	$975.00

Mold 715, ca. 1912, character, sleep eyes, closed mouth

15"	$300.00	$685.00

Mold 717, ca. 1920, character, sleep eyes, closed mouth

15"	$325.00	$650.00
17"	$700.00* flapper body, boxed	

Mold 728, ca. 1928, character, sleep eyes, open mouth

16"	$250.00	$500.00
20"	$350.00	$700.00

All-celluloid toddler body

18"	$425.00*	

Kestner

Mold 203, character baby

12"	$450.00*	

Kewpie: see that section.

König & Wernicke (K&W)

Toddler

15"	$165.00	$325.00
19"	$250.00	$500.00

Max and Moritz, each

7"	$150.00	$300.00

Parsons-Jackson (stork mark)

Baby

12"	$100.00	$200.00
14"	$150.00	$285.00

Toddler

15"	$200.00	$385.00

Black

14"	$250.00	$485.00

Petitcolin

18"	$150.00	$250.00

Provencial costume

15"	$85.00	$165.00

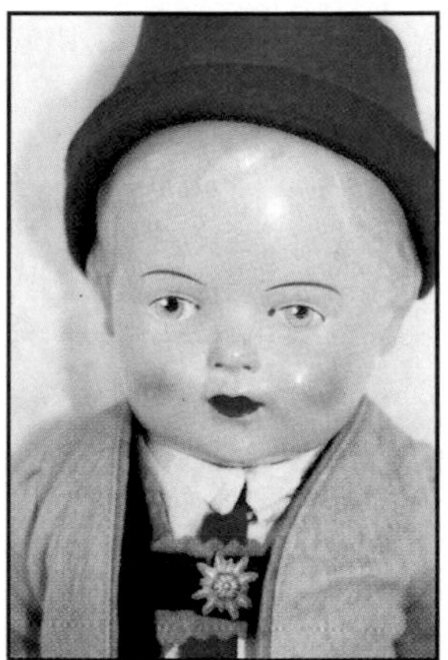

14" Rheinische Gummi und Celluloid Fabrik Co., with the turtle mark, molded painted hair, painted blue eyes, closed mouth, celluloid toddler body, original Tyrolean costume, green felt hat, circa 1950s, $150.00. Courtesy Marilyn Cross.

Century Doll Co.

1909 – 1930, New York City. Founded by Max Scheuer and sons; used bisque heads on many later dolls. In about 1929, Century merged with Domec to become the Doll Corporation of America. Some heads were made by Kestner, Herm Steiner, and other firms for Century.

* at auction

16" bisque Kestner Century Baby, marked "Century Doll Co.//Kestner Germany," solid dome flange head, blue sleep eyes, softly blushed brows, painted upper and lower lashes, open/closed mouth with two upper teeth, molded tongue, lightly molded painted hair, cloth body with non-working crier, composition hands, disk-jointed hips, possibly original pink organdy dress, matching bonnet, booties, three handmade dresses, sweater, matching bonnet, bib, two blankets, circa 1926, $500.00. Courtesy McMasters Doll Auctions.

Mark:

CENTURY DOLL C°.
Kestner Germany

Chuckles Mark on back:
"CHUCKLES//A CENTURY DOLL"

First price is for doll in good condition, but with flaws; second price for doll in excellent condition, with original clothes or appropriately dressed. More for boxed, tagged, or labeled exceptional doll.

Bisque

Baby, ca. 1926, by Kestner

Bisque head, molded painted hair, sleep eyes, open/closed mouth, cloth body

17"	$550.00	$750.00

Mold 275, solid dome, glass eyes, closed mouth, cloth body, composition limbs

14"	$715.00	$950.00

Child

Mold 285, by Kestner, bisque socket head, glass eyes, open mouth, wig, ball jointed body

23"	$575.00	$750.00

Composition

Chuckles, 1927 – 1929

Composition shoulder head, arms, and legs, cloth body with crier, open mouth, molded short hair, painted or sleep eyes, two upper teeth, dimples in cheeks. Came as a bent-leg baby or toddler.

16"	$85.00	$325.00

Mama dolls, ca. 1922+

Composition head, tin sleep eyes, cloth body, with crier, swing legs and arms of composition

16"	$70.00	$250.00
23"	$120.00	$475.00

Chase: see Cloth dolls.

China

Ca. 1840+. Most china shoulder head dolls were made in Germany by various firms. Prior to 1880, most china heads were pressed into the mold; later ones poured. Pre-1880, most china heads were sold separately with purchaser buying commercial body or making one at home. Original commercial costumes are rare; most clothing was homemade.

Early unusual features are glass eyes or eyes painted brown. After 1870, pierced ears and blond hair were found and, after 1880, more child chinas, with shorter hair and shorter necks were popular. Most common in this period were flat tops and low brows and the latter were made until the mid-1900s. Later innovations were china arms and legs with molded boots. Most heads are unmarked or with size or mold number only, usually on the back shoulder plate.

Identification tips: Hair styles, color, complexion tint, and body help date the doll.

First price indicates doll in good condition with some flaws; second price indicates doll in excellent condition with original or appropriate clothes. More for exceptional quality.

CHILD

Swivel neck, shoulder plate, may have china lower limbs

14"	$2,100.00	$2,850.00

Child or boy

Short black or blond hairdo, curly with exposed ears

13"	$195.00	$260.00
21"	$275.00	$365.00

French

Glass or painted eyes, open crown, cork pate, wig, kid body, china arms

14"	$2,350.00	$3,150.00
21"	$3,300.00*	

Japanese, ca. 1910 – 1920

Marked or unmarked, black or blond hair

10"	$110.00	$125.00
15"	$140.00	$190.00

K.P.M. (Königliche Porzellanmanufaktur Berlin), 1840s – 1850s+

Made china doll heads marked KPM inside shoulder plate.

Nymphenburg portrait, circa 1901

16"	$1,500.00*	

Pink tint lady w/Latchmann 1874 body

19"	$5,100.00*	

Brown hair man, 1869, marked

23"	$7,000.00*	

Pink tint Morning Glory, 1860s

24"	$10,250.00*	

Brown hair lady with bun, 1860s, marked

17"	$3,375.00	$4,500.00

Kling, marked with bell and number

13"	$265.00	$350.00
16"	$325.00	$435.00
22"	$400.00	$525.00

Man with curls

19"	$1,400.00	$1,850.00

30", pink tint, Covered Wagon hairstyle, unmarked, molded painted black hair with white center part, 11 vertical curls, painted brown eyes, red accent line, single stroke brows, closed mouth, cloth body with leather lower arms, joints at hips and knees made similar to fivet joints on kid bodies, rose print two-piece outfit, antique underclothing, socks and black leather shoes, circa 1840s, $1,350.00. Courtesy McMasters Doll Auctions.

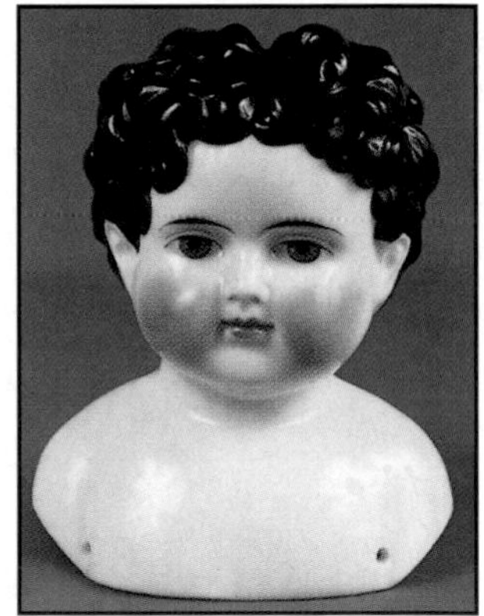

5", brown eyed, illegible marks inside rear of shoulder plate, molded painted black short curly hair, exposed ears, painted brown eyes, red accent line, single stroke brows, accented nostrils, closed mouth with accent line between lips, slightly turned head, circa 1860s, $325.00. Courtesy McMasters Doll Auctions.

* at auction

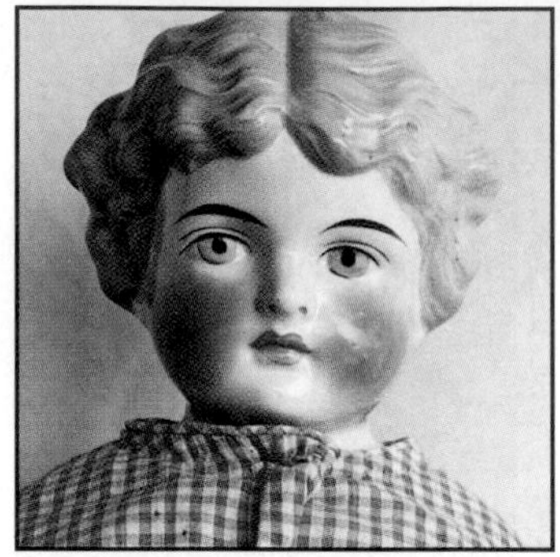

22" pink tinted C.F. Kling & Co. shoulder head, marked "180//(bell)//7," molded painted blond hair with loose waves and center part, painted blue eyes, molded eyelids, closed mouth, rosy cheeks, original cloth sawdust filled body, china lower arms and legs with decorated shoes, pink and white checked outfit, circa 1860+, $200.00. Courtesy Travis Cannon.

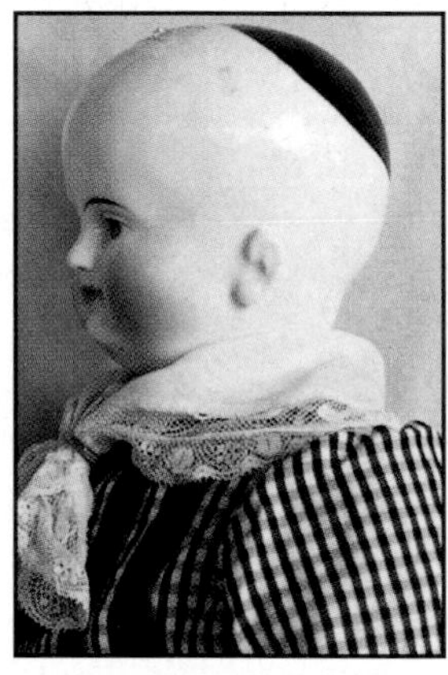

24" bald head, glazed china with black spot, formerly called Biedermier, round face with double chin, blue eyes with white highlights, molded ears, closed smiling mouth, human hair wig, china arms and feet, decorated boots, replaced cloth body, re-dressed, circa 1950s, $400.00. Courtesy Travis Cannon.

Man or boy, glass eyes

17"	$1,975.00	$2,650.00

Pierced ears, various common hair styles

14"	$365.00	$485.00
18"	$475.00	$635.00

Pierced ears, with elaborate hair style

17"	$1,164.00	$1,550.00+

Queen Victoria, young

16"	$1,195.00	$1,600.00
23"	$1,875.00	$2,500.00

Sophia Smith

Straight sausage curls ending in a ridge around head, rather than curved to head shape

19"	$985.00	$1,325.00+

Spill Curls

With or without headband, a lot of single curls across forehead, around back to ringlets in back

13"	$325.00	$435.00
20"	$550.00	$750.00
26"	$650.00	$850.00

Swivel neck, flange type

10"	$1,550.00	$2,100.00
13"	$2,025.00	$2,700.00

1840 Styles

China shoulder head with long neck, painted features, black or brown molded hair, may have exposed ears and pink complexion, with red-orange facial detail, may have bust modeling, cloth, leather, or wood body, nicely dressed, good condition.

Early marked china (Nuremberg, Rudolstadt)

14"	$1,700.00	$2,275.00+
17"	$2,125.00	$2,835.00

Brown hair, bun

16"	$2,650.00	$3,500.00

Boy, pressed china, smiling, side-parted brown hair

21"	$3,450.00	$4,600.00

Too few in database for reliable range.

Covered Wagon

Center part, combed back to form sausage curls

10"	$200.00	$275.00
14"	$300.00	$400.00
17"	$350.00	$475.00
20"	$425.00	$550.00
25"	$525.00	$700.00
31"	$650.00	$900.00+

Wood body

9"	$1,200.00	$1,575.00
13"	$1,600.00	$2,150.00
17"	$2,125.00	$2,850.00+

Pink tone, bun or coronet

15"	$2,100.00	$2,825.00

1850 Styles

China shoulder head, painted features, bald with black spot or molded black hair, may have pink complexion, cloth, leather, or wood body, china arms and legs, nicely dressed, good condition.

Alice in Wonderland, snood, headband

12"	$225.00	$300.00
16"	$300.00	$400.00
20"	$375.00	$500.00

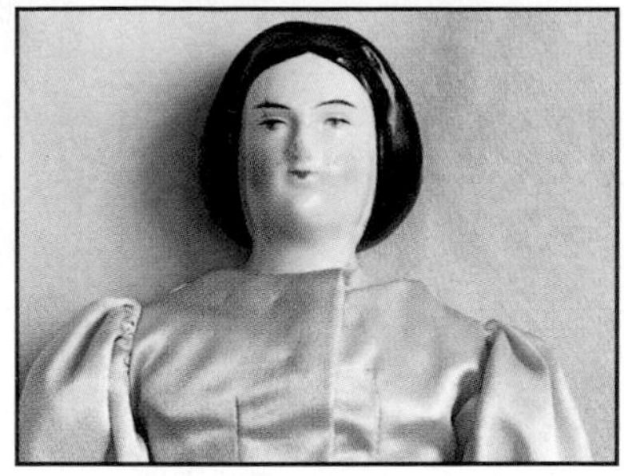

14" unmarked black-haired version of Mary Todd Lincoln, painted hair with headband and snood, blue painted eyes, original sawdust filled cloth body, china arms with spoon hands, china legs with brown shoes and blue bows as garters, antique dress, slip, petticoat, and bloomers, circa 1860s, $300.00. Courtesy Travis Cannon.

Bald head, glazed china with black spot

Formerly called Biedermeir, human hair or mohair wig

12"	$475.00	$650.00
14"	$550.00	$750.00
21"	$800.00	$1,050.00

Bald head, with black spot, glass eyes, wig

14"	$1,250.00	$1,675.00
21"	$1,975.00	$2,650.00

Frozen Charlies or Charlottes: See that section.

Greiner-type with painted black eyelashes, various hairdos

Painted eyes

15"	$500.00	$750.00
18"	$900.00	$1,200.00

Glass eyes

13"	$1,850.00	$2,450.00
16"	$2,400.00	$3,200.00
21"	$2,975.00	$4,000.00

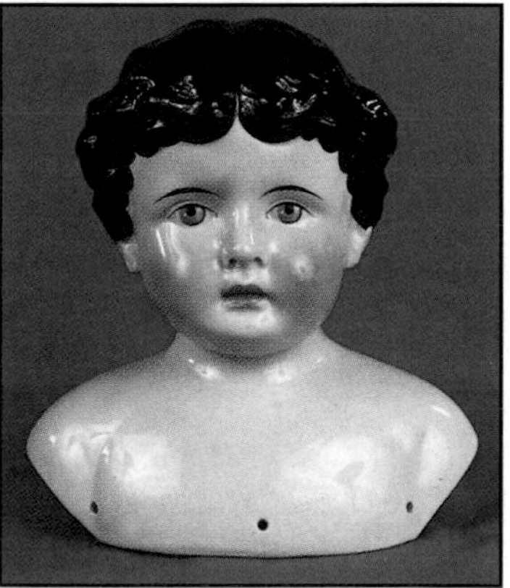

9" pink tint Kling mold 189 shoulder head, marked "Germany//189 14" on back of shoulder plate, painted blue eyes, black lash line, single stroke brows, closed mouth, molded painted black wavy hair with partially exposed ears, deeply molded shoulder plate with shoulder creases, three sew holes front and back, circa 1885, $240.00. Courtesy McMasters Doll Auctions.

1860 Styles

China shoulder head, center part, smooth black curls, painted features, seldom brushmarks or pink tones, all-cloth bodies or cloth with china arms and legs, may have leather arms. Decorated chinas with fancy hair styles embellished with flowers, ornaments, snoods, bands, ribbons, may have earrings.

Flat top Civil War

Black hair, center part, with flat top, curls on sides and back

7"	$75.00	$100.00
10"	$125.00	$165.00
14"	$180.00	$245.00
18"	$225.00	$300.00
22"	$280.00	$365.00
26"	$355.00	$475.00
34"	$465.00	$625.00

21" Alt, Beck & Gottschalck shoulderhead doll marked "1008//8," well molded blond curls, center part, painted blue eyes, molded eyelids, cloth body, legs, and hands with stitched fingers, antique satin dress, slip, bloomers, red lace-up corset, circa 1890s, $175.00. Courtesy Travis Cannon.

24" unmarked Jenny Lind, so-called because of her hairstyle, black painted molded hair puffed at the sides, drawn back into a braided bun, blue painted eyes, cloth body and legs, leather arms, antique cotton dress and white jacket, circa 1870s, $500.00. Courtesy Travis Cannon.

Swivel neck

15"	$750.00	$1,000.00

Molded necklace

21"	$525.00	$700.00+

Too few in database for reliable range.

Highbrow, curls, high forehead, round face

15"	$400.00	$535.00
19"	$525.00	$700.00
22"	$600.00	$800.00+

Grape Lady

With cluster of grape leaves and blue grapes

15"	$1,000.00	$1,325.00
18"	$1,500.00	$2,000.00

Mary Todd Lincoln

Black hair, gold snood, gold luster bows at ears

15"	$475.00	$625.00
21"	$650.00	$850.00

Blond with snood

21"	$1,300.00	$1,800.00

Too few in database for reliable range.

Morning Glory with flowers behind the ears

21"	$4,200.00	$5,600.00

Too few in database for reliable range.

1870 Styles

China shoulder head, poured, finely painted, well molded, black or blond hair, cloth or cloth and leather bodies, now with pink facial details instead of earlier red-orange.

14"	$185.00	$275.00
18"	$225.00	$325.00
24"	$300.00	$400.00

Adelina Patti

Hair pulled up and away, center part, brush-stroked at temples, partly exposed ears, ringlets across back of head

14"	$215.00	$325.00
20"	$400.00	$550.00
25"	$450.00	$600.00

Bangs, full cut across forehead, sometimes called Highland Mary

Black hair

14"	$225.00	$300.00
19"	$325.00	$425.00

Blond hair

14"	$265.00	$325.00

Jenny Lind, black hair pulled back into a bun or coronet

15"	$1,150.00	$1,550.00

1880 Styles

Now may also have many blond as well as black hair examples, more curls, and overall curls, narrower shoulders, fatter cheeks, irises outlined with black paint, may have bangs. China legs have fat calves and molded boots.

15"	$225.00	$325.00
22"	$375.00	$475.00
27"	$550.00	$675.00

Dolley Madison

Black molded hair, two separate clusters of curls on forehead, molded ribbon and bow across top, ears partially exposed, painted blue eyes, irises and eyes outlined with black, black eyebrows

14"	$275.00	$375.00
18"	$350.00	$475.00
24"	$475.00	$635.00

1890 Styles

Shorter fatter arms and legs, may have printed body with alphabet, emblems, flags

Common or low brow

Black or blond center part wavy hairdo that comes down low on forehead

10"	$85.00	$115.00
14"	$115.00	$155.00
19"	$150.00	$215.00
23"	$200.00	$300.00
27"	$250.00	$350.00
36"	$355.00	$475.00

With jewel necklace

14"	$175.00	$225.00
20"	$245.00	$325.00

Pet Names, ca. 1899 – 1930+

Agness, Bertha, Daisy, Dorothy, Edith, Esther, Ethel, Florence, Helen, Mabel, Marion, Pauline, and Ruth

Made for Butler Brothers by various German firms. China head and limbs on cloth body. Molded blouse marked in front with name in gold lettering, molded blond or black allover curls.

9"	$80.00	$110.00
14"	$165.00	$225.00
17"	$185.00	$275.00
21"	$250.00	$325.00

Cloth

First price is for doll in good condition, but with some wear or soiled; second price is for doll in very good condition and clean with good color. Exceptional doll may be more.

Alabama Indestructible Dolls

Ca. 1900 – 1925, Roanoke, Alabama. Ella Gauntt Smith, made all-cloth dolls with painted features; jointed at shoulders and hips. Head construction may include round "monk's cap" on top of head. Painted feet varied, some with stitched toes, but most had one-button slippers or low boots. Shoes were painted black, brown, pink, or blue; came in seven heights, from 12" to 27".

24" Saalfield Publishing Co. Golden Locks Girl, marked on fabric tied around middle "Copyright//1908//by the Saalfield Pub. Co.//Akron, Ohio," lithographed cloth, painted blond hair with red bow on side, painted smiling mouth, painted white ruffled blouse, red leather shoes, circa 1908, $165.00. Courtesy Elizabeth Fielding.

Art Fabric Mills Marks:
"ART FABRIC MILLS, NY, PAT. FEB. 13TH, 1900" on shoe or bottom of foot.

17" Dutch girl designed by Maud Tousey Fangel for Georgene Averill, printed features on stuffed cloth body, yellow painted hair with yellow yarn hair at bottom, wooden shoes, circa 1930s, $650.00. Courtesy Joan Sickler.

Alabama Indestructible Dolls Marks:
"MRS. S.S. SMITH//MANUFACTURER AND DEALER IN// THE ALABAMA INDESTRUCTIBLE DOLL// ROANOKE, ALA.// PATENTED//SEPT. 26, 1905."

Baby		
12"	$750.00	$1,500.00
22"	$3,600.00*	
Black Baby		
20"	$3,200.00	$6,200.00
Barefoot Baby, rare		
23"	$1,500.00	$3,000.00
Child		
15"	$800.00	$1,600.00
22"	$1,200.00	$2,400.00
Black Child		
18"	$3,100.00	$6,200.00
23"	$3,400.00	$6,800.00

ART FABRIC MILLS

1899 – 1910+, New York, New Haven, and London. Lithographed in color, made cloth cut-out dolls

Improved Life Size Doll, with printed underwear		
20"	$75.00	$275.00
30"	$100.00	$400.00
Punch and Judy, pair		
27"	$200.00	$800.00

BABYLAND RAG

1893 – 1928. A. Bruckner made Babyland Rag Dolls, with oil-painted or lithographed faces for E.I. Horsman.

Lithographed		
14½"	$175.00	$335.00
16½"	$200.00	$400.00
24"	$275.00	$550.00
Black		
14½"	$240.00	$480.00
16½"	$275.00	$550.00
24"	$400.00	$800.00
Molded painted faces		
13"	$350.00	$700.00
Flat painted faces		
16½"	$450.00	$900.00
Buster Brown		
17"	$300.00	$550.00
Black		
16½"	$490.00	$975.00
20"	$590.00	$1,180.00
30"	$885.00	$1,770.00

* at auction

Beecher, Julia Jones

Ca. 1893 – 1910, Elmira, New York. Wife of Congregational Church pastor Thomas K., sister-in-law of Harriet Beecher Stowe. Made Missionary Ragbabies, of old silk jersey underwear, with flat hand-painted and needle sculpted features. All proceeds used for missionary work. Sizes 16" to 23" and larger.

Missionary Ragbabies		
16"	$1,725.00	$3,450.00
23"	$2,500.00	$5,000.00
Black		
16"	$1,750.00	$3,500.00
23"	$2,800.00	$5,600.00
Beecher-type		
20"	$550.00	$2,200.00

17" Babyland Rag Buster Brown, by E.I. Horsman, face lithographed on flesh-colored sateen, blue eyes, blond wig, cloth body, red knicker suit, white collar and cuffs, black tam, black stockings, lace shoes, circa 1904 – 1920, $550.00. Courtesy Betty Warder.

Bing Art

Bing Werke, Germany, 1921 – 1932. All-cloth, felt or composition head with cloth body, molded face, oil-painted features, wigged or painted hair, pin-jointed cloth body, seams down front of legs, mitt hands.

Painted hair, cloth or felt, unmarked or "Bing" on bottom of foot

13"	$275.00	$550.00
15"	$325.00	$650.00
Wigged		
10"	$175.00	$350.00
16"	$325.00	$650.00
Composition head		
8"	$40.00	$145.00
12"	$45.00	$175.00
16"	$60.00	$225.00

Black, 1830+

Black cloth doll patterns in *American Girls Book*, describe how to make dolls of black silk or crepe, gingham or calico dress, apron, and cap. Beecher, Brückner, Chad Valley, Chase, and Lenci made black cloth dolls. Horsman advertised black cloth Topsy and Dinah cloth dolls, ca. 1912. Black cloth dolls were made ca. 1921 by Grace Cory for Century Doll Co. Many cloth dolls were homemade and one-of-a-kind. Patterns were available to make mammy doll toaster covers during the 1940s.

Mammy-style, with painted or embroidered features, 1910 – 1920s

12"	$65.00	$200.00
16"	$85.00	$285.00
1930s		
15"	$55.00	$165.00+

20" Beecher Missionary Baby, stockinette head, painted and needle sculptured features, applied ears, looped yarn hair, stockinette body jointed at shoulders, hips, and knees, antique white baby dress, knit wool knee high socks, crocheted bonnet. Julia Jones Beecher made Missionary Ragbabies of old silk jersey underwear and proceeds were used for missionary work, circa 1893 – 1910, $2,000.00. Courtesy McMasters Doll Auctions.

10" Norah Wellings Baby, mask face with painted blue side-glancing eyes, painted hair, closed mouth, velvet body, pink and white knitted jacket with hood, white dress with lace trim, pink knitted booties, circa 1930+, $300.00. Courtesy Sharon Kolibaba.

10½" Norah Wellings character with molded painted features, painted blue eyes, smiling mouth, red velvet pants for legs, matching red velvet hat, black sewn on shirt with white buttons and cuffs, black shoes for feet, circa 1926+, $100.00. Courtesy Stephanie Thomson.

Brownie Mark:
"Copyright 1892 by Palmer Cox" on right foot.

Brückner Mark:
On shoulder, "Pat'd July 8, 1901."

Chad Valley Marks:
Usually on sole of foot, "THE CHAD VALLEY CO. LTD//(BRITISH ROYAL COAT OF ARMS)//TOY-MAKER TO//H.M." or "HYGIENIC TOYS//MADE IN ENGLAND BY//CHAD VALLEY CO. LTD."

Topsy-Turvy

Cloth dolls with two heads, some with black doll under one skirt, which when turned over reveals white doll under other skirt.

Oil-painted		$200.00	$650.00
Printed		$150.00	$425.00
Brückner Topsy Turvy			
	13"	$250.00	$875.00
	13"	$950.00*	

Brownies by Palmer Cox

1892 – 1907. Printed cloth dolls based on copyrighted figures of Palmer Cox; 12 different figures, including Canadian, Chinaman, Dude, German, Highlander, Indian, Irishman, John Bull, Policeman, Sailor, Soldier, and Uncle Sam.

Single Doll		
	7½"	$100.00
Set of three, uncut		
	7½"	$350.00
Set of 12 with book		$825.00*

Brückner, Albert

Ca. 1901 – 1930+, Jersey City. Obtained patent for cloth dolls using printed, molded mask face. Made dolls for Horsman.

14"	$165.00	$325.00

Chad Valley

1917 – 1930+, Harbourne, England. Founded by Johnson Bros., made all types of cloth dolls, early ones had stockinette faces, later felt, with velvet body, jointed neck, shoulders, hips, glass or painted eyes, mohair wig. Mabel Lucie Atwell was an early designer.

Animals

Cat			
	12"	$75.00	$215.00+

Bonzo, cloth dog with painted eyes, almost closed and smile

4"	$65.00	$210.00
13"	$110.00	$415.00

* at auction

Bonzo, eyes open

5½"	$80.00	$275.00
14"	$150.00	$575.00

Dog, plush

12"	$65.00	$260.00

Characters

Captain Blye, Fisherman, Long John Silver, Pirate, Policeman, Train Conductor, etc.

Glass eyes

18"	$325.00	$1,000.00
20"	$375.00	$1,300.00

Painted eyes

18"	$225.00	$775.00
20"	$250.00	$875.00

Ghandi/India

13"	$175.00	$675.00

Rahmah-Jah

26"	$225.00	$900.00

Child

Glass eyes

14"	$165.00	$625.00
16"	$200.00	$725.00
18"	$225.00	$775.00

Painted eyes

9 – 10"	$40.00	$150.00
12"	$65.00	$225.00
15"	$115.00	$425.00
18"	$160.00	$625.00

Royal Family, all with glass eyes, 16" – 18"

Princess Alexandra

$400.00	$1,500.00

Prince Edward, Duke of Windsor

$400.00	$1,500.00

Princess Elizabeth

$425.00	$1,700.00

Princess Margaret Rose

$400.00	$1,500.00

Story Book Dolls

Dong Dell

14"	$125.00	$475.00

My Elizabeth, My Friend

14"	$165.00	$675.00

Snow White & Dwarfs

12", 6½"	$4,500.00*	

Red Riding Hood

14"	$125.00	$500.00

Martha Chase

Ca. 1889 – 1930+, Pawtucket, Rhode Island. Heads were made from stockinette

19" Georgene Averill Teardrop Baby, tagged "A Georgene Doll//Teardrop Baby//Georgene Novelties, Inc.//New York, N.Y.//Made in U.S.A.," painted blue eyes, open closed frowning mouth with painted teeth, one teardrop painted on cheek, white bonnet and baby dress, all original, circa 1940s, $225.00. Courtesy Joan Sickler.

10 – 12" Richard Krueger child, cloth mask face, yellow yarn hair, painted side-glancing blue eyes, closed smiling mouth, cloth body, green flower print outfit, yellow felt shovel, plastic watering can, circa 1930s – 1940s, $125.00. Courtesy Sandy Johnson Barts.

25" Martha Chase Hospital Mannequin, stamped "Chase//Hospital Doll//Trade Mark//Pawtucket, R.I.//Made in U.S.A." under left arm, oil painted stockinette head, painted hair, blue eyes, single stroke brows, thick upper lashes, pierced nostrils painted red, closed mouth, applied ears, cloth body tab jointed at shoulders, hips, stitch jointed at elbows, knees, smocked dotted Swiss dress, matching bonnet, holes from "shots" on rear torso, circa 1889+, $475.00. Courtesy McMasters Doll Auctions.

Martha Chase Marks:
"CHASE STOCKINET DOLL" on left leg or under left arm. Paper label, if there, reads "CHASE//HOSPITAL DOLL// TRADE MARK/ / PAWTUCKET, RI// MADE IN U.S.A."

covered masks reproduced from bisque dolls, heavily painted features including thick lashes, closed mouth, sometimes nostrils, painted textured hair, jointed shoulder, elbows, knees, and hips; later dolls only at shoulders and hips.

First price indicates doll in good condition with some flaws; second price indicates doll in excellent condition with original or appropriate clothes.

Baby

16"	$425.00	$575.00
19"	$495.00	$700.00
24"	$625.00	$875.00

Hospital-type

20"	$500.00*	
29"	$450.00	$575.00

Child

Molded bobbed hair

12"	$900.00	$1,200.00
16"	$1,200.00	$1,600.00
22"	$1,650.00	$2,200.00

Solid dome, simple painted hair

15"	$365.00	$485.00
18"	$475.00	$625.00

Unusual hairdo, molded bun

15"	$2,200.00*

Characters

Alice in Wonderland, character, circa 1905, set of six dolls, including Alice, Duchess, Tweedledee and Tweedledum, Mad Hatter, and Frog Footman, 12" tall excluding hats, hard pressed muslin, with oil painted features, stitch-jointed limbs, rare to find as a group

12"	$67,000.00* set of six

Benjamin Franklin

15"	$6,875.00*

Too few in database to give reliable range.

Later Dolls

Baby

14"	$150.00	$200.00
15"	$190.00	$250.00
19"	$300.00	$400.00

Child

15"	$215.00	$285.00
20"	$300.00	$400.00

* at auction

Columbian Doll, 1891+, Oswego, NY

Emma E. Adams made rag dolls, distributed by Marshall Field & Co., and won awards at the 1893 Chicago World Fair. Succeeded by her sister, Marietta Adams Ruttan. Cloth dolls had hand-painted features, stitched fingers and toes.

Columbian Doll Marks: "COLUMBIAN DOLL, EMMA E. ADAMS, OSWEGO, NY"

14"	$4,600.00*	
15"	$2,225.00	$4,500.00
19"	$2,850.00	$5,700.00
Columbian-type		
16"	$650.00	$1,280.00
22"	$1,100.00	$2,200.00

Comic Characters

15"	$150.00	$450.00

Deans Rag Book Co.

1905+, London. Subsidiary of Dean & Son, Ltd., a printing and publishing firm, used "A1" to signify quality, made Knockabout Toys, Tru-to-life, Evripoze, and others. An early designer was Hilda Cowham.

Child		
10"	$100.00	$285.00
16"	$185.00	$550.00
17"	$250.00	$750.00
Lithographed face		
9"	$30.00	$85.00
15"	$55.00	$165.00
16"	$75.00	$225.00
Mask face, velvet, with cloth body and limbs		
12"	$45.00	$125.00
18"	$90.00	$265.00
24"	$125.00	$385.00
30"	$155.00	$475.00
34"	$185.00	$565.00
40"	$225.00	$695.00
Golliwogs (English black character doll)		
13"	$85.00	$250.00
15"	$150.00	$450.00

Drayton, Grace

1909 – 1929, Philadelphia, Pennsylvania. An illustrator, her designs were used for cloth and other dolls. Made printed dolls with big eyes, flat faces.

Chocolate Drop, 1923, Averill Mfg. Corp., brown cloth, printed features, three tufts yarn hair

10"	$135.00	$400.00
14"	$185.00	$550.00

13" Georgene Averill Czechoslovakia, painted mask face, short curly hair, painted side-glancing eyes, painted upper lashes, closed smiling mouth, cloth body, green pants, yellow shirt, red vest with gold rick-rack trim, brown boots, all original and tagged, mint, circa 1940s, $200.00. *Courtesy Pat Graff.*

14" Mollye's Snow White by Mollye Goldman, velvet face with painted blue side-glancing eyes, black mohair wig, closed mouth, rosy cheeks, cloth body with tag sewn in leg seam, white dress with blue bodice and cuffs, circa 1950s, $250.00. *Courtesy Pat Graff.*

* at auction

4" thread wrapped Tiny Town Doll, red wig, painted features, pink thread-wrapped arms and legs, pink dress with blue trim, painted metal feet, in box that says "Tiny Town Dolls//San Francisco, California," circa 1940s, $25.00 – $75.00. Courtesy Barbara Hull.

Dolly Dingle, 1923, Averill Mfg. Corp., cloth, printed features, marked on torso

11"	$115.00	$385.00
15"	$165.00	$550.00

Double face or topsy turvy

15"	$190.00	$625.00

Hug Me Tight, 1916, Colonial Toy Mfg. Co., printed cloth with boy standing behind girl, one-piece

12"	$75.00	$250.00
16"	$150.00	$435.00

Kitty Puss, all-cloth, cat face, wired posable limbs and tail

15"	$135.00	$400.00

Peek-A-Boo, Horsman, 1913 – 1915, printed features

9"	$55.00	$175.00
12"	$75.00	$225.00
15"	$90.00	$275.00

Fangel, Maud Tousey

1920 – 1930+. Designed cloth dolls, with flat printed faces, some with mitten hands. Some had three-piece heads and feet.

Baby

13"	$150.00	$425.00
17"	$200.00	$600.00

Child, Peggy Ann, Rosy, Snooks, Sweets

9"	$100.00	$300.00
12"	$165.00	$500.00
15"	$200.00	$625.00
21"	$250.00	$800.00

Farnell, J.K. & Co. Ltd. 1871 – 1968, London

Baby

15"	$150.00	$475.00
18"	$200.00	$600.00

Child

10"	$85.00	$250.00
15"	$165.00	$500.00

King George VI, "H.M. The King"

Set of three

14"	$1,200.00*	

Palace Guard, "Beefeater"

15"	$225.00	$700.00

Gund

Circa 1898 on, CT & NY. Adolph Gund founded the company making stuffed toys and novelties. Later made teddy bears and dolls including Disney characters.

Character, cloth mask face, painted features

19"	$75.00	$300.00

*Gund Marks:
"A Gund Product, A Toy of Quality and Distinction."
From World War II on: Stylized "G" with rabbit ears and whiskers.
Mid 1960s – 1987: Bear's head above the letter "U"
From 1987 on: "GUND"*

*Kamkins Marks:
Heart-shaped sticker: KAMKINS// A DOLLY MADE TO LOVE // PATENTED//FROM// L.R. KAMPES//STUDIOS// ATLANTIC CITY//N.J.*

*Kreuger Marks:
"KRUEGER NY//REG. U.S. PAT. OFF/ /MADE IN U.S.A." on body or clothing seam.*

* at auction

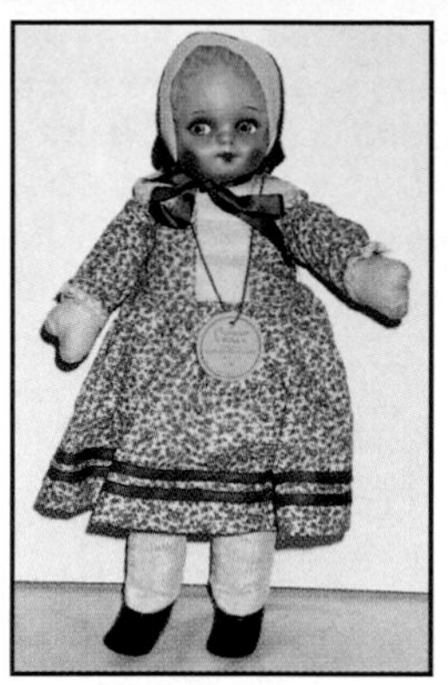

14" Silk Novelty Corp. character girl, "British #65" and "Character//Doll//created by//Silk Novelty Corp.//N.Y.C.//Made in U.S.A." on tag, blond yarn wig, cloth mask face, painted blue side-glancing eyes, closed mouth, rosy cheeks, cloth body, floral print dress with blue ribbon trim, matching bonnet, round paper tag, all original, mint-in-box, circa 1939, $175.00. Courtesy Pat Graff.

19" Kamkins made by Louise R. Kampes Studio, "Kamkins//A Dolly Made..//Patented By..//Atlantic City, N.J." (part of mark missing) stamped on back of head, faint heart on upper left torso, original mohair wig, oil painted face with blue eyes, closed mouth, cloth body tab jointed at shoulders, stitch jointed at hips, pink ruffled organdy dress, pink organdy bonnet, white lace-trimmed teddy, pink socks, white shoes, circa 1919 – 1928, $475.00. Courtesy McMasters Doll Auctions.

KAMKINS

1919 – 1928. Cloth doll made by Louise R. Kampes Studio, made by cottage industry workers at home. All-cloth, molded mask face, painted features, swivel head, jointed shoulders, hips, mohair wig

19"	$600.00	$1,600.00

KRUSE, KÄTHE: See that section.

KRUEGER, RICHARD

1917+. Made many cloth dolls, some of oilcloth or with oilcloth clothing, oil painted mask face, yarn or mohair wig, label.

Child

12"	$40.00	$135.00
16"	$60.00	$195.00
20"	$80.00	$240.00

Walt Disney and other characters

Dwarf

12½"	$65.00	$200.00

Pinocchio

16"	$125.00	$425.00+

LENCI: See that section.

MOLLY-'ES

1929 – 1930+. Trademark used by Mollye Goldman of International Doll Co. of Philadelphia, PA. Made clothes for cloth dolls with masked faces (and composition dolls), dressed in international costumes.

Child

13"	$90.00	$130.00
17"	$45.00	$150.00
22"	$65.00	$200.00
27"	$85.00	$275.00

Lady, in long dresses or gowns

16"	$55.00	$175.00
21"	$75.00	$250.00

Internationals

13"	$30.00	$90.00
15"	$45.00	$135.00
27"	$100.00	$300.00

14" Ronnaug Petterssen boy and girl, pressed felt swivel heads, painted brown eyes, single stroke brows, closed mouths, original mohair wigs, cloth bodies jointed at shoulders and hips, original elaborate embroidered Norwegian clothing by Ronnaug Petterssen of Oslo, original socks and shoes, girls dress tagged "Ronnaug Petterssen" on round label, circa 1934 – 1950s, $815.00 pair. *Courtesy McMasters Doll Auctions.*

13" Dollywood Studios Miss Catalina, unmarked except for printed ribbon around neck, large painted blue eyes, brown embroidered yarn hair on forehead, painted upper lashes and eyebrows, red heart-shaped lips, red dots for nose, gussets under arms, firmly stuffed body, blue soled shoes sewn on feet, thumbs on cloth mitt hands, wears floral print bathing suit and red bandana on head, seam open in crotch, circa 1946, $100.00. *Courtesy Carol Van Verst-Rugg.*

Princess, Thief of Bagdad

Blue painted Oriental-style eyes, harem outfit

14"	$100.00	$300.00

Peterssen, Ronnaug

1901 – 1980, Norway. Made cloth dolls, pressed felt head, usually painted side-glancing eyes, cloth bodies, intricate costumes, paper tags.

8"	$20.00	$40.00
14½"	$350.00	$700.00

Petzold, Dora

Germany, 1919 – 1930+. Made and dressed dolls, molded head, painted features, wig, stockinette body, sawdust filled, short torso, free-formed thumbs, stitched fingers, shaped legs.

18"	$200.00	$600.00
22"	$225.00	$775.00

Philadelphia Babies, J.B. Sheppard & Co.

Ca. 1860 – 1935. Shoulder head, stockinette rag doll with molded eyelids, stitched fingers and toes, painted features, sizes 18" – 22", also known as Sheppard Dolls.

18"	$1,200.00	$3,500.00
22"	$1,320.00	$4,000.00
21"	$4,730.00*	

Printed Cloth

Ca. 1876+. Made by various firms such as Arnold Print Works, North Adams, MA (some marked Cocheco Manufacturing Co.), Art Fabric Mills (see previous listing), and other lesser or unknown firms who printed fabric for making cutout dolls, to be sewn together and stuffed.

Aunt Jemima

Set of four dolls $100.00 each

Black Child

16"	$150.00	$425.00

Cream of Wheat, Rastus

16"	$40.00	$125.00

Printed underwear, Dolly Dear, Flaked Rice, Merry Marie, etc.

> *Printed Cloth Marks:*
> *Cloth label usually on sole of the foot reads: "MADE IN ENGLAND//BY//NORAH WELLINGS."*
>
> *Raynal Trademark: POUPEES RAYNAL.*
>
> *Santa Claus/St. Nicholas Marks: "Pat. Dec 18, 1886//Made by E.S.Peck NY"*

* at auction

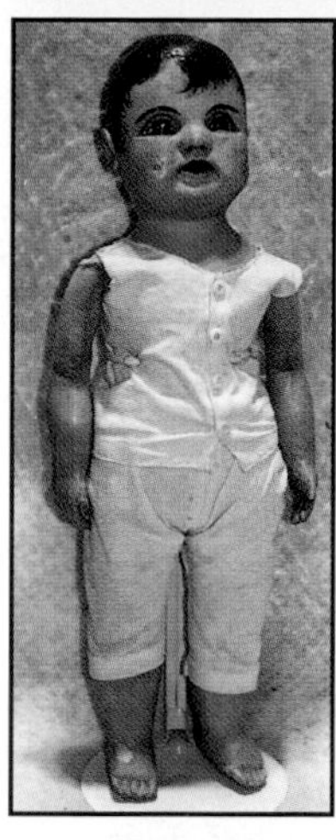

21" all-cloth J.B. Sheppard & Co. Philadelphia Baby, shoulder-type pressed oil painted head and lower limbs, brown hair, well molded and painted facial features, blue eyes, heavy molded eyelids, molded ears, stockinette body, closed mouth, stitched fingers and toes, white shirt and pants, circa 1900, $750.00. Courtesy Joan Radke.

Cut and sewn		
7"	$35.00	$95.00
16"	$60.00	$175.00
Uncut		
7"	$125.00	
19"	$275.00	

21" Hol-le Toy Co. Eloise, a literary character from book by Kay Thompson about little girl who lived at NY Plaza Hotel; tagged "Eloise©//© Eloise, Ltd.//Hol-le Toy Co.//NY/ /10//NY," painted features, rosy cheeks, yellow yarn hair, red bow on top of head, stuffed cloth body, original tagged blue skirt and white blouse, black oilcloth shoes, box says "ELOISE DOLL//Style 60/22E//Presented to Mfg. By Hol-Le Toy Co.//New York 10 NY," mint-in-box, circa 1955 – 1958+, $400.00. Courtesy Elizabeth Surber.

With printed clothing, ca. 1903

Cut and sewn		
14"	$65.00	$200.00
19"	$115.00	$325.00
Uncut		
Cocheco Darkey, 17" x 24"		$250.00*
Our Soldier Boys, 17" x 24"		$175.00*
Red Riding Hood, 18" x 24"		$300.00*

Santa Claus/St. Nicholas

Cut and sewn		
15"	$100.00	$325.00
Uncut		
15"	$600.00	

RALEIGH, JESSIE MCCUTCHEON

Shoebutton Sue, flat face, painted spit curls, mitten hands, sewn on red shoes, shown in 1921 Sears catalog

15" $1,900.00*

RAYNAL

1922 – 1930+, Paris. Edouard Raynal made dolls of felt, cloth, or with celluloid heads with widely spaced eyebrows. Dressed, some resemble Lenci, except fingers were together or their hands were of celluloid; marked *"Raynal"* on soles of shoes and/or pendant.

14½"	$125.00	$450.00
17"	$175.00	$600.00

ROLLINSON, GERTRUDE F.

Ca. 1916 – 1929 Holyoke, Massachusetts. Designed and made cloth dolls with molded faces treated to be washable, painted features. Dolls were produced by Utley Co., distributed by Borgfeldt, L. Wolf and Strobel, and Wilken.

Molded painted hair		
20"	$400.00	$1,150.00
Wigged, stamped body		
26"	$1,500.00	$2,000.00

*Rollinson Marks:
Cloth torso has diamond stamp, "ROLLINSON DOLL//HOLYOKE, MASS."*

*Russian Marks:
"MADE IN SOVIET UNION."*

*Izannah Walker Marks:
Some marked, "PATENTED NOV. 4, 1873."*

* at auction

Russian

Ca. 1920+. All-cloth, molded painted stockinette head, hands, in regional costumes

7"	$25.00	$70.00
15"	$50.00	$150.00
18"	$60.00	$180.00

Steiff: See that section.

Walker, Izannah

Ca. late 1800s, Central Fall, Rhode Island. Made cloth stockinette dolls, with pressed mask face, oil-painted features, applied ears, brush-stroked or corkscrew curls, stitched hands and feet, some with painted boots.

First price indicates very worn; second price for good condition. More for unusual hair style.

20"	$6,600.00*

Wellings, Norah

Victoria Toy Works, 1926 – 1930+, Wellington, Shropshire, England. Chief designer for Chad Valley, she and brother, Leonard, started their own factory. Made cloth dolls of velvet, velveteen, plush, and felt, specializing in sailor souvenir dolls for steamship lines. The line included children, adults, blacks, ethnic, and fantasy dolls.

6½" Raggedy Doodle, marked "Raggedy Doodle//U.S./ /Parachute//Trooper design//pat.," painted blue side-glancing eyes, yellow cloth eye mask, camoflauge body, sheepskin collar around neck, parachute, circa 1940s, $125.00. Courtesy Art Mock.

Baby

Molded face, oil painted features, some papier-mâché covered by stockinette, stitched hip and shoulder joints

15"	$200.00	$600.00
22"	$300.00	$900.00

Child, painted eyes

13"	$125.00	$400.00
18"	$200.00	$600.00
22"	$235.00	$700.00
28"	$300.00	$900.00

Glass eyes

15"	$175.00	$550.00
18"	$275.00	$850.00
22"	$425.00	$1,300.00

Characters in uniform, regional dress

Mounties, Policemen, others

13"	$125.00	$385.00
17"	$250.00	$750.00
24"	$350.00	$1,100.00

Black Islander or Scot

9"	$30.00	$90.00
13"	$61.00	$185.00
16"	$75.00	$225.00

Figures of various materials made especially for religious scenes such as the Christmas manger scene. Usually not jointed, some with elaborate costumes. Some early created

* at auction

Creche

figures were gesso over wood head and limbs, fabric covered bodies with wire frames, later figures made of terra-cotta or other materials. Some with inset eyes.

Man, wood shoulder head, glass eyes, wire body

8"	$115.00

Lady, carved shoulder head, glass eyes, wire body

10½"	$350.00

Lady, gesso over wood, glass eyes, wire frame

14½"	$500.00

Too few in database for reliable range.

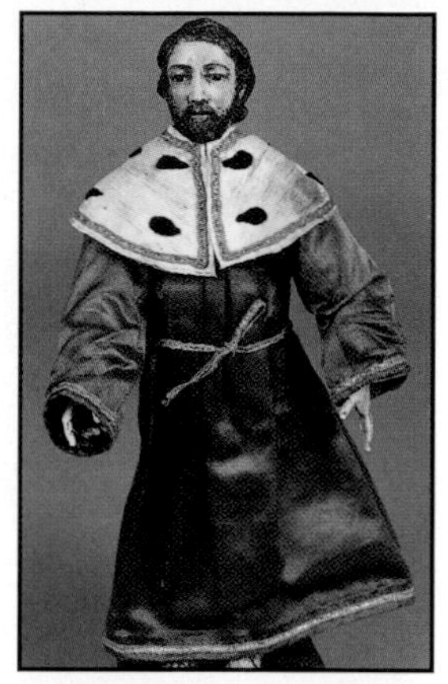

14½" composition glass-eyed man by unknown maker, painted molded hair, beard, molded fingers, molded painted bare feet, green robe, white collar with gold braid trim, $175.00. Courtesy McMasters Doll Auctions.

DEP

The "DEP" mark on the back of bisque heads stands for the French "Depose" or the German "Deponirt," which means registered claim. Some dolls made by Simon & Halbig have the "S&H" mark hidden above the "DEP" under the wig. Bisque head, swivel neck, appropriate wig, paperweight eyes, open or closed mouth, good condition, nicely dressed on French style wood and composition body.

First price is for doll in good condition, but with flaws; second price indicates doll in excellent condition with original or appropriate clothing.

Mark:
DEP
(Size number)

32" bisque child, marked "DEP," human hair wig, brown glass eyes, multi-stroke eyebrows, painted lashes above and below eyes, red accent dots inner eyes and nostrils, open mouth with upper teeth, re-dressed, $1,400.00. Courtesy McMasters Doll Auctions.

Closed mouth		
15"	$1,600.00	$2,150.00
19"	$1,900.00	$2,550.00
23"	$2,300.00	$3,150.00
Open mouth		
13"	$625.00	$825.00
18"	$875.00	$1,200.00
23"	$1,300.00	$1,725.00
28"	$1,900.00	$2,550.00

Dollhouse Dolls

Small dolls generally under 8" usually dressed as member of a family or in household-related occupations, often sold as a group. Made of any material, but usually bisque head by 1880.

First price is for doll in good condition, but with flaws; second price is for doll in excellent condition with original clothes.

3¼" bisque unknown German miniature woman dollhouse doll, blond floss hair, painted features, silk ribbon around wire body, white blouse, black skirt, circa 1930s, $65.00. Private collection.

Bisque

Adult, man or woman, painted eyes, molded hair, wig

6" $125.00 $225.00

Glass eyes, molded hair

6" $300.00 $400.00

Glass eyes, wigged

6" $400.00 $600.00

Black man or woman, molded hair, original clothes

6" $360.00 $475.00

Chauffeur, molded cap

6" $200.00 $285.00

Grandparents, or with molded on hats

6" $200.00 $265.00

Military man, mustache, original clothes

6" $435.00 $575.00+

With molded-on helmet

6" $525.00 $700.00+

Children, all-bisque

4" $40.00 $75.00

China

With early hairdo

4" $225.00 $300.00

With low brow or common hairdo, ca. 1900s+

4" $115.00 $150.00

Composition, Papier-mâché, plaster, etc.

5" $150.00 $225.00

Door of Hope

1901 – 1950, Shanghai, China. Cornelia Bonnell started the Door of Hope Mission in Shanghai, to help poor girls sold by families. As a means to learn sewing skills, the girls dressed carved pearwood heads from Ning-Po. The heads and hands were natural finish, stuffed cloth bodies were then dressed in correct representation for 26 different Chinese classes. Carved wooden head with cloth or wooden arms, original handmade costumes, in very good condition.

First price indicates doll with faded clothing or soiled; second price is for doll in excellent condition with clean, bright clothing. Exceptional dolls could be higher.

11" wooden Bride, painted black eyes, closed mouth, carved, painted hair, back view shows an elaborate all original bridal costume of China, cloth body, circa 1901 – 1950, $1,050.00. Courtesy McMasters Doll Auctions.

ADULT, MAN, WOMAN, OR CHILD

12"	$400.00	$600.00

Bride

11"	$1,050.00* elaborate dress	
12"	$350.00	$750.00

Groom

12"	$325.00	$650.00

Bridal couple in traditional dress

12"	$1,000.00*	

Amah with Baby

	$375.00	$750.00

Manchu Lady or Man

12"	$500.00	$1,000.00

Mourner

	$325.00	$750.00

Policeman

	$325.00	$750.00

Schoolchild

8"	$200.00	$550.00

Dressel, Cuno & Otto

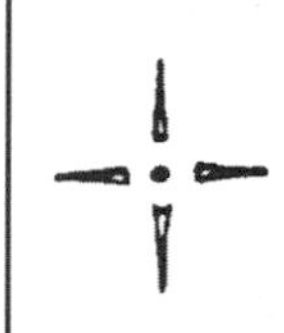

Ca. 1873 – 1945, Sonnenberg, Thüringia, Germany. The Dressels made wood, wax, wax-over-composition, papier-mâché, composition, china, and bisque heads for their dolls which they produced, distributed, and exported. Their bisque heads were made by Simon & Halbig, Armand Marseille, Ernst Heubach, Schoenau & Hoffmeister, and others.

BISQUE

Baby, 1910+, character face

Marked "C.O.D.," more for toddler body

13"	$225.00	$325.00
15"	$375.00	$475.00
19"	$450.00	$600.00

Child, mold 1912, open mouth, jointed composition body

14"	$225.00	$300.00
18"	$400.00	$475.00
22"	$450.00	$550.00

Child, character face, closed mouth, jointed child or toddler body

Painted eyes

13"	$1,200.00	$1,625.00
14"	$1,850.00	$2,450.00
18"	$2,300.00	$3,000.00

Glass eyes

15"	$2,000.00	$2,500.00
18"	$2,400.00	$3,400.00
23"	$3,100.00*	

17" bisque socket head, brown glass eyes, real lashes, painted lashes above and below eyes, human hair wig, feathered brows, pierced ears, open mouth with upper teeth, marked 1349, $425.00. Courtesy McMasters Doll Auctions.

12" character socket head, painted eyebrows, black eyeliner above eye, human hair wig, painted eyes, closed pouty mouth, regional dress, $800.00. Courtesy McMasters Doll Auctions.

Heubach•Köppelsdorf
Jutta-Baby
Dressel
Germany
1922
10

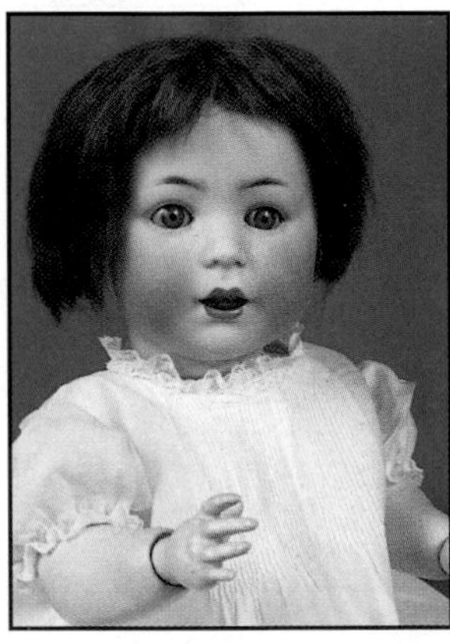

19" bisque mold 1914 Jutta, blue sleep eyes, open mouth with two upper teeth, mohair wig, bent-leg composition body with jointed wrists, small hairline, circa 1914, $375.00. Courtesy McMasters Doll Auctions.

Flapper

Closed mouth, five-piece composition body with thin legs and high heel feet, painted on hose up entire leg, mold 1469

12"	$2,500.00	$3,300.00
15"	$2,850.00	$3,800.00

Jutta

Baby open mouth, bent-leg body

16"	$400.00	$550.00
21"	$600.00	$800.00
24"	$1,000.00	$1,400.00

Child, 1906 – 1921, open mouth, marked with "Jutta" or "S&H" mold 1914, 1348, 1349, etc.

14"	$300.00	$425.00
17"	$450.00	$625.00
21"	$575.00	$775.00
25"	$800.00	$950.00
29"	$900.00	$1,300.00

Toddler

8"	$400.00	$550.00
15"	$500.00	$675.00
18"	$700.00	$950.00
23"	$975.00	$1,400.00
27"	$1,400.00	$1,900.00

Portrait dolls, 1896+

Bisque head, glass eyes, composition body

Admiral Dewey, Admiral Byrd

8"	$500.00	$700.00
12"	$1,150.00	$1,550.00

Buffalo Bill

10"	$575.00	$765.00

Farmer, Old Rip, Witch

8"	$475.00	$650.00
12"	$600.00	$800.00

Father Christmas

12"	$1,125.00	$1,500.00+

Uncle Sam

13"	$750.00	$1,000.00
15½"	$900.00	$1,400.00

COMPOSITION

Holz-Masse, 1875+. Composition shoulder head, wigged or molded hair, painted or glass eyes, cloth body, composition limbs, molded on boots

Molded hair

13"	$65.00	$250.00
17"	$100.00	$400.00
24"	$150.00	$565.00

* at auction

Wigged

16"	$80.00	$325.00
24"	$110.00	$425.00

E.D.

E.D. Bébés marked with *"E.D."* and a size number and the word *"Depose"* were made by Etienne Denamure, ca. 1890s, Paris. Other marked E.D. dolls with no Depose mark were made when Emile Douillet was director of Jumeau and should be priced as Jumeau Tête face dolls. Denamure had no relationship with the Jumeau firm and his dolls do not have the spiral spring used to attach heads used by Jumeau. Denamure bébés have straighter eyebrows, the eyes slightly more recessed, large lips, and lesser quality bisque. Smaller sizes of Denamure E.D. bébés may not have the Depose mark.

First price is for doll in good condition, but with some flaws; second price indicates doll in excellent condition, more for original costumes.

19" bisque Bebe, marked "E 8 D//Depose" on back of head, original human hair wig, set brown eyes, painted lashes, heavy feathered brows, open mouth, six upper teeth, pierced ears, wood and composition French body with jointed wrists, lace and ribbon trimmed factory chemise, pink crocheted socks, old cloth shoes, circa 1890s, $800.00. Courtesy McMasters Doll Auctions.

Closed mouth		
11"	$2,800.00*	
18"	$2,200.00	$2,900.00
25"	$3,000.00	$4,000.00
27"	$3,100.00	$4,250.00
Open mouth		
14"	$975.00	$1,300.00
16"	$1,200.00	$1,600.00
21"	$1,650.00	$2,200.00
27"	$2,100.00	$2,700.00

Eden Bébé

1890 – 1899, made by Fleischmann & Bloedel; 1899 – 1953, made by Société Francaise de Fabrication de Bébés & Jouet (S.F.B.J.). Dolls had bisque heads, jointed composition bodies.

First price indicates doll in good condition, but with some flaws; second price indicates doll in excellent condition, with original clothes or appropriately dressed.

Closed mouth, pale bisque		
15"	$1,800.00	$2,375.00
18"	$2,200.00	$2,800.00
22"	$2,300.00	$3,100.00
Closed mouth, high color, five-piece body		
13"	$900.00	$1,200.00
19"	$1,200.00	$1,600.00
22"	$1,450.00	$1,950.00

Mark:
EDEN BEBE
PARIS

* at auction

Open mouth

15"	$1,125.00	$1,500.00
18"	$1,250.00	$1,800.00
26"	$1,950.00	$2,600.00

Walking, Talking, Kissing

Jointed body, walker mechanism, head turns, arm throws a kiss, heads by Simon & Halbig using mold 1039 and others, bodies assembled by Fleischmann & Bloedel. Price for perfect working doll.

21"	$1,600.00

Too few in database for reliable range.

Fashion Type

19" unmarked Francois Gaultier fashion-type, bisque shoulder plate, blue paperweight eyes, blond human hair wig, closed mouth, pierced ears, kid body including hands, appropriately dressed in a gold dress, circa 1870s, $3,000.00. Courtesy Sharon Kolibaba.

COLLECTOR ALERT:
French fashion types are being reproduced, made to look old. Collectors need to arm themselves with knowledge before purchasing. Quality information is available to members and research is continuing by the United Federation of Doll Clubs (UFDC). See Collectors' Network at back of book.

French Poupee, 1869+. Glass eyes, doll modeled as an adult lady, with bisque shoulder head, stationary or swivel neck, closed mouth, earrings, kid or kid and cloth body, nicely dressed, good condition. Add more for original clothing, jointed body, black, or exceptional doll.

UNMARKED OR WITH SIZE NUMBER ONLY

12"	$1,250.00	$1,700.00
14"	$1,500.00	$2,000.00
16"	$1,600.00	$2,200.00
18"	$1,900.00	$2,500.00
21"	$2,600.00	$3,400.00
27"	$3,500.00	$4,600.00

Painted eyes, kid body

14"	$1,900.00

Wooden articulated body, glass eyes

13"	$2,300.00	$2,900.00
15"	$3,500.00	$4,500.00
18"	$4,000.00	$5,000.00

BARROIS (E.B.): See that category.

BLACK: See that section.

26" bisque F.G. Gaultier Fashion-type Poupee, marked "9" head and right shoulder, "F.G." on left shoulder, coarse human hair wig, blue paperweight eyes, closed mouth, pierced ears, kid fashion body with gussets at elbows, hips, knees, individually stitched fingers and toes, factory chemise with lace and ribbon trim, antique teal blue outfit with skirt, black velvet trimmed jacket, quilted cape, stockings, leather high button boots, circa 1860+, $2,300.00. Courtesy McMasters Doll Auctions.

Bru: See that category.

F. G.: See Gaultier and Gesland categories.

Fortune Teller Dolls

Fashion-type head with swivel neck, glass or painted eyes, kid body, skirt made to hold many paper "fortunes." Exceptional doll may be more.

Closed mouth		
15"	$3,450.00	$4,100.00+
Open mouth		
18"	$2,150.00	$3,100.00+
China, glazed finish, 1870 – 1880 hairstyle		
15"	$1,250.00	$1,700.00
Wood, German, with tuck comb		
16"	$2,300.00	$3,100.00

Gesland, marked F.G.: See that category.

Huret: See that category.

Jumeau: See that category.

Rohmer: See that category.

Accessories

Dress	$500.00+
Shoes marked by maker	$500.00+
unmarked	$250.00
Trunk	$250.00+
Wig	$250.00+

Frozen Charlie or Charlotte

Ca. 1860 – 1940. Most porcelain factories made all-china dolls in one-piece molds with molded or painted black or blond hair, and usually undressed. Sometimes called Bathing Dolls, they were dubbed "Frozen Charlotte" from a song about a girl who went dancing dressed lightly and froze in the snow. Victorians found them immoral. They range in size from under 1" to over 19". Some were reproduced in Germany in the 1970s. Allow more for pink tint, extra decoration, or hairdo.

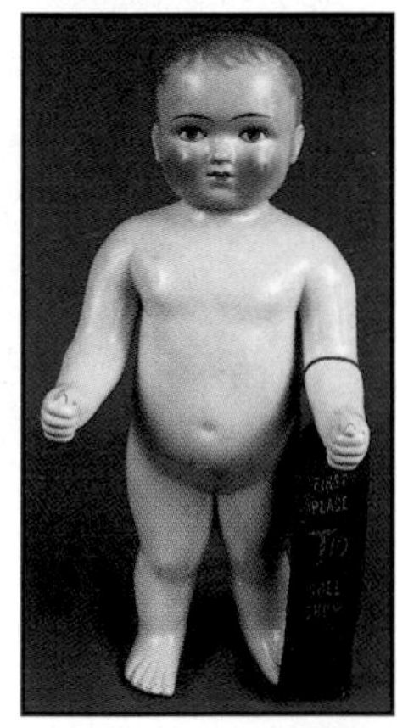

16" pink tint china, unmarked, lightly molded and painted blonde hair with brush strokes around face, painted blue eyes, lightly feathered brows, closed mouth, rosy cheeks, untinted china body with arms out in front, hands closed, nails outlined on fingers and toes, circa 1880s – 1890s, $425.00. Courtesy McMasters Doll Auctions.

All china		
2"	$50.00	$70.00
5"	$85.00	$135.00
7"	$150.00	$200.00
9"	$200.00	$275.00
15"	$350.00	$500.00
Black china		
6"	$200.00	$275.00
8"	$275.00	$375.00
Blonde hair, flesh tones head and neck		
9"	$300.00	$400.00
12"	$400.00	$550.00
Jointed shoulders		
5"	$110.00	$145.00
7"	$165.00	$225.00

Frozen Charlie or Charlotte

Molded boots		
4"	$150.00	$225.00
8"	$200.00	$275.00
Molded clothes or hats		
3"	$185.00	$250.00
6"	$225.00	$300.00
8"	$325.00	$425.00
Pink tint, hairdo		
3"	$200.00	$225.00
5"	$300.00	$375.00
Pink tint, bonnet-head		
3"	$350.00	$400.00
5"	$425.00	$500.00
Stone bisque, molded hair, one piece		
3"	$20.00	$25.00
6"	$30.00	$40.00
Parian-type, ca. 1860		
5"	$150.00	$200.00
7"	$200.00	$250.00

Fulper Pottery Co.

1918 – 1921, Flemington, NJ. Made dolls with bisque heads and all-bisque dolls. Sold dolls to Amberg, Colonial Toy Mfg. Co., and Horsman. "M.S." monogram stood for Martin Stangl, in charge of production.

Mark:

First price indicates doll in good condition, with flaws; second price indicates doll in excellent condition with original or appropriate clothes.

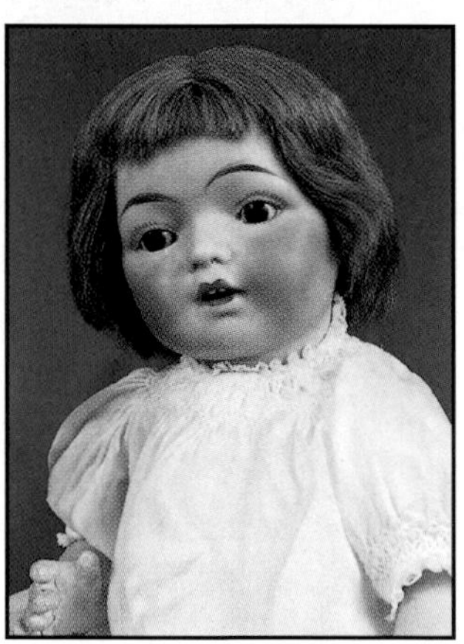

19" bisque Baby, marked "Fulper (vertical)//Made In//USA//A 11" on back of socket head, antique human hair wig, set brown eyes, painted lashes, feathered brows, open mouth, two upper teeth, composition baby body, old white baby dress with smocking around top, underclothing, socks, and shoes, circa 1918 – 1921, $225.00. Courtesy McMasters Doll Auctions.

Baby, bisque socket head, glass eyes, open mouth, teeth, mohair wig, bent-leg body

15"	$300.00	$500.00
19"	$500.00	$700.00

Toddler, straight-leg body

16"	$700.00*	
19"	$625.00	$825.00+
25"	$750.00	$1,000.00+

Gans & Seyfarth

Mark:
Germany
G. & S
3

1908 – 1922, Waltershausen, Germany. Made bisque dolls; had a patent for flirty and googly eyes. Partners separated in 1922, Otto Gans opened his own factory.

Baby, bent-leg baby, original clothes or appropriately dressed

16"	$375.00	$525.00
20"	$465.00	$625.00
25"	$575.00	$775.00

Child, open mouth, composition body, original clothes, or appropriately dressed

15"	$375.00	$500.00
21"	$500.00	$675.00
28"	$675.00	$900.00

Gaultier, Francois

1860 – 1899. After 1899, became part of S.F.B.J., located near Paris, they made bisque doll heads and parts for lady dolls and for bébés and sold to many French makers of dolls. Also made all-bisque dolls marked "F.G."

Bébé (child), "F.G." in block letters, 1879 – 1887

Closed mouth, excellent quality bisque socket head, glass eyes, pierced ears, cork pate

Composition and wood body with straight wrists

11"	$2,975.00	$3,950.00
13"	$3,100.00	$4,100.00
15"	$3,200.00	$4,250.00
20"	$4,200.00	$5,600.00
28"	$5,000.00	$7,000.00

Kid body, may have bisque forearms

15"	$3,300.00	$4,450.00
17"	$3,800.00	$5,000.00

16" bisque, marked "F.G.(in scroll)" on back of head, "Jumeau/ /Medaille d'Or//Paris" on lower back, replaced wig, large blue paperweight eyes, painted lashes, feathered brows, closed mouth, pierced ears, jointed wood and composition body, straight wrists, separate balls at hips and knees, white eyelet dress with new ribbons and lace, new socks and underclothing, old shoes, arms replaced, circa 1887 – 1900, $500.00. Courtesy McMasters Doll Auctions.

Bébé (child), "F.G." in scroll letters, 1887 – 1900

Composition body, closed mouth

12"	$1,000.00	$1,325.00
17"	$2,225.00	$2,975.00
23"	$2,825.00	$3,725.00
28"	$3,400.00	$4,500.00

With padded metal armature

40"	$26,000.00*	

Composition body, open mouth

11"	$475.00	$650.00
16"	$1,350.00	$1,800.00
24"	$2,000.00	$2,700.00

Fashion-type Poupee, 1860+

Marked one-piece shoulder head, glass eyes, kid body

13½"	$1,125.00	$1,500.00
17"	$1,800.00	$2,400.00
21"	$2,000.00	$2,750.00

Mark:

* at auction

Gaultier, Francois

Painted eyes

11"	$600.00	$800.00
15"	$825.00	$1,100.00
18½"	$1,025.00	$1,350.00

F.G., marked swivel head on bisque shoulder plate, kid body

May have bisque lower arms, glass eyes

12"	$1,200.00	$1,600.00
15"	$1,700.00	$2,250.00
18½"	$2,100.00	$2,775.00
20½"	$2,300.00	$3,100.00

Wood body

16"	$3,000.00	$4,250.00
20"	$3,600.00	$4,750.00

Gesland

1860 – 1928, Paris. Made, repaired, exported, and distributed dolls, patented a doll body, used heads from Francois Gaultier with "F.G." block or scroll mark. Gesland's unusual body had metal articulated armature covered with padding and stockinette, with bisque or wood/composition hands and legs.

Bébé (child) on marked Gesland body

Closed mouth

12"	$2,900.00	$3,900.00
17"	$3,375.00	$4,500.00
20"	$3,750.00	$5,000.00

Poupee (fashion-type) Gesland

Stockinette covered metal articulated fashion-type body, bisque lower arms and legs

17"	$4,400.00	$5,800.00
23"	$4,950.00	$6,600.00

Gladdie

1928 – 1930+. Tradename of doll designed by Helen Webster Jensen, made in Germany, body made by K&K, for Borgfeldt. Flange heads made of bisque and biscaloid, an imitation bisque and composition that is like a terra-cotta ceramic, with molded hair, glass or painted eyes, open/closed mouth with two upper teeth and laughing expression, composition arms, lower legs, cloth torso, some with crier and upper legs. Mark *"copyriht"* (misspelled).

Mark:

Gladdie
Copyriht By
Helen W. Jensen
Germany

21" biscaloid Gladdie, marked "Gladdie//Copyright by//Helen W. Jensen//Germany//1005/1420-4" on back of head, molded painted hair under original human hair wig, set blue eyes, feathered brows, open/closed laughing mouth, molded tongue and teeth, cloth body, composition arms and legs, red dress with white pique collar and cuffs, underclothing, socks, black center snap shoes, circa 1928 – 1930, $415.00. Courtesy McMasters Doll Auctions.

* at auction

Biscaloid ceramic head

18"	$875.00	$1,150.00
20"	$1,050.00	$1,400.00

Bisque head

14"	$2,000.00	$3,000.00
18"	$3,000.00	$4,000.00
21"	$4,000.00	$5,000.00

Goebel, Wm. and F. & W.

1871 – 1930 on, Oeslau, Bavaria. Made porcelain and glazed china dolls, as well as bathing dolls, Kewpie-types, and others. Earlier mark was triangle with half moon.

First price indicates doll in good condition, with flaws; second price indicates doll in excellent condition, appropriately dressed or original clothes. Exceptional dolls may be more.

16" porcelain Hummel Girl, On Holiday, heavily molded painted hair, painted brown eyes, open/closed mouth, painted teeth, red skirt and scarf, black and white top, carrying basket of flowers, hang tag, gold tag, circa 1970+, $200.00. Courtesy Glenda Koenigsberg.

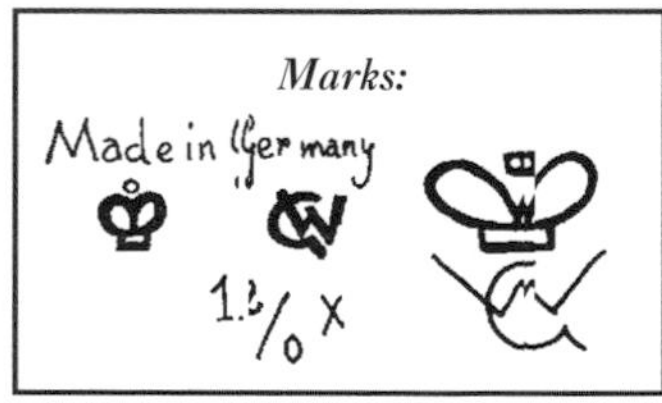

Character Baby, after 1909

Open mouth, sleep eyes, five-piece bent-leg baby body

15"	$365.00	$485.00
18"	$450.00	$600.00

Toddler body

14"	$425.00	$550.00
16"	$750.00*	

Child, 1895

Socket head, open mouth, composition body, sleep or set eyes

12"	$200.00	$275.00
17"	$350.00	$475.00

Child, open/closed mouth, shoulder plate, wig, molded teeth, kid body, bisque hands

17"	$625.00	$850.00
20"	$850.00	$1,150.00

Character Child, after 1909

Mold 120, circa 1921 – 1932, sleep eyes, open mouth, wigged

12½"	$300.00	$400.00
18"	$550.00* all original	

Mold 521, circa 1921 – 1932, sleep eyes, open mouth, wigged

19"	$400.00	$525.00

Molded hair

May have flowers or ribbons, painted features, with five-piece papier-mâché body

6"	$200.00	$275.00
9"	$325.00	$425.00

Molded on bonnet or hat

Closed mouth, five-piece papier-mâché body, painted features

9"	$400.00	$525.00

* at auction

7" bisque Armand Marseille mold 323 Googly, marked "Germany//323//A. 11/0 M." on back of head, mohair wig, large brown sleep eyes to side, painted lashes, closed smiling mouth, five-piece composition body, molded painted socks and shoes, original print dress with lace trim, panties, and white hat, all original, circa 1914 – 1925, $750.00. Courtesy McMasters Doll Auctions.

(Side-glancing eyes.) Sometimes round, painted, glass, tin, or celluloid, when they move to side they are called flirty eyes. Popular 1900 – 1925, most doll manufacturers made dolls with googly eyes. With painted eyes, they could be painted looking to side or straight ahead; with inserted eyes, the same head can be found with and without flirty eyes. May have closed smiling mouth, composition or papier-mâché body, molded hair or wigged.

First price is for doll in good condition with flaws; second price is for doll in excellent condition appropriately dressed or with original clothes. Exceptional dolls can be more.

All-Bisque

Jointed shoulders, hips, molded shoes, socks

Rigid neck, glass eyes

3"	$200.00	$275.00
5"	$365.00	$465.00

Painted eyes

3"	$150.00	$200.00
5"	$275.00	$350.00

Swivel neck, glass eyes

5"	$425.00	$575.00
7"	$650.00	$875.00

With jointed elbows, knees

5"	$1,725.00	$2,300.00
7"	$2,100.00	$2,750.00

Too few in database for reliable range.

Marked by maker, Mold 189, 292

5"	$675.00	$900.00
7"	$1,050.00	$1,400.00

Mold 217, 330, 501

5"	$500.00	$650.00
7"	$600.00	$800.00

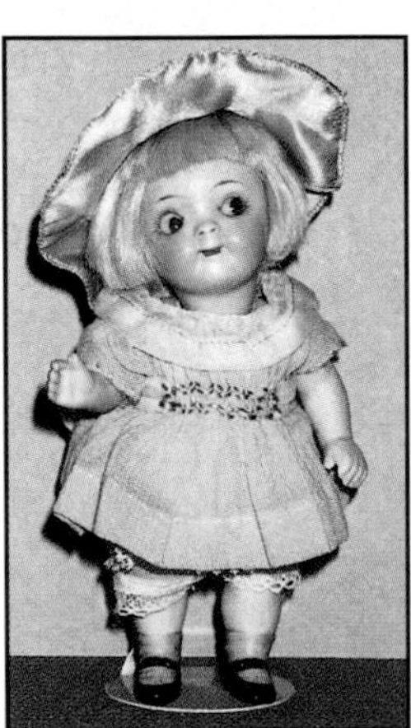

4½" all-bisque Kestner mold 189 Googly, side-glancing sleep eyes, blond wig, closed smiling mouth, painted blue socks and black shoes, dress with matching hat, circa 1910, $850.00. Courtesy Betty Fronefield.

Bähr & Pröschild

Marked *"B.P."*

Mold 686, ca. 1914, Baby

16"	$1,400.00	$1,800.00

Mold 686, Child

13"	$1,850.00	$2,500.00
15"	$2,250.00	$3,000.00

Demacol, made for Dennis Malley & Co., London

Bisque socket head, closed watermelon mouth, mohair wig, five-piece composition toddler body

13"	$900.00	$1,200.00

Handwerck, Max

Marked *"Elite,"* bisque socket head, molded helmet

14"	$1,350.00	$1,800.00

7½" bisque Recknagel Googly, marked "R-45-A," socket head, painted side-glancing eyes, closed painted mouth, molded painted blond hair, five-piece composition and papier-mâché body, blue/white striped shirt trimmed in lace, matching beret, blue short pants, white socks and shoes, circa 1914, $4,500.00. *Courtesy Elizabeth Fielding.*

Hertel Schwab & Co.

Mold 163, ca. 1914, solid dome, molded hair, closed smiling mouth

16"	$6,250.00*	

Mold 165, ca. 1914, socket head, closed smiling mouth

11"	$4,100.00*	

Mold 172, ca. 1914, solid dome, closed smiling mouth

15"	$4,875.00	$6,500.00

Mold 173, ca. 1914, solid dome, closed smiling mouth

16"	$4,350.00	$5,800.00

Mold 222, Our Fairy, all-bisque, wigged, glass eyes

7"	$800.00	$1,200.00
11"	$1,350.00	$1,800.00

Painted eyes, molded hair

8"	$650.00	$850.00
12"	$1,100.00	$1,500.00

Heubach, Ernst

Mold 262, ca. 1914, "EH" painted eyes, closed mouth

Mold 264, ca. 1914, character

8"	$300.00	$400.00
11"	$375.00	$500.00

Mold 291, ca. 1915, "EH" glass eyes, closed mouth

9"	$1,000.00	$1,350.00

Mold 318, ca. 1920, "EH" character, closed mouth

11"	$960.00	$1,285.00
14"	$1,500.00	$2,050.00

Mold 319, ca. 1920, "EH" character, tearful features

8"	$425.00	$575.00
11"	$850.00	$1,150.00

Mold 322, ca. 1915, character, closed smiling mouth

10"	$600.00	$750.00

Mold 417, Mold 419

8"	$400.00	$525.00
13"	$900.00	$1,200.00

Heubach, Gebrüder

9"	$600.00	$800.00
13"	$1,250.00	$1,700.00

Mold 8556

15"	$6,000.00	$8,000.00

Mold 8676

9"	$650.00	$850.00
11"	$775.00	$1,050.00

Mold 8723, 8995, glass eyes

13"	$2,200.00	$2,900.00

* at auction

*14" bisque Kammer & Reinhardt mold 131 Googly, with large blue glass side-glancing eyes, closed mouth and impish grin, original mohair wig, fully jointed wood and composition toddler body with diagonal hip joints, dressed in old white dress with blue flowers, old underclothing, new crocheted socks, old shoes, marked "K*R//Simon Halbig//131" circa 1914, $12,000.00.* Courtesy McMasters Doll Auctions.

13" bisque Kestner socket head, mold # 221, large glass eyes, multi-stroke eyebrows, painted lashes above eyes, blond mohair wig, closed smiling mouth, $5,000.00 – 7,500.00. Courtesy McMasters Doll Auctions.

Mold 8764, Einco, shoulder head, closed mouth

For Eisenmann & Co.

20" $11,500.00*

Too few in database for reliable range.

Mold 9056, ca. 1914, square, painted eyes closed mouth

8" $525.00 $700.00

Too few in database for reliable range.

Mold 9573

7" $675.00 $900.00

11" $1,050.00 $1,400.00

Mold 9578, Mold 11173, "Tiss Me," ca. 1914

10" $1,050.00 $1,450.00

14" $1,200.00 $1,600.00

Mold 9743

Sitting, open/closed mouth, top-knot, star shaped hands

7" $450.00 $600.00

Winker, one eye painted closed

14" $1,600.00 $2,200.00

Too few in database for reliable range.

Kämmer & Reinhardt

Mold 131, ca. 1914, *"S&H//K*R,"* closed mouth

8½" $6,500.00* toddler

13" $4,150.00 $5,500.00

15" $12,000.00*

Kestner

Mold 221, ca. 1913, *"JDK ges. gesch"*

Character, smiling closed mouth

12" $4,500.00 $6,000.00

14" $12,000.00*

Kley & Hahn

Mold 180, ca. 1915

"K&H" by Hertel Schwab & Co. for Kley & Hahn, character, laughing open/closed mouth

15" $2,025.00 $2,700.00

17" $2,550.00 $3,400.00

Lenci: See Lenci category.

Limbach

Marked with crown and cloverleaf, socket head, large round glass eyes, pug nose, closed smiling mouth

7" $1,600.00*

10" $1,050.00 $1,400.00

Armand Marseille

Mold 200, *"AM 243,"* ca. 1911, closed mouth

8" $950.00 $1,250.00

11" $1,500.00 $2,000.00

* at auction

Mold 210, *"AM 243,"* ca. 1911, character, solid-dome head, painted eyes, closed mouth

8"	$1,400.00	$1,850.00
13"	$1,000.00*	

Mold 223, ca. 1913, character, closed mouth

7"	$550.00	$750.00
11"	$725.00	$950.00

Mold 240, ca. 1914, "AM" dome, painted, closed mouth

10"	$2,400.00*	
11"	$2,100.00	$2,600.00

Mold 252, *"AM 248,"* ca. 1912

Solid dome, molded tuft, painted eyes, closed mouth

9"	$1,350.00	$1,800.00
12"	$1,800.00	$2,400.00

Mold 253, *"AM Nobbikid Reg. U.S. Pat. 066 Germany,"* ca. 1925

6"	$750.00	$1,000.00
10"	$2,000.00	$2,500.00

Mold 254, ca. 1912, *"AM"* dome, painted eyes, closed mouth

10"	$500.00	$700.00

Mold 310, *"AM//JUST ME"* 1929, for Geo. Borgfeldt

9"	$1,200.00	$1,600.00
12"	$1,350.00	$1,800.00

Mold 310, painted bisque, *"Just Me"*

9"	$525.00	$700.00
12"	$825.00	$1,100.00

Mold 320, *"AM 255,"* ca. 1913, dome, painted eyes

9"	$575.00	$775.00
12"	$700.00	$950.00

Mold 322, *"AM,"* ca. 1914, dome, painted eyes

8"	$500.00	$675.00
11"	$650.00	$875.00

Mold 323, 1914 – 1925, glass eyes, also composition

7½"	$800.00	$1,100.00
11"	$1,200.00	$1,500.00
13"	$1,700.00	$2,200.00

Mold 323, baby body

13"	$800.00	$1,200.00

Mold 323, painted bisque baby

11"	$350.00	$475.00

Mold 325, ca. 1915, character, closed mouth

9"	$548.00	$725.00
14"	$750.00	$1,000.00

16" composition Freundlich unmarked GooGoo Eye Dutch boy, molded painted curly hair, cloth body and hands, red Dutch-style pants, checked shirt, cap, wooden shoes, circa 1937, $100.00. Courtesy Thelma Williams.

* at auction

P.M. Porzellanfabrik Mengersgereuth, ca. 1926

"PM" character, closed mouth. Previously thought to be made by Otto Reinecke.

Mold 950

11"	$3,100.00*	
15"	$1,200.00	$1,600.00

S.F.B.J.

Mold 245

8"	$1,800.00*	

Fully jointed body

10"	$1,200.00	$1,600.00

Steiner, Herm

Mold 133, ca. 1920, "HS" closed mouth, papier-mâché body

8"	$500.00	$700.00

Strobel & Wilkin

Mold 405

7"	$1,400.00*	

Walter & Sohn

Mold 208, ca. 1920, "W&S" closed mouth

Five-piece papier-mâché body, painted socks/shoes

8"	$525.00	$700.00
9"	$1,100.00*	

Greiner, Ludwig

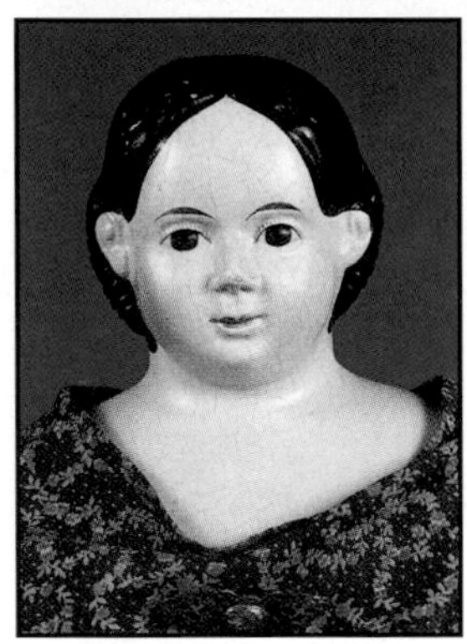

37" papier-mâché shoulder head, marked "Greiner's//Improved//Patent Heads//Pat. March 30, 1859" on rear shoulder plate label, molded painted hair with 11 vertical curls, exposed ears, painted upper lashes and dark eyes with blue around pupil, single stroke brows, closed mouth, cloth body, imitation leather lower arms and shoes, new calico dress, old underclothing, stockings, circa 1858+, $450.00. Courtesy McMasters Doll Auctions.

1840 – 1874. Succeeded by sons, 1890 – 1900, Philadelphia, PA. Papier-mâché shoulder head dolls, with molded hair, painted/glass eyes, usually made up to be large dolls, 13" – 38".

Mark:
GREINER'S
PATENT HEADS.
No. 0.
Pat. March 30th, '58.

First price is for doll in good condition with flaws; second price is for doll in excellent condition appropriately dressed or with original clothes.

With "1858" label

17"	$400.00	$750.00
23"	$600.00	$1,100.00
25"	$2,500.00*	
30"	$750.00	$1,400.00
35"	$750.00	$1,500.00
38"	$1,000.00	$2,000.00

Glass eyes

21"	$1,200.00	$1,600.00
26"	$1,725.00	$2,300.00

With "1872" label

18"	$225.00	$450.00
21"	$265.00	$525.00
26"	$425.00	$750.00
30"	$550.00	$1,075.00

Pre Greiner, unmarked, ca. 1850

Papier-mâché shoulder head, cloth body, leather, wood, or cloth limbs, painted hair, black glass eyes, no pupils

18"	$900.00	$1,200.00
26"	$1,200.00	$1,600.00
30"	$1,425.00	$1,900.00
Painted eyes		
18"	$335.00	$450.00
26"	$475.00	$650.00
30"	$600.00	$825.00

Handwerck, Heinrich

1876 – 1930, Gotha, Germany. Made composition dolls' bodies, sent Handwerck molds to Simon & Halbig to make bisque heads. Trademarks included an eight-point star with French or German wording, a shield, and "Bébé Cosmopolite," "Bébé de Reclame," and "Bébé Superior." Sold dolls through Gimbels, Macy's, Montgomery Wards, and others. Bodies marked *"Handwerk"* in red on lower back torso. Patented a straight wrist body.

Mark:

119 - 13
HANDWERCK
5
Germany

First price is for doll in good condition with flaws; second price is for doll in excellent condition appropriately dressed or with original clothes. Exceptional dolls may be more.

29" bisque girl, marked "14.//Germany//99//DEP//Handwerck//5½" on head, "Heinrich Handwerck//Germany" stamped on lower back, "5½//H.H. (in heart)" on bottom of shoes, original blond curly mohair wig, blue sleep eyes, painted lashes, open mouth, four upper teeth, pierced ears, jointed wood and composition Handwerck body, pale blue organdy lace trimmed dress, blue taffeta lining, underpants, original socks, blue satin shoes, circa 1900, $1,000.00. Courtesy McMasters Doll Auctions.

Child with Molds 69, 89, 99, or No Mold Number

Open mouth, sleep or set eyes, ball-jointed body, bisque socket head, pierced ears, appropriate wig, nicely dressed

11"	$400.00	$500.00
15"	$450.00	$575.00
21"	$550.00	$700.00
24"	$575.00	$775.00
28"	$775.00	$1,050.00
30"	$825.00	$1,100.00
32"	$1,000.00	$1,400.00
36"	$1,500.00	$2,000.00
40"	$2,500.00	$3,100.00

Child with mold number, open mouth

Molds 79, 109, 119, 139, 199

13"	$400.00	$500.00
15"	$475.00	$625.00

18"	$525.00	$725.00
22"	$625.00	$825.00
25"	$675.00	$900.00
29"	$750.00	$1,000.00
32"	$1,050.00	$1,350.00
36"	$1,550.00	$2,100.00
40"	$2,650.00	$3,400.00
Kid body, shoulder head, open mouth		
14"	$175.00	$235.00
17"	$250.00	$330.00
24"	$350.00	$475.00
Mold 79, 89 closed mouth		
15"	$1,300.00	$1,800.00
18"	$1,700.00	$2,200.00

Too few in database for reliable range.

Mold 189, open mouth

15"	$600.00	$800.00
18"	$700.00	$950.00
22"	$900.00	$1,200.00

Bébé Cosmopolite

28" $1,500.00* boxed

Handwerck, Max

17" bisque mold 421, marked "421//7/ /Germany//Handwerck" on back of socket head, stamped in red "Handwerck" on right hip, original mohair wig, blue sleep eyes, feathered brows, painted lashes, open mouth, four upper teeth, pierced ears, jointed wood and composition body, antique white dress with lacy ruffle around neck, socks and old shoes, red "straw" bonnet, circa 1900+, $300.00. Courtesy McMasters Doll Auctions.

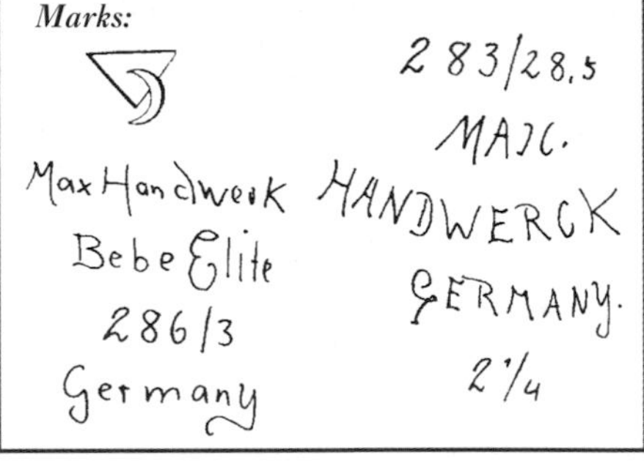

1899 – 1930, Walthershausen, Germany. Made dolls and doll bodies, registered trademark, "Bébé Elite." Used heads made by Goebel.

Child

Bisque socket head, open mouth, sleep or set eyes, jointed composition body

Mold 283, 286, 291, 297, 307, and others

23"	$400.00	$550.00

Bébé Elite, ca. 1900

Bisque socket head, mohair wig, glass sleep eyes, mohair lashes, open mouth, pierced ears, jointed composition/wood body

Marks: "Max Handwerck Bébé Elite 286 12 Germany" on back of head.

15"	$425.00	$575.00
20"	$600.00	$800.00
27"	$750.00	$975.00

Bébé Elite, flange neck, cloth body

15"	$350.00	$445.00
20"	$475.00	$650.00

Googly: See Googly category.

Hartmann, Carl

1889 – 1930, Neustadt, Germany. Made and exported bisque and celluloid dolls, especially small dolls in regional costumes, called Globe Babies. Kämmer & Reinhardt made heads for Hartmann.

Mark:

Globe Baby
DEP
Germany
C 3 H

Child

Bisque socket head, open mouth, jointed composition and wood body

22"	$225.00	$375.00

Globe Baby

Bisque socket head, glass sleep eyes, open mouth, four teeth, mohair or human hair wig, five-piece papier-mâché or composition body with painted shoes and stockings

8"	$315.00	$450.00
9"	$375.00	$500.00

Hartmann, Karl

1911 – 1926, Stockheim, Germany. Doll factory, made and exported dolls. Advertised ball-jointed dolls, characters, and papier-mâché dolls.

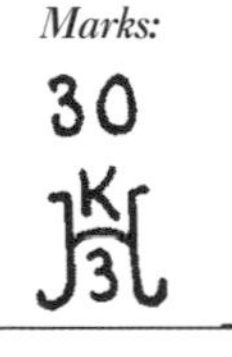

Child

Bisque socket head, open mouth, glass eyes, composition body

18"	$350.00	$500.00
22"	$400.00	$600.00
32"	$700.00	$875.00

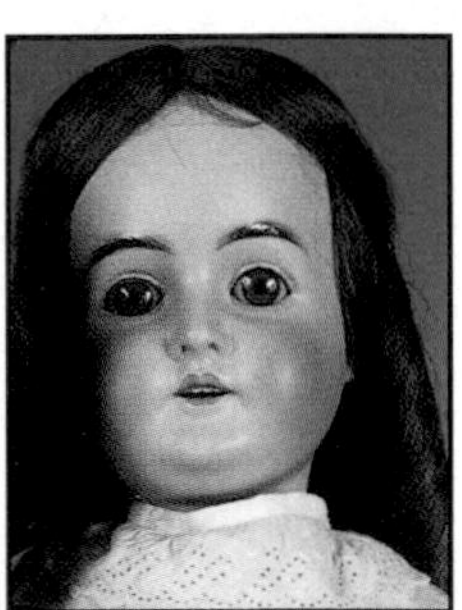

27" bisque socket head, open mouth with teeth, multi-stroke brown brows, painted lashes, red accent dots, human hair wig, composition and wood ball-jointed body, antique white dress, $375.00. Courtesy McMasters Doll Auctions.

Hertel Schwab & Co.

1910 – 1930+, Stutzhaus, Germany. Founded by August Hertel and Heinrich Schwab, both designed doll heads, used by Borgfelt, Kley and Hahn, König & Wernicke, Louis Wolf, and others. Made china and bisque heads as well as all-porcelain; most with character faces. Molded hair or wig, painted blue or glass eyes (often blue-gray), open mouth with tongue or closed mouth, socket or shoulder heads. Usually marked with mold number and *"Made in Germany,"* or mark of company that owned the mold.

Mark:

Made
in
Germany
151/0

* at auction

Hertel Schwab & Co.

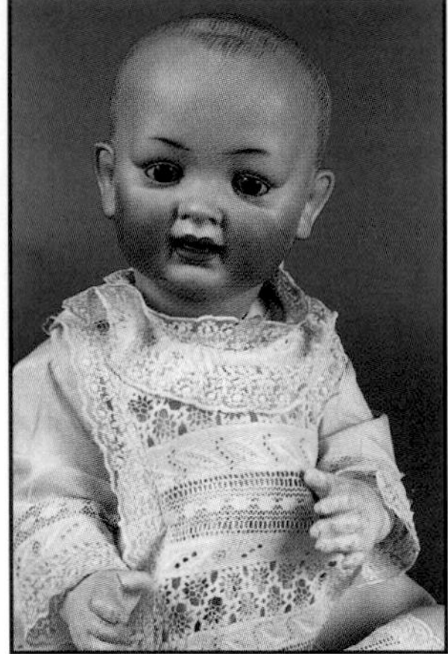

21" bisque mold 151 character baby, marked "151//13," blue sleep eyes, open mouth, two upper teeth, molded tongue, lightly molded and brush stroked hair, composition bent-limb baby body, antique christening dress with elaborate lace and cutwork panel, antique slip, circa 1912, $450.00. Courtesy McMasters Doll Auctions.

Baby

Bisque head, molded hair or wig, open or open/closed mouth, teeth, sleep or painted eyes, bent-leg baby composition body

Mold 130, 142, 150, 151, 152

9"	$250.00	$325.00
11"	$335.00	$450.00
16"	$475.00	$650.00
22"	$675.00	$900.00
24"	$700.00	$950.00

Toddler body

14"	$400.00	$600.00
20"	$600.00	$800.00

Child

Mold 127, ca. 1915, character face, solid dome with molded hair, sleep eyes, open mouth, Patsy-type

15"	$1,000.00	$1,350.00
17"	$1,500.00	$2,000.00

Mold 131, ca. 1912, character face, solid dome, painted closed mouth

18" $1,300.00*

Mold 134, ca. 1915, character face, sleep eyes, closed mouth

15" $15,000.00*

Mold 136, ca. 1912, *"Made in Germany,"* character face, open mouth

24" $700.00 $1,000.00

Mold 140, ca. 1912, character, glass eyes, open/closed laughing mouth

12" $2,550.00 $3,400.00

Mold 141, ca. 1912, character, painted eyes, open/closed mouth

12"	$2,400.00	$3,200.00
18"	$10,200.00*	

Mold 149, ca. 1912, character, glass eyes, closed mouth, ball-jointed body

17" $9,500.00*

Mold 154, ca. 1912, character, solid dome, molded hair, glass eyes, open mouth

20" $1,900.00*

Mold 159, ca. 1911, two faces

10" $850.00*

Mold 167, ca. 1912, "K&H" character, open/closed or closed mouth, made for Kley & Hahn

15" $2,000.00*

Googly: See Googly category.

Heubach, Ernst

1886 – 1930+, Köppelsdorf, Germany. In 1919, the son of Armand Marseille married the daughter of Ernst Heubach and merged the two factories. Mold numbers range from 250 to 452. They made porcelain heads for Dressel (Jutta), Revalo, and others.

* at auction

Baby

Open mouth, glass eyes, socket head, wig, five-piece bent-leg composition body, add more for toddler body, flirty eyes

Mold 267, 300, 320, 321, 342

11"	$190.00	$250.00
14"	$300.00	$400.00
20"	$400.00	$550.00
27"	$725.00	$975.00

Baby, Newborn, ca. 1925+

Solid dome, molded, painted hair, glass eyes, closed mouth, cloth body, composition or celluloid hands

Mold 338, 339, 340, 348, 349, 399

12"	$300.00	$425.00
14"	$425.00	$575.00
15"	$525.00	$700.00
17"	$600.00	$800.00

Black, mold 444

12"	$300.00	$400.00

Child, 1888+

Mold 1900 with Horseshoe Mark

Open mouth, glass eyes, kid or cloth body

12"	$115.00	$150.00
18"	$210.00	$275.00
22"	$310.00	$415.00
26"	$500.00	$650.00

Painted bisque

12"	$125.00	$175.00
16"	$175.00	$225.00

Mold 250, 251, 275 (shoulder head), 302, open mouth, kid body

9"	$130.00	$200.00
13"	$150.00	$250.00
16"	$200.00	$300.00
19"	$325.00	$425.00
23"	$400.00	$525.00
27"	$500.00	$675.00
32"	$650.00	$900.00
36"	$900.00	$1,100.00

20" bisque mold 300, marked "Heubach Koppelsdorf//300 – 1-//Germany" on back of socket head, old mohair wig, blue sleep eyes, painted lashes, feathered brows, open mouth, four upper teeth, jointed composition body with separate balls at shoulders and elbows, faded blue antique dress with blue ribbon trim, antique underclothing, old socks, replaced shoes, straw bonnet, circa 1920, $500.00. Courtesy McMasters Doll Auctions.

Mark:

Heubach, Gebrüder

1820 – 1945, Lichte, Thüringia, Germany. Made bisque heads and all-bisque dolls, characters after 1910, either socket or shoulder head, molded hair or wigs, sleeping or intaglio eyes, in heights from 4" to 26". Mold numbers from 556 to 10633. Sunburst or square marks; more dolls with square marks.

Marked *"Heubach,"* no mold number

Open/closed mouth, dimples

18"	$3,300.00	$4,450.00
24"	$4,700.00	$6,300.00

13" bisque mold 8420 character baby, marked "8420" at crown, "5//Heubach (in square) //41//Germany" on back of neck, "Made in Germany" stamped in red at top of back, mohair wig, blue sleep eyes, multi-stroke brows, painted upper and lower lashes, closed pouty mouth, composition bent-limb baby body, blue check romper with white bodice, matching cap, socks, old leatherette baby shoes, circa 1912, $925.00. Courtesy McMasters Doll Auctions.

Adult, open mouth, glass eyes

14"	$3,350.00	$4,500.00

Smile, painted eyes

15"	$2,700.00	$3,500.00

Marked Heubach Googly: See Googly category.

Character child, shoulder head

Mold 6688, ca. 1912, solid dome, molded hair, intaglio eyes, closed mouth

10"	$450.00	$625.00

Mold 6692, ca. 1912, sunburst, intaglio eyes, closed mouth

14"	$650.00	$875.00

Mold 6736, ca. 1912, square, painted eyes, laughing mouth

13"	$800.00	$1,100.00
16"	$1,400.00	$1,900.00

Mold 7345, ca. 1912, sunburst, pink-tinted closed mouth

17"	$1,150.00

Too few in database for reliable range.

Mold 7644, ca. 1910, sunburst or square mark, painted eyes, open/closed laughing mouth

14"	$650.00	$865.00
17"	$875.00	$1,200.00

Mold 7847, solid dome shoulder head, intaglio eyes, closed smiling mouth, teeth

20"	$2,100.00*

Too few in database for reliable range.

Mold 7850, ca. 1912, "Coquette," open/closed mouth

11"	$550.00	$750.00
15"	$800.00	$1,100.00

17½" bisque Dolly Dimple, marked "6//Heubach(in square)//Germany" on head, "American Beauty//Copyright by Sears Roebuck And Co.//Germany" on label on front of body, old replacement wig, brown sleep eyes, painted lashes, feathered brows, open mouth, four upper teeth, dimples in cheeks, kid body with rivet joints at elbows, composition lower arms, antique white organdy dress, underclothing, old black socks, new shoes, circa 1913, $375.00. Courtesy McMasters Doll Auctions.

* at auction

Mold 7925, ca. 1914, **Mold 7926,** ca. 1912, shoulder head, glass eyes, smiling open mouth, lady

15"	$1,500.00	$2,000.00
20"	$3,700.00, mold 7925*	

Too few in database for reliable range.

Mold 7972, intaglio eyes, closed mouth

20"	$1,500.00	$2,000.00

Too few in database for reliable range.

Mold 8221, square, dome, intaglio eyes, open/closed mouth

14"	$500.00	$675.00

Too few in database for reliable range.

Mold 9355, ca. 1914, square mark, glass eyes, open mouth

13"	$650.00	$850.00
19"	$925.00	$1,250.00

Character Baby or Child, Socket Head

Mold 5636, ca. 1912, glass eyes, open/closed laughing mouth, teeth

13"	$1,500.00	$2,000.00
15"	$1,800.00	$2,400.00

Mold 5689, ca. 1912, sunburst mark, open mouth

14"	$1,350.00	$1,800.00
17"	$1,700.00	$2,250.00
22"	$2,200.00	$2,900.00

Mold 5730, "Santa," ca. 1912, sunburst mark, made for Hamburger & Co.

16"	$1,250.00	$1,700.00
19"	$1,900.00	$2,500.00
26"	$2,100.00	$2,800.00

Mold 5777, "Dolly Dimple," ca. 1913, open mouth, for Hamburger & Co.

14"	$1,725.00	$2,300.00
16"	$1,900.00	$2,500.00
24"	$2,600.00	$3,450.00

Mold 6894, 6897, 7759, all ca. 1912, sunburst or square mark, intaglio eyes, closed mouth, molded hair

7"	$275.00	$375.00
9"	$375.00	$500.00
12"	$525.00	$700.00

Mold 6969, ca. 1912, socket head, square mark, glass eyes, closed mouth

12"	$1,600.00	$2,000.00
16"	$2,500.00	$3,000.00

Mold 6970, ca. 1912, sunburst, glass eyes, closed mouth

10"	$1,300.00	$1,800.00
13"	$1,700.00	$2,300.00
19"	$4,100.00*	

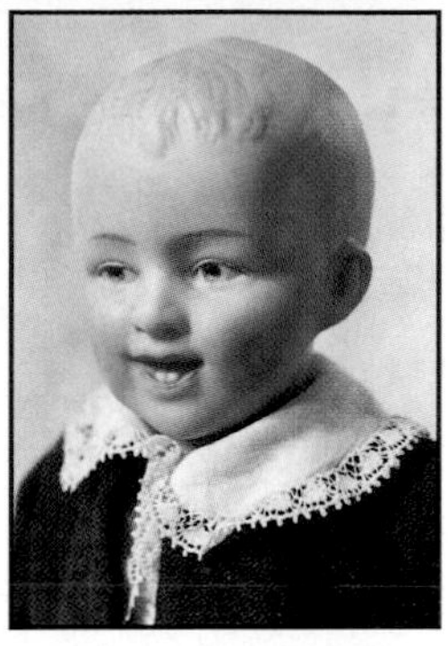

9½" bisque mold 6897 character laughing boy, domed head, painted blue eyes, open/closed laughing mouth with two lower teeth, composition and wood jointed body, black jacket and short pants, circa 1912, $600.00. Courtesy Ruth Brown.

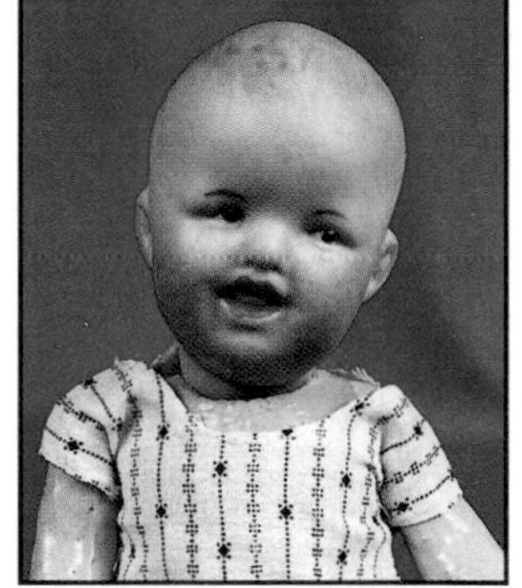

7" bisque character, marked "Heubach (in square)//5/0 D//Germany" on back of solid dome socket head, molded painted hair, blue intaglio eyes, single stroke brows, open/closed mouth with two upper teeth and tongue, crude five-piece composition body, black and white print pants and shirt, circa 1912+, $350.00. Courtesy McMasters Doll Auctions.

* at auction

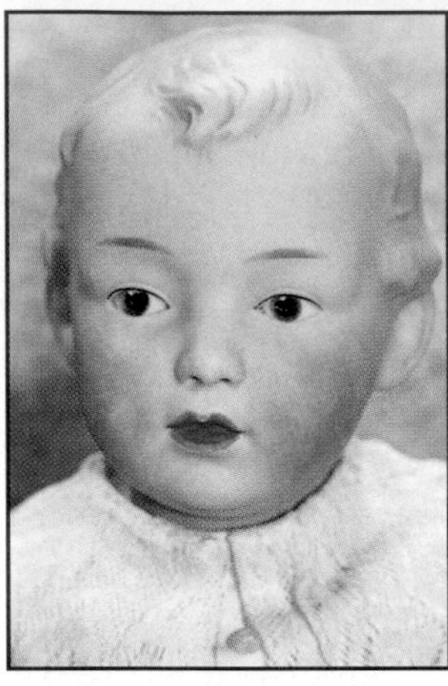

16" bisque mold 7622 character boy, painted intaglio eyes, molded painted hair, open/closed mouth, French-type body, toe damage, circa 1912, $975.00. Courtesy Sharon Kolibaba.

Mold 6971, ca. 1912, intaglio eyes, closed smiling mouth in original costume box

11"	$1,200.00*	

Mold 7246, 7248, ca. 1912, sunburst or square mark, closed mouth

16"	$975.00	$1,300.00

Mold 7247, ca. 1912, glass eyes, closed mouth

15"	$2,700.00	$3,500.00

Mold 7268, square, glass eyes, closed mouth

12"	$5,000.00*	

Mold 7407, character, glass eyes, open/closed mouth

18"	$2,500.00	$3,000.00

Mold 7602, 7603, ca. 1912, molded hair tufts, intaglio eyes

15"	$750.00	$1,000.00

Mold 7604, ca. 1912, open/closed mouth, intaglio eyes

12"	$550.00	$725.00
Baby		
15"	$525.00	$700.00

Mold 7622, 7623, ca. 1912, intaglio eyes, closed or open/closed mouth

16"	$800.00	$1,200.00
18"	$1,000.00	$1,400.00

Mold 7681, dome, intaglio eyes, closed mouth

10"	$650.00*	

Mold 7711, ca. 1912, glass eyes, open mouth, flapper body

10"	$525.00	$700.00

Mold 7759, ca. 1912, dome, painted eyes, closed mouth

12"	$900.00*	

Mold 7911, ca. 1912, intaglio eyes, laughing open/closed mouth

9"	$525.00	$700.00
15"	$900.00	$1,200.00

Mold 7975, "Baby Stuart," ca. 1912, glass eyes, removable molded bisque bonnet

13"	$1,425.00	$1,900.00

Mold 7977, "Baby Stuart," ca. 1912, molded bonnet, closed mouth, painted eyes

8"	$600.00	$800.00
11"	$1,000.00	$1,400.00

Mold 8191, "Crooked Smile," ca. 1912, square mark, intaglio eyes, laughing mouth

11½"	$500.00*	
14"	$375.00	$500.00

Mold 8192, ca. 1914, sunburst or square mark, sleep eyes, open mouth

13"	$675.00	$900.00
20"	$1,250.00*	

* at auction

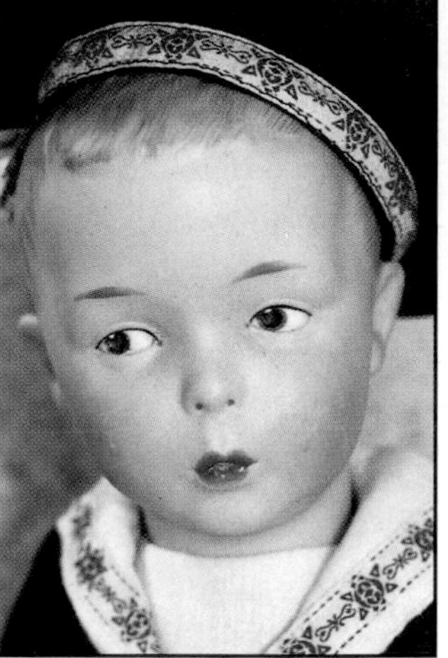

14" bisque Whistler, mold 8774, marked "5//87(Heubach square)74//Germany," intaglio eyes, molded painted hair, mouth drawn together, cloth body with a bellow, navy jacket with red trim, matching hat, circa 1914, $1,250.00. Courtesy Sharon Koliba-ba.

Mold 8316, "Grinning Boy," ca. 1914, wig, open/closed mouth, eight teeth, glass eyes

16"	$2,500.00	$3,400.00
19"	$3,600.00	$4,800.00

Mold 8381, "Princess Juliana," molded hair, ribbon, painted eyes, closed mouth

14"	$5,000.00	$6,600.00+

Mold 8413, ca. 1914, wig, sleep eyes, open/closed mouth, molded tongue, upper teeth

8"	$550.00	$850.00

Too few in database for reliable range.

Mold 8420, ca. 1914, square mark, glass eyes, closed mouth

15"	$2,100.00	$2,800.00

Too few in database for reliable range.

Mold 8429, square mark, closed mouth

15"	$2,500.00*

Too few in database for reliable range.

Mold 8686, glass eyes, open/closed mouth

14"	$3,200.00*

Too few in database for reliable range.

Mold 8774, "Whistling Jim," ca. 1914, smoker or whistler, square mark, flange neck, intaglio eyes, molded hair, cloth body, bellows

13"	$900.00	$1,200.00

Too few in database for reliable range.

Mold 8819, square, intaglio eyes, open/closed mouth

9"	$1,050.00*

Too few in database for reliable range.

Mold 8950, laughing girl, blue hairbow

18"	$7,000.00*

Mold 9027, dome, intaglio eyes, closed mouth

13"	$900.00	$1,200.00

Too few in database for reliable range.

Mold 9055, intaglio eyes, closed mouth

11"	$275.00	$375.00

Too few in database for reliable range.

Mold 9457, ca. 1914, square mark, dome, intaglio eyes, closed mouth, Eskimo

15"	$1,875.00	$2,500.00
18"	$3,000.00	$4,000.00

Mold 9746, square, painted eyes, closed mouth

7½"	$600.00	$800.00

Too few in database for reliable range.

Mold 10532, ca. 1920, square mark, open mouth

13½"	$450.00	$600.00
25"	$1,125.00	$1,500.00

Mold 11010, "Revalo," ca. 1922, sleep eyes, open mouth, for Gebr. Ohlhaver

19"	$525.00	$700.00
24"	$650.00	$850.00

* at auction

Heubach, Gebrüder

Mold 11173, "Tiss Me," socket head, wig

8"	$1,500.00	$2,000.00

Too few in database for reliable range.

FIGURINES

Square or Sunburst mark, all at auction

Seated Baby, dog	4½"	$525.00
Dutch pair	6"	$750.00
Coquette	16"	$1,900.00

Piano Baby, Mold 7287, 9693, and others

5"	$400.00	$525.00
9"	$525.00	$700.00
13"	$1,000.00*	

Hulss, Adolph

Mark:

1915 – 1930+, Waltershausen, Germany. Made dolls with bisque heads, jointed composition bodies. Trademark: "Nesthakchen," "h" in mold mark often resembles a "b." Made babies, toddlers, and child dolls with ball joints.

BABY

Bisque socket head, sleep eyes, open mouth, teeth, wig, bent-leg baby, composition body, add more for flirty eyes.

Mold 156

14"	$425.00	$575.00
19"	$850.00	$1,125.00

Toddler

16"	$625.00	$800.00
20"	$775.00	$1,000.00

CHILD

Bisque socket head, wig, sleep eyes, open mouth, teeth, tongue, jointed composition body

Mold 176

15"	$575.00	$750.00
22"	$925.00	$1,250.00

Huret, Maison

1812 – 1930+, France. May have pressed, molded bisque, or china heads, painted or glass eyes, closed mouths, bodies of cloth, composition, gutta-percha, kid, or wood, sometimes metal hands. Used fur or mohair for wigs, had fashion type body with defined waist.

What to look for: Dolls with beautiful painting on eyes and face; painted eyes are more common than glass, but the beauty of the painted features and/or wooden bodies increases the price.

Bisque shoulder head, kid body with bisque lower arms, glass eyes

15"	$4,500.00	$6,000.00
17"	$6,100.00	$8,000.00

17" china shoulder head man, marked "Brevet D'Inv:SCDG, Maison Huret, Boulevard Montmartre, 22, Paris; Exposition Universelle de 1855, Napoleon III Empereur" stamped on body, gutta percha body, $17,500.00. Courtesy McMasters Doll Auctions.

* at auction

Round face, painted blue eyes, cloth body

16"	$8,722.00*	

Wood body

17"	$21,000.00*	

Too few in database for reliable range.

China shoulder head, kid body, china lower arms

17"	$5,000.00	$7,000.00

Metal hands, swivel neck, glass eyes

15"	$10,550.00* (presumed Huret)	

Too few in database for reliable range.

Pressed bisque shoulder head, wood body, painted eyes, labeled body

17"	$21,000.00*	

Too few in database for reliable range.

Gutta-percha stamped body

17"	$17,500.00*	

Pressed bisque, doll, marked articulated body, with provenance

18"	$62,000.00*	

Too few in database for reliable range.

Painted eyes, marked kid body

17"	$16,500.00*	

Too few in database for reliable range.

Painted eyes, open/closed mouth, fashion body

* Only one reported, extremely rare

Jullien

1827 – 1904, Paris, Conflans, St. Leonard. Had a porcelain factory, won some awards, purchased bisque heads from Francois Gaultier.

CHILD

Bisque socket head, wig, glass eyes, pierced ears, open mouth with teeth or closed mouth, on jointed composition body

Closed mouth

19"	$2,850.00	$3,800.00
24"	$3,175.00	$4,250.00

Open mouth

18"	$1,200.00	$1,600.00

Jumeau

1842 – 1899, Paris and Monttreuil-sous-Bois; succeeded by S.F.B.J. through 1958. Founder Pierre Francois Jumeau made fashion dolls with kid or wood bodies; head marked with size number; bodies stamped *"JUMEAU/ /MEDAILLE D'OR/ /PARIS."* Early Jumeau heads were pressed pre-1890. By 1878, son Emile Jumeau was head of the company and made Bébé Jumeau, marked on back of head, on chemise, band on arm of dress. Tête Jumeaus have poured heads. Bébé Protige and Bébé Jumeau registered trademarks in 1886; Bee Mark in 1891; Bébé Marcheur in 1895, Bébé Francaise in 1896.

Mold numbers of marked EJs and Têtes approximate the following heights: 1 – 10", 2 – 11", 3 – 12", 4 – 13", 5 – 14", 6 – 16", 7 – 17", 8 – 18", 9 – 20", 10 – 21", 11 – 24", 12 – 26", 13 – 30".

* at auction

22" bisque Portrait fashion-type, marked "6" on back of head, swivel head on shoulder plate, set pale blue eyes, feathered brows, painted lashes, closed mouth, pierced ears into head, original human hair wig on cork pate, kid body with gussets at elbows, hips, and knees, individually stitched fingers, antique light blue fashion dress, antique underclothing, socks, shoes, bronze silk and beige velvet hat with lace trim, circa 1870+, $2,200.00. Courtesy McMasters Doll Auctions.

16½" bisque marked "E.D.," marked "E. 6. D//(red & black artist marks)" on head, "Bebe Jumeau" on back, auburn mohair wig, blue paperweight eyes, painted lashes, heavy feathered brows, closed mouth, pierced ears, jointed wood and composition body, jointed wrists, nicely re-dressed in elaborate peach silk dress, matching bonnet with lace and ribbon trim, made by Jumeau firm when Emile Douillet was director, circa 1892 – 1899, $2,500.00. Courtesy McMasters Doll Auctions.

First price is for doll in good condition, but with some flaws; second price is for doll in excellent condition, nicely wigged, and with appropriate clothing. Exceptional doll may be much more.

Fashion-type Jumeau

Marked with size number on swivel head, closed mouth, paperweight eyes, pierced ears, stamped kid body, add more for original clothes.

11"	$2,000.00	$2,600.00
17"	$3,050.00	$3,800.00
20"	$4,000.00	$4,600.00

Wood body, bisque lower arms

16"	$3,800.00	$5,100.00

Jumeau Portrait

21"	$4,850.00	$6,600.00

Wood body

20"	$6,300.00	$8,500.00

Almond eye

13½"	$8,500.00	$12,500.00
17"	$13,000.00	$17,500.00
20"	$20,000.00	$25,000.00

E.J. Bébé, 1881 – 1886

Mark:
E.J. Bébé
1881 – 86
6
E.J.

Earliest "EJ" mark above with number over initials, pressed bisque socket head, wig, paperweight eyes, pierced ears, closed mouth jointed body with straight wrists

17"	$7,200.00	$10,250.00
20"	$9,000.00	$12,000.00
26"	$15,000.00*	

EJ/A marked Bébé

17"	$20,000.00+	

**Too few in database for reliable range.*

Mark:
Mid EJ mark has size number centered between E and J
(E 8 J)

Mid "EJ" mark has size number centered between E and J (E 8 J)

15"	$4,700.00	$6,200.00
17"	$4,900.00	$6,600.00
20"	$5,400.00	$7,200.00
23"	$6,000.00	$8,000.00
26"	$6,750.00	$9,000.00

Later "EJ" mark is preceded by DEPOSE (DEPOSE/E 8 J)

15"	$3,800.00	$5,000.00
19"	$4,300.00	$5,850.00
23"	$5,025.00	$6,625.00
26"	$6,000.00	$8,000.00

* at auction

21½" bisque Tete Jumeau marked "Depose//Tete Jumeau//10" on head, "Bebe Jumeau//Bte S.G.D.G.//Depose" stamped on back, "10//Paris/ /(bee)//Depose" on shoes, blond mohair wig, blue paperweight eyes, long painted lashes, heavy feathered brows, closed mouth, pierced ears, jointed wood and composition body, jointed wrists, original flowered factory dress, antique underclothing, antique blue socks, marked shoes, circa 1885+, $3,300.00. Courtesy McMasters Doll Auctions.

19" bisque mold 1907 socket head, with red Tete Jumeau mark, blue paperweight eyes, painted upper and lower lashes, open mouth, six upper teeth, red human hair wig, pierced ears, jointed wood and composition body with jointed wrists, nicely re-dressed in beige dress, underclothing, new socks and shoes, old rose velvet hat, circa 1907, $1,700.00. Courtesy McMasters Doll Auctions.

Depose Jumeau, ca. 1886 – 1889

Poured bisque head marked, *"Depose Jumeau,"* and size number, pierced ears, closed mouth, paperweight eyes, composition and wood body with straight wrists marked *"Medaille d'Or Paris"*

14"	$3,750.00	$5,000.00
18"	$4,400.00	$5,900.00
23"	$5,200.00	$6,900.00

Long Face Triste Bébé, 1879 – 1886

Head marked with number only, pierced applied ears, closed mouth, paperweight eyes, straight wrists on umeau marked body

27" $15,000.00*

Too few in database for reliable range.

Tête Jumeau, ca. 1885+

Poured bisque socket head, red stamp on head, stamp or sticker on body, wig, glass eyes, pierced ears, closed mouth, jointed composition body with straight wrists. May also be marked E.D. with size number when Douillet ran factory, uses tête face.

The following sizes were used for Têtes: 1–10", 2–11", 3–12", 4–13", 5–14½", 6–16", 7–17", 8–19", 10–21½", 11–24", 12–26", 13–29", 14–31", 15–33", 16–34" – 35".

Bébé (Child), closed mouth

10"	$4,000.00	$5,500.00
12"	$2,700.00	$3,500.00
17"	$3,000.00	$4,100.00
19"	$3,500.00	$4,650.00
23"	$3,800.00	$5,000.00
26"	$4,000.00	$5,200.00
30"	$4,650.00	$6,200.00
32"	$6,000.00	$8,000.00

Trouseau/provenance

19" $13,500.00*

* at auction

17" bisque girl, marked "758//7" on head, "Bebe Jumeau//Diplome d'Honneur" on lower back, human hair wig, blue sleep eyes, painted lower lashes, heavy feathered brows, open mouth, six upper teeth, pierced ears, jointed wood and composition body, jointed wrists, non-working or missing voice box, green silk dress with net overlay, matching bonnet, underclothing, socks, antique cloth shoes, circa 1892+, $875.00. Courtesy McMasters Doll Auctions.

24" composition, "Jumeau//Medaille d'Or//Paris" stamped on lower back, socket head, original human hair wig, blue paperweight eyes, heavy feathered brows, painted upper and lower lashes, open mouth, six upper teeth, jointed composition body with straight wrists, antique white dress with lace inserts, antique underclothing, replaced socks, antique red leather shoes, circa 1880s+, $550.00. Courtesy McMasters Doll Auctions.

Adult body, open mouth

15"	$1,875.00	$2,500.00
17"	$2,100.00	$2,800.00
21"	$2,400.00	$3,200.00
25"	$2,600.00	$3,500.00
28"	$2,700.00	$3,700.00
32"	$3,100.00	$4,200.00

Rare pressed brown bisque swivel head, "Madagascar"

24½" $89,270.00*

"1907," Child, ca. 1907

Some with Tête Jumeau stamp, sleep or set eyes, open mouth, jointed French body

14"	$975.00	$1,850.00
17"	$1,800.00	$2,500.00
20"	$2,150.00	$2,900.00
23"	$2,350.00	$3,200.00
26"	$2,650.00	$3,600.00
29"	$2,950.00	$3,900.00
32"	$3,100.00	$4,150.00

B. L. Bébé, ca. 1880s

Marked *"B. L."* for the Louvre department store, socket head, wig, pierced ears, paperweight eyes, closed mouth, jointed composition body.

20" $3,800.00 $4,200.00

Too few in database for reliable range.

R.R. Bébé, ca 1880s

Wig, pierced ears, paperweight eyes, closed mouth, jointed composition body with straight wrists

22" $3,825.00 $5,100.00

Too few in database for reliable range.

Character Child

Mold 203, 208, and other 200 series

$50,000.00+

Too few in database for reliable range.

Mold 221, Great Ladies

10" $400.00 $600.00

Mold 230, open mouth

16" $1,100.00 $1,500.00

20" $1,350.00 $1,800.00

Too few in database for reliable range.

Two-Faced Jumeau

18" $14,500.00*

Too few in database for reliable range.

Phonograph Jumeau

Bisque head, open mouth, phonograph in torso, working condition

24" $19,000.00*

25" $7,800.00*

Too few in database for reliable range.

* at auction

PRINCESS ELIZABETH

Made after Jumeau joined SFBJ and adopted Unis label, mark will be *"71 Unis//France 149//306//Jumeau//1938//Paris."* Bisque socket head with high color, closed mouth, flirty eyes, jointed composition body

Mold 306

18"	$1,600.00	$2,100.00
30"	$2,900.00	$3,500.00

Too few in database for reliable range.

ACCESSORIES

Marked shoes

5 – 6"	$225.00	$300.00
7 – 10"	$450.00	$600.00

Kämmer & Reinhardt

1886 – 1930+, Waltershausen, Germany. Registered trademark K*R, Majestic Doll, Mein Leibling, Die Kokette, Charakterpuppen (character dolls). Designed doll heads, most bisque were made by Simon & Halbig; in 1918, Schuetzmeister & Quendt also supplied heads; Rheinische Gummi und Celluloid Fabrik Co. made celluloid heads for Kämmer & Reinhardt. Kämmer & Reinhardt dolls were distributed by Bing, Borgfeldt, B. Illfelder, L. Rees & Co., Strobel & Wilken, and Louis Wolf & Co. Also made heads of wood and composition, later cloth and rubber dolls.

*11" bisque baby, marked "K*R//29" on back of head, "W" on forehead at crown, original mohair wig, blue sleep eyes, remnants of real lashes, painted lashes, feathered brows, open mouth, two upper teeth, spring tongue, bent-limb composition baby body, old baby dress, knit sweater, flannel diaper, newer booties, circa 1900+, $435.00.* Courtesy McMasters Doll Auctions.

Mold numbers identify heads starting with 1) bisque socket heads; 2) shoulder heads, as well as socket heads of black or mulatto babies; 3) bisque socket heads or celluloid shoulder heads; 4) heads having eyelashes; 5) googlies, black heads, pincushion heads; 6) mulatto heads; 7) celluloid heads, bisque head walking dolls; 8) rubber heads; 9) composition heads, some rubber heads. Other letters refer to style or material of wig or clothing.

Marks:

First price indicates doll in good condition, but with some flaws. Second price indicates doll in excellent condition well dressed. Exceptional dolls may be more.

CHILD, DOLLY FACE

Mold 191, ca. 1900, open mouth, sleep eyes, jointed child body

17"	$650.00	$865.00
30"	$1,100.00	$1,500.00

Mold 192, ca. 1900, open mouth, sleep eyes, jointed child's body

9"	$750.00	$1,000.00
18"	$825.00	$1,100.00
22"	$975.00	$1,300.00

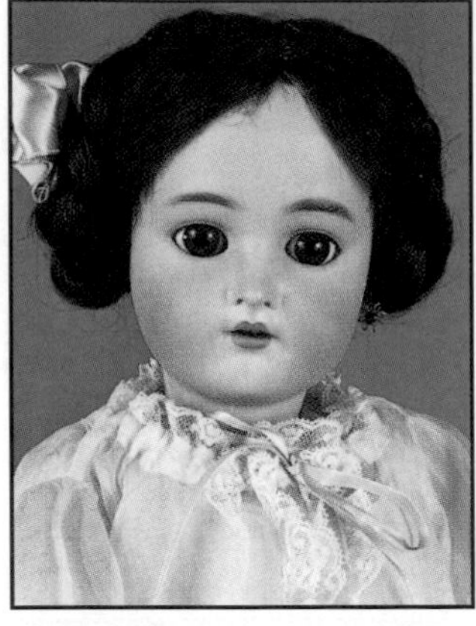

*24" bisque girl marked "Halbig//K*R//62" on back of head, human hair wig, brown sleep eyes, missing real lashes, painted lashes, molded feathered brows, open mouth, four upper teeth, pierced ears, jointed wood and composition body, lace-trimmed organdy dress with blue sash, antique underclothing, old socks and shoes, circa 1886+, $325.00.* Courtesy McMasters Doll Auctions.

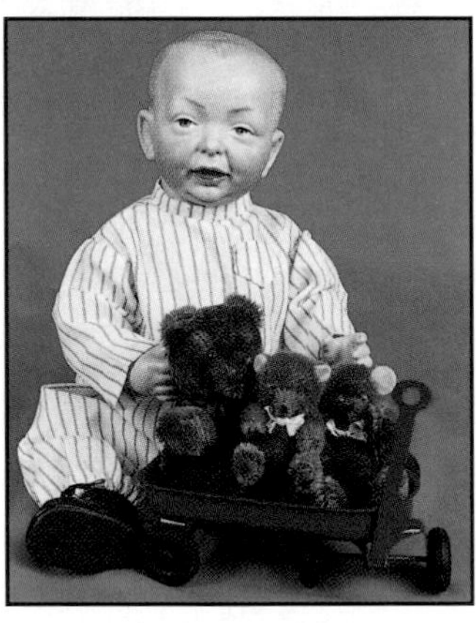

*14½" bisque mold 100 character baby marked "36//K*R//100" on solid dome socket head, lightly molded brush stroked hair, blue intaglio eyes, single stroke brows, open/closed mouth, composition bent-limb baby body, brown and white striped romper, new brown socks and black shoes, circa 1909, $250.00.* Courtesy McMasters Doll Auctions.

With trunk

9"	$1,800.00*	

Closed mouth

18"	$2,100.00	$2,800.00

No mold numbers, or marked only *"K*R"* or size number in centimeters, or mold 401, 402, 403, socket head, glass eyes, open mouth

12"	$375.00	$500.00
19"	$550.00	$750.00
25"	$825.00	$1,100.00

Closed mouth, flapper body

14"	$2,400.00*	

Characters

Mold 100, ca. 1909

Once called Kaiser Baby, but no connection has been found. Character baby, with dome head, jointed bent-leg body, intaglio eyes, open/closed mouth, appropriate dress, good condition

12"	$375.00	$575.00
15"	$575.00	$775.00
20"	$750.00	$1,100.00

Mold 101, Peter or Marie, ca. 1909, painted eyes, closed mouth, jointed body

7 – 8"	$1,200.00	$1,700.00
12"	$2,125.00	$2,800.00
15"	$2,500.00	$3,200.00+
18"	$3,700.00	$4,900.00+
19"	$8,725.00*	

Glass eyes

18"	$8,000.00*	

Too few in database for reliable range.

Mold 102, Elsa or Walter, ca. 1900, painted eyes, molded hair, closed mouth, very rare

14"	$32,000.00

Too few in database for reliable range.

Mold 103, ca. 1909, painted eyes, closed mouth

19"	$60,000.00+

Too few in database for reliable range.

Mold 104, ca. 1909, painted eyes, laughing closed mouth, very rare

18"	$65,000.00+

Too few in database for reliable range.

Mold 105, ca. 1909, painted eyes, open/closed mouth, very rare

21"	$170,956.00*

Too few in database to give reliable range.

Mold 106, ca. 1909, painted intaglio eyes to side, closed mouth, very rare

22"	$144,886.00* w/wrong body

Too few in database for reliable range.

Mold 107, Carl, ca. 1909, painted intaglio eyes, closed mouth

21"	$46,000.00*

Too few in database for reliable range.

Mold 108, ca. 1909, only one example reported

$275,000.00+*

Mold 109, Elise, ca. 1909, painted eyes, closed mouth

14"	$5,500.00	$7,000.00
24"	$20,000.00*	

Too few in database for reliable range.

Mold 112, ca. 1909, painted open/closed mouth

13"	$8,000.00* with provenance

Mold 112X, flocked hair

17"	$16,500.00*

Too few in database for reliable range.

Mold 114, Hans or Gretchen, ca. 1909, painted eyes, closed mouth

9"	$1,350.00	$1,800.00
13"	$2,450.00	$3,275.00
18"	$4,200.00	$5,700.00
25"	$19,500.00*	

Glass eyes

9"	$5,900.00*
15"	$9,250.00*

Mold 115, ca. 1911, solid dome, painted hair, sleeping eyes, closed mouth, toddler

15"	$4,250.00	$5,750.00

Mold 115A, ca. 1911, sleep eyes, closed mouth, wig

Baby, bent-leg body

13"	$2,000.00	$3,000.00
19"	$5,000.00*	

Toddler, composition, jointed body

15 – 16"	$3,750.00	$5,000.00
18"	$4,200.00	$5,500.00

Mold 116, ca. 1911, dome head, sleep eyes, open/closed mouth, bent-leg baby body

17"	$3,200.00*

Mold 116A, ca. 1911, sleep eyes, open/closed mouth or open mouth, wigged, bent-leg baby body

15"	$2,250.00	$2,950.00

Toddler body

16"	$2,600.00	$3,400.00

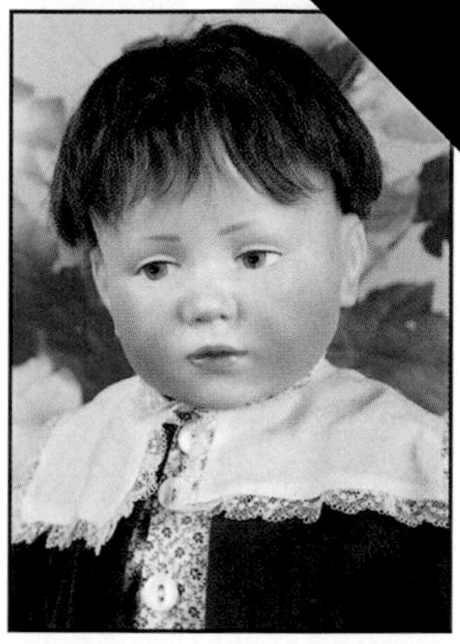

*18½" bisque mold 101 socket head, marked "K*R//101//46" on back of head, painted blue eyes, single stroke brows, closed pouty mouth, brown mohair wig, jointed wood and composition body, nicely re-dressed in two-piece blue velvet suit, blue print shirt with large lace-trimmed collar, socks and shoes, circa 1909, $2,700.00. Courtesy McMasters Doll Auctions.*

*8½" bisque mold 114 Gretchen, marked "K*R//114//23" on back of head, mohair wig in coiled braids, painted blue eyes with black lash line, single stroke brows, closed pouty mouth, five-piece composition body with molded painted white socks and brown two-strap shoes, dressed in original factory chemise trimmed with red embroidery, circa 1909, $1,175.00. Courtesy McMasters Doll Auctions.*

* at auction

16" bisque mold 117A, marked "K (star) R//Simon & Halbig//117/A//39" on back of head, mohair lashes, closed pouty mouth, jointed wood and composition body, antique blue dress with white embroidered trim, antique underclothing, replaced socks and shoes, circa 1911, $1,850.00. Courtesy McMasters Doll Auctions.

*Left: 19" bisque mold 127n, marked "Germany//Simon & Halbig//K*R//36//127n," solid dome head, sleep eyes, open mouth, two upper teeth, molded brush stroked hair, jointed wood and composition teenage body, antique suit, circa 1914, $725.00; Right: 19" bisque Kammer & Reinhardt mold 117n Mein Neuer Liebling, marked "K*R//Simon & Halbig//117n//46," sleep eyes, open mouth/four teeth, replaced wig, jointed wood and composition body, antique dress, hat, circa 1916, $425.00. Courtesy McMasters Doll Auctions.*

Mold 117 Mein Liebling (My Darling), ca. 1911, glass eyes, closed mouth

15" $3,325.00 $4,400.00
18" $4,100.00 $5,400.00
23" $5,100.00 $6,850.00

Mold 117A, ca. 1911, glass eyes, closed mouth

8" $1,800.00 $2,300.00
20" $3,500.00 $4,700.00
28" $6,500.00 $8,500.00

Flapper body

8" $3,500.00*

Mold 117N, Mein Neuer Liebling (My new Darling), ca. 1916, flirty eyes, open mouth

16" $1,100.00 $1,500.00
20" $1,450.00 $1,900.00
28" $2,400.00 $2,900.00

Mold 117X, ca. 1911, socket head, sleep eyes, open mouth

42" $4,800.00*

Mold 118, 118A, sleep eyes, open mouth, baby body

15" $1,125.00 $1,500.00
18" $1,700.00 $2,275.00

Mold 119, ca. 1913, sleep eyes, open/closed mouth, marked *"Baby,"* five-piece baby body

25" $16,000.00*

Mold 121, ca. 1912, sleep eyes, open mouth, baby body

10" $450.00 $600.00
16" $700.00 $900.00
24" $950.00 $1,300.00

Toddler body

14" $750.00 $1,100.00
18" $1,850.00*

Mold 122, ca. 1912, sleep eyes, bent-leg baby body

11" $525.00 $700.00
16" $635.00 $850.00
20" $825.00 $1,100.00

Original wicker layette basket and accessories

22" $2,800.00*

Toddler body

13" $825.00 $1,100.00
19" $975.00 $1,300.00
22" $1,025.00 $1,400.00

Mold 123 Max and Mold 124 Moritz, ca. 1913, flirty sleep eyes, laughing/closed mouth

16" each $14,500.00*
16" pair $37,400.00*

* at auction

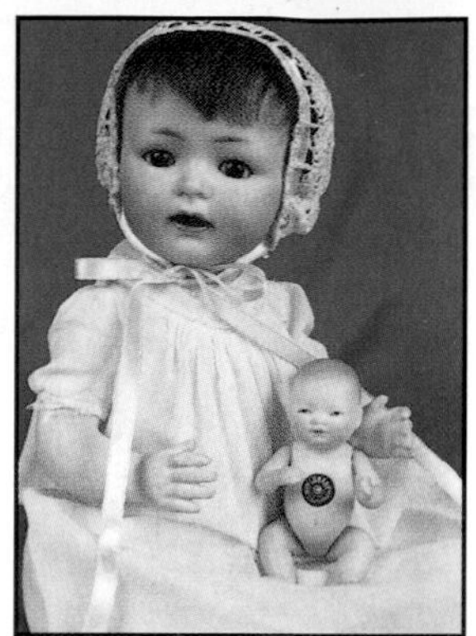

*15½" bisque mold 122 Baby, marked "K*R//Simon & Halbig//122//36" on head, old human hair wig, sleep eyes, painted lashes, open mouth, one upper tooth, three lower teeth, spring tongue, composition baby body, white dress, booties, crocheted bonnet, circa 1912, $175.00, holding 5" all bisque Bye-Lo Baby, marked "Bye-Lo Baby//©//Germany//G.S. Putnam" on label on chest, jointed at shoulders, hips, circa 1923, $400.00. Courtesy McMasters Doll Auctions.*

Mold 126 Mein Liebling Baby (My Darling Baby), ca. 1914

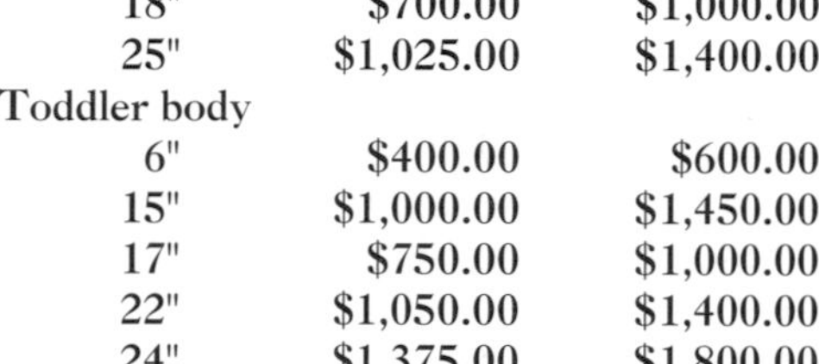

Sleep or flirty eyes, bent-leg baby, 1914 – 1930s

14"	$500.00	$700.00
18"	$700.00	$1,000.00
25"	$1,025.00	$1,400.00

Toddler body

6"	$400.00	$600.00
15"	$1,000.00	$1,450.00
17"	$750.00	$1,000.00
22"	$1,050.00	$1,400.00
24"	$1,375.00	$1,800.00

Mold 127, 127N, ca. 1914, domed head-like mold 126, bent-leg baby body, add more for flirty eyes

14"	$800.00	$1,200.00
18"	$1,200.00	$1,600.00

Toddler body

20"	$1,650.00	$2,200.00
26"	$1,950.00	$2,600.00

27" bisque mold 121 toddler, circa 1912+ $1,900.00; 12" early Steiff bear, $950.00. Courtesy McMasters Doll Auctions.

Mold 128, ca. 1914, sleep eyes, open mouth, baby body

13"	$925.00	$1,250.00

Original clothes, with layette in wicker basket

10"	$1,600.00*

Mold 131: See Googly category.

Mold 135, ca. 1923, sleep eyes, open mouth, baby body

13"	$625.00	$850.00

Toddler body

18"	$1,150.00	$1,550.00

Mold 171 Klein Mammi (Little Mammy), ca. 1925, dome, open mouth

18"	$1,500.00*

Too few in database for reliable range.

Mold 214, ca. 1909, shoulder head, painted eyes, closed mouth, similar to mold 114, muslin body

12"	$2,600.00*

Too few in database for reliable range.

Kestner, J.D.

1805 – 1930+, Waltershausen, Germany. Kestner was one of the first firms to make dressed dolls. Supplied bisque heads to Catterfelder Puppenfabrik. Borgfeldt, Butler Bros., Century Doll Co., Horsman, R.H. Macy, Sears, Siegel Cooper, F.A.O. Schwarz, and others were distributors for Kestner. Besides

* at auction

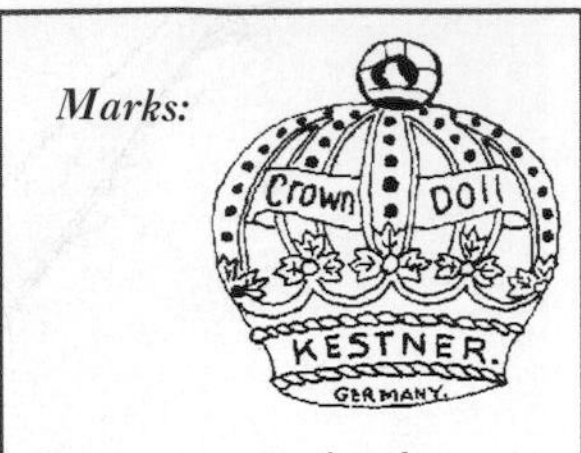

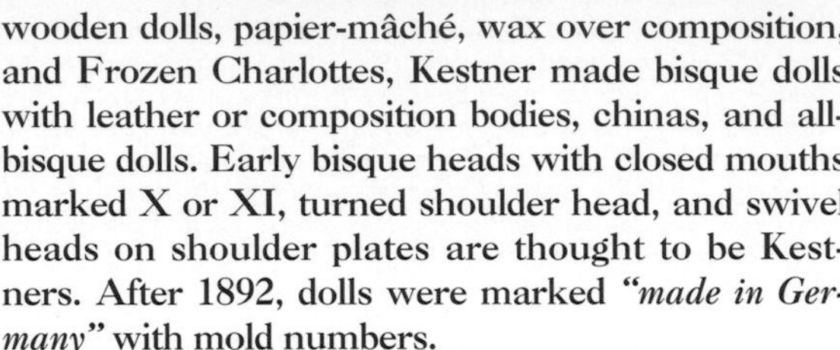
wooden dolls, papier-mâché, wax over composition, and Frozen Charlottes, Kestner made bisque dolls with leather or composition bodies, chinas, and all-bisque dolls. Early bisque heads with closed mouths marked X or XI, turned shoulder head, and swivel heads on shoulder plates are thought to be Kestners. After 1892, dolls were marked *"made in Germany"* with mold numbers.

Bisque heads with early mold numbers are stamped *"Excelsior DRP No. 70 685"*; heads of 100 number series are marked *"dep."* Some early characters are unmarked or only marked with the mold number. After "211" on, it is believed all dolls were marked *"JDK"* or *"JDK, Jr."* Registered the "Crown Doll" (Kronen Puppe) in 1915, used crown on label on bodies and dolls.

The Kestner Alphabet is registered in 1897 as a design patent. It is possible to identify the sizes of doll heads by this key. Letter and number always go together: B/6, C/7, D/8, E/9, F/10, G/11, H/12, H¾/12¾, J/13, J¾/13¾, K/14, K½/14½, L/15, L½/15½, M/16, N/17. It is believed all dolls with plaster pates were made by Kestner.

First price is for doll in good condition with some flaws; second price is for doll in excellent condition with original clothes or appropriately dressed. Exceptional dolls may be more.

23" bisque solid dome baby, marked "J.D.K.//made in 18 Germany" on back of socket head, molded and brush stroked hair, blue sleep eyes, feathered brows, painted lashes, open mouth, two lower teeth, composition baby body, antique long baby dress, old baby shoes, circa 1912, $550.00; holding five blown glass Russian Christmas ornaments, $65.00. Courtesy McMasters Doll Auctions.

Early Baby

Unmarked, or only *"JDK," "made in Germany"* or with size number, solid dome bisque socket head, glass sleep eyes, molded and/or painted hair, composition bent-leg baby body. Add more for body with crown label and/or original clothes.

16"	$700.00	$950.00
20"	$750.00	$1,000.00
Baby Jean, solid dome, fat cheeks		
15"	$1,050.00	$1,400.00
23"	$1,500.00	$2,000.00

Early Child

Bisque shoulder head, ca. 1880s

Closed or open/closed mouth, plaster pate, may be marked with size numbers only, glass eyes, may sleep,

22½" bisque mold 154 dolly face, marked "Dep. 19.(number is incomplete)154" on back of shoulder head, original human hair wig, brown sleep eyes, real lashes, painted lashes, molded feathered brows, open mouth, four upper teeth, kid body with jointed wood and composition arms, rivet joints at hips and knees, antique white dress trimmed with lace and tucks, antique underclothing, black socks, new black leather shoes, circa 1897, $300.00. Courtesy McMasters Doll Auctions.

* at auction

kid body, bisque lower arms, appropriate wig and dress, in good condition, more for original clothes.

15"	$525.00	$700.00
17"	$600.00	$800.00
19"	$1,050.00*	

Open mouth, ca. 1892+, Mold 145, 147, 148, 154, 166, 195

17"	$300.00	$400.00
21"	$350.00	$500.00
24"	$500.00	$650.00

Mold 154, all original, unplayed-with condition

22"	$950.00*	

Turned shoulder head, ca. 1880s closed mouth, size number only

16"	$550.00	$750.00
18"	$650.00	$850.00
22"	$650.00	$900.00
25"	$750.00	$1,000.00
28"	$2,700.00*	

Bisque socket head

Open mouth, glass eyes, Kestner ball-jointed body, add more for square cut teeth on body marked only with number and letter.

Mold 142, 144, 146, 164, 167, 171

8"	$500.00	$700.00
18"	$700.00	$950.00
24"	$950.00	$1,000.00
42"	$4,100.00*	

Mold 171, 18" size only called "Daisy"

18"	$850.00	$1,150.00

A.T. type, closed mouth, glass eyes, mohair wig over plaster pate, early composition and wood ball-jointed body with straight wrists. Marked only with size number such as 15 for 24".

21"	$17,000.00*	

Mold XI, 103 pouty closed mouth

16"	$3,500.00*	
20"	$1,950.00	$2,600.00
23"	$2,625.00	$3,500.00

Mold 128, 169, pouty closed mouth, glass eyes, composition and wood ball-jointed body, wigged

9"	$2,500.00* original costume	
15"	$900.00	$1,000.00
20"	$1,100.00	$1,400.00

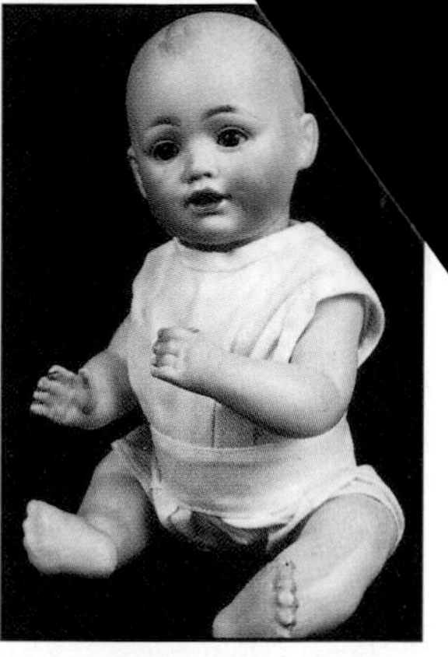

11" bisque Baby Jean, marked "J.D.K.//made in 6 Germany" on back of head, "Made in Germany" stamped in red at back of neck, solid dome socket head, brown sleep eyes, real lashes, feathered brows, painted upper and lower lashes, open mouth, two upper teeth, molded tongue, lightly molded and brush-stroked hair, composition bent-limb baby body, new white romper, has new two-piece outfit with pants and tunic-type top, circa 1910+, $675.00. Courtesy McMasters Doll Auctions.

16" bisque Hilda, marked "H. Made in 12//Germany//245//J.D.K. jr//1914//©//Hilda//ges. gesch. N. 1070" on back of head, human hair wig, brown sleep eyes, painted lashes, feathered brows, open mouth, two upper teeth, tongue, composition baby body, antique white baby dress with pink/blue smocking, slip, diaper, new booties, old knit bonnet, circa 1914, $1,600.00. Courtesy McMasters Doll Auctions.

* at auction

11" bisque mold 211 character toddler, marked "A. made in Germany 5//211//J.D.K." on back of socket head, blue leep eyes, feathered brows, painted lashes, pen/closed mouth, original blond mohair g, fully jointed toddler body, two-piece out- agged Helen Huchison 1953, cotton socks, eatherette shoes, near mint, circa 1910+, 950.00. Courtesy McMasters Doll Auctions.

9" bisque child marked "Germany//A. 10/0 M." on back of head, original mohair wig in original set, brown sleep eyes, painted lashes, open mouth, four upper teeth, five-piece composition child body, painted socks and shoes, factory original dress trimmed with red ribbon, matching bonnet, underclothing, near mint in unplayed with condition, circa 1880+, $310.00. Courtesy McMasters Doll Auctions.

12" bisque mold 143, marked "B made in//Germany 6" on back of head, "Excelsior//Germany//2/0" stamped on body, synthetic wig, blue sleep eyes, feathered brows, painted upper and lower lashes, open mouth, two upper teeth, jointed wood and composition body, white dress, underclothing, new socks and shoes, circa 1897, $750.00. Courtesy McMasters Doll Auctions.

Mold 129, 130, 149, 160, 161, 168, 173, 174, 196, 214, open mouth, glass eyes, composition wood jointed body, add more for fur eyebrows

12"	$450.00	$600.00
15"	$500.00	$675.00
19"	$700.00	$950.00
23"	$800.00	$1,100.00
28"	$1,100.00	$1,400.00
33"	$1,700.00*	

Mold 143, ca. 1897, open mouth, glass eyes, jointed body

8"	$475.00	$700.00
9"	$625.00	$850.00
13"	$750.00	$1,000.00
18"	$900.00	$1,250.00

Mold 155, ca. 1897, open mouth, glass eyes, five-piece or fully jointed body

7½"	$700.00	$925.00

Character Baby, 1910+

Socket head with wig or solid dome with painted hair, glass eyes, open mouth with bent-leg baby body. More for toddler body.

Mold 211, 226, 236, 260, 262, 263

8"	$650.00	$800.00
12"	$600.00	$775.00
16"	$675.00	$900.00
18"	$750.00	$1,000.00
24"	$1,050.00	$1,450.00+
26"	$1,250.00	$1,650.00

Mold 210, ca. 1912, Mold 234, 235, ca. 1914, shoulder head, solid dome, sleep eyes, open/closed mouth or open mouth

12"	$550.00	$700.00
14"	$1,300.00*	

Too few in database for reliable range.

* at auction

Mold 220, sleep eyes, open/closed mouth

14"	$3,225.00	$4,300.00

Toddler

19"	$4,650.00	$6,200.00
26½"	$10,000.00*	

Mold 237, 245 (Mold 1070, bald solid dome), **ca. 1914.** Hilda, sleep eyes, open mouth

13"	$1,800.00	$2,400.00
15"	$2,400.00	$3,200.00
17"	$2,500.00	$3,400.00
25"	$5,795.00*	

Mold 243, ca. 1914, Oriental baby, sleep eyes, open mouth

13"	$3,000.00	$4,000.00
15"	$3,900.00	$5,400.00
19"	$4,950.00	$6,600.00

Mold 247, ca. 1915, socket head, open mouth, sleep eyes

15"	$1,425.00	$1,900.00

Mold 249, ca. 1915, socket head, open mouth, sleep eyes

14"	$1,300.00*	

Too few in database for reliable range.

Mold 255, ca. 1916, marked *"O.I.C. made in Germany,"* solid dome flange neck, glass eyes, large open/closed screamer mouth, cloth body

10½"	$750.00	$1,000.00

Too few in database for reliable range.

Mold 257, ca. 1916, socket head, sleep eyes, open mouth

10"	$450.00	$650.00
14"	$675.00	$900.00
17"	$775.00	$1,025.00
23"	$1,050.00	$1,400.00
25"	$1,800.00	$2,400.00

Toddler body

16"	$700.00	$950.00
24"	$1,350.00	$1,800.00

CHARACTER CHILD, CA. 1910+

Socket head, wig, closed mouth, glass eyes, composition and wood jointed body; add more for painted eyes.

13" bisque child, marked "9" on back of socket head, brown sleep eyes, feathered brows, painted upper and lower lashes, closed mouth, blond mohair wig on plaster pate, jointed wood and composition body, jointed wrists, separate balls at shoulders and hips, original maroon wool and velvet dress, factory chemise trimmed with pleats, lace, and maroon trim, original maroon socks and leather shoes, circa late 1800s, $2,500.00. Courtesy McMasters Doll Auctions.

20" bisque Gibson Girl, no marks visible, original mohair wig over plaster pate, brown sleep eyes, real lashes, painted lower lashes, single stroke brows, closed mouth, kid body with rivet joints at elbows, hips, and knees, bisque lower arms, antique eyelet blouse, white skirt, black velvet ribbon at waist, slip, pants, socks, and antique black leather shoes, black hat with glass fruit decoration, circa 1900, $1,400.00. Courtesy McMasters Doll Auctions.

* at auction

30" bisque mold 171, marked "Made in//Germany//171" on back of head, long curled human hair wig, blue sleep eyes, real lashes, feathered brows, painted upper and lower lashes, open mouth, teeth, dimple in chin, jointed wood and composition body, white lace dress, bonnet, ribbons in hair, circa 1900, $2,000.00. Courtesy JoAnn Threadgill.

Mold 175, 176, 177, 178, 179, 180, 181, 182, 184, 185, 187, 188, 189, 190

15"	$3,000.00	$4,000.00
20"	$3,750.00	$5,000.00

Mold 206, ca. 1910, fat cheeks, closed mouth, glass eyes child or toddler

15"	$6,700.00	$8,900.00

Too few in database for reliable range.

Mold 208, ca. 1910, glass eyes, for all-bisque, see that category

16"	$6,750.00	$9,000.00

Too few in database for reliable range.

Mold 208, painted eyes

12"	$2,500.00	$3,300.00
20"	$7,000.00	$9,300.00

Too few in database for reliable range.

Mold 239, ca. 1914, socket head, open mouth, sleep eyes

Toddler, also comes as baby

16"	$2,325.00	$3,100.00

Too few in database for reliable range.

Mold 241, ca. 1914, socket head, open mouth, sleep eyes

18"	$3,900.00	$5,200.00

Too few in database for reliable range.

Adult

Mold 162, ca. 1898, bisque, open mouth, glass eyes, composition body, slender waists and molded breasts

18"	$1,150.00	$1,525.00
20"	$1,800.00*	

Mold 172, ca. 1900, Gibson Girl, shoulder head, closed mouth, glass eyes, kid body, bisque forearms

10"	$650.00	$850.00
18"	$2,000.00	$2,700.00
20"	$2,200.00	$3,000.00

Wunderkind

Set includes doll body with four interchangeable heads, some with extra apparel, one set includes heads with mold numbers 174, 178, 184, and 185.

11"	$7,500.00	$10,000.00
15"	$9,475.00	$12,600.00

Kewpie

1912+, designed by Rose O'Neill. Manufactured by Borgfeldt, later Joseph Kallus, and then Jesco in 1984, and various companies with special license, as well as unlicensed companies. They were made of all-bisque, celluloid, cloth, composition, rubber, vinyl, zylonite, and other materials. Kewpie figurines (action Kewpies) have mold numbers 4843 through 4883. Kewpies were also marked with a round paper sticker on back, *"KEWPIES DES. PAT. III, R.*

* at auction

1913; Germany; REG. US. PAT. OFF." On the front, was a heart-shaped sticker marked *"KEWPIE//REG. US. // PAT. OFF."* May also be incised on the soles of the feet, *"O'Neill."*

First price indicates doll in good condition, with some flaws; second price indicates doll in excellent condition with no chips. Add more for label, accessories, original box, or exceptional doll.

All-Bisque

Immobiles

Standing, legs together, immobile, no joints, blue wings, molded painted hair, painted side-glancing eyes

2"	$55.00	$110.00
2½"	$70.00	$135.00
4½"	$75.00	$150.00
5"	$90.00	$175.00
6"	$150.00	$275.00

Jointed shoulders

2"	$50.00	$95.00
4½"	$65.00	$130.00
6"	$100.00	$195.00
8½"	$200.00	$400.00
10"	$350.00	$625.00

Carnival chalk Kewpie with jointed shoulders

13"	$50.00	$165.00

Jointed shoulders with any article of molded clothing

2½"	$100.00	$200.00
4½"	$2,600.00* pirate	
6"	$115.00	$330.00
8"	$190.00	$375.00

With Mary Jane shoes

6½"	$250.00	$500.00

Jointed hips and shoulders

5"	$815.00*	
7"	$375.00	$750.00
10"	$500.00	$1,000.00
12½"	$650.00	$1,300.00

Bisque Action Figures

Arms folded

6"	$300.00	$600.00

Aviator

8½"	$425.00	$850.00

Back, laying down, kicking one foot

4"	$100.00	$200.00

Basket and ladybug, Kewpie seated

4"	$900.00	$1,800.00

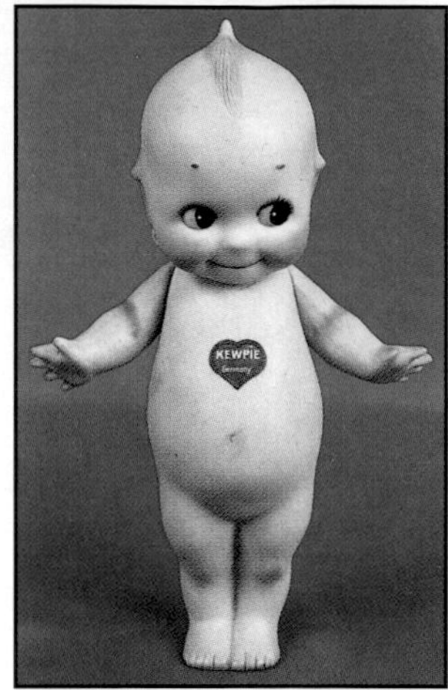

9" all-bisque, "O'Neill" incised on bottom of feet, "Kewpie//Germany" on paper heart label on chest, "Design//Patented" on partial round label on back, stiff neck, painted black side-glancing eyes, dash brows, thick painted upper lashes, closed smiling mouth, molded painted tufts of hair, jointed at shoulders only, molded blue wings at shoulders, circa 1912+, $235.00. Courtesy McMasters Doll Auctions.

Marks:

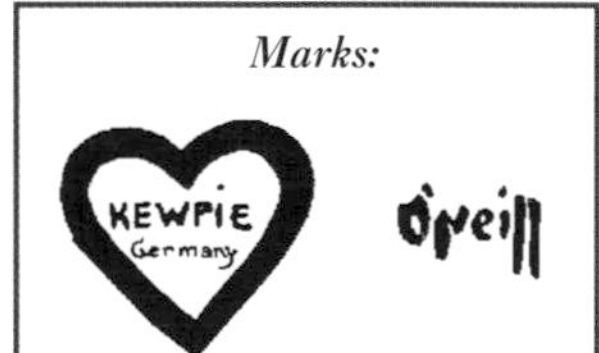

* at auction

10" all-bisque Bride & Groom pair, original crepe paper costume, side-glancing eyes, painted molded blond tufts of hair, $1,300.00+. Courtesy McMasters Doll Auctions.

Bear holding Kewpie		
3½"	$110.00	$220.00
"Blunderboo," Kewpie falling down		
1¾"	$240.00	$465.00
Bottle, green beverage, Kewpie standing, kicking out		
2½"	$330.00	$660.00
Bottle stopper		
2"	$75.00	$150.00
Box, heart shaped, with Kewpie kicker atop		
4"	$440.00	$880.00
Bride and Groom		
3½"	$175.00	$350.00
Boutonniére		
1½"	$55.00	$110.00
2"	$70.00	$135.00
Candy container		
4"	$250.00	$500.00
Card holder		
2"	$250.00	$500.00
With label		
2¼"	$330.00	$660.00
Carpenter, wearing tool apron		
8½"	$550.00	$1,100.00
Cat, black with Kewpie		
2¼"	$150.00	$300.00
Cat, gray on lap of seated Kewpie		
2¼"	$850.00*	
Cat, gray with Kewpie on back		
3"	$275.00	$525.00
Cat, tan with Kewpie		
3"	$150.00	$300.00
Cat, white with Kewpie		
3"	$220.00	$440.00
Chick with seated Kewpie		
2"	$300.00	$600.00
Cowboy		
10"	$400.00	$800.00
Dog, with Kewpie on stomach		
3"	$3,400.00*	
Dog, with Red Cross Kewpie		
4"	$300.00	
Doodle Dog alone		
1½"	$350.00	$700.00
3"	$625.00	$1,350.00
Doodle Dog with Kewpie		
2½"	$125.00	$250.00
Drum on brown stool, with Kewpie		
3½"	$1,200.00	$2,400.00

* at auction

Farmer		
6½"	$450.00	$900.00
Flowers, Kewpie with bouquet in right hand		
5"	$475.00	$935.00
Fly on foot of Kewpie		
3"	$300.00	$600.00
Governor		
2½"	$150.00	$275.00
3¼"	$250.00	$500.00
Hottentot, black Kewpie		
3½"	$225.00	$425.00
5"	$300.00	$575.00
9"	$450.00	$950.00
12"	$4,500.00+	
Huggers		
2½"	$65.00	$125.00
3½"	$75.00	$150.00
4½"	$100.00	$200.00
Inkwell, with writer Kewpie		
4½"	$250.00	$500.00
Jack-O-Lantern between legs of Kewpie		
2"	$250.00	$500.00
Jester, with white hat on head		
4½"	$300.00	$575.00
Kneeling		
4"	$375.00	$750.00
Mandolin, green basket and seated Kewpie		
2"	$150.00	$275.00
Mandolin held by Kewpie in blue chair		
4"	$475.00	$925.00
Mandolin, with Kewpie on moon swing		
2½"	$4,400.00*	
Mayor, seated Kewpie in green wicker chair		
4½"	$475.00	$950.00
Minister		
5"	$125.00	$250.00
Nursing bottle, with Kewpie		
3½"	$300.00	$600.00
Reader Kewpie seated with book		
2"	$125.00	$250.00
3½"	$165.00	$325.00
4"	$250.00	$500.00
Sack held by Kewpie with both hands		
4½"	$1,430.00*	
Salt Shaker		
2"	$165.00	
Seated in fancy chair		
4"	$200.00	$400.00
Soldier bursting out of egg		
4"	$6,900.00*	

4" all-bisque Farmer, incised "O'Neill" on bottom of feet, "Copyright//Rose O'Neill" on round label on back, eyes painted to side, dash brows, tiny painted upper lashes, closed smiling mouth, molded bisque straw hat, molded blue wings, right hand molded to hold rake (missing), left arm molded behind back, unjointed body, stiff neck, circa 1912+, $405.00. Courtesy McMasters Doll Auctions.

* at auction

Soldier, Confederate

4"	$200.00	$400.00

Soldier in egg

3½"	$6,600.00*	

Soldier taking aim with rifle

3½"	$500.00	$990.00

Soldier vase

6½"	$330.00	$660.00

Soldier with black hat, sword, and rifle

4½"	$200.00	$385.00

Soldier with helmet

2¾"	$300.00	$400.00
4½"	$300.00	$600.00

Soldier with red hat, sword, and rifle

3½"	$150.00	$300.00
5¼"	$415.00	$825.00

Stomach, Kewpie laying flat, arms and legs out

4"	$225.00	$450.00

Thinker

4 – 5"	$150.00	$275.00

Traveler with dog and umbrella

3½"	$1,300.00*	

Traveler with umbrella and bag

4"	$175.00	$350.00
5"	$300.00	$600.00

Vase with card holder and Kewpie

2½"	$165.00	$330.00

Vase with Doodle dog & Kewpie

4½"	$2,600.00*	

Vase with huggers

3¾"	$325.00	$650.00

Writer, seated Kewpie with pen in hand

2"	$255.00	$475.00
4"	$265.00	$550.00

Bisque Shoulder head

Cloth, or stockinette body

7"	$285.00	$565.00

Head only

3"	$165.00+	

Celluloid

Bride and Groom

4"	$15.00	$40.00

Jointed arms, heart label on chest

12"	$175.00	$325.00

China

Perfume holder, one piece with opening at back of head

4½"	$550.00	$1,100.00

Salt Shaker

1¼"	$85.00	$165.00

* at auction

10" cloth Richard Krueger Cuddle Kewpie, tagged "Kewpie//Reg. U.S. Pat Off.//Rose O'Neill//©//Krueger N.Y./ /Reg. U.S. Pat. Off.//Made in U.S.A." on right side seam, cloth mask face, painted eyes to side, dash brows, painted upper lashes, painted button nose, closed smiling mouth, blushed cheeks, red satin all-cloth body with shaped wings, near mint condition, circa 1929 – 1930+, $135.00. Courtesy McMasters Doll Auctions.

Dishes

Service for 4	$650.00	$900.00
Service for 6	$975.00	$1,200.00

Cloth

Richard Krueger "Cuddle Kewpie," silk screened face, sateen body, tagged

13"	$325.00	$500.00

Plush, with stockinette face, tagged

8"	$115.00	$225.00

Composition

Hottentot, all-composition, heart decal to chest, jointed arms, red winks, ca. 1946

11"	$300.00	$575.00

All-composition, jointed body, blue wings

11"	$125.00	$375.00
13"	$200.00	$450.00

Composition head, cloth body, flange neck, composition forearms tagged floral dress

11"	$250.00	$875.00

Talcum container

One-piece composition talcum shaker with heart label on chest

7"	$35.00	$65.00

Hard Plastic

Original box, ca. 1950, Kewpie design

8½"	$200.00	$385.00

Sleep eyes, five-piece body with starfish hands

14"	$150.00	$300.00

Metal

Figurine, cast steel on square base, excellent condition

5½"	$30.00	$55.00

Soap

Kewpie soap figure with cotton batting

Colored label with rhyme, marked *"R.O. Wilson, 1917"*

4"	$55.00	$110.00

Kley & Hahn

1902 – 1930+, Ohrdruf, Thüringia, Germany. Bisque heads, jointed composition or leather bodies, exporter; bought heads from Kestner (Walkure) and Hertel Schwab & Co. Also made composition and celluloid head dolls.

First price indicates doll in good condition, but with some flaw; second price indicates doll in excellent condition, with original clothes, or appropriately dressed.

Character Baby

Mold 133, 135, 138, 158, 160, 161, 167, and 571

Mold 133 (made by Hertel Schwab & Co.), solid-dome, painted eyes, closed mouth

Mold 135 (made by Hertel Schwab & Co.), solid-dome, painted eyes, open/closed mouth

Mold 138 (made by Hertel Schwab & Co.), solid-dome, painted eyes, open/closed mouth

Mold 158 (made by Hertel Schwab & Co.), painted eyes, open mouth

Mold 160 (made by Hertel Schwab & Co.), sleep eyes, open/closed mouth

Mold 161 (made by Hertel Schwab & Co.), character face, sleep eyes, open/closed mouth

Mold 167 (made by Hertel Schwab & Co.), sleep eyes, open/closed or open mouth

Mold 571, "K&H" (made by Bähr & Pröschild) character, solid-dome, glass eyes, open/closed mouth, laughing, giant baby

13"	$450.00	$575.00
16"	$500.00	$675.00
19"	$600.00	$800.00
22"	$750.00	$1,025.00
Toddler body		
21"	$1,050.00	$1,400.00
26"	$1,300.00	$1,750.00

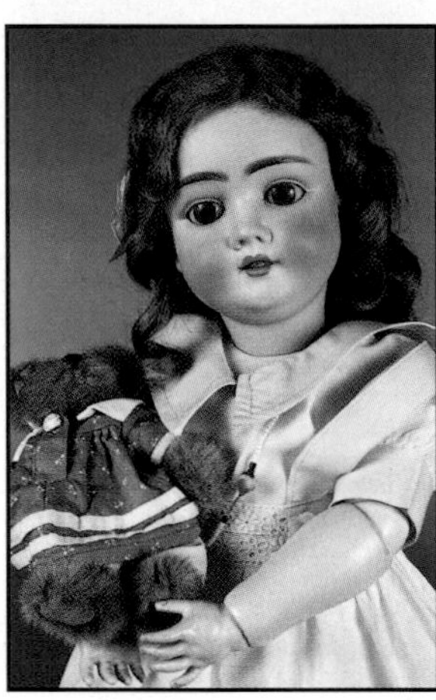

25" bisque mold 250 dolly face Walkure, marked "250//K.H./ /Walkure//4 3/4//Germany," human hair wig, blue sleep eyes, painted upper and lower lashes, open mouth with four teeth, jointed wood and composition body, antique two-piece blue and white outfit, antique underclothing, new socks and shoes, circa 1920, $475.00. *Courtesy McMasters Doll Auctions.*

Mold 567 (made by Bähr & Pröschild) character multi-face, laughing face, glass eyes, open mouth; crying face, painted eyes, open/closed mouth

15"	$1,475.00	$1,950.00
17"	$1,875.00	$2,500.00
19"	$2,550.00	$3,400.00

Mold 680, *"K & CO K&H"* with *"266 K&H,"* ca. 1920, made by Kestner, character, sleep eyes, open mouth

17"	$700.00	$925.00
Toddler		
19"	$975.00	$1,300.00

Child

Mold 250, 282, or Walkure, circa 1920 (made by J.D. Kestner, Jr.), dolly face, sleep eyes, open mouth

21"	$475.00	$625.00
28"	$700.00	$925.00
33"	$900.00	$1,200.00

Mold 325, "Dollar Princess," open mouth

25"	$325.00	$525.00

Character Child

Mold numbers 154, 166, 169, ca. 1912

Mold 154, 166 (made by Hertel Schwab & Co.), solid-dome, glass eyes, closed mouth

Mold 169 (made by Hertel Schwab & Co.), sleep eyes, closed or open/closed mouth

17"	$2,000.00	$2,600.00
19"	$2,175.00	$2,900.00
27"	$2,600.00	$3,500.00
Baby body with bent legs		
12"	$1,785.00*	

Mold 162, ca. 1912 (made by Hertel Schwab & Co.), open mouth, voice cut out

17"	$1,100.00	$1,500.00

Too few in database for reliable range.

Mold 178, ca. 1918 (made by Hertel Schwab & Co.), dome, molded hair, googly, open mouth

Mold 180, ca. 1915 (made by Hertel Schwab & Co.), googly, open/closed mouth

17"	$2,550.00	$3,400.00

Too few in database for reliable range.

Mold 292, 520, 525, 526, 531, character face

Mold 292 *"KH 1930,"* ca. 1930 (made by J. D. Kestner, Jr.), character face

Mold 520 *"K&H,"* ca. 1910 (made by Bähr & Pröschild), painted eyes, closed mouth

Mold 525 *"K & H,"* ca. 1912 (by Bähr & Pröschild), dome, painted eyes, open/ closed mouth

Mold 526 *"K&H,"* ca. 1912 (made by Bähr & Pröschild), painted eyes, closed mouth (see photo in *Doll Values, 3rd Edition*)

Mold 531 *"K&H,"* ca. 1912 (made by Bähr & Pröschild), solid dome, painted eyes, open/closed mouth

12" bisque mold 525 character baby, marked "K&H (in banner)//525//4" on back of solid dome socket head, "Germany" stamped on left shoulder, blue intaglio eyes, molded lids, feathered brows, open/closed mouth, lightly molded and brush-stroked hair, composition bent-limb baby body, pink knit outfit with matching bonnet, white shoes, circa 1912, $300.00. Courtesy McMasters Doll Auctions.

Baby bent-leg body

9½"	$250.00	$325.00

Child

14"	$3,700.00* Mold 520	
17"	$2,200.00* Mold 531	
21"	$2,250.00	$3,000.00

Mold 546, 549, ca. 1912, character face

Mold 546 *"K&H"* (made by Bähr & Pröschild), glass eyes, closed mouth, child body

Mold 549 *"K&H"* (made by Bähr & Pröschild), painted eyes, closed mouth, also in celluloid

16"	$3,150.00	$4,200.00
18"	$3,375.00	$4,500.00

Marks:

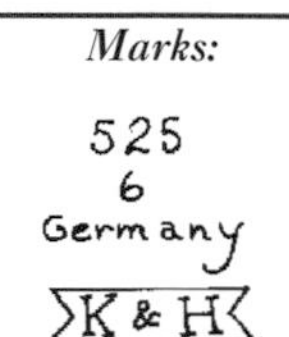

Mold 554, 568, ca. 1912, character face

Mold 554 *"K&H"* (made by Bähr & Pröschild), glass eyes, open/closed mouth

20" bisque mold 546 character face child, mohair wig, applied ears, blue glass eyes, closed eyes, jointed composition child body, antique hat and shoes are replacements, white dress with white pinafore trimmed in lace, circa 1912, $5,000.00. Courtesy Allyson Flagg-Miller.

* at auction

Kley & Hahn

Mold 568 (made by Bähr & Pröschild), solid dome, sleep eyes, smiling

21"	$1,400.00*

Too few in database for reliable range.

Kling, C.F. & Co.

Mark:

1836 – 1930+ Ohrdruf, Thüringia, Germany. Porcelain factory that made china, bisque, and all-bisque dolls, and snow babies. Often mold number marks are followed by size number.

First price indicates doll in good condition, but with some flaws; second price indicates doll in excellent condition, with original clothes, or appropriately dressed, more for exceptional doll with elaborate molded hair or bodice.

Bisque Shoulder Head

Painted eyes, wig or molded hair, cloth or kid body

15"	$300.00	$400.00
19"	$465.00	$575.00
21"	$475.00	$650.00

Glass eyes

13"	$400.00	$525.00

Mold 123, 124, ca. 1880, incised with bell mark, glass eyes, closed mouth, shoulder head

15"	$650.00	$850.00

Mold 131, 167, 178, 182, 189, ca. 1885

Mold 131, incised bell, shoulder head, glass eyes, closed mouth
Mold 167, incised bell, solid dome, with wig, closed mouth
Mold 178, shoulder head, molded hair, glass eyes, closed mouth
Mold 182, shoulder head, molded hair, painted eyes, closed mouth
Mold 189, shoulder head, molded hair, painted eyes, closed mouth

15"	$800.00	$1,075.00

Mold 135, ca. 1885, molded bodice, flower in molded hair

21"	$825.00	$1,200.00

Mold 370, 372, 373, 377, ca. 1900, sleep eyes, open mouth

15"	$375.00	$500.00
21"	$525.00	$700.00

Bisque socket head, open mouth, jointed body

13"	$300.00	$400.00
17"	$425.00	$550.00
21"	$550.00	$725.00

China Shoulder Head

Mold numbers 131, 188, 189, 202, ca. 1880s

Cloth or kid body, china limbs, blond or black molded hair
Mold 131, painted eyes, closed mouth
Mold 188, molded hair, glass eyes, closed mouth
Mold 189, molded hair, painted eyes, closed mouth
Mold 202, molded hair, painted eyes, closed mouth

13"	$200.00	$275.00
18"	$335.00	$450.00
21"	$375.00	$500.00

* at auction

Knoch, Gebrüder

1887 – 1918+, Neustad, Thüringia, Germany. Made bisque doll heads and doll joints, with cloth or kid body. Succeeded in 1918 by Max Oscar Arnold.

Mark:
GK N
Made in Germany
Ges N. 216 Gesch
15/0

Shoulder Head

Mold 203, 205, ca. 1910

Mold 203, character face, painted eyes, closed mouth, stuffed cloth body

Mold 205, "GKN" character face, painted eyes, open/closed mouth, molded tongue

12"	$600.00	$800.00
14"	$750.00	$1,000.00

Too few in database for reliable range.

Mold 223, "GKN GES. NO. GESCH," ca. 1912

Character face, solid-dome or shoulder head, painted eyes, molded tears, closed mouth

Too few in database for reliable range.

Socket Head

Mold 179, 181, 190, 192, 193, 201, ca. 1900

(Mold 201 also came as black), dolly face, glass eyes, open mouth

13"	$185.00	$250.00
17"	$300.00	$425.00

Mold 204, 205, ca. 1910, character face

15"	$865.00	$1,150.00

Mold 206, ca. 1910, "DRGM" solid dome, intaglio eyes, open/closed mouth

11"	$750.00*

Mold 216, ca. 1912, "GKN" solid dome, intaglio eyes, laughing, open/closed mouth

12"	$315.00*

Too few in database for reliable range.

229: See All-Bisque category.

230, ca. 1912, molded bonnet, character shoulder head, painted eyes, open/closed mouth laughing

232, ca. 1912, molded bonnet, character shoulder head, laughing

13"	$675.00	$900.00
15"	$1,200.00	$1,600.00

König & Wernicke

1912 – 1930+, Waltershausen, Germany. Had doll factory, made bisque or celluloid dolls with composition bodies, later dolls with hard rubber heads.

Mark:
K&W
HARTGUMMI
555 0
GERMANY

Bisque Baby

Mold 98, 99, ca. 1912, *"made in Germany"* (made by Hertel Schwab & Co.), character, socket head, sleep eyes, open mouth, teeth, tremble tongue, wigged, composition bent-leg baby body

9"	$275.00	$375.00
18"	$500.00	$675.00
22"	$600.00	$800.00

* at auction

König & Wernicke

20" bisque character child, marked "K & W//9" on back of head, human hair wig, blue sleep eyes, real lashes, painted lower lashes, feathered brows, open mouth, two upper teeth, tongue, jointed composition body with straight wrists, antique white dress with tucks and lace inserts, antique underclothing, new socks and shoes, circa 1912+, $650.00. Courtesy McMasters Doll Auctions.

Mold 1070, ca. 1915, socket head, open mouth, bent-leg baby body

12"	$400.00	$550.00
16"	$500.00	$650.00

Toddler

17"	$1,000.00	$1,400.00
19"	$1,150.00	$1,575.00

Composition Child

Composition head on five-piece or fully-jointed body, open mouth, sleep eyes, add more for flirty eyes.

14"	$225.00	$300.00
16"	$350.00	$450.00

Kruse, Käthe

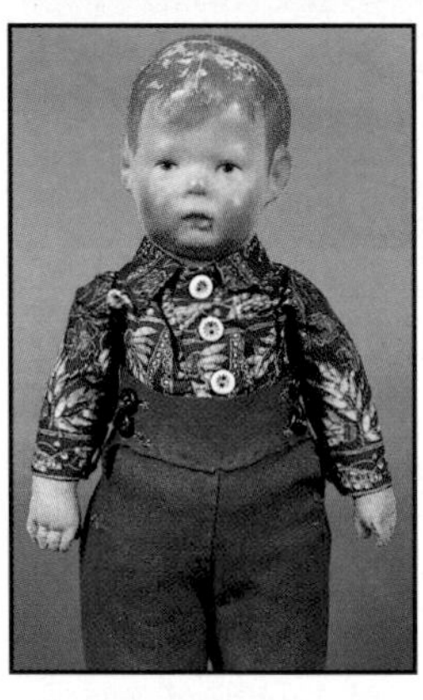

16" cloth Doll I, wide hips, applied thumbs, some light soil, paint rubs, 1910+ $2,300.00. Courtesy McMasters Doll Auctions.

1910 – 1980 on, Prussia, after W.W.II, Bavaria. Made dolls of waterproof muslin, wool, and stockinette with heads, hair, and hands oil painted. The skeleton frame was rigid with movable parts; early dolls are stuffed with deer hair. Early thumbs are part of the hand; after 1914 they are attached separately, later again, they're part of the hand. Marked on the bottom of the left foot with number and name *"Käthe Kruse,"* in black, red, or purple ink. After 1929, dolls had wigs, but some still had painted hair. Original doll modeled after Dutch bust sculpture "Fiammingo," by Francois Duquesnois.

Cloth

Doll I Series, 1910 – 1929

All-cloth, jointed shoulders, wide hips, painted eyes and hair

Three vertical seams in back of head, marked on left foot

17"	$1,700.00	$4,800.00

Ball-jointed knees, 1911 variant produced by Kämmer & Reinhardt

17"	$5,500.00+

Too few in database for reliable range.

Doll I Series, later model, 1929+, now with slim hips

17"	$1,600.00	$3,100.00

Doll IH Series, wigged version, 1929+

17"	$1,600.00	$3,000.00

Bambino, a doll for a doll, circa 1915 – 1925

8"	$500.00+

Too few in database for reliable range.

Mark:

Doll II Series, "Schlenkerchen," ca. 1922 – 1936

Smiling baby, open/closed mouth, stockinette covered body and limbs, one seam head

13"	$10,400.00*	

Too few in database for reliable range.

Doll V, VI, Sandbabies Series, 1920s+

"Traumerchen" (closed eyes) and "Du Mein" (open eyes) were cloth dolls with painted hair, weighted with sand or unweighted, with or without belly buttons, in 19⅝" and 23⅝" sizes. One- or three-seam heads, or cloth over cardboard. Later heads were made in the 1930s from a heavy composition called magnesit.

19⅝"	$2,000.00	$3,900.00

Magnesit head, circa 1930s+

20"	$350.00	$1,500.00
40"	$2,650.00	$3,500.00

Doll VII Series, circa 1927 – 1952

Two versions were offered.

A smaller 14" Du Mein open eye baby, painted hair or wigged, three-seam head, wide hips, sewn on thumbs, 1927 – 1930

14"	$1,500.00	$2,800.00

Too few in database for reliable range.

A smaller Doll I version, with wide hips, separately sewn on thumbs, painted hair or wigged, after 1930 – 1950s slimmer hips and with thumbs formed with hand

14"	$1,000.00	$2,000.00

20" cloth boy marked "Kathe Kruse//40740" on left foot, oil painted cloth swivel head, painted blue eyes, single stroke brows, accented nostrils, closed mouth, original wig, five-piece cloth body, original red/white shorts and shirt, tie, underwear, socks, and shoes, original paper hang tag, circa 1929+, $950.00. Courtesy McMasters Doll Auctions.

Doll VIII Series, Deutsche Kind, the "German child," 1929+

Modeled after Kruse's son, Friedebald, hollow head, swivels, one verticle seam in back of head, wigged, disk-jointed legs, later made in plastic during the 1950s

20"	$1,300.00	$2,500.00

Doll IX Series, "The Little German Child," 1929+

Wigged, one seam head, a smaller version of Doll VIII

14"	$1,000.00	$1,800.00

Doll X Series, 1935+

Smaller Doll I with turning one-seam head

14"	$1,200.00	$2,400.00

Doll XII Series, 1930s

Hampelchen with loose legs, three vertical seams on back of head, painted hair, button and band on back to make legs stand. The 14" variation has head of Doll I; the 16" variation also has the head of Doll I, and is known after 1940s as Hempelschatz, Doll XIIB.

14"	$800.00	$1,200.00
16"	$900.00	$1,500.00
18"	$1,100.00	$2,100.00

* at auction

XIIH, wigged version

18" $1,200.00 $2,200.00

XII/I, 1951+, legs have disc joints

18" $300.00 $650.00

U.S. Zone, after World War II, circa 1946+

Cloth

14" $300.00 $600.00

Magnesit (heavy composition)

14" $400.00 $800.00

HARD PLASTIC, 1952 – 1975 (CELLULOID AND OTHER SYNTHETICS)

Turtle Dolls, 1955 – 1961, synthetic bodies

14" $125.00 $325.00

16" $150.00 $400.00

18" $200.00 $500.00

Glued-on wigs, sleep or painted eyes, pink muslin body

18" $200.00 $600.00

21" $250.00 $750.00

1975 to date, marked with size number in centimeters, B for baby, H for hair, and G for painted hair

10" $100.00 $200.00

13" $175.00

Kuhnlenz, Gebrüder

16" bisque Belton-type, marked "G.K.//13.27" on back of head, bisque socket head with flat top, two small stringing holes, antique human hair wig, blue paperweight eyes, heavy feathered brows, blush over eyes, painted lashes, closed mouth, pieced-in ears, jointed wood and composition body with separate balls at shoulders, elbows, hips, and knees, blue/white factory chemise, antique underclothing, socks, and shoes, circa 1885+, $1,800.00. Courtesy McMasters Doll Auctions.

1884 – 1930, Kronach, Bavaria. Made dolls, doll heads, movable children, and swimmers. Butler Bros. and Marshall Field distributed their dolls.

Mark:

Gbr K
44-17
Bavaria

Mold 28, 31, 32, ca. 1890, bisque socket head, closed mouth, glass eyes, pierced ears, wig, wood and composition jointed body

19" $1,800.00 $2,400.00

23" $2,100.00 $2,800.00

Mold 34, Bru type, paperweight eyes, closed mouth, pierced ears, composition jointed body

12½" $1,650.00 $2,200.00

Mold 38, solid dome turned shoulder head, closed mouth, pierced ears, kid body

20" $900.00 $1,200.00

Mold 41, solid dome socket head, open mouth, glass eyes

16" $900.00 $1,125.00

Mold 44, small dolls marked Gbr. K in sunburst, socket head, glass eyes, open mouth, five-piece composition body, molded painted socks and shoes

7" $250.00 $325.00

9" $1,500.00* pr in presentation box

* at auction

Kuhnlenz, Gebruder

Mold 165, ca. 1900, socket head, sleep eyes, open mouth, teeth

22"	$350.00	$450.00
33"	$525.00	$650.00

Lanternier, A. & Cie.

1915 – 1924, Limoges, France. Porcelain factory, made dolls and heads, including heads marked *"Caprice," "Cherie," "Favorite," "La Georgienne," "Lorraine,"* and *"Toto."* Lady dolls were dressed in French provincial costumes, bodies by Ortyz; dolls were produced for Association to Aid War Widows.

Adult, ca. 1915

Marked *"Caprice," "Cherie," "Favorite," "La Georgienne," "Lorraine,"* or *"Toto,"* bisque socket head, open/closed mouth with teeth, composition adult body

17"	$700.00	$1,000.00
22"	$1,000.00*	

Painted eyes

12½"	$1,975.00*

Child

Bisque socket head, open mouth with teeth, wig, composition jointed body

17"	$525.00	$725.00
23"	$700.00	$950.00

Leather

Leather was an available resource for Native Americans to use for making doll heads, bodies, or entire dolls. Some examples of Gussie Decker's dolls were advertised as "impossible for child to hurt itself" and leather was fine for teething babies.

12" $275.00

Too few in database for reliable range.

25" $325.00

Too few in database for reliable range.

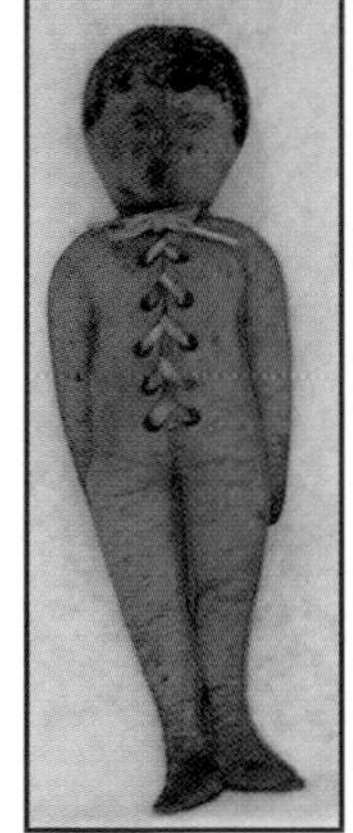

12¼" all-leather cotton stuffed teething doll that laces up the front, painted features and hair, designed by Gussie Decker for M.S. Davis Co. and distributed by Butler Bros. advertised as "impossible to hurt themselves — will last several generations," circa 1902 – 1909, $275.00. Courtesy Jennifer Scott.

Lenci

1918 – 80+, Turine, Italy. Trademark and name of firm started by Enrico and Elenadi Scavini, that made felt dolls with pressed faces, also made composition head dolls, wooden dolls, and porcelain figurines and dolls. Early Lenci dolls have tiny metal button, hang tags with *"Lenci//Torino//Made in Italy."* Ribbon strips marked *"Lenci//Made in Italy"* were found in the clothes ca. 1925 – 1950. Some, but not all dolls have Lenci marked in purple or black ink on the sole of the foot. Some with original paper tags may be marked with a model number in pencil.

Mark:

* at auction

9" felt girl, red hair, surprise eyes, surprise "O" shaped mouth, molded and pressed face, red dress, holding white felt pig, scarf around hair, wooden shoes, circa 1930s, $375.00. Courtesy Nancy Lazenby.

16" felt, mohair wig, oil painted features including side-glancing brown eyes, two-tone painted lips with highlights on lower lips, accent dots at nose, yellow organdy original dress, scalloped socks and felt shoes, marked "Lenci" on bottom of left foot, circa 1930s, $500.00+. Courtesy Patrice Hunker.

Dolls have felt swivel heads, oil-painted features, often side-glancing eyes, jointed shoulders and hips, sewn together third and fourth fingers, sewn-on double felt ears, often dressed in felt and organdy original clothes, excellent condition. May have scalloped socks.

The most sought after are the well-constructed early dolls from the 1920s and 1930s, when Madame Lenci had control of the design and they were more elaborate with fanciful well-made accessories. They carried animals of wood or felt, baskets, felt vegetables, purses, or bouquets of felt flowers. This era of dolls had eye shadow, dots in corner of eye, two-tone lips, with lower lip highlighted and, depending on condition, will command higher prices.

The later dolls of the 1940s and 1950s have hard cardboard-like felt faces, with less intricate details, like less elaborate appliqués, fewer accessories, and other types of fabrics such as taffeta, cotton, and rayon, all showing a decline in quality and should not be priced as earlier dolls. The later dolls may have fabric covered cardboard torsos. Model numbers changed over the years, so what was a certain model number early, later became another letter or number.

Identification Tips:

Lenci characteristics include double layer ears, scalloped cotton socks. Early dolls may have rooted mohair wig, 1930s dolls may have "frizzed" played-with wigs. Later dolls are less elaborate with hard cardboard-type felt faces.

First price indicates doll in poor condition, perhaps worn, soiled, or faded, price in this condition should reflect 25 percent value of doll in excellent condition; second price indicates doll in excellent condition, clean, with colors still bright. Deduct for dolls of the 1940s and 1950s or later. Add more for tags, boxes, or accessories. Exceptional dolls and rare examples may go much higher.

Baby

13"	$375.00	$1,500.00
16"	$1,700.00*	
22"	$2,000.00	$3,200.00

Child, 1920s – 1930s, softer face, more elaborate costume

13"	$500.00	$1,750.00
17"	$650.00	$2,500.00
21"	$750.00	$2,750.00

1940s – 1950s+, hard face, less intricate costume

13"	$75.00	$400.00
15"	$100.00	$500.00
17"	$125.00	$600.00

* at auction

14" cloth girl, unmarked, pressed felt swivel head, original blond mohair wig, painted blue eyes to side, molded single stroke brows, painted lashes, closed mouth, applied felt ears, cloth torso, felt arms and legs, original pink organdy dress with ruffles, felt flowers, faded pink felt vest, hat, and shoes, original underclothing and socks, circa 1930s, $375.00. Courtesy McMasters Doll Auctions.

9" cloth Mascotte, "Lenci//Torino//Made in Italy" on round paper tag, "Lenci//Made in Italy" on cloth tag, pressed felt swivel head, original mohair wig, painted brown eyes, single stroke brows, painted upper lashes, open/closed mouth, applied felt ears, cloth body, felt arms, jointed at shoulders and hips, original felt and organdy dress, felt jacket and hat, original organdy underclothing, socks, and shoes, circa 1920s, $170.00. Courtesy McMasters Doll Auctions.

SMALL DOLLS

Miniatures, 9"

Child	$125.00	$400.00
Tyrol Boy	$100.00	$375.00
Young Flower Merchant		$1,300.00*
10 – 11"	$125.00	$500.00

Mascottes, 8½", have swing legs like Mama dolls, may have loop on neck

8½"	$80.00	$325.00

In rare outfit, carrying accessories

8½"	$115.00	$450.00

FADETTE

With adult face, flapper or boudoir body with long slim limbs

17"	$265.00	$1,050.00
32"	$650.00	$2,600.00
48"	$1,250.00	$5,000.00

CELEBRITIES

Bach

17"	$715.00	$2,850.00

Jack Dempsey

18"	$875.00	$3,500.00

Tom Mix

18"	$875.00	$3,500.00

Mendel

22"	$925.00	$3,700.00

Mozart

14"	$3,000.00*

Pastorelle

14"	$3,000.00*

CHARACTERS

Aladdin

14"	$1,925.00	$7,750.00

Athlete, Golfer, ca. 1930

17" $2,700.00 *a few moth holes

* at auction

20" cloth Modestina, pressed felt swivel head, original curly mohair wig, large blue painted surprise "O" shaped eyes to the side, painted upper lashes, open/closed two-tone mouth, five-piece body with cloth torso, upper torso felt-covered, felt arms and legs, original felt dress with colorful plaid skirt, felt-trimmed organdy sleeves and bloomers with ruffles, gold felt flower-trimmed bonnet, green felt shoes, white cotton socks, circa 1925+, $1,000.00. Courtesy McMasters Doll Auctions.

Aviator, girl with felt helmet

18"	$800.00	$3,200.00

Benedetta

19"	$300.00	$1,100.00

Court Gentleman

18"	$400.00	$1,600.00

Cupid

17"	$1,300.00	$5,200.00

Devil

9"	$1,500.00*	

Fascist Boy, rare

14"	$750.00	$1,500.00
17"	$1,800.00*	

Flower Girl, ca. 1930

20"	$250.00	$1,000.00

Henriette

26"	$625.00	$2,500.00

Indian

17"	$900.00	$3,600.00

Squaw with papoose

17"	$1,050.00	$4,200.00

Laura

16"	$250.00	$950.00

Lucia 48, ca. 1930

14"	$200.00	$800.00

Merry Widow

20"	$350.00	$1,450.00

Pan, hooved feet

8"	$1,000.00*	

Pierrot

21"	$1,500.00	$2,000.00

Salome, ca. 1920, brown felt, ball at waist allows doll to swivel

17"	$850.00	$3,500.00

Series 300 Children

Eastern European boy

17"	$275.00	$1,100.00

Turkish boy

17"	$375.00	$1,500.00

Smoker

Painted eyes

28"	$600.00	$2,400.00

* at auction

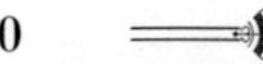

Glass eyes		
24"	$975.00	$3,900.00
Sport Series Boy		
17"	$4,000.00*	
Val Gardena		
19"	$225.00	$900.00
Winking Bellhop with Love Letter		
11"	$200.00	$750.00
ETHNIC OR REGIONAL COSTUME		
Bali dancer		
15"	$375.00	$1,500.00
Eugenia		
25"	$275.00	$1,100.00
Chinese Boy, ca. 1925		
16"	$1,700.00*	
Madame Butterfly, ca. 1926		
17"	$800.00	$3,200.00
25"	$1,200.00	$4,800.00
Marenka, Russian girl, ca. 1930		
14"	$1,100.00*	
Scottish girl, ca. 1930		
14"	$175.00	$700.00
Spanish girl, ca. 1930		
14"	$200.00	$800.00
17"	$250.00	$1,000.00
Tyrol boy or girl, ca. 1935		
14"	$200.00	$800.00
EYE VARIATIONS		
Glass eyes		
16"	$400.00	$1,600.00
22"	$750.00	$3,000.00
Flirty glass eyes		
15"	$550.00	$2,200.00
20"	$700.00	$2,800.00
Surprise eye, Widow, "O" shaped eyes and mouth		
19"	$1,500.00*	
MODERN, CA. 1979+		
13"	$65.00	$125.00
21"	$100.00	$200.00
26"	$125.00	$250.00
ACCESSORIES		
Lenci Catalogs	$900.00 – 1,200.00	
Lenci Dog	$100.00 – 150.00	
Purse	$175.00	$225.00

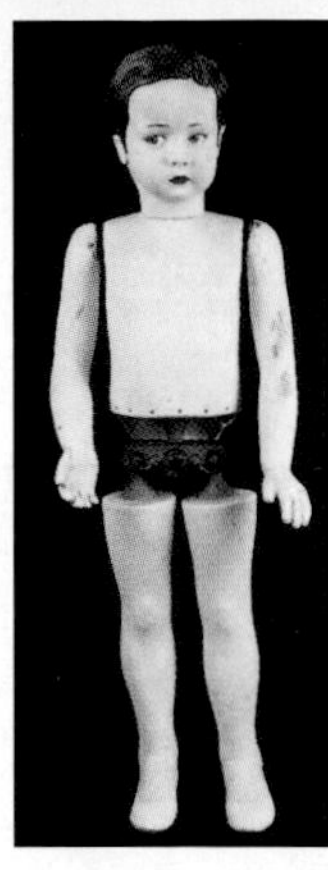

39" cloth Mannequin, marked "Lenci//Turin Italy" on torso, "Kirsh & Reale Inc.//167 Madison Ave.//New York City" on metal plate, pressed felt swivel head, painted brown side-glancing eyes, closed mouth, applied ears, mohair rooted into felt for hair, felt covered wooden torso, felt covered metal or wooden arms/legs, wooden balls from torso and legs pivot for posing, antique shirt, checkered two-piece suit with short pants, circa 1920s, $1,650.00. Courtesy McMasters Doll Auctions.

Lenci-Type

1920 – 1950. These were made by many English, French, or Italian firms like Gre-Poir or Raynal from felt with painted features, mohair wig, original clothes. These must be in very good condition, tagged or unmarked. Usually Lenci-types have single felt ears or no ears.

* at auction

Lenci-Type

Child

15" $35.00 $145.00

Regional costume

8" $15.00 $45.00

Smoker

16" $100.00 $400.00

Gre Poir, France, New York City, ca. 1927 – 1930s; Eugenie Poir made felt or cloth mask dolls, unmarked on body, no ears, white socks with three stripes, hang tag

Cloth

17 – 18" $150.00 $525.00

Felt

19½" $150.00 $500.00

11" cloth Alma Company girl, marked "Alma//Made in Italy" on bottom of left foot, swivel socket head strung with elastic, brown painted side-glancing eyes, tiny closed mouth, blond mohair wig, five-piece felt body jointed at shoulders and hips, mitten hands, white felt dress and hat trimmed with blue, silhouette of cat playing with ball appliquéd on skirt, white organdy underwear combination, white felt shoes, circa late 1920s – early 1930s, $200.00. Courtesy McMasters Doll Auctions.

Limbach

1772 – 1927+, Alsbach, Thüringia, Germany. This porcelain factory made bisque head dolls, china dolls, bathing dolls, and all-bisque dolls. Usually marked with three leaf clover.

All-Bisque

Child, small doll, molded hair or wigged, painted eyes, molded painted shoes and socks, may have mark *"8661,"* and cloverleaf. More for exceptional dolls.

6" $100.00 $175.00

8" $185.00 $275.00

Glass eyes

6" $200.00 $275.00

Baby

Mold 8682, character face, bisque socket head, glass eyes, clover mark, bent-leg baby body, wig, open/closed mouth

8½" $450.00*

Child

May have name above mold mark, such as Norma or Rita, bisque socket head, glass eyes, clover mark, wig, open mouth

20" $700.00 $950.00

Marottes

Ca. 1860 on and earlier. Doll's head on wooden or ivory stick, sometimes with whistle; when twirled some play music. Bisque head on stick made by various French and German companies. Add more for marked head.

* at auction

Bisque, open mouth

14" $625.00 $1,025.00

Marseille, Armand, Mold 3200, open mouth

13" $1,000.00 $1,300.00

Mold 600, closed mouth, squeaker mechanism

13" $900.00 $1,200.00

Schoenau & Hoffmeister, mold 4700, circa 1905

15" $800.00* pristine

Celluloid

11" $190.00 $250.00

Marseille, Armand

1885 – 1930+, Sonneberg, Köppelsdorf, Thüringia, Germany. One of the largest suppliers of bisque doll heads, ca. 1900 – 1930, to such companies as Amberg, Arranbee, Bergmann, Borgfeldt, Butler Bros., Dressel, Montgomery Ward, Sears, Steiner, Wiegand, Louis Wolf, and others. Made some doll heads with no mold numbers, but names, such as Alma, Baby Betty, Baby Gloria, Baby Florence, Baby Phyllis, Beauty, Columbia, Duchess, Ellar, Florodora, Jubilee, Mabel, Majestic, Melitta, My Playmate, Nobbi Kid, Our Pet, Princess, Queen Louise, Rosebud, Superb, Sunshine, and Tiny Tot. Some Indian dolls had no mold numbers. Often used Superb kid bodies, with bisque hands.

First price indicates doll in good condition with flaws; second price indicates doll in excellent condition, appropriately dressed. Add $50.00 more for composition body; add $100.00 more for toddler body; more for original clothes or exceptional doll.

NEWBORN BABY

Newborn, bisque solid-dome socket head or flange neck, may have wig, glass eyes, closed mouth, cloth body with celluloid or composition hands

Mold 341, My Dream Baby, 351, ca. 1926, Rock-A-Bye Baby, marked *"AM"* in original basket with layette; head circumference:

10" $185.00 $250.00

12" $225.00 $325.00

15" $350.00 $475.00

Mold 345, Kiddiejoy, ca. 1926, 352, bisque solid-dome socket head or flange neck, may have wig, glass eyes, closed mouth, cloth body with celluloid or composition hands, head circumference:

8" $150.00 $225.00

11" $200.00 $275.00

16" $350.00 $525.00

With toddler body

28" $900.00 $1,200.00

Mold 372 Kiddiejoy, ca. 1925, shoulder head, molded hair, painted eyes, open/closed mouth, two upper teeth, kid body

12" $300.00 $400.00

18" $500.00 $650.00

21" $775.00 $1,025.00

Marks:

Armand Marseille
Germany
390
A. 4. M.

Made in Germany
Florodora
A 5 M

Queen Louise
Germany
7.

* at auction

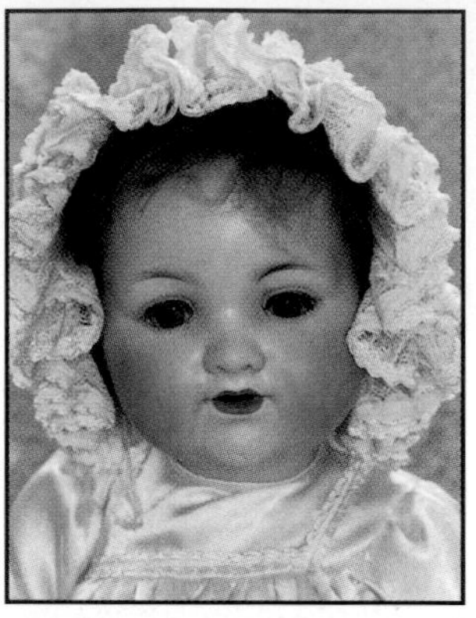

20" bisque mold 990 character baby, marked "Armand Marseille/ /Germany//990//A. 10. M." on back of head, blue sleep eyes, real lashes, painted upper and lower lashes, open mouth, auburn wig, bent-limb baby body, white satin dress with ruffled bonnet, circa 1925, $700.00. Courtesy Deborah Baron.

Character Baby

Baby Betty, usually found on child composition body, some on bent-leg baby body

16"	$500.00*	

Baby Gloria, solid dome, open mouth, painted hair

15"	$500.00	$675.00

Baby Phyllis, head circumference

	$300.00	$450.00
9"	$275.00	$450.00
13"	$300.00	$500.00

Fany, mold 230, 231, ca. 1912, can be child, toddler, or baby, more for molded hair

#231

16"	$6,300.00*	
17"	$3,150.00	$4,200.00

Mold 256, 259, 326, 327, 328, 329, 360a, 750, 790, 900, 927, 970, 971, 975, 980, 984, 985, 990, 991, 992 Our Pet, 995, 996, bisque solid-dome or wigged socket head, open mouth, glass eyes, composition bent-leg baby body, add more for toddler body or flirty eyes or exceptional doll

12"	$225.00	$300.00
15"	$300.00	$425.00
17"	$400.00	$550.00
21"	$525.00	$750.00
24"	$600.00	$800.00

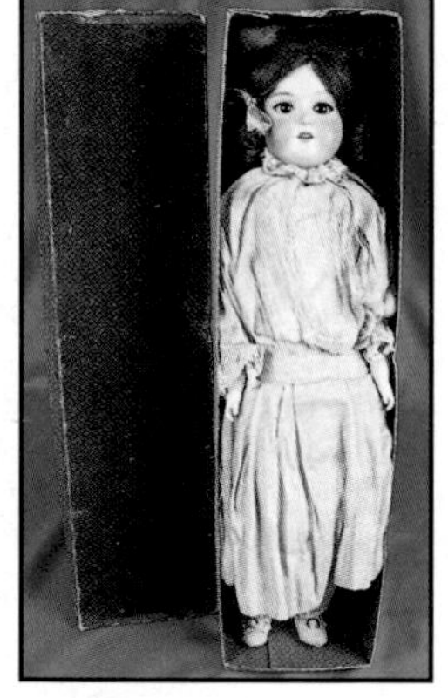

20" bisque mold 370 Floradora, marked "370//A.M. – 1-DEP//Armand Marseille/ /Made in Germany" on back of shoulder plate, "Real Hair//Florodora//Germany" on label on front of body, original human hair wig, brown sleep eyes, real lashes, open mouth, four upper teeth, kid body, bisque lower arms, fragile original pink silk dress, pink cloth shoes, unplayed with in original labeled box, box reads "Auburn Hair//Brown Eyes//Florodora," circa 1911+, $425.00. Courtesy McMasters Doll Auctions.

Child

No mold number, or just marked *"A.M.,"* bisque socket head, open mouth, glass eyes, wig, composition jointed body

17"	$300.00	$400.00
32"	$700.00	$925.00
42"	$1,500.00	$2,000.00

Mold 1890, 1892, 1893 (made for Cuno & Otto Dressel), 1894, 1897, 1898 (made for Cuno & Otto Dressel), 1899, 1900, 1901, 1902, 1903, 1909, and 3200, kid body, bisque shoulder or socket head, glass eyes, open mouth with teeth, wig. Add more for original clothes, labels.

12"	$125.00	$150.00
16"	$135.00	$225.00
19"	$210.00	$280.00
22"	$255.00	$350.00
26"	$330.00	$450.00

Composition body

8"	$245.00	$325.00
10"	$200.00	$275.00
16"	$550.00* original	
18"	$350.00	$450.00
21"	$375.00	$500.00
24"	$465.00	$624.00

* at auction

Mold 370, 390, ca. 1900, Duchess, Florodora, Lilly, Mabel, My Playmate, open mouth, glass eyes

Kid body

12"	$125.00	$165.00
15"	$190.00	$255.00
18"	$245.00	$325.00
22"	$525.00	$700.00

composition body

10"	$375.00* original costume	
13"	$200.00	$270.00
18"	$285.00	$375.00
21"	$375.00	$450.00
24"	$425.00	$525.00
27"	$550.00	$700.00
33"	$750.00	$1,025.00

Alma, Beauty, Columbia, Melitta, My Companion, Princess, Queen Louise, Rosebud

Kid body

15"	$150.00	$200.00
23"	$375.00	$450.00

composition body

13"	$225.00	$325.00
17"	$285.00	$375.00
22"	$425.00	$565.00
28"	$475.00	$650.00
31"	$775.00	$1,075.00

Character Child

Mold 225, ca. 1920, bisque socket head, glass eyes, open mouth, two rows of teeth, composition jointed body

14"	$2,700.00	$3,600.00
19"	$3,500.00	$4,650.00

Mold 250, ca. 1912, domed

9"	$400.00*	
15"	$450.00	$600.00
18"	$750.00	$1,000.00

Mold 251, ca. 1912, socket head, open/closed mouth

13"	$1,100.00	$1,450.00
17"	$1,500.00	$2,000.00

Open mouth

14"	$600.00	$800.00

Mold 253: See Googly.

Mold 310, Just Me, ca. 1929, bisque socket head, wig, flirty eyes, closed mouth, composition body

7½"	$800.00	$1,100.00
9"	$1,000.00	$1,400.00
11"	$1,300.00	$1,700.00
13"	$1,600.00	$2,100.00

* at auction

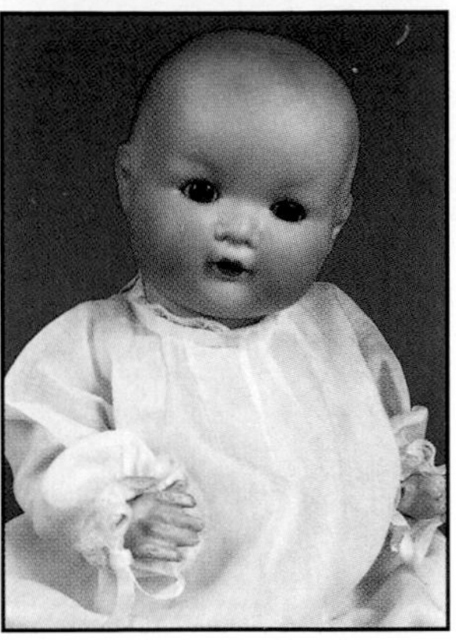

16" bisque mold 518, marked "A.M.//Germany//518//5½K" on back of solid dome flange head, lightly molded painted hair, brown sleep eyes, painted lashes, softly blushed brows, open mouth, two upper teeth, composition baby body, antique baby dress, slip, diaper, socks, and booties, circa 1920s, $340.00. Courtesy McMasters Doll Auctions.

22" bisque mold 992 Our Pet, marked "Armand Marseille/ /Germany//992//A. 12. M." on head, old human hair wig, sleep eyes, real lashes, painted lashes, open mouth, two upper teeth, composition baby body, new mint green baby dress, lace trim, booties, circa 1930, $260.00, holding seven Russian cotton Christmas ornaments, $145.00. Courtesy McMasters Doll Auctions.

25" bisque Queen Louise, marked "28.8//Queen Louise//Germany//7," brown sleep eyes, molded feathered brows, painted lashes, open mouth, four upper teeth, replaced mohair wig, jointed wood and composition body, redressed in ecru antique-style dress with blue ribbon trim, tatted shawl, underclothing, new socks and shoes, black antique hat, circa 1910, $350.00. Courtesy McMasters Doll Auctions.

10" painted bisque Just Me, marked "Just Me//Registered//Germany//A 310/5/0 M," blue side-glancing sleep eyes, closed mouth, human hair wig, five-piece composition Patsy-type body with bent right arm, pink dotted Swiss dress, panties, new socks, pink shoes with buckles, circa 1929, $600.00. Courtesy McMasters Doll Auctions.

Painted bisque, with Vogue labeled outfits

8"	$625.00	$850.00
10"	$750.00	$1,000.00

Mold 350, ca. 1926, glass eyes, closed mouth

16"	$1,650.00	$2,250.00
20"	$2,100.00	$2,850.00

Mold 360a, ca. 1913, open mouth

12"	$300.00	$400.00

Too few in database for reliable range.

Mold 400, 401, ca. 1926, glass eyes, closed mouth

13"	$1,100.00	$1,400.00

Flapper body, thin limbs

16"	$1,800.00	$2,300.00

Mold 449, ca. 1930, painted eyes, closed mouth

13"	$475.00	$635.00
18"	$900.00	$1,200.00

Painted bisque

11"	$250.00	$350.00
15"	$575.00	$765.00

Mold 450, glass eyes, closed mouth

14"	$550.00	$725.00

Mold 500, 620, 630, ca. 1910, domed shoulder head, molded/painted hair, painted intaglio eyes, closed mouth

17"	$750.00	$1,000.00

Mold 520, ca. 1910, domed head, glass eyes, open mouth

composition body

12"	$575.00	$775.00
19"	$1,625.00	$2,175.00

Kid body

16"	$700.00	$1,000.00
20"	$1,125.00	$1,500.00

Mold 550, ca. 1926, domed, glass eyes, closed mouth

14"	$1,400.00*	

Too few in database for reliable range.

Mold 560, ca. 1910, character, domed, painted eyes, open/closed mouth or **560A**, ca. 1926, wigged, glass eyes, open mouth

14"	$600.00	$850.00

Mold 570, ca. 1910, domed, closed mouth

12"	$1,400.00	$1,850.00

Mold 590, ca. 1926, sleep eyes, open/closed mouth

9"	$375.00	$500.00
16"	$1,050.00*	

* at auction

Mold 600 (dome), #640, ca. 1910, character, painted eyes, closed mouth

10"	$625.00	$850.00
17"	$1,350.00	$1,800.00

Mold 700, ca. 1920, closed mouth

Painted eyes

12½"	$1,500.00	$1,870.00

Glass eyes

14"	$4,200.00*	

Too few in database for reliable range.

Mold 701, 711, ca. 1920, socket or shoulder head, sleep eyes, closed mouth

16"	$1,835.00	$2,450.00

Too few in database to give reliable range.

Mold 800, ca. 1910, socket head, 840 shoulder head

18"	$1,800.00	$2,400.00

Too few in database for reliable range.

11½" bisque mold 500, marked "500//Germany//A.0M.//DRGM (sideways)" on back of solid dome socket head, molded painted hair, blue intaglio eyes, black lash line, single stroke brows, closed mouth, jointed wood and composition body, straight wrists, blue velvet two-piece suit, lace trimmed shirt, socks, and handmade shoes, circa 1910, $225.00. Courtesy McMasters Doll Auctions.

Metal Heads

Ca. 1850 – 1930+. Often called Minerva, because of a style of metal shoulder head widely distributed in the United States. Dolls with metal heads were made by various manufactures, including Buschow & Beck, Alfred Heller, who made Diana metal heads, and Karl Standfuss who made Juno metal heads. In the United States, Art Metal Works made metal head dolls. Various metals used were aluminum, brass, and others, and they might be marked with just a size and country of origin or unmarked.

Metal shoulder head, cloth or kid body, molded painted hair, glass eyes, more for wigged.

16"	$160.00	$215.00
18"	$215.00	$290.00
21"	$250.00	$335.00

Painted eyes

14"	$100.00	$140.00
20"	$185.00	$250.00

Child, all metal or with composition body, metal limbs

15"	$335.00	$445.00
20"	$475.00	$625.00

Swiss: See Bucherer in Modern Section.

19" brass Alfred Heller doll marked "DRGM 160?" on front shoulder plate, "Lam?//6//DEP," brown glass eyes, open/closed mouth, yellow painted hair, dressed in white shirt with tan vest, circa 1888, $250.00+. Courtesy Debbie Hamilton.

* at auction

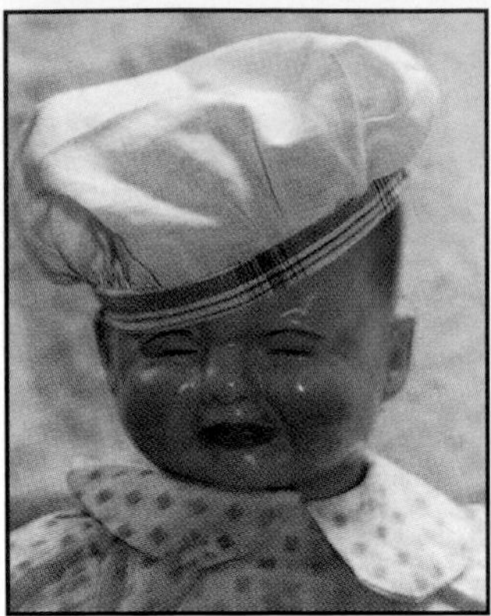

17" composition Ideal Soozie Smiles, unmarked, one face crying, one face smiling, painted eyes, painted hair, head turns on flange neck, red dots inside nostrils, composition lower arms, soft cotton-stuffed body and legs, crying voice when put down, happy "mama" voice when picked up, checked gingham rompers, circa 1923, $325.00. Courtesy Betty Warder.

1866 – 1930+. Various firms made dolls with two or more faces, or more than one head.

Bisque

French

Bru, Surprise poupee, awake/asleep faces

12" $9,500.00

Too few in database for reliable range.

Jumeau, crying, laughing faces, cap hides knob

18" $15,950.00*

Too few in database for reliable range.

German

Bergner, Carl, bisque socket head, three faces, sleeping, laughing, crying, molded tears, glass eyes, on composition jointed body may have molded bonnet or hood, marked *"C.B."* or *"Designed by Carl Bergner"*

12"	$900.00	$1,200.00
15"	$1,050.00	$1,400.00

Kestner, J. D., ca. 1900+, Wunderkind, bisque doll with set of several different mold number heads that could be attached to body, set of one doll and body with additional three heads and wardrobe

With heads 174, 178, 184 & 185

11" $10,000.00*

With heads, 171, 179, 182 & 183

14½" $12,650.00*

Kley & Hahn, solid-dome bisque socket head, painted hair, smiling baby and frowning baby, closed mouth, tongue, glass eyes, baby body

13" $1,100.00*

Simon & Halbig, smiling, sleeping, crying, turn ring at top of head to change faces, glass/painted eyes, closed mouth

14½" $935.00*

Cloth

Topsy-Turvy: one black, one white head. See Cloth section.

Composition

Berwick Doll Co., Famlee Dolls, ca. 1926+, composition head and limbs, cloth body with crier, neck with screw joint, allowing different heads to be screwed into the body, painted features, mohair wigs and/or painted molded hair. Came in sets of two to 12 heads, with different costumes for each head.

Seven-head set including baby, girl in fancy dress, girl in sports dress, Indian, and clown

16" $600.00 $800.00+

Effanbee, Johnny Tu Face

16" $275.00

Too few in database for reliable range.

Ideal, 1923, Soozie Smiles, compositionsition, sleep or painted eyes on happy face, two faces, smiling, crying, cloth body, composition hands, cloth legs, original romper and hat

15½" $300.00 $400.00

* at auction

Multi-Face, Multi-Head Dolls

Three in One Doll Corp., 1946+, Trudy, composition head with turning knob on top, cloth body and limbs, three faces, "Sleepy, Weepy, Smiley," dressed in felt or fleece snowsuit, or sheer dresses, more for exceptional doll

15½"	$85.00	$300.00

PAPIER MÂCHÉ

Smiling/crying faces, glass eyes, cloth body, composition lower limbs

19"	$550.00	$700.00

WAX

Smiling/crying faces, glass eyes, carton body, crier

15"	$400.00	$600.00

Munich Art Dolls

1908 – 1920s. Marion Kaulitz hand painted heads designed by Marc-Schnur, Vogelsanger, and Wackerle, dressed in German or French regional costumes. Usually composition heads and bodies distributed by Cuno & Otto Dressell and Arnoldt Doll Co.

Composition, painted features, wig, composition body, unmarked

17"	$5,750.00*

Ohlhaver, Gebrüder

1913 – 1930, Sonneberg, Germany. Had Revalo (Ohlhaver spelled backwards omitting the two H's) line; made bisque socket and shoulder head and composition dolls. Ernst Heubach supplied some heads to Ohlhaver.

Baby or Toddler, character face, bisque socket head, glass eyes, open mouth, teeth, wig, composition and wood ball-jointed body (bent-leg for baby)

Mark:

.Revalo.
Germany

Baby

16"	$425.00	$575.00
20"	$525.00	$750.00

Toddler

14"	$750.00	$975.00

Child, Mold 150, ca. 1920

Bisque socket head, open mouth, sleep eyes, composition body

17"	$500.00	$675.00

Coquette-type

Bisque solid dome with molded painted hair, ribbon, eyes, composition and wood body

13"	$550.00	$800.00+

Oriental Dolls

ALL-BISQUE

Heubach, Gebrüder, Chin-Chin

4"	$250.00	$350.00

Kestner

6"	$1,050.00	$1,400.00
8"	$1,200.00	$1,600.00

Simon & Halbig

5"	$550.00	$750.00
7"	$750.00	$1,000.00

* at auction

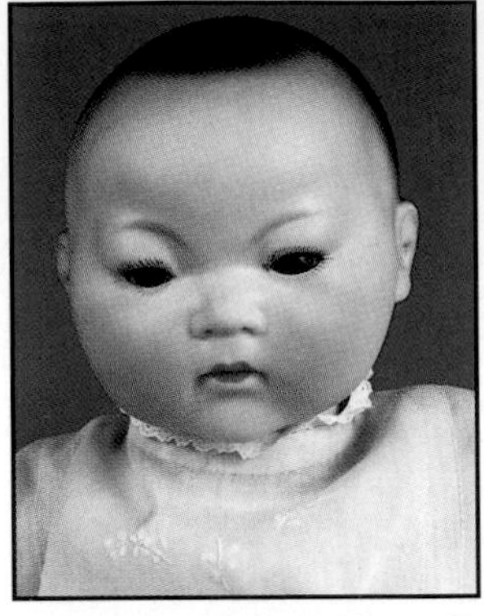

16" bisque Armand Marseille mold 353, marked "A.M.//Germany/ /353//4" on back of solid dome flange head, painted black hair, dark brown sleep eyes, painted lashes, softly blushed brows, closed mouth, cloth body with "frog" legs, celluloid hands, old blue embroidered baby dress, matching slip, undershirt, diaper and blue booties, circa 1925, $760.00. Courtesy McMasters Doll Auctions.

14" bisque unknown boy, glass sleep eyes, open mouth with teeth, stone bisque body, patterned rust silk top with purple and tan flowers, matching hat with purple brim and two strands of beads hanging, purple silk pants, circa 1900+, $1,000.00. Private collection.

Unmarked or unknown maker, presumed German or French

6" $400.00 $550.00

European Bisque

Bisque head, jointed body

Amusco, mold 1006

17" $900.00 $1,200.00

Belton-type, mold 193, 206

10" $1,550.00 $2,075.00
14" $2,000.00 $2,700.00

Bru, pressed bisque swivel head, glass eyes, closed mouth

20" $26,000,00*

Too few in database for reliable range.

Kestner, J. D., 1899 – 1930+, mold 243, bisque socket head, open mouth, wig, bent-leg baby body, add more for original clothing

14" $3,600.00 $4,700.00
16" $4,600.00 $6,100.00

Solid dome, painted hair

15" $3,750.00 $5,000.00

Armand Marseille, ca. 1925

Mold 353, solid-dome bisque socket head, glass eyes, closed mouth

Baby body

7½" $900.00 $1,200.00
14" $925.00 $1,225.00
16" $1,050.00 $1,400.00

Toddler

16" $975.00 $1,300.00

Painted bisque

7" $350.00*

Schmidt, Bruno, marked *"BSW"*

Mold 500, ca. 1905, glass eyes, open mouth

14" $1,600.00 $2,100.00
18" $2,200.00*

Schoenau & Hoffmeister

Mold 4900, bisque socket head, glass eyes, open mouth, tinted composition wood jointed body

10" $375.00 $500.00

Simon & Halbig

Mold 1199, ca. 1898, bisque socket head, glass eyes, open mouth, pierced ears

16" $9,000.00*

Mold 1079, 1129, 1159, 1329, bisque socket head, glass eyes, open mouth, pierced ears, composition wood jointed body

13" $1,350.00 $1,800.00
18" $2,100.00 $2,600.00

* at auction

Unknown maker, socket head, jointed body, closed mouth

14"	$975.00	$1,300.00
20"	$2,200.00	$2,800.00

Japanese Bisque

Various makers including Morimura, Yamato, marked *"FY,"* and others marked *"Nippon"* or *"J.W."* made dolls when doll production was halted in Europe during World War I.

Baby, marked *"Japan"* or *"Nippon"* or by other maker

11"	$135.00	$180.00
15"	$225.00	$300.00
19"	$400.00	$525.00

Child, marked *"Nippon"* or *"Japan"* or other maker

14"	$195.00	$250.00
17"	$250.00	$330.00
22"	$415.00	$550.00

11" gofun Chinese man, tagged "OTA Shanghai," carved painted features, long wooden fingers, heavily embroidered orange and gold coat, matching headdress, circa early 1930s, $250.00+. Courtesy Mary Alice Scheflow.

Composition

Child, unmarked, original outfit

16"	$65.00	$200.00

Effanbee

Butin-nose, in basket with wardrobe, painted Oriental features including black bobbed hair, bangs, side-glancing eyes, excellent color and condition

8"	$125.00	$500.00

Patsy, painted Oriental features, including black bangs, straight across the forehead, brown side-glancing eyes, dressed in silk Chinese pajamas and matching shoes, excellent condition

14"	$250.00	$800.00

Horsman

Baby Butterfly, ca. 1911 – 1913, composition head, hands, cloth body, painted hair, features

13"	$175.00	$650.00

Quan-Quan Co., California

Ming Ming Baby, all-composition jointed baby, painted features, original costume, yarn que, painted shoes

11"	$75.00	$250.00

16" bisque Simon & Halbig mold 1199 child, marked "S&H 1199," socket head, yellow tinted bisque, slanted brown glass eyes, pierced ears, open mouth, teeth, composition body, original silk outfit and headdress, circa 1898, $8,000.00. Courtesy Allyson Flagg-Miller.

Traditional Chinese

Man or woman, composition type head, cloth-wound bodies, may have carved arms and feet, in traditional costume

11"	$115.00	$350.00
14"	$175.00	$525.00

Traditional Japanese

Ichimatsu, 1870s on, a play doll made of papier-mâché-type material with gofun finish of crushed oyster shells, swivel head, shoulder plate, cloth midsection, upper arms, and legs. Limbs and torso are papier mâché, glass eyes, pierced nostrils. Early dolls may have jointed

26" gofun-finish Japanese child, inset black glass eyes, closed mouth, black human hair wig, cloth body with squeaker in center, gofun legs and hands, wearing red multicolor flower print kimono, orange brocade sash, circa 1944 – 1945, $300.00 – $400.00. *Courtesy Patricia Christlieb.*

10" composition unmarked Chinese lady with child on back, painted features, black braided hair on both, pink kimono top, blue pants, red painted shoes, circa 1950s, $100.00. Courtesy Isobel Grover.

wrists and ankles, in original dress. Later 1950s+ dolls imported by Kimport.

Traditional, Meiji era, ca. 1870s –1912		
10"	$300.00	$600.00+
16"	$475.00	$950.00+
22"	$675.00	$1,400.00+
Traditional child, painted hair, 1920s		
12"	$225.00	$450.00
18"	$350.00	$675.00
24"	$475.00	$900.00
Traditional child, 1930s		
14"	$80.00	$155.00
19"	$150.00	$300.00
Traditional child, 1940s on		
15"	$50.00	$100.00
Traditional Lady, 1920s – 1930s		
14"	$135.00	$270.00
16"	$165.00	$325.00
Traditional Lady, 1940s – 1950s		
14"	$50.00	$95.00
16"	$70.00	$135.00
Emperor or Empress, seated, ca. 1890s		
8"	$285.00	$575.00
Ca. 1920s		
6"	$90.00	$180.00
8"	$115.00	$225.00
Warrior, 1880 – 1890s		
16"	$500.00	$650.00
Too few in database for reliable range.		
On horse		
15"	$1,100.00+	
Too few in database for reliable range.		
Warrior, 1920s		
15"	$400.00	
Too few in database for reliable range.		

9½" gofun-finish unmarked Japanese lady, glass eyes, black wig, closed mouth, orange multicolored kimono carrying pink parasol, circa 1950s, $125.00. *Courtesy Nelda Shelton.*

On horse

13"	$850.00+	

Japanese baby, ca. 1920s, bisque head, sleep eyes, closed mouth, papier mâché body

8"	$50.00	$70.00
14"	$65.00	$90.00

Glass eyes

8"	$95.00	$125.00
14"	$200.00	$265.00

Japanese baby, gofun finish of crushed oyster-shell head, painted flesh color, papier mâché body, glass eyes and original clothes

8"	$25.00	$50.00
14"	$45.00	$95.00
18"	$95.00	$185.00

Wood

Door of Hope: See that section.

Schoenhut: See that section.

Papier Mâché

Pre-1600 on. Varying types of composition made from paper or paper pulp could be mass produced in molds for heads after 1810. It reached heights of popularity by mid-1850s and was also used for bodies. Papier mâché shoulder head, glass or painted eyes, molded and painted hair, sometimes in fancy hairdos. Usually no marks.

First price indicates doll in good condition with flaws, less if poorly repainted; second price is for doll in excellent condition, nicely dressed. More for exceptional examples.

Early Type Shoulder head, ca. 1840s – 1860s

Cloth body; wooden limbs; with topknots, buns, puff curls, or braids; dressed in original clothing or excellent copy; may have some wear; more for painted pate

Painted eyes

9"	$225.00	$450.00
12"	$340.00	$675.00
18"	$525.00	$1,050.00
21"	$575.00	$1,150.00
26"	$1,500.00	$1,750.00
32"	$1,000.00	$2,000.00

Glass eyes

18"	$1,000.00	$1,700.00
24"	$1,100.00	$2,200.00

Long curls

14"	$375.00	$750.00
16"	$775.00	$1,550.00

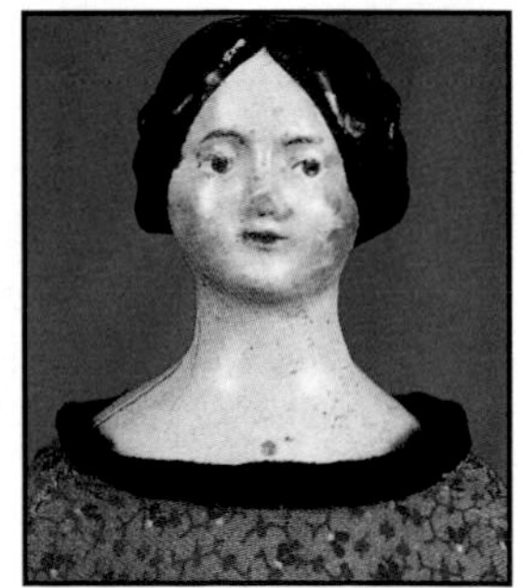

13½" papier mâché unmarked Milliner's Model-type shoulder head, molded painted black hair, side hair brought back to molded braided bun, painted brown eyes, closed mouth, kid body with wooden lower arms and lower legs, dress in old pink print dress, old pants, circa 1820 – 1860s, $475.00. Courtesy McMasters Doll Auctions.

Milliner's Models type, ca. 1820 – 1860s

Many collectors may use this term "Milliner's models" to describe dolls with molded hair, a shapely waist, kid body, and wooden limbs.

* at auction

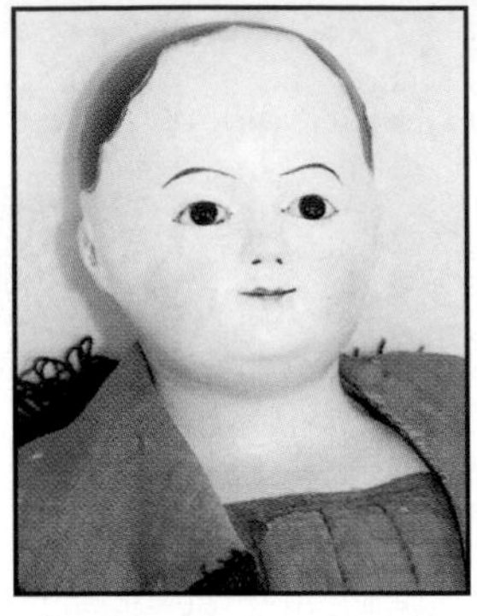

25" lady, painted hair, glass eyes, closed mouth, long green dress, matching coat with black fringe trim, circa 1850+, $1,500.00. Courtesy Sharon Kolibaba.

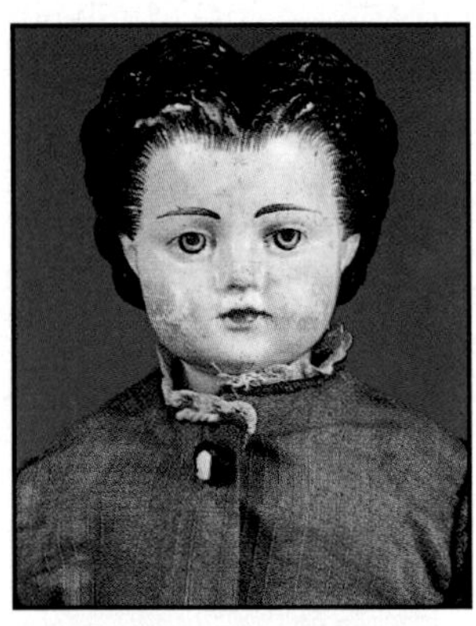

19" M. & S. Superior lady, marked "2018//M & S//Superior" on label on back of shoulder plate, molded painted with brush strokes around face, painted blue eyes, multi-stroke brows, closed mouth, cloth body with leather lower arms, red and white striped lower legs, red leather boots, original green dress trimmed with brown, old underclothing, circa 1844 – 1892, $425.00. Courtesy McMasters Doll Auctions.

Apollo top knot (beehive), side curls

10"	$425.00	$850.00
14"	$2,200.00*	
16"	$1,050.00	$2,125.00

Braided bun, side curls

9"	$400.00	$800.00
15"	$800.00	$1,600.00

Center part, molded bun

9"	$325.00	$650.00
13"	$550.00	$1,100.00

Center part, sausage curls

14"	$275.00	$575.00
21"	$450.00	$950.00

Coiled braids over ears, braided bun

11"	$550.00	$1,000.00
21"	$1,150.00	$2,300.00

Covered Wagon or Flat Top hair style

10"	$175.00	$325.00
14"	$250.00	$500.00
16"	$300.00	$600.00

Molded bonnet, kid body, wood limbs, bonnet painted to tie under chin, very rare

15"	$1,700.00

Too few in database for reliable range.

Molded comb, side curls, braided coronet

16"	$1,650.00	$3,300.00

Too few in database for reliable range.

French Type, ca. 1835 – 1850

Painted black hair, brush marks, solid-dome, shoulder head, some have nailed on wigs, open mouth, bamboo teeth, kid or leather body, appropriately dressed

Glass eyes

13"	$750.00	$1,000.00
18"	$1,500.00	$1,750.00
28"	$4,200.00*	

Painted eyes

12"	$375.00	$750.00
16"	$500.00	$1,000.00

Wooden jointed body

8"	$385.00	$765.00

German Type

1844 – 1892

"M & S Superior," Muller & Strasburger, Sonneberg, Germany, shoulder head, with blond or molded hair, painted blue or brown eyes, cloth body, with kid or leather arms and boots. Mold numbers on stickers reported are

* at auction

Mold 1020, 2020, 2015, and 4515

17"	$225.00	$425.00
22"	$365.00	$675.00
27"	$425.00	$850.00
Glass eyes		
12"	$300.00	$500.00
16"	$500.00	$700.00
Wigged		
13"	$675.00	$900.00

24" unknown German girl, marked "2" on shoulder head, long braided hair, blue glass eyes, cloth straw-filled body, white dress and matching bonnet, circa 1880s, $600.00. Courtesy Debbie Hamilton.

1879 – 1900s

Patent washable shoulder head with mohair wig, open or closed mouth, glass eyes, cloth body, composition limbs.

Better quality

15"	$275.00	$550.00
18"	$400.00	$700.00
22"	$550.00	$900.00
Lesser quality		
10"	$75.00	$150.00
16"	$125.00	$250.00

Turned shoulder head, solid dome, glass eyes, closed mouth, cloth body, composition forearms

16"	$350.00	$700.00
22"	$465.00	$925.00

M & S Superior or unmarked, ca. 1880 – 1910, Germany, shoulder head

15"	$150.00	$300.00
18"	$200.00	$400.00

Left: 16" unmarked Russian Father Christmas, painted eyes, molded painted brows, closed smiling mouth, unjointed figure with long robe, painted red fringed belt, brown cane, arms molded to body, holding decorated Christmas tree, circa 1930s – 1940s, $95.00; right: 16" painted composition Russian girl, sleep eyes, open mouth/upper teeth, molded painted hair, five-piece composition body, taffeta dress, net body suit, oilcloth shoes, circa 1930s – 1940s, $85.00. Courtesy McMasters Doll Auctions.

1920+

Head has brighter coloring, wigged, child often in ethnic costume, stuffed cloth body and limbs, or papier mâché arms

French

9"	$65.00	$125.00
13"	$100.00	$200.00
15"	$150.00	$300.00
German		
10"	$40.00	$80.00
15"	$90.00	$165.00
Unknown maker		
8"	$30.00	$60.00
12"	$60.00	$115.00
16"	$90.00	$175.00

Clowns, papier mâché head, with painted clown features, open or closed mouth, molded hair or wigged, cloth body, composition or

* at auction

papier mâché arms, or five-piece jointed body

8"	$120.00	$235.00
14"	$245.00	$485.00
20"	$395.00	$785.00
26"	$460.00	$925.00

Eden Clown, socket head, open mouth, blue glass eyes, blond mohair wig, five-piece jointed body, all original with labeled box

16"	$4,000.00*

Parian-Type Untinted Bisque

Ca. 1850 – 1900+, Germany. Refers to very white color of untinted bisque dolls, often with molded blond hair, some with fancy hair arrangements and ornaments or bonnets; can have glass or painted eyes, pierced ears, may have molded jewelry or clothing. Occasionally solid dome with wig. Cloth body, nicely dressed in good condition.

First price indicates doll in good condition, but with flaws; second price indicates doll in excellent condition, appropriately dressed. Exceptional examples may be much higher.

Mark: Seldom any mark; may have number inside shoulder plate.

25" German, ornate hair style with molded bows, painted blue eyes, rosy cheeks, pierced ears, detailed painted shoulder plate with lace and beading, china spoon hands/arms, kid body, red leather sewn-on boots with blue tassels, red and white striped socks, lace and white milk glass beading and full-sleeved dress, circa 1870s, $2,800.00. Courtesy Allyson Flagg-Miller.

Lady

Common hair style

Undecorated, simple molded hair

10"	$125.00	$175.00
15"	$225.00	$300.00
21"	$325.00	$425.00
25"	$400.00	$525.00

Fancy hair style

With molded combs, ribbons, flowers, bands, or snoods, cloth body, untinted bisque limbs, more for very elaborate hairstyle

Painted eyes, pierced ears

16"	$685.00	$900.00
22"	$1,300.00	$1,700.00

Painted eyes, ears not pierced

13"	$550.00	$700.00

Glass eyes, pierced ears

15"	$1,200.00	$1,600.00
20"	$2,100.00	$2,700.00

Swivel neck, glass eyes

15"	$2,000.00	$2,700.00

Alice in Wonderland, molded headband or comb

16"	$475.00	$625.00
19"	$550.00	$750.00

Countess Dagmar, no mark, head band, cluster curls on forehead

21"	$750.00	$950.00

Dolly Madison

22"	$1,000.00	$1,600.00

22" unmarked German, fancy blond painted molded hairdo with rolls on top and crown, curls on forehead and loose curls extending down neck, black ribbon molded necklace with gold luster and black bowtie in back, painted blue eyes, pierced ears with earrings, original cloth body/legs, brown leather arms with stitched fingers, new dress and underwear, bloomers, all hand sewn, creamy pale flesh toned bisque, circa 1850+, $325.00. Courtesy Travis Cannon.

Empress Eugenie, headpiece snood

25"	$500.00	$750.00

Irish Queen, Limbach, clover mark, #8552

14"	$350.00	$575.00

Mary Todd Lincoln, headband, snood

25"	$400.00	$700.00

Molded bodice, fancy trim

17"	$600.00	$800.00

Molded hat, blond or black painted hair

Painted eyes

16"	$1,700.00	$2,300.00
19"	$2,150.00	$2,900.00

Glass eyes

14"	$1,850.00	$2,400.00
17"	$2,250.00	$3,000.00

Necklace, jewels, or standing ruffles

17"	$9,700.00+	

Too few in database for reliable range.

Men or Boys

Center or side-part hair style, cloth body, decorated shirt and tie

Painted eyes

13"	$575.00	$775.00
17"	$750.00	$1,000.00

Glass eyes

16"	$2,100.00	$2,825.00

Piano Babies

Ca. 1880 – 1930+, Germany. These all-bisque figurines were made by Gebrüder Heubach, Kestner, Dressel, Limbach, and others. May have molded on clothes; came in a variety of poses. Some were reproduced during the 1960s and 1970s and the skin tones are paler than the others.

First price indicates figurine in good condition with flaws; second price indicates figurine in excellent condition.

Excellent quality or marked "*Heubach*," fine details

4"	$235.00	$300.00
6"	$350.00	$475.00
7½"	$600.00* with sunburst mark	
9"	$525.00	$700.00
16"	$850.00	$1,125.00

* at auction

Piano Babies

6½" all-bisque Gebruder Heubach figurine, marked "(sunburst)//GH//DEP//3841" on back of baby's chair, unjointed, sitting in wicker baby chair, leaning forward and pulling off sock, blue intaglio eyes, molded lids, single stroke brows, open/closed mouth, molded clothing with blue ruffled bonnet, pastel clothing of green, pink, and white, purple pillow or blanket behind baby in chair, circa 1920s, $375.00. *Courtesy McMasters Doll Auctions.*

Black

5"	$300.00	$425.00
9"	$375.00	$500.00
14"	$675.00	$900.00

With animal, pot, flowers, chair, or other items

5"	$195.00	$260.00
8"	$315.00	$425.00
10"	$400.00	$525.00
15"	$750.00	$1,000.00

Medium quality, unmarked, may not have painted finish on back

4"	$75.00	$100.00
8"	$150.00	$200.00
12"	$225.00	$300.00

Pincushion or Half-Dolls

Ca. 1900 – 1930s, Germany, Japan. Half dolls can be made of bisque, china, composition, or papier mâché, and were used not only for pincushions but on top of jewelry or cosmetic boxes, brushes, and lamps. The hardest to find have arms molded away from the body as they were easier to break with the limbs in this position and thus fewer survived.

First price is for doll in good condition, with flaws; second price is for doll in excellent condition; add more for extra attributes. Rare examples may bring more.

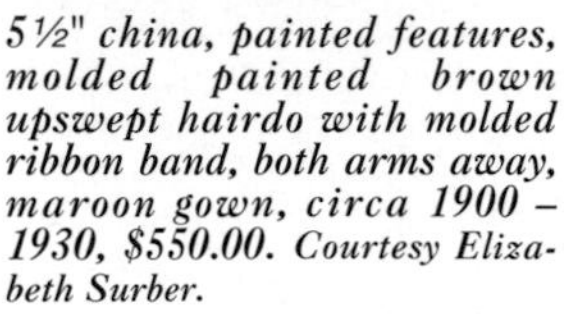

5½" china, painted features, molded painted brown upswept hairdo with molded ribbon band, both arms away, maroon gown, circa 1900 – 1930, $550.00. Courtesy Elizabeth Surber.

Arms Away

China or bisque figure, bald head with wig

4"	$105.00	$140.00
6"	$155.00	$210.00

Goebel mark, dome head, wig

5"	$195.00*	

Holding items, such as letter, flower

4"	$135.00	$185.00
6"	$200.00	$275.00

Marked by maker or mold number

4"	$150.00	$200.00
6"	$225.00	$300.00
8"	$300.00	$400.00
12"	$675.00	$900.00

Arms In

Close to figure, bald head with wig

4"	$55.00	$80.00
6"	$80.00	$115.00

* at auction

Left: 3½" marked "22674" near base, "16" inside, molded painted hair with curls by face and bun on top with black ribbon, painted eyes, arms away, delicate fingers; right: 4" marked "15271//Germany" near base, molded painted curls down on neck, ribbon and flowers in hair, arms held away to side, circa 1900 – 1930, $285.00 for both. Courtesy McMasters Doll Auctions.

4½" china, marked "Germany//15509," black flapper style painted hair with spit curls, arms away to one side with hands clasped together, chip on base, circa 1920s, $130.00. Private collection.

Hands attached		
3"	$20.00	$35.00
5"	$30.00	$45.00
7"	$45.00	$70.00
Decorated bodice, necklace, fancy hair or holding article		
3"	$85.00	$125.00
5"	$105.00	$145.00
Marked by maker or mold number		
5"	$80.00	$135.00
6"	$110.00	$155.00
With legs, dressed, fancy decorations		
5"	$225.00	$300.00
7"	$300.00	$400.00
Papier Mâché or composition		
4"	$25.00	$35.00
6"	$60.00	$80.00
JOINTED SHOULDERS		
China or bisque, molded hair		
5"	$110.00	$145.00
7"	$150.00	$200.00
Solid dome, mohair wig		
4"	$165.00	$220.00
5¾"	$685.00*	
6"	$330.00	$400.00
MAN OR CHILD		
4"	$90.00	$120.00
6"	$120.00	$160.00
MARKED GERMANY		
4"	$150.00	$200.00
6"	$375.00	$500.00

6" German, china dressed as a Spanish senorita, cream mantilla, maroon dress, marked "10016," one arm attached to waist, the other arm away, but close to body, circa 1910+ $600.00. Courtesy Patricia Wright.

* at auction

Pincushion or Half-Dolls

Marked Japan

3"	$10.00	$15.00
6"	$38.00	$50.00

Other Items

Brush, with porcelain figurine for handle, molded hair, may be holding something

9"	$55.00	$75.00

Dresser box, unmarked, with figurine on lid

7"	$265.00	$350.00
9"	$345.00	$450.00

Dresser box, marked with mold number, country, or manufacturer

5"	$210.00	$285.00
6"	$275.00	$350.00

Perfume bottle, stopper is half-doll, skirt is bottle

6½"	$165.00*	

Rabery & Delphieu

1856 – 1930 and later, Paris. Became S.F.B.J. in 1899. Some heads pressed (pre-1890) and some poured, purchased heads from Francois Gaultier.

First price indicates doll in good condition, but with some flaws; second price indicates doll in excellent condition, appropriately dressed. Exceptional dolls may be more.

Child

Closed mouth, bisque socket head, paperweight eyes, pierced ears, mohair wig, cork pate, French composition and wood jointed body

11"	$3,000.00	$4,500.00
12½"	$7,000.00* with presentation box	
17"	$3,800.00*	
23"	$4,200.00	$5,600.00

Mark:

R.3. D

Open mouth, row of upper teeth

18"	$1,075.00	$1,400.00
24"	$1,250.00	$1,650.00
26"	$1,700.00	$2,300.00

Recknagel

1886 – 1930+, Thüringia, Germany. Made bisque heads of varying quality, incised or raised mark, wigged or molded hair, glass or painted eyes, open or closed mouth, flange neck or socket head.

Baby

Mold 23, 121, 126, 1924, bent-limb baby body, painted or glass eyes

6½"	$225.00	$300.00
8"	$250.00	$375.00

9" bisque Recknagel sockethead with glass eyes, dark brows, open mouth, teeth, mohair wig, on crude composition five-piece body, paint missing, re-dressed, marked "1914//Dep//R14 0 A," circa 1914, $100.00. Private collection.

* at auction

Bonnet head baby, painted eyes, open/closed mouth, teeth
Mold 22, 28, 44, molded white boy's cap, bent-leg baby body

8"	$425.00*	
11"	$600.00	$800.00

Oriental baby, solid-dome bisque socket head
Sleep eyes, closed mouth five-piece yellow tinted body

11"	$2,300.00*	

Mold 137, Newborn, ca. 1925, flange neck, sleep eyes, closed mouth, cloth body, boxed

13"	$545.00*	

Mark:
RXA
RIX·72/0

CHILD

Dolly face, 1890s – 1914

Mold 1907, 1909, 1914, open mouth, glass eyes

7"	$85.00	$110.00
12"	$150.00	$200.00
15"	$250.00	$325.00
21"	$400.00	$525.00

Character face, ca. 1910+, may have crossed hammer mark

7"	$300.00	$400.00
12"	$550.00	$750.00

Mold 31, 32, Max and Moritz

8"	$500.00	$650.00

Rohmer

1857 – 1880, Paris. Mme. Rohmer held patents for doll bodies, made dolls of various materials.

First price is for doll in good condition, but with flaws; second price is for doll in excellent condition, appropriately dressed; may be much more for exceptional dolls.

FASHION-TYPE

Bisque or china glazed shoulder or swivel head on shoulder plate, closed mouth, kid body with green oval stamp, bisque or wood lower arms

Mark:
MME ROHMER
BREVETE SGDG PARIS

Glass eyes

14"	$3,400.00*	
17"	$7,200.00	$9,500.00

Painted eyes

14"	$4,200.00	$5,600.00
18"	$5,400.00* pink tint	

Untinted bisque swivel head, lined shoulder plate, cobalt glass eyes, kid over wood arms, kid gusseted body, original costume

16"	$7,400.00*	

China head, painted eyes

17"	$2,800.00	$3,700.00

Schmidt, Bruno

1900 – 1930+, Waltershausen, Germany. Made bisque, composition, and wooden head dolls, after 1913 also celluloid. Acquired Bähr & Pröschild in 1918. Often used a heart-shaped tag.

* at auction

19½" bisque mold 2072 toddler, marked "B & P//0" at top of back of head, "BSW (in heart)//2072//5" on back of head, original mohair wig, brown sleep eyes, painted lashes, closed mouth, fully jointed wood and composition toddler body with diagonal hip joints, old knit outfit with knit top, sweater, pants, cap, socks, and replaced shoes, circa 1912, $750.00. Courtesy McMasters Doll Auctions.

Character Baby

Bisque socket head, glass eyes, composition bent leg body

Mold 2092, ca. 1920, **Mold 2097,** ca. 1911

13"	$375.00	$475.00
15"	$450.00	$600.00
21"	$675.00	$900.00

Mold 2097, toddler

15"	$500.00	$700.00
21"	$750.00	$1,000.00

Child,

BSW, no mold numbers

Bisque socket head, jointed body, sleep eyes, open mouth, add $50.00 more for flirty eyes.

14"	$335.00	$450.00
18"	$475.00	$625.00
23"	$625.00	$850.00

Character

Oriental, mold 500, ca. 1905, yellow tint bisque socket head, glass eyes, open mouth, teeth, pierced ears, wig, yellow tint composition jointed body

11"	$1,100.00	$1,450.00
18"	$1,450.00	$1,900.00

Mold 529, "2052," ca. 1912, painted eyes, closed mouth

20"	$2,800.00	$4,000.00

Mark:

BS W

5

Mold 539, "2023," ca. 1912, solid dome or with wig, painted eyes, closed mouth

24"	$2,250.00	$3,500.00

Mold 537, "2033," ca. 1912, sleep eyes, closed mouth

13½"	$14,000.00*

Too few in database for reliable range.

Mold 2048, ca. 1912**, Tommy Tucker, 2094, 2096,** ca. 1920, solid dome, molded painted hair or wig, sleep eyes, open or closed mouth, composition jointed body

Open mouth

12"	$650.00	$900.00
18"	$950.00	$1,250.00
28"	$1,400.00	$2,000.00

Closed mouth

16"	$1,560.00	$2,050.00

Mold 2072, ca. 1920, sleep eyes

Closed mouth

16"	$2,550.00*

Too few in database for reliable range.

Schmidt, Franz

1890 – 1930+, Georgenthal, Germany. Made, produced, and exported dolls with bisque, composition, wood, and celluloid heads. Used some heads made by Simon & Halbig.

* at auction

Heads marked *"S & C,"* mold 269, 293, 927, 1180, 1310

Heads marked *"F.S. & C,"* mold 1250, 1253, 1259, 1262, 1263, 1266, 1267, 1270, 1271, 1272, 1274, 1293, 1295, 1296, 1297, 1298, 1310

Walkers: mold 1071, 1310

Baby

Bisque head, solid dome or cut out for wig, bent-leg body, sleep or set eyes, open mouth, some pierced nostrils. Add more for flirty eyes.

Mold 1271, 1272, 1295, 1296, 1297, 1310

10"	$325.00	$400.00
13"	$375.00	$500.00
18"	$500.00	$650.00
24"	$850.00	$1,100.00
Toddler		
10"	$750.00	$1,000.00
18"	$975.00	$1,300.00
23"	$1,100.00	$1,475.00
25"	$1,325.00	$1,800.00

Character Face

Mold 1266, 1267, ca. 1912, *marked "F.S. & Co.,"* solid dome, painted eyes, closed mouth

14"	$2,150.00	$2,850.00
19"	$2,900.00	$3,900.00

Mold 1270, ca. 1910, solid dome, painted eyes, open/closed mouth

9"	$475.00	$650.00
13"	$1,350.00	$1,800.00

With two faces

16"	$1,075.00	$1,450.00

Child

Dolly face, Mold 269, ca. 1890s, **Mold 293**, ca. 1900, *marked "S & C,"* open mouth, glass eyes

7"	$200.00	$300.00
19"	$500.00	$650.00
23"	$625.00	$800.00
27"	$800.00	$1,050.00

Mold 1259, ca. 1912, *marked "F.S. & Co."* character, sleep eyes, pierced nostrils, open mouth

15"	$300.00	$500.00

Mold 1262, 1263, ca. 1910, *marked "F.S. & Co."* painted eyes, closed mouth

14"	$4,350.00	$5,800.00

Too few in database for reliable range.

Mold 1272, ca. 1910, *marked "F.S. & Co.,"* solid dome or wig, sleep eyes, pierced nostrils, open mouth

9½"	$700.00	$950.00

Too few in database for a reliable range.

19" bisque mold 1272 baby, marked "F.S. & Co.//1272/50 Z//Deponiert," socket head, blue sleep eyes, pierced nostrils, open mouth, two upper teeth, lightly molded and brush-stroked hair, composition bent-limb baby body, red, white, and blue dress, matching hat, booties, circa 1910, $625.00, holding bisque F.G. candy container marked "F.G.(in scroll)," set brown eyes, mohair wig, papier-mâché jointed arms, cardboard body separates to hold candy, $2,050.00. Courtesy McMasters Doll Auctions.

* at auction

Schmitt & Fils

1854 – 1891, Paris. Made bisque and wax-over-bisque, or wax-over-composition dolls. Heads were pressed. Used neck socket like on later composition Patsy dolls.

First price is for doll in good condition, but with flaws; second price is for doll in excellent condition, appropriately dressed; more for exceptional doll with wardrobe or other attributes.

Mark:

Shield on head, "SCH" in shield on bottom of flat cut derriere.

Child

Pressed bisque head, closed mouth, glass eyes, pierced ears, mohair or human hair wig, French composition and wood eight ball-jointed body with straight wrists.

Early round face

12"	$7,875.00	$10,500.00
13"	$12,000.00* trousseau, box	
18"	$16,000.00*	
24"	$12,850.00	$17,125.00

Long face modeling

19"	$9,000.00	$13,000.00
24"	$12,500.00	$16,500.00

Wax over papier mâché, swivel head, cup and saucer type neck, glass eyes, closed mouth, eight ball-jointed body

16"	$1,125.00	$1,500.00
22"	$1,300.00	$1,700.00

Schmitt body only, eight ball joints, straight wrists, separated fingers, marked "*SCH*" in shield

15"	$1,400.00*

Schoenau & Hoffmeister

1901 – 1953, Sonneberg, and Burggrub, Bavaria. Had a porcelain factory, produced bisque heads for dolls, also supplied other manufacturers, including Brückner, Dressel, E. Knoch, and others.

First price is for doll in good condition with flaws; second price is for doll in excellent condition, appropriately dressed. More for exceptional dolls.

Baby

Bisque solid-dome or wigged socket head, sleep eyes, teeth, composition bent-leg body, closed mouth, newborn, solid dome, painted hair, cloth body, may have celluloid hands, add more for original outfit.

Mark:

9" pair	$950.00* pair	
13"	$625.00	$825.00
15"	$700.00	$950.00
Toddler		
15"	$600.00	$800.00
21"	$1,100.00	$1,500.00

Mold 169, ca. 1930, open mouth, composition bent-leg body, wigged

23"	$385.00	$500.00
25"	$425.00	$575.00

* at auction

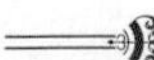

Mold 170, ca. 1930, open mouth, composition five-piece toddler body

19"	$350.00	$475.00

Hanna, sleep eyes, open/closed mouth, bent-leg baby body, $100.00 more for toddler

13"	$375.00	$500.00
18"	$600.00	$800.00
24"	$1,000.00	$1,350.00

Princess Elizabeth, ca. 1929, socket head, sleep eyes

Smiling open mouth, chubby leg toddler body

16"	$1,450.00	$1,950.00
22"	$1,925.00	$2,550.00

CHILD

Dolly face, bisque socket head, open mouth with teeth, sleep eyes, composition ball-jointed body

Mold 1906, 1909, 2500, 4000, 4600, 4700, 5500, 5700, 5800

14"	$250.00	$325.00
18"	$350.00	$450.00
26"	$650.00	$850.00

Mold 914, ca. 1925, character

30"	$625.00*	

Mold 4900, ca. 1905, Oriental, dolly-face

10"	$350.00	$475.00

25" bisque mold 4000, marked "SPB(in star)//4000 – 10" on back of socket head, original mohair wig, brown sleep eyes, painted lashes, heavy feathered brows, open mouth, four upper teeth, jointed composition body, pale green silk dress with pink flowers, new underclothing, socks, and shoes, circa 1901+, $550.00. Courtesy McMasters Doll Auctions.

Schoenhut, A. & Co.

1872 – 1930+, Philadelphia, PA. Made all-wood dolls, using spring joints, had holes in bottoms of feet to fit into stands. Later made elastic strung with cloth bodies. Carved or molded painted hair or wigged, intaglio or sleep eyes, open or closed mouth. Later made composition dolls.

First price is for doll in good condition, but with some flaws, perhaps touch-up; second price is for doll in excellent condition, appropriately dressed; more for exceptional doll.

Mark:

SCHOENHUT DOLL
PAT. JAN. 17th 1911
U.S.A.

INFANT

Graziano Infants, circa May 1911 – 1912

Schnickel – Fritz, carved hair, open/closed grinning mouth, four teeth, large ears, toddler

15"	$2,250.00	$3,000.00

14" wood Toddler Walker, marked "Schoenhut//©//1913" on round label on head, "Schoenhut Doll//Pat. Jan. 17th 1911//U.S.A." on oval label on back, socket head, original blond mohair wig, painted blue eyes, single stroke brows, closed mouth, wooden toddler body jointed at shoulders and hips with construction that helps the doll walk, possibly original navy two-piece dress and jacket, old replaced socks and shoes, circa 1913, $575.00. Courtesy McMasters Doll Auctions.

* at auction

19" wood 19/308 girl, marked "Schoenhut Doll//Pat. Jan 17, 11 U.S.A.//& Foreign Countries," mohair wig, brown intaglio eyes, closed pouty mouth, spring-jointed wooden body, joints at shoulders, elbows, wrists, hips, knees, and ankles, re-dressed in blue/white check dress, white leather shoes, circa 1912 – 1916, $900.00; Russian Christmas ornament, blown glass, unmarked, $45.00. Courtesy McMasters Doll Auctions.

16" wood baby marked "H.E. Schoenhut//©//1913" on round label on back of head, "Schoenhut Doll//Pat. Jan. 17th 1911//U.S.A." on oval label on back, socket head, painted eyes, blond mohair wig, bent-limb baby body, white romper, replaced socks, shoes, circa 1913, $350.00; holding 10" unmarked stuffed mohair plush Steiff bear, black shoebutton eyes, black floss nose, mouth, jointed at shoulders, hips, elongated arms, hump, oversize feet, circa 1905+, $650.00. Courtesy McMasters Doll Auctions.

Tootsie Wootsie, carved hair, open/closed mouth, two upper teeth, large ears on child body

15"	$2,600.00	$3,400.00

Too few in database for reliable range.

Model 107, 107W (walker)

Baby, nature (bent) limb, 1913 – 1926		
13"	$375.00	$550.00
Toddler, 1917 – 1926		
11"	$550.00	$700.00
Toddler, 1913 – 1926		
14"	$575.00	$750.00
Toddler, elastic strung, 1924 – 1926		
14"	$575.00	$750.00
Toddler, cloth body with crier		
14"	$475.00	$600.00

Model 108, 108W (walker)

Baby, nature (bent) limb, 1913 – 1926		
15"	$450.00	$600.00
Toddler, 1917 – 1926		
17"	$650.00	$850.00
Toddler, elastic strung, 1924 – 1926		
17"	$475.00	$725.00
Toddler, cloth body, crier, 1924 – 1928		
17"	$425.00	$550.00

Model 109 W, 1921 – 1923

Baby, nature (bent) limb, sleep eye, open mouth		
13"	$350.00	$500.00
Toddler, sleep eye		
14"	$575.00	$800.00

Too few in database for reliable range.

Model 110 W, 1921 – 1923

Baby, nature (bent) limb, sleep eye, open mouth		
15"	$475.00	$625.00
Toddler		
17"	$675.00	$900.00

Too few in database for reliable range.

Bye-Lo Baby, *"Grace S. Putnam"* stamp, cloth body, closed mouth, sleep eyes,

13" $2,400.00*

Child

Graziano Period, 1911 – 1912, dolls may have heavily carved hair or wigs, painted intaglio eyes, outlined iris. All with wooden spring-jointed bodies and are 16" tall, designated with 16 before the model number, like "16/100."

Model 100, girl, carved hair, solemn face

Model 101, girl, carved hair, grinning, squinting eyes

Model 102, girl, carved hair, bun on top

Model 103, girl, carved hair, loose ringlets

Model 200, boy, carved hair, short curls

Model 201, boy, carved hair, based on K*R 114

Model 202, boy, carved hair, forelock

Model 203, boy, carved hair, grinning, some with comb marks

Carved hair dolls of this early period; add more if excellent condition, original clothes

16" $2,200.00 $3,000.00+

Too few in database for reliable range.

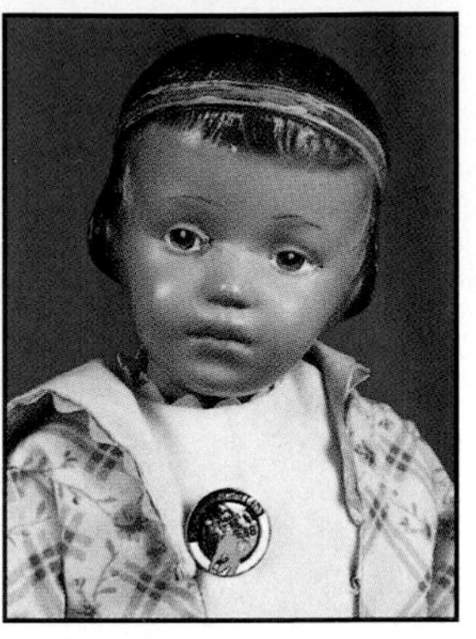

16", wooden sockethead, incised on back "Schoenhut Doll//Pat. Jan. 17, '11 U.S.A.//& Foreign Countries," carved and painted brown hair with carved pink ribbon, brown intaglio eyes, multi-stroke brows, closed mouth, spring-jointed wooden body, nicely re-dressed in Schoenhut-style dress, slip, knit union suit, socks, and shoes, circa 1911+, $900.00. Courtesy McMasters Doll Auctions.

Model 300, girl, long curl wig, face of 102

Model 301, girl, bobbed wig with bangs, face of 300

Model 302, girl, wig, bases on K*R 101

Model 303, girl, short bob, no bangs, grinning, squinting eyes

Model 304, girl, wig in braids, ears stick out

Model 305, girl, snail braids, grinning, face of 303

Model 306, girl, wig, long curls, face of 304

Model 307, girl, short bob, no bangs, "dolly-type" smooth eye

Model 400, boy, short bob, K*R 101 face

Model 401, boy, side part bob, face of 300/301

Model 402, boy, side part bob, grin of 303

Model 403, boy, dimple in chin

Wigged dolls, with intaglio eyes, outlined iris of this period, more if original costume and paint

16" $750.00 $1,500.00

Transition Period, 1911 – 1912, designs by Graziano and Leslie, dolls may no longer have outlined iris, some models have changed, still measure 16", now have a groove above knee for stockings

Model 100, girl, same, no iris outline

Model 101, girl, short carved hair, bob/bow, round eyes/smile

Model 102, girl, braids carved around head

Model 103, girl, heavy carved hair in front/fine braids in back

Model 104, girl, fine carved hair in front/fine braids in back

Model 200, boy, carved hair, same, no iris outline

Model 201, boy, carved hair, same, iris outline, stocking groove

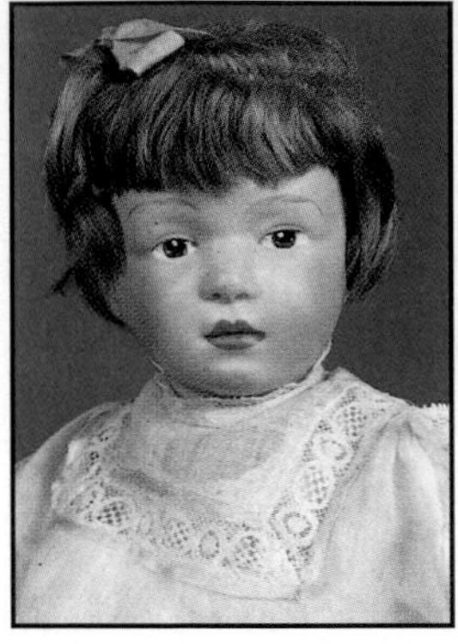

16" wood girl, marked "Schoenhut Doll//Pat. Jan. 17th 1911//U.S.A." on oval label on back, blue intaglio eyes with white highlights, feathered brows, closed pouty mouth, full lips, original mohair wig, wooden body spring jointed at shoulders, elbows, wrists, hips, knees, and ankles, white lace and ribbon trimmed dress, antique underclothing, black cotton socks, brown leather sandals, circa 1911 – 1924, $1,900.00. *Courtesy McMasters Doll Auctions.*

Model 202, boy, carved hair, same, smoother

Model 203, boy, smiling boy, round eyes, no iris outline

Model 204, boy, carved hair brushed forward, serious face

Carved hair is smoother, may no longer have outlined iris, some with stocking groove; more for excellent condition and original costume

16"	1,800.00	$2,400.00

Model 300, girl, long curl wig, dimple in chin

Model 301, girl, bob wig, face of 102

Model 302, girl, wig, same like K*R 101

Model 303, girl, wig, similar to 303G, smiling, short bob, no bangs

Model 304, girl, wig, braids, based on K*R

Model 305, girl, wig, braids, face of 303

Model 306, girl, long curl wig, same face as 304

Model 307, girl, smooth eyeball

Model 400, boy, same (like K*R 101)

Model 401, boy, like K*R 114 (304)

Model 402, boy, smiling, round eyes

Model 403, boy, same as 300 with side part bob

Model 404, boy, same as 301, side part bob

Wigged boy or girl, similar to earlier models with some refinements; more for excellent condition, original costume.

16"	$1,000.00	$1,500.00

Classic Period, 1912 – 1923

Some models discontinued, some sizes added, those marked with* were reissued in 1930

Model 101, girl, short carved hair bob, no iris outline

1912 – 1923*	14"	$1,600.00	$2,200.00
1911 – 1916	16"	$1,800.00	$2,400.00

Model 102, girl, heavy carved hair in front, fine braids in back

1912 – 1923*	14"	$1,300.00	$1,900.00
1911 – 1923*	16"	$1,400.00	$2,000.00
1912 – 1916	19 – 21"	$1,500.00	$2,100.00

Model 105, girl, short carved hair bob, carved ribbon around head

1912 – 1923*	14 – 16"	$1,100.00	$1,900.00
1912 – 1916	19 – 21"	$1,300.00	$2,100.00

Model 106, girl, carved molded bonnet on short hair, 1912 – 1916

14"	$1,500.00	$2,200.00
16"	$1,950.00	$2,600.00
19"	$2,100.00	$2,800.00

Model 203, 16" boy, same as transition

Model 204, 16" boy, same as transition*

Model 205, carved hair boy, covered ears

1912 – 1923

14" – 16" $1,800.00 $2,400.00

1912 – 1916

19 – 21" $2,000.00 $2,600.00

Model 206, carved hair boy, covered ears, 1912 – 1916

19" $2,000.00 $2,600.00

Model 207, carved short curly hair boy, 1912 – 1916

14" $1,800.00 $2,400.00

Model 300, 16" wigged girl, same as transition period, 1911 – 1923

Model 301, 16" wigged girl, same as transition, 1911 – 1924

Model 303, 16" wigged girl, same as transition 305, 1911 – 1916

Model 307, long curl wigged girl, smooth eye, 1911 – 1916

16" $625.00 $850.00

21" wood Miss Dolly, label on back (not incised), original blond wig, blue sleep eyes, open mouth with teeth, wooden spring-jointed body with jointed wrists, original stockings and shoe (missing one shoe), lace-trimmed slip, circa 1921 – 1928, $600.00. Courtesy Pat Graff.

Model 308, girl, braided wig, 1912 – 1916

14" $575.00 $800.00

Bobbed hair, 1912 – 1924

19" $650.00 $900.00

Bob or curls, 1917 – 1924

19 – 21" $650.00 $900.00

Model 309, wigged girl, two teeth, long curls, bobbed hair, 1912 – 1913

16" $650.00 $825.00

1912 – 1916

19 – 21" $675.00 $875.00

Model 310, wigged girl, same as 105 face, long curls, 1912 – 1916

14 – 16" $625.00 $775.00

19 – 21" $675.00 $825.00

Model 311, wigged girl, heart shape 106 face, bobbed wig, no bangs, 1912 – 1916

14 – 16" $650.00 $825.00

1912 – 1913

19" $675.00 $850.00

Model 312, wigged girl, bobbed, 1912 – 1924; bobbed wig or curls, 1917 – 1924

14" $625.00 $775.00

Model 313, wigged girl, long curls, smooth eyeball, receding chin, 1912 – 1916

14 – 16" $650.00 $800.00

19 – 21" $675.00 $825.00

Model 314, wigged girl, long curls, wide face, smooth eyeball, 1912 – 1916

19" $575.00 $725.00

Model 315, wigged girl, long curls, four teeth, triangular mouth, 1912 – 1916

21" $675.00 $825.00

Model 403, 16" wigged boy, same as transition, bobbed hair, bangs, 1911 – 1924

* at auction

Model 404, 16" wigged boy, same as transition, 1911 – 1916

Model 405, boy, face of 308, bobbed wig, 1912 – 1924

14"	$450.00	$650.00
19"	$850.00*	

Model 407, wigged boy, face of 310 girl, 1912 – 1916

19 – 21"	$625.00	$825.00

MISS DOLLY

Model 316, open mouth, teeth, wigged girl, curls or bobbed wig, painted or decal eyes, all four sizes, circa 1915 – 1925

15 – 21"	$500.00	$675.00

Model 317, sleep eyes, open mouth, teeth, wigged girl, long curls or bob, sleep eyes, four sizes, 1921 – 1928

15 – 21"	$525.00	$700.00

Manikin

Model 175, man with slim body, ball-jointed waist, circa 1914 – 1918

19"	$2,400.00*

VARIATIONS

Circus performers, rare figures may be much higher

Bisque head, Bareback Lady Rider or Ringmaster

9"	$650.00* all original

Clowns

8"	$150.00 – $300.00
32"	$4,500.00* store display

Lion Tamer

8½"	$300.00 – $450.00

Ringmaster

8"	$225.00 – $325.00

Animals *some rare animals may be much higher

Gorilla

8"	$2,185.00*

Kangaroo

$1,250.00*

Quacky Doodles, Daddy and children

$1,239.00*

Bandwagon

$7,000.00*

Seven Bandsmen

$14,000.00*

Cartoon Characters

Maggie and Jiggs, from cartoon strip "Bringing up Father"

7 – 9"	$525.00 each

7½" bisque acrobat and 9" bisque head Lady Rider, swivel heads, molded painted hair, painted blue eyes, open/closed mouths, molded teeth (man has mustache), wooden bodies jointed at shoulders/hips, open hands to grip display items, man is dressed in green wool suit with braid trim, lady is dressed in red velvet dress with braid and rhinestone trim, both have large wooden feet, both re-dressed, man has grooves in feet for high wire, circa 1906+, $175.00. Courtesy McMasters Doll Auctions.

* at auction

Max and Moritz, carved figures, painted hair, carved shoes

8"	$625.00 each	
14"	$8,500.00*	

Pinn Family, all wood, egg-shaped head, original costumes

Mother, and four children

	$667.00*	

Baby

5"	$133.00*	

Rolly-Dolly figures

9 – 12"	$350.00	$850.00

Teddy Roosevelt

8"	$800.00	$1,600.00

Schuetzmeister & Quendt

1889 – 1930+, Boilstadt, Gotha, Thüringia. A porcelain factory that made and exported bisque doll heads, all-bisque dolls, and Nankeen dolls. Used initials "S & Q," mold 301 was sometimes incised *"Jeannette."*

Baby

Character face, bisque socket head, sleep eyes, open mouth, bent-leg body

Mold 201, 204, 300, 301, ca. 1920

14"	$335.00	$450.00
19"	$450.00	$600.00

Mold 252, ca. 1920, character face, black baby

15"	$575.00	

Too few in database for reliable range.

Mark:

201

S&Q

Germany

Child

Mold 101, 102, ca. 1900, dolly face

17"	$350.00	$400.00
22"	$375.00	$500.00

Mold 1376, ca. 1900, character face

19"	$550.00	

Too few in database for reliable range.

S.F.B.J.

Société Francaise de Fabrication de Bebes & Jouets, 1899 – 1930+, Paris and Montreuil-sous-Bois. Competition with German manufacturers forced many French companies to join together including Bouchet, Fleischmann & Bloedel, Gaultier, Rabery & Delphieu, Bru, Jumeau, Pintel & Godchaux, Remignard and Wertheimer, and others. This alliance lasted until the 1950s. Fleischman owned controlling interest.

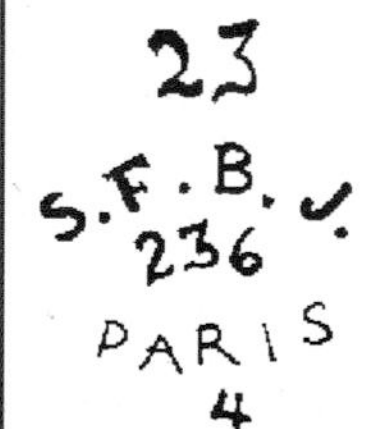

First price indicates doll in good condition, but may have flaws; second price indicates doll in excellent condition, appropriately dressed; more for exceptional dolls.

Child

Bisque head, glass eyes, open mouth, pierced ears, wig, composition jointed French body

* at auction

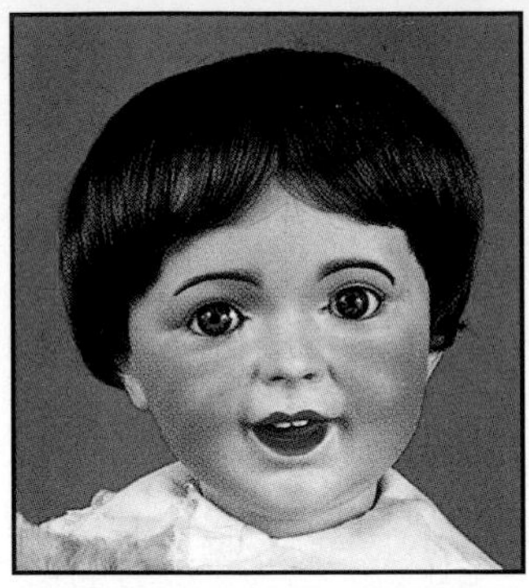

24" bisque S.F.B.J. mold 236 baby, marked "S.F.B.J.//236//Paris//12" on back of head, replaced wig, blue sleep eyes, feathered brows, painted upper and lower lashes, open/closed mouth, two molded upper teeth, composition baby body, white ruffled shirt, brown velvet shorts, socks, circa 1920s, $300.00. Courtesy McMasters Doll Auctions.

22½" bisque mold 301 marked "25//France//S.F.B.J.//301//Paris//10" on back of head, replaced wig, blue sleep eyes, real lashes, painted lower lashes, molded feathered brows, open mouth, four upper teeth, pierced ears, jointed wood and composition walking, kiss-throwing body, redressed in light blue French-style dress, antique underclothing, new black socks and shoes, circa 1920+, $525.00. Courtesy McMasters Doll Auctions.

Bluette, circa 1905 – 1960

This premium doll was first made in bisque and later in composition for a weekly children's periodical, *La Semanine De Suzette* (The Week of Suzette), that also produced patterns for Bleuette. **Premiere Bleuette** was a bisque socket head, Tete Jumeau, marked only with a "1" superimposed on a "2," and 10⅝" tall. She had set blue or brown glass eyes, open mouth with four teeth, wig, and pierced ears. The composition jointed body was marked "2" on back and "1" on the sole of each foot. This mold was made only in 1905. **S.F.B.J.,** a bisque socket head, began production in 1905, using a Fleischmann and Bloedel mold marked "6/0," blue or brown glass eyes, wig, open mouth, and teeth. S.F.B.J. mold marked "SFBJ 60" or "SFBJ 301 1" bisque socket head, open mouth with teeth, wig, and blue or brown glass eyes. All Bleuettes were 10⅝" tall prior to 1933, after, all Bleuettes were 11⅜".

Bleuette, mold 60, 301, and 71 Unis/France 149//301

10⅝"	$650.00	$900.00
11⅜"	$725.00	$975.00

Mold 301

6"	$225.00	$300.00
16"	$625.00	$850.00
24"	$850.00	$1,150.00

Mold 301, Kiss Thrower

24"	$1,650.00*

Lady body

22"	$1,250.00	$1,700.00

Jumeau type, no mold number, open mouth

13"	$675.00	$900.00
20"	$1,250.00	$1,650.00
24"	$1,500.00	$2,050.00
28"	$1,875.00	$2,700.00

CHARACTER FACES

Bisque socket head, wigged or molded hair, set or sleep eyes, composition body, some with bent baby limb, toddler or child body. Mold number 227, 235, and 236 may have flocked hair. Add $100.00 for toddler body.

Mold 226, glass eyes, closed mouth

20"	$1,800.00	$2,400.00

* at auction

31" bisque Jumeau type, marked "21//R//S.F.B.J./ /Paris//14" on back of socket head, human hair wig, set brown eyes, real lashes, feathered brows, painted lower lashes, open mouth, six upper teeth, pierced ears, jointed wood and composition French body, ecru silk dress, embroidered jacket, antique slip, replaced shoes and stockings, circa 1900+, $675.00. Courtesy McMasters Doll Auctions.

Mold 227, open mouth, teeth, glass eyes

14"	$1,125.00	$1,500.00
17"	$1,425.00	$1,900.00
21"	$1,750.00	$2,350.00

Mold 230, glass eyes, open mouth, teeth

12"	$850.00	$1,100.00
22"	$1,500.00	$2,000.00

Mold 233, ca. 1912, crying mouth, glass eyes

14"	$7,400.00*	

Mold 234

18"	$2,400.00	$3,250.00

Too few in database for reliable range.

Mold 235, glass eyes, open/closed mouth

18"	$1,350.00	$1,800.00
21"	$2,300.00*	

Mold 236, glass eyes, toddler

13"	$875.00	$1,150.00
15"	$1,000.00	$1,350.00

Mold 237, glass eyes, open/closed mouth

16"	$1,300.00	$1,700.00

Mold 238, small open mouth

18"	$1,800.00	$2,400.00

Mold 239, ca. 1913, designed by Poulbot

14"	$4,000.00	$6,000.00

Mold 242, ca. 1910, nursing baby

15"	$3,000.00	

Too few in database for reliable range.

Mold 247, glass eyes, open/closed mouth

13"	$1,050.00	$1,400.00
16"	$1,300.00	$1,800.00

Mold 248, ca. 1912, glass eyes, lowered eyebrows, very pouty closed mouth

12"	$7,500.00*	

Mold 250, open mouth with teeth

12"	$3,300.00* trousseau box	

Mold 251, open/closed mouth, teeth, tongue

15"	$1,125.00	$1,500.00

Mold 252, closed pouty mouth, glass eyes

15"	$3,000.00	$4,000.00
26"	$10,750.00*	

Simon & Halbig

1869 – 1930+, Hildburghausen and Grafenhain, Germany. Porcelain factory, made heads for Jumeau (200 series); bathing dolls (300 series); porcelain figures (400 series); perhaps doll house or small dolls (500 – 600 series); bisque head dolls (700 series); bathing and small dolls (800 series); more bisque head dolls (900 – 1000 series). The earliest models of a series had the last digit of their model number ending with an 8; socket heads ended with 9; shoulder heads ended with 0; and models using a shoulder plate for swivel heads ended in 1.

* at auction

22" bisque mold 550 dolly face marked "550//Germany//G//Simon & Halbig//S&H" on back of socket head, "Gimbel Bros.//Germany" stamped in red on right hip, synthetic wig, brown sleep eyes, feathered brows, painted upper and lower lashes, open mouth, full lips, four upper teeth, jointed wood and composition body, lace-trimmed blue dress with white dots, underclothing, new white socks and white leather shoes, circa 1890+, $400.00. Courtesy McMasters Doll Auctions.

Marks:

1079
HALBIG
S&H
Germany

S&H. 1249
DEP
Germany
SANTA

Germany
S&H 13-1010 DEP.

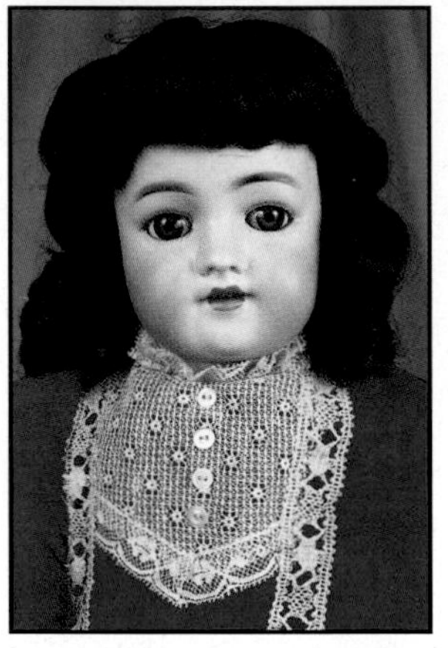

21" bisque mold 570 dolly face, marked "570//Germany//Simon & Halbig" on back of socket head, "Heinrich Handwerck//Germany" stamped on left hip, synthetic wig, blue sleep eyes, feathered brows, painted upper and lower lashes, open mouth, four upper teeth, jointed wood and composition body, redressed in red taffeta dress with ecru lace overlay, underclothing, new socks and white leather shoes, circa 1890+, $300.00. Courtesy McMasters Doll Auctions.

First price indicates doll in good condition, with flaws; second price indicates doll in excellent condition, appropriately dressed. Original or exceptional dolls may be more.

Baby, character face, 1910+

Molded hair or wig, painted or glass eyes, open or closed mouth, bent-leg baby body. Add more for flirty eyes or toddler body.

Mold 1294, ca. 1912, glass eyes, open mouth

16"	$550.00	$750.00
19"	$800.00	$1,100.00

Mold 1294, clockwork mechanism moves eyes

26"	$1,575.00*

Mold 1428, ca. 1914, glass eyes, open/closed mouth

13"	$1,200.00	$1,600.00

Toddler

16"	$1,725.00	$2,300.00

Mold 1488, ca. 1920, glass eyes, open/closed or open mouth

20"	$3,375.00	$4,500.00+

Mold 1489, "Baby Erika," ca. 1925, glass eyes, open mouth, tongue

20"	$4,200.00*

Mold 1498, ca. 1920, solid dome, painted or sleep eyes, open/closed mouth

24"	$3,700.00*

Child

Shoulder head, 1870s

Molded hair, marked *"S&H,"* no mold number

19"	$1,275.00	$1,700.00

Mold 530, 540, 550, 570, ca. 1910, **927, ca. 1913, Baby Blanche**

19"	$500.00	$685.00
22"	$600.00	$800.00

* at auction

Oily bisque

22" $1,100.00*

Mold 719, ca. 1886, sleep eyes, closed mouth, pierced ears, composition wood jointed body

18" $2,800.00 $3,700.00

Open mouth

18" $1,400.00 $1,850.00

Edison phonograph mechanism in torso

23" $4,800.00*

Mold 739, ca. 1888, open or closed mouth, glass eyes, pierced ears, composition/wood jointed body, add more for closed mouth

15" $1,575.00 $2,100.00

Mold 758, 759, 769, ca. 1888, **979,** ca. 1887

20" $1,575.00 $2,100.00

36" $3,300.00*

Mold 905, ca. 1888, closed mouth; **908, ca. 1888,** open or closed mouth

Closed mouth

17" $1,800.00*

Open mouth

18" $1,350.00 $1,800.00

22" $1,025.00 $2,200.00

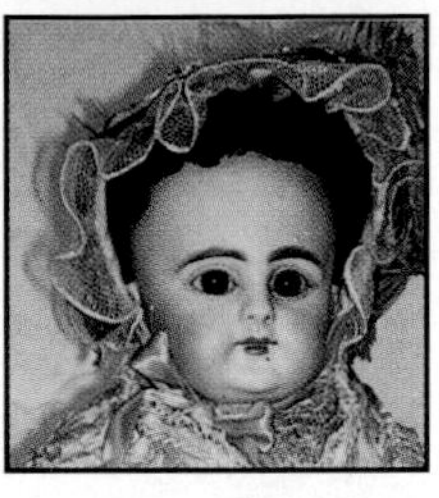

20" bisque mold 749, human hair wig, bulgy paperweight eyes, composition and wood jointed body, silk bonnet, peach silk with ecru silk lace and matching umbrella, all original, circa 1888, $2,800.00. Courtesy Allyson Flagg-Miller.

Mold 1009, ca. 1889, sleep eyes, open mouth, teeth, pierced ears, wig, add more for closed mouth

Kid body

19" $350.00 $525.00

Jointed body

15" $575.00 $750.00

25" $1,125.00 $1,500.00

Mold 1010, 1040, 1170, 1080 (shoulder heads), 1029 (socket head)

18" $425.00 $575.00

25" $600.00 $800.00

28" $675.00 $900.00

Mold 1039, 1049, 1059, 1069, 1078, 1079, 1099 (Oriental), bisque socket or swivel head with bisque shoulder plate, pierced ears, open mouth, glass eyes, composition/wood or papier mâché body; less for shoulder plate with kid or cloth body, more for walkers or original outfit

9" $375.00 $500.00

17" $550.00 $725.00

23" $750.00 $1,000.00

34" $1,400.00 $1,800.00

44" $4,200.00*

Pull-string eyes

18" $1,000.00+

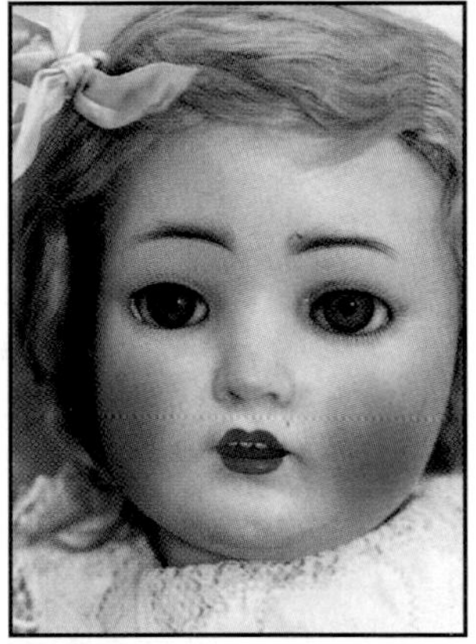

23" bisque mold 927 dolly face, marked "Simon//Halbig//927 – 1x," for Franz Schmidt & Co., blond mohair wig, blue sleep eyes, open mouth with teeth, redressed, circa 1913, $2,000.00. Courtesy Joan Rice.

* at auction

29" bisque mold 949, marked "S 15 H//949" on back of head, "10" on arms, human hair wig, brown sleep eyes, heavy feathered brows, painted upper and lower lashes, open mouth with two upper teeth, one lower square tooth, pierced ears, kid body, bisque lower arms, pin joints at elbows, gussets at hips and knees, old beige and pale green silk French style dress, antique pants, antique leather shoes with rosettes, three ankle straps, circa 1888, $700.00. Courtesy McMasters Doll Auctions.

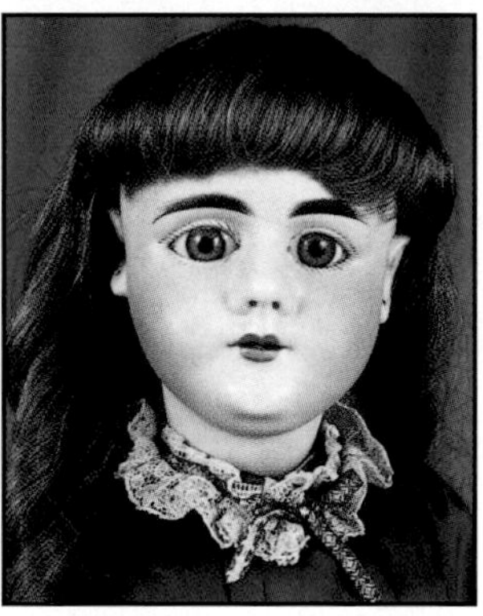

22½" bisque mold 979, marked "11//979" on back of socket head, human hair wig, set blue eyes, painted upper and lower lashes, heavy feathered brows, open mouth, two upper and one lower square cut teeth, pierced ears, French-type wood and composition walking body with working crier, straight legs, blue satin dress trimmed with lace, underclothing, old socks and leatherette shoes, circa 1888, $500.00. Courtesy McMasters Doll Auctions.

* at auction

Mold 1079, Asian child, yellow tint bisque

8"	$1,900.00*	

Mold 1079, Ondine, swimming doll

16"	$1,600.00*	

Mold 1109, ca. 1893, open mouth, glass eyes, dolly face

13"	$500.00	$750.00
18"	$800.00	$1,050.00

Mold 1159, circa 1894, glass eyes, open mouth, Gibson Girl

20"	$2,200.00	$2,950.00

Mold 1248, 1249 "Santa," ca. 1898, open mouth, glass eyes

6"	$500.00	$650.00
10½"	$525.00	$700.00
18"	$900.00	$1,200.00
24"	$1,200.00	$1,600.00

Mold 1250, 1260, open mouth, glass eyes, shoulder head, kid body

16"	$500.00	$625.00
19"	$600.00	$800.00
23"	$800.00	$1,075.00

Mold 1269, 1279, sleep eyes, open mouth

14"	$1,100.00	$1,500.00
16"	$3,500.00* MIB	
25"	$2,550.00	

Character Face, 1910+

Mold 150, ca. 1912, intaglio eyes, closed mouth

21"	$15,500.00*	

Too few in database for reliable range.

Mold 151, ca. 1912, painted eyes, closed laughing mouth

15"	$3,750.00	$5,000.00

Too few in database for reliable range.

Mold 153, ca. 1912, molded hair, painted eyes, closed mouth

17"	$27,000.00	

Too few in database for reliable range.

Mold 600, ca. 1912, sleep eyes, open mouth

17"	$900.00*	

Too few in database for reliable range.

Mold 720, ca. 1887, dome shoulder head, glass eyes, closed mouth, wig, bisque lower arms, kid body

17"	$1,000.00*	

Mold 729, ca. 1888, laughing face, glass eyes, open/closed mouth

16"	$1,900.00	$2,550.00

Mold 740, ca. 1888, dome shoulder head, glass eyes, closed mouth, cloth or kid body

11"	$1,700.00*	
18"	$1,200.00	$1,600.00

Mold 749, ca. 1888, socket head, glass eyes, pierced ears

Closed mouth

21"	$2,325.00	$3,100.00

Open mouth

13"	$825.00	$1,100.00

Mold 759, ca. 1888, open mouth

17"	$900.00*	

Mold 919, ca. 1888, glass eyes, closed mouth

15"	$5,700.00	$7,600.00
19"	$6,400.00	$8,550.00

Too few in database for reliable range.

Mold 929, ca. 1888, glass eyes, open/closed or closed mouth

14"	$1,725.00	$2,300.00
23"	$2,850.00	$3,800.00
25"	$6,600.00*	

Mold 939, ca. 1888, bisque socket head, pierced ears, glass eyes

Open mouth

11"	$700.00	$925.00
16"	$1,300.00	$1,800.00

Closed mouth

16"	$1,600.00	$2,100.00
18"	$2,400.00	$3,000.00
20"	$3,400.00*	

Mold 940, 950, ca. 1888, socket or shoulder head, open or closed mouth, glass eyes

Kid body

14"	$485.00	$650.00
18"	$1,200.00	$1,575.00

Jointed body

8"	$415.00	$550.00
15"	$985.00	$1,300.00
21"	$1,700.00	$2,300.00

Mold 949, ca. 1888, glass eyes, open or closed mouth

Closed mouth

10"	$2,000.00*	
16"	$1,750.00	$2,350.00
21"	$2,000.00	$2,700.00
31"	$3,200.00	$4,250.00

Open mouth

15"	$1,050.00	$1,350.00
19"	$1,400.00	$1,800.00
24"	$1,700.00	$2,250.00

* at auction

22" bisque mold 1009 dolly face, marked "S 9 H 1009//DEP//Germany" on head, socket head on bisque shoulder plate, brown sleep eyes, painted lashes, open mouth with four upper teeth, pierced ears, replaced wig, kid body with cloth torso, bisque lower arms, gussets at hips and knees, nicely dressed in beige silk dress with lavender bows, antique underclothing, new socks and leather shoes, circa 1889, $275.00. Courtesy McMasters Doll Auctions.

16" bisque mold 1039 in ethnic dress, marked "SH 1039//4 DEP," bisque socket head on bisque shoulder plate, original mohair wig, set dark brown eyes, feathered brows, painted upper and lower lashes, open mouth, four upper teeth, pierced ears, cloth body with bisque lower arms, stitch-jointed at hips and knees, original ethnic-type outfit, original underclothing, black socks and shoes, circa 1891, $650.00. Courtesy McMasters Doll Auctions.

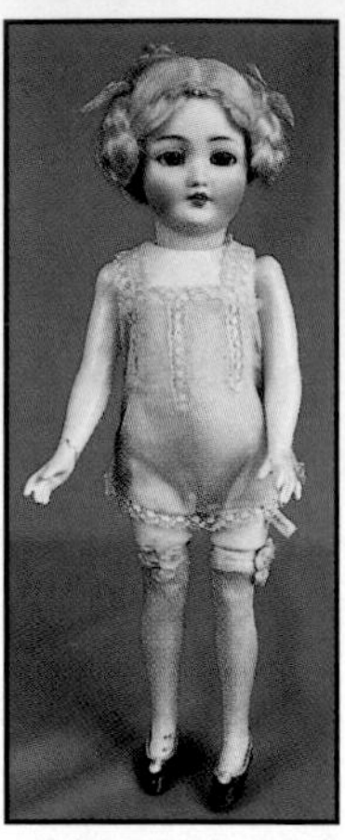

13" bisque mold 1159 Gibson Girl, marked "1159//Simon & Halbig//S & H//5" head, "Made in Germany" on paper tag on bottom of left leg opening, blue sleep eyes, painted upper and lower lashes, feathered brows, open mouth, four upper teeth, blond mohair wig in coiled braids, composition flapper body, high knee joints, silk stockings, ribbon garters, black high heels shoes with silk covered buttons, blue silk ribbons in hair, all original, circa 1894, $1,600.00. Courtesy McMasters Doll Auctions.

Mold 969, ca. 1887, open smiling mouth

19"	$5,700.00	$7,600.00

Too few in database for reliable range.

Mold 1019, ca. 1890, laughing, open mouth

14"	$4,275.00	$5,700.00

Too few in database for reliable range.

Mold 1246, ca. 1898, bisque socket head, sleep eyes, open mouth

18"	$2,400.00*

Mold 1250, ca. 1898, dolly face, shoulder head

15"	$425.00	$550.00
23"	$600.00	$800.00

Mold 1299, ca. 1912, marked *"S&H"*

13"	$1,200.00	$1,600.00

Mold 1304, ca. 1902, closed mouth

14"	$4,500.00	$6,000.00

Too few in database for reliable range.

Mold 1448, ca. 1914, bisque socket head, sleep eyes, closed mouth, pierced ears, composition, wood ball-jointed body

16"	$17,500.00*

Too few in database for reliable range.

Mold 1478, ca. 1920, closed mouth

15"	$6,750.00	$9,000.00

Too few in database for reliable range.

Adults

Mold 1303, ca. 1902, lady face, glass eyes, closed mouth

14"	$5,815.00*

Too few in database for reliable range.

Mold 1305, ca. 1902, old woman, glass eyes, open/closed laughing mouth

18"	$10,035.00*

Too few in database for reliable range.

Mold 1308, ca. 1902, old man, molded mustache/dirty face, may be solid dome

18"	$4,200.00	$5,600.00

Too few in database for reliable range.

Mold 1388, ca. 1910, glass eyes, closed smiling mouth, teeth, wig

20"	$24,000.00*

Mold 1469, ca. 1920, flapper, glass eyes, closed mouth

15"	$2,625.00	$3,500.00

Portrait, Mary Pickford

40"	$34,000.00*

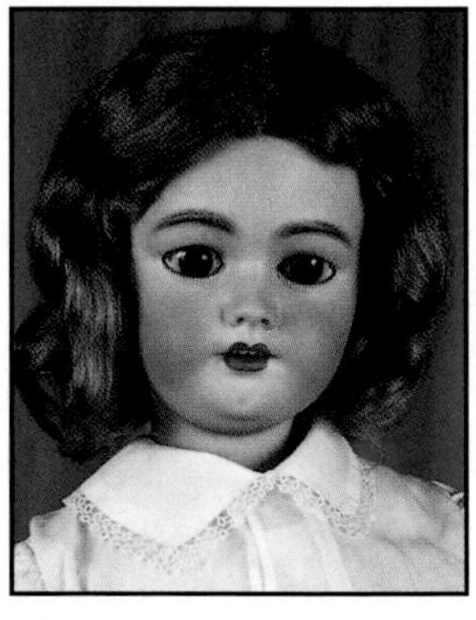

27" bisque mold 1078, marked "1078//Germany//Simon & Halbig/ /S&H//13," original mohair wig, brown sleep eyes, real lashes, molded feathered brows, painted lower lashes, open mouth, four upper teeth, pierced ears, jointed wood and composition body, re-dressed in antique white dress with ribbon at waist, antique underclothing, socks, and black leatherette tie shoes, circa 1892, $575.00. Courtesy McMasters Doll Auctions.

* at auction

MECHANICALS

Walker, mold #1039, bisque, glass eyes, open mouth, wig, composition walking body

13"	$1,500.00	$2,000.00+

Walker, mold #1078, glass eyes, open mouth, pierced ears, clockwork mechanism in torso

23"	$2,200.00	$2,900.00

SMALL DOLLS — DOLLS UNDER 9" TALL

Mold 749, ca. 1888, glass sleep eyes, open mouth, teeth, pierced ears, wig, composition/wood jointed body

5½"	$375.00	$550.00
9"	$700.00	$950.00

Mold 852, ca. 1880, all-bisque, Oriental, swivel head, yellow tint bisque, glass eyes, closed mouth, wig, painted shoes and socks

5½"	$825.00	$1,100.00

Mold 886, ca. 1880, all-bisque swivel head, glass eyes, open mouth, square cut teeth, wig, peg jointed, painted shoes and socks

7"	$1,600.00* in presentation box	
8"	$600.00	$800.00

Mold 950, ca. 1888, shoulder head, closed mouth

8"	$375.00	$500.00

Mold 1078, ca. 1892, glass eyes, open mouth, teeth, mohair wig, five-piece body, painted shoes and socks

8"	$400.00	$550.00

Mold 1078, pair Marquis and Marquise, original costume

8½"	$650.00 each*	

Flapper body

9"	$400.00	$600.00

Mold 1079, ca. 1892, open mouth, glass eyes, five-piece body

8"	$400.00	$600.00

Yellow tinted bisque, glass eyes, open mouth, teeth, five-piece papier mâché body

8"	$1,900.00*	

Mold 1160, Little Women, ca. 1894, shoulder head, glass eyes, closed mouth

7"	$265.00	$350.00

Snow Babies

1901 – 1930+. All-bisque dolls covered with ground porcelain slip to resemble snow, made by Bähr & Pröschild & Proschild, Hertwig, C.F. Kling, Kley & Hahn, and others, Germany. Mostly unjointed, some jointed at shoulders and hips. The Eskimos named Peary's daughter Marie, born in 1893, Snow Baby, and her mother published a book in which she called her daughter Snow Baby and showed a picture of a little girl in white snowsuit. These little figures have painted features, various poses.

First price indicates figure in good condition, but with flaws or lessor quality; second price is for figure in excellent condition. More for exceptional figures.

SINGLE SNOW BABY

1½"	$40.00	$55.00
3"	$130.00	$175.00

* at auction

1¾" bisque German Snow Baby on skis, marked "Germany," painted features, closed mouth, arms outstretched, full suit, standing on yellow skis, circa 1901 – 1930s, $125.00 to $175.00. Courtesy *Debra Ruberto.*

On bear		
	$225.00	$300.00
On sled		
2"	$150.00	$200.00
Pulled by dogs		
3"	$275.00	$375.00
With reindeer		
2½"	$225.00	$300.00
Jointed hips, shoulders		
4"	$215.00	$290.00
5"	$275.00	$375.00
With Broom		
4½"	$400.00	$550.00
Two Snow Babies, molded together		
1½"	$100.00	$125.00
3"	$185.00	$250.00
On sled		
2½"	$200.00	$275.00

Mold 3200, Armand Marseille, candy container, two Snow Babies on sled

11"	$3,100.00*	

Three Snow Babies, molded together		
3"	$190.00	$350.00
On sled		
2½"	$190.00	$350.00
Six Snow Babies, band with instruments		
2"	$275.00*	

New Snow Babies

Today's commercial reproductions are by Dept. 56 and are larger and the coloring is more like cream. Dept. 56 Snow Babies and their Village Collections are collectible on the secondary market. Individual craftsmen are also making and painting reproductions that look more like the old ones. As with all newer collectibles, items must be mint to command higher prices.

First price for Dept 56 Snow Babies is issue price; second price will be upper market price. Secondary market prices are extremely volatile; some markets may not bring upper prices. Usually offered in limited production, prices may rise when production is closed.

Dept 56	Issue Price	Current Price
1986		
Snowbaby Winged clip ornament	$61.00	
Climbing on Snowball, w/candle	$14.00	$118.00
Snowbaby on Brass Ribbon	$153.00*	
1987		
Snowbaby Adrift		$125.00*
Winter Surprise		$27.00*
1988		
Snowbaby on Votive		$65.00*
Pony Express	$22.00	$90.00

* at auction

1989

All Fall Down, set 4	$36.00	$85.00
Finding Falling Star	$32.50	$200.00
Penquin Parade	$25.00	$70.00

1990

A Special Delivery	$15.00	$50.00
Twinkle Twinkle Little Star, set 2	$37.50	$65.00
Who Are You?	$32.50	$140.00

Reproduction crafted Snow Babies, set of ten in various poses

1 – 1½" $25.00

Sonnenberg, Taufling

(Motschmann-type) 1851 – 1900+, Sonneberg, Germany. Various companies made an infant doll with special separated body with bellows and voice mechanism. Motschmann is erroneously credited with the body style; but he did patent the voice mechanism. Some bodies stamped "Motschmann" refer to the voice mechanism. The Sonneberg Taufling is a wax-over-papier mâché head with wood body with twill cloth covered bellows, "floating" twill covered upper joints with lower joints of wood or china.

They have glass eyes, closed mouth, painted hair, or wigged. Other variations include papier mâché or wax over composition. The body may be stamped.

Bisque: See also Steiner, Jules.

China

China solid dome, shoulder plate, lower torso, arms, feet, padded twill body separates china portion, bellows crier

9½" $2,750.00*

Too few in database for reliable range.

Papier-Mâché

Brown swivel head, flock-painted hair, black glass eyes, closed mouth, papier mâché shoulder plate, muslin body, working squeak crier, original outfit

5½" $2,600.00*

Too few in database for reliable range.

Wax Over Papier-Mâché

Solid dome wax over papier mâché, closed mouth, papier mâché torso, wood arms and legs, original outfit

12" $750.00 $1,000.00

Wood

Carved wooden socket head, closed mouth, twill and wood torso, nude

17" $1,000.00*

Steiff, Margarete

1877 – 1930+, Giengen, Wurtembur, Germany. Known today for their plush stuffed animals, Steiff made clothes for children, dolls with mask heads in 1889, clown dolls by 1898. Most Steiff dolls of felt, velvet, or plush have seam down the center of the face, but not all. Registered trademark button in ear in 1905. Button type eyes, painted features, sewn-on ears, big feet/shoes enables them to stand alone, all in excellent condition.

Mark:

Button in ear

* at auction

Steiff, Margarete

16" vinyl Clownie, brown glass eyes, painted clown face, large nose and ears, blond hair around sides and back of head, velvet body, large white felt hands, large black felt feet, marked "Steiff-Original-Marke, Clownie" on round paper tag with yellow bear head, "Mottenecht Durch, Eulan, Bayer" in blue circle on tag, original clown outfit, red/white shirt, blue platched pants, red felt suspenders, black felt hat, red ribbon tie, circa late 1950s, $575.00. Courtesy McMasters Doll Auctions.

Prices are for older dolls, newer dolls are much less. First price is for doll in good condition, but with some flaws (for soiled, ragged, or worn dolls, use 25% or less of this price); second price is for doll in excellent condition.

Adults

14½" $1,400.00 $2,000.00
18" $1,875.00 $2,500.00

Characters

Man with pipe, some moth holes, some soil
17" $1,300.00*

Alphonse & Garton (Mutt & Jeff), circa 1915
13 – 18" $4,700.00* pair

Happy Hooligan, moth holes
15" $2,500.00*

Children

14" $1,000.00 $1,300.00

Military

Men in uniform and conductors, firemen, etc.
10½" $1,275.00 $1,700.00
18" $3,200.00 $4,275.00

Made in U.S. Germany, glass eyes
12" $575.00 $750.00

Steiner, Hermann

1909 – 1930+, near Coburg, Germany. Porcelain and doll factory. First made plush animals, then made bisque, composition, and celluloid head dolls. Patented the Steiner eye with moving pupils.

Baby

No mold number, entertwined HS mark
12" $1,050.00* pair of toddlers

Mold 240, circa 1925, newborn, solid dome, closed mouth, sleep eyes
16" $450.00 $600.00

Mold 246, circa 1926, character, solid dome, glass eyes, open/closed mouth, laughing baby, teeth, cloth or composition body
15" $475.00 $625.00

Too few in database for reliable range.

Mary Ann & Her Baby Walker
6¾" $200.00*

Child

Mold 128, character bisque socket head, sleep eyes, open mouth, teeth, wig, composition/wood jointed body
9" $700.00*

Too few in database for reliable range.

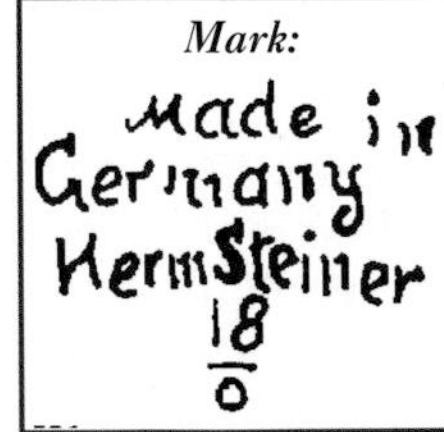

* at auction

Mold 401, shoulder head, solid dome, painted eyes, open/closed laughing mouth, teeth, molded tongue

15"	$350.00	$475.00

Steiner, Jules

1855 – 1891+, Paris. Made dolls with pressed heads, wigs, glass eyes, pierced ears on jointed composition bodies. Advertised talking, mechanical jointed dolls and bébés. Some sleep eyes were operated by a wire behind the ear, marked *"J. Steiner."* May also carry the Bourgoin mark.

First price is for doll in good condition, but with flaws; second price is for doll in excellent condition, appropriately dressed. Add more for original clothes, rare mold numbers.

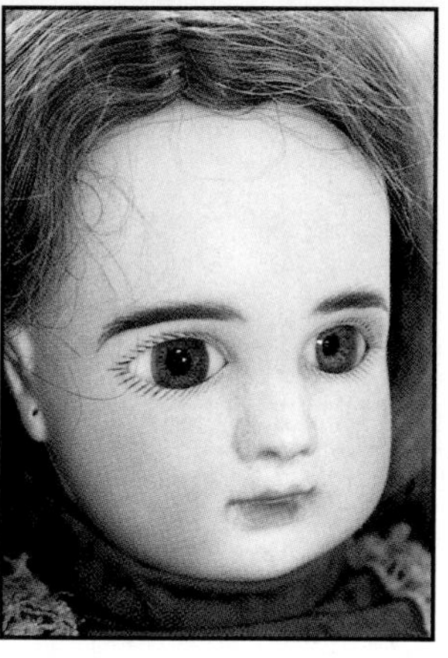

17" bisque Series A, marked "J.S. Steiner//B.TE SGDG//Paris//F.RE A 9," blue paperweight eyes, closed mouth, human hair wig, composition body, repaired near eye, circa 1885, $3,500.00. Private collection.

Bebe with Taufling (Motschmann) type body

Solid dome bisque head, shoulders, hips, lower arms and legs, with twill body in-between, closed mouth, glass eyes, wig

14"	$3,600.00	$4,800.00
19"	$3,000.00*	

Gigoteur, "Kicker"

Crying bébé, key-wound mechanism, solid dome head, glass eyes, open mouth, two rows tiny teeth, pierced ears, mohair wig, papier mâché torso

18"	$1,650.00	$2,200.00

Early unmarked Bebe

Round face, ca. 1870s, pale pressed bisque socket head, rounded face, pierced ears, bulgy paperweight eyes, open mouth, two rows teeth, pierced ears, wig, composition/wood jointed body

18"	$4,500.00	$6,000.00

Closed mouth, round face, dimples in chin

18"	$8,250.00	$11,000.00

Bebe with series marks, ca. 1880s

Bourgoin red ink, Caduceus stamp on body, pressed bisque socket head, cardboard pate, wig, pierced ears, closed mouth, glass paperweight eyes, French composition/wood jointed body with straight wrists. Series C and A more common. Marked with series mark: Sie and letter and number; rare Series E and G models may be valued much higher.

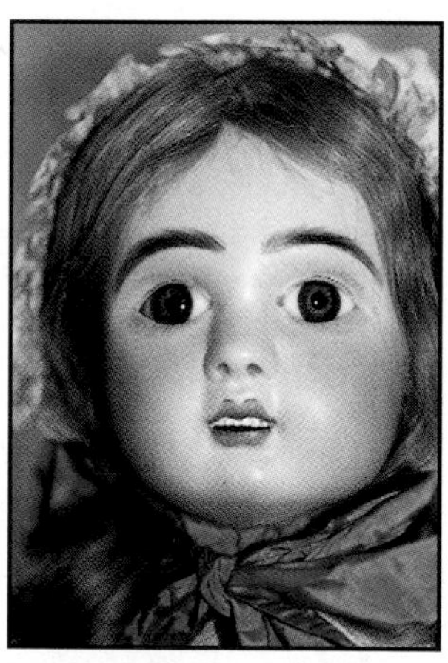

23" bisque Figure A Bebe, original Figure A stamped body, bisque socket head, blue glass eyes, open mouth with teeth, human hair wig, bonnet with blue ribbon ties under chin, circa 1880s, $3,100.00. Courtesy Sharon Kolibaba.

Series A, C, E, G

8"	$4,200.00* presentation case	
14"	$4,500.00	$6,000.00
22"	$6,400.00	$8,500.00
27"	$7,125.00	$9,500.00

* at auction

22" bisque Figure A Bebe marked "Steiner//Paris//Fre A – 14" on back of socket head, replaced human hair wig, blue paperweight eyes, painted lashes, feathered brows, closed mouth, pierced ears, jointed composition body with jointed wrists and slender fingers, antique white dress trimmed with tucks on the bodice and hem, new underclothing, socks, antique leather shoes, circa 1887+, $3,100.00. Courtesy McMasters Doll Auctions.

Series C

34 – 38"	$9,750.00	$13,000.00+

Series E

24"	$22,000.00*

Series G

19"	$17,000.00*

Bebe with figure marks, ca. 1887+

Bisque socket head, pierced ears, closed mouth, glass eyes, wig, composition/wood jointed French body. May use body marked *"Le Petit Parisien."* Marked figure: *"Flre"* and letter and number, usually "A" or "C."

Closed mouth

13"	$2,625.00	$3,500.00
16"	$3,700.00	$4,900.00
23"	$4,400.00	$5,900.00
23"	$7,750.00*	Figure C with stamped body
34"	$8,000.00	$12,000.00

Open/closed mouth, dimple in chin

16"	$2,500.00	$3,500.00
27"	$3,275.00	$4,500.00

Bebe le Parisien, ca. 1895+

Bisque socket head, cardboard pate, wig, paperweight eyes, closed or open mouth, pierced ears, wig, composition jointed body. Head marked with letter, number, and Paris; body stamped in red, *"Le Parisien."*

Mark:

BÉBÉ "LE PARISIEN"
Médaille d'Or
PARIS

10"	$2,700.00	$3,600.00
21"	$3,075.00	$4,100.00
27"	$4,000.00	$5,250.00

Swaine & Co.

1910 – 1927, Huttensteinach, Thüringia, Germany. Made porcelain doll heads. Marked *"S & Co.,"* with green stamp. May also be incised *"DIP"* or *"Lori."*

Baby

Baby Lori, marked *"Lori,"* solid dome, open/closed mouth molded hair, sleep eyes

18"	$1,200.00	$1,600.00
23"	$1,870.00	$2,500.00

Mold 232, Lori variation, open mouth

12"	$750.00	$1,000.00
21"	$1,300.00	$1,750.00

DI, solid dome, intaglio eyes, closed mouth

11"	$600.00	$800.00
16"	$2,100.00* toddler	

DV, solid dome, sleep eyes, closed mouth

15"	$1,125.00	$1,500.00

Marks:

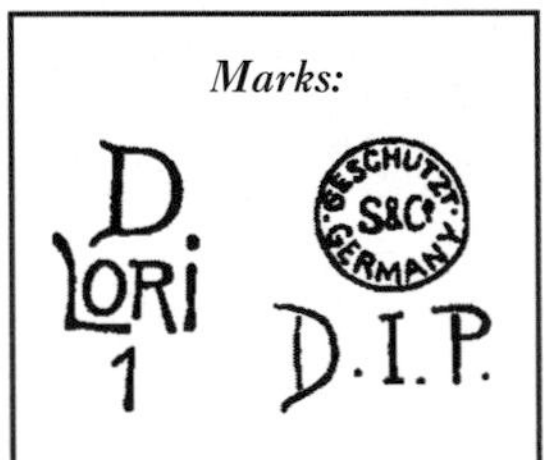

* at auction

FP, S&C, socket head, sleep eyes, closed mouth

8"	$750.00*	

Too few in database for reliable range.

Child

AP, socket head, intaglio eyes, closed mouth

15"	$5,200.00*	

BP, socket head, open/closed smiling mouth, teeth, painted eyes

14½"	$3,400.00*	

Too few in database for reliable range.

DIP, S&C, socket head, sleep eyes, closed mouth

14"	$1,400.00	$1,700.00

Thuiller, A.

1875 – 1893, Paris. Made bisque head dolls with composition, kid, or wooden bodies. Some of the heads were reported made by Francoise Gaultier. Bisque socket head, or swivel on shoulder plate, glass eyes, closed mouth with white space, pierced ears, cork pate, wig, nicely dressed, in good condition. First price is for doll in good condition, but with flaws; second price is for doll in excellent condition, appropriately dressed. Exceptionally beautiful dolls may run more.

Child

Closed mouth

13"	$23,250.00	$31,000.00
17"	$24,000.00*	
26 – 28"	$30,000.00	$40,000.00+

**See *1997 Doll Values* for photo of A.Thuiller

Mark:
A.14.T

Unis France

1916 – 1930+. Mark used by S.F.B.J. (Société Francaise de Fabrication de Bebes & Jouets) is Union Nationale Inter-Syndicale.

Child

Mold 60, 301, bisque head, jointed composition/wood body, wig, sleep eyes, open mouth

9"	$350.00	$475.00
11½"	$1,050.00* trunk, wardrobe	
16"	$400.00	$600.00
21"	$600.00	$800.00

Mold 247, 251, toddler body

15"	$1,050.00	$1,400.00
27"	$1,650.00	$2,200.00

16" bisque socket head, mold 301, glass eyes, feathered brows, red accent dots at inner eyes, painted and real lashes, open mouth with teeth, wood and composition jointed body, circa 1916 – 1930+, $225.00. Courtesy McMasters Doll Auctions.

Wagner & Zetszche

1875 – 1930+, Ilmenau, Thüringia. Made dolls, doll parts, and doll clothes and shoes; used heads by Gebrüder Heubach, Armand Marseille, and Simon & Halbig.

* at auction

Wagner & Zetszche

Child

Bisque head, kid body, bisque lower arms, cloth lower legs

Mark:

W.u.Z
y.
Germany

Closed mouth

21"	$675.00	$900.00

Open mouth

14"	$265.00	$350.00

Too few in database for reliable range.

Inge, character, bisque solid dome, closed mouth, kid body

14½" $1,300.00*

Composition-type swivel head, painted eyes, closed mouth, kid body

16" $525.00*

Too few in database for reliable range.

Wax

11" unmarked Crimean War Water Carrier, original mohair wig in ringlets, set blue eyes, single stroke brows, closed mouth, cloth body with wax over papier-mâché lower arms and lower legs, molded orange boots, dressed in original uniform, circa 1854+, $225.00. Courtesy McMasters Doll Auctions.

Ca. 1850 – 1930. Made by English, German, French, and other firms, reaching heights of popularity ca. 1875. Seldom marked, wax dolls were poured, some reinforced with plaster, and less expensive, but more durable with wax over papier mâché or composition. English makers included Montanari, Pierotti, and Peck. German makers included Heinrich Stier.

First price indicates doll in good condition, but with flaws; second price is for doll in excellent condition, original clothes, or appropriately dressed. More for exceptional dolls; much less for dolls in poor condition.

Poured Wax

Baby, shoulder head, painted features, glass eyes, English Montanari type, closed mouth, cloth body, wig, or hair inserted into wax

17"	$1,125.00	$1,500.00
25"	$1,700.00	$2,250.00

Infant nurser, slightly turned shoulder head, set glass eyes, open mouth, inserted hair wig, cloth body, wax limbs, nicely dressed

26" $1,320.00*

Child, shoulder head, inserted hair, glass eyes, wax limbs, cloth body

13"	$825.00	$1,100.00
27"	$1,100.00	$1,400.00
24"	$2,600.00* by Lucy Peck	

Lady

8"	$575.00	$770.00
15"	$825.00	$1,100.00

Bride, rose wax shoulder head, blue glass eyes, closed mouth, wig, kid jointed fashion body

15" $1,650.00*

* at auction

Wax over Composition or Reinforced

Child, ca. 1860 – 1890, early poured wax reinforced with plastic, inserted hair, glass eyes, cloth body

14"	$750.00	$1,000.00

Child, wax over socket head, glass eyes

16"	$1,500.00*

Child, later wax over composition shoulder head, open or closed mouth, glass eyes, cloth body

11"	$165.00	$225.00
17"	$250.00	$350.00
23"	$425.00	$575.00

Molded hair, wax over composition, shoulder head, glass eyes, cloth body, wooden limbs, molded shoes

15"	$225.00	$300.00
23"	$350.00	$475.00

Alice in Wonderland style, with molded headband

16"	$400.00	$525.00
19"	$475.00	$625.00

Slit-head wax, English, ca. 1830 – 1860s, wax over composition shoulder head, glass eyes may use wire closure

14"	$750.00	$1,000.00
18"	$900.00	$1,300.00
25"	$1,700.00	$2,300.00

Too few in database for reliable range.

Mechanical Baby, dome over papier mâché, painted hair, glass eyes, open mouth, papier mâché torso with bellows mechanism

18"	$2,000.00*

Two-faced doll, ca. 1880 – 1890s, one laughing, one crying, body stamped *"Bartenstein"*

15"	$675.00	$900.00

Bonnethead

Child, 1860 – 1880, with molded cap

16"	$250.00	$325.00

Lady with poke bonnet

25"	$3,000.00*

Too few in database for reliable range.

Man, turned shoulder head, molded top hat, set eyes, cloth body, wooden arms

17"	$1,000.00*

Too few in database for reliable range.

17½" pour wax shoulder head doll, ummarked, original mohair inserted into wax, set blue eyes, painted upper and lower lashes, feathered brows, closed mouth, cloth body, poured wax lower limbs attached with grommets, original white dress trimmed with eyelet and lace, underwear, not socks or shoes, blue velvet ribbon at waist, circa 1850s+, $400.00. Courtesy McMasters Doll Auctions.

25" wax over papier mâché unmarked shoulder head, original mohair wig in sausage curls, blue sleep eyes, single stroke brows, closed smiling mouth, cloth body, wax over papier mâché lower arms and lower legs, original organdy dress with ruffle trim, underclothing, socks, and shoes, circa 1860s – 1870s, $625.00. Courtesy McMasters Doll Auctions.

Wislizenus, Adolf

1850 – 1930+, Walterhausen, Thüringia, Germany. Doll and toy factory that specialized in ball-jointed bodies and used Bähr & Pröschild, Simon &

* at auction

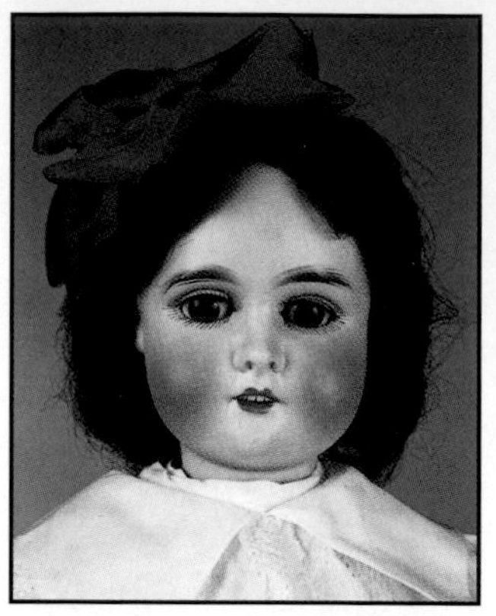

25" bisque A.W. Special marked "29//A.W.//Special//Germany," socket head, original human hair wig, blue sleep eyes, real and painted lashes, open mouth, four upper teeth, jointed wood and composition body, re-dressed in white antique style dress, underclothing, new socks and lace-up boots, circa 1890+, $350.00. Courtesy McMasters Doll Auctions.

Mark:

AW
W
DR G M
421481

Halbig, and Ernst Heubach bisque heads for dolls they made.

Child

AW, bisque socket head, sleep eyes, open mouth, jointed body, original regional costume

23" $950.00*

AW Special, 101 My Sweetheart, open mouth, sleep eyes

22 – 23" $375.00 $500.00

Mold #110, socket head, glass eyes, open/closed mouth with teeth

16" $2,400.00*

Mold #115, solid dome, open/closed mouth, painted eyes

12" $1,200.00* toddler

Wolf, Louis & Co.

1870 – 1930+, Sonneberg, Germany, Boston, and New York City. They made and distributed dolls, also distributed dolls made for them by other companies such as Hertel Schwab & Co. and Armand Marseille. They made composition as well as bisque dolls and specialized in babies and Red Cross nurses before World War I. May be marked *"L.W. & C."*

Mark:

152
L.W. & C°
12

Baby, open or closed mouth, sleep eyes

12" $360.00 $475.00

Sunshine Baby, solid dome, cloth body, glass eyes, closed mouth

15" $1,000.00*

Wooden

1600s – 1700s+, England, Germany, Switzerland, Russia, United States, and other countries.

English

William & Mary Period, 1690s – 1700

Carved wooden head, tiny multi-stroke eyebrow and eyelashes, colored cheeks, human hair or flax wig, wooden body, fork-like carved wooden hands, jointed wooden legs, cloth upper arms, medium to fair condition

19¾" $36,350.00*

21¾" $45,500.00*

Too few in database for reliable range.

Queen Anne Period, early 1700s

Dotted eyebrows, eyelashes, painted or glass eyes, no pupils, carved oval-

* at auction

shaped head, flat wooden back and hips, nicely dressed, good condition

14"	$7,500.00	$10,000.00
18"	$11,000.00	$14,900.00
24"	$18,000.00	$24,000.00

Too few in database for reliable range.

Georgian Period, 1750s – 1800

Round wooden head, gesso coated, inset glass eyes, dotted eyelashes and eyebrows, human hair or flax wig, jointed wooden body, pointed torso, medium to fair condition

13"	$2,300.00	$3,000.00
15¾"	$2,750.00	$3,650.00
24"	$3,100.00	$4,200.00

1800 – 1840

Gesso coated wooden head, painted eyes, human hair or flax wig, original clothing comes down below wooden legs

12 – 13"	$900.00	$1,200.00
15"	$1,400.00	$1,875.00
20"	$2,100.00	$2,800.00

German

1810 – 1850s

Delicately carved painted hair style, spit curls, some with hair decorations, all wooden head and body, pegged or ball-jointed limbs

7"	$475.00	$650.00
12 – 13"	$1,050.00	$1,400.00
28¼"	$16,000.00* peg, disk jointed	

1850s – 1900

All wood with painted plain hair style; may have spit curls

5"	$95.00	$125.00
8"	$150.00	$200.00
14"	$300.00	$400.00

Wooden shoulder head, fancy carved hair style, wood limbs, cloth body

12"	$375.00	$500.00
16"	$1,000.00* man, carved hair	
23"	$650.00	$875.00

1900+

Turned wooden head, carved nose, painted hair, lower legs with black shoes, peg jointed

11"	$60.00	$80.00

Child, all-wood, fully-jointed body, glass eyes, open mouth

15"	$335.00	$450.00
18"	$450.00	$625.00
23"	$600.00	$825.00

Grodner Tal

1700s – 1930s, originally Austrian town, later Italian

Wooden dolls have been carved in this town for years. The Colemans report 2,000 carvers in the 1870s, plus painters making wooden dolls, jointed and unjointed, in sizes from ½" to 24".

Carved one-piece head and torso, dowel jointed limbs, dressed

5"	$165.00	$220.00
17"	$725.00	$975.00

* at auction

Carved hair in bun

8½" $1,050.00*

Character

24" $5,250.00*

Ca. 1810

Molded bosom, painted chemise, dowel pin, eight ball-jointed body

14½" $2,750.00*

Ca. 1820

Small (up to 5") peg-jointed dolls, period costumes

Set of 7 $4,361.00*

Matryoskia — Russian Nesting Dolls, 1900+

Set of wooden canisters that separate in the middle, brightly painted with a glossy finish to represent adults, children, storybook, or fairytale characters and animals. These come in sets usually of five or more related characters, the larger doll opening to reveal a smaller doll nesting inside, and so on.

Set pre 1930s

4"	$70.00	$100.00
7"	$115.00	$150.00
9"	$175.00	$230.00

Set new

5"	$20.00
7"	$30.00

Political set: Gorbachev, Yeltsin

5"	$35.00
7"	$60.00

Swiss, 1900+

Carved wooden dolls with dowel jointed bodies, joined at elbow, hips, knees, some with elaborate hair

12"	$315.00	$425.00
16"	$475.00	$635.00

Ellis, Joel

Cooperative Manufacturing Co., 1873 – 74, Springfield, VT. Manufactured wooden dolls patented by Joel Ellis. The head was cut into a cube, steamed until it softened, then compressed in hydraulic press to form features. Metal hands and feet painted black or blue, painted black molded hair sometimes blond. Similar type Springville wooden dolls were made by Joint Doll Co. and D. M. Smith & Co. have cut out hip joints.

12"	$700.00	$950.00
15"	$975.00	$1,300.00

Fortune Tellers

Wooden half or full doll with folded papers with fortunes printed on them making up the skirt

18" $2,600.00 $3,500.00

Too few in database for reliable range.

Hitty: See Artist Dolls.

Schoenhut: See that section.

* at auction

Modern Dolls

16" composition Arranbee Nancy Lee, blue plastic sleep eyes, eyeshadow, real lashes, painted lashes below, closed mouth, brown mohair wig, original black dot on white long dress with pink flower and feather trim, gold and round blue foil hang tag reads "Nancy Lee//R&B//Quality Doll," no other marks noted, boxed, circa 1940s, $650.00. Courtesy Kay Walimaa.

20" composition Arranbee My Dream Baby, tagged "RandB QUALITY DOLL//My//Dream//Baby//LIKE A TOT OF YOUR OWN," molded painted dark brown hair, blue sleep eyes, real lashes, painted lower lashes, open mouth with teeth, composition arms, legs, cloth body, blue baby dress and matching bonnet trimmed with lace and net, white shoes, circa 1927+, $475.00. Courtesy Sandra Tripp.

16" hard plastic Terri Lee, with brown synthetic wig, brown painted eyes, painted lashes, one stroke brown eyebrows, red dots at nostrils, bright red lips, wearing rose colored velveteen coat and matching hat, fur gloves attached to coat with ribbon, white socks, black shoes, circa 1951 – 1962, $450.00. Courtesy Diane Vigne.

7½" hard plastic Danish Knorr Dolls for Knorr Soup, a Best Foods product, blue sleep eyes, European look faces with full lips, jointed, will stand alone, the dolls came in pairs, a boy and a girl dressed in costumes representing several countries, circa 1963 – 1964, $15.00. Courtesy Betty Strong.

Aunt Jemima, cloth, stained

16" $95.00 *

Bell Telephone "Pioneers of America" Bell

15" $30.00 $75.00

Buster Brown Shoes

Composition head, cloth body, tag reads *"Buster Brown Shoes"*

15" $256.00*

Capezio Shoes

"Aida, Toe Dancing Ballerina Dolls"

$40.00 $150.00

Colgate Fab Soap Princess Doll, ca. 1951

5½" $5.00 $15.00

Gerber Baby, 1936+

An advertising and trademark doll for Gerber Products, a baby food manufacturer located in Fremont, Michigan. First price is for doll flawed, nude, or re-dressed, second price is for all original with package. More for black or special sets with accessories.

1936, cloth one-piece doll, printed, holds can

8" $400.00 $500.00

Sun Rubber Company, 1955 – 1958, designed by Bernard Lipfert, vinyl

12" $50.00 $150.00

18" $35.00 $100.00

Arrow Rubber & Plastic Co., 1965, vinyl

14" $40.00 $150.00

Amsco, Milton Bradley, 1972 – 1973, vinyl

10" $60.00 $100.00

14", 16", 18" $35.00 $50.00

Atlanta Novelty, 1979 – 1985, vinyl, flirty eyes, cloth body

17" $25.00 $90.00

Talker

17" $25.00 $100.00

Collector Doll, christening gown, basket

12" $25.00 $100.00

Porcelain, limited edition

17" $75.00 $350.00

Lucky Ltd. 1989 – 1992, vinyl

6" $5.00 $15.00

11" $10.00 $40.00

14 – 16" $10.00 $40.00

Toy Biz, Inc. 1994 – 1996, vinyl

8" $4.00 $15.00

15" $7.50 $25.00

Battery operated

12 – 13" $10.00 $25.00

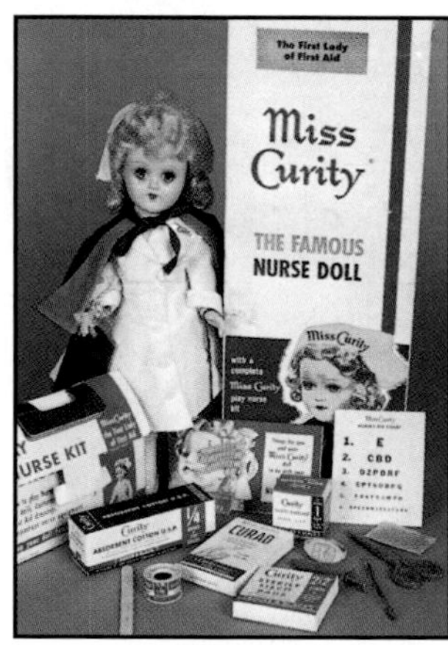

14" all hard plastic Ideal Miss Curity, blue sleep eyes, five-piece body, includes play nurse kit, tagged nurse uniform, unplayed with condition in original box, circa 1953, $650.00. Courtesy McMasters Doll Auctions.

* at auction

12 – 13" set of three cloth Kellogg Premium dolls, sold for 10 cents plus a boxtop. 2nd set of this kind, missing Baby Bear, lithographed, came as sheet of fabric, had to be sewn together, some wear, $75.00 each. Courtesy Harold Tanner.

Talker

14"	$10.00	$40.00
17"	$10.00	$50.00

Green Giant, Sprout, 1973

10½"	$7.50	$25.00

Jolly Joan, Portland, Oregon, restaurant

11"	$35.00	$125.00

Kellogg's cereals

Corn Flakes & Pep "Red Riding Hood," cloth

13½"	$40.00	$150.00

Goldilocks & Three Bears, set of four

12 – 15"	$80.00	$225.00

Korn Krisp cereal

"Miss Korn-Krisp," ca. 1900, cloth marked body

24"	$60.00	$225.00

Lustre Créme, original dress, patterns

7½"	$78.00*	

Nabisco cereal "Your Overseas Doll"

8½"	$7.50	$25.00

Texaco Cheerleader

Vinyl, boxed with wardrobe, ca. 1970s

11½"	$20.00	$75.00

Madame Alexander

In 1912, Beatrice and Rose Alexander, known for making doll costumes, began the Alexander Doll Co. They began using the "Madame Alexander" trademark in 1928. Beatrice A. Behrman became a legend in the doll world with her long reign as head of the Alexander Doll Company. Alexander made cloth, composition, and wooden dolls, and eventually made the transition to hard plastic and vinyl. Dolls are listed by subcategories of the material of which the head is made.

First price is for doll in good condition with flaws, may have soiled or worn clothing; second price is for complete beautiful doll in mint condition with original clothes, tag, labels, etc. Unusual dolls with presentation cases or rare costumes may be much more.

* at auction

13" cloth Susie-Q and Bobby-Q, marked "Susie Q (Bobby Q)//by Madame Alexander, N.Y.//All Rights Reserved" on tags on clothing, both also with cardboard tags, mask faces, painted side-glancing eyes, painted upper lashes, closed mouths, rosy cheeks, yarn hair, cloth bodies jointed at shoulders, mitten hands, striped fabric on legs for stockings, black felt feet for shoes, original matching outfits, unplayed with condition, circa 1940 – 1942, $1,600.00. Courtesy McMasters Doll Auctions.

9" composition Little Betty, marked "Mme. Alexander," red mohair wig, painted blue eyes, painted shoes and socks, original pink and white checked dress, bonnet, circa 1935 – 1943, $250.00. Courtesy Barbara Hull.

Cloth, ca. 1930 – 1950+

All-cloth head and body, mohair wig, flat or molded mask face, painted side-glancing eyes

Alice in Wonderland, ca. 1930
Flat face $200.00 $875.00
Mask face
16" $200.00 $675.00

Animals $70.00 $275.00
Dogs $75.00 $290.00
Baby
13" $75.00 $300.00
17" $125.00 $475.00

Clarabell, the Clown, 1951 – 1953
19" $100.00 $350.00

Dionne Quintuplets, ca. 1935 – 1936
16" $250.00 $900.00
24" $450.00 $1,200.00

David Copperfield or other boys, ca. 1930s
16" $200.00 $800.00+

Funny, 1963 – 1977
18" $10.00 $70.00

Little Shaver, 1940 – 1944, yarn hair
15" $150.00 $600.00
22" $175.00 $650.00

Little Women, ca. 1930 – 1936
16" $125.00 $700.00+

Muffin, ca. 1965
14" $25.00 $95.00

So Lite Baby or Toddler, ca. 1930s – 1940s
20" $100.00 $375.00+

Suzie Q, 1940 – 1942
$175.00 $650.00

Teeny Twinkle, 1946, disc floating eyes
$150.00 $525.00

Tiny Tim, ca. 1930s
$230.00 $725.00

Composition, ca. 1930 – 1950

Baby

Baby Genius, cloth body, sleep eyes, marked *"Alexander"*
22" $550.00* wrist tag, yellow taffeta tagged gown

Baby Jane, 1935
16" $325.00 $950.00+

Pinky, 1937 – 1939, composition
23" $100.00 $300.00

Princess Alexandria, 1937 only
24" $95.00 $300.00

* at auction

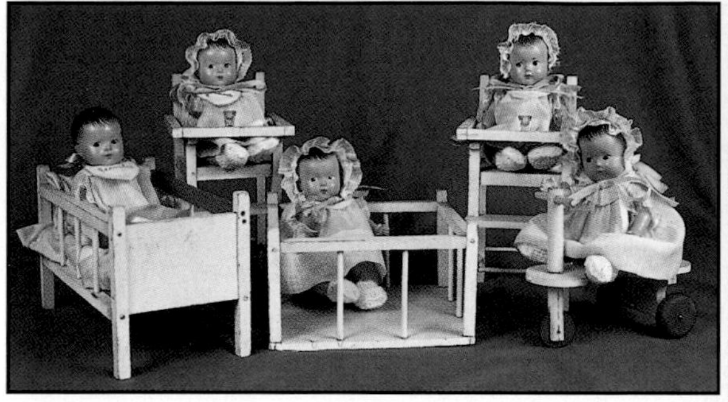

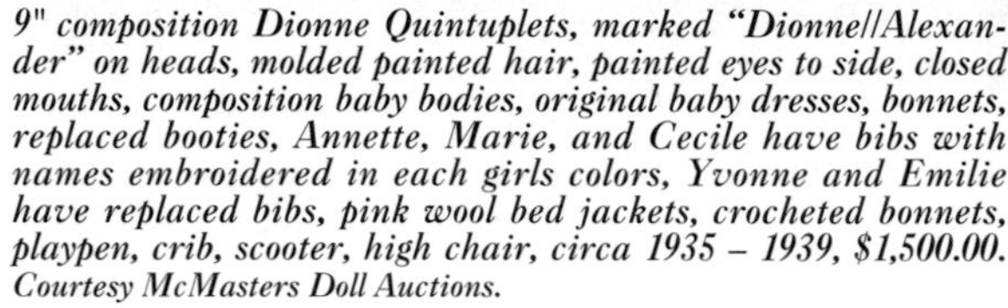

9" composition Dionne Quintuplets, marked "Dionne//Alexander" on heads, molded painted hair, painted eyes to side, closed mouths, composition baby bodies, original baby dresses, bonnets, replaced booties, Annette, Marie, and Cecile have bibs with names embroidered in each girls colors, Yvonne and Emilie have replaced bibs, pink wool bed jackets, crocheted bonnets, playpen, crib, scooter, high chair, circa 1935 – 1939, $1,500.00. *Courtesy McMasters Doll Auctions.*

16¾" hard plastic possibly Madame Alexander Bride, dark blond wig, sleep eyes, real lashes, painted lashes below, eyeshadow, closed mouth, jointed hard plastic body, white gown with netting over gown, two ruffles at hem, netting is torn, matching veil, lace ruffle at neck, long net sleeves, bouquet tied with ribbon and netting attached to hand, circa 1950s, $150.00. *Courtesy Carol Van Verst-Rugg.*

Child

Alice in Wonderland, 1930s, swivel waist

13" $125.00 $425.00

Babs Skater, 1948, marked *"ALEX"* on head, clover tag

18" $400.00 $1,250.00+

Bride and Bridesmaids, Wendy Ann, 1935 – 1943

15" $100.00 $350.00

18" $125.00 $450.00

Butch, 1942 – 1946, cloth body

12" $40.00 $150.00

1950, vinyl, cloth body

14" $45.00 $175.00

1965 – 1966, vinyl, cloth body

12" $35.00 $125.00*

Carmen Miranda-type

7" $350.00* near mint

14" $125.00 $450.00

Dionne Quintuplets, ca. 1935 – 1945, all-composition, swivel head, jointed toddler or baby body, painted molded hair or wigged, sleep or painted eyes. Outfit colors: Annette, yellow; Cecile, green; Emilie, lavender; Marie, blue; Yvonne, pink. Add more for extra accessories or in layette.

Baby 8" $75.00 $300.00

Set of five

Toddler 8" $275.00 $1,300.00

11" $400.00 $2,200.00

14" $500.00 $2,500.00

20" $700.00 $4,200.00

Set of five with wooden nursery furniture

8" $1,750.00*

* at auction

19" composition McGuffey Ana marked "Princess Elizabeth/ /Alexander Doll Co" on head, "McGuffey Ana//Madame Alexander, N.Y. U.S.A.//All Rights Reserved" on dress tag, human hair wig, brown sleep eyes, real lashes, painted lashes, open mouth, four upper teeth, five-piece composition body, red/white dotted Swiss dress, rickrack trim, red taffeta jacket, straw hat, snap shoes, all original with box, School House wrist tag, circa 1937 – 1943, $1,075.00. Courtesy McMasters Doll Auctions.

20"composition Fairy Princess, "Fairy Princess/ /Madame Alexander, N.Y. U.S.A.//All Rights Reserved" on dress tag, wig in original set, brown sleep eyes, real lashes, eye shadow, painted lower lashes, feathered brows, five-piece composition body, original rosy gold satin gown, trimmed with lace and sequins, pink slip and panties, socks, silver tie shoes, crown of gold braid and pale pink sequins, all original in box, circa 1939, also 1944 – 1946, $775.00. Courtesy McMasters Doll Auctions.

* at auction

Set of five in basket with extra dresses

8" $3,800.00*

11" $560.00 $2,300.00

Dr. Dafoe, 1937 – 1939

14" $525.00 $1,600.00+

Nurse

13" $250.00 $900.00+

Fairy Queen, ca. 1940 – 1946, clover wrist tag, tagged gown

14" $200.00 $700.00

18" $225.00 $800.00

Flora McFlimsey, 1938, freckles, marked *"Princess Elizabeth"*

16" $135.00 $550.00+

22" $250.00 $800.00

Flower Girl, 1939 – 1947, marked *"Princess Elizabeth"*

20" $175.00 $650.00+

Happy Birthday, set of 12, side-glancing eyes

7" $2,700.00* all original

Jane Withers, 1937 – 1939, green sleep eyes, open mouth, brown mohair wig

15" $425.00 $1,300.00

20" $800.00 $1,600.00

Jeannie Walker, tagged dress, closed mouth, mohair wig

13" $175.00 $675.00+

Judy, original box, wrist tag, Wendy-Ann face, eyeshadow

21" $3,200.00+

Karen Ballerina, blue sleep eyes, closed mouth, *"Alexander"* on head

15" $275.00 $900.00+

18" $325.00 $1,200.00+

Kate Greenaway, yellow wig, marked *"Princess Elizabeth"*

13" $200.00 $750.00

24" $275.00 $900.00

Little Betty, 1939 – 1943, side-glancing painted eyes

9" $85.00 $325.00

9" $550.00* Alice in Wonderland

Little Colonel

17" $200.00 $750.00

Little Genius, blue sleep eyes, cloth body, closed mouth, clover tag

12" $75.00 $200.00

16" $100.00 $250.00

17" composition Sonja Henie, marked "Madame Alexander//Sonja//Henie" on head, human hair wig in original set, brown sleep eyes, real lashes, painted lower lashes, single stroke brows, open mouth, six upper teeth, five-piece composition body, original red skating dress with white bodice, red taffeta panties, white skates, circa 1939 – 1942, $625.00. Courtesy McMasters Doll Auctions.

Little Women, Meg, Jo, Amy, Beth

Set of four

7"	$325.00	$1,200.00
9"	$300.00	$1,100.00

Madelaine DuBain, 1937 – 1944

14"	$185.00	$550.00
17"	$250.00	$675.00

Marcella, ca. 1936, open mouth, wig, sleep eyes

24"	$200.00	$900.00+

Margaret O'Brien, 1946 – 1948

21"	$300.00	$1,250.00+

McGuffey Ana, 1935 – 1937, sleep eyes, open mouth, tagged dress

13"	$175.00	$675.00
15"	$200.00	$650.00
23"	$2,100.00* original	

Marionettes by Tony Sarg

12"	$125.00	$475.00

Princess Elizabeth, ca. 1937 – 1941

Closed mouth

13"	$185.00	$625.00+

Open mouth

15"	$200.00	$750.00+
28"	$275.00	$1,000.00+

Scarlett, ca. 1937 – 1946, add more for rare costume

14"	$200.00	$750.00
18"	$400.00	$1,200.00

Snow White, 1939 – 1942, marked *"Princess Elizabeth"*

14"	$150.00	$475.00
18"	$200.00	$750.00

Sonja Henie, 1939 – 1942, open mouth, sleep eyes

13"	$1,000.00* twist waist, MIB	
15"	$200.00	$750.00
21"	$350.00	$1,200.00

Tiny Betty, 1934 – 1943, side-glancing painted eyes

7"	$75.00	$275.00

W.A.A.C. (Army), W.A.A.F. (Air Force), W.A.V.E. (Navy), ca. 1943 – 1944

14"	$200.00	$750.00

Wendy-Ann, 1935 – 1948, more for special outfit

11"	$150.00	$575.00
14"	$100.00	$400.00
18"	$150.00	$600.00

17" composition Scarlett, "Scarlett O'Hara//Madame Alexander, N.Y. U.S.A.//All Rights Reserved" on dress tag, black human hair wig, original set, green sleep eyes, real lashes, eye shadow, painted lashes, feathered brows, closed mouth, five-piece composition body, original flower print with striped skirt dress, green velvet bodice, matching bonnet with plume, hoop slip, matching pantalettes, socks, green leatherette snap shoes, circa 1939 – 1946, $1,050.00. Courtesy McMasters Doll Auctions.

* at auction

16" composition Snow White, marked "Princess Elizabeth//Alexander Doll Co." on head, original human hair wig, green sleep eyes, painted lashes, closed mouth, five-piece composition body, original pink taffeta dress, black velvet bodice, pink velvet cape, stockings, black shoes with pointed toes and pink bows, wrist tag "Walt Disney's//Snow White//Dolls//by Madame Alexander//New York, U.S.A.," unplayed with condition, circa 1939 – 1940, $85.00. Courtesy McMasters Doll Auctions.

14" painted hard plastic Kathy (Maggie face), braided hair, sleep eyes, real lashes, jointed hard plastic body, tagged blue bodysuit, pink skirt, socks, shoes, missing roller skates, circa 1949 – 1951, $450.00. Courtesy Harlene Soucy.

Hard Plastic, 1948+, and Vinyl

Alexander-kins, 1953+

1953, 7½" – 8", straight leg nonwalker

Nude	$60.00	$225.00
Jumper, one-piece bodysuit		$375.00
Garden Party long gown		$1,300.00+

1954 – 1955, straight leg walker

Basic	$35.00	$200.00
Cotton school dress		$425.00
Day in Country		$875.00
Maypole Dance		$550.00
Riding habit	$375.00+	
Sailor dress	$875.00+	

1956 – 1965, bent-knee walker, after 1963 marked "*Alex*"

Nude	$45.00	$125.00
Carcoat set	$850.00	
Flowergirl	$850.00	
Skater		$575.00
Swim suit	$85.00	$325.00

1965 – 1972, bent-knee non-walker

Nude	$40.00	$125.00
Party dress, long	$200.00	$800.00

1973 – 1975

Ballerina, straight leg		$80.00
Bride, straight leg		$100.00

1976 – 1994, straight leg non-walker, marked "*Alexander*"

Ballerina	$25.00	$85.00
Bride	$30.00	$100.00

Babies

Baby Angel, #480, tagged tulle gown

8" $950.00*

Baby Brother or Sister, 1977 – 1982, vinyl

14"	$20.00	$85.00

Baby Clown, #464, seven-piece walker, leashed dog, Huggy

8"	$300.00	$1,200.00+

Baby Ellen, 1965 – 1972, vinyl, rigid vinyl body, marked "*Alexander 1965*"

14"	$75.00	$125.00

Baby Precious, 1975, vinyl, cloth body

14"	$25.00	$100.00

Bonnie Toddler, 1954 – 1955, vinyl

19"	$35.00	$125.00

Happy, 1970 only, vinyl

20"	$60.00	$225.00

Hello Baby, 1962 only

22"	$40.00	$175.00

* at auction

Honeybun, 1951, vinyl

19"	$55.00	$200.00

Huggums, Big, 1963 – 1979

25"	$25.00	$100.00

Huggums, Lively, 1963

25"	$35.00	$150.00

Little Bitsey, 1967 – 1968, all-vinyl

9"	$35.00	$150.00

Little Genius, ca. 1956 – 1962, hard plastic, varies with outfit, nude

8"	$25.00	$100.00

Littlest Kitten, vinyl, nude

8"	$30.00	$125.00

Mary Cassatt, 1969 – 1970, vinyl

14"	$50.00	$175.00
20"	$80.00	$250.00

Pussy Cat, ca. 1965 – 1985, vinyl

14"	$20.00	$65.00

Pussy Cat, black

14"	$35.00	$75.00

Rusty, 1967 – 1968 only, vinyl

20"	$80.00	$300.00

Sweet Tears, 1965 – 1974

9"	$20.00	$100.00

With layette, 1965 – 1973

	$50.00	$175.00

Victoria, 1967 – 1989

20"	$20.00	$100.00

Bible Character Dolls, 1954 only

Hard plastic, original box made like Bible

8"	$1,500.00	$7,000.00+

Cissette, 1957 – 1963

10", hard plastic head, synthetic wig, pierced ears, closed mouth, seven-piece adult body, jointed elbows and knees, high-heeled feet, mold later used for other dolls. Marks: None on body, clothes tagged *"Cissette."*

Ballgown	$125.00	$475.00+
Ballerina	$100.00	$375.00
Beauty Queen	$90.00	$300.00
Bride	$100.00	$375.00
Doll only	$40.00	$125.00
Day dress	$85.00	$275.00
Formal	$150.00	$475.00
Gibson Girl	$250.00	$800.00+
Jacqueline	$160.00	$650.00+
Margot	$135.00	$475.00+
Portrette	$125.00	$450.00
Renoir	$135.00	$450.00
Scarlett	$135.00	$475.00

19" hard plastic Snow White, Margaret face, black saran wig, sleep eyes, real lashes, painted lower lashes, closed mouth, hard plastic jointed body, long print gown, gold lamé vest with laces, ribbon in hair, circa 1952, $850.00. Courtesy Carol Van Verst-Rugg.

17" hard plastic Alice in Wonderland, Maggie face, blond styled wig, blue sleep eyes, real lashes, painted lashes below, eyeshadow, closed mouth, jointed hard plastic body, pink nylon dress with white organdy pinafore, trimmed in lace, white stockings, black shoes, circa 1949 – 1950, $650.00. Courtesy Carol Van Verst-Rugg.

19" hard plastic Wendy Bride (Margaret face), red rooted hair, blue sleep eyes, closed mouth, jointed hard plastic body, white wedding gown, hat with lace and veil, white bouquet of flowers in one hand, carrying pink hat box, mint in box, circa 1951, $950.00. Courtesy Sharon Kolibaba.

Sleeping Beauty (1959 only)

	$100.00	$375.00
Tinkerbell	$125.00	$475.00+

Cissy, 1955 – 1959

20", hard plastic, vinyl arms, jointed elbows and knees, high-heeled feet. Clothes are tagged *"Cissy."*

Ballgown	$225.00	$850.00+
Bride	$200.00	$700.00+
Bridesmaid	$350.00	$1,000.00

Miss Flora McFlimsey, 1953 only (Cissy), vinyl head, inset eyes

15"	$150.00	$600.00
Formal	$400.00	$1,400.00
Southern Belle, #2244		$2,835.00*

Agatha from "Me and My Shadow," #2035F, in rose taffeta gown $3,675.00*

Princess	$275.00	$1,000.00
Queen	$400.00	$1,200.00

Scarlett, rare white organdy dress

	$500.00	$2,000.00+
Street dress	$115.00	$385.00
Pantsuits	$250.00	$275.00*

17" hard plastic Princess Margaret Rose, marked "Alexander" on head, "Margaret Rose//Madame Alexander, New York, U.S.A.//All Rights Reserved" on dress tag, mohair wig, blue sleep eyes, real lashes, eye shadow, painted lower lashes, single stroke brows, closed mouth, five-piece hard plastic body, original yellow nylon dress with lace and ribbon trim, long rayon stockings, black snap shoes, straw bonnet, circa 1949 – 1953, $375.00. Courtesy McMasters Doll Auctions.

Others

Alice in Wonderland, 1949 – 1952, Margaret and/or Maggie

15"	$120.00	$450.00
23"	$200.00	$800.00

American Girl, 1962 – 1963, #388, seven-piece walker body, became McGuffey Ana in 1964 – 1965

8"	$100.00	$375.00

Annabelle, ca. 1952, Maggie head

20"	$250.00	$875.00+

Aunt Pitty-Pat, ca. 1957, #435, seven-piece body

8" $1,700.00+

Babs Skater, 1948 – 1950, hard plastic, Margaret

15"	$250.00	$1,000.00+
18"	$350.00	$1,250.00+

Bill/Billy, ca. 1960, seven-piece walker body

8"	$150.00	$475.00+

Binnie Walker, 1954 – 1955, Cissy

15"	$175.00	$325.00
Skater	$650.00*	

Only in formals, 1955

25"	$125.00	$500.00+

* at auction

Bitsey, ca. 1950, cloth body, molded hair, more for wigged version

11"	$75.00	$275.00

Brenda Starr, 1964 only, 12" hard plastic, vinyl arms, red wig

Ballgown	$75.00	$375.00
Bride	$75.00	$300.00
Raincoat/hat/dress	$65.00	$225.00
Street dress	$50.00	$225.00

Caroline, ca. 1961, #131, vinyl

15"	$90.00	$375.00

Cinderella, 1950, Margaret face, 14", hard plastic

Ballgown

14"	$225.00	$850.00+

Poor Cinderella, gray dress, original broom

14"	$300.00	$600.00

Ballgown

18"		$750.00*

Lissy, 1966

12"	$250.00	$950.00

1970 – 1986, vinyl body, ballgown (pink and blue)

14"	$40.00	$125.00

Cynthia, 1952 only, hard plastic

15"	$300.00	$850.00+
18"	$200.00	$850.00+
23"	$400.00	$1,200.00

Davy Crockett, ca. 1955, hard plastic, straight leg walker, coonskin cap

8"	$225.00	$700.00+

Edith, The Lonely Doll, 1958 – 1959, vinyl head, hard plastic body

8"	$250.00	$750.00+
16"	$175.00	$375.00

Elise, 1957 – 1964, 16", hard plastic body, vinyl arms, jointed ankles and knees

Ballerina	$200.00	$375.00+
Ballgown	$350.00	$700.00+
Street clothes	$100.00	$400.00+

Elise, 1963 only, 18", hard plastic, vinyl arms, jointed ankles and knees

Riding Habit	$175.00	$350.00
Bouffant hairstyle	$200.00	$425.00

Elise, 1966 – 1972, 17", hard plastic, vinyl arms, jointed ankles and knees

Street dress	$75.00	$275.00
Trousseau/Trunk	$175.00	$650.00+
Bride, 1966 – 1987	$40.00	$175.00

Estrella, 1953, Maggie face, walker body, tagged lilac gown, hard plastic body

18"	$600.00	$1,200.00+

9" hard plastic Prince Charles, #397 (Wendy Ann), auburn wig, blue sleep eyes, real lashes, painted lashes below, closed mouth, jointed hard plastic body, blue jacket, short pants, matching hat, white socks, shoes, made in 1957 only, $650.00. Courtesy Joan Radke.

9" hard plastic Princess Ann, #396 (Wendy Ann), auburn wig, blue sleep eyes, painted lashes below, jointed hard plastic body, white lace dress with pink ribbons, matching hat, made in 1957 only, $450.00. Courtesy McMasters Doll Auctions.

17" hard plastic Bride, marked "Alexander" on back of head, "Madame Alexander//All Rights Reserved//New York, U.S.A." on dress tag, original wig, blue sleep eyes, real lashes, painted lower lashes, single stroke brows, closed mouth, five-piece hard plastic walking body, head attached to walking mechanism, original bride dress, flower-trimmed hat, panties, stockings, shoes, circa 1949 – 1955, $375.00. Courtesy McMasters Doll Auctions.

Fairy Queen, 1948 – 1950, Margaret face
14" $225.00 $750.00

Fashions of a Century, 1954 – 1955, 14" – 18", Margaret face, hard plastic
$900.00 $1,800.00+

First Ladies, 1976 – 1990
Set 1, 1976 – 1978
$150.00 ea. $1,000.00 set
Set 2, 1979 – 1981
$125.00 ea. $800.00 set
Set 3, 1982 – 1984
$125.00 ea. $800.00 set
Set 4, 1985 – 1987
$125.00 ea. $700.00 set
Set 5, 1988
$125.00 ea. $700.00 set
Set 6, 1989 – 1990
$125.00 ea. $700.00 set

Fischer Quints, 1964 only, vinyl, hard plastic body (Little Genius), 1 boy, 4 girls
7" $25.00 $75.00
Set of five $550.00

Flower Girl, ca. 1954, hard plastic, Margaret
15" $275.00 $550.00

Glamour Girl Series, 1953 only, hard plastic, Margaret head, auburn wig, straight leg walker
18" $800.00 $1,000.00+

Godey Bride, 1950 – 1951, Margaret, hard plastic
1950
14" $500.00 $1,000.00+
1950 – 1951
18" $700.00 $1,400.00

Godey Groom, 1950 – 1951, Margaret, hard plastic
1950, curls over ears
14" $475.00 $975.00
1950 – 1951
18" $600.00 $1,200.00

Godey Lady, 1950 – 1951, Margaret, clover wrist tag, hard plastic
1950
14" $500.00 $1,000.00

21" hard plastic Cissy, marked "Alexander" on back of head, original wig in elaborate curls cascading down back of head, blue sleep eyes, real lashes, painted lower lashes, feathered brows, closed mouth, pierced ears, hard plastic lady body, vinyl arms jointed at elbows, high heel feet, red taffeta gown tagged "Cissy//by Madame Alexander" with polka dot tulle scarf, pearl drop earrings, choker necklace, pearl ring, circa 1955 – 1958, $650.00. Courtesy McMasters Doll Auctions.

1950 – 1951

18"	$750.00	$1,500.00

Gold Rush, 1963 only, hard plastic, Cissette

10"	$400.00	$1,600.00

Grandma Jane, 1970 – 1972, #1420, Mary Ann, vinyl body

14"	$125.00	$250.00

Groom, 1949 – 1951, Margaret, hard plastic

14" – 16"	$375.00	$750.00+

Groom, 1953 – 1955, Wendy-Ann, hard plastic

7½"	$225.00	$450.00+

Jacqueline, 1961 – 1962, 21", hard plastic, vinyl arms

Street dress	$325.00	$650.00+
Ballgown	$425.00	$850.00+

Janie, 1964 – 1966, #1156, toddler, vinyl head, hard plastic body, rooted hair

12"	$75.00	$275.00

Jenny Lind, 1969 – 1970, hard plastic head

14"	$100.00	$375.00
21"	$450.00	$1,400.00

John Robert Powers Model, ca. 1952, with oval beauty box, hard plastic

14"	$800.00	$1,650.00

Kathy, 1949 – 1951, Maggie, has braids

15" – 18"	$350.00	$700.00

Kelly, 1959 only, hard plastic, Lissy

12"	$250.00	$475.00

Kelly, 1958 – 1959, hard plastic, Marybel

15" – 16"	$150.00	$325.00

Leslie (black Polly), 1965 – 1971, 17", vinyl head, hard plastic body, vinyl limbs, rooted hair

Ballerina	$200.00	$375.00
Bride	$190.00	$375.00

Lissy, 1956 – 1958, 12", jointed knees and elbows, hard plastic

Ballerina	$215.00	$425.00
Bridesmaid	$325.00	$650.00
Street dress	$175.00	$350.00
Formal	$250.00	$500.00

Little Shaver, 1963 – 1965, painted eyes, vinyl body

12"	$75.00	$250.00

Little Women, 1947 – 1956, Meg, Jo, Amy, Beth, plus Marme, Margaret, and Maggie faces

14" – 15"	$225.00	$450.00

9" hard plastic Cowboy and Cowgirl with Wendy Ann face from Americana/Storybook Series, blue sleep eyes, molded lashes, painted lower lashes, single stroke brows, closed mouths, original wigs, dressed in tagged cowboy and cowgirl clothing, brown felt hats, black boots on boy, brown boots with red metal stars on girl, circa 1967 – 1970, $345.00 for pair. Courtesy McMasters Doll Auctions.

14" hard plastic Polly Pigtails left and Annabelle right, both with blue sleep eyes, real lashes, closed mouths, original wigs, tagged dresses, five-piece hard plastic bodies, Polly Pigtails dressed in original red plaid romper with skirt, replaced socks, black side snap shoes, circa 1949 – 1951, $305.00; Annabelle dressed in original white dress, red rickrack trim, red sweater monogrammed "Annabelle," replaced socks, shoes, circa 1951 – 1952, $280.00. Courtesy McMasters Doll Auctions.

* at auction

19" vinyl Madeline, blond synthetic wig in original set, blue sleep eyes, hard plastic body with extra joints at elbows, wrists, and knees, original white dress with red stripes, matching bonnet, carrying hat box, white socks, red shoes, circa 1953, $595.00. Courtesy Rita Mauze.

Set of five	$1,100.00	$2,200.00
Set of five	$5,900.00* original box, tags	

1955, Meg, Jo, Amy, Beth, plus Marme, Wendy-Ann, straight-leg walker

8"	$200.00	$375.00
Set of five	$900.00	$1,800.00

1956 – 1959, Wendy-Ann, bent-knee walker

8"	$225.00	$250.00
Set of five	$600.00	$1,300.00

1974 – 1992, straight leg, #411 – #415

8"	$40.00	$75.00
Set of five	$200.00	$375.00

1957 – 1958, Lissy, jointed elbows and knees

12"	$200.00	$375.00
Set	$850.00	$1,900.00

1959 – 1968, Lissy, one-piece arms and legs

12"	$125.00	$250.00
Set	$300.00	$1,500.00

Lovey-Dove Ringbearer, 1951, hard plastic, five-piece toddler body, mohair wig, satin top, shorts

12"	$325.00	$650.00+

Maggie Mixup, 1960 – 1961, 8", hard plastic, freckles

Angel	$325.00	$750.00
Overalls	$325.00	$750.00
Riding Habit	$225.00	$550.00
Roller Skates	$325.00	$750.00

Maggie Teenager, 1951 – 1953, hard plastic

15" – 18"	$300.00	$600.00

Margaret O'Brien, 1949 – 1951, hard plastic

14"	$250.00	$475.00

Margot Ballerina, 1953 – 1955, Margaret and Maggie, dressed in various colored outfits

15" – 18"	$325.00	$750.00

Mary Ellen, 1954 only, rigid vinyl walker

31"	$300.00	$600.00+

Mary Ellen Playmate, 1965 only, bendable vinyl body

17"	$175.00	$325.00

Mary Martin, 1948 – 1952, South Pacific character Nell, two-piece sailor outfit, hard plastic

14" – 17"	$475.00	$975.00

Marybel, "The Doll That Gets Well," 1959 – 1965, rigid vinyl, in case

16"	$175.00	$350.00

McGuffey Ana, 1948 – 1950, hard plastic, Margaret

21"	$700.00	$1,400.00

1956 only, hard plastic, #616, Wendy Ann face

8"	$325.00	$750.00

21" vinyl Melanie (Coco), blond synthetic wig in original set, blue sleep eyes, closed mouth, rigid vinyl body, pleated blue formal with wide lace down sides, satin slippers, panties, ring, necklace, hair adornments, mint-in-box, circa 1966, $1,950.00. Courtesy Rita Mauze.

9" vinyl Little Genius, blond hair, blue sleep eyes, closed mouth, hard plastic body, dressed in dressy lacy outfit with matching bonnet, circa 1956 – 1962, $295.00. Courtesy McMasters Doll Auctions.

1963 only, hard plastic, rare doll, Lissy face
12" $1,000.00 $2,000.00+

Melanie, 1955 – 1956, #633, hard plastic, Wendy Ann Scarlett Series, lavender lace
8" $25.00 $100.00+

1966, "Coco," #2050, blue gown
21" $1,100.00 $2,200.00+

Melinda, 1962 – 1963, plastic/vinyl, cotton dress
14" – 22" $185.00 $375.00+

Nancy Drew, 1967 only, vinyl body, Literature Series
12" $165.00 $325.00

Nina Ballerina, 1949 – 1951, Margaret head, clover wrist tag
14" $300.00 $575.00+
19" $425.00 $850.00+
23" $400.00 $800.00

Peter Pan, 1953 – 1954, Wendy Ann Quiz-kin
8" $400.00 $850.00+

1969, 14" Wendy (Mary Ann head), 12" Peter, Michael (Jamie head), 10" Tinker Bell (Cissette head)
Set of four $1,000.00

Pink Champagne/Arlene Dahl, hard plastic, red hair, pink lace, rhinestone bodice gown
18" $2,750.00 $5,500.00+

Polly, 1965 only, 17"
Street dress $150.00 $275.00

Polly Pigtails, 1949 – 1951, Maggie, hard plastic
14" $250.00 $500.00
17" $300.00 $625.00

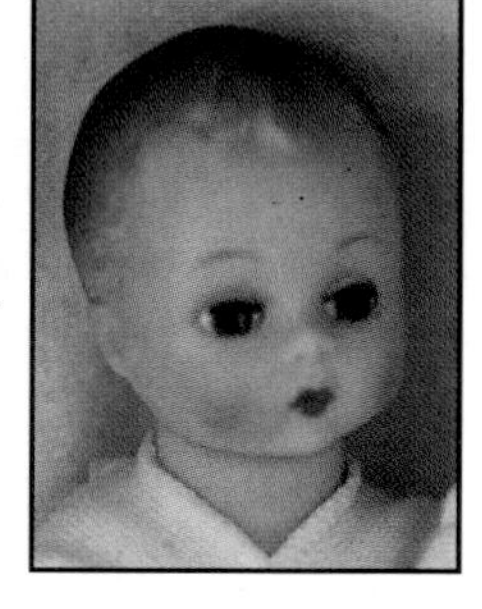

7" hard plastic Fischer Quints, sleep eyes, molded painted hair, open mouths for bottles, vinyl bent-leg baby bodies, white baby shirts/diapers, pink blanket, "QUINTUPLETS//by//Madame Alexander//Manufacturer of ORIGINAL QUINTUPLET Dolls" on box, all original in box, circa 1964, $550.00. Courtesy Deborah Baron.

Portraits, 1960+

Marked *"1961,"* Jacqueline, 21", early dolls have jointed elbows, later one-piece.

Agatha	1967 – 1980	#2171	$900.00
Cornelia	1972	#2191	$450.00
Gainsborough	1968 – 1978	#2184	$650.00
Godey, Coco	1966	#2063	$2,300.00
Godey, Jacqueline	1969,	#2195	$600.00
Goya	1968	#2183	$550.00
Jenny Lind	1969 – 1970	#2193	$1,400.00
Lady Hamilton	1968	#2182	$475.00
Madame	1966	#2060	$2,200.00
Madame Pompadour	1970	#2197	$1,200.00
Melanie (Coco)	1966	#2050	$2,200.00
Melanie	1970	#2196	$550.00
Magnolia	1977	#2299	$500.00
Queen	1965 – 1968	#2150	$750.00

Renoir	1965	#2154	$700.00
Scarlett	1965	#2152	$1,900.00+
Scarlett (Coco), white gown		#2061	$2,700.00+
Southern Belle	1965	#2155	$1,200.00
Southern Belle	1967	#2170	$625.00

Prince Charles, 1957 only, #397, hard plastic, blue jacket, cap, shorts
8" $325.00 $750.00+

Prince Charming, 1948 – 1950, hard plastic, Margaret face, brocade jacket, white tights
14" $350.00 $700.00

Princess Margaret Rose, 1949 – 1953, hard plastic, Margaret face
18" $425.00 $975.00

1953 only, #2020B, hard plastic, Beaux Arts Series, pink taffeta gown with red ribbon, tiara, Margaret face
18" $600.00 $1,700.00

Queen, 1953 only, #2025, hard plastic, Beaux Arts Series, white gown, long velvet cape trimmed with fur, Margaret
18" $900.00 $1,800.00

Queen, Me and My Shadow Series, 1954 only, hard plastic
8" $500.00 $1,000.00+
18" $600.00 $1,200.00

Quiz-Kin, ca. 1953, hard plastic, back buttons, nods yes or no
8" $250.00 $475.00

21" composition Judy, amber sleep eyes, real lashes, mauve eye shadow, multi-stroke brows, painted lashes at corners, closed mouth, original mohair wig, flower decoration, five-piece body, dressed in long peach taffeta gown with pinch-pleated insets at bottom of skirt, pink half slip, panties, and pink satin shoes, flower bouquet, foil wrist tag, marked "Alexander" on back, circa 1945 – 1947, $2,500.00. Courtesy McMasters Doll Auctions.

Renoir Girl, 1967 – 1968, vinyl body, Portrait Children Series
14" $100.00 $195.00

Scarlett, 1950s, hard plastic, more for rare costumes, bent-knee walker
8" $650.00 $1,300.00+
21" $650.00 $1,300.00+

Shari Lewis, 1958 – 1959
14" $325.00 $650.00
(Cissy)
21" $700.00 $1,400.00

Sleeping Beauty, ca. 1959, Disneyland Special
10" $200.00 $355.00
16" $325.00 $650.00
21" $425.00 $850.00+

Smarty, 1962 – 1963, vinyl body
12" $175.00 $325.00

Snow White, ca. 1952, gold vest, Walt Disney edition
15" $325.00 $750.00
21" $600.00 $1,200.00

Sound of Music, 1965 – 1970 (large), **1971 – 1973** (small), vinyl
Brigitta
10" $95.00 $175.00
14" $95.00 $195.00

Friedrich	8"	$115.00	$225.00
	10"	$150.00	$275.00
Gretl	8"	$90.00	$175.00
	10"	$100.00	$195.00
Liesl	10"	$125.00	$250.00
	14"	$150.00	$275.00
Louisa	10"	$140.00	$275.00
	14"	$140.00	$275.00
Maria	12"	$150.00	$300.00
	17"	$150.00	$300.00
Marta	8"	$115.00	$225.00
	10"	$95.00	$195.00
Set/seven small		$625.00	$1,250.00
Set/seven large		$700.00	$1,200.00

Southern Belle, hard plastic

1956 – 1963			
	8"	$375.00	$750.00
1968 – 1973			
	10"	$150.00	$450.00
1965 – 1981			
	21"	$400.00	$1,200.00

Timmy Toddler, 1960 – 1961, vinyl head, hard plastic body

	23"	$50.00	$150.00
1960 only	30"	$85.00	$250.00

Tommy Bangs, 1952 only, hard plastic, Little Men Series

11"	$450.00	$875.00

Wendy, Wendy-Ann, Wendy-kin, see Alexander-kins

Winnie Walker, 1953, Cissy, hard plastic

15"	$140.00	$275.00
18"	$175.00	$350.00
25"	$275.00	$550.00

Souvenir Dolls, UFDC, Limited Edition

Little Emperor, **1992,** limit 400

8" $500.00

Miss Unity, **1991,** limit 310

10" $400.00

Sailor Boy, limit 260

8" $750.00

Turn of Century Bathing Beauty, **1992,** R9 Conference, limit 300

10" $275.00

Columbian 1893 Sailor, **1993**

12" $250.00

Gabrielle, **1998,** limit 400

10" $325.00

American Character Doll Co.

1919 – 1963, New York City. Made composition dolls; in 1923 began using Petite as a tradename for mama and character dolls; later made cloth, hard plastic, and vinyl dolls. In 1960 advertised as American Doll & Toy Co.

First price is for dolls in good condition, but with some flaws; second price is

19" composition Petite Sally, marked "Petite Sally," wig, blue sleep eyes, closed mouth, composition arms and legs, cloth body, original orange coat and hat, circa 1931 – 1934, $350.00. Courtesy Janet Hill.

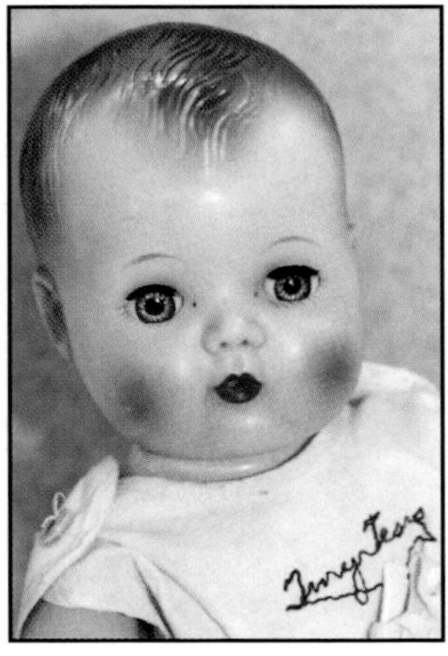

12½" vinyl Tiny Tears, molded painted hair, blue sleep eyes, holes for tears, open mouth for bottle, rosy cheeks, five-piece bent-leg baby body, white sunsuit, circa 1950s, $185.00. Courtesy Sharon Kolibaba.

for dolls in excellent condition, in original clothes. Exceptional dolls may be more. All vinyl and hard plastic dolls should have original tagged clothes, wrist tags, etc.

CLOTH

Eloise, ca. 1950s, cloth character, orange yarn hair, crooked smile

15"	$150.00	$260.00
Christmas dress	$90.00	$360.00
21"	$100.00	$425.00
Christmas dress	$135.00	$515.00

COMPOSITION

"A. C." or "Petite" marked baby

Composition head, limbs, cloth bodies, original clothes, good condition

14"	$50.00	$185.00
18"	$65.00	$225.00

"A. C." or "Petite" marked mama doll

Composition head, limbs, sleep eyes, mohair or human hair wig, cloth body with crier, swing legs, original clothes

16"	$75.00	$275.00
24"	$100.00	$385.00

Bottletot, 1926

Composition head, bent limbs, cloth body with crier, sleep eyes, painted hair, open mouth, composition arm formed to hold bottle, original outfit

13"	$75.00	$250.00
18"	$125.00	$325.00

1936 – 1938, rubber drink, wet doll with bottle, original diaper

11"	$35.00	$75.00
15"	$40.00	$95.00

Campbell Kids, 1928

All-composition, jointed neck, shoulders, hips, curl in middle of forehead. *Marks: "A Petite Doll"*

Allow more for original dress with label reading *"Campbell Kid."*

12"	$95.00	$350.00

Carol Ann Beery, 1935

All-composition Patsy-type, sleep eyes, closed mouth, braided cornet, celebrity doll, named for daughter of Hollywood actor, Wallace Beery. Originally came with two outfits such as a playsuit and matching dress. *Marks: "Petite Sally" or "Petite"*

13"	$100.00	$415.00
16½"	$150.00	$615.00
19½"	$200.00	$785.00

Chuckles, 1930s – 1940s

Composition head, open mouth, sleep eyes, cloth body. *Marks: "AM/Character"*

20"	$250.00	$350.00

Puggy, 1928

All-composition, jointed neck, shoulders, hip, pug nose, scowling expression, side-glancing painted eyes, painted molded hair. Original costumes include Boy Scout, cowboy, baseball player, and newsboy. *Marks: "A //Petite// Doll"; tag on clothing: "Puggy// A Petite Doll"*

13"	$200.00	$500.00

Sally, 1930, a Patsy-look-alike

Composition head, arms, legs, cloth or composition body, crier, painted or sleep eyes

Marks: "Sally//A Petite Doll"

12½"	$60.00	$225.00
14"	$100.00	$400.00
16"	$115.00	$450.00
19"	$125.00	$500.00

Sally, 1934, Shirley Temple look-alike

Ringlet curls and bangs, composition shoulder plate, cloth body, sleep eyes, open mouth. Some dressed in Shirley Temple-type costumes.

24"	$100.00	$375.00

Sally Joy, 1934

Composition shoulder plate, cloth body, sleep eyes, open mouth, curly wig

Marks: "Petite; Amer Char. Doll Co."

24"	$100.00	$400.00

Hard Plastic and Vinyl

Baby

Hard plastic head, vinyl body, bottle, boxed

12"	$60.00	$250.00

Vinyl head, marked *"American Character"*

20"	$20.00	$80.00

Tiny Tears, 1950 – 1962, hard plastic and vinyl

8"	$17.50	$75.00
13"	$65.00	$225.00
16"	$100.00	$400.00

Mint-in-box, with accessories, ca. 1954

12"	$1,045.00*	

1963, all-vinyl

9"	$20.00	$80.00
12"	$40.00	$150.00+
16"	$50.00	$200.00+

Toodles, ca. 1960, box, wardrobe, accessories

11"	$75.00	$285.00
29"	$150.00	$350.00

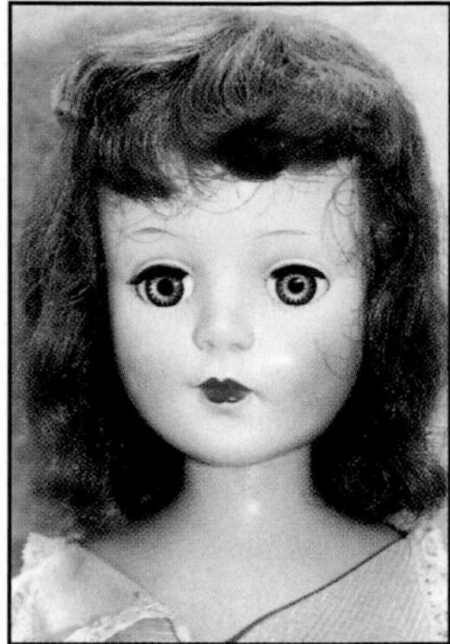

21" hard plastic Sweet Sue, saran hair, sleep eyes, real lashes, painted lower lashes, closed mouth, jointed hard plastic body, jointed elbows, wearing long formal with pink skirt and blue top trimmed with lace, circa 1950s, $225.00. Courtesy Rose Pitzer.

13" vinyl Ricky Jr., from "I Love Lucy" TV sitcom, molded painted hair, blue sleep eyes, hole in mouth for bottle, jointed baby body, in blue romper with hood, circa 1954 – 1956, $30.00. Courtesy Jeanne M. Perkins.

* at auction

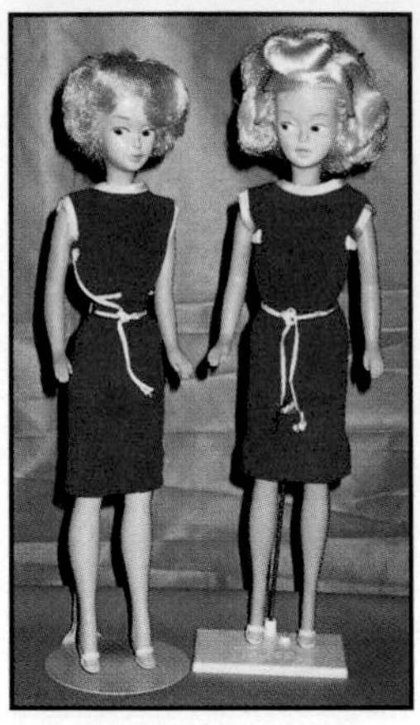

11½" vinyl Mary Make Up on left, with beige eyeliner, not a grow hair doll, straight legs, circa 1965 – 1966, $75.00; right, Magic Make Up Face Tressy blue eyeliner, grow hair feature, bendable legs, circa 1965 – 1966, $100.00. Courtesy Debby L. Davis.

19½" vinyl Whimsie Wheeler the Dealer, marked "Whimsies//19©60//American//Doll & Toy," one-piece stuffed vinyl body with molded head, molded painted slightly closed eyes, painted mustache, closed smiling mouth, black pants, red polka dot short sleeve shirt, red vest, black pants, circa 1961, $65.00. Courtesy Joan Sickler.

Toddler, with eight additional pieces of clothing, box #2503

24"	$150.00	$400.00

Child or Adult

Annie Oakley, hard plastic walker, embroidered on skirt

14"	$125.00	$400.00

Betsy McCall, 1957: See Betsy McCall category.

Cartwrights, Ben, Hoss, Little Joe, ca. 1966, TV show *Bonanza.*

8"	$40.00	$140.00

Freckles, 1966, face changes

13"	$10.00	$40.00

Little Miss Echo, 1964, talker

30"	$75.00	$300.00

Miss America, 1963

	$15.00	$60.00+

Ricky Jr., 1954 – 1956, *I Love Lucy* TV show, starring Lucille Ball and Desi Arnez, vinyl, baby boy

12"	$300.00*	
20"	$50.00	$225.00

Sally Says, 1965, plastic and vinyl, talker

19"	$20.00	$70.00

Sweet Sue, 1953 – 1961, hard plastic

Some walkers, some with skull caps, some with extra joints at knees, elbows, and/or ankles, some hard plastic and vinyl, excellent condition, good cheek color, original clothes.

Marks: "A.C.," "Amer. Char. Doll," or "American Character" in circle

15"	$75.00	$275.00
22"	$85.00	$350.00

Sweet Sue Sophisticate, vinyl head, tag, earrings

19"	$65.00	$275.00
Bride	$85.00	$325.00
Sunday Best	$100.00	$375.00

Talking Marie, 1963, record player in body, battery operated

18"	$25.00	$50.00

Toni, vinyl head, ca. 1958, rooted hair

10½"	$50.00	$195.00
20"	$190.00* box	

Toodle-Loo, 1961, rooted blond hair, painted eyes, closed mouth, fully-jointed, "Magic Foam" plastic body

18"	$50.00	$190.00

Tressy, her family and friends, 1963 – 1966, grow hair, 1963 – 1965

* at auction

Tressy, all-vinyl high heel doll, marked *"American Doll & Toy Corp.//19C.63"* in circle on head

	11"	$40.00	$115.00
Black Tressy			
	11"	$150.00	$300.00+

Pre-teen Tressy, 1963 only, vinyl, marked *"Am.Char.63"* on head

14"	$75.00	$300.00

Cricket, 1964 – 1966, all-vinyl pre-teen sister of Tressy, bendable legs, marked *"Amer Char//1964"* on head

9"	$75.00	$200.00

Magic Make Up, 1965 – 1966, vinyl, bendable legs, grow hair, not marked

11½"	$40.00	$75.00

Mary Make Up, 1965 – 1966, vinyl, Tressy's friend, high-heeled doll, no grow hair, not marked

11"	$40.00	$75.00

Whimette/Little People, ca. 1963, Pixie, Swinger, Granny, Jump'n, Go-Go

7½"	$6.00	$30.00

Whimsie, 1960, stuffed vinyl, painted on features, tag reads: *"Whimsie"* with name of doll, Bessie the Bashful Bride, Dixie the Pixie, Fanny (angel), Hedda-Get-Bedda, Hilda the Hillbilly, Lena the Cleaner, Miss Take, Monk, Polly the Lolly, Raggie, Simon, Strong Man, Suzie the Snoozie, Tillie the Talker, Wheeler the Dealer, Zack the Sack, and Zero (a football player)

Bessie the Bashful Bride, box, tag	$100.00	$225.00
Devil, or Hilda the Hillbilly	$75.00	$150.00
Hedda Get Bedda	$65.00	$125.00
Trixie the Pixie	$100.00	$225.00
Zack, the Sack	$75.00	$140.00
Zero, the Hero	$100.00	$250.00

Annalee Mobilitee Doll Co.

1934+, Meredith, NH. Decorative cloth dolls, early labels were white with woven red lettering; then white rayon tags with red embroidered lettering. In about 1969, white satin tags with red lettering were used, after 1976 gauze type cloth was used. Until 1963, the dolls had yarn hair, ca. 1960 – 1963, it was orange or yellow chicken feathers, after 1963, hair was synthetic fur. Collector's Club started in 1983.

First price is issue price, if known; second price for doll in excellent condition on secondary market. Remember secondary market prices are volatile and fluctuate.

10" felt, #3164, retired '92, tagged "Annalee '92//MADE ONLY//IN MEREDITH//NEW HAMPSHIRE//U.S.A.," $55.00. Courtesy Martha Cramer.

Celebrities, 10", all-cloth

Johnny Appleseed		
1984	$80.00	$1,000.00
Annie Oakley		
1985	$90.00	$700.00

Mark Twain		1986	$117.50	$500.00
Abraham Lincoln		1989	$119.50	$500.00
Christopher Columbus		1991	$119.50	$300.00
Logo Kids, all with collector's club logo				
Christmas, with Cookie		1985	$675.00	
Sweetheart		1986	$150.00	
Naughty		1987	$300.00	
Raincoat		1988	$150.00	
Christmas Morning		1989	$125.00	
Clown		1991	$125.00	
Reading		1992	$100.00	
Back to School		1993	$50.00	
Ice Cream		1994	$50.00	
Dress Up Santa		1994	$50.00	
Goin' Fishing		1995	$25.00	
Little Mae Flower	7"	1996	$25.00	
Clowns – A. Thorndike				
Clown, 1956	10"	1987	$80.00	
Clown	18"	1978	$225.00	
Clown with Balloon	18"	1985	$150.00	
Hot Air Balloon with 10" Clown		1985	$150.00	
Halloween – A. Thorndike				
Baby Witch with Diaper	3"	1987	$125.00	
Scarcrow Kid 3058	7"	1992	$55.00	
Trick or Treat Mouse 3005	7"	1977	$45.00	
Bat 2980	10"	1991	$80.00	
Pumpkin (medium) 3027	10"	1987	$165.00	
Witch Mouse on Broom 3030	12"	1980	$95.00	
Pumpkin (solid) 3025	14"	1986	$125.00	
Trick or Treat Bunny Kid	18"	1990	$150.00	
Witch (flying) 3008	18"	1989	$100.00	
Others				
Annalee self-portrait			$290.00*	
Betsy Ross		1990	$200.00*	
Bob Cratchet, w/ Tim, 7"	18"	1974	$11.95	$425.00
Elf Pixie		1964	$200.00*	
Girl Hiker with backpack			$1,111.00*	
Mr. & Mrs. Fireside Couple	18"	1970	$7.45	$300.00
Holly Hobby	22"	1973		$1,000.00
Bellhop	24"	1963	$13.95	$1,750.00
Woman	26"	1955		$6,500.00
Woman Golfer			$356.00*	
Mr. Santa Mouse with sack	29"	1977	$49.95	$800.00
Mrs. Snow Woman, holder	29"	1972	$19.95	$700.00
Santa in chair, two 18" kids	30"	1984	$169.95	$1,200.00
Scarecrow	42"	1977	$61.95	$2,050.00
Santa	48"	1978	$49.95	$1,450.00

* at auction

1922 – 1958, New York. Some of their bisque dolls were made by Armand Marseille and Simon & Halbig. Made composition baby, child, and mama dolls; early dolls have an eight-sided tag. Sold to Vogue Doll Co. which used molds until 1961.

Marks:
ARRANBEE//DOLL
Co. or R & B

First price is for soiled, faded, or without complete costume dolls; second price is for perfect dolls, with good color, complete costume, more for MIB.

Composition

Baby, 1930s – 1940s

Cloth body, original clothes or appropriately dressed

16"	$50.00	$150.00

My Dream Baby, 1925

Bisque solid dome heads made by Armand Marseille, painted hair, sleep eyes, open or closed mouth, cloth body, composition hands

Marks: "A.M. 341," "351," or "ARRANBEE"

See Marseille, Armand for prices.

Dream Baby, 1927+, composition, cloth body

14"	$65.00	$250.00
19"	$125.00	$475.00+

Child, 1930s – 1940s, all-composition

Marks: "Arranbee" or "R & B"

9"	$45.00	$125.00
15"	$85.00	$300.00+

Debu' Teen, circa late 1930s, 1940

Usually all-composition, some cloth body, mohair or human hair wig, closed mouth, original costumes, unmarked or marked Arranbee. Hang tags or paper labels read *"Debu'Teen//R & B Quality Doll."*

14"	$100.00	$375.00
17"	$125.00	$425.00

Ice Skater, 1945, some with Debu' Teen tag

14"	$70.00	$275.00
17"	$100.00	$300.00
21"	$115.00	$425.00

Kewty, circa 1934 – 1936, all-composition with molded hair, several faces used form the marked Kewty body.

Mark: "KEWTY"

14"	$100.00	$300.00

Nancy, 1930, a Patsy look-alike

Molded hair, or wig, sleep eyes, open mouth

Marks: "ARRANBEE" or "NANCY"

12"	$100.00	$300.00
19"	$150.00	$600.00
21"	$175.00	$750.00

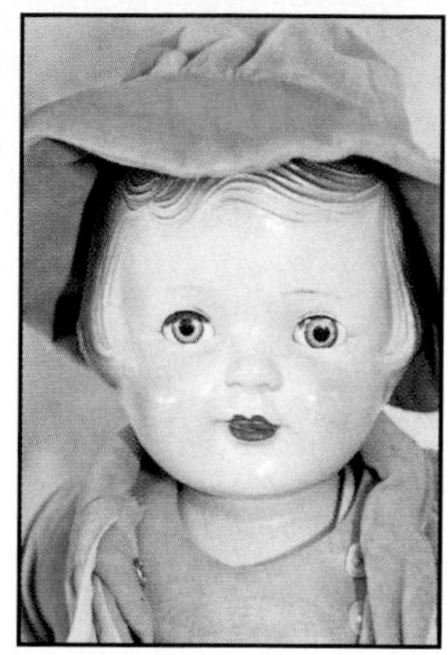

16½" composition Nancy, a Patsy look-a-like, marked "Nancy" on back of head, molded painted hair, blue tin sleep eyes, open mouth with teeth, green coat and matching hat, dress, shoes, socks, trunk with wardrobe, circa 1930, $300.00. Courtesy Donna Hadley.

26" composition Nannette, brown glassine sleep eyes, eye shadow, real lashes, painted lashes, open mouth, two upper teeth, blond human hair wig, original tagged aqua cotton dress and matching hat, red, white, and blue tag reads, "Nannette//Walking//and//Talking//doll//An R&B Quality Product" no marks noted on body, circa 1940s, $650.00. Courtesy Harlene Soucy.

10½" vinyl Littlest Angel, blue sleep eyes, molded lashes, single stroke brows, painted lower lashes, closed mouth, rooted saran hair, hard plastic body with jointed knees, original panties, socks, and shoes, two original booklets, wrist tag, boxed red and white check play outfit, shoes and hat, circa 1961 – 1963, marketed by Vogue, $300.00. Courtesy McMasters Doll Auctions.

14" composition Debu'Teen, blond human hair wig, sleep eyes, eyeshadow, closed mouth, jointed composition body, all original in long pink satin gown trimmed with lace, fur jacket, with all original wardrobe including skis, riding boots, ski boots, long and short slips, jodphurs, flower print dress, vest, shirt, jumpsuit, hats, doll and outfits near mint condition, circa 1939, $750.00. Courtesy Pat Graff.

Nancy Lee, 1939+

Sleep eyes, mohair, or human hair wig, original clothes

12" $75.00 $300.00

17" $100.00 $400.00

Storybook Dolls, 1930s, Nursery Rhyme Characters

Little Bo-Peep, ca. 1935, with papier-mâché lamb

8½" $100.00 $225.00

Little Boy Blue, ca. 1935, in decorated case, silver horn

8½" $125.00 $500.00

HARD PLASTIC AND VINYL

Cinderella, ca. 1952, silver/pink dress, silver cords on both wrists

20" $421.00* not mint

Darling Daisy Bride, tagged

18" $65.00 $325.00

Lil' Imp, 1960, hard plastic, red hair and freckles

10" $20.00 $75.00

Littlest Angel, 1956+, hard plastic walker, *"R&B"* marked torso and seven-piece body

11" $100.00 $275.00

Vinyl head, original dress, brochure

11½" $15.00 $50.00

Red hair/freckles, 1960

10" $20.00 $70.00

Miss Coty, ca. 1958, vinyl, *"10½R"* under right arm, high heels

10½" $35.00 $175.00

My Angel, 1961, hard plastic and vinyl

17" $10.00 $45.00

22" $20.00 $70.00

36" $45.00 $165.00

Walker, 1957 – 1959

30" $40.00 $150.00

1959, vinyl head, oilcloth body

22" $15.00 $60.00

Nancy, 1951 – 1952 vinyl head, arms, hard plastic torso, wigged

14" $40.00 $150.00

18" $50.00 $190.00

Walker

24" $75.00 $285.00

Nancy Lee, 1950 – 1959, hard plastic

14" $125.00 $500.00

17" $135.00 $550.00

20" $900.00* skater, mint-in-box

* at auction

Nancy Lee Baby, 1952, painted eyes, crying look

15"	$70.00	$145.00

Nanette, 1949 – 1959, hard plastic, synthetic wig, sleep eyes, closed mouth, original clothes

14"	$100.00	$350.00
17"	$125.00	$400.00

Nannette Walker, 1957 – 1959

17"	$125.00	$450.00
20"	$135.00	$500.00

Taffy, 1956, looks like Alexander's Cissy

23"	$45.00	$165.00

Artist Dolls

Original, one-of-a-kind, limited edition, or limited production dolls of any medium (cloth, porcelain, wax, wood, vinyl, or other material) made for sale to the public.

Cloth

Barrie, Mirren

Historical children $95.00

Heiser, Dorothy, soft sculpture

Early dolls $400.00+

Queens $1,100.00+

Wright, R. John, cloth

7½" Elfin girl $800.00

Adult characters $1,500.00

Children $900.00 – $1,300.00

Christopher Robin with Winnie the Pooh

$750.00 $2,500.00

Winnie the Pooh, 1987

14"	$550.00 – $700.00
18"	$1,000.00 – $1,300.00

19" cloth St. Agnes Academy is Having a Fortieth Reunion by Jane Darin, hand needle sculptured and painted face made from 100% Swiss pima cotton knit, 14" x 19" wooden base, the figures are both self-portraits wearing a combination of cottons and wools, glasses, charms, the mirror is a wire armature covered with batting, nylons, wooden beads, Fimo clay grapes, peacock, clock, shasta mirror, inspired by the artist's 40th high school reunion, circa 1997, $5,400.00. Courtesy Jane Darin.

Other Media

Baker, Betsy, Sculpey

$250.00 $500.00+

Baron, Cynthia, resin plymer clay

$100.00 $2,500.00+

Blackeley, Halle, high-fired clay lady dolls

$550.00 – $750.00

Bollenbach, Cheryl, Cernit

$600.00 $1,200.00+

Cochran, Dewees, circa 1950s, latex composition

Peter Ponsett

18" $2,500.00

Commissioned Portraits

20" $2,500.00

Child

15 – 16" $500.00 $900.00

Florian, Gertrude, ceramic/composition dressed ladies

$300.00

24" paper clay Iris by Yvonne Flipse of Maskerade in Holland, one-of-a-kind, handmade wig, side-glancing eyes, handmade outfit, paper clay and papier-mâché body, circa 2000, $4,400.00. Photo courtesy Yvonne Flipse.

14" porcelain Sona by Atelier Bets van Boxel, human hair wig, handcrafted crystal eyes, closed pouty mouth, gold sweater, cap, green pants, circa 2000, $1,500.00. Photo courtesy Atelier Bets van Boxel.

Goodnow, June
Chocolate Delight, resin, cloth
14" $920.00
Indian, Singer Drummer, one-of-a-kind, cernit
14" $3,000.00
The Quilter, resin, cloth
18" $500.00

Hopkins, Lillian, Paperclay over gourd
$500.00 $800.00+

Huston, Marilynn, Sculpey
$300.00 $700.00+

Parker, Ann, historical character
$150.00 – $200.00

Poole, Daryl, Sculpey
$700.00 $1,000.00+

Russell, Sarah, wax over fimo
$1,800.00+

Simonds, Sandy, Creall-therm
$1,000.00 $1,500.00+

PORCELAIN AND CHINA

Armstrong-Hand, Martha, porcelain babies, children $1,200.00+

Brandon, Elizabeth, porcelain children
$300.00 – $500.00

Campbell, Astry, porcelain
Ricky & Becky, pair $850.00

Clear, Emma, porcelain, china, shoulder head dolls $350.00 – $500.00

Dunham, Susan, porcelain babies, children/adults $75.00 – $1,000.00+

Hoskins, Dorothy
Lilabeth Rose, one-of-a-kind porcelain
$6,000.00+

Kane, Maggie Head, porcelain
$400.00 – $450.00

Oldenburg, Maryanne, porcelain children
$200.00 – $250.00

Redmond, Kathy, porcelain ladies
$400.00 – $450.00

Roche, Lynn and Michael, porcelain
17" children $1,100.00 – $1,500.00

Sutton, Linda Lee
Babies, children $400.00 – $1,000.00

Thompson, Martha, porcelain
Betsy $900.00
Little Women, ea. $800.00 – $900.00
Queen Anne $2,300.00
Princess Caroline, Prince Charles, Princess Anne ea
$900.00

24" porcelite resin Madison by Pat Moulton, brown human hair wig, painted brown eyes, closed mouth, holding brown plush bear, plaid dress trimmed in black, black ribbon in hair, black stockings and shoes, limited edition of 20, circa 2001, $450.00. Courtesy Pat Moulton.

14" wood carved Buffalo Man by W. Harry Perzyk, kneeling, handmade glass eyes, silk hair fastened to the head by individual hairs, handmade clothes, one-of-a-kind, circa 1987, $3,500.00. Courtesy Bernard P. Perzyk.

Princess Margaret, Princess Grace
ea. $1,500.00 – $2,000.00
Young Victoria $2,300.00
Thorpe, Ellery, porcelain children
$300.00 – $500.00
Tuttle, Eunice, miniature porcelain children
$700.00 – $800.00
Angel Baby $400.00 – $425.00
Walters, Beverly, porcelain miniature fashions
$500.00+
Wick, Faith, porcelain, other materials
$2,500.00+
Wyffels, Berdine, porcelain
Girl, glass eyes
6" $195.00
Zeller, Fawn, porcelain
One-of-a-kind $2,000.00+
Angela $800.00 – $900.00
Polly Piedmont, 1965 $800.00 – $900.00
Holly, U.S. Historical Society
$500.00 – $600.00
Polly II, U.S. Historical Society
$200.00 – $225.00

VINYL

Good-Krueger, Julie, vinyl
20" – 21" $150.00 $225.00
Hartman, Sonja, 1981+, vinyl and porcelain
Porcelain 20" $300.00
Vinyl, Odette 23" $375.00
Schrott, Rotrout, vinyl
Child $375.00
Spanos, FayZah, vinyl
Baby $250.00

22" porcelain Linda Lee Sutton black Ipsy, limited to 12 worldwide, black hair with bangs, brown paperweight eyes, open smiling mouth with teeth, holding two birds, white dress with puff sleeves, embroidered flowers on bodice, ribbons in hair, circa 2001, $850.00. Courtesy Linda Lee Sutton.

12" and 14" polymer clay Native American Couple by Susan Ware, hand-sculpted one-of-a-kind pair, both with dark hair, handmade deerskin clothing, girl holding matching mocassins, circa 2000, $800.00. *Courtesy Susan Ware.*

Wax

Gunzel, Hildegard, wax over porcelain
$1,500.00 – $2,000.00

Park, Irma, wax-over-porcelain miniatures
$125.00+

Sorensen, Lewis
Father Christmas $1,200.00
Toymaker $800.00

Vargas family, wax ethnic figures
10" – 11" $350.00 – $700.00

Wood

Beckett, Bob and June, carved wood children
$300.00 – $450.00

Bringloe, Frances, carved wood
American Pioneer Children
$600.00

Bullard, Helen, carved wood
Holly $125.00
American Family Series (16 dolls)
ea. $250.00

Hale, Patti, NIADA 1978, hand-carved character dolls, wooden heads, stuffed wired cloth bodies can pose; some all-wood jointed dolls
$200.00+

JANCI, Nancy Elliott, Jill Sanders
$400.00+

Sandreuter, Regina $550.00 – $650.00

Smith, Sherman, simple carved wood
5 – 6" $65.00 $100.00
With finer details, souvenir dolls, etc.
5 – 6" $235.00 $300.00

Hitty

Reproduced by modern artists to represent the small 6¼" – 6⅜" wooden doll from the literary character in Rachel Field's 1929 book, *Hitty, Her First 100 Years*. Original doll now resides in Stockbridge Library in Massachusetts.

Judy Brown $195.00
Ruth Brown $150.00
Helen Bullard $350.00
DeAnn Cote $400.00+

17" cloth R. John Wright Christopher Robin & 7" Winnie-the-Pooh, tagged "Christopher Robin & Pooh//Bedtime//No. 317/500//R.John Wright Dolls Inc.//©Disney, Based on the "Winnie-the-Pooh" works//©A.A. Milne and E.H. Shepard," "RJW" on gold buttons, made exclusively for the 1998 Disney convention, felt swivel heads, jointed felt bodies, Christopher has painted eyes, mohair wig, PJs, robe, slippers, Pooh has glass eyes, floss nose, mouth, mint in original case, $625.00. *Courtesy McMasters Doll Auctions.*

David Greene	$310.00	
Patti Hale	$300.00	
JANCI	$300.00	
Lonnie Lindsay	$205.00	
Jeff Scott	$175.00	
Mary Lee Sundstrom/Sandy Reinke	$500.00+	
Larry Tycksen, son-in-law of Sherman Smith	$65.00+	

Ashton Drake

Niles, IL. Markets via mail order and through distributors, has a stable of talented artists producing porcelain collector dolls. Many of these dolls are available on the volatile secondary markets with prices fluctuating widely. See Gene category for Ashton Drakes' hottest collectible.

Diana, The People's Princess

	18"	$50.00	$200.00

Elvis: Legend of a Lifetime, 1991

68 Comeback Special	$75.00	

Fairy Tale Heroines, designed by Diann Effner

Snow White	$65.00	

Mother Goose Series, designed by Yolanda Bello

Mary, Mary, Diane Effner	$90.00	
Miss Muffet, Yolanda Bello	$50.00	

Picture Perfect Babies, designed by Yolanda Bello

Jason	$100.00	$475.00
Heather	$25.00	$50.00
Jennifer	$25.00	$50.00
Matthew	$25.00	$50.00
Jessica	$25.00	$50.00
Lisa	$25.00	$50.00
Emily	$25.00	$75.00
Danielle	$25.00	$50.00
Amanda	$25.00	$50.00
Michael	$55.00	$100.00
Sarah	$30.00	$60.00

Precious Memories of Motherhood, designed by Sandra Kuch

Loving Steps	$65.00	

Barbie®

Mattel, Inc., 1959+, Hawthorne, CA.

First price indicates mint doll, no box; second price (or one price alone) is for mint never-removed-from-box doll. Doll alone, without box, would be less, and soiled or played-with dolls, much, much less. Even though Barbie is over 40 years old, she is still considered a newer doll by seasoned collectors.

In pricing newer dolls, the more perfect the doll has to be with mint color, condition, rare pristine outfit, complete with all accessories, retaining all tags, labels, and boxes to command the highest prices. This is not a complete listing of every Barbie doll, her friends, or accessories, but some of the more popular items.

11½" vinyl #1 Ponytail Barbie, brunette hair in original topknot, tiny ringlets for bangs, red lips, nostril paint, white irises with dark blue eyeliner, straight legs, high arched eyebrows, holes in bottom of feet with copper tubing in legs, heavy solid body, original black/white striped swimsuit, hoop earrings, black open toe shoes, pink cover Barbie booklet in box, very good condition, in original box, circa 1959, $8,700.00. Courtesy McMasters Doll Auctions.

11½" vinyl #2 Ponytail Barbie, blond hair with tiny ringlets for bangs, white irises with dark blue eyeliner, faded red lips, high arched brows, heavy solid body, finger paint, wearing black silk sheath with bow accent, added white nylon short gloves, white open toe shoes, hoop earrings, black wire stand, marked "Barbie™//Pats. Pend.//©MCMLVIII//by Mattel//Inc.," circa 1959, $2,200.00. Courtesy McMasters Doll Auctions.

11½" vinyl #3 Brunette, Ponytail Barbie heavy vinyl body, blue irises, curved eyebrows, no holes in feet, soft ponytail, all original in box, if mint, $1, 200.00. Courtesy McMaster Doll Auction.

Marks:
1959 – 1962
BARBIE™
PATS. PEND.
©MCMLVIII
BY//MATTEL, INC.
1963 – 1968
MIDGE™©1962
Barbie®/©1958
BY//MATTEL, INC.
1964 – 1966
©1958//MATTEL, IN.
U.S. PATENTED
U.S. PAT. PEND.
1966 – 1969
©1966//MATTEL, INC.
U.S. PATENTED//
U.S. PAT. PEND//
MADE IN JAPAN

Number One Barbie, 1959

11½", heavy vinyl solid body, faded white skin color, white irises, pointed eyebrows, soft ponytail, brunette or blond only, black and white striped bathing suit, holes with metal cylinders in balls of feet to fit round-pronged stand, gold hoop earrings

#1 Blond Ponytail Barbie
$3,500.00 $7,100.00
#1 Brunette Ponytail Barbie
$4,000.00 $7,500.00
#1 Barbie stand $350.00
#1 Barbie shoes $20.00
#1 Barbie earrings $65.00

Number Two Barbie, 1959 – 1960

11½", heavy vinyl solid body, faded white skin color, white irises, pointed eyebrows, no holes in feet, some with pearl earrings, soft ponytail, brunette or blond only

#2 Blond Ponytail Barbie
$3,000.00 $6,500.00
#2 Brunette Ponytail Barbie
$3,500.00 $6,325.00

Number Three Barbie, 1960

11½", heavy vinyl solid body, some fading in

11½" vinyl #4 Ponytail Barbie, blond hair in original topknot, red lips, nostril paint, finger and toe paint, straight legs, wearing #976 Sweater Girl outfit, orange sleeveless knit shell, matching sweater with button accents, gray flannel skirt, "How to Knit" book, metal scissors, wooden bowl with yellow, orange, and green yarn, two needles, black open toe shoes, in box, circa 1960, $650.00. Courtesy McMasters Doll Auctions.

11½" vinyl # 5 Ponytail Barbie, light blond hair in ponytail, blue painted eyes, blue eyeshadow, nostril paint, red lips, straight legs, original black and white striped one piece strapless swimsuit, black open toe shoes, white rimmed glasses, near mint condition, marked "Barbie®//Pats. Pend//©MCMLVIII//by//Mattel//Inc.," circa 1961, $270.00. Courtesy McMasters Doll Auctions.

11½" vinyl #6 Ponytail Barbie, titian hair, blue painted side-glancing eyes, blue eyeshadow, coral lips, fingernail and toenail paint, wearing #1669 Dreamland orange nylon long nightgown with lace accent, white open toe shoes with orange pompon, white plastic comb and brush, also includes red nylon one-piece swimsuit with red open toe shoes, black wire stand, marked "Midge T.M.//© 1962//Barbie®//© 1958//by//Mattel," circa 1962 – 1964, $205.00. Courtesy McMasters Doll Auctions.

skin color, blue irises, curved eyebrows, no holes in feet, soft ponytail, brunette or blond only

#3 Blond Ponytail Barbie	$600.00	$1,100.00+
#3 Brunette Ponytail Barbie	$650.00	$1,150.00+

Number Four Barbie, 1960

11½", same as Number Three, but solid body of skin-toned vinyl, soft ponytail, brunette or blond only

#4 Ponytail Barbie	$250.00	$665.00+

Number Five Barbie, 1961

11½", vinyl head, now less heavy, hard plastic hollow body, firmer texture, saran ponytail, can now be redhead, has arm tag

#5 Ponytail Barbie	$185.00	$560.00
#5 Redhead Ponytail Barbie	$320.00	$640.00+

Number Six Barbie, 1962

11½", same features and markings as Number Five Barbie except for a wider variety of hair and lip color, wears a different red jersey swimsuit, chubbier appearance to face

#6 Ponytail Barbie	$250.00	$525.00

More Basic Barbies

Listed alphabetically, year of issue and value. First price indicates doll in excellent condition, no box; second price indicates mint-in-box doll. Never-removed-from-box (NRFB) dolls would be more; played-with dolls would be less.

Bendable Leg

American Girl, side part

1965	$1,900.00	$3,000.00

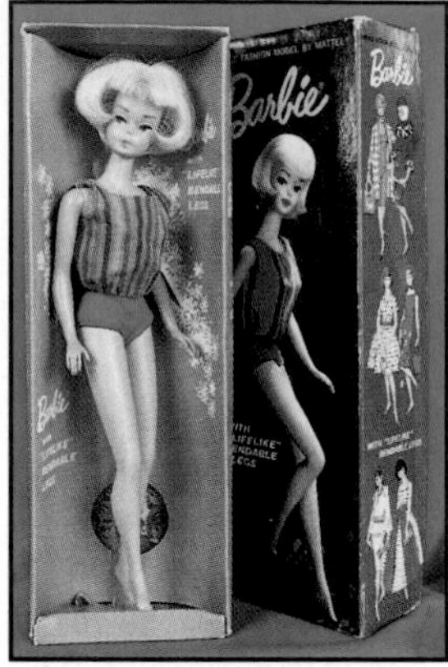

11½" vinyl American Girl Barbie, pale blond hair, blue eyes to side, beige lips with tint of orange, fingernail paint, bendable legs, wearing striped swimsuit with aqua bottoms, in box with gold wire stand, aqua open toe shoes, wrist tag, box is age discolored and worn along edges, circa 1965 – 1966, $600.00. Courtesy McMasters Doll Auctions.

11½" vinyl Swirl Ponytail Barbie, blond hair, gold lips with tint of peach, blue irises, fingernail and toenail paint, straight legs, wearing #917 Apple Print Sheath, black #1 open toe shoes with holes, hair has been reset, marked "Midge™//©1962//Barbie®//©1958//by//Mattel, Inc.//Patented," circa 1964 – 1965, $175.00. Courtesy McMasters Doll Auctions.

American Girl, 1070

1965	$500.00	$1,500.00

American Girl, 1070

1966	$1,200.00	$2,500.00

Bubble Cut, 1961 – 1967

Brown	$450.00	$1,000.00
White Ginger	$300.00	$875.00
Other	$150.00	$425.00

Color Magic

Blond, cardboard box

1966	$375.00	$2,500.00

Blond, plastic box

1966	$375.00	$1,300.00

Midnight, plastic box

1966	$1,450.00	$2,700.00

Fashion Queen

1963 – 1964	$125.00	$320.00

Swirl Ponytail

1964 – 1965	$200.00	$475.00

Swirl Platinum

1964	$400.00	$1,000.00

Twist 'N Turn

1967	$175.00	$475.00

Redhead

1967	$475.00	$850.00

Other Barbie Dolls

First price is for doll only in excellent condition; second price is for mint-in-box.

Angel Face		
1983	$16.00	$45.00
Ballerina		
1976	$35.00	$95.00
Barbie Baby-sits		
1974	$20.00	$60.00
Beach Party		
1980	$25.00	$75.00
Beautiful Bride		
1976	$95.00	$240.00
Beauty Secrets		
1980	$20.00	$$55.00
Bicyclin'		
1994	$15.00	$40.00
Busy Barbie		
1972	$95.00	$260.00
Dance Club		
1989	$15.00	$40.00
Day-To-Night		
1985	$25.00	$75.00
Doctor		
1988	$22.50	$65.00

Dream Barbie		
1995	$20.00	$55.00
Fashion Jeans, black		
1982	$16.00	$45.00
Fashion Photo		
1978	$22.50	$65.00
Free Moving		
1975	$55.00	$150.00
Gold Medal Skater		
1975	$32.50	$90.00
Golden Dream w/coat		
1981	$32.50	$90.00
Growin' Pretty Hair		
1971	$125.00	$350.00
Hair Fair		
1967	$75.00	$200.00
Hair Happenin's		
1971	$375.00	$1,150.00
Happy Birthday		
1981	$17.50	$50.00
Ice Capades, 50th		
1990	$15.00	$40.00
Kellogg Quick Curl		
1974	$25.00	$65.00
Kissing		
1979	$15.00	$40.00
Live Action on Stage		
1971	$100.00	$270.00
Living Barbie		
1970	$110.00	$290.00
Loving You		
1983	$25.00	$65.00
Magic Curl		
1982	$17.50	$50.00
Magic Moves		
1986	$25.00	$65.00
Malibu (Sunset)		
1971	$25.00	$65.00
My First Barbie		
1981	$10.00	$30.00
My Size		
1993	$55.00	$150.00
Newport the Sport's Set		
1973	$62.50	$165.00
Peaches 'n Cream		
1985	$15.00	$40.00
Pink & Pretty		
1982	$15.00	$40.00
Rappin' Rockin'		
1992	$22.50	$60.00
Rocker		
1986	$20.00	$45.00

11½" vinyl Swirl Ponytail Barbie, brunette hair in original set with hairpin/yellow ribbon, beige lips/hint of peach color, blue irises, fingernail/toenail paint, straight legs, wearing #874 Arabian Nights, pink satin blouse, long satin and chiffon skirt with gold trim, matching chiffon sari, gold foil slippers, gold/turqouise necklace, plastic bracelets, gold dangle earrings, paper theatre program, booklet, plastic lamp, in box, circa 1964 – 1965, $550.00. Courtesy McMasters Doll Auctions.

11½" vinyl Fashion Queen Barbie, molded painted dark brown hair with a blue vinyl headband, blue irises, light pink lips, eyeshadow, wearing original gold lamé and white striped swimsuit with matching turban, pearl earrings, wrist tag, in box with three interchangeable wigs and a white wig stand, white cover booklet and white open toe shoes in cellophane bag, black wire stand, near mint, circa 1963, $285.00. Courtesy McMasters Doll Auctions.

11½" vinyl American Girl Barbie, titian hair, blue eyes to side, beige lips, fingernail paint, bendable legs, wearing #1615 Saturday Matinee, brown tweed jacket with fur trim, matching skirt and hat, brown open toe shoes, brown nylon short gloves, foil purse with fur trim, chain strap and gold leaf accent, near mint, circa 1965 – 1966, $610.00. Courtesy McMasters Doll Auctions.

Roller Skating			
	1980	$22.50	$60.00
Secret Hearts			
	1993	$12.50	$35.00
Sensations			
	1988	$25.00	$60.00
Sun Lovin' Malibu			
	1979	$16.00	$45.00
Sun Valley – The Sport's Set			
	1973	$32.50	$85.00
Super Fashion Fireworks			
	1976	$45.00	$125.00
Super Size, 18"			
	1977	$100.00	$265.00
Superstar Promotional			
	1978	$32.50	$90.00
Talking			
	1968	$130.00	$370.00
Talking Busy			
	1972	$130.00	$365.00
Twinkle Lights			
	1993	$25.00	$60.00
Walking Lively			
	1972	$90.00	$245.00
Western (3 hairstyles)			
	1981	$25.00	$55.00
Ward's Issue			
	1972	$275.00	$700.00

Gift Sets

Mint-in-box prices; add more for NRFB (never removed from box), less for worn or faded.

Barbie Hostess		
	1966	$4,750.00
Beautiful Blues, Sears		
	1967	$3,300.00
Color Magic Gift Set, Sears		
	1965	$4,000.00
Fashion Queen Barbie & Friends		
	1963	$2,250.00
Fashion Queen & Ken Trousseau		
	1963	$2,600.00
Little Theatre Set		
	1964	$5,500.00

On Parade	1960	$2,350.00
Party Set	1960	$2,300.00
Pink Premier	1969	$1,600.00
Round the Clock	1964	$5,000.00
Sparkling Pink	1964	$2,500.00
Travel in Style, Sears	1964	$2,400.00
Trousseau Set	1960	$2,850.00
Wedding Party	1964	$3,000.00

Custom or Exclusive Barbie Dolls

Often the most sought after are the first editions of a series, or exclusive Barbie dolls such as those produced for Disney, FAO Schwarz, WalMart, Target, and others. These types of Barbie dolls usually increase in price because the number made is less than others, so they are not as easily found.

Prices indicate mint-in-box.

Bob Macke Barbie Dolls

Gold	1990	$560.00
Starlight Splendor	1991	$670.00
Platinum	1991	$690.00
Neptune Fantasy	1992	$810.00
Empress Bride	1992	$830.00
Masquerade Ball	1993	$450.00
Queen of Hearts	1994	$300.00
Goddess of the Sun	1995	$205.00
Moon Goddess	1996	$110.00
Madame Du Barbie	1997	$250.00

Happy Holiday Series

Holiday, red gown	1988	$775.00
International Holiday	1988	$580.00
Holiday, white gown	1989	$240.00
Holiday, fuchsia gown	1990	$160.00
Holiday, green gown	1991	$185.00
Holiday, silver gown	1992	$150.00
Holiday, red/gold gown	1993	$150.00
Holiday (black), fuchsia	1990	$105.00
Holiday (black), green gown	1991	$120.00
Holiday (black), silver gown	1992	$110.00
Holiday (black), red/gold	1993	$70.00

Classique Series

Benefit Ball, Carol Spenser	1992	$165.00
City Styles, Janet Goldblatt	1993	$145.00
Opening Night, Janet Goldblatt	1994	$95.00
Evening Extravaganza, Perkins	1994	$85.00

11½" vinyl Color Magic Barbie, blond hair with blue barrette, original plaid nylon headband, blue irises and very heavy eye makeup, red lips, nostril paint, finger paint, bendable legs, plaid color magic dress, circa 1966 – 1967, $525.00. Courtesy McMasters Doll Auctions.

11½" vinyl Twist 'n Turn Barbie, brunette hair, pink lips, cheek blush, rooted eyelashes, finger paint, bendable legs, waist that twists back and forth, wearing #1453 Flower Wower print dress, wrist tag, clear plastic stand, circa 1968, $205.00. Courtesy McMasters Doll Auctions.

Uptown Chic, Perkins	1994	$90.00
Midnight Gala, Abbe Littleton	1995	$110.00
Store Specials or Special Editions		
Avon, Winter Velvet	1996	$60.00
Ballroom Beauties, Starlight Waltz	1995	$75.00
Billy Boy, Feeling Groovy	1986	$290.00
Bloomingdales, Savvy Shopper	1994	$165.00
Disney,		
Euro Disney	1992	$70.00
Disney Fun	1993	$55.00
FAO Schwarz		
Golden Greetings	1989	$225.00
Winter Fantasy	1990	$235.00
Night Sensation	1991	$200.00
Madison Avenue	1991	$245.00
Rockette	1993	$260.00
Silver Screen	1994	$275.00
Jeweled Splendor	1995	$335.00
Great Eras		
Gibson Girl	1993	$130.00
Flapper	1993	$200.00
Southern Belle	1994	$125.00
Hallmark		
Victorian Elegance	1994	$115.00
Sweet Valentine	1996	$75.00
Hills		
Party Lace	1989	$45.00
Evening Sparkle	1990	$45.00
Moonlight Rose	1991	$60.00
Blue Elegance	1991	$55.00
Hollywood Legends		
Scarlett O'Hara, red	1994	$70.00
Dorothy, Wizard of Oz	1995	$260.00
Glinda, Good Witch	1995	$105.00
Home Shopping Club		
Evening Flame	1991	$160.00
J.C. Penney		
Evening Elegance	1990	$105.00
Enchanted Evening	1991	$105.00
Golden Winter	1993	$70.00
Night Dazzle, blond	1994	$65.00
K-Mart		
Peach Pretty	1989	$40.00
Pretty in Purple	1992	$35.00
Mattel Festival		
35th Anniversary, brunette	1994	$520.00
Festival Banquet	1994	$225.00
Happy Holidays, brunette	1994	$1,120.00
Snow Princesss	1994	$830.00

Mervyns		
Ballerina	1983	$75.00
Fabulous Fur	1986	$70.00
Montogmery Ward		
#1 Replica, shipping box	1972	$710.00
#1 Replica, pink box	1972	$840.00
Prima Ballerina Music Box		
Swan Lake, music box	1991	$205.00
Nutcracker, music box	1992	$285.00
Sears		
Celebration, 100th Anniversary	1986	$90.00
Star Dream	1987	$70.00
Blossom Beautiful	1992	$315.00
Ribbons & Roses	1995	$60.00
Service Merchandise		
Blue Rhapsody	1991	$185.00
Satin Nights	1992	$80.00
City Sophisticate	1994	$110.00
Spiegel		
Sterling Wishes	1991	$140.00
Regal Reflections	1992	$250.00
Royal Invitation	1993	$120.00
Theatre Elegance	1994	$180.00
Target		
Gold 'n Lace	1989	$40.00
Party Pretty	1990	$30.00
Cute 'n Cool	1991	$30.00
Golden Evening	1991	$45.00
Toys R Us		
Dance Sensation	1985	$60.00
Pepsi Spirit	1989	$80.00
Vacation Sensation	1989	$80.00
Radiant in Red	1992	$70.00
Moonlight Magic	1993	$90.00
Harley-Davidson, #1	1997	$475.00
Firefighter	1995	$55.00
WalMart		
Pink Jubilee, 25th Anniversary	1987	$75.00
Frills & Fantasy	1988	$55.00
Dream Fantasy	1990	$50.00
Wholesale Clubs		
Party Sensation	1990	$65.00
Fantastica	1992	$70.00
Royal Romance	1992	$115.00
Very Violet	1992	$75.00
Season's Greetings	1994	$75.00
Winter Royale	1994	$75.00
After the Walk, Sam's Club	1997	$75.00
Country Rose, Sam's Club	1997	$100.00

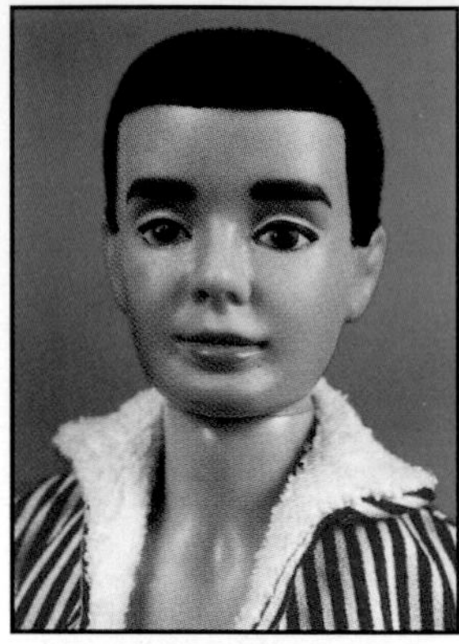

12" vinyl Ken, brunette flocked hair, beige lips, straight legs, wearing red and white striped jacket, red swim trunks, cork sandals with red straps, yellow terry towel, light blue cover Barbie/Ken booklet, black wire stand, circa 1961, $110.00. Courtesy McMasters Doll Auctions.

11½" vinyl Midge, titian hair, painted blue eyes, pink lips, freckles, finger and toe paint, straight legs, wearing original two-piece nylon chartreuse and orange swimsuit, black wire stand, circa 1963, $70.00. Courtesy McMasters Doll Auctions.

Woolworths

Special Expressions, white

1989 $30.00

Sweet Lavender

1992 $25.00

Barbie Related Dolls, Friends and Family

First price indicates doll in good condition, no box; second price indicates mint-in-box.

Allan, 1964 – 1967

Bendable legs $175.00 $525.00

Straight legs $60.00 $120.00

Bild Lilli, not Mattel

German doll made prior to Barbie, clear plastic cylinder case $500.00 $600.00

Casey, Twist 'N Turn

1967 $75.00 $150.00

Chris, brunette, bendable leg

1967 $90.00 $185.00

Francie

Bendable leg

1966 $120.00 $300.00

Straight leg

1966 $125.00 $320.00

Twist 'N Turn

1967 $175.00 $385.00

Twist 'N Turn, black

1967 $900.00 $1,500.00

Malibu 1971 $40.00 $50.00

Growin' Pretty Hair

1971 $150.00 $250.00

Jamie, Walking

1970 $185.00 $385.00

Julia, Twist 'N Turn

1969 $125.00 $245.00

Talking 1969 $120.00 $215.00

Kelly, Quick Curl

1973 $65.00 $150.00

Yellowstone

1974 $150.00 $275.00

Ken, #1, straight leg, blue eyes, hard plastic hollow body, flocked hair, 12"

Mark: "Ken® MCMLX//by//Mattel//Inc."

1961 $100.00 $185.00

Molded hair

1962 $55.00 $150.00

Bendable legs

1965 $125.00 $350.00

Midge, straight leg

1963 $90.00 $175.00

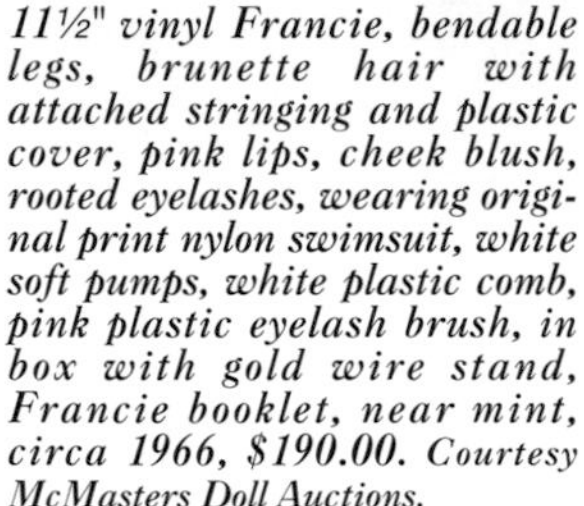

11½" vinyl Francie, bendable legs, brunette hair with attached stringing and plastic cover, pink lips, cheek blush, rooted eyelashes, wearing original print nylon swimsuit, white soft pumps, white plastic comb, pink plastic eyelash brush, in box with gold wire stand, Francie booklet, near mint, circa 1966, $190.00. Courtesy McMasters Doll Auctions.

9" vinyl Skipper, straight legs, brunette hair with metal hairband, pink lips, painted blue eyes, wearing original red and white one-piece swimsuit, red flat shoes, circa 1964, $70.00. Courtesy McMasters Doll Auctions.

11" hard plastic German-made Bild-Lilli, blond hair tied on top and bottom curl with beige string, black plastic hair bow, painted eyes to side, painted black earrings, red lips, painted fingernails, painted black pumps, dotted white nylon shirt, floral print skirt with attached black corset with string ties, in plastic tube with white plastic base with protruding metal rods that fit into the dolls leg, round plastic lid, near mint, circa 1950s, $3,200.00. Courtesy McMasters Doll Auctions.

No freckles		
1963	$225.00	$385.00
Bendable legs		
1965	$275.00	$500.00
P.J.		
Talking		
1970	$110.00	$225.00
Twist 'N Turn		
1970	$60.00	$260.00
Live Action/Stage		
1971	$90.00	$255.00
Ricky, straight legs		
1965	$55.00	$160.00
Skipper		
Straight leg		
1964	$65.00	$175.00
Bendable leg		
1965	$70.00	$250.00
Twist 'N Turn		
1968	$135.00	$195.00
Skooter, straight leg		
1965	$65.00	$125.00
Bendable leg		
1966	$100.00	$290.00

Stacey, talking	1968	$150.00	$300.00
Twist 'N Turn	1968	$160.00	$325.00
Todd, bendable, poseable	1966	$90.00	$180.00
Tutti, bendable, poseable	1967	$90.00	$145.00
Twiggy, Twist 'N Turn	1967	$165.00	$320.00

Barbie Accessories

Animals

All American (horse)	1991	$35.00
Blinking Beauty (horse)	1988	$25.00
Champion (horse)	1991	$40.00
Dancer (horse)	1971	$100.00
Fluff (kitten)	1983	$20.00
Ginger (giraffe)	1988	$30.00
Prancer (horse)	1984	$35.00
Prince (poodle)	1985	$35.00
Snowball (dog)	1990	$35.00
Tahiti (bird w/cage)	1985	$20.00

Cases

Fashion Queen, black, zippered	1964	$150.00
Fashion Queen, round hatbox	1965	$250.00
Miss Barbie, zippered	1964	$160.00
Vanity, Barbie & Skipper	1964	$200.00

Clothing

Name of outfit, stock number; price for mint in package, much less for loose.

Aboard Ship	1631	$550.00
All That Jazz	1848	$350.00
Arabian Knights	874	$495.00
Barbie in Japan	821	$500.00
Beautiful Bride	1698	$2,100.00
Benefit Performance	1667	$1,400.00
Black Magic Ensemble	1609	$420.00
Bride's Dream	947	$350.00
Busy Gal	981	$450.00
Campus Sweetheart	1616	$1,750.00
Cinderella	872	$550.00
Commuter Set	916	$1,400.00
Country Club Dance	1627	$490.00
Dancing Doll	1626	$525.00
Debutante Ball	1666	$1,300.00
Dog 'n Duds	1613	$350.00
Drum Majorette	875	$265.00
Easter Parade	971	$4,500.00
Evening Enchantment	1695	$595.00
Fabulous Fashion	1676	$595.00
Formal Occasion	1697	$550.00
Fashion Editor	1635	$850.00
Formal Luncheon	1656	$1,400.00
Garden Wedding	1658	$575.00
Gay Parisienne	964	$4,500.00

Glimmer Glamour	1547	$5,000.00
Gold 'n Glamour	1647	$1,750.00
Golden Glory	1645	$495.00
Here Comes the Bride	1665	$1,200.00
Holiday Dance	1639	$625.00
International Fair	1653	$500.00
Intrigue	1470	$425.00
Invitation to Tea	1632	$600.00
Junior Prom	1614	$695.00
Knitting Pretty, pink	957	$450.00
Let's Have a Ball	1879	$325.00
Little Red Riding Hood	880	$625.00
Magnificence	1646	$625.00
Make Mine Midi	1861	$350.00
Masquerade	944	$250.00
Maxi 'n Midi	1799	$375.00
Midnight Blue	1617	$850.00
Miss Astronaut	1641	$700.00
On the Avenue	1644	$575.00
Open Road	985	$385.00
Pajama Pow	1806	$300.00
Pan American Stewardess	1678	$5,000.00
Patio Party	1692	$375.00
Picnic Set	967	$365.00
Plantation Belle	966	$600.00
Poodle Parade	1643	$985.00
Rainbow Wraps	1798	$350.00
Reception Line	1654	$600.00
Red Fantastic, Sears	1817	$850.00
Riding in the Park	1668	$625.00
Roman Holiday	968	$5,000.00
Romantic Ruffles	1871	$250.00
Satin 'n Rose	1611	$395.00
Saturday Matinee	1615	$950.00
Sears Pink Formal	1681	$2,450.00
Shimmering Magic	1664	$1,750.00
Sleeping Pretty	1636	$375.00
Smasheroo	1860	$275.00
Sorority Meeting	937	$300.00
Suburban Shopper	969	$350.00
Sunday Visit	1675	$595.00
Swirley-Cue	1822	$300.00
Trailblazers	1846	$250.00
Travel Togethers	1688	$300.00
Tunic 'n Tights	1859	$300.00
Under Fashions	1655	$695.00
Velveteens, Sears	1818	$850.00
Weekenders, Sears	1815	$950.00
Wedding Wonder	1849	$375.00
Wild 'n Wonderful	1856	$300.00

Furniture, Suzy Goose		
Canopy Bed, display box	1960s	$250.00
Chifferobe, cardboard box	1960s	$250.00
Queen Size Bed, pink	1960s	$600.00
Vanity, pink		$75.00
Vehicles		
Austin Healy, beige	1964	$3,300.00
Beach Bus	1974	$45.00
Mercedes, blue-green	1968	$450.00
Speedboat, blue-green	1964	$1,100.00
Sport Plane, blue	1964	$3,000.00
Sun 'n Fun Buggy	1971	$150.00
United Airlines	1973	$75.00

Betsy McCall

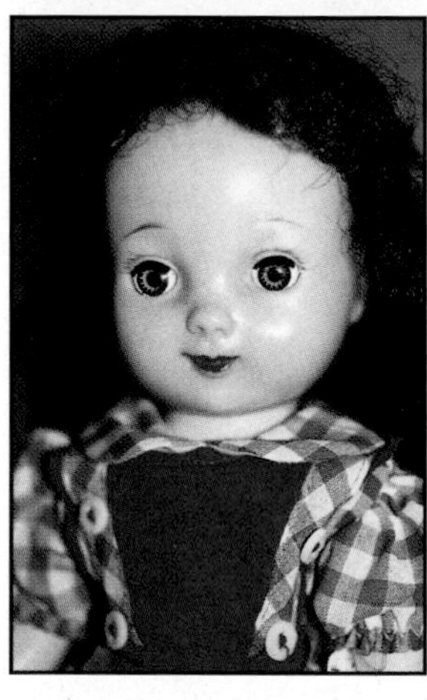

14" vinyl Ideal Betsy McCall, marked "McCall Corp®" on head, "Ideal Doll//P-90" on body, designed by Bernard Lipfert, black rooted hair, brown sleep eyes, watermelon smile, strung hard plastic Toni body, original gray and white checked dress with red front, original black shoes, circa 1952 – 1953, $165.00. Courtesy Judie Conroy.

Ideal Doll Company, 1952 – 1953

Based on May 1951 *McCall* magazine paper doll, designed by Bernard Lipfert, vinyl head, watermelon smile, strung hard plastic Toni body, rooted saran wig.

Mark: "McCall Corp.®" on head; "IDEAL DOLL//P 90" on back

14"	$65.00	$250.00

American Character, 1957 – 1963

In 1957, American Character introduced an 8", hard plastic doll, with rigid vinyl arms, sleep eyes, single stroke eyebrows, molded eyelashes, metal barrettes in hair; first year dolls had mesh base wig, plastic peg-joined knees. Second year and later dolls had saran hair rooted in rubber-type skullcap, metal pin-jointed knees; the company advertised as American Doll & Toy Co. circa 1960. Marked in circle on back waist "*McCall © Corp.*" One hundred costumes available. First price for doll with flaws, perhaps nude, poor color. Second price for doll in basic chemise with great color. Double price for mint-in-box.

	8"	$175.00	$350.00
Sunday Best, MIB			$985.00*

Accessories: complete costume, more for rare or NRFP

Town & Country	$75.00
Black vinyl shoes	$25.00
Red vinyl shoes	$85.00

1958, vinyl, four hair colors, rooted hair, flat feet, slim body, round sleep eyes, may have swivel waist or one-piece torso

Mark: "McCall 19©58 Corp." in circle

14"	$250.00	$500.00

* at auction

1959, vinyl, rooted hair, slender limbs, some with flirty eyes, one-piece torso

Mark: "McCall 19©58 Corp." in a circle

19 – 20"	$250.00	$500.00
19"	$1,250.00*	

1959, vinyl, rooted hair (Patti Playpal style body)

Mark: "McCall Corp//1959" on head

36"	$60.00	$325.00

1961, vinyl, five colors of rooted hair, jointed wrists, ankles, waist, blue or brown sleep eyes, four to six outfits available

Mark: "McCall 19©61 Corp." in a circle

22"	$30.00	$250.00
29"	$50.00	$300.00

Linda McCall (Betsy's cousin)

1959, vinyl, Betsy face, rooted hair

Mark: "McCall Corp//1959" on head

36"	$50.00	$350.00

Sandy McCall (Betsy's brother)

1959, vinyl, molded hair, sleep eyes, red blazer, navy shorts

Mark: "McCall 1959 Corp."; tag reads "I am Your Life Size Sandy McCall"

39"	$50.00	$350.00

Uneeda

1964, vinyl, rooted hair, rigid vinyl body, brown or blue sleep eyes, slim pre-teen body, wore mod outfits, some mini-skirts, competitor of Ideal's Tammy.

Mark: None

11½"	$25.00	$95.00+

Horsman

1974, vinyl with rigid plastic body, sleep eyes, came in Betsy McCall Beauty Box with extra hair piece, brush, bobby pins on card, eye pencil, blush, lipstick, two sponges, mirror, and other accessories

Mark: "Horsman Doll Inc.//19©67" on head; "Horsman Dolls Inc." on torso

12½"	$25.00	$50.00

1974, vinyl with rigid plastic teen type body, jointed wrists, sleep eyes, lashes, rooted hair with sidepart (some blond with ponytails), closed mouth, original clothing marked *"BMc"* in two-tone blue box marked *"©1974//Betsy McCall – she WALKS with you"*

Marks: "Horsman Dolls 1974"

29"	$75.00	$275.00

McCall Heirloom Tradition Figurines

Circa 1984, 12 one-piece procelain figurines in box, includes Back to School, Introducing Betsy McCall, Betsy McCall Gives a Tea Party, and Most Christmacy, match paper dolls published in *McCalls* magazine

4"	$5.00	$20.00

14" vinyl American Character Betsy McCall, marked "McCall © Corp" in a circle, rooted saran hair, blue sleep eyes, closed smiling mouth, wearing long pink gown with ruffle around hem, black top, pink shawl across front attached with "diamond" brooch, with trunk with extra outfit and robe, circa 1957 – 1963, $725.00. Courtesy Sharon Kolibaba.

9" vinyl Robert Tonner Tiny Betsy McCall, rooted hair, plastic sleep eyes, real lashes, painted lashes below, closed smiling mouth, jointed vinyl body, jointed knees, wearing Betsy McCall Makes a Wish, style # BM CL 8103, pink dress with pink flower print, pink satin belt, white collar with lace trim, gloves, white nylon socks, pink one-strap shoes, outfit only, $23.99, circa 2001, doll in chemise with shoes and socks, $39.95. Courtesy Robert Tonner Doll Company.

Betsy McCall

ROTHCHILD

1986, 35th anniversary Betsy, hard plastic, sleep eyes, painted lashes below eyes, single stroke eyebrows, tied ribbon emblem on back

Marks: Hang tag reads "35th Anniversary//BetsyMcCall//by Rothschild (number) 'Betsy Goes to a Tea Party,' or 'Betsy Goes to the Fair'." Box marked "Rothchild Doll Company//Southboro, MA 01722."

8"	$15.00	$35.00
12"	$20.00	$45.00

ROBERT TONNER

1996+, vinyl (some porcelain), rooted hair, rigid vinyl body, glass eyes, closed smiling mouth

Mark: "Betsy McCall//by//Robert Tonner//©Gruner & Jahr USA PUB."

14"	$69.00 retail	
Limited Editions		
Mouseketeer	$225.00*	
Tonner Birthday	$145.00*	
Kimono Betsy	$175.00	
Roy Rogers Betsy	$225.00	

Buddy Lee

13" hard plastic Buddy Lee, molded painted hair, painted black eyes, brown eyebrows, eyelashes, marked "Buddy Lee" on back, wearing tan Phillips 66 gas station attendant uniform with orange and black Phillips shield patch and matching cap with visor, circa 1950s, $600.00. Courtesy Odessa Tiefel.

Ca. 1920 – 1963. Trademark doll of H.D. Lee Co., Inc., who made uniforms and work clothes, first made of composition; ca. 1948 made in hard plastic, some marked "*Buddy Lee.*" Engineer had Lee label on hat and overalls; cowboy hat band printed, *"Ride 'Em in Lee Rider Overalls."*

First price for played-with, incomplete outfit; second price for mint doll, more for rare uniform.

Composition		
Coca-Cola	$125.00	$625.00
Cowboy	$90.00	$400.00
Engineer	$95.00	$400.00
Engineer	$860.00*	
Gas station	$175.00	$650.00
Hard Plastic		
Coca-Cola	$275.00	$650.00
Cowboy	$200.00	$425.00
Engineer	$200.00	$425.00
Gas station	$300.00	$800.00+

Bucherer

1921 – 1930+, Armiswil, Switzerland. Made metal bodied dolls with composition head, hands, and feet, some with changeable heads — Charlie Chaplin, Mutt and Jeff, regional costumes, and others.

6½" – 7½		
Regional	$100.00	$285.00
Mutt and Jeff, ea.	$175.00	$600.00+

* at auction

1978+, Babyland General Hospital, Cleveland, GA. Cloth, needle sculpture

"A" blue edition	1978	$1,500.00+
"B" red edition	1978	$1,200.00+
"C" burgundy edition	1979	$900.00+
"D" purple edition	1979	$800.00+
"X" Christmas edition	1979	$1,200.00+
"E" bronze edition	1980	$1,200.00+
Preemie edition	1980	$650.00+
Celebrity edition	1980	$600.00+
Christmas edition	1980	$600.00+
Grand edition	1980	$750.00+
New Ears edition	1981	$125.00+
Ears edition	1982	$150.00+
Green edition	1983	$400.00+
"KP" dark green edition	1983	$550.00+
"KPR" red edition	1983	$550.00+
"KPB" burgundy edition	1983	$200.00
Oriental edition	1983	$850.00
Indian edition	1983	$850.00
Hispanic edition	1983	$750.00
"KPZ" edition	1983 – 1984	$175.00
Champagne edition	1983 – 1984	$900.00
"KPP" purple edition	1984	$250.00
Sweetheart edition	1984	$250.00
Bavarian edition	1984	$250.00
World Class edition	1984	$175.00
"KPF," "KPG," "KPH," "KPI," "KPJ" editions		
	1984 – 1985	$100.00 – 200.00+
Emerald edition	1985	$200.00 – 250.00

Coleco Cabbage Patch Kids

1983, have powder scent and black signature stamp

Boys and Girls	$95.00
Bald babies	$50.00 – $75.00
With freckles	$100.00
Black boys or girls	
With freckles	$175.00
Without freckles	$75.00
Red Hair boys, fuzzy hair	$175.00
Tsukuda	$200.00*

1984 – 1985, green signature stamp in 1984; blue signature stamp in 1985. Most dolls are only worth retail price, exceptions are

Single tooth, brunette with ponytail	$165.00+
Popcorn hairdos, rare	$200.00
Gray-eyed girls	$165.00
Freckled girl, gold hair	$95.00

Other

Baldies, popcorn curl with pacifier, red popcorn curls, single tooth, freckled girls, and gold braided hair are valued at retail to $65.00. Still easily obtainable for collectors are a host of other Cabbage Patch Kids, including ringmaster, clown, baseball player, astronaut, travelers, twins, babies, Splash Kid, Cornsilk Kid, valued at $30.00 – $50.00.

White Popcorn Girl $295.00*

Cameo Doll Co.

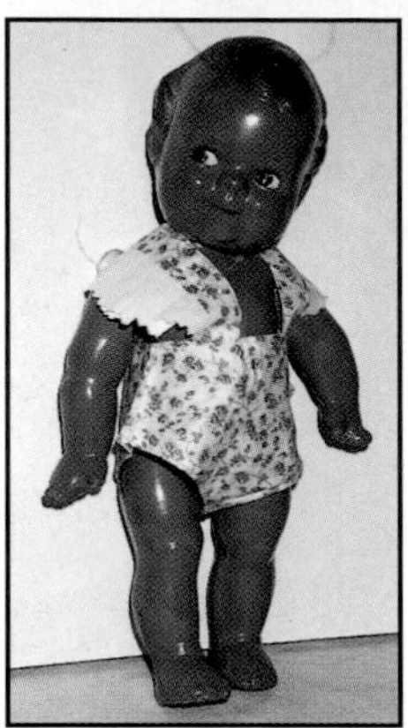

12" composition brown Scootles, unmarked, molded painted brown hair, painted brown side-glancing eyes, closed smiling mouth, fully jointed composition body, original romper, circa 1935, $650.00. Courtesy Pat Graff.

1922 – 1930+, New York City, Port Allegheny, PA. Joseph L. Kallus's company made composition dolls, some with wood segmented bodies and cloth bodies. First price for played-with dolls; second price for mint dolls.

Bisque

Baby Bo Kaye, 1925

Bisque head, made in Germany, molded hair, open mouth, glass eyes, cloth body, composition limbs, good condition. *Mark: "J.L. Kallus: Copr. Germany// 1394/30"*

17"	$1,875.00	$2,500.00
20"	$2,100.00	$2,800.00

All-bisque, molded hair, glass sleep eyes, open mouth, two teeth, swivel neck, jointed arms and legs, molded pink or blue shoes, socks, unmarked, some may retain original round sticker on body

5"	$700.00	$1,500.00
6"	$900.00	$1,800.00

Celluloid

Baby Bo Kaye

Celluloid head, made in Germany, molded hair, open mouth, glass eyes, cloth body

12"	$200.00	$400.00
15"	$350.00	$750.00

Composition

Annie Rooney, 1926

Jack Collins, designer, all-composition, yarn wig, legs painted black, molded shoes

12"	$125.00	$475.00+
17"	$175.00	$700.00+

Baby Blossom, 1927, *"DES, J.L.Kallus"*

Composition upper torso, cloth lower body and legs, molded hair, open mouth

19"	$300.00	$1,100.00

Baby Bo Kaye

Composition head, molded hair, open mouth, glass eyes, light crazing

14"	$350.00	$675.00

Bandy, 1929

Composition head, wood segmented body, marked on hat *"General Electric/ Radio"* designed by J. Kallus

18½"	$600.00	$1,000.00

Betty Boop, 1932

Composition head character, wood segmented body, molded hair, painted features, label on torso

11"	$200.00	$650.00
13½"	$200.00	$850.00

* at auction

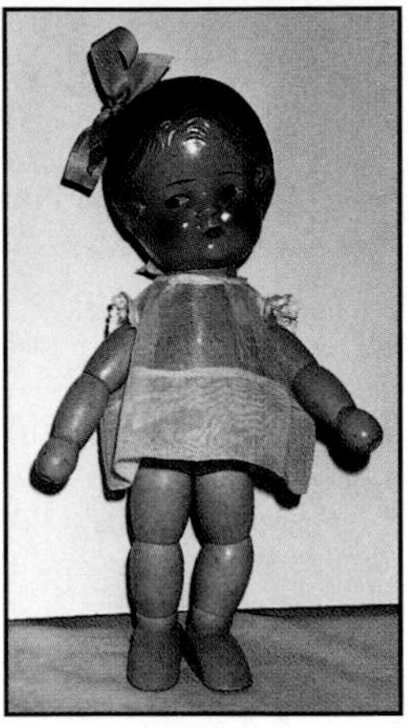

10" composition child, stamped "Cameo" on bottom of one foot, designed by Joseph Kallus for Cameo, molded painted hair with molded loop for ribbon, painted side-glancing eyes, rosy cheeks, wood body with segmented limbs, possibly original dress, blue silk ribbon added to hair, circa 1930s, $300.00. Courtesy Pat Graff.

Champ, 1942

Composition with freckles

16"	$175.00	$585.00

Giggles, 1946, "Giggles Doll, A Cameo Doll"

Composition with molded loop for ribbon

12"	$90.00	$350.00
14"	$150.00	$600.00

Ho-Ho, 1940, painted plaster, laughing mouth

5½"	$50.00	$200.00

Joy, 1932

Composition head character, wood segmented body, molded hair, painted features, label on torso

10"	$75.00	$300.00
15"	$125.00	$475.00

Margie, 1929

Composition head character, wood segmented body, molded hair, painted features, label on torso

5½"	$65.00	$250.00
9½"	$75.00	$285.00
15"	$75.00	$350.00

Pete the Pup, 1930 – 1935

Composition head character, wood segmented body, molded hair, painted features, label on torso

9"	$70.00	$265.00

Pinkie, 1930 – 1935

Composition head character, wood segmented body, molded hair, painted features, label on torso

10"	$100.00	$375.00

Composition body

10"	$75.00	$285.00

Popeye, 1935

Composition head character, wood segmented body, molded hair, painted features, label on torso

14"	$75.00	$300.00

Pretty Bettsie

Composition head, molded hair, painted side-glancing eyes, open/closed mouth, composition one-piece body and limbs, wooden neck joint, molded and painted dress with ruffles, shoes, and socks, triangular red tag on chest marked *"Pretty Bettsie//Copyright J. Kallus"*

18"	$125.00	$500.00

Scootles, 1925+

Rose O'Neill design, all-composition, no marks, painted side-glancing eyes, paper wrist tag

8"	$200.00	$975.00* all original with hang tag
13"	$135.00	$425.00
15"	$185.00	$650.00
22"	$375.00	$1,500.00

Composition, sleep eyes

15"	$175.00	$700.00

Black composition

12"	$750.00*	

Cameo Doll Co.

"The Selling Fool," 1926

Wood segmented body, hat represents radio tube, composition advertising doll for RCA Radiotrons

16"	$200.00	$800.00

Hard Plastic and Vinyl

Baby Mine, 1962 – 1964

Vinyl and cloth, sleep eyes

16"	$25.00	$100.00
19"	$35.00	$125.00

On Miss Peep hinged body

16"	$35.00	$135.00

Ho Ho, *"Rose O'Neill,"* laughing mouth, squeaker, tag

White, 7"	$35.00	$200.00
Black, 7"	$65.00	$275.00

Miss Peep, 1957 – 1970s+

Pin jointed shoulders and hips, vinyl

15"	$35.00	$75.00
18"	$50.00	$100.00

Black

18"	$65.00	$125.00

1970s+, ball-jointed shoulders, hips

17"	$12.50	$50.00
21"	$25.00	$70.00

Miss Peep, Newborn, 1962, vinyl head and rigid plastic body

18"	$10.00	$40.00

Pinkie, 1950s

10 – 11"	$75.00	$150.00

Scootles, 1964, vinyl

14"	$50.00	$195.00
27"	$135.00	$535.00
Boxes 16"		$405.00*

Composition

American, unknown maker, or little known manufacturer.

First price is for poorer quality, worn doll; second price is for excellent doll original or appropriate dress. More for exceptional dolls with elaborate costume or accessories.

Baby, 1910+

Wigged or molded hair, painted or sleep eyes, composition or cloth body with bent legs

12"	$65.00	$225.00
18"	$75.00	$300.00

Dionne Quintuplets, ca. 1934+, all-composition, jointed five-piece baby or toddler body, molded hair or wig, with painted or sleep eyes, closed or open mouth

7 – 8"	$35.00	$140.00
13"	$65.00	$250.00

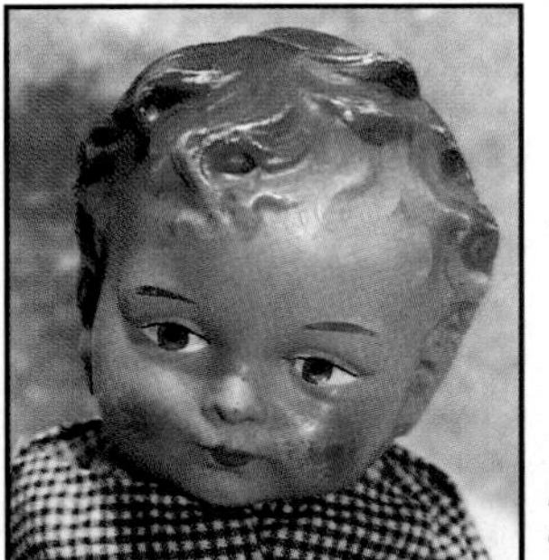

14" unmarked child, flange head, heavily molded and painted hair, painted blue eyes, closed mouth, composition lower arms, cloth body, brown and white striped cloth legs, jointed with outside disks, brown boots, brown checked dress, circa 1900 – 1910, $95.00. Courtesy Barbara J. Andresen.

* at auction

Child

Costumed in ethnic or theme outfit, all composition, sleep or painted eyes, mohair wig, closed mouth, original costume

Lesser quality

9 – 11"	$15.00	$75.00

Better quality

9 – 11"	$25.00	$145.00

Dream World, ca. 1939, painted eyes

9 – 11"	$45.00	$185.00

Early child, ca. 1910 – 1920, unmarked, cork-stuffed cloth body, painted features, may have molded hair

12"	$35.00	$145.00
18"	$50.00	$200.00

Early Child, character face, ca. 1910 – 1920

12"	$50.00	$200.00
18"	$75.00	$300.00

MaMa doll, ca. 1922+, wigged or painted hair, sleep or painted eyes, cloth body, with crier and swing legs, lower composition legs and arms

16"	$70.00	$250.00
20"	$90.00	$350.00
24"	$115.00	$450.00

Patsy-type girl, 1928+, molded, painted bobbed hair, sleep or painted eyes, closed pouty mouth, composition or hard stuffed cloth body

14"	$70.00	$250.00
19"	$80.00	$300.00

With molded hair loop

15"	$50.00	$200.00

Shirley Temple-type girl, 1934+, all-composition, five-piece jointed body, blond curly wig, sleep eyes, open mouth, teeth, dimples

16"	$100.00	$400.00
19"	$125.00	$450.00

Others

Animal head doll, ca. 1930s, all-composition on Patsy-type five-piece body, could be wolf, rabbit, cat, monkey

9½"	$55.00	$210.00

Denny Dimwitt, Toycraft Inc, ca. 1948, all-composition, nodder, painted clothing

11½"	$65.00	$225.00

Jackie Robinson, complete in box

13"	$300.00	$1,000.00

Kewty, 1930, made by Domec of Canada, all-composition Patsy-type, molded bobbed hair, closed mouth, sleep eyes, bent left arm

13½"	$80.00	$350.00

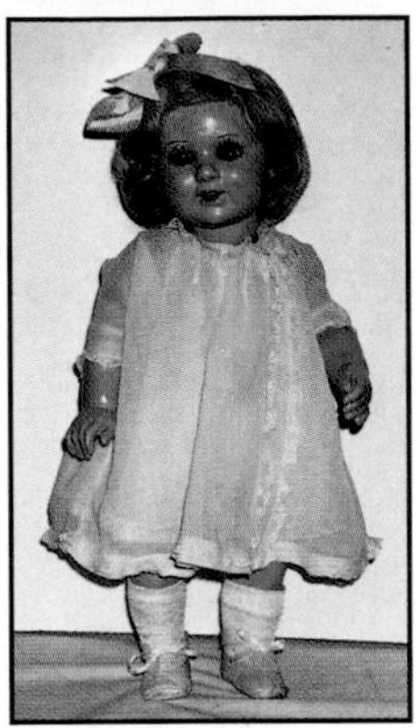

19" Jesse McCutcheon Raleigh child, blond mohair wig, celluloid covered sleep eyes, open/closed mouth with two painted upper teeth, painted lashes, five-piece spring-jointed composition toddler body, re-dressed in old doll dress, original shoes, circa 1919, $575.00. Courtesy Pat Graff.

15½" unmarked Patsy-type girl, molded painted yellow hair with molded headband, painted side-glancing heart shaped eyes, painted upper lashes, closed watermelon mouth, white muslin dress with brown flower print and yellow bias tape trim, white socks, black shoes, circa 1930s – 1940s, $100.00. Courtesy Janet Hill.

13" Allied Grand Doll Mfg. Co. toddler, unmarked, blond mohair wig in pigtails, painted blue side-glancing eyes, closed mouth, jointed composition toddler body, red flower print dress, matching bonnet, white pinafore, white socks, black shoes, all original, circa 1949, $175.00. Courtesy Pat Graff.

Lone Ranger, *"TLR Co, Inc.//Doll Craft Novelty Co. NYC,"* cloth body, hat marked

20" $1,400.00* in original box

Louis Vuitton, 1955, ceramic, type composition with labeled case and wardrobe

19" $2,200.00*

Maiden America, *"1915, Kate Silverman,"* all-composition, patriotic ribbon

8½" $45.00 $185.00

Miss Curity, composition, eye shadow, in nurse's uniform

18" $150.00 $500.00

Monica Studios, See that category.

Pinocchio, composition and wood character

16½" $125.00 $425.00

Puzzy, 1948, *"H of P"*

15" $100.00 $400.00

Raleigh, Jessie McCutcheon, 1916 – 1920, Chicago, IL. All-composition, painted or sleep eyes, painted and molded hair or wigged, cloth or composition bodies, some with metal spring joints, unmarked

Baby

11½" $100.00 $400.00
13½" $125.00 $500.00

Child

16½" $165.00 $650.00
18½" $235.00 $950.00

Refugee, Madame Louise Doll Co. ca. 1945, represents victims of WWII

20" $550.00* MIB

Reliable Toy Company Limited, 1920 – 1991, Toronto, Canada

Made composition, hard plastic, and vinyl dolls, some dolls with license from American doll manufacturers. First price for dolls with flaws; second price for all-original dolls, near mint. Add more for unusual characters.

Child

12" $50.00 $175.00
17" $65.00 $250.00

Santa Claus, composition molded head, composition body, original suit, sack

19" $150.00 $500.00

Sizzy, 1948, *"H of P"*

14" $75.00 $300.00

Thumbs-Up, to raise money for ambulances during WWII, see photo '97 edition

8" $50.00 $175.00

Uncle Sam, various makers

All original, cloth body

13" $900.00*

11" Dream World Doll, blond mohair wig, painted side-glancing blue eyes, painted upper lashes, closed mouth, jointed composition body, costumed in long white dress with red, white, and blue trim, blue apron with white stars, blue hat, all original, circa 1940s, $75.00 – 100.00. Courtesy Michele Newby.

* at auction

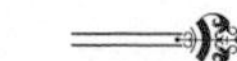

Ca. 1918, straw-filled

30" $450.00*

Whistler, composition head, cotton body, composition arms, open mouth

14½" $125.00 $225.00

GERMAN

Composition head, composition or cloth body, wig or painted molded hair, closed or open mouth with teeth, dressed. May be Amusco, Sonneberger Porzellanfabrik, or others.

Character Baby

Cloth body

18" $95.00 $350.00

Composition baby body, bent limbs

16" $125.00 $425.00

Child

Composition shoulder head, cloth body, composition arms

20" $150.00 $300.00

Socket head, all-composition body

19" $125.00 $425.00

21" $175.00 $500.00

Petzold, Dora made character child, ca. 1920s, cloth body

19" $175.00 $575.00

NEAPOLITAN

Adult, finely modeled character face, stick or wire bodies, elaborately dressed

13 – 14" $1,300.00 $1,800.00

16" $1,700.00 $2,000.00

Cosmopolitan

Ginger, ca. 1955, hard plastic, bent knees

7½" $40.00 $150.00

Straight leg

7½" $50.00 $200.00

Little Miss Ginger, ca. 1957, vinyl, rooted hair, sleep eyes, teen doll, tagged clothes

10½" $50.00 $190.00

Deluxe Reading

Deluxe Topper, Deluxe Premium, also uses names Topper Toys and Topper Corp. Made mechanical dolls, battery operated, ca. 1955 – 1972. These play dolls are collectible because so few survived intact.

First price is for played-with doll, second price is for complete doll, in excellent-to-mint condition.

HARD PLASTIC OR VINYL

Baby

Baby Boo, 1965, battery operated

21" $120.00 $200.00

Baby Catch A Ball, 1969, battery operated

18" $15.00 $55.00

* at auction

7" vinyl Suzy Cute, marked "Deluxe Reading Corp.//©1964//229/4" on body, and "Deluxe Reading Corp.//©1964 67//X" on head, rooted blond hair, blue stationary eyes, drink and wet feature, push her arms down then press her chest and her arms come up "reaching for mommy," in a plastic yellow crib, mint-in-box with three boxed outfits, circa 1964, $400.00. Courtesy Sharon Kolibaba.

9" vinyl Penny Brite with ten MIP outfits, rooted blond hair, painted side-glancing eyes, mint-in-plastic box, circa 1963+, $725.00 with extra outfits. Courtesy Sharon Kolibaba.

Baby Magic, 1966, blue sleep eyes, rooted saran hair, magic wand has magnet that opens/closes eyes

18" $100.00 $200.00

Baby Peek 'N Play, 1969, battery operated

18" $12.00 $45.00

Baby Tickle Tears

14" $9.00 $35.00

Suzy Cute, move arm and face changes expressions

7" $15.00 $90.00

Child or Adult

Betty Bride, 1957, also called Sweet Rosemary, Sweet Judy, Sweet Amy, one-piece vinyl body and limbs, more if many accessories

30" $25.00 $90.00

Candy Fashion, 1958, made by Deluxe Premium, a division of Deluxe Reading, sold in grocery stores, came with three dress forms, extra outfit

21" $23.00 $85.00

Dawn Series, circa 1969 – 1970s, all-vinyl doll with additional friends, Angie, Daphne, Denise, Glori, Jessica, Kip, Long Locks, Majorette, Maureen, black versions of Van and Dale. Accessories available, included Apartment, Fashion Show, outfits

Dawn

6" $15.00 $200.00 MIB

Car

$150.00*

Glori, ponytail, not MIB

6" $1,525.00*

Dawn & other outfits

Loose, but complete $10.00+

NRFP $25.00+

Fashion Show Stage in box

$50.00 $75.00

Go Gos

Private Ida, 1965, one of the Go Gos

6" $6.00 $45.00

Tom Boy, 1965, one of the Go Gos

6" $12.00 $45.00

Little Miss Fussy, battery operated

18" $6.00 $35.00

Little Red Riding Hood, 1955, vinyl, synthetic hair, rubber body, book, basket

23" $50.00 $125.00

Penny Brite, circa 1963+, all-vinyl, rooted blond hair, painted eyes, bendable and straight legs, extra outfits, case, furniture available

* at auction

Marks: "A – 9/B150 (or B65) DELUXE READING CORP.//c. 1963."

8"	$40.00	$125.00
Outfit, NRFP	$25.00	$40.00
Kitchen set	$100.00	

Suzy Homemaker, 1964, hard plastic and vinyl, jointed knees

Mark: *"Deluxe Reading Co."*

21"	$12.00	$45.00

Suzy Smart, ca. 1962, vinyl, sleep eyes, closed mouth, rooted blond ponytail, hard plastic body, The Talking School Doll, desk, chair, easel

25"	$50.00	$300.00

Eegee

1917+, Brooklyn, NY. E.G. Goldberger made composition and cloth dolls, imported bisque heads from Armand Marseille, made character head composition, mama dolls, babies, carnival dolls, and later the company made hard plastic and vinyl dolls.

First price for played-with doll, second price for completely original excellent condition doll.

> *Marks:*
> *Trademark, EEGEE,*
> *or circle with the words,*
> *"TRADEMARK*
> *//EEGEE//Dolls//MADE*
> *IN USA"*
> *Later changed to just*
> *initials, E.G.*

Composition

Add more for exceptional doll, tagged, extra outfits, or accessories.

Baby, cloth body, bent limbs

16"	$25.00	$100.00

Child, open mouth, sleep eyes

14"	$40.00	$160.00
18"	$55.00	$210.00

MaMa Doll, ca. 1920s – 1930s, composition head, sleep or painted eyes, wigged or molded hair, cloth body with crier, swing legs, composition lower arms and legs

16"	$75.00	$250.00
20"	$100.00	$350.00

Miss Charming, 1936, all-composition, Shirley Temple look-alike

19"	$125.00	$450.00
Miss Charming, pin-back button		$50.00

Hard Plastic and Vinyl

Andy, 1963, vinyl, teen-type, molded painted hair, painted eyes, closed mouth

12"	$9.00	$35.00

Annette, 1963, vinyl, teen-type fashion, rooted hair, painted eyes

11½"	$15.00	$55.00

Child, 1966, marked *"20/25 M/13"*

19"	$10.00	$50.00

Child, walker, all-vinyl rooted long blond hair, or short curly wig, blue sleep eyes, closed mouth

25"	$15.00	$50.00
28"	$20.00	$65.00
36"	$25.00	$85.00

* at auction

Babette, 1970, vinyl head, stuffed limbs, cloth body, painted or sleep eyes, rooted hair

15"	$10.00	$40.00
25"	$18.00	$65.00

Baby Care, 1969, vinyl, molded or rooted hair, sleep or set glassine eyes, drink and wet doll, with complete nursery set

18"	$12.00	$45.00

Baby Carrie, 1970, rooted or molded hair, sleep or set glassine eyes with plastic carriage or carry seat

24"	$15.00	$60.00

Baby Luv, 1973, vinyl head, rooted hair, painted eyes, open/closed mouth, marked *"B.T. Eegee,"* cloth body, pants are part of body

14"	$10.00	$35.00

Baby Susan, 1958, marked *"Baby Susan"* on head

8½"	$4.00	$20.00

Baby Tandy Talks, 1963, pull string activates talking mechanism, vinyl head, rooted hair, sleep eyes, cotton and foam-stuffed body and limbs

14"	$10.00	$35.00
20"	$20.00	$65.00

Ballerina, 1964, vinyl head and hard plastic body

31"	$25.00	$100.00

1967, vinyl head, foam-filled body

18"	$8.00	$30.00

Barbara Cartland, painted features, adult

15"	$15.00	$52.00

Beverly Hillbillies, Clampett family from 1960s TV sitcom

Car	$80.00	$350.00

Granny Clampett, gray rooted hair

14"	$20.00	$65.00

Fields, W. C., 1980, vinyl ventriloquist doll by Juro, division of Goldberger

30"	$65.00	$210.00

Flowerkins, 1963

Marked "F-2" on head; seven dolls in series.

Boxed	16"	$15.00	$60.00

Gemmette, 1963, rooted hair, sleep eyes, jointed vinyl, dressed in gem colored dress, includes child's jeweled ring, Misses Amethyst, Diamond, Emerald, Ruby, Sapphire, and Topaz

15½"	$15.00	$50.00

Georgie, Georgette, 1971, vinyl head, cloth bodies, redheaded twins

22"	$12.00	$50.00

Gigi Perreau, 1951, early vinyl head, hard plastic body, open/closed smiling mouth

17"	$175.00	$700.00

Karena Ballerina, 1958, vinyl head, rooted hair, sleep eyes, closed mouth, hard plastic body, jointed knees, ankles, neck, shoulders, and hips, head turns when walks

21"	$12.00	$45.00

Little Debutantes, 1958, vinyl head, rooted hair, sleep eyes, closed mouth, hard plastic body, swivel waist, high-heeled feet

18"	$15.00	$50.00
20"	$20.00	$75.00

My Fair Lady, 1958, all-vinyl, fashion type, swivel waist, fully jointed

20"	$15.00	$75.00

Parton, Dolly, 1978

11½"	$5.00	$25.00
18"	$12.00	$45.00

Posi Playmate, 1969, vinyl head, foam-filled vinyl body, bendable arms and legs, painted or rooted hair, sleep or painted eyes

12"	$5.00	$20.00

Puppetrina, 1963+, vinyl head, cloth body, rooted hair, sleep eyes, pocket in back for child to insert hand to manipulate doll's head and arms

22"	$45.00	$90.00

Shelly, 1964, Tammy-type, grow hair

12"	$5.00	$18.00

Sniffles, 1963, vinyl head, rooted hair, sleep eyes, open/closed mouth, marked *"13/14 AA-EEGEE"*

12"	$5.00	$20.00

Susan Stroller, ca. 1955, vinyl head, hard plastic walker body, rooted hair, closed mouth

20"	$35.00	$75.00
23"	$45.00	$90.00
26"	$50.00	$100.00

Tandy Talks, 1961, vinyl head, hard plastic body, freckles, pull string talker

20"	$15.00	$55.00

Effanbee

Effanbee Doll Company, 1910+, New York, NY. Bernard E. Fleischaker and Hugo Baum founders. Trademark *"EFFANBEE DOLLS//THEY WALK//THEY TALK//THEY SLEEP"* registered in 1918. Made dolls in composition and later hard plastic and vinyl. The new management recently introduced limited edition collectible dolls such as Patsy Joan, Skippy, Wee Patsy, and others.

First price indicates played-with doll in good condition, but with flaws; second price indicates doll in excellent condition with appropriate or original clothes. More for exceptional doll with wardrobe or accessories.

Marks: Some marked on shoulder plate, "EFFANBEE //BABY DAINTY" or "EFFANBEE //DOLLS//WALK, TALK, SLEEP" in oval

Bisque

Mary Jane, ca. 1920

Some with bisque heads, others all-composition; bisque head, manufactured by Lenox Potteries, NJ, for Effanbee, sleep eyes, composition body, wooden arms and legs, wears Bluebird pin

20"	$525.00	$700.00

Early Composition

Babies

Baby Bud, 1918+

All-composition, painted features, molded hair, open/closed mouth, jointed arms, legs molded to body. One finger goes into mouth.

6"	$50.00	$195.00
Black	$65.00	$225.00

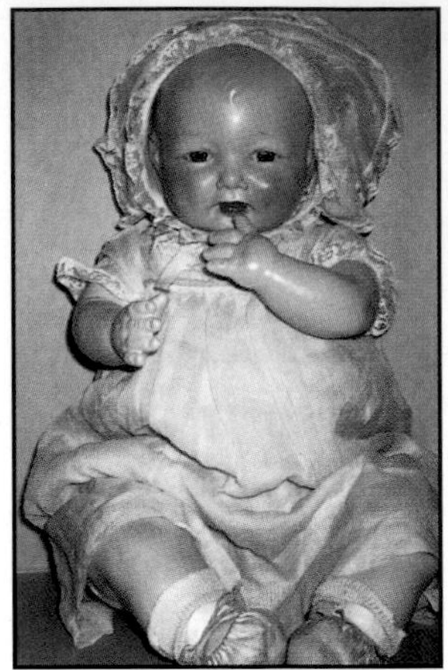

25" composition Bubbles, molded and painted blond hair, blue sleep eyes, dark blond painted eyebrows, open closed mouth, fingers on hand molded to position up to mouth, dimples in cheeks, wonderful rosy color on cheeks, hands, elbows, and knees, all original in organdy and lace trimmed gown and bonnet with pink ribbon trim, leatherette shoes, marked "EFFANBEE//BUBBLES//C OPR. 1924//MADE IN USA" with labeled box, circa 1924+, $750.00. Courtesy Irene Grundtvig.

Baby Dainty, 1912+

Name given to a variety of dolls, with composition heads, cloth bodies, some toddler types, some mama-types with crier

12 – 14"	$80.00	$245.00
15"	$125.00	$400.00

Vinyl

10"	$10.00	$40.00

Baby Effanbee, ca. 1925

Composition head, cloth body

12 – 13"	$45.00	$165.00

Baby Evelyn, ca. 1925

Composition head, cloth body

17"	$75.00	$275.00

Baby Grumpy, 1915+, also later variations

Composition character, heavily molded painted hair, frowning eyebrows, painted intaglio eyes, pin-jointed limbs, cork-stuffed cloth body, gauntlet arms, pouty mouth

Mold #172, 174, 176

11½"	$85.00	$325.00
14½"	$125.00	$425.00

Baby Grumpy Gladys, 1923, composition shoulder head, cloth body

Marked in oval, "Effanbee//Baby Grumpy// copr. 1923"

15"	$85.00	$350.00

Grumpy Aunt Dinah, black, cloth body, striped stocking legs

14½"	$110.00	$425.00

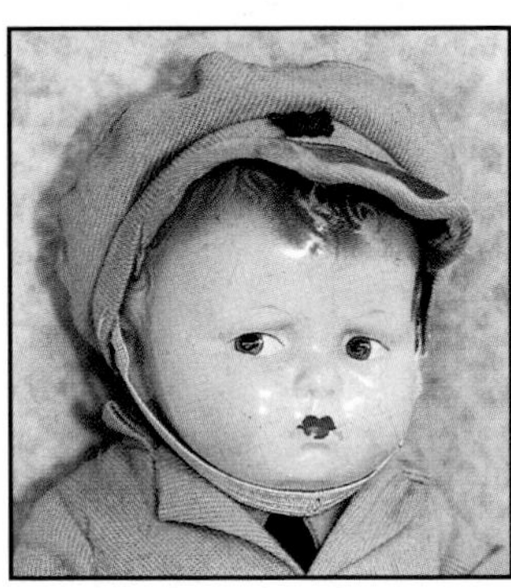

11½" composition Grumpykins Soldier, heavily molded and painted hair, frowning eyebrows, painted blue side-glancing eyes, pouty mouth, dressed in soldier's uniform, circa 1940, $350.00. Courtesy Janet Hill.

Grumpykins, 1927, composition head, cloth body, composition arms, some with cloth legs, others with composition legs

12"	$75.00	$300.00
Black	$85.00	$375.00

Grumpykins, Pennsylvania Dutch Dolls, ca. 1936, dressed by Marie Polack in Mennonite, River Brethren and Amish costumes

12"	$85.00	$300.00

Bubbles, ca. 1924+

Composition shoulder head, open/closed mouth, painted teeth, painted molded hair, sleep eyes, cloth body, bent-cloth legs, some with composition toddler legs, composition arms, finger of left hand fits into mouth, wore heart necklace. *Various marks including "Effanbee//Bubbles//Copr. 1924//Made in U.S.A."*

16"	$100.00	$375.00
22"	$125.00	$525.00
25"	$200.00	$750.00

14½" composition Harmonica Joe, molded and painted blond hair, painted eyes, painted eyelashes above, open mouth to receive metal harmonica, cloth body and legs, original clothes, bluebird pin, advertised in 1924 Playthings*, $350.00. Private collection.*

21" composition Barbara Lou from the American Children collection designed by Dewees Cochran, marked "Effanbee//American//Children" on head, "Effanbee//Anne Shirley" on body, blond human hair wig, brown sleep eyes, open mouth with four teeth, jointed composition body, separated fingers, red dress jumper with white shirt and apron, white socks trimmed with red, leather tie shoes, wrist tag reads "I am one of//AMERICA'S CHILDREN//Barbara//Lou," circa 1936 – 1939+, $1,000.00. Courtesy Janet Hill.

Lamkin, ca. 1930+

Composition molded head, sleep eyes, open mouth, cloth body, crier, chubby composition legs, with feet turned in, fingers curled, molded gold ring on middle finger

16"	$150.00	$475.00

Pat-o-pat, 1925+

Composition head, painted eyes, cloth body with mechanism which, when pressed causes hands to clap

13"	$50.00	$150.00
15"	$80.00	$200.00

Characters, 1912+

Composition, heavily molded hair, painted eyes, pin-jointed cloth body, composition arms, cloth or composition legs. *Some marked "Deco"*

Cliquot Eskimo, ca. 1920

Painted eyes, molded hair, felt hands, mohair suit

18"	$150.00	$525.00

Coquette, Naughty Marietta, ca. 1915+

Composition girl, molded bow in hair, side-glancing eyes, cloth body

12"	$100.00	$400.00

Harmonica Joe, 1923

Cloth body, with rubber ball when squeezed, provides air to open mouth with harmonica

15"	$85.00	$350.00

Irish Mail Kid, 1915, or Dixie Flyer

Composition head, cloth body, arms sewn to steering handle of wooden wagon

10"	$125.00	$350.00

Johnny Tu-face, 1912

Composition head with face on front and back, painted features, open/closed crying mouth, closed smiling mouth, painted molded hair, cloth body, red striped legs, cloth feet, dressed in knitted romper and hat

16"	$150.00	$325.00

22" composition Betty Bee, brown sleep eyes, open mouth with teeth, auburn wig, pink silk dress, all original with box, circa 1932, $425.00. Courtesy Martha Sweeney.

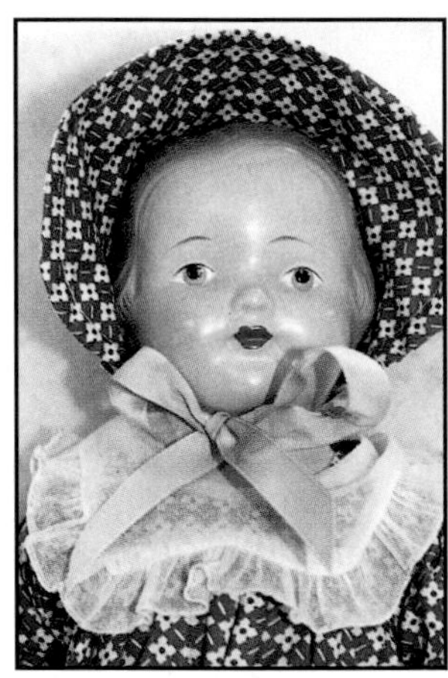

16" composition Baby Dainty, molded painted hair, painted blue eyes, closed mouth, composition arms and legs, cloth body, original blue and white flowered dress and matching hat, white socks and shoes, circa 1929, $400.00. Courtesy Janet Hill.

Pouting Bess, 1915

Composition head with heavily molded curls, painted eyes, closed mouth, cloth cork stuffed body, pin jointed. *Mark: "166" on back of head*

15" $85.00 $350.00

Whistling Jim, 1916

Composition head, with heavily molded hair, painted intaglio eyes, perforated mouth, cork stuffed cloth body, black sewn-on cloth shoes, wears red striped shirt, blue overalls. *Mark, label: "Effanbee/ /Whistling Jim//Trade Mark"*

15" $85.00 $350.00

LATE COMPOSITION

American Children, 1936 – 1939+

All-composition, designed by Dewees Cochran, open mouth, separated fingers can wear gloves. *Marks: heads may be unmarked, "Effanbee//Anne Shirley" on body*

Barbara Joan

15" $350.00 $700.00

Barbara Ann

17" $1,400.00* MIB

Barbara Lou

21" $450.00 $900.00

Closed mouth, separated fingers, sleep or painted eyes. *Marks: "Effanbee//American//Children" on head; "Effanbee//Anne Shirley" on body*

Boy

17" $400.00 $1,600.00

Gloria Ann, paper purse tag reads *"Gloria Ann"*

18½" $400.00 $1,600.00

Peggy Lou, paper purse tag, holds gloves, reads, *"Peggy Lou"*

20½" $500.00 $1,800.00

Anne Shirley, 1936 – 1940

Never advertised as such, same mold used for Little Lady. All-composition, more grown-up body style. *Mark: "EFFANBEE//ANNE SHIRLEY"*

14" $75.00 $300.00

21" $125.00 $425.00

27" $150.00 $625.00

Movie Anne Shirley, 1935 – 1940

1934 RKO movie character, Anne Shirley from *Anne of Green Gables* movie. All-composition, marked *"Patsy"* or other Effanbee doll, red braids, wearing Anne Shirley movie costume and gold paper hang tag stating *"I am Anne Shirley."* The Anne Shirley costume changes the identity of these dolls.

Mary Lee/Anne Shirley, open mouth, head marked *"©Mary Lee,"* on marked *"Patsy Joan"* body

16" $250.00 $500.00

Patsyette/Anne Shirley, body marked *"Effanbee// Patsyette// Doll"*

9½" $150.00 $325.00

Patricia/Anne Shirley, body marked *"Patricia"*

15" $200.00 $550.00

Patricia-kin/Anne Shirley, head marked *"Patricia-kin,"* body marked *"Effanbee//Patsy Jr.,"* hang tag reads *"Anne Shirley"*

11½" $175.00 $375.00

27" composition Little Lady, with paper heart tag and hairstyle booklet, yarn hair, pink chifffon formal, very good condition, some light crazing, $400.00. Courtesy McMasters Doll Auctions.

Brother or Sister, 1943

Composition head, hands, cloth body, legs, yarn hair, painted eyes

Brother

6" $60.00 $235.00

Sister

12" $45.00 $175.00

Butin-nose: See Patsy family, and vinyl.

Candy Kid, 1946+

All-composition, sleep eyes, toddler body, molded painted hair, closed mouth

13½" $75.00 $300.00

Black

13½" $150.00 $600.00

Charlie McCarthy, 1937

Composition head, hands, feet, painted features, mouth opens, cloth body, legs, *marked: "Edgar Bergen's Charlie McCarthy//An Effanbee Product"*

15" $125.00 $550.00

17 – 19" $175.00 $775.00

19" $2,000.00* in box, top hat, tails

Happy Birthday Doll, ca. 1940

Music box in body, heart bracelet

17" $1,050.00*

Historical Dolls, 1939+

All-composition, jointed body, human hair wigs, painted eyes, made only three sets of 30 dolls depicting history of apparel, 1492 – 1939, very fancy original costumes, metal heart bracelet. *Head marked "Effanbee//American//Children," on body, "Effanbee//Anne Shirley."*

21" $650.00 $1,500.00+

Too few in database for reliable range.

Historical Replicas, 1939+

All-composition, jointed body, copies of sets above, but smaller, human hair wigs, painted eyes, original costumes

14" $250.00 $600.00

15½" composition Little Lady, sleep eyes, closed mouth, lovely color, auburn mohair wig, magnet hands can hold metal heart Effanbee Durable Dolls bracelet or metal accessories, original outfit, circa 1940, $350.00. Courtesy Lee Ann Beaumont.

* at auction

14" compostion Suzanne, marked with name on body, mohair wig, sleep eyes, closed mouth, jointed composition body, white dress with black lace trim, all original, circa 1940, $325.00. Courtesy Pat Graff.

Honey, ca. 1947 – 1948

All-composition jointed body, human hair wig, sleep eyes, closed mouth

18"	$80.00	$300.00
21"	$100.00	$400.00

All hard plastic, ca. 1949 – 1955, see Vinyl and Hard Plastic later in this category.

Howdy-Doody, 1947 – 1949

Composition head, brown sleep eyes, open/closed mouth, painted molded teeth, cloth body, plaid shirt, personalized neck scarf, *"HOWDY DOODY,"* jeans and boots, cowboy hat

Effanbee gold heart paper hang tag reads *"I AM AN//EFFANBEE //DURABLE DOLL//THE DOLL//SATIN-SMOOTH//SKIN."*

20"	$65.00	$275.00
23"	$75.00	$300.00

Ice Queen, 1937+

Composition, open mouth, skater outfit

17"	$200.00	$850.00

Little Lady, 1939+

Used Anne Shirley mold. All-composition, wigged, sleep eyes, more grown-up body, separated fingers, gold paper hang tag. Many in formals, as brides, or fancy gowns with matching parasol. During war years yarn hair was used; may have gold hang tag with name, like Gaye or Carole.

15"	$365.00* box	
18"	$95.00	$325.00
21"	$125.00	$425.00
27"	$150.00	$625.00

14" composition Historical Replica New York Settlement 1625, marked "EFFANBEE" on body, human hair wig, closed mouth, jointed composition body, metal heart bracelet, all original with box, circa 1939+, $600.00. Courtesy Pat Graff.

Lovums, ca. 1928

Composition swivel head, shoulder plate, and limbs, cloth body, sleep eyes, painted molded hair or wigged, can have bent baby legs or toddler legs

16"	$100.00	$400.00
20"	$125.00	$450.00

Mae Starr, ca. 1928

Talking doll, composition shoulder head, cloth body, open mouth, four teeth, with cylinder records

Marked: "Mae//Starr// Doll"

29"	$200.00	$750.00

MaMa Dolls, ca. 1921+

Composition shoulder head, painted or sleep eyes, molded hair or wigged, cloth body, swing legs, crier, with composition arms and lower legs

18"	$75.00	$350.00
24"	$125.00	$400.00

* at auction

Marionettes, 1937+

Puppets designed by Virginia Austin, composition, painted eyes

Clippo, clown

15" $85.00 $300.00

Emily Ann

14" $85.00 $300.00

Lucifer, black

15" $525.00* mint-in-box

Marilee, ca. 1924

Mama doll, with composition shoulder head, sleep eyes, open mouth, cloth body, crier, swing legs

Marked on shoulder plate: "Effanbee//Marilee// Copyr.//Doll" in oval

24" $150.00 $550.00

27" $175.00 $600.00

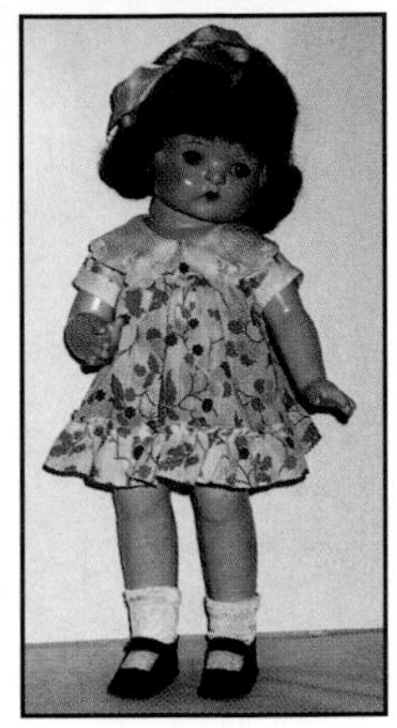

19" composition Patsy Ann, marked "Effanbee//"Patsy-Ann"//©//Pat. #1283558," auburn wig, sleep eyes, jointed composition body, white dress with blue floral print may be original, white socks, black one-strap shoes, pink silk hair ribbon added, circa 1929, $600.00. Courtesy Pat Graff.

Portrait Dolls, ca. 1940

All-composition, Bo-Peep, Ballerina, Bride, Groom, Gibson Girl, Colonial Maid, etc.

12" $65.00 $250.00

Rosemary, 1926

Marks: "EFFANBEE//ROSEMARY//WALK/ /TALK//SLEEP" in oval "MADE IN US"

18" $100.00 $350.00

24" $150.00 $425.00

Suzanne, ca. 1940

All-composition, jointed body, sleep eyes, wigged, closed mouth, may have magnets in hands to hold accessories. More for additional accessories or wardrobe.

14" $100.00 $325.00

Suzette, ca. 1939

All-composition, fully jointed, painted side-glancing eyes, closed mouth, wigged

11" $75.00 $265.00

Sweetie Pie, 1939+

Also called Baby Bright Eyes, Tommy Tucker, Mickey, composition bent limbs, sleep eyes, caracul wig, cloth body, crier. Issued again in 1952+ in hard plastic, cloth body, and vinyl limbs, painted hair or synthetic wigs. Wore same pink rayon taffeta dress with black and white trim as Noma doll.

16" $75.00 $300.00

20" $85.00 $350.00

24" $100.00 $400.00

W. C. Fields, 1929+

Composition shoulder head, painted features, hinged mouth, painted teeth. In 1980 made in vinyl. See Legend Series.

16" composition Sister Twins, marked "Effanbee/ /Made in U.S.A." on back of flange heads, brown flirty sleep eyes, real lashes, multi-stroke brows, painted lower lashes, closed mouths, human hair wigs, cloth bodies, non-working criers, composition arms and lower legs, original pink rompers, original beige snowsuits with brown velvet collars, cuffs and brims on hats, socks, suede baby shoes, metal heart bracelet on one doll, circa 1930s, $700.00. Courtesy McMasters Doll Auctions.

* at auction

14" composition Patsy marked "Effanbee//Patsy" on head, "Effanbee//Patsy//Doll" on back, sleep eyes, closed mouth, molded painted hair, five-piece composition body, circa 1928+, $200.00; and 14" composition Skippy, marked "Effanbee//Skippy//©//P.L. Crosby" on back of head, original Skippy button, painted eyes to side, closed mouth, molded painted hair, cloth torso, composition arms and legs, both with original outfits, circa 1929+, $625.00. Courtesy McMasters Doll Auctions.

9" composition Patsyette, marked "Effanbee//Patsyette//Doll" on back, painted brown side-glancing eyes, single stroke brows, painted upper lashes, closed rosebud mouth, molded painted bobbed hair, five-piece composition body with bent right arm, original yellow organdy lace-trimmed dress, matching slip, romper and bonnet, white rayon shoes, black side snap shoes with silver buckle, circa 1931, $160.00. Courtesy McMasters Doll Auctions.

Marked: "W.C. Fields//An Effanbee Product"

17½"	$250.00	$950.00

Patsy Family, 1928+

Composition through 1947, later issued in vinyl and porcelain. Many had gold paper hang tag and metal bracelet that read *"Effanbee Durable Dolls."* More for black, special editions, costumes, or with added accessories.

Babies

Patsy Baby, 1931

Painted or sleep eyes, wigged or molded hair, composition baby body, advertised as Babykin, came also with cloth body, in pair, layettes, trunks

Marks: on head, "Effanbee//Patsy Baby"; on body, "Effanbee //Patsy// Baby"

10 – 11"	$125.00	$350.00
11"	$475.00* boxed	

Patsy Babyette, 1932

Sleep eyes

Marked on head "Effanbee"; on body, "Effanbee//Patsy //Babyette"

9"	$100.00	$325.00

Patsy Baby Tinyette, 1934

Painted eyes, bent-leg composition body

Marked on head, "Effanbee"; on body, "Effanbee//Baby/ /Tinyette"

6½"	$90.00	$300.00

Quints, 1935

Set of five Patsy Baby Tinyettes in original box, from FAO Schwarz, organdy christening gowns and milk glass bottles, excellent condition.

Set of five

6½"	$450.00	$1,750.00

Children

Patsy, ca. 1924, cloth body, composition legs, open mouth, upper teeth, sleep eyes, painted or human hair wig, with composition legs to hips. *Marked in half oval on back shoulder plate:"Effanbee//Patsy"*

15"	$100.00	$300.00

* at auction

16" composition Patricia, marked "Effanbee//"Patricia" on back, "Effanbee//Durable//Dolls" on metal heart bracelet, original human hair wig, green sleep eyes, real lashes, painted lashes, single stroke brows, closed mouth, five-piece composition body, red print dress with faded tag, matching romper, replaced rayon socks, center snap shoes, circa 1935, $250.00. Courtesy McMasters Doll Auctions.

22" composition Patsy Lou, marked "Effanbee//Patsy Lou" on back, molded painted hair, green sleep eyes, real lashes, painted lashes, feathered brows, closed mouth, five-piece composition body with bent right arm, original pale blue organdy dress trimmed with ruffles and lace, blue organdy slip and teddy, matching bonnet, rayon socks, blue-green leatherette shoes with buckles, circa 1930, $600.00. Courtesy McMasters Doll Auctions.

Patsy, ca. 1926, mama doll, open mouth, upper teeth, sleep eyes, human hair wig, cloth body with crier and swing legs, composition arms and lower legs. *Marked on shoulder plate in oval: "Effanbee //Patsy//Copr.// Doll"*

22"	$100.00	$400.00
29"	$150.00	$550.00

Patsy, 1928, all-composition jointed body, painted or sleep eyes, molded headband on red molded bobbed hair, or wigged, bent right arm, with gold paper hang tag, metal heart bracelet. *Marked on body: "Effanbee//Patsy//Pat. Pend.//Doll"*

14"	$225.00	$550.00

Patsy, Oriental with black painted hair, painted eyes, in fancy silk pajamas and matching shoes

14"	$350.00	$750.00

Patsy, 1946, all-composition jointed body, bright facial coloring, painted or sleep eyes, wears pink or blue checked pinafore

14"	$200.00	$450.00

Patsy Alice, ca. 1933, advertised in Effanbee's *Patsytown News* for two years

24"	$400.00	$1,200.00

**No doll with this name has been positively identified.*

Patsy Ann, 1929, all-composition, closed mouth, sleep eyes, molded hair, or wigged. *Marked on body: "Effanbee//'Patsy-Ann'//©//Pat. #1283558"*

19"	$275.00	$600.00
19"	$875.00* boxed, tagged	

Patsy Ann, 1959, all-vinyl, full jointed, rooted saran hair, sleep eyes, freckles across nose. *Head marked "Effanbee// Patsy Ann//©1959"; body marked "Effanbee//Official Girl Scout"*

15"	$75.00	$250.00

Patsy Ann, 1959, limited edition, vinyl, sleep eyes, white organdy dress, with pink hair ribbon

Marked "Effanbee//Patsy Ann//©1959" on head; "Effanbee" on body

15"	$100.00	$285.00

* at auction

9" composition Tinyettes, painted side-glancing eyes, painted hair, closed mouths, gold paper hang tag, "Kit & Kat//Dutch Twins" in original Dutch outfits, circa 1934, $450.00. Courtesy Gay Smedes.

14" composition Patsy, marked "Effanbee//Patsy//Pat. Pend.//Doll," molded painted hair with molded headband, painted side-glancing eyes, jointed composition body with bent right arm, blue and white checked outfit trimmed with red, all original with box, unplayed with condition, circa 1946, $750.00. Courtesy Ellen Sturgess.

Patsyette, 1931, composition

9½" $150.00 $425.00

Black, Dutch, Hawaiian

9½" $200.00 $650.00+

Patsy Fluff, 1932

All-cloth, with painted features, pink checked rompers and bonnet

16" $500.00 $1,000.00

Too few examples in database for reliable range.

Patsy Joan, 1931, composition

16" $225.00 $550.00

Patsy Joan, 1946

Marked *"Effandbee"* on body, with extra "d" added

17" $200.00 $500.00

Patsy Jr., 1931

All-composition, advertised as Patsykins. *Marks: "Effanbee//Patsy Jr.//Doll"*

11½" $150.00 $400.00

Patsy Lou, 1930

All-composition, molded red hair or wigged. *Marks: "Effanbee//Patsy Lou" on body*

22" $275.00 $625.00

Patsy Mae, 1934

Shoulder head, sleep eyes, cloth body, crier, swing legs. *Marks: "Effanbee//Patsy Mae" on head; "Effanbee//Lovums//c//Pat. No. 1283558" on shoulder plate*

29" $700.00 $1,400.00

Patsy Ruth, 1934

Shoulder head, sleep eyes, cloth body, crier, swing legs. *Marks: "Effanbee//Patsy Ruth" on head; "Effanbee//Lovums//©//Pat. No. 1283558" on shoulder plate*

26" $650.00 $1,300.00+

Patsy Tinyette Toddler, ca. 1935

Painted eyes. *Marks: "Effanbee" on head; "Effanbee// Baby/ /Tinyette" on body*

7¾" $100.00 $325.00+

29" composition Patsy Mae, marked "Effanbee//Patsy Mae" on back of head, "Effanbee//Lovums//©//Pat. No. 1283659" on shoulder plate, human hair wig, brown sleep eyes, real lashes, painted lashes, feathered brows, closed rosebud mouth, cloth body, composition arms and legs, original blue-gray dress with red print, metal heart bracelet, blue-gray romper, matching slip, rayon socks, replaced red leather shoes, circa 1934, $900.00. Courtesy McMasters Doll Auctions.

26" composition Patsy Ruth, marked "Effanbee//Patsy Ruth" with composition shoulderplate marked "Effanbee Lovums/ /©//Pat. No. 123558," green sleep eyes, real lashes, feathered brows, painted upper and lower lashes, accented nostrils, closed mouth, mohair wig, cloth mama doll body, composition arms and lower legs, re-dressed in copy of original dress, metal heart bracelet, circa 1934, $900.00. Courtesy McMasters Doll Auctions.

Tinyette Toddler, tagged *"Kit & Kat"*

In Dutch costume

$800.00 for pair

Wee Patsy, 1935

Head molded to body, molded painted shoes and socks, jointed arms and hips, advertised only as "Fairy Princess," pinback button. *Marks on body: "Effanbee//Wee Patsy"*

5¾"	$150.00	$475.00
In trousseau box		
	$250.00	$650.00+

Related items

Metal heart bracelet, reads *"Effanbee Durable Dolls"* $25.00

(original bracelets can still be ordered from Shirley's Doll House)

Metal personalized name bracelet for Patsy family

$65.00

Patsy Ann, Her Happy Times, c. 1935, book by Mona Reed King $75.00

Patsy For Keeps, c 1932, book by Ester Marian Ames $125.00

Patricia Series, 1935, all sizes advertised in *Patsytown News*

All-composition slimmer bodies, sleep eyes, wigged, later WWII-era Patricias had yarn hair and cloth bodies

Patricia, wig, sleep eyes, marked, *"Effanbee Patricia"* body

15"	$225.00	$525.00

Patricia Ann, wig, marks unknown

19"	$375.00	$750.00

Too few in database for reliable range.

Patricia Joan, wig, marks unknown, slimmer legs

16"	$325.00	$650.00

Too few in database for reliable range.

Patricia-Kin, wig. *Mark: "Patricia-Kin" head; "Effanbee//Patsy Jr." body*

11½"	$275.00	$450.00

Patricia Lou, wig, marks unknown

22"	$300.00	$600.00

Too few in database for reliable range.

* at auction

11" composition Effanbee Patsy Babykin, blue sleep eyes, real lashes, painted upper and lower lashes, closed mouth, molded painted hair, composition bent-limb baby body, original tagged organdy dress with lace trim, matching bonnet, slip, flannel diaper, marked "Effanbee//Patsy Baby" on head and back, "Effanbee Durable Dolls//Made in U.S.A." on dress tag, "Effanbee Patsy Babykin" on metal heart bracelet, circa 1931, $325.00. Courtesy McMasters Doll Auctions.

9" composition Patsy Babyette Twins, marked "Effanbee//Patsy//Babyette," molded painted hair, blue sleep eyes, closed mouths, five-piece composition baby bodies, blue outfits with matching hats, hang tags read "I AM//Babyette//An//EFFANBEE//DURABLE//DOLL," all original with box, circa 1940s, $900.00. Courtesy Ellen Sturgess.

Patricia Ruth

Head marked: "Effanbee//Patsy Ruth," no marks on slimmer composition body

27"	$700.00	$1,350.00
27"	$3,600.00*	

PATSY RELATED DOLLS AND VARIANTS

Betty Bee, tousel head, 1932

All-composition, short tousel wig, sleep eyes. *Marked on body: "Effanbee//Patsy Lou"*

22"	$250.00	$400.00

Betty Bounce, tousel head, 1932+

All-composition, sleep eyes, used Lovums head on body, *marked: "Effanbee//'Patsy Ann'//©//Pat. #1283558"*

19"	$200.00	$350.00

Betty Brite, 1932

All-composition, short tousel wig, sleep eyes, some marked: *"Effanbee//Betty Brite"* on body and others marked on head *"© Mary-Lee"*; on body, *"Effanbee Patsy Joan"*

Gold hang tag reads *"This is Betty Brite, The lovable Imp with tiltable head and movable limb, an Effanbee doll."*

16"	$175.00	$300.00

Butin-nose, ca. 1936+

All-composition, molded painted hair, features, distinct feature is small nose, usually has regional or special costume; name "button" misspelled to "Butin"

8"	$85.00	$275.00

Cowboy outfit

8"	$95.00	$325.00

Dutch pair, with gold paper hang tags reading: *"Kit and Kat"*

8"	$250.00	$525.00

Oriental, with layette

8"	$250.00	$525.00

Mary Ann, 1932+

Composition, sleep eyes, wigged, open mouth. *Marked: "Mary Ann" on head; "Effanbee//Patsy Ann'//©//Pat. #1283558" on body*

19"	$200.00	$350.00

Mary Lee, 1932

Composition, sleep eyes, wigged, open mouth. *Marked: "©//Mary Lee" on head; "Effanbee//Patsy Joan" on body.*

16½"	$225.00	$325.00

* at auction

7" composition Baby Tinyette, marked "Effanbee" on head, "Effanbee//Baby Tinyette" on back, molded painted hair, painted blue eyes to side, painted upper lashes, single stroke brows, closed mouth, composition bent-leg baby body, original pale blue organdy baby dress, matching bonnet, underclothing, socks with ribbon trim, circa 1934, $335.00. Courtesy McMasters Doll Auctions.

MiMi, 1927

All-composition, blue painted eyes, prototype of 1928 Patsy, but name change indicates a very short production run. *Marked on body: "Effanbee//MiMi//Pat.Pend//Doll"*

14"	$250.00	$600.00

Patsy/Patricia, 1940

Used a marked Patsy head on a marked Patricia body, all-composition, painted eyes, molded hair, may have magnets in hands to hold accessories. *Marked on body: "Effanbee//'Patricia'"*

15"	$300.00	$600.00

Skippy, 1929

Advertised as Patsy's boyfriend, composition head, painted eyes, painted molded blond hair, composition or cloth body, with composition molded shoes and legs. *Marked on head: "Effanbee//Skippy//©//P. L. Crosby"; on body, "Effanbee//Patsy//Pat. Pend// Doll"*

14"	$275.00	$600.00

White Horse Inn, with pin

$1,400.00*

Rubber

Dy-Dee, 1934+

Hard rubber head, sleep eyes, jointed rubber bent-leg body, drink/wet mechanism, molded painted hair. Early dolls had molded ears, after 1940 had applied rubber ears, nostrils, and tear ducts. Later made in hard plastic and vinyl.

Marked: "Effanbee//Dy-Dee Baby" with four patent numbers

16" hard plastic Honey, marked "Effanbee" on head, saran wig, sleep eyes, real lashes, painted lower lashes, closed mouth, hard plastic jointed body, red plaid dress with white corduroy jacket with matching plaid ruffles, matching plaid hat, white socks, red shoes, circa 1949 – 1955, $325.00. Courtesy Harlene Soucy.

Dy-Dee Wee

9"	$75.00	$300.00

Dy-Dee-ette, Dy-Dee Ellen

11"	$50.00	$200.00

Dy-Dee Kin

13"	$65.00	$225.00

Dy-Dee Baby, Dy-Dee Jane

15"	$100.00	$400.00

Dy-Dee Lou, Dy-Dee Louise

20"	$125.00	$450.00

Dy-Dee in layette trunk, with accessories

15"	$150.00	$475.00

Dy-Dee Accessories

Dy-Dee marked bottle

	$7.50	$15.00

Dy-Dee pattern pajamas

	$8.00	$25.00

Dy-Dee book, *Dy-Dee Doll's Days*, c 1937, by Peggy Vandegriff, with black and white pictures

5½" x 6¾"	$25.00	$55.00

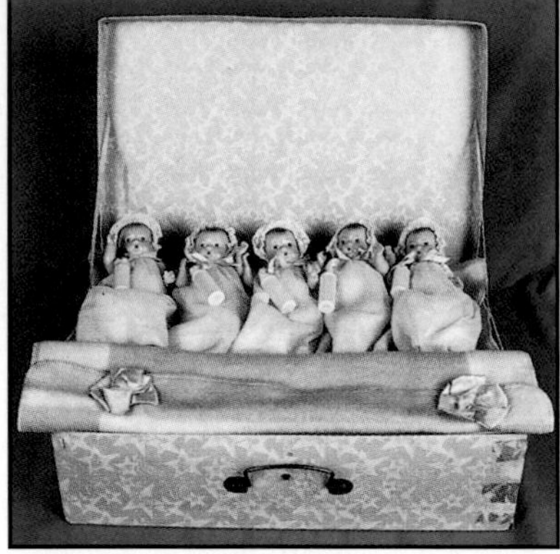

Set of five 7" composition Quints, painted brown eyes, single stroke brows, painted upper lashes, closed mouths, molded painted hair, composition bent-limb baby bodies, dressed in original long white organdy baby dresses, slips, birdseye diapers, organdy lace trimmed bonnets, original glass bottles with black rubber nipple and pink ribbon, original FAO Schwarz marked case, pink/white blanket with pink ribbon rosettes, circa 1934, $1,200.00.
Courtesy McMasters Doll Auctions.

Hard Plastic and Vinyl

Alyssa, ca. 1960 – 1961

Vinyl head, hard plastic jointed body, walker, including elbows, rooted saran hair, sleep eyes

23"	$90.00	$225.00

Armstrong, Louis, 1984 – 1985, vinyl

15½"	$25.00	$85.00

Baby Lisa, 1980

Vinyl, designed by Astri Campbell, represents a three-month-old baby, in wicker basket with accessories

11"	$50.00	$150.00

Baby Lisa Grows Up, 1983

Vinyl, toddler body, in trunk with wardrobe

	$50.00	$150.00

Button Nose, 1968 – 1971

Vinyl head, cloth body

18"	$9.00	$35.00

Champagne Lady, 1959

Vinyl head and arms, rooted hair, blue sleep eyes, lashes, hard plastic body, from Lawrence Welk's TV show, Miss Revlon-type

21"	$75.00	$275.00
23"	$85.00	$300.00

Churchill, Sir Winston, 1984, vinyl

	$20.00	$75.00

Currier & Ives, vinyl and hard plastic

12"	$12.00	$45.00

Disney dolls, 1977 – 1978

Snow White, Cinderella, Alice in Wonderland, and Sleeping Beauty

14"	$45.00	$185.00
16½"	$85.00	$325.00

Fluffy, 1954+, all-vinyl

	10"	$10.00	$35.00
Black	$12.00	$45.00	
Girl Scout	$15.00	$75.00	

Gumdrop, 1962+

Vinyl, jointed toddler, sleep eyes, rooted hair

16"	$9.00	$35.00

Hagara, Jan

Designer, all-vinyl, jointed, rooted hair, painted eyes

Christina, 1984

	15"	$50.00	$200.00
Larry, 1985		$25.00	$95.00
Laurel, 1984	15"	$40.00	$150.00
Lesley, 1985		$20.00	$85.00

19" vinyl black Susie Sunshine, from A Touch of Velvet Collection, rooted dark brown hair, brown sleep eyes, closed mouth, fully jointed vinyl body, maroon dress, matching ribbon in hair, white pinafore, mint-in-box, circa 1977, $100.00. Courtesy Pat Graff.

Half Pint, 1966 – 1983

All-vinyl, rooted hair, sleep eyes, lashes

11"	$8.00	$30.00

Happy Boy, 1960

Vinyl, molded hair, tooth, freckles, painted eyes

11"	$10.00	$45.00

Hibel, Edna

Designer, 1984 only, all-vinyl

Flower Girl

11"	$40.00	$165.00
Contessa	$50.00	$185.00

Honey, 1949 – 1958

Hard plastic (see also composition), saran wig, sleep eyes, closed mouth

Marked on head and back, "Effanbee," had gold paper hang tag that read: "I am//Honey//An//Effanbee//Sweet//Child"

Honey, ca. 1949 – 1955, all hard plastic, closed mouth, sleep eyes

14"	$250.00	$500.00
17"	$300.00	$600.00

Honey Walker, 1952+

All hard plastic with walking mechanism; Honey Walker Junior Miss, 1956 – 1957, hard plastic, extra joints at knees and ankles permit her to wear flat or high-heeled shoes. Add $50.00 for jointed knees, ankles.

14"	$65.00	$350.00
19"	$175.00	$425.00

Humpty Dumpty, 1985

	$25.00	$75.00

Katie, 1957, molded hair

8½"	$15.00	$50.00

Legend Series, vinyl

1980, W.C. Fields,		$40.00	$200.00
1981, John Wayne, cowboy		$50.00	$300.00
1982, John Wayne, cavalry		$50.00	$350.00
1982, Mae West		$25.00	$100.00
1983, Groucho Marx		$20.00	$95.00
1984, Judy Garland, Dorothy		$20.00	$90.00
1985, Lucille Ball		$40.00	$120.00
1986, Liberace		$17.50	$95.00
1987, James Cagney		$15.00	$70.00

Lil Sweetie, 1967

Nurser with no lashes or brow	16"	$25.00	$45.00

Limited Edition Club, vinyl

1975, Precious Baby		$115.00	$350.00
1976, Patsy Ann		$85.00	$300.00
1977, Dewees Cochran		$40.00	$135.00
1978, Crowning Glory		$35.00	$105.00
1979, Skippy		$75.00	$265.00

1980, Susan B. Anthony		$35.00	$75.00
1981, Girl with Watering Can		$25.00	$70.00
1982, Princess Diana		$25.00	$100.00
1983, Sherlock Holmes		$40.00	$150.00
1984, Bubbles		$25.00	$100.00
1985, Red Boy		$25.00	$85.00
1986, China head		$17.50	$60.00
1987 – 1988, Porcelain Grumpy (2,500)		$125.00	
Vinyl Grumpy		$50.00	

Martha and George Washington, 1976 – 1977

All-vinyl, fully jointed, rooted hair, blue eyes, molded lashes

	11" pair	$40.00	$155.00

Mickey, 1956 – 1972

All-vinyl, fully jointed, some with molded hat, painted eyes

	10"	$20.00	$75.00

Miss Chips, 1966 – 1981

All-vinyl, fully jointed, side-glancing sleep eyes, rooted hair

	17"	$9.00	$35.00
Black	17"	$12.00	$45.00

Noma, The Electronic Doll, ca. 1950

Hard plastic, cloth body, vinyl limbs, battery-operated talking doll wore pink rayon taffeta dress with black and white check trim

	27"	$125.00	$375.00

Polka Dottie, 1954

Vinyl head, with molded pigtails on fabric body, or with hard plastic body

	21"	$60.00	$165.00
Latex body			
	11"	$30.00	$120.00

Presidents, 1984+

Abraham Lincoln			
	18"	$15.00	$50.00
George Washington			
	16"	$15.00	$50.00
Teddy Roosevelt			
	17"	$17.50	$75.00
Franklin D. Roosevelt, 1985			
		$15.00	$75.00

Prince Charming or Cinderella, Honey

All-hard plastic

	16"	$165.00	$425.00

Pun'kin, 1966 – 1983

All-vinyl, fully jointed toddler, sleep eyes, rooted hair

	11"	$15.00	$30.00

Rootie Kazootie, 1954

Vinyl head, cloth or hard plastic body, smaller size has latex body

	11"	$30.00	$120.00
	21"	$60.00	$165.00

Roosevelt, Eleanor, 1985, vinyl

	14½"	$15.00	$70.00

Santa Claus, 1982+, designed by Faith Wick

"Old Fashioned Nast Santa," No. 7201, vinyl head, hands, stuffed cloth body, molded painted features, *marked "Effanbee//7201 c//Faith Wick"*

18"	$25.00	$75.00

Suzie Sunshine, 1961 – 1979

Designed by Eugenia Dukas, all-vinyl, fully jointed, rooted hair, sleep eyes, lashes, freckles on nose. Add $25.00 more for black.

18"	$25.00	$60.00

Sweetie Pie, 1952, hard plastic

27"	$65.00	$325.00

Tintair, 1951, hard plastic, hair color set, to compete with Ideal's Toni

15"	$250.00	$400.00

Twain, Mark, 1984, all-vinyl, molded features

16"	$20.00	$70.00

Wicket Witch, 1981 – 1982, designed by Faith Wick

No. 7110, vinyl head, blond rooted hair, painted features, cloth stuffed body, dressed in black, with apple and basket. *Head marked: "Effanbee//Faith Wick//7110 19cc81"*

18"	$25.00	$75.00

Ethnic

This category describes dolls costumed in regional dress to show different nationalities, facial characteristics, or cultural background. Examples are dolls in regional costumes that are commonly sold as souvenirs to tourists. A well-made beautiful doll with accessories or wardrobe may be more.

13" composition Skookum Indian and papoose, designed by Mary McAboy, black mohair wigs, painted features, painted side-glancing eyes, red headband, cloth figure wrapped in Indian blanket, folds representing arms holding child, linen boots, beads around neck, circa 1950s, $175.00. *Courtesy Carol Van Verst-Rugg.*

Celluloid

8"	$20.00	$55.00
15"	$65.00	$150.00

Cloth

8"	$50.00	$175.00
13"	$65.00	$200.00

Composition Child

8"	$65.00	$185.00
13"	$75.00	$250.00

Native American Indian

8"	$65.00	$225.00
13"	$75.00	$300.00
23"	$85.00	$350.00

Skookum, 1913+ designed by Mary McAboy, painted features, with side-glancing eyes, mohair wigs, cloth figure wrapped in Indian blanket, with folds representing arms, wooden feet, later plastic, label on bottom of foot. Box marked *"Skookum Bully Good."*

First price indicates incomplete, but still very good; second price is excellent to mint with box.

6"	$25.00	$75.00
10 – 12"	$135.00	$230.00
16 – 18"	$150.00	$300.00
33"	$950.00	$1,550.00+

Ethnic

Hard Plastic, regional dress, unmarked or unknown maker

7"	$5.00	$15.00
12"	$7.50	$30.00

Baitz, Austria, 1970s, painted hard plastic, painted side-glancing eyes, open "o" mouth, excellent quality, tagged and dressed in regional dress

8"	$40.00	$75.00

Vinyl

6"	$10.00	$35.00
12"	$15.00	$65.00

Freundlich

12" composition, painted and molded blond hair, round blue iris eyes with round black pupils, closed mouth, red dress, white collar, Little Orphan Annie and her dog Sandy, hang tag, $575.00. Courtesy McMasters Doll Auctions.

Ralph A. Freundlich, 1923+, New York City. Formerly Jeanette Doll Co, then Ralph Freundlich, Inc. Made composition dolls, some with molded caps in military uniform.

Baby Sandy, ca. 1939 – 1942, all-composition, jointed toddler body, molded hair, painted or sleep eyes, smiling mouth

8"	$75.00	$300.00
12"	$100.00	$400.00
15"	$125.00	$500.00

Dummy Dan, ventriloquist doll, Charlie McCarthy look-alike

15"	$40.00	$150.00
21"	$90.00	$350.00

General Douglas MacArthur, ca. 1942, all-composition, jointed body, bent arm salutes, painted features, molded hat, jointed, in khaki uniform, with paper tag

18"	$85.00	$350.00

Military dolls, ca. 1942+, all-composition, molded hats, painted features, original clothes, with paper tag

Soldier, Sailor, WAAC, or WAVE

15"	$65.00	$275.00

Orphan Annie and her dog, Sandy

12"	$85.00	$325.00

Pinocchio, composition and cloth, with molded hair, painted features, brightly colored cheeks, large eyes, open/closed mouth

Tagged: "Original as portrayed by C. Collodi"

16"	$125.00	$500.00

Red Riding Hood, Wolf, Grandma, 1930s, composition, set of three, in schoolhouse box, original clothes

9½"	$250.00	$800.00

Trixbe, 1930s, all-composition, painted features, unmarked body, in original box

11½"	$75.00	$150.00

The Lone Ranger Series

Vinyl action figures with horses, separate accessory sets available.

Dan Reed on Banjo, blond hair, figure on palomino horse

9"	$15.00	$50.00

Butch Cavendish on Smoke, black hair, mustache, on black horse

9"	$20.00	$80.00

Lone Ranger on Silver, masked figure on white horse

9"	$25.00	$100.00

Little Bear, Indian boy

6"	$25.00	$100.00

Red Sleeves, vinyl Indian figure, black hair, wears shirt with red sleeves

9"	$25.00	$100.00

Tonto on Scout, Indian on brown and white horse

9"	$20.00	$80.00

Gene

15½" vinyl Madra Unsung Melody, painted eyes, rooted synthetic wig, bendable knees and elbows, jointed fashion-type body, dressed in a seafoam green satin gown dramatically cut through with a black satin inset panel, matching wrap around neck, earrings, black purse, circa 2001, $110.00. Photo courtesy Ashton-Drake Galleries.

1995. Designed by Mel Odom marketed through Ashton Drake.

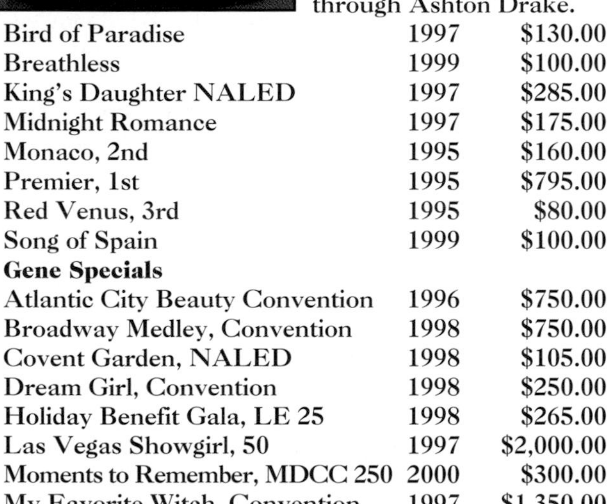

Bird of Paradise	1997	$130.00
Breathless	1999	$100.00
King's Daughter NALED	1997	$285.00
Midnight Romance	1997	$175.00
Monaco, 2nd	1995	$160.00
Premier, 1st	1995	$795.00
Red Venus, 3rd	1995	$80.00
Song of Spain	1999	$100.00
Gene Specials		
Atlantic City Beauty Convention	1996	$750.00
Broadway Medley, Convention	1998	$750.00
Covent Garden, NALED	1998	$105.00
Dream Girl, Convention	1998	$250.00
Holiday Benefit Gala, LE 25	1998	$265.00
Las Vegas Showgirl, 50	1997	$2,000.00
Moments to Remember, MDCC 250	2000	$300.00
My Favorite Witch, Convention	1997	$1,350.00

15½" vinyl Gene in Brunch With Katie, marked "Gene ™//© 1995 Mel Odom" on head, painted eyes, rooted synthetic wig, jointed fashion-type body, bendable knees, dressed in a sheath style white dress with sky blue pinstripes, has a sash in front with a hip drape that hangs from the side, pink flower accents, white hat, short gloves, blue and white high heel shoes, earrings, circa 2001, $44.95 retail, costume only; doll $49.95. Courtesy Ashton-Drake Galleries.

Gene

Night at Versailles, FAO Schwarz	1997	$250.00
On the Avenue, FAO Schwarz	1998	$180.00
On the Avenue, FAO Schwarz	1998	$180.00
Santa Fe Celebration, 250	1999	$600.00
TeaTime at the Plaza, FAO Schwarz	1999	$100.00
The King's Daughter, Special LE 5000	1999	$285.00
On the Set, UFDC Convention	1999	$400.00

Gibbs, Ruth

Marks: RG on back shoulder blade Box labeled: "GODEY LITTLE LADY DOLLS," Dolls designed by Herbert Johnson.

Ca. 1940s+, Flemington, NJ. Made dolls with china and porcelain heads and limbs, pink cloth bodies. Dolls designed by Herbert Johnson.

Godey's Lady Book Dolls

Pink-tint shoulder head, cloth body

Boxed

7" $75.00 $210.00

Caracul wig, original outfit

9½" $200.00 $295.00

Hard plastic, mint-in-box, with identification

11" $200.00

Gilbert Toys

Honey West, 1965, vinyl, vinyl arms, hard plastic torso and legs, rooted blond hair, painted eyes, painted beauty spot near mouth, head marked *"K73"* with leopard

11½" $60.00 $125.00

The Man From U.N.C.L.E. characters from TV show of the 1960s. Other outfits available. (For photo, see *Doll Values, third edition.*)

Ilya Kuryakin (David McCallum)

12¼" $25.00 $100.00

Napoleon Solo (Robert Vaughn)

12¼" $25.00 $100.00

James Bond, Secret Agent 007, character from James Bond movies

12¼" $20.00 $75.00

Costume only $180.00*

Girl Scout Dolls

1920+, listed chronologically. First price for played-with doll missing accessories; second price is for mint doll.

1920s Girl Scout doll in Camp Uniform

Pictured in Girls Scout 1920 handbook, all-cloth, mask face, painted features, wigged, gray green uniform

13" $250.00 $600.00+

Too few in database for reliable range.

Grace Corry, Scout 1929

Composition shoulder head, designed by Grace Cory, cloth body with crier, molded hair, painted features, original uniform

Mark on shoulder plate: "by Grace Corry"; body stamped "Madame Hendren Doll//Made in USA"

13" $350.00 $700.00+

Too few in database for reliable range.

* at auction

Averill Mfg. Co, ca. 1936

Believed to be designed by Maud Tousey Fangel, all-cloth, printed and painted features

16" $100.00 $400.00+

Too few in database for reliable range.

Georgene Novelties, ca. 1940

All-cloth, flat-faced painted features, yellow yarn curls, wears original silver green uniform, with red triangle tie

Hang tag reads: "Genuine Georgene Doll//A product of Georgene Novelties, Inc., NY//Made in U.S.A."

15" $100.00 $400.00

Georgene Novelties, ca. 1949 – 1954

All-cloth, mask face, painted features and string hair

13½" $75.00 $250.00

1954 – 1958

Same as previous listing, but now has a plastic mask face

13½" $35.00 $100.00

Terri Lee, 1949 – 1958

Hard plastic, felt hats, oilcloth saddle shoes

16" $125.00 $450.00

Outfit only $160.00*

Tiny Terri Lee, 1956 – 1958

Hard plastic, walker, sleep eyes, wig, plastic shoes

10" $65.00 $225.00

19" cloth Rag Doll Brownie, with frizzy reddish yarn hair, painted features, mitt hands with thumb, wears brown jumper, blue shirt, beanie cap, label in left body seam, available in white or African American, $27.50 retail. Courtesy Pidd Miller.

Ginger, ca. 1956 – 1958, made by Cosmopolitan for Terri Lee, hard plastic, straight-leg walker, synthetic wig

7½" – 8" $100.00 $250.00

7½" $385.00*

Vogue, 1956 – 1957+

Ginny, hard plastic, straight-legged walker with sleep eyes and painted eyelashes; in 1957 had bending leg and felt hat

8" $225.00 $325.00

Brownie, boxed

8" $1,124.00*

Uneeda, 1959 – 1961

Ginny look-alike, vinyl head, hard plastic body, straight-leg walker, Dynel wig, *marked "U" on head*

8" $50.00 $150.00

Effanbee, Patsy Ann, 1959+

All-vinyl jointed body, saran hair, with sleep eyes, freckles on nose, Brownie or Girl Scout

15" $95.00 $350.00

Effanbee Suzette, ca. 1960

Jointed vinyl body, sleep eyes, saran hair, thin body, long legs

15" $95.00 $350.00

* at auction

Effanbee Fluffy, 1964 – 1972

Vinyl dolls, sleep eyes, curly rooted hair, Brownie had blond wig; Junior was brunette. Box had clear acetate lid, printed with Girl Scout trademark, and catalog number

8"	$65.00	$175.00

Effanbee Fluffy Cadette, 1965

11"	$75.00	$300.00

Effanbee Pun'kin Jr., 1974 – 1979+

All-vinyl, sleep eyes, long straight rooted hair Brownie and Junior uniforms

11½"	$25.00	$75.00

Hallmark, 1979

All-cloth, Juliette Low, from 1916 handbook, wearing printed 1923 uniform

6½"	$25.00	$65.00

Jesco, ca. 1985, Katie

All-vinyl, sleep eyes, long straight rooted hair, look-alike Girl Scout, dressed as Brownie and Junior

9"	$25.00	$75.00

Madame Alexander, 1992

Vinyl, unofficial Girl Scout, sleep eyes

8"	$15.00	$60.00

Hard Plastic

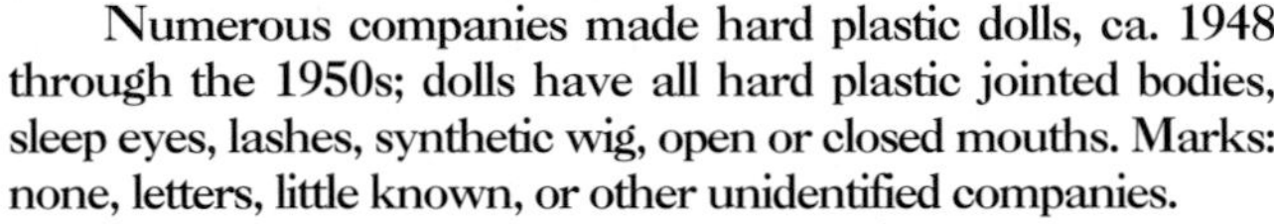

19" Eugenia Doll Co. Personality Playmate Barbara, made for Montgomery Ward, mohair wig, brown sleep eyes, closed mouth, jointed hard plastic body, white blouse, gray skirt with black ribbon trim, black bow in hair, white stockings, black shoes, added black purse, circa 1948, $200.00. Courtesy Pat Graff.

Numerous companies made hard plastic dolls, ca. 1948 through the 1950s; dolls have all hard plastic jointed bodies, sleep eyes, lashes, synthetic wig, open or closed mouths. Marks: none, letters, little known, or other unidentified companies.

14"	$65.00	$250.00
18"	$75.00	$300.00
24"	$85.00	$325.00

ADVANCE DOLL & TOY COMPANY

Ca. 1954+. Made heavy walking hard plastic dolls, metal rollers on molded shoes, named Winnie and Wanda. Later models had vinyl heads.

19"	$45.00	$150.00
24"	$75.00	$200.00

ARTISAN NOVELTY COMPANY,

Ca. 1950s, hard plastic, wide crotch

Raving Beauty

19"	$85.00	$275.00

DUCHESS DOLL CORPORATION

Ca. 1948 – 1950s. Made small hard plastic adult dolls, mohair wigs, painted or sleep eyes, jointed arms, stiff or jointed neck, painted molded shoes, about 7 – 7½" tall, costumes stapled on to body. Elaborate costumed, exceptional dolls may be more.

7"	$5.00	$15.00

FORTUNE DOLL COMPANY

Pam, hard plastic, sleep eyes, synthetic wig, closed mouth

8"	$20.00	$65.00

Furga, Italy

Child with sleep eyes, original simple outfit, more for elaborate dress

16½"	$125.00	$225.00

Imperial Crown Toy Col (Impco)

Ca. 1950s, made hard plastc or vinyl dolls, rooted hair, synthetic wigs

Vinyl

16"	$35.00	$85.00

Hard plastic

20"	$75.00	$200.00

Kendall Company

Miss Curity, ca. 1953

Hard plastic, jointed only at shoulders, blond wigs, blue sleep eyes, molded-on shoes, painted stockings, uniform sheet vinyl, *"Miss Curity"* marked in blue on hat

7½"	$20.00	$75.00

25" Paris Doll Company Rita, saran hair, blue sleep eyes, painted lashes below eyes, eyeshadow, open mouth with teeth, five-piece hard plastic body, long blue formal with net and lace trim, circa 1951 – 1953, $125.00. Courtesy Diane Vigne.

Roddy of England, ca. 1950 – 1960s

Made by D.G. Todd & Co. Ltd., Southport, England. Hard plastic walker, sleep or set eyes.

12½"	$25.00	$100.00

Walking Princess, tagged

11½"	$15.00	$50.00

Rosebud of England, ca. 1950s – 1960s

Started in Raunds, Northamptonshire, England, by T. Eric Smith shortly after WWII.

Miss Rosebud, hard plastic, various shades of blue sleep eyes, glued-on mohair wig, jointed at the neck and hips. Marked *"Miss Rosebud"* in script on her back and head and *"MADE IN ENGLAND"* on her upper back. More for rare examples or mint-in-box dolls.

7½"	$35.00	$85.00

Ross Products

Tina Cassini, designed by Oleg Cassini. Hard plastic, marked on back torso, *"TINA CASSINI";* clothes tagged *"Made in British Crown Colony of Hong Kong."*

12"	$50.00	$200.00

Hartland Industries

1950s+. Made action figures and horses; many figures from Warner Brothers television productions.

Television or Movie Characters, 8"

Annie Oakley, 1953 – 1956, by Gail Davis in *Annie Oakley*

8" $200.00* with horse

Bret Maverick, ca. 1958, by James Garner in *Maverick*

8" $510.00* with horse

Captain Chris Colt, 1957 – 1960, by Wade Preston in *Colt 45*

8"	$135.00	$250.00

Cheyenne Bodie, 1955 – 1963, by Clint Walker in *Cheyenne*

8" $315.00* with horse

Clint Bonner, 1957 – 1959, by John Payne in *The Restless Gun*

8" $135.00 $250.00

Colonel Ronald MacKenzie, ca. 1950s, by Richard Carlson, in *MacKenzies' Raiders*

8" $810.00* with horse

Dale Evans, ca. 1958, #802, with horse, Buttermilk in *The Roy Rogers Show*

8" $375.00* MIB

Gil Favor, ca. 1950s, in *Rawhide*

8" $685.00* with horse

Josh Randall, ca. 1950s, by Steve McQueen in *Wanted Dead or Alive*

8" $615.00* with horse

Major Seth Adams, 1957 – 1961, #824, by Ward Bond in *Wagon Train*

8" $200.00* with horse

Marshall Johnny McKay, *"Lawman"*

8" $520.00*

Paladin, 1957 – 1963, by Richard Boone in *Have Gun, Will Travel*

8" $610.00* with horse

Roy Rogers, ca. 1955, and Trigger in *The Roy Rogers Show*

8" $485.00* MIB with Trigger

Sgt. William Preston, ca. 1958, #804, by Richard Simmons in *Sgt. Preston of the Yukon*

8" $700.00* with horse

Wyatt Earp, 1955 – 1961 by Hugh O'Brien in *Life and Legend of Wyatt Earp*

8" $190.00* with horse

Other 8" Figures

8" $380.00*

Brave Eagle, #812, and his horse, White Cloud
Buffalo Bill, #819, Pony Express Rider
Chief Thunderbird, and horse, Northwind
Cochise, #815, with pinto horse from *Broken Arrow*
Jim Bowie, #817, with horse, Blaze
General George Custer, #814, and horse, Bugler
General George Washington, #815 and horse, Ajax
General Robert E. Lee, #808, and horse, Traveler
Lone Ranger, #801, and horse, Silver
Tonto, #805, and horse, Scout

All others 8" $125.00 $225.00

Baseball 8" Figures

Dick Groat with bat & hat	$1,000.00*
Duke Snider	$255.00*
Ernie Banks, #920	$430.00*
Hank Aaron, #912	$245.00*
Harvey Keunn	$325.00*
Willie Mays	$245.00*
Yogi Berra, boxed	$280.00*
Ted Williams	$135.00*

* at auction

Ca. 1960s+, Hassenfeld Bros. Toy manufacturer, also makes plastic or plastic and vinyl dolls and action figures.

First price for doll in played with condition, or missing some accessories; second price for mint doll.

Marks:
1964 – 1965
Marked on right lower back:
G.I. Joe ™//COPYRIGHT 1964//BY HASBRO ®//PATENT PENDING//MADE IN U.S.A.//GIJoe®
1967
Slight change in marking: COPYRIGHT 1964//BY HASBRO ®//PATENT PENDING// MADE IN U.S.A.// GIJoe®
This mark appears on all four armed service branches, excluding the black action figures.

Adam, 1971, Boy for "World of Love" Series, all-vinyl, molded painted brown hair, painted blue eyes, red knit shirt, blue denim jeans. *Mark: "Hasbro//U.S. Pat Pend//Made in//Hong Kong"*

9"	$5.00	$18.00

Aimee, 1972, rooted hair, amber sleep eyes, jointed vinyl body, long dress, sandals, earrings

18"	$25.00	$85.00

Dolly Darling, 1965

4½"	$15.00	$60.00

Flying Nun

5"	$135.00*	

Jem: See Jem section, following this category.

Leggie, 1972

10"	$7.50	$30.00
Black	$10.00	$40.00

Little Miss No Name, 1965

15"	$100.00	$250.00

Mamas and Papas, 1967

	$12.00	$45.00

Show Biz Babies, 1967

	$12.00	$50.00
Mama Cass	$15.00	$50.00

Monkees, set of four

4"	$28.00	$110.00

Real baby, 1984, J. Turner

18"	$35.00	$70.00

Storybook, 1967, 3"

Goldilocks	$12.50	$50.00
Prince Charming	$15.00	$60.00
Rumpelstiltskin	$15.00	$55.00
Sleeping Beauty	$12.50	$50.00
Snow White and Dwarfs		
	$20.00	$75.00

Sweet Cookie, 1972, vinyl, with cooking accessories

18"	$35.00	$125.00

That Kid, 1967

21"	$22.50	$95.00

World of Love Dolls, 1971

White 9"	$5.00	$18.00
Black 9"	$5.00	$20.00

16" vinyl Little Miss No Name with hard plastic body, oversized brown glassene eyes with molded tear, pouty mouth, all original, circa 1965 $100.00. Courtesy Kathy & Roy Smith.

* at auction

11½" hard plastic G.I. Joe mint in box with dogtags, brochure, circa 1964 – 1979, $300.00. *Courtesy Jeff Jones.*

G.I. Joe

G.I. Joe Action Figures, 1964

Hard plastic head with facial scar, painted hair and no beard. First price indicates doll lacking accessories or nude; second price indicates mint doll in package. Add more for pristine package.

G.I. Joe Action Soldier, flocked hair, Army fatigues, brown jump boots, green plastic cap, training manual, metal dog tag, two sheets of stickers

11½" $120.00 $450.00

Painted hair, red

$140.00 $300.00

Black, painted hair

$325.00 $1,300.00

Green Beret

Teal green fatigue jacket, four pockets, pants, Green Beret cap with red unit flashing, M-16 rifle, 45 automatic pistol with holster, tall brown boots, four grenades, camouflage scarf, and field communication set

11" $275.00 $1,500.00

G.I. Joe Action Marine

Camouflage shirt, pants, brown boots, green plastic cap, metal dog tag, insignia stickers, and training manual

11" $80.00 $300.00

G.I. Joe Action Sailor

Blue chambray work shirt, blue denim work pants, black boots, white plastic sailor cap, dog tag, rank insignia stickers

$75.00 $250.00

G.I. Joe Action Pilot

Orange flight suit, black boots, dog tag, stickers, blue cap, training manual

$125.00 $300.00

Dolls only $50.00 $95.00

G.I. Joe Action Soldier of the World, 1966

Figures in this set may have any hair and eye color combination, no scar on face, hard plastic heads

Australian Jungle Fighter	$255.00	$1,050.00
British Commando, boxed	$300.00	$1,150.00
French Resistance Fighter	$150.00	$1,200.00
German Storm Trooper	$400.00	$1,200.00
Japanese Imperial Soldier	$175.00	$1,400.00
Russian Infantryman		
Boxed	$350.00	$1,100.00
Doll, no box	$75.00	$250.00

Talking G.I. Joe, 1967 – 1969

Talking mechanism added, excluding black figure, semi-hard vinyl head
Marks: "G.I. Joe®//Copyright 1964//By Hasbro®//Pat. No. 3,277,602//Made in U.S.A.

Talking G.I. Joe Action Soldier

Green fatigues, dog tag, brown boots, insignia, stripes, green plastic fatigue cap, comic book, insert with examples of figure's speech

	$150.00	$300.00

Talking G.I. Joe Action Sailor

Denim pants, chambray sailor shirt, dog tag, black boots, white sailor cap, insignia stickers, Navy training manual, illustrated talking comic book, insert examples of figure's speech

	$200.00	$1,000.00

Talking G.I. Joe Action Marine

Camouflage fatigues, metal dog tag, Marine training manual, insignia sheets, brown boots, green plastic cap, comic, and insert

	$60.00	$800.00

Talking G.I. Joe Action Pilot

Blue flight suit, black boots, dog tag, Air Force insignia, blue cap, training manual, comic book, insert

	$150.00	$1,000.00

G.I. Joe Action Nurse, 1967

Vinyl head, blond rooted hair, jointed hard plastic body, nurse's uniform, cap, red cross armband, white shoes, medical bag, stethoscope, plasma bottle, two crutches, bandages, splints. *Marks: "Patent Pending®//1967 Hasbro//Made in Hong Kong"*

Boxed	$1,200.00	$1,850.00
Dressed	$200.00	$1,000.00
Nude	$40.00	$150.00

G.I. Joe, Man of Action, 1970 – 1975

Flocked hair, scar on face, dressed in fatigues with Adventure Team emblem on shirt, plastic cap. *Marks: "G.I. Joe®//Copyright 1964//By Hasbro®// Pat. No. 3, 277, 602//Made in U.S. A."*

	$15.00	$75.00
Talking	$45.00	$175.00

G.I. Joe, Adventure Team

Marks: "©1975 Hasbro ®//Pat. Pend. Pawt. R.I." Flocked hair and beard, six team members:

Air Adventurer, orange flight suit

	$75.00	$285.00

Astronaut, talking, white flight suit, molded scar, dog tag pull string

	$115.00	$450.00

Land Adventurer, black, tan fatigues, beard, flocked hair, scar

	$90.00	$350.00

Land Adventurer, talking, camouflage fatigues

	$115.00	$450.00

Sea Adventurer, light blue shirt, navy pants

	$75.00	$300.00

Talking Adventure Team Commander, flocked hair, beard, green jacket, and pants

	$115.00	$450.00

G.I. Joe Land Adventurer, flocked hair, beard, camouflage shirt, green pants

	$70.00	$150.00

G. I. Joe Negro Adventurer, flocked hair

	$175.00	$750.00

G. I. Joe, "Mike Powers, Atomic Man"

	$25.00	$55.00

G.I. Joe Eagle Eye Man of Action

	$40.00	$125.00

G.I. Joe Secret Agent, unusual face, mustache

	$115.00	$450.00

Sea Adventurer w/King Fu Grip

	$80.00	$145.00

Bulletman, muscle body, silver arms, hands, helmet, red boots

	$55.00	$125.00

Others

G.I. Joe Air Force Academy, Annapolis, or West Point Cadet

11"	$125.00	$400.00

G.I. Joe Frogman, Underwater Demolition Set

11"		$300.00*

G.I. Joe Secret Service Agent, limited edition of 200

11"		$275.00*

Accessory Sets, mint, no doll included

Adventures of G.I. Joe

Adventure of the Perilous Rescue	$250.00
Eight Ropes of Danger Adventure	$200.00
Fantastic Free Fall Adventure	$275.00
Hidden Missile Discovery Adventure	$150.00
Mouth of Doom Adventure	$150.00
Adventure of the Shark's Surprise	$200.00

Accessory Packs or Boxed Uniforms and Accessories

Air Force, Annapolis, West Point Cadet	$200.00
Action Sailor	$350.00
Astronaut	$250.00
Crash Crew Fire Fighter	$275.00
Deep Freeze with Sled	$250.00
Deep Sea Diver	$250.00
Frogman Demolition Set	$375.00
Fighter Pilot, no package	$285.00*
Green Beret	$450.00
Landing Signal Officer	$250.00
Marine Jungle Fighter	$850.00
Marine Mine Detector	$275.00
Military Police	$325.00
Pilot Scramble Set	$275.00
Rescue Diver	$350.00
Secret Agent	$150.00
Shore Patrol	$300.00
Ski Patrol	$350.00

G.I. Joe Vehicles and Other Accessories, mint in package

Amphibious Duck, green plastic, Irwin	$600.00
Armored Car, green plastic, one figure	$150.00

* at auction

Crash Crew Fire Truck, blue	$1,400.00
Desert Patrol Attack Jeep, tan, one figure	$1,400.00
Footlocker, with accessories	$400.00+
Iron Knight Tank, green plastic	$1,400.00
Jet Aeroplane, dark blue plastic	$550.00
Jet Helicopter, green, yellow blades	$350.00
Motorcycle and Side Car, by Irwin	$225.00
Personnel Carrier and Mine Sweeper	$700.00
Sea Sled and Frogman	$400.00
Space Capsule and Suit, gray plastic	$425.00
Staff Car, four figures, green plastic, Irwin	$900.00

Jem, 1986 – 1987

Jem dolls were patterned after characters in the animated television Jem series, ca. 1985 – 1988, and include a line of 27 dolls. All-vinyl fashion type with realistically proportioned body, jointed elbows, wrists, and knees, swivel waist, rooted hair, painted eyes, open or closed mouth and hole in bottom of each foot.

Marks:
On head:
"HASBRO, INC."
On back:
"COPYRIGHT 1985 (or 1986 or 1987) HASBRO, INC." followed by either "CHINA" or "MADE IN HONG KONG."
Not all are marked on head.

12" vinyl Rio maroon pants, lavender jacket, yellow and green shirt is Truly Outrageous packaged with a music cassette, stock #4015, mint-in-box, circa 1985, $45.00. Courtesy Cornelia Ford.

All boxes say *"Jem"* and *"Truly Outrageous!"* Most came with cassette tape of music from Jem cartoon, plastic doll stand, poster, and hair pick. All 12½" tall, except Starlight Girls, 11".

First price is for excellent to near mint doll wearing complete original outfit; anything less is of lower value. Second price is for never removed from box doll (NRFB) which includes an excellent quality box. For an "Audition Contest" labeled box, add $10.00. A rule of thumb to calculate loose dolls which have been dressed in another outfit is the price of the mint/complete outfit plus the price of mint loose nude doll.

Jem and Rio	**Stock No.**	**Mint**	**NRFB**
Jem/Jerrica 1st issue	4000	$30.00	$40.00
Jem/Jerrica, star earrings	4000	$35.00	$45.00
Glitter 'n Gold Jem	4001	$60.00	$125.00
Rock 'n Curl Jem	4002	$20.00	$30.00
Flash 'n Sizzle Jem	4003	$30.00	$40.00
Rio, 1st issue	4015	$25.00	$35.00
Glitter 'n Gold Rio	4016	$25.00	$35.00
Glitter 'n Gold Rio, pale vinyl	4016	$125.00	$150.00
Holograms			
Synergy	4020	$45.00	$60.00
Aja, 1st issue	4201/4005	$45.00	$60.00
Aja, 2nd issue	4201/4005	$90.00	$125.00

12" vinyl Pizzazz has yellow hair, painted features, black zebra stripe top with chartreuse tie, a Truly Outrageous costume, music cassette and guitar, mint-in-box, stock #4206, circa 1985, $50.00. *Courtesy Cornelia Ford.*

Kimber, 1st issue	4202/4005	$40.00	$50.00
Kimber, 2nd issue	4202/4005	$75.00	$90.00
Shana, 1st issue	4203/4005	$125.00	$175.00
Shana, 2nd issue	4203/4005	$225.00	$300.00
Danse	4208	$45.00	$60.00
Video	4209	$25.00	$35.00
Raya	4210	$150.00	$175.00
Starlight Girls, 11", no wrist or elbow joints			
Ashley	4211/4025	$40.00	$55.00
Krissie	4212/4025	$35.00	$65.00
Banee	4213/4025	$25.00	$40.00
Misfits			
Pizzazz, 1st issue	4204/4010	$50.00	$65.00
Pizzazz, 2nd issue	4204/4010	$55.00	$75.00
Stormer, 1st issue	4205/4010	$50.00	$65.00
Stormer, 2nd issue	4205/4010	$60.00	$75.00
Roxy, 1st issue	4206/4010	$50.00	$65.00
Roxy, 2nd issue	4206/4010	$50.00	$65.00
Clash	4207/4010	$25.00	$35.00
Jetta	4214	$40.00	$55.00
Accesories			
Glitter 'n Gold Roadster		$150.00	$250.00
Rock 'n Roadster		$65.00	$90.00
KJEM Guitar		$25.00	$40.00
New Wave Waterbed		$35.00	$50.00
Backstager		$25.00	$35.00
Star Stage		$30.00	$45.00
MTV jacket (promo)		$90.00	$125.00

Jem Fashions

Prices reflect NRFB (never removed from box or card), with excellent packaging. Damaged boxes or mint and complete, no packaging prices are approximately 25 percent less.

On Stage Fashions, 1st year, "artwork" on card

Award Night	4216/4040	$30.00
Music is Magic	4217/4040	$30.00
Dancin' the Night Away	4218/4040	$25.00
Permanent Wave	4219/4040	$25.00
Only the Beginning	4220/4040	$20.00
Command Performance	4221/4040	$35.00
Twilight in Paris	4222/4040	$25.00
Encore	4223/4040	$35.00

On Stage Fashions, 2nd year, "photo" on card		
Award Night	4216/4040	$35.00
Music is Magic	4217/4040	$35.00
Permanent Wave	4219/4040	$30.00
Encore	4223/4040	$30.00
Friend or Stranger	4224/4040	$50.00
Come On In	4225/4040	$55.00
There's Melody Playing	4226/4040	$280.00
How You Play Game	4227/4040	$30.00
Love's Not Easy	4228/4040	$100.00
Set Your Sails	4229/4040	$35.00
Flip Side Fashions, 1st year "artwork" on box		
Up & Rockin'	4232/4045	$20.00
Rock Country	4233/4045	$35.00
Gettin' Down to Business	4234/4045	$40.00
Let's Rock this Town	4235/4045	$30.00
Music in the Air	4236/4045	$35.00
Like a Dream	4237/4045	$30.00
Sophisticated Lady	4238/4045	$30.00
City Lights	3129/4045	$20.00
Flip Side Fashions, 2nd year "photo" on box		
Gettin' Down to Business	4234/4045	$45.00
Let's Rock This Town	4235/4045	$35.00
Music in the Air	4236/4045	$40.00
Sophisticated Lady	4238/4045	$35.00
Putting it All Together	4240/4045	$75.00
Running Like the Wind	4241/4045	$125.00
We Can Change It	4242/4045	$125.00
Broadway Magic	4243/4045	$200.00
She Makes an Impression	4244/4045	$90.00
Lightnin' Strikes	4245/4045	$45.00
Smashin' Fashions, 1st year "artwork" on card (includes Rio fashions)		
Rappin'	4248/4051	$40.00
On the Road with Jem	4249/4051	$25.00
Truly Outrageous	4250/4051	$125.00
Makin' Mischief	4251/4050	$30.00
Let the Music Play	4252/4050	$30.00
Outta My Way	4253/4050	$15.00
Just Misbehavin'	4254/4050	$65.00
Winning is Everything	4255/4050	$15.00
Smashin' Fashions, 2nd year, "photo" on card (Misfits fashions only)		
Let the Music Play	4252/4050	$35.00
Just Misbehavin'	4254/4050	$75.00
Gimme, Gimme, Gimme	4256/4050	$25.00
You Can't Catch Me	4257/4050	$35.00
We're Off & Running	4258/4050	$35.00
You Gotta' Be Fast	4259/4050	$45.00
There Ain't Nobody Better	4260/4050	$50.00
Designing Woman	4261/4050	$35.00

Rio Fashion, 2nd year only, "photo" on card

Rappin'	4248/4051	$45.00
On the Road with Jem	4249/4051	$30.00
Truly Outrageous	4250/4051	$150.00
Time is Running Out	4271/4051	$25.00
Share a Little Bit	4272/4051	$125.00
Congratulations	4273/4051	$30.00
Universal Appeal	4274/4051	$25.00
It Takes a Lot	4275/4051	$25.00
It all Depends on Mood	4276/4051	$15.00

Glitter 'n Gold Fashions, 2nd year only, "photo" on boxes

Fire and Ice	4281/4055	$55.00
Purple Haze	4282/4055	$30.00
Midnight Magic	4283/4055	$30.00
Gold Rush	4284/4055	$60.00
Moroccan Magic	4285/4055	$75.00
Golden Days/Diamond Nights	4286/4055	$50.00

Music is Magic Fashion, 2nd year only, "photo" on boxes

Rock'n Roses	4296/4060	$35.00
Splashes of Sound	4297/4060	$25.00
24 Carat Sound	4298/4060	$35.00
Star Struck Guitar	4299/4060	$85.00
Electric Chords	4300/4060	$25.00
Rhythm & Flash	4301/4060	$35.00

Horsman, E.I.

1865 – 1980+, New York City. Founded by Edward Imeson Horsman, distributed, assembled, and made dolls, merged with Aetna Doll and Toy Co., and in 1909 obtained first copyright for a complete doll with his Billiken. Later made hard plastic and vinyl dolls.

Marks: "E.I. H.//CO." and "CAN'T BREAK 'EM"

Composition

First price is for played-with doll, or missing some clothing or accessories; second price is for doll in excellent condition, add more for exceptional doll.

Baby, 1930s – 1940s

15"	$50.00	$125.00

Baby Bumps, 1910 – 1917

Composition head, cloth cork stuffed body, blue and white cloth label on romper, copy of K*R #100 Baby mold

11"	$65.00	$250.00
Black	$75.00	$300.00

Baby Butterfly, ca. 1913

Oriental baby, composition head, hands, painted features

13"	$225.00	$650.00

Billiken, 1909

Composition head, molded hair, slanted eyes, smiling closed mouth, on stuffed mohair or velvet body. *Marks: Cloth label on body. "Billiken" on right foot.*

12"	$100.00	$400.00

Betty Ann, rubber arms and legs

19"	$100.00	$350.00

Betty Jane, all-composition

25"	$100.00	$300.00

Betty Jo, all-composition

16"	$65.00	$225.00

Body Twist, 1930, all-composition, with jointed waist

11"	$65.00	$225.00

Bright Star, 1937 – 1946, all-composition

19"	$75.00	$300.00

Campbell Kids, 1910+

By Helen Trowbridge, based on Grace Drayton's drawings, composition head, painted molded hair, side-glancing painted eyes, closed smiling mouth, composition arms, cloth body and feet. *Mark: "EIH a 1910;" cloth label on sleeve, "The Campbell Kids// Trademark by //Joseph Campbell// Mfg. by E.I. Horsman Co."*

14"	$85.00	$325.00+

1930 – 1940s, all-composition

13"	$100.00	$350.00

Child, all-composition

14"	$65.00	$185.00

Cotton Joe, black

13"	$100.00	$400.00

Dimples, 1927 – 1930+

Composition head, arms, cloth body, bent-leg body, or bent-limb baby body, molded dimples, open mouth, sleep or painted eyes, *marked "E.I. H."*

16 – 18"	$70.00	$250.00
20 – 22"	$90.00	$350.00

Laughing Dimples, open/closed mouth with painted teeth

22"	$710.00*	

Dimples, toddler body

20"	$100.00	$385.00
24"	$150.00	$425.00

Dolly Rosebud, 1926 – 1930

Mama doll, composition head, limbs, dimples, sleep eyes

18"	$50.00	$175.00

Ella Cinders, 1928 – 1929

Based on a cartoon character, composition head, black painted hair or wig, round painted eyes, freckles under eyes, open/closed mouth, cloth body. Also came as all-cloth. *Mark: "1925//MNS"*

14"	$100.00	$400.00
18"	$175.00	$650.00

Gene Carr Kids, 1915 – 1916

Composition head, molded, painted hair, painted eyes, open/closed smiling mouth with teeth, big ears,

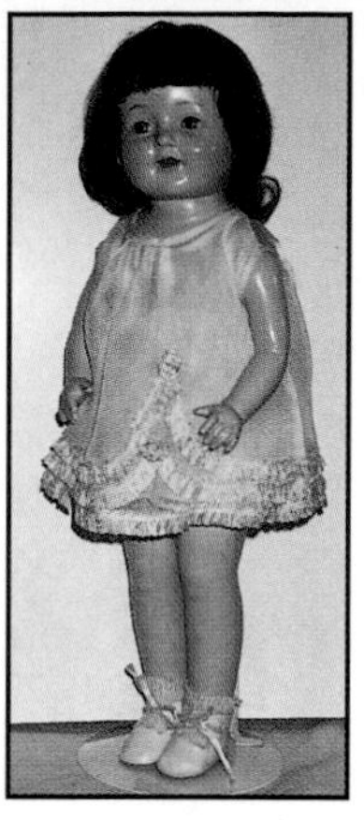

20" composition Rosebud, marked "Rosebud" on back of socket head, human hair wig, sleep eyes, real lashes, painted lashes, open mouth with three upper teeth, cloth torso, composition shoulder plate, arms, and legs, original ruffled white organdy dress, underclothing, socks, and leatherette shoes, circa 1926 – 1930, $300.00. Courtesy Pat Graff.

19" composition Gold Medal Baby, tagged "GOLD//MEDAL//Baby//HORSMAN//SUPER QUALITY," blond wig, blue sleep eyes, real lashes, painted lower lashes, eyeshadow, open mouth with teeth, tilting turning head, jointed toddler body, blue dotted Swiss dress, white coat and matching hat, white socks and white baby shoes, with Horsman box, circa 1939 – 1940, $300.00. Courtesy Sandra Tripp.

19" composition Nan, unmarked, molded painted hair, sleep eyes, closed mouth, dimple in chin, jointed composition body, original floral print dress with matching bonnet, underwear, replaced white socks and black one-strap shoes, circa 1931, $275.00. Courtesy Pat Graff.

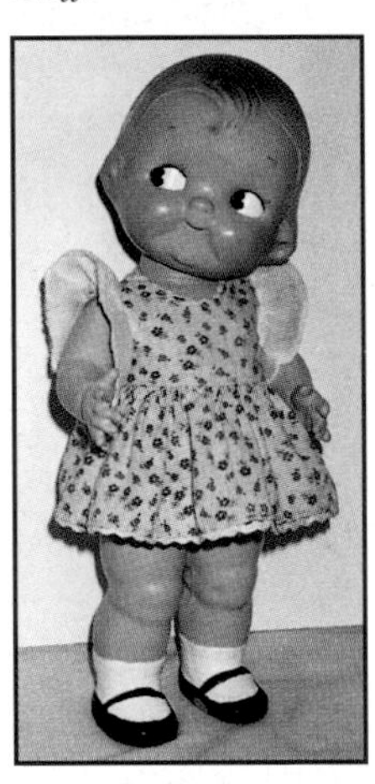

12" composition Campbell Kid, unmarked, character head, molded painted hair, painted side-glancing eyes, closed smiling mouth, five-piece composition body with molded painted white socks and black one-strap shoes, original flower print dress, circa 1930s – 1940s, $300.00. Courtesy Pat Graff.

cloth body, composition hands, original outfit. *Marks: Cloth tag reads: "MADE GENE CARR KIDS U.S.A.//FROM NEW YORK WORLD'S //LADY BOUNTIFUL COMIC SERIES//By E.I. HORSMAN CO. NY. 13½""*

Blink	$90.00	$360.00
Carnival Kids	$75.00	$300.00
Lizzie	$90.00	$360.00
Mike	$90.00	$360.00
Skinney	$90.00	$360.00
Snowball, black	$135.00	$550.00
Polly Pru, 13"	$85.00	$325.00

Gold Medal doll, 1930s, composition head and limbs, upper and lower teeth, cloth body

21"	$50.00	$200.00

HEbee-SHEbees, 1925 – 1927

Based on drawings by Charles Twelvetrees, all-bisque or all-composition, painted features, molded undershirt and booties or various costumes. *Marks: on all-bisque, "Germany," and paper sticker on tummy, "COPYRIGHT BY//HEbee SHEbe//TRADEMARK//CHAS. TWELVETREES"*

Composition

10½"	$125.00	$450.00

Jackie Coogan, "The Kid," 1921 – 1922

Composition head, hands, molded hair, painted eyes, cloth body, turtleneck sweater, long gray pants, checked cap. *Button reads: "HORSMAN DOLL// JACKIE// COOGAN// KID// PATENTED"*

13½"	$135.00	$465.00+
15½"	$160.00	$550.00+

Jeanie Horsman, 1937

Composition head and limbs, painted molded brown hair, sleep eyes, cloth body, *mark: "Jeanie© Horsman"*

14"	$65.00	$225.00

Jo Jo, 1937

All-composition, blue sleep eyes, wigged, over molded hair, toddler body. *Mark: "HORSMAN JO JO//©1937"*

13"	$75.00	$250.00

Mama Dolls, 1920+

Composition head, arms, and lower legs, cloth body with crier and stitched hip joints so lower legs will swing, painted or sleep eyes, mohair or molded hair

14 – 15"	$50.00	$185.00
19 – 21"	$75.00	$285.00
Rosebud	$75.00	$275.00

Peggy Ann $85.00 $350.00

Naughty Sue, 1937, composition head, jointed body

16"	$100.00	$400.00

Peterkin, 1914 – 1930+

Cloth or composition body, character face, molded hair, painted or sleep eyes, closed smiling mouth, rectangular tag with name *"Peterkin"*

11"	$75.00	$300.00
13½"	$85.00	$350.00

Roberta, 1937, all-composition

16"	$115.00	$450.00

Sweetums, cloth body, drink and wet, box, accessories

15"	$75.00	$225.00

Tynie Baby, ca. 1924 – 1929

Bisque or composition head, sleep or painted eyes, cloth body, some all-bisque

Marks: "a 1924//E.I. HORSMAN//CO. INC." or "E.I.H. Co. 1924" on composition or "a 1924 by//E I Horsman Co. Inc//Germany// 37" incised on bisque head

All-bisque, with wardrobe, cradle

6"	$1,785.00*	
9"	$1,800.00	$2,500.00

Bisque, head circumference

9"	$150.00	$600.00
12"	$200.00	$800.00

Composition

15"	$75.00	$300.00

16" hard plastic Cindy, marked "Horsman" on neck, mohair wig, sleep eyes, open mouth with teeth, jointed hard plastic body, original peach dress, new hair ribbon, white socks, tie shoes, circa 1950s, $175.00+. Courtesy Pat Graff.

Hard Plastic and Vinyl

First price is for doll in excellent condition, but with flaws; second price is for mint-in-box doll. Add more for accessories or wardrobe.

Angelove, 1974, plastic/vinyl made for Hallmark

12"	$10.00	$25.00

Answer Doll, 1966, button in back moves head

10"	$8.00	$15.00

Baby First Tooth, 1966

Vinyl head, limbs, cloth body, open/closed mouth with tongue and one tooth, molded tears on cheeks, rooted blond hair, painted blue eyes. *Mark: "©Horsman Dolls Inc. //10141"*

16"	$20.00	$40.00

Baby Tweaks, ca. 1967

Vinyl head, cloth body, inset eyes, rooted saran hair. *Mark: "54//HORSMAN DOLLS INC.//Copyright 1967/67191" on head*

20"	$15.00	$30.00

Ballerina, 1957, vinyl, one-piece body and legs, jointed elbows

18"	$15.00	$50.00

Betty, 1951, all-vinyl, one-piece body and limbs

14"	$15.00	$60.00

17" vinyl Poor Pitiful Pearl, blue sleep eyes, rosy cheeks, red scarf, flowered dress, black stockings, mint-in-box, circa 1959 – 1963, $195.00. Courtesy Betty Strong.

* at auction

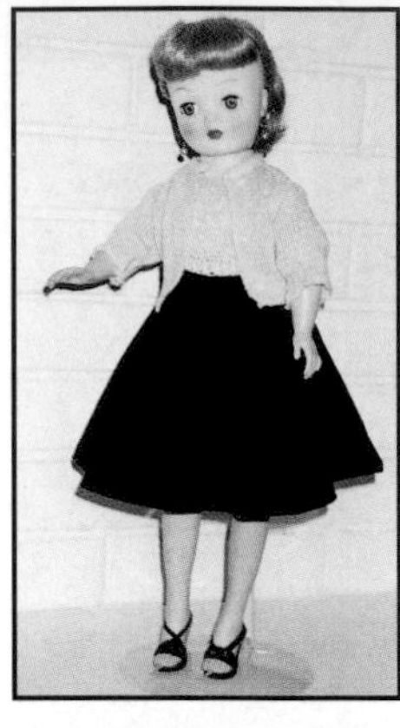

16" hard vinyl Cindy, the Couturier Doll, marked "Horsman" on neck, blond wig, sleep eyes, closed mouth, pierced ears, jointed lady body with swivel waist, peach sweater set, black skirt, black high-heel sandals, all original, circa 1959, $100.00. Courtesy Pat Graff.

Vinyl head, hard plastic body

16"	$15.00	$25.00

Betty Ann, vinyl head, hard plastic body

19"	$15.00	$60.00

Betty Jane, vinyl head, hard plastic body

25"	$20.00	$75.00

Betty Jo, vinyl head, hard plastic body

16"	$15.00	$30.00

Bright Star, ca. 1952+, all hard plastic

15"	$125.00	$450.00

Bye-Lo Baby, 1972

Reissue, molded vinyl head, limbs, cloth body, white nylon organdy bonnet dress. *Mark: "3 (in square)//HORSMAN DOLLS INC.//©1972"*

14"	$15.00	$55.00

1980 – 1990s

14"	$8.00	$25.00

Celeste, portrait doll, in frame, eyes painted to side

12"	$10.00	$35.00

Christopher Robin

11"	$10.00	$35.00

Cinderella, 1965, vinyl head, hard plastic body, painted eyes to side

11½"	$8.00	$30.00

Cindy, 1950s, all hard plastic, *"170"*

15"	$50.00	$175.00+
17"	$65.00	$200.00+

1953, early vinyl

18"	$20.00	$60.00

1959, lady-type with jointed waist

19"	$25.00	$95.00

Walker

16"	$60.00	$225.00

Cindy Kay, 1950s+, all-vinyl child with long legs

15"	$25.00	$80.00
20"	$35.00	$125.00
27"	$60.00	$225.00

Crawling Baby, 1967, vinyl, rooted hair

14"	$8.00	$25.00

Disney Exclusives, 1981

Cinderella, Snow White, Mary Poppins, Alice in Wonderland

8"	$10.00	$40.00

Elizabeth Taylor, 1976

11½"	$15.00	$45.00

Floppy, 1958, vinyl head, foam body and legs

18"	$8.00	$25.00

Flying Nun, 1965, TV character portrayed by Sally Field

12"	$50.00	$125.00

Gold Medal Doll, 1953, vinyl, molded hair

26"	$45.00	$185.00

1954, vinyl, boy

15"	$20.00	$75.00

Hansel & Gretel, 1963

Vinyl head, hard plastic body, rooted synthetic hair, closed mouth, sleep eyes *Marks: "MADE IN USA" on body, on tag, "HORSMAN, Michael Meyerberg, Inc.," "Reproduction of the famous Kinemins in Michael Myerberg's marvelous Technicolor production of Hansel and Gretel"*

15"	$50.00	$200.00

Jackie, 1961

Vinyl doll, rooted hair, blue sleep eyes, long lashes, closed mouth, high-heeled feet, small waist, nicely dressed. Designed by Irene Szor who says this doll named Jackie was not meant to portray Jackie Kennedy. *Mark: "HORSMAN//19a61//BC 18"*

25"	$35.00	$125.00

Lullabye Baby, 1967 – 1968, vinyl bent-leg body, rooted hair, inset station blue eyes, drink and wet feature, musical mechanism, Sears 1968 catalog, came on suedette pillow, in terry-cloth p.j.s. *Mark: "2580//B144 8 //HORSMAN DOLLS INC//19©67"*

12"	$4.00	$15.00

Mary Poppins, 1965

12"	$9.00	$35.00
16"	$20.00	$70.00
26", '66	$50.00	$200.00
36"	$90.00	$350.00

In box with Michael and Jane, 1966

12" and 8"	$150.00

Police Woman, ca. 1976, vinyl, plastic fully articulated body, rooted hair

9"	$10.00	$35.00

Poor Pitiful Pearl, 1963

From cartoon by William Steig. *Marked on neck*: "*Horsman 1963*."

11"	$40.00	$145.00
17"	$45.00	$175.00*

Tynie Baby, ca. 1950s, vinyl, boxed

15"	$30.00	$110.00

Mary Hoyer Doll Mfg. Co.

1937+, Reading, PA. Designed by Bernard Lipfert, all-composition, later hard plastic, then vinyl, swivel neck, jointed body, mohair or human hair wig, sleep eyes, closed mouth, original clothes, or knitted from Mary Hoyer patterns.

Marks:
"THE MARY HOYER DOLL" or "ORIGINAL MARY HOYER DOLL"

Composition, less for painted eyes

14"	$115.00	$450.00

Hard Plastic

14"	$125.00	$525.00

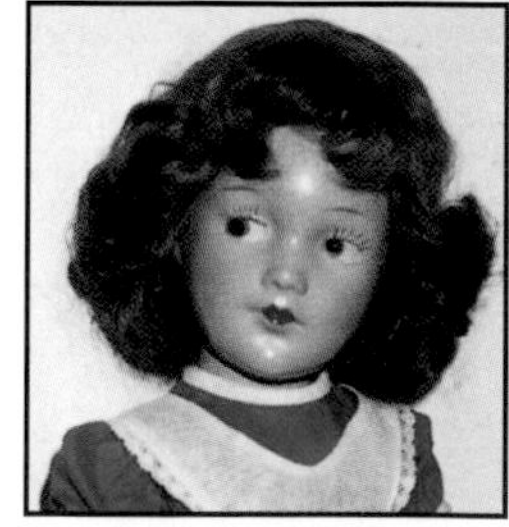

14" composition girl, unmarked, auburn wig, painted blue side-glancing eyes, painted lashes, closed mouth, jointed composition body, green dress with white pinafore, circa 1937, $200.00. Courtesy Pat Graff.

Mary Hoyer Doll Mfg. Co.

14" hard plastic, marked "Original Mary//Hoyer Doll" in circle, red mohair wig, blue sleep eyes, eyeshadow, closed mouth, yellow crocheted outfit, matching hat, white socks/shoes, circa mid 1940s to 1950, $300.00. *Courtesy Barbara Hull.*

Gigi, circa 1950, with round Mary Hoyer mark found on 14" dolls, only 2,000 made by the Frisch Doll Company

18"	$1,000.00	$2,000.00

Vinyl, circa 1957+

Vicky, all-vinyl, high-heeled doll, body bends at waist, rooted saran hair, two larger sizes 12" and 14" were discontinued

10½"	$25.00	$100.00

Margie, circa 1958, toddler, rooted hair, made by Unique Doll Co.

10"	$15.00	$75.00

Cathy, circa 1961, infant, made by Unique Doll Co.

10"	$10.00	$25.00

Janie, circa 1962, baby

8"	$10.00	$25.00

Ideal Novelty and Toy Co.

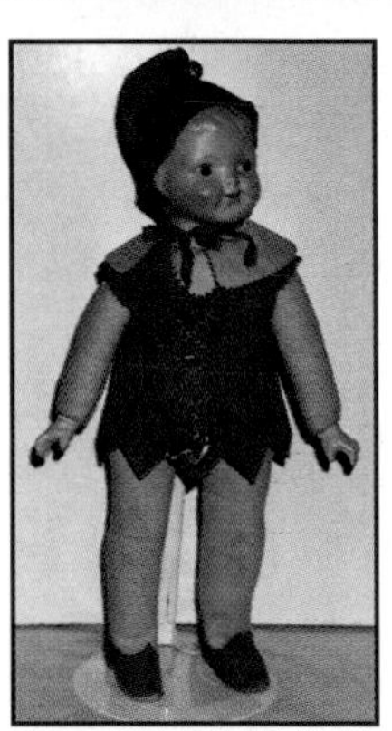

17" composition Peter Pan, marked "Ideal" in diamond on neck, molded painted hair, painted eyes, closed mouth, composition hands, cloth body and feet, red and yellow felt suit, felt hat with bell, vest, hat, collar, and shoes are removable, all original, circa 1928, $150.00. *Courtesy Pat Graff.*

1906 – 1980+, Brooklyn, NY. Produced their own composition dolls in early years.

Marks:
Various including "IDEAL" (in a diamond), "US of A: IDEAL NOVELTY," and "TOY CO. BROOKLYN, NEW YORK," and others.

Cloth

Dennis the Menace, 1976

All-cloth, printed doll, comic strip character by Hank Ketcham, blond hair, freckles, wearing overalls, striped shirt

7"	$5.00	$15.00
14"	$7.50	$20.00

Peanuts Gang, 1976 – 1978

All-cloth, stuffed printed dolls from Peanuts cartoon strip by Charles Schulz, Charlie Brown, Lucy, Linus, Peppermint Patty, and Snoopy

7"	$5.00	$20.00
14"	$8.00	$25.00

Snow White, 1938

Cloth body, mask face, painted eyes, black human hair wig, variation of red and white dress with small cape, Snow White and Seven Dwarfs printed on it. No other marks.

16"	$150.00	$550.00

Strawman, 1939

All-cloth, scarecrow character portrayed by Ray Bolger in *Wizard of Oz* movie. Yarn hair, all original, wearing dark jacket and hat, tan pants, round paper hang tag

17"	$250.00	$1,000.00
21"	$400.00	$1,500.00

Composition

Composition Baby Doll, 1913+

Composition head, molded hair or wigged, painted or sleep eyes, cloth or composition body. May have Ideal diamond mark or hang tag. Original clothes.

12"	$25.00	$100.00+
16"	$40.00	$150.00+
20"	$50.00	$200.00+
24"	$65.00	$250.00+

Composition Child or Toddler, 1915+

Composition head, molded hair, or wigged, painted or sleep eyes, cloth or composition body. May have Ideal diamond mark or hang tag. Original clothes.

13"	$35.00	$125.00+
15"	$40.00	$150.00+
18"	$50.00	$200.00+

11" composition Snow White, on marked Shirley Temple body, black mohair wig, flirty glass eyes, open mouth, four teeth, dimple in chin, jointed composition body, red velvet bodice, rayon taffeta skirt pictures seven dwarfs, all original, circa 1938, $500.00. Courtesy Pat Graff.

Composition Mama Doll, 1921+

Composition head and arms, molded hair or wigged, painted or sleep eyes, cloth body with crier and stitched swing leg, lower part composition

16"	$50.00	$250.00+
20"	$75.00	$300.00+
24"	$85.00	$350.00+

Buster Brown, 1929

Composition head, hands, legs, cloth body, tin eyes, red outfit. *Mark: "IDEAL" (in a diamond)*

16"	$75.00	$300.00

Charlie McCarthy, 1938 – 1939

Hand puppet, composition head, felt hands, molded hat, molded features, wire monocle, cloth body, painted tuxedo

Mark: "Edgar Bergen's//©CHARLIE MCCARTHY//MADE IN U.S.A."

8"	$15.00	$60.00

Cinderella, 1938 – 1939

All-composition, brown, blond, or red human hair wig, flirty brown sleep eyes, open mouth, six teeth, same head mold as Ginger, Snow White, Mary Jane with dimple in chin, some wore formal evening gowns of organdy and taffeta, velvet cape, had rhinestone tiara, silver snap shoes. Sears catalog version has Celanese rayon gown. *Marks: none on head; "SHIRLEY TEMPLE//13" on body*

13"	$85.00	$325.00
16"	$90.00	$350.00
20"	$95.00	$375.00
22"	$100.00	$400.00
25"	$105.00	$425.00
27"	$110.00	$450.00

Cracker Jack Boy, 1917

Composition head, gauntlet hands, cloth body, molded boots, molded hair, wears blue or white sailor suit, cap, carries package of Cracker Jacks

14"	$100.00	$375.00

20" composition Deanna Durbin, marked "Deanna Durbin//Ideal Doll" on head, "Ideal Doll" on back, "Genuine//Deanna Durbin//Doll//Ideal Novelty & Toy Co.//A Universal Star//Made in U.S.A." on jacket tag, human hair wig, sleep eyes, gray eyeshadow, open mouth, six upper teeth, five-piece composition body, original blue velvet skirt, white blouse, plaid jacket, matching hat, original box with Deanna Durbin label, left hand missing three fingers, circa 1938 – 1941, $400.00. Courtesy McMasters Doll Auctions.

Deanna Durbin, 1938 – 1941

All-composition, fully jointed, dark brown human hair wig, brown sleep eyes, open mouth, six teeth, felt tongue, original clothes, pin, reads: *"DEANNA DURBIN//A UNIVERSAL STAR."* More for fancy outfits. *Marks: "DEANNA DURBIN//IDEAL DOLL" on head; "IDEAL DOLL//21" on body*

15"	$125.00	$550.00
18"	$190.00	$800.00
21"	$200.00	$900.00
25"	$225.00	$1,100.00

Flexy, 1938 – 1942

Composition head, gauntlet hands, wooden torso and feet, flexible wire tubing for arms and legs, original clothes, paper tag. *Marks: "IDEAL DOLL//Made in U.S. A." or just "IDEAL DOLL" on head.*

Black Flexy, molded painted hair, painted eyes, closed smiling mouth, tweed patched pants, felt suspenders

13½"	$85.00	$325.00

Baby Snooks, based on a character by Fannie Brice, designed by Kallus, painted molded hair, painted eyes, open/closed mouth with teeth

13½"	$70.00	$275.00

Clown Flexy, looks like Mortimer Snerd, painted white as clown

13½"	$60.00	$225.00

Mortimer Snerd, Edgar Bergen's radio show dummy, molded painted blond hair, smiling closed mouth, showing two teeth

13½"	$70.00	$275.00

Soldier, closed smiling mouth, molded painted features, in khaki uniform

13½"	$65.00	$250.00

Sunny Sam and Sunny Sue, molded painted hair, girl bobbed hair, pouty mouth, boy as smiling mouth

13½"	$65.00	$250.00

20" composition Miss Liberty, using Deanna Durbin mold for face, body is Judy Garland teenage mold, marked "IDEAL DOLL (over backwards 21)," blond mohair wig, sleep eyes, real lashes, painted lower lashes, open mouth with six upper teeth, tongue, six-piece fully jointed body, white organdy skirt and sleeves, faded red satin bodice, missing satin crown, from Ideal's patriotic WWII series, circa 1943, $375.00. Courtesy Pat Graff.

Flossie Flirt, 1924 – 1931

Composition head, limbs, cloth body, crier, tin flirty eyes, open mouth, upper teeth, original outfit, dress, bonnet, socks and shoes

Mark: "IDEAL" in diamond with "U.S. of A"

14"	$60.00	$225.00+
18"	$65.00	$250.00+
20"	$70.00	$275.00+
22"	$75.00	$300.00+
24"	$80.00	$350.00+
28"	$100.00	$400.00+

Jiminy Cricket, 1940

8½", composition head and wood segmented body, yellow suit, black coat, blue felt trim on hat, felt collar, ribbon necktie, carries a wooden umbrella

Marks: "JIMINY CRICKET//IDEAL" and "BY IDEAL NOVELTY & TOY CO." on foot

9"	$125.00	$500.00

Judy Garland, 1939 – 1940, as Dorothy from *The Wizard of Oz*

All-composition, jointed, wig with braids, brown sleep eyes, open mouth, six teeth, designed by Bernard Lipfert, blue or red checked rayon jumper, white blouse

Marks: "IDEAL" on head plus size number, and "USA" on body

13"	$250.00	$1,000.00+
15½"	$300.00	$1,200.00+
18"	$350.00	$1,400.00+

Judy Garland, 1940 – 1942

Teen, all-composition, wig, sleep eyes, open mouth, four teeth, original long dress. *Hang tag reads: "Judy Garland// A Metro Goldwyn Mayer//Star//in// 'Little Nellie//Kelly.'" Original pin reads "JUDY GARLAND METRO GOLDWYN MAYER STAR."*

Marks: "IN U.S.A." on head, "IDEAL DOLLS," a backwards "21" on body

15"	$175.00	$700.00
21"	$250.00	$1,000.00

Liberty Boy, 1918+ (Dough Boy)

All-composition, molded Army uniform, painted features, molded hair, felt hat with gold cord, Ideal diamond mark on back

12"	$65.00	$250.00

Pinocchio, 1939

Composition head, wood segmented body, painted features, clothes, yellow felt cap. *Marks: "PINOCCHIO//Des. a by Walt Disney //Made by Ideal Novelty & Toy Co" on front, "© W.D.P./ /ideal doll//made in USA" on back*

8"	$75.00	$300.00
11"	$115.00	$450.00
20"	$125.00	$550.00

12" composition Flexy Soldier and Flexy Fanny Brice, marked "Ideal Doll" on heads, molded painted hair/eyes, composition hands, wooden feet, wire mesh arms/legs, wooden torso, soldier has closed smiling mouth, original khaki uniform, black tie, jacket and hat, Fanny Brice represents Baby Snooks character she portrayed, open/closed laughing mouth, lower teeth indicated, original blue print dress, matching pants, white organdy collar/belt, circa 1938 – 1942, $125.00 each. Courtesy McMasters Doll Auctions.

Princess Beatrix, 1938 – 1943

Represents Princess Beatrix of the Netherlands, composition head, arms, legs, cloth body, flirty sleep eyes, fingers molded into fists, original organdy dress and bonnet

14"	$45.00	$175.00
16"	$50.00	$200.00
22"	$65.00	$250.00
26"	$75.00	$300.00

Seven Dwarfs, 1938

Composition head and cloth body, or all-cloth, painted mask face, head turn, removable clothes, each dwarf has name on cap, pick, and lantern

Cloth

12"	$50.00	$175.00

Composition

12"	$65.00	$250.00

Dopey, 1938

One of Seven Dwarfs, a ventriloquist doll, composition head and hands, cloth body, arms, and legs, hinged mouth with drawstring, molded tongue, painted eyes, large ears, long coat, cotton pants, felt shoes sewn to leg, felt cap with name, can stand alone. *Mark: "IDEAL DOLL" on neck*

20"	$200.00	$800.00

Snoozie, 1933+

Composition head, painted hair, hard rubber hands and feet, cloth body, open yawning mouth, molded tongue, sleep eyes, designed by Bernard Lipfert. *Marks: "©B. Lipfert//Made for Ideal Doll & Toy Corp. 1933" or "©by B. Lipfert" or "IDEAL SNOOZIE//B. LIPFERT" on head*

14"	$40.00	$150.00
16"	$65.00	$250.00
18"	$75.00	$300.00
20"	$90.00	$350.00

Snow White, 1938+

All-composition, jointed body, black mohair wig, flirty glass eyes, open mouth, four teeth, dimple in chin, used Shirley Temple body, red velvet bodice, rayon taffeta skirt pictures seven Dwarfs, velvet cape, some unmarked. *Marks: "Shirley Temple/18" or other size number on back*

11½"	$125.00	$500.00
13 – 14"	$135.00	$550.00
19"	$150.00	$600.00
22"	$165.00	$650.00
27"	$175.00	$700.00

Snow White, 1938 – 1939, as above, but with painted molded bow and black hair, painted side-glancing eyes. Add 50 percent more for black version. *Mark: "IDEAL DOLL" on head*

14½"	$50.00	$200.00
17½"	$100.00	$400.00
19½"	$150.00	$600.00

Soozie Smiles, 1923

Two-headed composition doll with smiling face, sleep or painted eyes, and crying face with tears, painted molded hair, cloth body and legs, composition arms, original clothes, tag, also in gingham check romper

15 – 17"	$75.00	$300.00

Tickletoes, 1928 – 1939

Composition head, rubber arms, legs, cloth body, squeaker in each leg, flirty sleep eyes, open mouth, two painted teeth, original organdy dress, bonnet, paper hang tag. *Marks: "IDEAL" in diamond with "U.S. of A." on head*

14"	$50.00	$275.00
17"	$75.00	$300.00
20"	$95.00	$325.00

Uneeda Kid, 1916

Advertising doll, carries package of Nabisco crackers, some have molded yellow hats, wears yellow rain coat, molded black boots

Painted eyes

11"	$75.00	$300.00

Sleep eyes

16"	$125.00	$475.00

ZuZu Kid, 1966 – 1967

Composition head, molded hair, composition hands, feet, cloth body, jointed hip, shoulders, girl in yellow with brown star clown costume, hat, holds small box ZuZu gingersnaps, licensed by National Biscuit Co.

15½"	$115.00	$450.00

HARD PLASTIC AND VINYL

Baby

11"	$15.00	$45.00
14"	$20.00	$65.00

Child

14"	$10.00	$35.00

April Shower, 1969

Vinyl, battery operated, splashes hands, head turns

14"	$8.00	$28.00

Baby Coos, 1948 – 1953, also Brother and Sister Coos

Designed by Bernard Lipfert, hard plastic head, stuffed magic skin body, jointed arms, sleep eyes, molded painted hair, closed mouth, or cloth and vinyl body. Many magic skin bodies deteriorated or tuned dark. *Marks on head, "16 IDEAL DOLL// MADE IN U.S. A." or unmarked*

14"	$15.00	$75.00
16"	$25.00	$100.00
18"	$30.00	$125.00
20"	$40.00	$150.00
22"	$45.00	$175.00
27"	$50.00	$200.00
30"	$55.00	$250.00

Baby Crissy, 1973 – 1976

All-vinyl, jointed body, legs and arms foam filled, rooted auburn grow hair, two painted teeth, brown sleep eyes. *Mark: "©1972//IDEAL TOY COPR.//2M 5511//B OR GHB-H-225" on back*

White	24"	$35.00	$150.00
	24"	$400.00*	

Baby Pebbles, 1963 – 1964

Character from the Flintstone cartoons, Hanna Barbera Productions, vinyl head, arms, legs, soft body, side-glancing blue painted eyes, rooted hair

* at auction

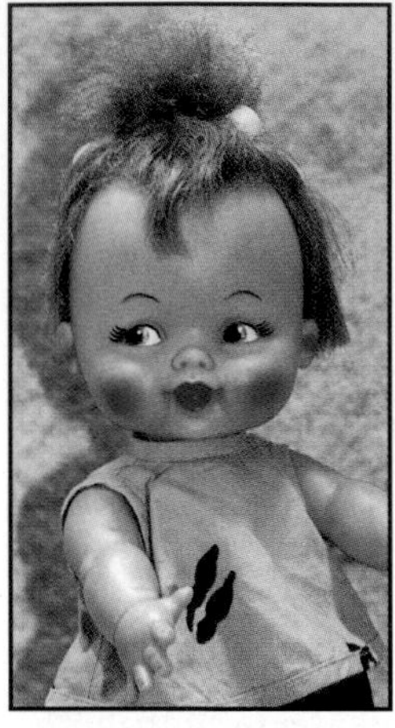

12" vinyl Tiny Pebbles, marked "©HANNA-BARBERA PRODUCTIONS, INC.," rooted saran hair with top knot and bone, painted side-glancing blue eyes, open/closed mouth, jointed vinyl body, leopard print outfit, circa 1964 – 1966, $75.00. Courtesy Karen McCarthy.

with topknot and bone, leopard print nightie and trim on flannel blanket. Also as an all-vinyl toddler, jointed body, outfit with leopard print.

Baby			
	14"	$75.00	$225.00
Toddler			
	16"	$50.00	$200.00
	16"	$365.00*	

Tiny Pebbles, 1964 – 1966, smaller version, came with plastic log cradle in 1965.

Toddler	12"	$40.00	$150.00

Bamm-Bamm, 1964

Character from Flintstone cartoon, Hanna Barbera Productions, all-vinyl head, jointed body, rooted blond saran hair, painted blue side-glancing eyes, leopard skin suit, cap, club

12"	$35.00	$150.00
16"	$50.00	$200.00

Belly Button Babies, 1971

Me So Glad, Me So Silly, Me So Happy, vinyl head, rooted hair, painted eyes, press button in belly to move arms, head, and bent legs; both boy and girl versions

White	9½"	$10.00	$35.00+
Black	9½"	$12.00	$45.00+

Betsy McCall, 1952 – 1953: See that section.

Betsy Wetsy, 1937 – 1938, 1954 – 1956, 1959 – 1962, 1982 – 1985

Hard rubber head, soft rubber body, sleep or painted eyes, molded hair, open mouth for bottle, drinks, wets, came with bottle, some in layettes. *Marks: "IDEAL" on head, "IDEAL" on body*

11"	$35.00	$125.00
13½"	$350.00*	
15"	$40.00	$150.00

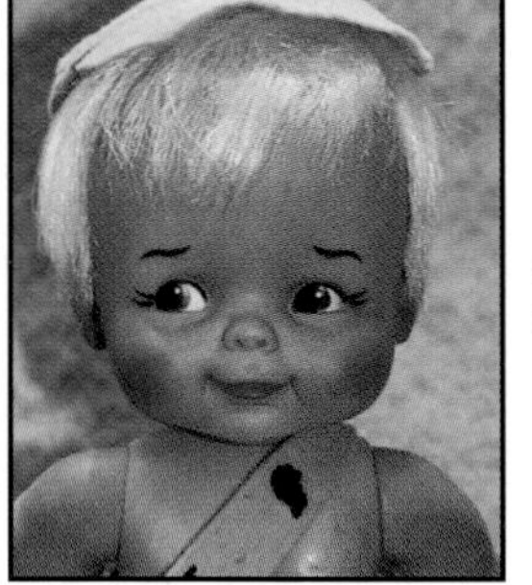

12" vinyl Tiny Bamm-Bamm, marked "©HANNA-BARBERA PRODUCTIONS, INC.," rooted blond saran hair, painted side-glancing brown eyes, closed smiling mouth, jointed vinyl body, leopard skin suit and hat, blue club, circa 1964 – 1966, $75.00. Courtesy Karen McCarthy.

Bizzie-Lizzie, 1971 – 1972

Vinyl head, jointed body, rooted blond hair, sleep eyes, plugged into power pack, she irons, vacuums, uses feather duster, two D-cell batteries

White	18"	$15.00	$60.00
Black	18"	$20.00	$75.00

Bonny Braids, 1951 – 1953

Comic strip character, daughter of Dick Tracy and Tess Trueheart, vinyl head, jointed arms, "Magic Skin" rubber one-piece body, open mouth, one tooth, painted yellow hair, two yellow saran pigtails, painted blue eyes, coos when squeezed, long white gown, bed jacket, toothbrush, Ipana toothpaste. *Mark: "©1951//Chi. Tribune//IDEAL DOLL//U.S.A." on neck*

Baby			
	11½"	$35.00	$125.00
	14"	$75.00	$150.00

* at auction

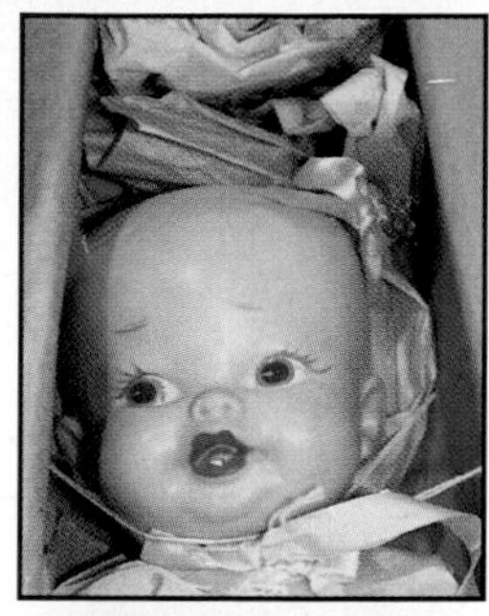

14" vinyl Bonnie Braids, painted blue eyes, open/closed mouth, one tooth, painted yellow hair, two pigtail tufts, magic skin latex rubber one-piece body, came with tube of Ipana toothpaste and toothbrush, wearing pink tagged gown, marked on back of neck "© 1951//CHI. Tribune//Ideal Doll//U.S.A." braids would grow to 4" according to letter included in box, daughter of comic strip Dick Tracy & Tess Truheart, circa 1953, $250.00+. Courtesy Geri Teeter.

Toddler, 1953, vinyl head, jointed hard plastic body, open/closed mouth with two painted teeth, walker

11½"	$35.00	$150.00
14"	$40.00	$200.00

Butterick Sew Easy Designing Set, 1953

Plastic mannequin of adult woman, molded blond hair, came with Butterick patterns and sewing accessories

14"	$20.00	$65.00

Captain Action® Superhero, 1966 – 1968

Represents a fictional character who changes disguises to become a new identity, vinyl articulated figure, dark hair and eyes

Captain Action 1967 Promo		
12"	$40.00	$250.00
Batman disguise		
	$40.00	$150.00
Capt. American disguise only		
	$50.00	$200.00
Capt. Flash Gordon accessories		
	$40.00	$150.00
Phantom disguise only		
	$50.00	$200.00
Steve Canyon disguise		
	$50.00	$200.00
Superman set w/dog		
	$45.00	$175.00
Lone Ranger outfit only		
	$40.00	$150.00
Spiderman disguise only		
	$40.00	$150.00
Tonto outfit only		
	$40.00	$150.00
Action Boy		
9"	$65.00	$250.00
Robin Accessories		
	$45.00	$150.00
Special Ed.	$75.00	$300.00
Dr. Evil	$50.00	$250.00
Dr. Evil Lab Set		
	$250.00	$2,000.00
Super Girl		
11½"	$75.00	$300.00

17" vinyl Posie, marked "IDEAL DOLL//VP – 17" on head, "IDEAL DOLL" on back, soft vinyl head, hard plastic body, jointed bent knees, walker, rooted saran hair, flirty blue sleep eyes, came with curlers, wears short blue dress, white socks/shoes, box says "Ideal's//Posie//Doll//with exclusive//MAGIC KNEE ACTION//The walking doll of a hundred life-like poses," mint-in-box, circa 1954 – 1956, $250.00. Courtesy Iva Mae Jones.

Chelsea, 1967 (Jet Set Doll)

Vinyl head, posable body, rooted straight hair, mod fashions, earrings, strap shoes

24" $15.00 $50.00

Clarabelle, 1954, clown from *Howdy Doody* TV show, mask face, cloth body, dressed in satin Clarabelle outfit with noise box and horn, later vinyl face

16" $25.00 $90.00

20" $30.00 $110.00

17½" vinyl Crissy marked "© Ideal Toy Corp.//GH 17 – 129" on head, vinyl body with swivel waist, growing hair, original dress and shoes, circa 1969 – 1974, $25.00. Courtesy Sharon Harrington.

Crissy®, Beautiful Crissy, 1969 – 1974

All-vinyl, dark brown eyes, long hair, turn knob in back to make hair grow, some with swivel waist (1971), pull string to turn head (1972), pull string to talk (1971). Reissued ca. 1982 – 1983. First year hair grew to floor length. More for black version.

1969, white

17½" $25.00 $110.00

17½" $365.00* w/extra wardrobe

Crissy's Friends & Family

Brandi, 1972 – 1973; Kerry, 1971; Tressy, 1970 (Sears Exclusive); Crissy's Friends, vinyl head, painted eyes, rooted growing hair, swivel waist

17½" $40.00 $150.00+

Cinnamon, Velvet's Little Sister, 1972 – 1974, vinyl head, painted eyes, rooted auburn growing hair, orange polka dotted outfit, additional outfits sold separately. *Marks: "©1971//IDEAL TOY CORP.//G-H-12-H18//HONG KONG//IDEAL 1069-4 b" head; "©1972//IDEAL TOY CORP.//U.S. PAT-3-162-976//OTHER PAT. PEND.//HONG KONG" on back*

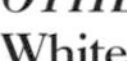

White

13½" $12.00 $50.00

Black

13½" $15.00 $55.00

Cricket, 1971 – 1972 (Sears Exclusive); Dina, 1972 – 1973; Mia, 1971, vinyl, members of the Crissy® family, growing hair dolls, painted teeth, swivel waist

15" $40.00 $150.00

Tara, 1976, all-vinyl black doll, long black rooted hair that "grows," sleep eyes, marked *"©1975//IDEAL TOY CORP//H-250//HONG KONG" on head and "©1970//IDEAL TOY CORP//GH-15//M5169-01//MADE IN HONG KONG" on buttock*

15½" $45.00 $170.00

Velvet, 1971 – 1973, Crissy's younger cousin, vinyl head, body, grow hair, talker, pull-string, marked *"©1969//IDEAL TOY CORP.//GH-15-H-157" on head ©1971//IDEAL TOY CORP.//TV15//US PAT 3162973//OTHER PATENTS PEND." on back*

15" $40.00 $150.00

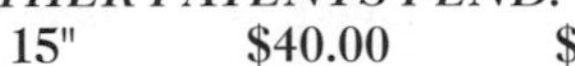

Velvet, 1974, non-talker, other accessories, gorw hair

15"	$9.00	$35.00

Daddy's Girl, 1961

Vinyl head and arms, plastic body, swivel waist, jointed ankles, rooted saran hair, blue sleep eyes, closed smiling mouth, preteen girl, label on dress reads *"Daddy's Girl." Marks: "IDEAL TOY CORP.//g-42-1" on head, "IDEAL TOY CORP.//G-42" on body*

38"	$300.00	$1,200.00
42"	$350.00	$1,400.00

Davy Crockett and his horse, 1955 – 1956

All-plastic, can be removed from horse, fur cap, buckskin clothes

4½"	$13.00	$50.00

Diana Ross, 1969

From the Supremes (singing group), all-vinyl, rooted black bouffant hairdo, gold sheath, feathers, gold shoes, or chartreuse mini-dress, print scarf, and black shoes

17½"	$75.00	$300.00
17½"	$535.00* MIB	

Dorothy Hamill, 1978

Olympic skating star, vinyl head, plastic posable body, rooted short brown hair, comes on ice rink stand with skates; also extra outfits available

11½"	$20.00	$75.00

Harnomy, ca. 1972

Vinyl, battery operated, makes music with guitar

21"	$105.00*	

Evel Knievel, 1974 – 1977

All-plastic stunt figure, helmet, more with stuntcycle

7"	$7.50	$25.00

Harriet Hubbard Ayer, 1953, Cosmetic doll

Vinyl stuffed head, hard plastic (Toni) body, wigged or rooted hair, came with eight-piece H. H. Ayer cosmetic kit, beauty table and booklet. *Marks: "MK 16//IDEAL DOLL" on head "IDEAL DOLL//P-91" on body*

14"	$60.00	$225.00
16"	$70.00	$250.00
19"	$75.00	$275.00
21"	$80.00	$325.00

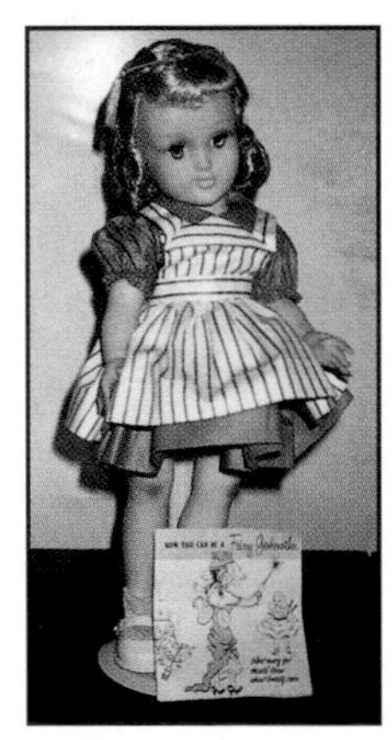

14" vinyl Harriet Hubbard Ayer uses Ideal Toni hard plastic body, special make-up face took three years to design, includes hang tag, all cosmetics, make-up desk, direction and Special gift for mother, circa 1953, $400.00. Courtesy Sally DeSmet.

Hopalong Cassidy, 1949 – 1950

Vinyl stuffed head, vinyl hands, molded painted gray hair, painted blue eyes, one-piece body, dressed in black cowboy outfit, leatherette boots, guns, holster, black felt hat. *Marked: "Hopalong Cassidy" on buckle*

18"	$20.00	$80.00
23"	$25.00	$100.00
27"	$40.00	$150.00

Plastic, with horse, Topper

4½"	$10.00	$40.00

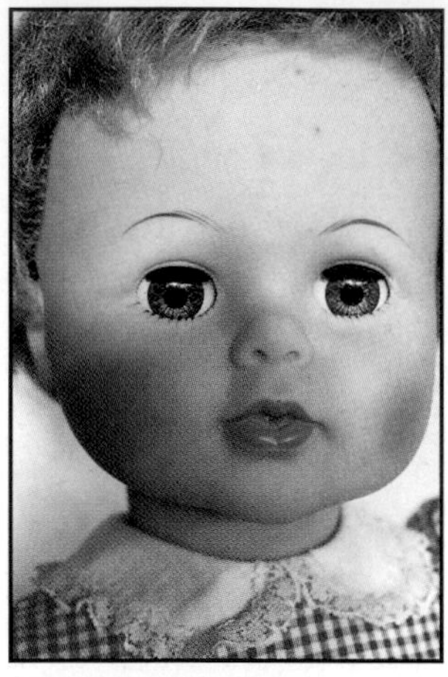

22" vinyl Kissy, marked "©IDEAL CORP.//K-21-L" on head, blue sleep eyes, rooted saran hair, jointed wrists, press hands together and mouth puckers up and makes a kiss with kissing sound, hard vinyl body, tagged red checked dress, red t-strap plastic shoes, all original, circa 1961 – 1964, $135.00. Courtesy Nelda Shelton.

Howdy Doody, 1950 – 1953

Television personality, hard plastic head, red painted molded hair, freckles, ventriloquist doll, mouth operated by pull string, cloth body and limbs, dressed in cowboy outfit, scarf reads *"HOWDY DOODY." Mark: "IDEAL" on head*

19"	$100.00	$200.00
24"	$125.00	$250.00

1954, with vinyl hands, wears boots, jeans

18"	$100.00	$200.00
20"	$125.00	$250.00
25"	$150.00	$300.00

Judy Splinters, 1949 – 1950

Vinylite TV character

18"	$75.00	$200.00

Kissy, 1961 – 1964

Vinyl head, rigid vinyl toddler body, rooted saran hair, sleep eyes, jointed wrists, press hands together and mouth puckers, makes kissing sound, original dress, panties, t-strap sandals. *Marks: "©IDEAL CORP.//K-21-L" on head "IDEAL TOY CORP.// K22//PAT. PEND." on body*

White

22½"	$40.00	$155.00

Black

22½"	$45.00	$175.00

Kissy Baby, 1963 – 1964, all-vinyl, bent legs

22"	$55.00	$240.00

Tiny Kissy, 1963 – 1968, smaller toddler, red outfit, white pinafore with hearts. *Marks: "IDEAL CORP.//K-16-1" on head "IDEAL TOY CORP./K-16-2" on body*

White

16"	$20.00	$80.00

Black

16"	$25.00	$90.00

Loni Anderson, 1981, star of TV sitcom, *WKRP in Cincinnati*

Vinyl, posable fashion doll packaged with picture of Loni Anderson. This doll was featured in Ideal's 1981 catalog in a red dress, white high heels, blond wig, unsure how many produced

11½"	$10.00	$50.00

Lori Martin, 1961, character from National Velvet TV show

All-vinyl, swivel waist, jointed body, including ankles, blue sleep eyes, rooted dark hair, individual fingers, dressed shirt, jeans, black vinyl boots, felt hat. *Marks: "Metro Goldwyn Mayer Inc.//Mfg. by//IDEAL TOY CORP//38" on head, "©IDEAL TOY CORP.//38" on back*

30"	$175.00	$750.00
38"	$200.00	$800.00
42"	$2,000.00 store display	

Magic Skin Baby, 1940, 1946 – 1949

Hard plastic head, one-piece molded latex body and legs, jointed arms, sleep eyes, molded painted hair, some with fancy layettes or trunks, latex usually darkened

13 – 14"	$25.00	$50.00
15 – 16"	$20.00	$75.00
17 – 18"	$25.00	$100.00
20"	$35.00	$125.00

Marama, 1940: See Shirley Temple section.

Mary Hartline, 1952, from TV personality on *Super Circus* show

Hard plastic, fully jointed, blond nylon wig, blue sleep eyes, lashes, black eyeshadow over and under eye, red, white, or green drum majorette costume and baton, red heart paper hang tag, with original box. *Marks: "P-91//IDEAL DOLL//MADE IN U.S.A." on head, "IDEAL DOLL//P-91 or IDEAL//16" on body*

7½"	$35.00	$125.00
16"	$300.00	$650.00
23"	$375.00	$750.00

16" hard plastic Mary Hartline, marked "P-91//Ideal Doll//Made in U.S.A." on back of head, "Ideal Doll//P-91" on back, original blond wig, blue sleep eyes, real lashes, eyeshadow, feathered brows, closed mouth, five-piece hard plastic body, original red dress with name and musical notes, attached slip, matching panties, majorette boots, circa 1952, $300.00. Courtesy McMasters Doll Auctions.

Miss Clairol, Glamour Misty, 1965 – 1966

Vinyl head and arms, rigid plastic legs, body, rooted platinum blond saran hair, side-glancing eyes, high-heeled feet. Teen doll had cosmetics to change her hair. All original. *Marks: "©1965//IDEAL TOY CORP//W-12-3" on neck, "©1965 IDEAL" in oval on lower rear torso*

12"	$10.00	$40.00

Miss Curity, 1953

Hard plastic, saran wig, sleep eyes, black eyeshadow, nurse's outfit, navy cape, white cap, Bauer & Black first aid kit and book, curlers, uses Toni body. *Mark: "P-90 IDEAL DOLL, MADE IN U.S.A." on head*

14½"	$300.00	$650.00

Miss Ideal, 1961

All vinyl, rooted nylon hair, jointed ankles, wrists, waist, arms, legs, closed smiling mouth, sleep eyes, original dress, with beauty kit and comb. *Marks: "©IDEAL TOY CORP.//SP-30-S" head; "©IDEAL TOY CORP.//G-30-S" back*

25"	$100.00	$375.00
30"	$125.00	$475.00

19" vinyl Miss Revlon, marked "VT18//IDEAL DOLL," rooted saran hair, sleep eyes, lashes, pierced ears, hang tag, hard plastic teenage body, jointed shoulders, waist, hips, high-heeled feet, in original box, circa 1956 – 1959, $405.00. Courtesy McMasters Doll Auctions.

Miss Revlon, 1956 – 1959

Vinyl, hard plastic teenage body, jointed shoulders, waist, hips, and knees, high-heeled feet, rooted saran hair, sleep eyes, lashes, pierced ears, hang tag, original

10½" vinyl Little Miss Revlon, strung body, rooted blond hair, sleep eyes, pierced ears, jointed body, swivel waist, high heeled feet, yellow top with blue and red rick-rack, red sash around waist, blue, white, green, and red striped pants, green high heel sandals, painted fingernails and toenails, in Style Show box, hang tag and brochure, circa 1958 – 1960, $175.00. Courtesy Cathy DeWolfe.

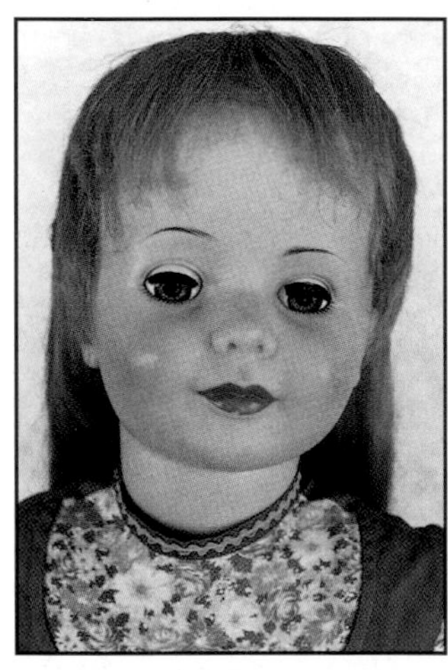

35" vinyl Patti Play Pal marked "Ideal Doll//G-35" on head, hard-to-find orange-red rooted saran hair with bangs, walker, wears original orange print and green school dress, circa 1960 – 1961, $500.00. Courtesy Cornelia Ford.

dress. Some came with trunks. *Mark: "VT 20//IDEAL DOLL"*

15"	$100.00	$350.00
18"	$150.00	$500.00
20"	$200.00	$600.00
23"	$225.00	$700.00
1957		
26"	$75.00	$300.00

Little Miss Revlon, 1958 – 1960

Vinyl head and strung body, jointed head, arms, legs, swivel waist, high-heeled feet, rooted hair, sleep eyes, pierced ears with earrings, original clothes, with box, many extra boxed outfits available

10½"	$75.00	$175.00

Mysterious Yokum, Li'l Honest Abe, 1953

Son of comic strip character, Li'l Abner, hard plastic head, body, "Magic Skin" arms and legs, painted eyes, molded hair, forelock, wears overalls, one suspender, knit cap and sock

	$20.00	$80.00

Palooka, Joan, 1953

Daughter of comic strip character, Joe Palooka, vinyl, head, "Magic Skin" body, jointed arms and legs, yellow molded hair, topknot of yellow saran, blue painted eyes, open/closed mouth, smells like baby powder, original pink dress with blue ribbons, came with Johnson's baby powder and soap. *Mark: "©1952//HAM FISHER//IDEAL DOLL" on head*

14"	$50.00	$250.00

Patti Playpal and related dolls, 1959 – 1962

All-vinyl, jointed wrists, sleep eyes, curly or straight saran hair, bangs, closed mouth, blue or red and white check dress with pinafore, three-year-old size, reissued in 1981 and 1982 from old molds, more for redheads. *Mark: "IDEAL TOY CORP.//G 35 OR B-19-1" on head*

White		
35"	$80.00	$350.00
Black		
35"	$90.00	$375.00

Pattite, 1960

All-vinyl, rooted saran hair, sleep eyes, red and white check dress, white pinafore with her name on it, looks like Patti Playpal

18"	$150.00	$300.00
18"	$1,226.00* red head, original, hang tags	

* at auction

Bonnie Play Pal, 1959

Patti's three-month-old sister, made only one year, vinyl, rooted blond hair, blue sleep eyes, blue and white check outfit, white shoes and socks

24"	$70.00	$275.00

Penny Play Pal, 1959

Vinyl jointed body, rooted blond or brown curly hair, blue sleep eyes, wears organdy dress, vinyl shoes, socks, Patti's two-year-old sister, made only one year. *Marks: "IDEAL DOLL//32-E-L" or "B-32-B PAT. PEND." on head, "IDEAL" on back*

32"	$75.00	$300.00

Johnny Play Pal, 1959

Vinyl, blue sleep eyes, molded hair, Patti's three-month-old brother

24"	$70.00	$275.00

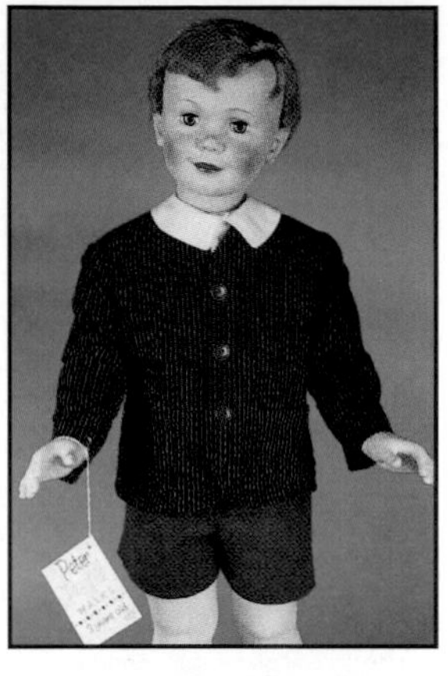

39" vinyl Peter Playpal, all original, blue sleep eyes, freckles, pug nose, closed smiling mouth, rooted hair, five-piece body, circa 1960 – 1961, $500.00. Courtesy McMasters Doll Auctions.

Peter Playpal, 1960 – 1961

Vinyl, gold sleep eyes, freckles, pug nose, rooted blond, brunette hair, original clothes, black plastic shoes. *Marks: "©DEAL TOY CORP.// BE-35-38" on head, "©IDEAL TOY CORP.//W-38//PAT. PEND." on body*

38"	$375.00	$850.00
Walker		
38"	$450.00	$900.00

Suzy Play Pal, 1959

Vinyl, jointed body, rooted curly short blond saran hair, blue sleep eyes, wears purple dotted dress, Patti's one-year-old sister

28"	$80.00	$325.00

Plassie, 1942

Hard plastic head, painted molded hair, composition shoulder plate, composition limbs, stuffed pink oilcloth body, blue sleep eyes, original dress, bonnet. *Mark: "IDEAL DOLL//MADE IN USA//PAT.NO. 225 2077" on head*

16"	$25.00	$100.00
19"	$35.00	$125.00
24"	$45.00	$175.00

Samantha, 1965 – 1966, from TV show *Bewitched*

Vinyl head, body, rooted saran hair, posable arms

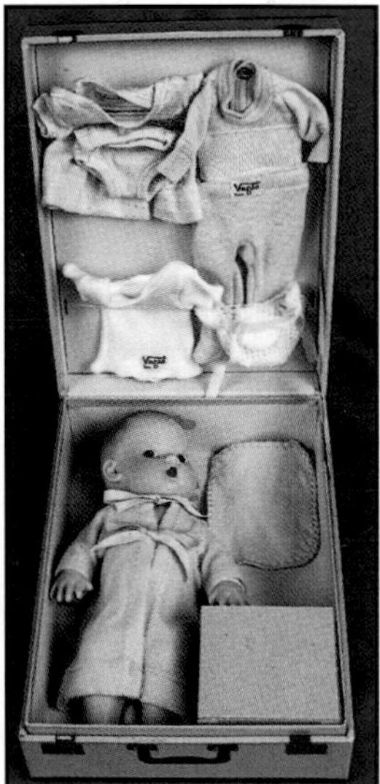

9½" vinyl Vicki Vanta, painted blue eyes to side, painted upper lashes, closed mouth, molded painted hair, "magic skin" body, green flannel gown trimmed with pink ribbons, labeled case with blue knit dress, matching panties, pink sleeper, bib, undershirt, knit blanket, original price tag of $5.00 from Macy's in San Francisco, marked "Ideal Doll" on head, "Vanta, Size 0" label on clothing, "Vicki Vanta, Mother Goose Special" on lid of case, circa 1950s, $175.00. Courtesy McMasters Doll Auctions.

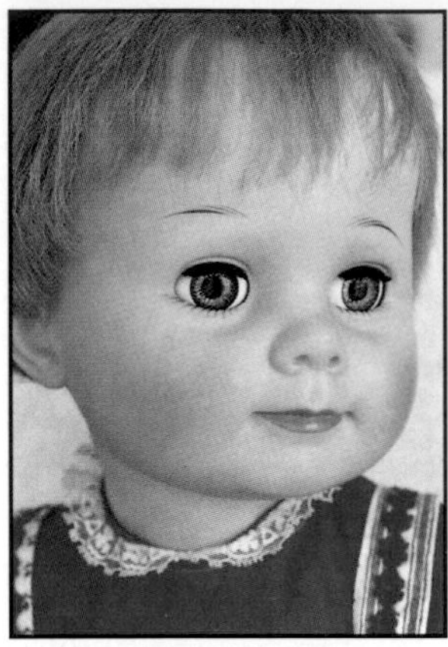

29" vinyl Saucy Walker, rooted blond saran hair, blue sleep eyes, closed smiling mouth, original red dress with marked pinafore, marked, head "Ideal Toy Corp.// T28X-60" "© Ideal Toy Crop, 1-28 Pat. Pend." circa 1960 – 1961, $175.00. Courtesy Cornelia Ford.

25" vinyl Talkytot, mask face, brown eyes, gold wool hair, dressed in plaid dress and hat, hand crank makes doll say phrases like "Rock-A-Bye Baby on a tree-top," mint-in-box, circa 1953, $85.00. Courtesy Leslie Tannenbaum.

and legs, wearing red witch's costume, with broom, painted side-glancing eyes, other costume included negligee. *Mark: "IDEAL DOLL//M-12-E-2" on head*

12"	$45.00	$175.00
All original, with broom		
	$300.00	$600.00
Mint-in-box	$1,500.00 – $2.000.00	

Tabitha, 1966, baby from TV show *Bewitched*, vinyl head, body, rooted platinum hair, painted blue side-glancing eyes, closed mouth, came in pajamas. *Mark: "©1965//Screen Gems, Inc.//Ideal Toy Corp.//T.A. 18-6//H-25" on head*

14"	$40.00	$150.00
All original	$150.00	$300.00
Mint-in-box	$1,000.00 – $1,500.00	

Saucy Walker, 1951 – 1955

All hard plastic, walks, turns head from side to side, flirty blue eyes, crier, open/closed mouth, teeth, holes in body for crier, saran wig, plastic curlers, came as toddler, boy, and "Big Sister"

16"	$60.00	$225.00
22"	$85.00	$325.00
Black		
16"	$50.00	$200.00
Big Sister, 1954		
25"	$40.00	$200.00

1960 – 1961

All-vinyl, rooted saran hair, blue sleep eyes, closed smiling mouth, walker, original print dress, pinafore, box. *Marks: "©IDEAL TOY CORP.//T28X-60" or "IDEAL TOY CO.//BYE S 285 B" on head, "IDEAL TOY CORP.//T-28 Pat. Pend." on body*

28"	$50.00	$200.00
32"	$65.00	$250.00

Smokey Bear, 1953+

Bakelite vinyl face and paws, rayon plush stuffed body, vinyl forest ranger hat, badge, shovel, symbol of US National Forest Service, wears Smokey marked belt, twill trousers, came with Junior Forest Ranger kit. Issued on 50th anniversary of Ideal's original teddy bear.

18"	$25.00	$100.00
25"	$35.00	$135.00
1957, Talking		
	$25.00	$100.00

Snoozie, 1949

1933 doll reissued in vinyl, cloth body with Swiss music box

11"	$20.00	$75.00
16"	$25.00	$100.00
20"	$40.00	$150.00

11½" vinyl black Taylor Jones, marked "1975//Ideal (in oval)//Hong Kong," rooted black hair, painted eyes, rooted eyelashes, change color of hair from red to black by twisting top of head, mint-in-box, circa 1976 – 1977, $50.00. Courtesy Pat Graff.

1958 – 1965

All-vinyl, rooted saran hair, blue sleep eyes, open/closed mouth, cry voice, knob makes doll wiggle, close eyes, crier, in flannel pajamas

14"	$12.00	$45.00

1964 – 1965

Vinyl head, arms, legs, soft body, rooted saran hair, sleep eyes, turn knob, she squirms, opens and closes eyes, and cries. *Marks: "©1965//IDEAL TOY CORP//YTT-14-E" on head, "IDEAL TOY CORP//U.S. PAT. NO. 3,029,552" on knob on back*

20"	$15.00	$60.00

Sparkle Plenty, 1947 – 1950

Hard plastic head, "Magic Skin" body may be dark, yarn hair, character from Dick Tracy comics

14"	$140.00	$300.00
14"	$700.00*	

Tammy and Her Family

Tammy, 1962+, vinyl head, arms, plastic legs and torso, head joined at neck base. *Marks: "©IDEAL TOY CORP.//BS12" on head, "©IDEAL TOY CORP.//BS-12//1" on back*

White	12"	$15.00	$55.00
NRFB	12"	$200.00*	
Pos'n	12"	$25.00	$65.00
Mom	12"	$20.00	$65.00
Ted	12"	$30.00	$100.00
Pepper	9"	$20.00	$55.00
Clothing (MIP)		$20.00	$75.00

12" vinyl Tammy , side-glancing painted eyes, rooted hair, closed mouth, marked on head "© Ideal Toy Corp," rigid plastic torso, played with condition, circa 1962+, $25.00. Courtesy Barbara Jones.

Thumbelina, 1961 – 1962

Vinyl head and limbs, soft cloth body, painted eyes, rooted saran hair, open/closed mouth, wind knob on back moves body, crier in 1962

16"	$125.00	$300.00
16"	$825.00* original box	

1982 – 1983

All-vinyl one-piece body, rooted hair, comes in quilted carrier, also black

7"	$20.00	$75.00

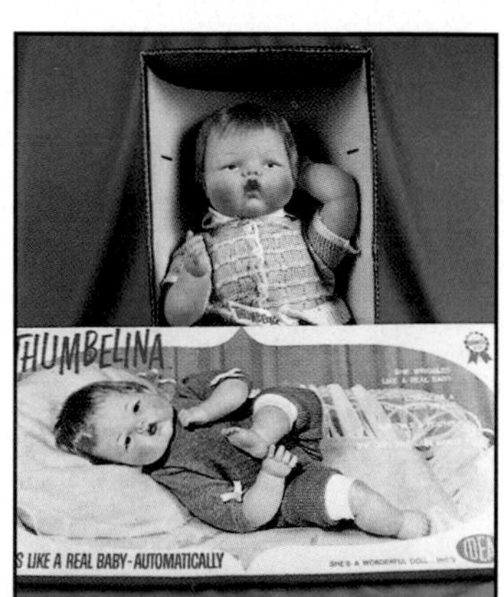

20" vinyl Thumbelina, rooted saran hair, painted eyes with three outer lashes, open/closed mouth, vinyl limbs, soft cloth body, wind the knob in her back and she moves her body and wriggles and cries, with box, circa 1962, $328.00. Courtesy McMasters Doll Auctions.

14" hard plastic Toni with blue/green plastic sleep eyes, eyeshadow, real and painted lashes, closed mouth, synthetic wig, marked on back of head "Ideal Doll//Made in USA" and on back "P-90//Ideal Doll//Made in USA," red leatherette center snap shoes, original white with red dot organdy dress, blue rickrack trim, over blue cotton slip, Toni hang tag, circa 1949, $350.00. Courtesy June Allgeier.

1982, 1985

Reissue from 1960s mold, vinyl head, arms, legs, cloth body, painted eyes, crier, open mouth, molded or rooted hair, original with box

18"	$8.00	$30.00

Thumbelina, Ltd. Production Collector's Doll, 1983 – 1985

Porcelain, painted eyes, molded painted hair, beige crocheted outfit with pillow booties, limited edition 1,000

18"	$20.00	$75.00
24"	$25.00	$100.00

Tiny Thumbelina, 1962 – 1968

Vinyl head, limbs, cloth body, painted eyes, rooted saran hair, wind key in back makes body head move, original tagged clothes

Marks: "IDEAL TOY CORP.//OTT 14" on head, "U.S. PAT. # 3029552" on body

14"	$465.00* MIB

Tiffany Taylor, 1974 – 1976

All-vinyl, rooted hair, top of head turns to change color, painted eyes, teenage body, high-heeled, extra outfits available

	19"	$20.00	$75.00+
Black	19"	$25.00	$85.00+

Toni, 1949, designed by Bernard Lipfert

All hard plastic, jointed body, Dupont nylon wig, usually blue eyes, rosy cheeks, closed mouth, came with Toni wave set and curlers in original dress, with hang tag. *Marks: "IDEAL DOLL//MADE IN U.S.A." on head, "IDEAL DOLL" and P-series number on body*

P-90	14"	$125.00	$475.00
P-91	16"	$175.00	$625.00
P-92	19"	$185.00	$675.00
P-93	21"	$200.00	$750.00
P-94	22½"	$225.00	$800.00

Tuesday Taylor, 1976 – 1977, vinyl, poseable body, turn head to change color of hair, clothing tagged *"IDEAL Tuesday Taylor"*

11½"	$20.00	$55.00

Whoopsie, 1978 – 1981, vinyl, reissued in 1981. *Marked: "22//©IDEAL TOY CORP//HONG KONG//1978//H298"*

13"	$10.00	$35.00

16" hard plastic Toni, marked "P-91//Ideal Doll//Made in U.S.A." on back of head, "Ideal Doll//P-91" on back, blue sleep eyes, real lashes, painted lower lashes, single stroke brows, closed mouth, original brunette wig, five-piece hard plastic body, original dress with pink pique bodice, blue/gold print skirt, matching draw string purse, attached white cotton half slip, panties, white socks, white leatherette center snap shoes, circa 1949 – 1953, $250.00. Courtesy McMasters Doll Auctions.

Ideal Novelty and Toy Co.

Wizard of Oz Series, 1984 – 1985

Tin Man, Lion, Scarecrow, Dorothy, and Toto, all-vinyl, six-piece posable bodies

9" $9.00 $35.00

Wonder Woman, Batgirl, Mera Queen of Atlantis, or Super Girl, 1967 – 1968

All-vinyl, posable body, rooted hair, painted side-glancing eyes, dressed in costume

MIB 11½" $900.00

Kenner

First price indicates played with or missing accessories doll; second price is for mint condition doll.

Baby Bundles

White 16" $4.00 $20.00

Baby Yawnie, 1974

Vinyl head, cloth body

15" $5.00 $20.00

Blythe, 1972

Pull string to change color of eyes, "mod" clothes

11½" $175.00 $700.00

11½" $1,585.00* NRFB

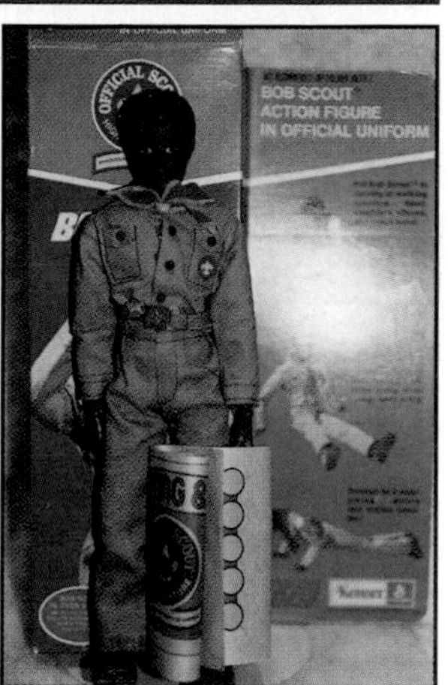

9" vinyl black Bob Scout, molded painted black hair, painted eyes, molded painted features, fully articulated vinyl body, wearing replica of genuine Boy Scouts of America uniform, in original box with Scout comic book, approved by the Boy Scouts of America, circa 1974, $75.00. Courtesy Joan Radke.

Bob Scout, 1974

9" $80.00* black, MIB

Butch Cassidy or Sundance Kid

4" $4.00 $15.00

Charlie Chaplin, 1973

All-cloth, walking mechanism

14" $25.00 $90.00

Cover Girls, 1978

Posable elbows and knees, jointed hands

Dana, black

12½" $30.00 $75.00

Darci, blond

12½" $35.00 $125.00

Darci, brunette

12½" $30.00 $90.00

Darci, redhead

12½" $20.00 $80.00

Erica, redhead

12½" $45.00 $150.00

Crumpet 1970, vinyl and plastic

18" $8.00 $30.00

Dusty, 1974, vinyl teenage doll

11" $10.00 $20.00

Skye, black, teenage friend of Dusty

11" $8.00 $25.00

12½" vinyl Erica from the Cover Girl Series, Darci's friend, rooted hair, painted eyes, smiling mouth with painted teeth, fashion type body with jointed wrists, posable elbows and knees, marked "74//HongKong//© GMFGI 1978," circa 1978, $50.00. Courtesy Pat Graff.

Gabbigale, 1972

White	18"	$10.00	$35.00
Black	18"	$12.00	$45.00

Garden Gals, 1972, hand bent to hold watering can

6½"	$3.00	$10.00

Hardy Boys, 1978, Shaun Cassidy, Parker Stevenson

12"	$15.00	$60.00

Indiana Jones, 1981

12"	$50.00	$150.00

International Velvet, 1976, Tatum O'Neill

11½"	$8.00	$25.00

Jenny Jones and baby, 1973, all-vinyl

Jenny, 9", Baby, 2½"

set	$8.00	$25.00

Rose Petal, 1984, scented

7"	$10.00	$20.00

Six Million Dollar Man Figures, 1975 – 1977

TV show starring Lee Majors

Bionic Man, Big Foot	13"	$7.00	$25.00
Bionic Man, Masketron Robot	13"	$8.00	$30.00
Bionic Woman, Robot	13"	$27.00	$85.00
Jaime Sommers, Bionic Woman	13"	$20.00	$75.00
Oscar Goldman, 1975 – 1977, with exploding briefcase	13"	$15.00	$50.00
Steve Austin, The Bionic Man, with equipment and accessories	13"	$20.00	$100.00
Steve Austin, Bionic Grip, 1977	13"	$25.00	$95.00

Star Wars Figures, 1974 – 1978

Large size action figures

First price indicates doll played with or missing accessories; second price is for mint-in-box/package doll. Complete doll in excellent condition would be somewhere in between. Never-removed-from-box would bring greater prices.

Ben-Obi-Wan Kenobi	12"	$25.00	$95.00
Boba Fett	13"	$55.00	$175.00
C-3PO	12"	$35.00	$135.00
Chewbacca	12"	$40.00	$145.00
Darth Vader	12"	$50.00	$200.00

* at auction

Han Solo
12" $125.00 $475.00
IG-88
15" $150.00 $600.00
Jawa
8½" $25.00 $100.00
Leia Organa
11½" $65.00 $275.00
Luke Skywalker
12" $65.00 $275.00
R2-D2, robot
7½" $45.00 $175.00
Stormtrooper
12" $50.00 $200.00

Steve Scout, 1974, black
9" $15.00 $55.00

Strawberry Shortcake, ca. 1980 – 1986
5" $6.00 $25.00
Peach Blush, mechanical $2,200.00*
Berry Happy Home $760.00*

Sweet Cookie, 1972
18" $8.00 $30.00

Terminator, Arnold Schwarzenegger, 1991, talks
13½" $15.00 $30.00

Klumpe

Caricature figures made of felt over wire armature with painted mask faces, produced in Barcelona, Spain, from about 1952 to the mid-1970s. Figures represent professionals, hobbyists, Spanish dancers, historical characters, and contemporary males and females performing a wide variety of tasks. Of the 200 or more different figures, the most common are Spanish dancers, bull fighters, and doctors. Some Klumpes were imported by Effanbee in the early 1950s. Originally the figures had two sewn-on identifying cardboard tags.

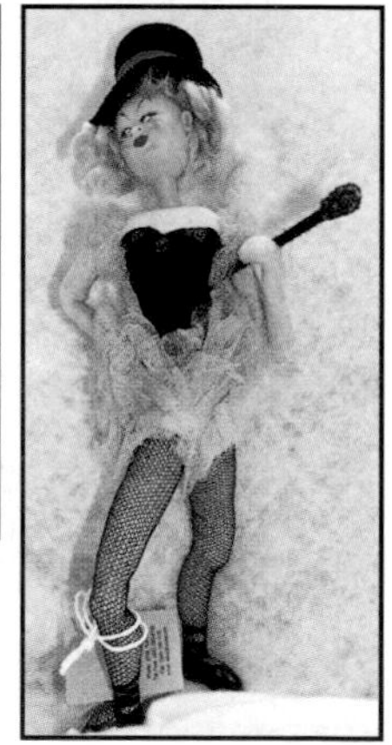

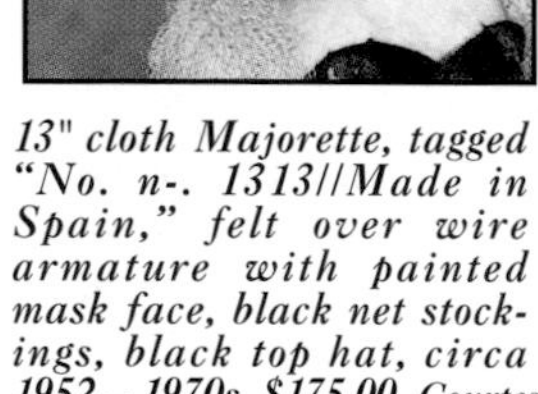

13" cloth Majorette, tagged "No. n-. 1313//Made in Spain," felt over wire armature with painted mask face, black net stockings, black top hat, circa 1952 – 1970s, $175.00. Courtesy Sharon Kolibaba.

Average figure
10½" $35.00 $125.00

Elaborate figure, MIB with accessories
10½" $250.00+

6" hard plastic brown Indian Boy, painted black side-glancing eyes, painted black hair, yellow fringed leather top and pants with red and black designs, circa 1950s, $35.00. Courtesy Carol Van Verst-Rugg.

6" hard plastic black Hawaiian Girl, marked "Knickerbocker" on back, painted side-glancing eyes, black mohair wig, green grass skirt, circa 1950s, $35.00. Private collection.

Cloth

Clown

17" $5.00 $25.00

Disney characters

Donald Duck, Mickey Mouse, etc., all-cloth

10½" $125.00 $425.00

Mickey Mouse, ca. 1930s, oil cloth eyes

15" $3,100.00*

Pinocchio, cloth and plush

13" $65.00 $250.00

Seven Dwarfs, 1939+

14" $65.00 $260.00

Snow White, all-cloth

16" $95.00 $365.00

Holly Hobby, 1970s, cloth, later vinyl

Cloth

9" $7.00 $25.00

26" $25.00 $100.00

Vinyl

16" $15.00 $35.00

Composition

"Blondie" comic strip characters

Composition, painted features, hair

Alexander Bumsted

9" $100.00 $375.00

Dagwood Bumsted

14" $175.00 $650.00

Child, 1938+

15" $55.00 $285.00

Mickey Mouse, 1930s – 1940s

Composition, cloth body

18" $300.00 $1,100.00

Jiminy Cricket, all-composition

10" $125.00 $495.00

Pinocchio, all-composition

13" $125.00 $400.00

14" $1,500.00* in original labeled box

Seven Dwarfs, 1939+

9" each $75.00 $275.00

Sleeping Beauty, 1939+, bent right arm

15" $100.00 $425.00

18" $130.00 $495.00

Snow White, 1937+, all-composition, bent right arm, black wig

15" $110.00 $435.00

20" $125.00 $475.00

Molded hair and ribbon. *Mark: "WALT DISNEY//1937//KNICKERBOCKER"*

13" $75.00 $360.00

* at auction

Set of seven Dwarfs, Snow White, mohair wigs, beards

9 – 11" $1,300.00*

Hard Plastic and Vinyl

Bozo Clown

14"	$7.00	$25.00
24"	$17.00	$60.00

Cinderella

Two faces, one sad; one with tiara

16"	$5.00	$20.00

Flintstone characters

6"	$3.00	$10.00
17"	$9.00	$43.00

Kewpies: See Antique Kewpie section.

Little House on the Prairie, 1978

12"	$6.00	$22.00

"Little Orphan Annie" comic strip characters, 1982

Little Orphan Annie, vinyl

6"	$5.00	$17.50

Daddy Warbucks

7"	$5.00	$17.50

Punjab

7"	$4.00	$18.00

Miss Hannigan

7"	$4.00	$18.00

Molly

5½"	$4.00	$12.00

Soupy Sales, 1966

Vinyl and cloth, non-removable clothes

13"	$35.00	$135.00

Two-faced dolls, 1960s

Vinyl face masks, one crying, one smiling

12"	$5.00	$18.00

Lawton Doll Co.

Wendy Lawton, 1979+, Turlock, CA.

Price indicates complete mint-in-box doll; dolls missing accessories or with flaws would be priced less.

Childhood Classics

Alice in Wonderland

1983		$3,000.00+

Anne of Green Gables

1986	14"	$1,600.00+

Hans Brinker

1985	14"	$850.00

Heidi

1984	14"	$850.00

Laura Ingalls

1986		$600.00

Little Eva

1988		$750.00

Lawton Doll Co.

Li'l Princess	1989	14"	$850.00
Pollyanna	1986	14"	$800.00
Christmas Dolls			
Christmas Joy	1988		$800.00
Noel	1989		$450.00
Christmas Angel	1990		$450.00
Yuletide Carole	1991		$450.00
Disney World Specials			
1st Main Street			$450.00
2nd Liberty Square (250)			$400.00
3rd Tish			$400.00
4th Karen (50)			$800.00
5th Goofy Kid (100)			$800.00
6th Melissa & Her Mickey			$750.00
7th Christopher, Robin, Pooh		12"	$750.00
Guild Dolls			
Ba Ba Black Sheep	1989		$750.00
Lavender Blue	1990		$450.00
Special Editions			
Marcella & Raggedy Ann	1988		$795.00
Flora McFlimsey	1993		$1,000.00
Other Specials			
Beatrice Louise, UFDC, 1998 Luncheon			$975.00*
Josephine, UFDC Regional		12"	$750.00
Little Colonel, Dolly Dears, Birmingham, AL			$425.00
1st WL Convention, Lotta Crabtree			$1,300.00+

Marx

8½" vinyl Archie and Jughead, comic characters, with their 1932 Ford Riverdale High roadster, ca. 1975, dolls with roadster $100.00. Courtesy Shirley Meade.

Archie and Friends

Characters from comics, vinyl, molded hair or wigged, painted eyes, in package

Archie	8½"	$10.00	$30.00
Betty	8½"	$10.00	$30.00
Jughead	8½"	$10.00	$30.00
Veronica	8½"	$10.00	$30.00

* at auction

Johnny Apollo Double Agent, vinyl, trench coat, circa 1970s

12" $25.00 $50.00

Miss Seventeen, 1961

Hard plastic, high heeled, fashion-type doll, modeled like the German Bild Lilli, Barbie doll's predecessor, came in black swimsuit, black box, fashion brochure pictures 12 costumes, she was advertised as "A Beauty Queen."

18" $175.00 $300.00

Costume only $155.00* MIP

Miss Marlene

Hard plastic, high heeled, Barbie-type, ca. 1960s, blond rooted wig

7" $170.00* in original box, costume

Miss Toddler

Also know as Miss Marx, vinyl, molded hair, ribbons, battery operated walker, molded clothing

18" $75.00 $155.00

Johnny West Family of Action Figures, 1965 – 1976

Adventure or Best of the West Series, rigid vinyl, articulated figures, molded clothes, came in box with vinyl accessories and extra clothes. Had horses, dogs, and other accessories available. First price indicates played with, missing some accessories; second price for complete in box; more if never-removed-from-box or special sets.

Bill Buck, brown molded-on clothing, 13 pieces, coonskin cap

11½" $35.00 $125.00

Captain Tom Maddox, blue molded-on clothing, brown hair, 23 pieces

11½" $25.00 $90.00

Chief Cherokee, tan or light color molded-on clothing, 37 pieces

11½" $25.00 $100.00

Daniel Boone, tan molded-on clothing, coonskin cap

11½" $30.00 $115.00

Fighting Eagle, tan molded-on clothes, with Mohawk hair, 37 pieces

11½" $45.00 $135.00

General Custer, dark blue molded-on clothing, yellow hair, 23 pieces

11½" $25.00 $85.00

Geronimo, light color molded-on clothing

11½" $50.00 $95.00

Orange body

11½" $50.00 $125.00

14½" vinyl Miss Seventeen, painted side-glancing eyes, blond hair, all original with black swimsuit, red cape, trophy cup, with box labeled "Miss Seventeen //Trademark A Beauty Queen"// moth-hole in swimsuit, circa 1961, $275.00. Courtesy Debbie Crume.

9" rigid vinyl articulated Janice West of the Johnny West Series molded on clothing, 14 pieces of vinyl clothing and accessories, box, circa 1965 – 1976, $75.00. Courtesy Chad Moyer.

* at auction

Jamie West, dark hair, molded-on tan clothing, 13 accessories

9"	$20.00	$45.00

Jane West, blond hair, turquoise molded on clothing, 37 pieces

11½"	$20.00	$50.00
Orange body	$25.00	$45.00

Janice West, dark hair, turquoise molded-on clothing, 14 pieces

9"	$20.00	$45.00

Jay West, blond hair, tan molded-on clothing, 13 accessories, later brighter body colors

9"	$20.00	$45.00

Jeb Gibson, c. 1973, black figure, molded-on green clothing

12"	$100.00	$200.00

Johnny West, brown hair, molded-on brown clothing, 25 pieces

12"	$25.00	$90.00

Johnny West, with quick draw arm, blue clothing

12"	$20.00	$55.00

Josie West, blond, turquoise molded-on clothing, later with bright green body

9"	$20.00	$45.00

Princess Wildflower, off-white molded-on clothing, with papoose in vinyl cradle, 22 pieces of accessories

11½"	$50.00	$130.00

Sam Cobra, outlaw, with 26 accessories

11½"	$25.00	$100.00

Sheriff Pat Garrett (Sheriff Goode in Canada), molded-on blue clothing, 25 pieces of accessories

11½"	$75.00	$125.00

Zeb Zachary, dark hair, blue molded-on clothing, 23 pieces

11½"	$30.00	$110.00

Knight and Viking Series, ca. 1960s

Action figures with accessories

Gordon, the Gold Knight, molded-on gold clothing, brown hair, beard, mustache

11½"	$35.00	$125.00

Sir Stuart, Silver Knight, molded-on silver clothing, black hair, mustache, goatee

11½"	$35.00	$125.00

Brave Erik, Viking with horse, ca. 1967, molded-on green clothing, blond hair, blue eyes

11½"	$50.00	$150.00

Odin, the Viking, ca. 1967, brown molded-on clothing, brown eyes, brown hair, beard

11½"	$50.00	$150.00

Sindy

Ca. 1963+, in England by Pedigree, a fashion-type doll, rooted hair, painted eyes, wires in limbs allow her to pose, distributed in U.S. by Marx c. 1978 – 1982.

11"	$50.00	$120.00
Pedigree	$75.00	$175.00
Pedigree Sindy Majorette, box		$480.00*

Gayle, Sindy's friend, black vinyl

11"	$50.00	$115.00
Outfits	$35.00	$100.00

Soldiers, ca. 1960s

Articulated action figures with accessories

Buddy Charlie, Montgomery Wards, exclusive, a buddy for GI Joe, molded-on military uniform, brown hair

11½"	$35.00	$100.00

Stony "Stonewall" Smith, molded-on Army fatigues, blond hair, 36-piece accessories

11½"	$25.00	$100.00

Others

Freddy Krueger, 1989, vinyl, pull string talker horror movie *Nightmare on Elm Street* character played by Robert England

18"	$20.00	$50.00

PeeWee Herman, 1987 TV character, vinyl and cloth, ventriloquist doll in gray suit, red bow tie

18"	$10.00	$30.00

PeeWee Herman, pull string talker

18"	$10.00	$36.00

Mattel

Baby Beans, 1971 – 1975

Vinyl head, bean bag dolls, terry cloth or tricot bodies filled with plastic and foam

12"	$8.00	$35.00

Talking

12"	$10.00	$40.00

Baby First Step, 1965 – 1967

Battery operated walker, rooted hair, sleep eyes, pink dress

18"	$90.00	$175.00

Talking

18"	$100.00	$335.00

Baby Go Bye-Bye and Her Bumpety Buggy, 1970

Doll sits in car, battery operated, 12 maneuvers

11"	$25.00	$100.00

Baby's Hungry, 1967 – 1968

Battery operated, eyes move and lips chew when magic bottle or spoon is put to mouth, wets, plastic bib

17"	$12.00	$45.00

Baby Love Light

Battery operated

16"	$5.00	$18.00

Baby Pattaburp, 1964 – 1966

Vinyl, drinks milk, burps when patted, pink jacket, lace trim

16"	$75.00	$250.00

19" vinyl Baby First Step, marked "Baby//First Step" on back torso, rooted blond hair, blue sleep eyes, closed mouth, pink dress with blue ribbon trim, battery operated walking doll, circa 1965, $75.00. Courtesy Patricia Crhistlieb.

16" vinyl Luv'n Touch Real Sister, designed by Martha Armstrong Hand, blond synthetic hair, blue eyes, open/closed smiling mouth, vinyl arms, cloth body and legs, all original in flower print outfit, circa 1979, $40.00. Courtesy Pat Graff.

10¾" vinyl Baby Small Talks Little Bo Peep, marked "1967//Mattel Inc.//U.S. for Pats Pend.//Mexico," blue eyes, blond hair, open mouth with teeth, hard plastic body, says eight phrases, child's voice, turquoise dress, gold shoes, circa 1968 – 1969, $15.00. Courtesy Bev Mitchell.

Baby Play-A-Lot, 1972 – 1973

Posable arms, fingers can hold things, comes with 20 toys, moves arm to brush teeth, moves head, no batteries, has pull string and switch

16" $5.00 $22.00

Baby Say 'N See, 1967 – 1968

Eyes and lips move while talking, white dress, pink yoke

17" $10.00 $35.00

Baby Secret, 1966 – 1967

Vinyl face and hands, stuffed body, limbs, red hair, blue eyes, whispers 11 phrases, moves lips

18" $25.00 $100.00

Baby Small Talk, 1968 – 1969

Says eight phrases, infant voice, additional outfits available

10¾" $10.00 $25.00

Black

10¾" $15.00 $30.00

In Nursery Rhyme outfit

10¾" $15.00 $50.00

Baby Tender Love, 1970 – 1973

Baby doll, realistic skin, wets, can be bathed

Newborn

13" $20.00 $75.00

Talking

16" $10.00 $40.00

Boxed

16" $180.00*

Molded hairpiece, 1972

11½" $9.00 $33.00

Brother, sexed

11½" $25.00 $80.00

Baby Walk 'n Play, 1968

11" $4.00 $12.00

Baby Walk 'n See

18" $5.00 $18.00

Barbie: See that section.

Bozo, 1964

18" $25.00 $100.00

Big Jim Series

Vinyl action figures, many boxed accessory sets available

Big Jim, black hair, muscular torso

9½" $20.00 $115.00

Big Josh, dark hair, beard

9½" $9.00 $35.00

Dr. Steele, bald head, silver tips on right hand

9½" $8.00 $32.00

20" vinyl Mrs. Beasley, painted blue eyes, closed smiling mouth, rooted hair, blue/white polka dot printed body for clothing with removable collar and skirt, large yellow flannel feet, vinyl hands, original glasses, pull ring talking mechanism on left hip, original pink cardboard box marked "©1967 Family Affair Company//©1966 Mattel, Inc.//Hawthorne, Calif.//Printed in U.S.A.," NRFB, circa 1967 – 1974, $230.00. *Courtesy McMasters Doll Auctions.*

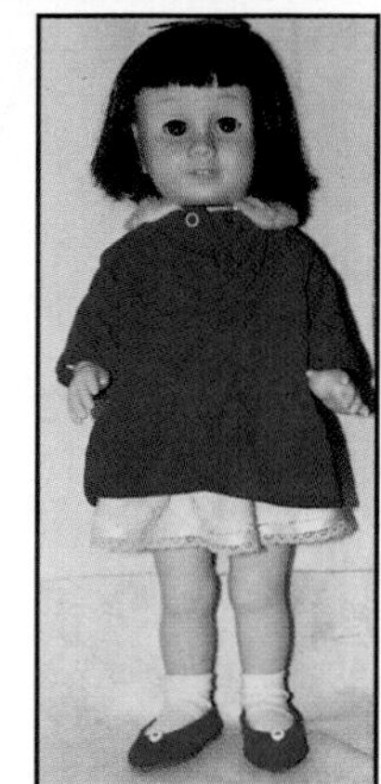

20" vinyl Chatty Cathy, soft vinyl head, brown sleep eyes, open/closed mouth with painted teeth, brunette rooted hair, hard plastic body, pull string activates voice, dressed in red velvet party coat with white fur collar, red shoes, circa 1960 – 1963, $250.00. *Courtesy Leslie Tannenbaum.*

Buffy and Mrs. Beasley, 1967 & 1974

Characters from TV sitcom, *Family Affair.*

Buffy, vinyl, rooted hair, painted features, holds small Mrs. Beasley, vinyl head, on cloth body

6½"	$75.00	$185.00

Talking Buffy, vinyl, 1969 – 1971, holds tiny 6" rag Mrs. Beasley

10¾"	$50.00	$400.00

Mrs. Beasley, 1967 – 1974, talking vinyl head, cloth body, square glasses, blue polka-dot dress

22"	$175.00	$550.00

Mrs. Beasley, 1973, non-talker

15½"	$25.00	$100.00

Captain Kangaroo, 1967

Sears only, talking character, host for TV kids program

19"	$20.00	$75.00

Captain Laser, 1967

Vinyl, painted features, blue uniform, silver accessories, batteries operate laser gun, light-up eyes

12"	$70.00	$265.00

Casper, the Friendly Ghost, ca. 1964

16"	$35.00	$100.00+

1971

5"	$15.00	$60.00

Chatty Cathy Series

Chatty Cathy, 1960 – 1963, vinyl head, hard plastic body, pull string activates voice, dressed in pink and white checked or blue party dresses, 1963 – 1965, says 18 new phrases, red velvet and white lace dress, extra outfits available

Blond

20"	$100.00	$350.00

Brunette, brown eyes

20"	$125.00	$400.00

Pink Peppermint

20"	$465.00*	

24" vinyl Charmin' Chatty Travels 'Round the World Set, boxed with accessories, circa 1963 – 1964, $200.00 – 400.00. Courtesy McMasters Doll Auctions.

Chatty Baby, 1962 – 1964, red pinafore over rompers

18" $20.00 $75.00

Charmin' Chatty, 1963 – 1964

Talking doll, soft vinyl head, closed smiling mouth, hard vinyl body, long rooted hair, long legs, five records placed in left side slot, one-piece navy skirt, white middy blouse, with red sailor collar, red socks and saddle shoes, glasses, five disks; extra outfits and 14 more disks available

24" $55.00 $200.00

Tiny Chatty Baby, 1963 – 1964

Smaller version of Chatty Baby, blue rompers, blue, white striped panties, bib with name, talks, other outfits available

15½" $20.00 $90.00

Black

15½" $25.00 $100.00

Tiny Chatty Brother, 1963 – 1964

Boy version of Tiny Chatty Baby, blue and white suit and cap, hair parted on side

15½" $20.00 $75.00

Cheerful Tearful, 1966 – 1967

Vinyl, blond hair, face changes from smile to pout as arm is lowered, feed her bottle, wets and cries real tears

7" $25.00 $100.00

Dancerina, 1969 – 1971

Battery operated, posable arms, legs, turns, dances with control knob on head, pink ballet outfit

24" $100.00 $275.00

Baby Dancerina, 1970

Smaller version, no batteries, turn-knob on head, white ballet outfit

16" $75.00 $150.00

Black

16" $85.00 $175.00

Teeny Dancerina

12" $8.00 $30.00

Debbie Boone, 1978

11½" $12.00 $40.00

Dick Van Dyke, 1969

As Mr. Potts in movie, *Chitty Chitty Bang Bang,* all-cloth, flat features, talks in actor's voice

Mark: "© Mattel 1969" on cloth tag

24" $18.00 $85.00

Drowsy, 1965 – 1974

Vinyl head, stuffed body, sleepers, pull-string talker

15½" $35.00 $175.00

15½" $200.00* MIB

30" vinyl Marie Osmond, long auburn rooted wig, painted brown eyes, open/closed smiling mouth with painted teeth, in original long pink dress, original stand and wardrobe with five patterns, circa 1977, $125.00. *Courtesy Maria Traver.*

Dr. Dolittle, 1968

Character patterned after Rex Harrison in movie version, talker, vinyl with cloth body

24"	$18.00	$55.00

All vinyl

6"	$6.00	$22.00

Gramma Doll, 1970 – 1973

Sears only, cloth, painted face, gray yarn hair, says ten phrases, talker, foam-filled cotton

11"	$5.00	$20.00

Grizzly Adams, 1971

10"	$10.00	$40.00

Guardian Goddesses, 1979

11½"	$40.00	$125.00

Herman Munster, 1965

Cloth doll, talking TV character, *The Munsters*

21"	$25.00	$125.00

Julia, 1969, TV character nurse, from *Julia*

Twist 'N Turn

11½"	$80.00	$250.00

Talking

11½"	$75.00	$200.00

Talking, new hairstyle

11½"	$65.00	$185.00

Liddle Kiddles, 1966+

Small dolls of vinyl over wire frame, posable, painted features, rooted hair and came with bright costumes and accessories, packaged on 8½" x 9½" cards.

Mark: "1965// Mattel Inc.// Japan" on back

First price is for complete doll and accessories, excellent condition; second price (or one price only) is for mint complete doll and accessories. Add more for mint in package (or card) and never-removed-from-package. Less for worn dolls with missing accessories.

1966, First Series

3501 Bunson Bernie	3"	$50.00	$60.00
3502 Howard "Biff" Boodle	3½"	$55.00	$75.00
3503 Liddle Diddle	2¾"	$45.00	$150.00
3505 Babe Biddle	3½"	$165.00	$225.00
3506 Calamity Jiddle	3"	$45.00	$160.00
3507 Florence Niddle	2¾"	$65.00	$75.00
3508 Greta Griddle	3"	$85.00	$95.00
3509 Millie Middle	2¾"	$45.00	$55.00
3510 Beat A Diddle	3½"	$155.00	$180.00

1967, Second Series

3513 Sizzly Friddle	3"	$50.00	$80.00
3514 Windy Fiddle	2¾"	$200.00	$225.00
3515 Trikey Triddle	2¾"	$140.00	$160.00
3516 Freezy Sliddle	3½"	$130.00	$150.00
3517 Surfy Skiddle	3"	$50.00	$60.00

3518 Soapy Siddle	3½"	$55.00	$75.00
3519 Rolly Twiddle	3½"	$180.00	$200.00
3548 Beddy Bye Biddle (with robe)		$60.00	$70.00
3549 Pretty Priddle	3½"	$50.00	$65.00
1968, Third Series			
3587 Baby Liddle	2¾"	$175.00	$200.00
3551 Telly Viddle	3½"	$50.00	$200.00
3552 Lemons Stiddle	3½"	$60.00	$75.00
3553 Kampy Kiddle	3½"	$50.00	$200.00
3554 Slipsy Sliddle	3½"	$60.00	$200.00
Storybook Kiddles, 1967 – 1968		$120.00	$260.00
Skediddle Kiddles, 1968 – 1970	4"	$75.00	
Playhouse Kiddles, 1970	3½"	$95.00	
Kiddles 'N Kars, 1969 – 1970	2¾"	$177.50*	
Tea Party Kiddles, 1970 – 1971	3½"	$135.00	
Lucky Locket Kiddles, 1967 – 1970	2"	$50.00+	
Kiddle Kolognes, 1968 – 1970	2"	$125.00	
Kola Kiddles, 1968 – 1969	2"	$75.00+	
Sweet Treat Kiddles, 1969 – 1970	2"	$125.00	
Liddle Kiddle Playhouses, 1966 – 1968		$75.00+	
Mork & Mindy	9"	$10.00	$45.00

2" vinyl Santa Kiddle, #3595, white beard, red santa suit and cap, in package, package says "Real Christmas Tree Ornament," circa 1968, $25.00. *Courtesy Adrienne Hagey.*

Osmond Family

Donny or Marie Osmond, 1978

12"	$12.00	$40.00

Jimmy Osmond, 1979

10"	$15.00	$65.00

Scooba Doo, 1964

Vinyl head, rooted hair, cloth body, talks in Beatnik phrases, blond or black hair, striped dress

23"	$25.00	$125.00

Shogun Warrior

All plastic, battery operated

23½"	$65.00	$250.00

Shrinkin' Violette, 1964 – 1965

Cloth, yarn hair, pull-string talker, eyes close, mouth moves

16"	$50.00	$250.00

Sister Belle, 1961 – 1963

Vinyl, pull string talker, cloth body

16"	$45.00	$100.00

Star Spangled dolls

Uses Sunshine Family adults, *marked "1973"*

Pioneer Daughter	$12.00	$45.00

Sunshine Family, The

Vinyl, posable, come with Idea Book, Father, Mother, Baby

Steve	9"	$10.00	$40.00
Stephie	7½"	$10.00	$40.00
Sweets	3½"	$10.00	$40.00

* at auction

Tatters, 1965 – 1967
Talking cloth doll, wears rag clothes

19"	$30.00	$125.00

Teachy Keen, 1966 – 1970
Sears only, vinyl head, cloth body, ponytail, talker, tells child to use accessories included, buttons, zippers, comb

16"	$9.00	$35.00

Tinkerbelle, 1969, talking, patter pillows

18"	$7.00	$22.00

Tippee Toes, 1968 – 1970
Battery operated, legs move, rides accessory horse, tricycle, knit sweater, pants

17"	$60.00	$100.00
Tricycle/horse	$10.00	$40.00

Welcome Back Kotter, 1973, characters from TV sitcom
Freddie "Boom Boom" Washington, Arnold Horshack

9"	$10.00	$40.00

Vinnie Barbarino (John Travolta)

9"	$25.00	$80.00

Gabe Kotter

9"	$8.00	$30.00

Zython, 1977
Has glow-in-the-dark head. Enemy in *Space 1999* series.

	$25.00	$100.00

Mego

Action Jackson, 1971 – 1972
Vinyl head, plastic body, molded hair, painted black eyes, action figure, many accessory outfits. *Mark: "©Mego Corp//Reg. U.S. Pat. Off.//Pat. Pend.//Hong Kong//MCMLXXI"*

8"	$12.00	$50.00

Black

8"	$20.00	$75.00

Dinah-mite, Black

	$7.50	$30.00

Batman, 1974

8"	$15.00	$45.00

Arch enemy

8"	$4.00	$15.00

Captain and Tennille
Daryl Dragon and Toni Tennille, 1977, recording and TV personalities, Toni Tennille doll has no molded ears

12½"	$20.00	$85.00

Cher, 1976
TV and recording personality, husband Sonny Bono, all-vinyl, fully jointed, rooted long black hair, also as grow-hair doll
Growing Hair Cher, 1976

12"	$60.00	$225.00
Frosted Feathers costume		$50.00 – 200.00+
Star Brite costume		$325.00*

Sonny Bono

12" $12.00 $45.00

CHiPs 1977

California Highway Patrol TV show, Jon Baker (Larry Wilcox), Frank "Ponch" Poncherello (Erik Estrada)

8" $5.00 $20.00

Diana Ross, 1977

Recording and movie personality, all-vinyl, fully jointed, rooted black hair, long lashes

12½" $55.00 $150.00

Farrah Fawcett, 1977

Model, movie, and television personality, starred as Jill in *Charlie's Angels,* vinyl head, rooted blond hair, painted green eyes

12½" $25.00 $60.00

Flash Gordon Series, ca. 1977+

Vinyl head, hard plastic articulated body

Dale Arden

9" $25.00 $100.00

Dr. Zarkov

9½" $25.00 $100.00

Flash Gordon

9½" $25.00 $100.00

Ming, the Merciless

9½" $25.00 $100.00

Happy Days Series, 1976

Characters from *Happy Days* TV sitcom, Henry Winkler starred as Fonzie, Ronnie Howard as Richie, Anson Williams as Potsie, and Donny Most as Ralph Malph

Fonzie

8" $15.00 $50.00

Richie, Potsie, Ralph

$7.50 $25.00

Jaclyn Smith, 1977

Vinyl

12½" $50.00 $170.00

Joe Namath, 1970

Football player, actor, soft vinyl head, rigid vinyl body, painted hair and features

12" $25.00 $100.00

Outfit, MIP $32.50

KISS, 1978

Rock group, with Gene Simmons, Ace Frehley, Peter Cris, and Paul Stanley, all-vinyl, fully jointed, rooted hair, painted features and makeup

12½" $100.00 $410.00, set of four

Kristy McNichol, 1978. Actress, starred in TV show, *Family.* All-vinyl, rooted brown hair, painted eyes. *Marked on head: "©MEGO CORP.//MADE IN HONG KONG." Marked on back: "©1977 MEGO CORP.//MADE IN HONG KONG."*

9" $15.00 $40.00

Laverne and Shirley, 1977

TV sitcom; Penny Marshall played Laverne, Cindy Williams played Shirley, also, from the same show, David Lander as Squiggy, and Michael McKean as Lenny, all-vinyl, rooted hair, painted eyes

	11½"	$25.00	$75.00

Our Gang, 1975

From *Our Gang* movie shorts, that replayed on TV, included characters Alfalpha, Buckwheat, Darla, Mickey, Porky, and Spanky

	6"	$7.00	$25.00

Planet of the Apes

Planet of the Apes Movie Series, ca. 1970s

Astronaut	8"	$30.00	$120.00
Ape Soldier	8"	$25.00	$100.00
Cornelius	8"	$35.00	$140.00
Dr. Zaius	8"	$40.00	$150.00
Zira	8"	$35.00	$140.00

Planet of the Apes TV Series, ca. 1974

Alan Verdon	8"	$40.00	$150.00
Galen	8"	$25.00	$100.00
General Urko	8"	$40.00	$150.00
General Ursus	8"	$50.00	$450.00
Peter Burke	8"	$40.00	$150.00

Star Trek

Star Trek TV Series, ca. 1973 – 1975

Captain Kirk	8"	$15.00	$60.00
Dr. McCoy	8"	$20.00	$75.00
Klingon	8"	$25.00	$100.00
Lt. Uhura	8"	$15.00	$60.00
Mr. Scott	8"	$20.00	$75.00
Mr. Spock	8"	$15.00	$60.00

Star Trek Movie Series, ca. 1979

Acturian	12½"	$25.00	$100.00
Captain Kirk	12½"	$15.00	$60.00
Ilia	12½"	$15.00	$60.00
Mr. Spock	12½"	$25.00	$100.00

Star Trek Aliens, ca. 1975 – 1976

Andorian	8"	$80.00	$325.00
Cheron	8"	$35.00	$130.00
Mugato	8"	$75.00	$300.00
Talos	8"	$65.00	$250.00
The Gorn	8"	$50.00	$200.00
The Romulan	8"	$150.00	$600.00

Starsky and Hutch, 1976

Police TV series, Paul Michael Glaser as Starsky, David Soul as Hutch, Bernie Hamilton as Captain Dobey, Antonio Fargas as Huggy Bear, also included a villain, Chopper, all-vinyl, jointed waists

	7½"	$12.00	$45.00

Suzanne Somers, 1978

Actress, TV personality, starred as Chrissy in *Three's Company,* all-vinyl, fully jointed, rooted blond hair, painted blue eyes, long lashes

	12½"	$15.00	$60.00

9" vinyl Mister Fantastic, a Marvel character, Les Extraordinaires Super Heroes, on card, NRFB, circa 1979, $50.00. Courtesy McMasters Doll Auctions.

Waltons, The, 1975

From TV drama series, set of two 8" dolls per package, all-vinyl

John Boy and Mary Ellen		
	$12.00	$45.00
Mom and Pop		
	$15.00	$50.00
Grandma and Grandpa		
	$10.00	$35.00

Wonder Woman Series, ca. 1976 – 1977

Vinyl head, rooted black hair, painted eyes, plastic body

Lt. Diane Prince		
12½"	$40.00	$150.00
Nubia		
12½"	$25.00	$100.00
Nurse		
12½"	$10.00	$40.00
Queen Hippolyte		
12½"	$25.00	$100.00
Steve Trevor		
12½"	$25.00	$100.00
Wonder Woman		
12½"	$40.00	$150.00

Molly'es

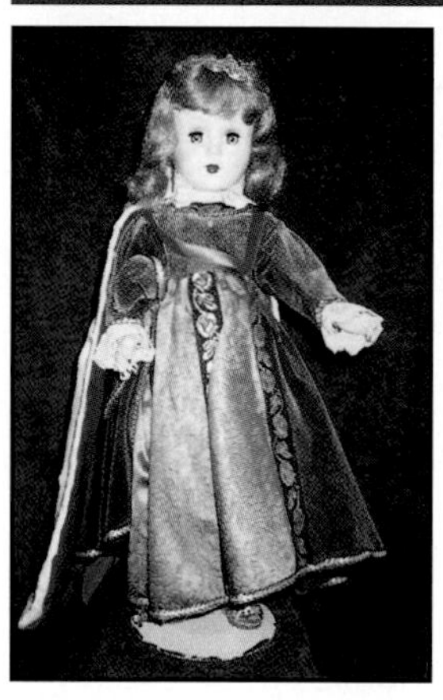

17" hard plastic Mollye Queen, blue sleep eyes, synthetic wig in original set, jointed hard plastic body, blue velvet and brocade dress, fur cape, gold sandals, tiara, sash with pin, circa 1950s, $695.00. Courtesy Rita Mauze.

Mollye Goldman, 1920+, International Doll Co., Philadelphia, PA. Designed and created clothes for cloth, composition, hard plastic, and vinyl dolls. Name marked only on vinyls; others may have had paper hang tags. She used dolls made by other companies. Also designed clothes for other makers.

First price is for doll in good condition, but with flaws; second price is for doll in excellent condition, original clothes. More for exceptional doll with fancy wardrobe or accessories.

Cloth, fine line painted lashes, pouty mouth

Child		
15"	$40.00	$150.00
18"	$45.00	$165.00
24"	$65.00	$215.00
29"	$85.00	$325.00
Internationals		
13"	$27.00	$95.00
15"	$45.00	$155.00
27"	$75.00	$300.00
Girl/Lady		
16"	$50.00	$195.00
21"	$75.00	$300.00

* at auction

Composition		
Baby		
15"	$40.00	$175.00
21"	$60.00	$250.00
Cloth body		
18"	$25.00	$100.00
Toddler		
15"	$50.00	$235.00
21"	$75.00	$295.00
Child		
15"	$50.00	$185.00
18"	$70.00	$265.00
Girl/Lady, add more for ball gown		
16"	$90.00	$365.00
21"	$130.00	$525.00
Hard Plastic		
Baby		
14"	$25.00	$95.00
20"	$40.00	$150.00
Cloth body		
17"	$25.00	$90.00
23"	$35.00	$140.00
Child		
14"	$50.00	$200.00+
18"	$75.00	$300.00+
23"	$100.00	$400.00+
Girl/Lady		
17"	$75.00	$315.00
20"	$80.00	$415.00
25"	$110.00	$465.00
Vinyl		
Baby		
8½"	$6.00	$22.00
12"	$5.00	$27.00
15"	$9.00	$43.00
Child		
8"	$7.00	$25.00
10"	$9.00	$35.00
15"	$15.00	$60.00
Girl/Lady		
Little Women		
9"	$9.00	$40.00

Monica Dolls

Ca. 1941 – 1951. Monica Dolls from Hollywood, designed by Hansi Share, made composition and later hard plastic with long face and painted or sleep eyes, eyeshadow, unique feature is very durable rooted human hair. Did not have high-heeled feet and unmarked, but wore paper wrist tag reading *"Monica Doll, Hollywood."* Composition dolls had pronounced widow's peak in center of forehead.

Monica Dolls

21" all-composition Monica, unmarked, identified by her unusual rooted human hair wig with widows peak, painted blue eyes, dark eyeliner above eyes, eyeshadow, soft rosy cheeks, closed mouth, five-piece composition body, original red and white dress, circa 1941 – 1949, $500.00. Courtesy Pat Graff.

Composition, 1941 – 1949

Painted eyes, Veronica, Jean, and Rosalind were names of 17" dolls produced in 1942.

11"	$75.00	$295.00
15"	$150.00	$525.00
17"	$175.00	$750.00
20 – 21"	$250.00	$950.00
24"	$300.00	$1,200.00

Hard plastic, 1949 – 1951, sleep eyes, Elizabeth, Marion, or Linda

14"	$150.00	$600.00
18"	$200.00	$800.00
20"	$250.00	$900.00

Nancy Ann Storybook

1936+, San Francisco, CA. Started by Rowena Haskin (Nancy Ann Abbott). Painted bisque, mohair wig, painted eyes, head molded to torso, jointed limbs, either sticker on outfit or hang tag, in box, later made in hard plastic.

First price for played-with or missing accessories doll; second price for mint or mint-in-box. Add 30 percent or more for black dolls. Selected auction prices reflect once-only extreme high prices and should be noted accordingly. Painted bisque baby prices vary with outfits.

Baby only, 1936+

Pink/blue mottled or sunburst box with gold label, gold foil sticker on clothes *"Nancy Ann Dressed Dolls," marked "87," "88," or "93," "Made in Japan,"* no brochure

Baby		
3½" – 4½"	$100.00	$400.00
with cradle		
3¾"	$1,525.00*	

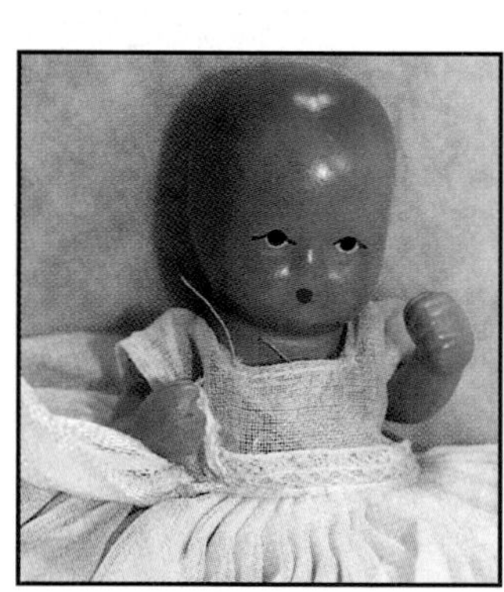

3½" painted bisque baby, marked "Story//Book//Doll//USA," painted hair, painted eyes, closed mouth, fist hands, long white dress, circa 1938+, $200.00. Courtesy Barbara Hull.

Baby or Child

1937

Child marked "Made in Japan," "1146," "1148," or "Japan" sunburst box with gold label, gold foil sticker on clothes read *"Nancy Ann Dressed Dolls,"* no brochure

Baby		
3½" – 4½"	$275.00	$700.00
Child		
5"	$500.00	$1,200.00

1938

Marked *"America"* (baby *marked "87," "88,"*

or "93" "Made in Japan"), colored box, sunburst pattern with gold label, gold foil sticker on clothes: *"Judy Ann,"* no brochure

Baby		
3½" – 4½"	$200.00	$325.00
Child		
5"	$200.00	$500.00

1938

Marked *"Judy Ann USA"* and *"Story Book USA"* (baby *marked "Made in USA"* and *"88, 89, and 93 Made in Japan"*), colored box, sunburst pattern with gold or silver label, gold foil sticker on clothes: *"Storybook Dolls,"* no brochure

3½"– 4½"	$225.00	$325.00
5"	$200.00	$300.00

Complete with teddy bear, dress tagged *"Judy Ann,"* blue box, silver dots, marked *"Japan 1146"*

5"	$160.00	$650.00
Judy Ann mold		
	$100.00	$500.00
Storybook mold		
	$100.00	$350.00

Jointed bisque

Pussy Cat, Pussy Cat, complete with pet

5"	$100.00	$300.00

1939

Child, molded socks and molded bangs (baby has star-shaped hands), colored box with small silver dots, silver label, gold foil sticker on clothes, *"Storybook Dolls,"* no brochure

Baby		
3½" – 4½"	$75.00	$150.00
Child		
5"	$125.00	$225.00

1940

Child has molded socks only (baby has star-shaped bisque hands), colored box with white polka dots, silver label, gold foil sticker on clothes, *"Storybook Dolls,"* has brochure

Baby		
3½" – 4½"	$60.00	$135.00
Child		
5"	$50.00	$200.00

1941 – 1942

Child has pudgy tummy or slim tummy; baby has star-shaped hands or fist, white box with colored polka dots, with silver label, gold foil bracelet with name of doll and brochure

5½" painted bisque, marked "Story//Book//Dolls//USA" on back, painted eyes, closed mouth, red mohair wig, long yellow flower print dress with black lace, straw hat, circa 1941+, $50.00. Courtesy Barbara Hull.

5½" painted bisque Little Betty Blue, #109, from the Storybook Series, blond mohair wig, painted eyes, one-piece head, body, and legs, blue and white check dress, blue bonnet, gold foil label, white box with blue polka dots, circa 1943 – 1947, $55.00. Private collection.

5½" painted bisque Friday's Child, #184, brunette mohair wig, painted eyes, one-piece head, body, and legs, long red print dress, white apron, white box with pink polka dots, brochure, circa 1943 – 1947, $55.00. *Private collection.*

5½" hard plastic Curly Locks, black sleep eyes, brown mohair wig, box marked Fairyland Series, "Curly Locks," pink felt hat, pink dotted Swiss dress and matching long pants, white box with polka dots, circa 1949, $55.00. *Courtesy Susana Auza-Smith.*

Baby
3½" – 4½" $65.00 $125.00
Child
5" $20.00 $75.00

1943 – 1947

Child has one-piece head, body, and legs, baby has fist hands, white box with colored polka dots, silver label, ribbon tie or pin fastener, gold foil bracelet with name of doll and brochure

Baby
3½" – 4½" $60.00 $125.00
Child
5" $25.00 $65.00

1947 – 1949

Child has hard plastic body, painted eyes, baby has bisque body, plastic arms and legs, white box with colored polka dots with *"Nancy Ann Storybook Dolls"* between dots, silver label, brass snap, gold foil bracelet with name of doll and brochure. More for special outfit.

Baby
3½" – 4½" $45.00 $90.00

Ca. 1949

Hard plastic, both have black sleep eyes, white box with colored polka dots and *"Nancy Ann Storybook Dolls"* between dots, silver label, brass or painted snaps, gold foil bracelet with name of doll and brochure

Baby
3½" – 4½" $40.00 $75.00
Child
5" $15.00 $50.00

Ca. 1953

Hard plastic, child has blue sleep eyes, except for 4½" girls; baby has black sleep eyes, white box with colored polka dots, some with clear lids, silver label, gripper snap, gold foil bracelet with name of doll and brochure

Baby
3½" – 4½" $40.00 $75.00*
only in christening dress
Child
5" $925.00*

SPECIAL DOLLS

Mammy and Baby, marked *"Japan 1146"* or America mold
5" $150.00 $1,200.00

Storybook USA
5" $125.00 $500.00

9" hard plastic Muffie, marked "Storybook Dolls//California//MUFFIE," saran wigs, sleep eyes, painted lashes, closed mouths, walkers, hard plastic bodies, with boxes, circa 1956, Left: blond Muffie, $335.00; right: brunette Muffie, $345.00. Courtesy McMasters Doll Auctions.

Topsy, bisque black doll, jointed leg

All-bisque	$75.00	$400.00
Plastic arms	$50.00	$150.00
Topsy, all plastic, painted or sleep eye	$30.00	$100.00

White boots, bisque jointed leg dolls

5"	Add $50.00	

Series Dolls, depending on mold mark

All-Bisque

Around the World Series

Chinese	$300.00	$1,200.00
English Flower Girl	$150.00	$400.00
Portuguese	$200.00	$450.00
Poland	$200.00	$450.00
Russia	$200.00	$1,200.00
Other Countries	$100.00	$400.00

Masquerade Series

Ballet Dancer	$200.00	$800.00
Cowboy	$200.00	$800.00
Pirate	$200.00	$800.00

Sports Series	$300.00	$1,200.00
Flower Series (bisque)	$175.00	$400.00

Margie Ann Series

Margie Ann	$60.00	$175.00
Margie Ann in other outfits	$125.00	$350.00

Powder & Crinoline Series	$60.00	$175.00

Bisque or Plastic

Operetta or Hit Parade Series	$60.00	$175.00

19" hard plastic Nancy Ann Style Show, brown synthetic wig in original set, sleep eyes, hard plastic body, original striped green formal with black velvet bodice, matching straw hat trimmed with flowers, circa 1952 – 1955, $200.00. Courtesy Rita Mauze.

Hard Plastic

Big and Little Sister Series, or Commencement Series (except baby)

$30.00 $100.00

Bridal, Dolls of the Day, Dolls of the Month, Fairytale, Mother Goose, Nursery Rhyme, Religious, and Seasons Series, painted or sleep eye

$20.00 $75.00

Other Dolls

Audrey Ann, toddler, marked *"Nancy Ann Storybook 12"*

6" $250.00 $975.00

Nancy Ann Style Show

Hard plastic, sleep eyes, long dress, unmarked

18" $300.00 $600.00

Wedding Day, boxed, hang tag

18" $1,903.00*

Vinyl head, plastic body, all original, complete

18" $300.00 $500.00

Muffie, 1953 – 1956

1953, hard plastic, wig, sleep eyes, strung straight leg, non-walker, painted lashes

8" $75.00 $350.00

1954, hard plastic walker, molded eyelashes, brows

8" $65.00 $185.00

1955 – 1956, vinyl head, molded or painted upper lashes, rooted saran wig, walker or bent-knee walker

8" $60.00 $165.00

Davy Crockett, 1955, walker, molded painted lashes, all original

8" $175.00*

Muffie, 1968+, reissued, hard plastic

8" $45.00 $105.00

Lori Ann

Vinyl

7½" $45.00 $175.00+

Debbie

Hard plastic in school dress, name on wrist tag/box

10" $100.00 $400.00 MIB

Vinyl head, hard plastic body

10" $25.00 $110.00 MIB

Hard plastic walker

10½" $40.00 $160.00 MIB

Vinyl head, hard plastic walker

10½" $23.00 $90.00 MIB

Little Miss Nancy Ann, 1959

Nude

8½" $25.00 $100.00 MIB

Day dress

$25.00 $50.00 MIB

Other outfits

$30.00 $75.00 MIB

* at auction

Miss Nancy Ann, 1959, marked *"Nancy Ann,"* vinyl head, rooted hair, rigid vinyl body, high-heeled feet

Nude	10½"	$25.00	$85.00 MIB
Day dress		$25.00	$50.00 MIB
Other outfits		$30.00	$75.00 MIB
Baby Sue Sue, 1960s, vinyl			
Doll only		$35.00	$1750.00+ MIB
Outfit		$50.00	$75.00 MIB

Old Cottage Dolls

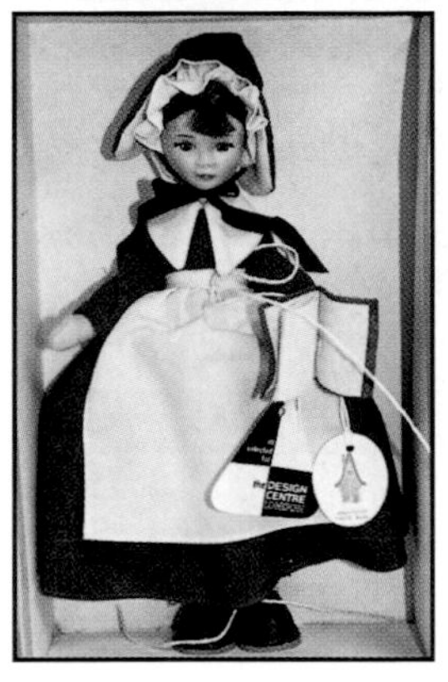

8¾" composition, brown mohair wig, painted features, blue eyes, closed mouth, cloth body, mitt hands, dark gray dress with white collar and apron, matching bonnet, holding book, "Old Cottage Toys" hang tag with house logo, all original with box, circa 1950+, $175.00. Courtesy Dorothy Bohlin.

9½" hard plastic, blond mohair wig in braids, painted features, blue eyes, closed mouth, cloth body, mitt hands, navy blue jumper, matching hat, white shirt, red tie and belt, red ribbons in hair, white socks, black shoes, "Old Cottage Toys" hang tag with house logo, circa 1960+, $125.00+. Courtesy Dorothy Bohlin.

8½" composition Spring Girl, dark blond mohair wig, painted features, blue eyes, closed mouth, cloth body, mitt hands, green flower print dress with white pinafore, purse, matching shoes, with "Old Cottage Toys" hang tag, all original with box marked "Spring Girl//in Kate Greenaway style//by//Old Cottage Toys//Made in England," circa 1950+, $175.00. Courtesy Dorothy Bohlin.

Late 1940s on, England.

Mrs. M.E. Fleischmann made dolls with hard composition type heads, felt body, some with wire armature, oval hang tag has trademark "Old Cottage Dolls," special characters may be more.

7½"	$35.00	$125.00+
9"	$50.00	$175.00+
Mary Stuart, MIB		$280.00*
Tweedle Dee or Tweedle Dum, circa 1968		
10"	$200.00	$350.00

Pleasant Company

1986+, Middleton, WI. Pleasant Rowland started the company by making

Pleasant Company

19" vinyl Josephina, American Girl Series, represents a Mexican American, brown sleep eyes, black hair in braid, cloth body, vinyl arms and legs, original costume white blouse, multicolor skirt, $82.00. Courtesy Marilyn Ramsey.

vinyl play dolls with cloth bodies, synthetic hair, and sleep eyes. Each doll was sold with a book placing it in a specific time perod. Each doll has many accessories, additional wardrobe, and books. The set includes Felecity, 1774, Williamsburg, Virginia; Kirsten, 1854, American frontier; Samantha, 1904, Victorian era; Josefina, 1824, a Hispanic in New Mexico; Addy, 1864, African American; Kit, 1934, Depression era; Molly, 1944, W.W.II; and the American Girl of Today that can be ordered with choice of hair, eye, and skin color. Mattel bought the company in 1998.

18" $55.00 $82.00 (retail)

Raggedy Ann & Andy

19" cloth Georgene Novelties Raggedy Ann & Andy, tagged "Johnny Gruelle's Own Raggedy Ann & Andy Dolls//Copyright P.F. Volland Co.//1918//1920//Renewed//Myrtle T. Gruelle//1945//1947" on side seam of each doll, black disk eyes circled by white, triangle noses, painted smiling mouths, red yarn hair, stitch jointed at shoulders, elbows, hips, knees, mitten hands, dressed in original clothing, original boxes, circa 1951, $850.00. Courtesy McMasters Doll Auctions.

1915+. Designed by Johnny Gruelle in 1915, made by various companies. Ann wears dress with apron; Andy, shirt and pants with matching hat.

P.J. Volland, 1920 – 1934

Early dolls marked *"Patented Sept. 7, 1915."* All-cloth, tin or wooden button eyes, painted features. Some have sewn knee or arm joints, sparse brown or auburn yarn hair, oversize hands, feet turned outward.

Raggedy Ann and Andy

15 – 16" $400.00 $1,700.00

Beloved Belindy, 1926 – 1930, painted face, **1931 – 1934,** print face

15" $600.00 $2,300.00

Pirate Chieftain and other Characters

18" $500.00 $2,500.00

18" $4,000.00 MIB

Exposition, 1935

Raggedy Ann, no eyelashes, no eyebrows, outline nose, no heart, satin label on hem of dress

18" $3,000.00*

Too few in database for reliable range.

Mollye Goldman, 1935 – 1938

Marked on chest *"Raggedy Ann and Andy Dolls Manufactured by Molly'es Doll Outfitters."* Nose outlined in black, red heart on chest,

* at auction

reddish-orange hair, multicolored legs, blue feet, some have oilcloth faces

15"	$225.00	$900.00
17"	$275.00	$1,100.00
21"	$350.00	$1,500.00

Did not make Beloved Belindy

Georgene Novelties, 1938 – 1962

Ann has orange hair and a top knot, six different mouth styles; early ones had tin eyes, later ones had plastic, six different noses, seams in middle of legs and arms to represent knees and elbows. Feet turn forward, red and white striped legs. All have hearts that say *"I love you"* printed on chest. Tag sewn to left side seam, several variations, all say *"Georgene Novelties, Inc."*

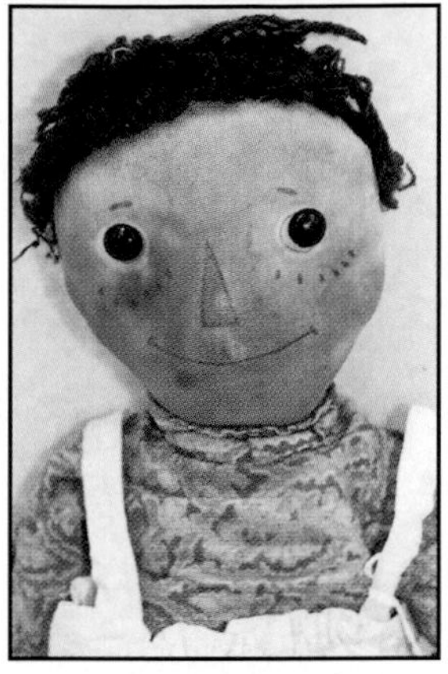

16" cloth Volland Raggedy Ann, black shoebutton eyes, single stroke brows, painted lower lashes, red triangle nose, closed smiling mouth, brown yarn hair, wooden heart in left side of chest, mitten hands, red and white striped legs, brown cloth feet turned outward, original flower print dress and white apron, soil on face, circa 1915 – 1920, $750.00. Courtesy Joan Sickler.

Raggedy Ann or Andy, 1930s – 1960s

1930s

15"	$90.00	$350.00
18"	$180.00	$750.00

Ca. 1938

19"	$4,350.00* pair	

1940s

13"	$1,665.00* pair	
18"	$85.00	$325.00
21"	$100.00	$400.00

1950s

18"	$50.00	$300.00

1960 – 1963

15"	$25.00	$110.00
18"	$35.00	$150.00

Awake/Asleep, pair

1940s

12"	$175.00	$650.00

Beloved Belindy, 1940 – 1944

18"	$125.00	$750.00

Knickerbocker, 1962 – 1982

Printed features, hair color change from orange to red; there were five mouth and five eyelash variations, tags were located on clothing back or pants seam.

Raggedy Ann or Andy, 1960s

15"	$75.00	$350.00
30 – 36"	$150.00	$600.00

Raggedy Ann Talking, 1960s

	$70.00	$265.00

Beloved Belindy, ca. 1965

15"	$1,600.00* MIB	

Raggedy Ann, 1970s

12"	$12.00	$45.00
15"	$15.00	$80.00

Size	Low	High
24"	$25.00	$135.00
30 – 36"	$50.00	$300.00

Talking, 1974

Size	Low	High
12"	$25.00	$100.00

Raggedy Ann, 1980s

Size	Low	High
16"	$7.00	$25.00
24"	$15.00	$55.00
30 – 36"	$35.00	$110.00

Camel with Wrinkled Knees

Size	Low	High
15"	$45.00	$175.00

Applause Toy Company, 1981 – 1983, Hasbro (Playskool), 1983+

Size	Low	High
8"	$2.00	$15.00
17"	$5.00	$50.00
48"	$25.00	$175.00

Nasco/Bobbs-Merrill, 1972

Cloth head, hard plastic doll body, printed features, apron marked *"Raggedy Ann"*

Size	Low	High
24"	$45.00	$150.00

Bobbs-Merrill Co., 1974

Ventriloquist dummy, hard plastic head, hands, foam body, printed face

Size	Low	High
30"	$50.00	$175.00

Ravca, Bernard

9" cloth Sam Houston, tagged "Sam Houston," sculptured stockinette face, cloth over wire arms, full fingers, blue wool suit, circa pre – 1930s, $250.00. Courtesy Nelda Shelton.

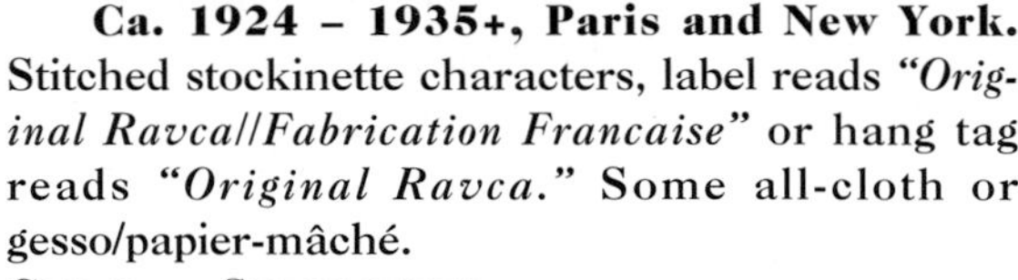

Ca. 1924 – 1935+, Paris and New York. Stitched stockinette characters, label reads *"Original Ravca//Fabrication Francaise"* or hang tag reads *"Original Ravca."* Some all-cloth or gesso/papier-mâché.

Cloth — Stockinette

Celebrities, Occupations, or Literary characters

Size	Low	High
7"	$38.00	$135.00
9½"	$40.00	$155.00
12"	$55.00	$210.00
17"	$75.00	$365.00

Queen Elizabeth

Size	Low	High
36"	$850.00*	Ravca cloth label on wrist

Military figures, such as Hitler, Mussolini

Size	Low	High
9"	$250.00	$1,300.00
20"	$450.00	$2,600.00
27"	$1,000.00	$5,000.00+

Peasants/Old People

Size	Low	High
7"	$23.00	$100.00
9"	$25.00	$135.00
12"	$35.00	$165.00
15"	$50.00	$235.00
23"	$75.00	$275.00

* at auction

Gesso — Papier-Mâché

12"	$100.00	$435.00
15"	$150.00	$625.00
17"	$250.00	$1,000.00
20"	$375.00	$1,525.00

Remco Industries

Ca. 1960 – 1974. One of the first companies to market with television ads. First price is for played-with doll; second price is for mint-in-box.

Addams Family

5½"	$5.00	$20.00

Baby Crawl-Along, 1967

20"	$7.00	$25.00

Baby Glad 'N Sad, 1967

Vinyl and hard plastic, rooted blond hair, painted blue eyes

14"	$5.00	$20.00

Baby Grow a Tooth, 1968

Vinyl and hard plastic, rooted hair, blue sleep eyes, open/closed mouth, one tooth, grows her own tooth, battery operated

	15"	$7.00	$25.00
Black			
	14"	$8.00	$30.00

Baby Know It All, 1969

17"	$4.00	$20.00

Baby Laugh A Lot, 1970

Rooted long hair, painted eyes, open/closed mouth, teeth, vinyl head, hands, plush body, push button, she laughs, battery operated

	16"	$5.00	$20.00
Black	16"	$8.00	$30.00

Baby Stroll A Long, 1966

15"	$4.00	$15.00

Beatles, 1964

Vinyl and plastic, Paul McCartney, Ringo Starr, George Harrison, and John Lennon. Paul 4⅞", all others 4½" with guitars bearing their names

Set of 4		$125.00	$525.00
John Lennon		$40.00	$150.00

Dave Clark Five, 1964

Set of five musical group, vinyl heads, rigid plastic bodies

Set		$50.00	
Dave Clark	5"	$8.00	$15.00
Other band members have name attached to leg			
	3"	$4.00	$10.00

Heidi and friends, 1967, in plastic case

Rooted hair, painted side-glancing eyes, open/closed mouth, all-vinyl, press button and dolls wave

Heidi			
	5½"	$13.00	$50.00
Herby			
	4½"	$3.00	$12.00

* at auction

6" vinyl Jan, marked "Remco Inc.//Heidi Doll//Jan," painted side-glancing eyes, open closed mouth with painted teeth, long black rooted braided hair, yellow dress, white shoes, circa 1967, $25.00. Courtesy Nelda Shelton.

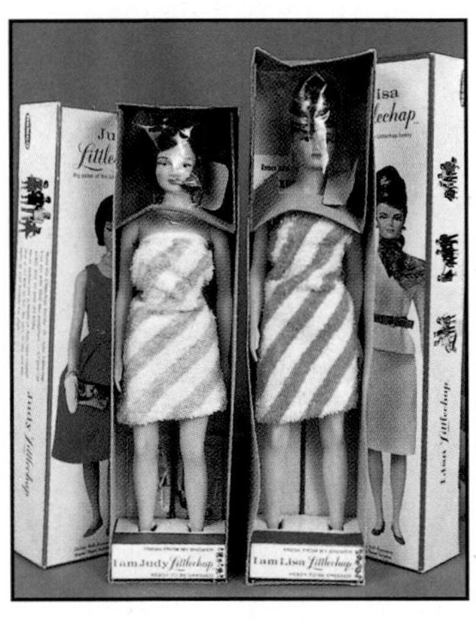

13½" vinyl Lisa Littlechap and 12" Judy Littlechap, pink lips, cheek blush, jointed hips, shoulders, and neck, painted eyes, closed mouths, Lisa has brunette/silver wig, wearing orange/white striped terry cloth towel, Judy has brunette wig, wearing pink/white striped terry cloth towel, both in original boxes with stands, booklets, cardboard foot inserts, plastic head covers, near mint, circa 1963, Lisa, $35.00, Judy, $40.00. Courtesy McMasters Doll Auctions.

Jan, Oriental
5½" $13.00 $50.00

Pip
5½" $13.00 $50.00

Winking Heidi, 1968
5½" $7.00 $35.00

Jeannie, I Dream of
6" $20.00 $65.00

Jumpsy, 1970, vinyl and hard plastic, jumps rope, rooted blond hair, painted blue eyes, closed mouth, molded-on shoes and socks
14" $5.00 $20.00

Black
14" $7.00 $25.00

Laurie Partridge, 1973
19" $50.00 $150.00

L.B.J., 1964
5½" $9.00 $25.00

Littlechap Family, 1963+

Vinyl head, arms, jointed hips, shoulders, neck, black molded painted hair, black eyes, box

Set of four $200.00 $480.00

Dr. John Littlechap
14½" $20.00 $85.00

Judy Littlechap
12" $25.00 $75.00

Libby Littlechap
10½" $35.00 $85.00

Lisa Littlechap
13½" $15.00 $50.00

Littlechap Accessories

Dr. John's Office
$75.00 $325.00 MIP

Bedroom
$25.00 $110.00 MIP

Family room
$25.00 $110.00 MIP

Dr. John Littlechap's outfits

Golf outfit $30.00 MIP

Medical $65.00 MIP

Suit $50.00 MIP

Tuxedo $70.00 MIP

Lisa's outfits

Evening dress $90.00 MIP

Coat, fur trim $50.00 MIP

Libby's, Judy's outfits

Jeans/sweater $30.00 MIP

Dance dress $45.00 MIP

* at auction

Mimi, 1973

Vinyl and hard plastic, battery operated singer, rooted long blond hair, painted blue eyes, open/closed mouth, record player in body, sings *I'd Like to Teach the World to Sing,* song used for Coca-Cola® commercial; sings in different languages

19"	$15.00	$50.00

Black

19"	$20.00	$60.00

Grandpa Munster, #1821, 1964, vinyl head, one-piece plastic body

4¾"	$65.00	$110.00

Orphan Annie, 1967

15"	$150.00* MIB

Sweet April, 1971

Vinyl

5½"	$2.50	$10.00

Black

5½"	$4.00	$15.00

Tippy Tumbles, 1968

Vinyl, rooted red hair, stationary blue eyes, does somersaults, batteries in pocketbook

16"	$14.00	$55.00

Tumbling Tomboy, 1969

Rooted blond braids, closed smiling mouth, vinyl and hard plastic, battery operated

17"	$5.00	$20.00

Richwood Toys Inc.

Sandra Sue, ca. 1940s, 1950s. Hard plastic, walker, head does not turn, slim body, saran wigs, sleep eyes. Some with high-heeled feet, only marks are number under arm or leg. All prices reflect outfits with original socks, shoes, panties, and accessories.

First price is for played with doll, incomplete costume; second price is for complete mint-in-box doll.

9" hard plastic Sandra Sue, sleep eyes, painted lower lashes, brunette synthetic wig, flat foot, non-walker, slim body, strung with elastic, plaid dress with yellow pinafore, circa 1952 – 1954, $225.00. Courtesy Peggy Millhouse.

Sandra Sue, 8"

Flat feet, in camisole, slip, panties, shoes, and socks

$55.00	$200.00

In school dress

$65.00	$225.00+

In party/Sunday dress

$95.00	$250.00

Special coat, hat, and dress, limited editions, Brides, Heidi, Little Women, Majorette

$85.00+	$250.00

Sport or play clothes

$45.00	$175.00

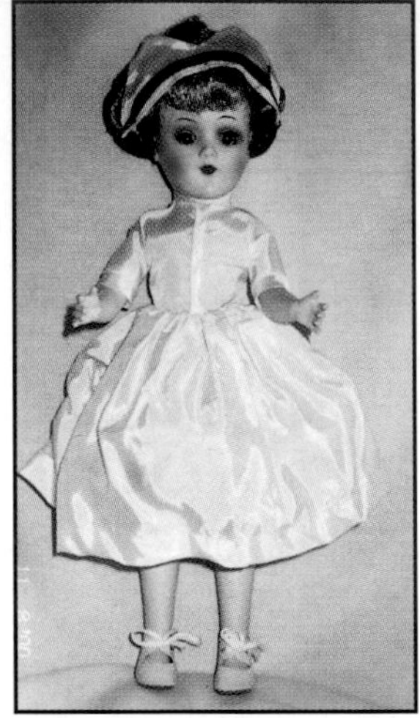

14" hard plastic Cindy Lou Nurse, auburn wig, sleep eyes, closed mouth, hard plastic jointed body, in original nurse uniform, circa 1950s, $300.00. Courtesy Sandy Johnson Barts.

MIB Twin Sandra Sues $395.00

Too few in database for reliable range.

High-heeled feet, camisole, slip, panties, shoes, socks

	$40.00	$150.00
In school dress		
	$40.00	$175.00+
In party/Sunday dress		
	$75.00	$200.00+

Special coat, hat and dress, limited editions, Brides, Heidi, Little Women, Majorette

	$75.00	$200.00+
Sport or play clothes		
	$40.00	$150.00
MIB Twin Sandra Sues		
		$350.00

Too few in database for reliable range.

Sandra Sue Outfits: mint, including all accessories

School dress	$5.00	$15.00
Party dress	$15.00	$25.00
Specials	$35.00	$50.00
Sport sets	$15.00	$25.00

Cindy Lou, 14"

Hard plastic, jointed dolls were purchased in bulk from New York distributor, fitted with double-stitched wigs by Richwood.

All prices include shoes, socks, panties, slips, and accessories.

In camisole, slip, panties, shoes, and socks

	$45.00	$165.00+
In school dress	$75.00	$175.00+
In party dress	$95.00	$225.00
In special outfits	$85.00+	$250.00
In sports outfits	$65.00	$175.00

Cindy Lou Outfits: mint, including all accessories

School dress	$35.00
Party dress	$45.00
Special outfit	$50.00
Sports clothes	$35.00

Roldan

Roldan characters are similar to Klumpe figures in many respects. They were made in Barcelona, Spain, from the early 1960s until the mid-1970s. They are made of felt over a wire armature with painted mask faces. Like Klumpe, Roldan figures represent professionals, hobbyists, dancers, historical characters, and contemporary males and females performing a wide variety of tasks.

Some, but not all Roldans, were imported by Rosenfeld Imports and Leora Dolores of Hollywood. Figures originally came with two sewn-on identifying cardboard tags. Roldan characters most commonly found are doctors,

Spanish dancers, and bull fighters. Roldan characters tend to have somewhat smaller heads, longer necks, and more defined facial features than Klumpe.

Common figures $30.00 $100.00+

Elaborate figure, MIB with accessories $250.00

Felt traveling lady, white paper tag, "Roldan," those with more accessories are more desirable, circa 1965, $125.00. Courtesy Sondra Gast.

Sasha

1965 – 1986+. Sasha dolls were created by Swiss artist, Sasha Morgenthaler, who handcrafted 20" children and 13" babies in Zurich, Switzerland, from the 1940s until her death in 1975. Her handmade studio dolls had cloth or molded bodies, five different head molds, and were hand painted by Sasha Morgenthaler. To make her dolls affordable as children's playthings, she licensed Gotz Puppenfabric (1964 – 1970) in Germany and Frido Trendon Ltd. (1965 – 1986) in England to manufacture 16" Sasha dolls in series. The manufactured dolls were made of rigid vinyl with painted features. Gotz Dolls, Inc. was granted a new license in 1994 and is currently producing them in Germany.

Left: 16" vinyl Sasha; right: 16" vinyl Sasha Gregor; and center: 11" vinyl Sasha Baby, made by Gotz Puppenfabrik licensed to produce Sasha in 1994 from estate of Sarah Morgenthaler, wrist tags, circa 1994+, Left: $165.00; right: $145.00; center: $105.00. Courtesy McMasters Doll Auctions.

Price range reflects rarity, condition, and completeness of doll, outfit, and packaging, and varies with geographic location. First price is for doll without original clothing and/or in less than perfect condition; second price is for mint-in-box (or tube).

Original Studio Sasha Doll, ca. 1940s – 1974

Made by Sasha Morganthaler in Switzerland. Some are signed on soles of feet, have wrist tags, or wear labeled clothing.

20" $2,000.00 $9,000.00 – $14,000.00

Gotz Sasha Doll, 1964 – 1970, Germany

Girls or boys, two face molds. Marked *"Sasha Serie"* in circle on neck and in three-circle logo on back. Three different boxes were used. Identified by wrist tag and/or booklet.

16" $600.00 $1,500.00

Frido-Trendon Ltd., 1965 – 1986, England

Unmarked on body, wore wrist tags and current catalogs were packed with doll

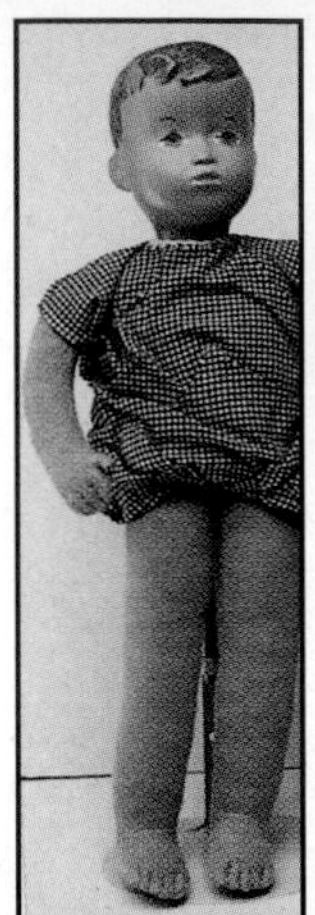

20" gypsum original boy, created by Sasha Morganthaler in Switzerland, a Type A Body with Type II molded head and rare molded hair, cloth body, stitched fingers and toes, arms and legs are sewn to the cloth torso, circa early 1940s, fine examples bring $9,000.00 – 14,000.00. Courtesy Dorisanne Osborne.

Child, 1965 – 1968, packaged in wide box

16" $100.00 $1,000.00

Child, 1969 – 1972, packaged in crayon tubes

16" $100.00 $600.00

Sexed Baby, 1970 – 1978, cradle, styrofoam cradles package or straw box and box

White or black

$100.00 $300.00

Unsexed Baby, 1978 – 1986, packaged in styrofoam wide or narrow cradles or straw basket and box

$100.00 $300.00

16" vinyl limited edition Princess, marked "Limited Edition//1986//297" on back of head, "Sasha//Serie//Made in England" on round wrist tag, blond human hair wig, painted brown eyes, painted upper lashes, single stroke brows, closed mouth, five-piece vinyl child body, orginal pink cotton ruffled dress, velvet coat lined with matching pink fabric, white socks, pink shoes, mint in original aged box with certificate, circa 1986, $495.00. Courtesy McMasters Doll Auctions.

Child, 1973 – 1975, packaged in shoe box style box

16" $100.00 $400.00

Child, 1975 – 1980, black, white, shoe box style box

16" $100.00 $300.00

Child, 1980 – 1986, black, white, packaged in photo box with flaps

$100.00 $250.00

#1 Sasha Anniversary doll

16" $175.00 $300.00

117S, Sasha "Sari" 1986, black hair, estimated only 400 produced before English factory closed January 1986

16" $450.00 $700.00

130E Sasha "Wintersport" 1986, blond hair

16" $400.00 $600.00

330E Gregor Sandy (hair) "Hiker"

16" $450.00 $750.00

Limited Editions

Made by Trendon Sasha Ltd. in England, packaged in box with outer sleeve picturing individual doll. Limited edition Sasha dolls marked on neck with date and number. Number on certificate matches number on doll's neck.

1981 "Velvet," girl, light brown wig, production number planned, 5,000

$300.00 $450.00

1982 "Pintucks" girl, blond wig, production number planned, 6,000

$300.00 $450.00

1983 "Kiltie" girl, red wig, production number planned, 4,000

	$350.00	$500.00

1984 "Harlequin" girl, rooted blond hair, production number planned 4,000

	$200.00	$350.00

1985 "Prince Gregor" boy, light brown wig, production number planned, 4,000

	$250.00	$400.00

1986 "Princess Sasha" girl, blond wig, production number planned, 3,500, but only 350 were made

	$1,000.00	$1,500.00

Gotz Dolls Inc., 1995 +, Germany

They received the license in September 1994; dolls introduced in 1995.

Child, 1995 – 1996

Marked *"Gotz Sasha"* on neck and *"Sasha Series"* in three circle logo on back. About 1,500 of the dolls produced in 1995 did not have mold mark on back. Earliest dolls packaged in generic Gotz box, currently in tube, wear wrist tag, Gotz tag, and have mini-catalog.

16½"	$300.00 retail

Baby, 1996

Baby, unmarked on neck, marked *"Sasha Series"* in three circle logo on back. First babies were packaged in generic Gotz box or large tube, currently packaged in small "Baby" tube. Wears Sasha wrist tag, Gotz booklet and current catalog.

12"	$150.00 retail

Shirley Temple

1934+, Ideal Novelty Toy Corp., New York. Designed by Bernard Lipfert, 1934 – 1940s. Composition head and jointed body, dimples in cheeks, green sleep eyes, open mouth, teeth, mohair wig, tagged original dress, center-snap shoes. Prototype dolls may have paper sticker inside head and bias trimmed wig.

First price is for incomplete or played-with doll. Second price is for doll in excellent to mint condition, all original. Add more for exceptional dolls or special outfits like Ranger or Wee Willie Winkie.

Composition

Shirley Temple

11"	$400.00	$975.00
13"	$350.00	$750.00
16"	$400.00	$800.00
17"	$200.00	$875.00
18"	$250.00	$975.00
20"	$300.00	$1,100.00
22"	$375.00	$1,200.00
27"	$450.00	$1,750.00

20" composition Ideal Shirley Temple in Captain January outfit, marked "SHIRLEY TEMPLE//Cop//Ideal//N&T Co." on head, "SHIRLEY TEMPLE//20" on body, mohair wig, hazel sleep eyes, open mouth, six upper teeth, dimples, five-piece composition body, designed by Bernard Lipfert, circa 1934+, $2,250.00. Courtesy Iva Mae Jones.

16" composition Ideal Shirley Temple Baby, marked "SHIRLEY TEMPLE" on head, molded painted hair, flirty sleep eyes, open mouth with two upper and three lower teeth, dimples, white and pink dress trimmed in lace, pink socks, white shoes, circa 1935, $1,500.00. Courtesy Sharon Kolibaba.

12" vinyl Ideal Shirley Temple, marked "Ideal Doll//ST – 12" on head, sleep eyes, synthetic rooted wig, open/closed mouth, teeth, dimples, rosy cheeks, green pants, matching hat, gray button up jacket with fur lining, white socks, black shoes, circa 1957, $395.00. Courtesy Iva Mae Jones.

Marks:
SHIRLEY TEMPLE//IDEAL NOV. & TOY on back of head and SHIRLEY TEMPLE on body. Some marked only on head and with a size.

Baby Shirley

18"	$400.00	$1,200.00
21"	$400.00	$1,500.00

Hawaiian, "Marama," Ideal used the composition Shirley Temple mold for this doll representing a character from the movie *Hurricane*, black yarn hair, wears grass skirt, Hawaiian costume

18"	$400.00	$950.00

Shirley at the Organ, special display stand with composition Shirley Temple at non-functioning organ, music provided by record

$3,500.00+

**Too few in database for reliable range.*

Accessories:

Button, three types	$125.00
Buggy, wood	$650.00
Buggy, wicker	$500.00
Dress, tagged	$125.00 – $175.00
Trunk	$175.00 – $225.00

Variants

Japanese, unlicensed Shirley dolls

All-bisque

6"	$65.00	$250.00

Celluloid

5"	$45.00	$185.00
8"	$65.00	$245.00

Celluloid, Dutch Shirley Temple, ca. 1937+. All-celluloid, open crown, metal pate, sleep eyes, dimples in cheeks. Marked: *"Shirley Temple"* on head, may have additional marks, dressed in Dutch costume.

13"	$90.00	$350.00
15"	$100.00	$400.00

Composition Japanese, heavily molded brown curls, painted eyes, open/closed mouth with teeth, body stamped *"Japan"*

7½"	$75.00	$300.00

Vinyl

First price indicates doll in excellent condition with flaws; second price is for excellent condition doll, original clothes, accessories. The newer the doll the more perfect it must be to command higher prices.

* at auction

1957

All-vinyl, sleep eyes, synthetic rooted wig, open/closed mouth, teeth, came in two-piece slip and undies, tagged Shirley Temple, came with gold plastic script pin reading *"Shirley Temple,"* marked on back of head: *"ST//12"*

12"	$135.00	$300.00+

1958 – 1961

Marked on back of head: *"S.T.//15," "S.T.//17,"* or *"S.T.//19,"* some had flirty ("Twinkle") eyes; add more for flirty eyes or 1961 Cinderella, Bo Peep, Heidi, and Red Riding Hood

15"	$100.00	$375.00
17"	$115.00	$450.00
19"	$125.00	$500.00

1960, Jointed wrists, marked *"ST-35-38-2"*

35 – 36"	$550.00	$2,100.00

1972, Montgomery Wards reissue, plain box

17"	$50.00	$225.00

1973, red dot "Stand Up and Cheer" outfit, box with Shirley pictures, extra outfits available

16"	$45.00	$165.00

1982 – 1983

8"	$8.00	$30.00
12"	$9.00	$35.00

1984, by Hank Garfinkle, *marked "Doll Dreams & Love"*

36"	$75.00	$250.00

1994+, Shirley Temple Dress-Up Doll, Danbury Mint, similar to 1987 doll; no charge for doll, get two outfits bimonthly

16"	$30.00	$60.00

1996 Danbury Mint, Little Colonel, Rebecca/Sunnybrook Farm, and Heidi

16" $25.00, retail at Target stores

Porcelain

1987+, Danbury Mint

16"	$65.00	$90.00

1990+, Danbury Mint, designed by Elke Hutchens, in costumes from *The Little Princess, Bright Eyes, Curly Top, Dimples,* and others. *Marked on neck: "Shirley Temple//1990."*

20"	$150.00	$240.00

1997 Toddler, Danbury Mint, designed by Elke Hutchens, porcelain head, arms, legs, cloth body, pink dress, more dolls in the toddler series include Flower Girl and others

20" $129.00 retail

12" vinyl Ideal Shirley Temple marked "Ideal Doll//ST – 12" on head, "ST – 12-N" on back, rooted hair in original set, hazel sleep eyes, molded lashes, open/closed mouth, six upper teeth, five-piece body, tagged black velvet dress, white nylon sleeves, socks, black plastic shoes, comes with seven extra outfits, flannel night coat and cap, tagged orange/white school dress, Captain January, Heide, Rebecca of Sunnybrook Farm, raincoat, Wee Willie Winkie, circa 1957, $475.00. *Courtesy McMasters Doll Auctions.*

Sun Rubber

Ca. 1930s+, Barberton, OH.

Betty Bows, 1953

Molded hair with loop for ribbon, drink and wet baby, jointed body

11"	$103.00*

Psyllium, 1937

Molded painted hard rubber, moving head, blue pants, white suspenders, black shoes and hat

10"	$3.00	$15.00

Ruth E. Newton, vinyl child, molded clothes, squeaker

8"	$75.00	$155.00

16" vinyl Sunny Tears with blue plastic eyes, open mouth with hole for bottle, rooted synthetic hair, original dress, plastic bib with name, circa 1957, $35.00. Courtesy Penny Reeve-Griffith.

Terri Lee

16" hard plastic black Patty Jo, marked "Terri Lee//Pat. Pending" on back, original coarse black wig, large painted brown eyes, painted lashes, heavy arched brows, closed mouth, five-piece brown hard plastic body, black polished cotton dress, tagged Terri Lee slip, cotton panties, rayon socks, white tie leatherette shoes, circa 1950 – 1951, $1,150.00. Courtesy McMasters Doll Auctions.

1946 – 1962, Lincoln, NE, and Apple Valley, CA. First dolls composition, then hard plastic and vinyl. Closed pouty mouth, painted eyes, wigged, jointed body.

Marks:
On torso,
'TERRI LEE" and
early dolls,
"PAT. PENDING."

First price indicates played-with doll or missing accessories; second price is mint-in-box. More for fancy costume, additional wardrobe.

Terri Lee

Composition, 1946 – 1947		
16"	$80.00	$375.00+
Painted hard plastic, 1947 – 1950		
16"	$125.00	$500.00
Hard plastic, 1951 – 1962		
16"	$150.00	$400.00
Terri Lee		
16"	$2,500.00* MIB	
Vinyl, less if sticky		
16"	$80.00	$250.00
Talking		
16"	$150.00	$600.00

Benji, painted plastic, brown, 1947 – 1958, black lamb's wool wig

16"	$150.00	$600.00

Connie Lynn, 1955, hard plastic, sleep eyes, caracul wig, bent-limb baby body

19"	$125.00	$400.00

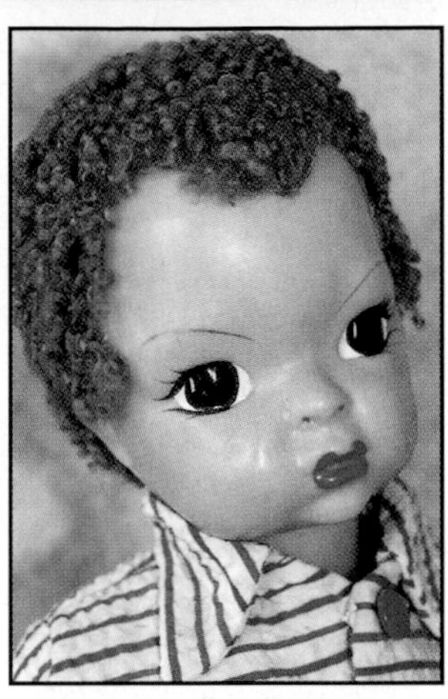
16" hard plastic Jerri Lee, painted brown eyes, caracul wig, cowboy clothing, circa 1950 – 1951, $200.00. Courtesy Betty Strong.

Gene Autry, 1949 – 1950, painted plastic
16" $450.00 $1,800.00

Jerri Lee, hard plastic, caracul wig
16" $125.00 $500.00
Vinyl16" $1,500.00

Linda Lee, 1950 – 1951, vinyl
12" $20.00 $75.00
1952 – 1958, vinyl baby
10" $45.00 $145.00

Mary Jane, Terri Lee look-alike, hard plastic walker
16" $50.00 $265.00

Patty Jo, Bonnie Lou,black
16" $150.00 $600.00
16" $3,825.00*

Tiny Terri Lee, 1955 – 1958
10" $50.00 $175.00

Accessories

Terri Lee Outfits:
Ball gown $150.00
Girl Scout/Brownie uniform $50.00
Heart Fund $325.00
School dress $150.00
Shoes $25.00 $100.00+

Jerri Lee Outfits:
Two-piece pant suit $100.00
Majorette $100.00
Gene Autrey $250.00

Robert Tonner

Ca. 1991.

Ann Estelle, 1999, a Mary Engelbreit character, hard plastic, blond wig, glasses
10" $69.00 retail

Betsy McCall, see Betsy McCall section.

Kripplebush Kids, 1997, hard plastic, Marni, Eliza, Hannah
8" $55.00 retail

Tyler Wentworth, 1999, fashion-type, long, straight, brunette, blond, or red hair
16" $79.99 retail

Kitty Collier, 2000, blond, brunette, or red head
18" $89.00 (retail)

19" vinyl Ann Estelle, new larger playmates, a Mary Engelbreit character, style #ME 7102 May Flowers, blond wig, blue eyes, closed mouth, gold rimmed eyeglasses, rigid vinyl body, blue overalls with cuffs, trimmed in red and white, white shirt with red rickrack trim, straw hat, red shoes, circa 2001, $124.99. Courtesy Robert Tonner Doll Company.

Trolls

Trolls portray supernatural beings from Scandinavian folklore. They have been manufactured by various companies including Helena and Martii Kuuslkoski who made Fauni Trolls, ca. 1952+ (sawdust filled cloth dolls); Thomas Dam, 1960+; and Scandia House, later Norfin®; Uneeda Doll and Toy Wishniks®; Russ Berrie; Ace Novelty; Treasure Trolls; Applause Toys; Magical Trolls; and many other companies who made lesser quality vinyl look-alikes, mostly unmarked, to take advantage of the fad. Most are all-vinyl or vinyl with stuffed cloth bodies.

Troll Figures

2½"	$3.00	$15.00
5"	$7.00	$25.00
7"	$10.00	$40.00
10"	$15.00	$55.00
12"	$17.00	$65.00
15"	$22.00	$85.00

Troll Animals

Cow, unmarked

6"	$50.00	$125.00

Donkey, Dam, 1964

9"	$40.00	$150.00

Monkey, Thomas Dam

7"		$230.00*

Mouse, Thomas Dam

5"		$170.00*

Tailed Troll, Thomas Dam

6½"		$190.00*

Uneeda

1917+, New York City. Made composition head dolls, including Mama dolls and made the transition to plastics and vinyl.

Composition

Rita Hayworth, as "Carmen," ca. 1948

From *The Loves of Carmen* movie, all-composition, red mohair wig, unmarked, cardboard tag

14"	$135.00	$565.00

Hard Plastic and Vinyl

Baby Dollikins, 1960

Vinyl head, hard plastic jointed body with jointed elbows, wrists, and knees, drink and wet

21"	$45.00	$200.00 MIB

Baby Trix, 1965

19"	$8.00	$30.00

Bareskin Baby, 1968

12½"	$5.00	$20.00

Blabby, 1962+

14"	$7.00	$28.00

Coquette, 1963+

16"	$7.00	$28.00

* at auction

21" vinyl Saranade, marked "Uneeda//Doll//1962," rooted blond ponytail, blue sleep eyes, closed mouth, fully jointed vinyl and hard plastic body, speaker in tummy, red dress with white trim, white socks and shoes, phonograph and records, can sing, tell stories, count, or say the alphabet, uses 9-volt battery, mint in box, $350.00. *Courtesy Michael Stitt.*

Black

16"	$9.00	$36.00

Dollikin, 1957+, multi-joints, *marked "Uneeda//2S"*

13"	$280.00*	
19"	$135.00	$225.00

Fairy Princess, 1961

32"	$40.00	$110.00

Freckles, 1960, vinyl head, rigid plastic body, *marked "22"* on head

32"	$25.00	$100.00

Freckles, 1973

Ventriloquist doll, vinyl head, hands, rooted hair, cotton stuffed cloth body

30"	$17.00	$70.00

11" composition Sweetums, unmarked, molded painted brown hair, brown sleep eyes, open/closed nurser mouth, drink and wet doll, composition arms and legs, cloth body, re-dressed in pink baby dress and matching bonnet, circa 1936, $250.00. *Courtesy Pat Graff.*

Jennifer, 1973

Rooted side-parted hair, painted features, teen body, mod clothing

18"	$7.00	$25.00

Magic Meg, w/Hair That Grows

Vinyl and plastic, rooted hair, sleep eyes

16"	$7.00	$25.00

Pir-thilla, 1958

Blows up balloons, vinyl, rooted hair, sleep eyes

12½"	$4.00	$12.00

Purty, 1973

Long rooted hair, vinyl and plastic, painted features

11"	$7.00	$25.00

Pollyanna, 1960, for Disney

11"	$9.00	$35.00
17"	$200.00* MIB	
31"	$40.00	$150.00

Saranade, 1962

Vinyl head, hard plastic body, rooted blond hair, blue sleep eyes, red and white dress, speaker in tummy, phonograph and records came with doll, used battery

21"	$15.00	$350.00

* at auction

Suzette (Carol Brent)

12"	$25.00	$125.00

Tiny Teen, 1957 – 1959

Vinyl head, rooted hair, pierced ears, six-piece hard plastic body, high-heeled feet to compete with Little Miss Revlon, wrist tag

10½"	$40.00	$135.00

Vinyl

16" S&P Doll & Toy Co. Nancy, comic figure, molded painted black hair with molded white ribbon, large side-glancing eyes, closed smiling mouth, magic skin one-piece body, marked "S&P" on head, red plaid skirt, white shirt, black vest, white socks, red shoes, all original, circa 1954, $200.00. Courtesy Pat Graff.

Ca. 1950s+. By the mid-1950s, vinyl (polyvinylchloride) was being used for dolls. Material that was soft to the touch and processing that allowed hair to be rooted were positive attractions. Vinyl became a desirable material and the market was soon deluged with dolls manufactured from this product. Many dolls of this period are of little known manufacturers, unmarked, or marked only with a number. With little history behind them, these dolls need to be mint-in-box and totally complete to warrant top prices. With special accessories or wardrobe values may be more.

UNKNOWN MAKER

Baby

Vinyl head, painted or sleep eyes, molded hair or wig, bent legs, cloth or vinyl body

12"	$2.50	$10.00
16"	$3.00	$12.00
20"	$5.00	$20.00

Child

Vinyl head, jointed body, painted or sleep eyes, molded hair or wig, straight legs

14"	$5.00	$14.00
22"	$6.00	$25.00

Adult

Vinyl head, painted or sleep eyes, jointed body, molded hair or wig, smaller waist with male or female modeling for torso

8"	$5.00	$25.00
18"	$20.00	$75.00

KNOWN MAKER

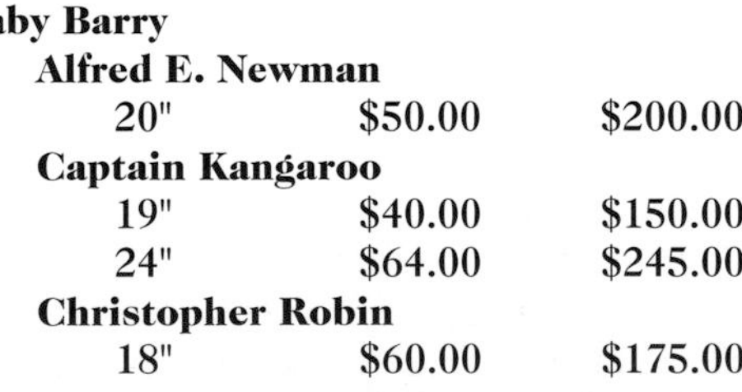

Baby Barry

Alfred E. Newman

20"	$50.00	$200.00

Captain Kangaroo

19"	$40.00	$150.00
24"	$64.00	$245.00

Christopher Robin

18"	$60.00	$175.00

11" Sayco Miss America, platinum rooted synthetic hair, blue sleep eyes, closed mouth, jointed vinyl body, knee joints, white dress with red trim, blue sash, red slippers, mint-in-box, with mint-in-package extra outfit, circa 1960s, $75.00. Courtesy Rita Mauze.

Daisy Mae

14"	$55.00	$190.00

Emmett Kelly (Willie the Clown)

15"	$45.00	$185.00
21"	$100.00	$325.00

Li'l Abner

14"	$50.00	$200.00
21"	$70.00	$265.00

Mammy Yokum, 1957

Molded hair

14"	$45.00	$175.00
21"	$70.00	$275.00

Yarn hair

14"	$50.00	$200.00
21"	$75.00	$300.00

Nose lights up

23"	$85.00	$325.00

Pappy Yokum, 1957

14"	$35.00	$135.00
21"	$65.00	$260.00

Nose lights up

23"	$85.00	$325.00

19" Royal Lilo, marked "14R," rooted platinum hair, blue sleep eyes, closed mouth, earrings, fully jointed vinyl body with twist waist, original black gown with net overskirt, matching net hairpiece, silver high-heel sandals, all original with wrist tag and box, circa 1950s, $75.00. Courtesy Pat Graff.

Dee & Cee, Canada

Marylee, 1967+, rigid vinyl, rooted hair, sleep eyes

17"	$75.00	$300.00

Glad Toy/BrookGlad

Poor Pitiful Pearl, circa 1955

Vinyl, some with stuffed one-piece vinyl bodies, others jointed

12"	$25.00	$85.00
17"	$200.00* MIB	

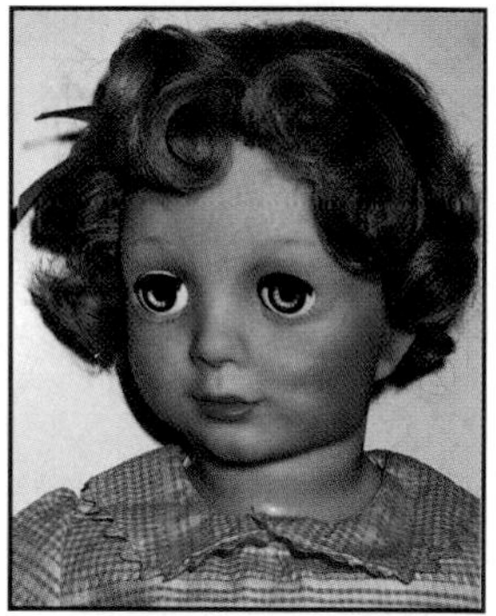

27" Fleischaker Little Girl of Today, stuffed vinyl rooted human hair, sleep eyes, closed mouth, cloth body, marked "Fleischaker" on shoulder plate, re-dressed in pink and white checked dress, circa 1951, $100.00. Courtesy Pat Graff.

Himstedt, Annette, 1986+

Distributed by Timeless Creations, a division of Mattel, Inc. Swivel rigid vinyl head with shoulder plate, cloth body, vinyl limbs, inset eyes, real lashes, molded eyelids, holes in nostrils, human hair wig, bare feet, original in box.

Barefoot Children, 1986, 26"

Bastian	$200.00	$800.00
Beckus	$400.00	$1,500.00
Ellen	$200.00	$900.00
Fatou	$275.00	$1,100.00
Kathe	$200.00	$800.00
Lisa	$200.00	$800.00
Paula	$175.00	$800.00

Blessed Are the Children, 1988, 31"

Friederike	$550.00	$2,200.00
Kasimir	$500.00	$2,000.00

* at auction

20" unmarked boy, molded painted hair, blue sleep eyes with lashes, painted lower lashes, closed mouth, Fairyland Toy Booklet, "No. 3//Made in USA" on shoes, white jacket trimmed in red, matching cap, gray pants, black shoes, circa 1950s+, $45.00. Courtesy Adrienne & Don Hagey.

Makimura	$350.00	$1,400.00
Malin	$350.00	$1,600.00
Michiko	$400.00	$1,500.00
Reflections of Youth, 1989 – 1990, 26"		
Adrienne	$200.00	$900.00
Ayoka	$550.00	$1,100.00
Janka	$200.00	$900.00
Kai	$215.00	$900.00

Playmates, 1985+

Made animated talking dolls using a tape player in torso powered by batteries. Extra costumes, tapes, and accessories available. More for black versions.

Amazing Amy, Maddy, circa 1998, vinyl, cloth body, interactive

20"	$69.95 retail	

Cricket, circa 1986+

25"	$50.00	$125.00

Corky, circa 1987+

25"	$50.00	$125.00

Sayco

An Adorable Doll, circa late 1950s, rooted hair, rigid vinyl body

15"	$40.00	$75.00

Shindana

1968 – 1983, Operation Bootstrap, Los Angeles, ethnic features

14"	$30.00	$65.00

Tomy

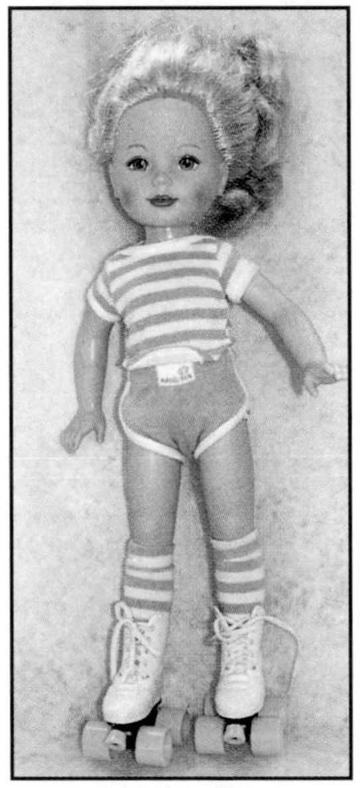

17" Tomy Kimberly, marked "Tomy," rooted blond hair pulled up in ponytail, painted blue eyes, closed mouth, jointed vinyl body, in pink and white striped shirt and matching socks, pink shorts, white skates, circa 1981 – 1985, $55.00. Courtesy Barbara Hull.

Kimberly, 1981 – 1985, closed mouth, more for black

17"	$25.00	$55.00

Getting Fancy Kimberly, 1984, open mouth with teeth

17"	$35.00	$65.00

Tristar

Poor Pitiful Pearl, circa 1955+, vinyl jointed doll came with extra party dress

11"	$222.00* MIB

World of Wonder, circa 1985 – 1987+

Fremont, CA. Made talking dolls and Teddy Ruxpin powered by batteries, had extra accessories, voice cards.

Pamela, The Living Doll, 1986+

21"	$45.00	$125.00

Julie, 1987+

24"	$50.00	$150.00
Extra costume	$5.00	$25.00

Teddy Ruxpin, 1985+, animated talking bear

20"	$15.00	$50.00

30" unmarked girl, rooted blond hair in ponytails with curly bangs, blue sleep eyes, rosy cheeks, closed mouth, rigid vinyl jointed body, original blue dress, white socks, black shoes, circa 1950s, $100.00. Courtesy Elizabeth Surber.

Vogue

1930s+, Medford, MA. Jennie Graves started the company and dressed "Just Me" and Arranbee dolls in the early years, before Bernard Lipfert designed Ginny. After several changes of ownership, Vogue dolls was purchased in 1995 by Linda and Jim Smith.

Ginny Family

Toddles

Composition, 1937 – 1948, name stamped in ink on bottom of shoe. Some early dolls which have been identified as "Toodles" (spelled with two o's) are blank dolls from various companies used by Vogue. Painted eyes, mohair wig, jointed body; some had gold foil labels reading *"Vogue."*

First price indicates doll in good condition, but with flaws; second price indicates doll in excellent condition with original clothes. More for fancy outfits such as Red Riding Hood or Cowboy/Cowgirl or with accessories.

8"	$125.00	$425.00

Ginny, painted hard plastic, 1948 – 1950

Marked *"Vogue"* on head, *"Vogue Doll"* on body, painted eyes, molded hair with mohair wig. Clothing tagged *"Vogue Dolls"* or *"Vogue Dolls, Inc. Medford Mass.,"* inkspot tag on white with blue letters.

8"	$100.00	$375.00

7" hard plastic molded lash Ginny, marked "Ginny//Vogue Dolls//Inc.//Pat. No. 2887954//Made in U.S.A." on back, original wig in braids, blue sleep eyes, molded lashes, closed mouth, hard plastic body with straight legs and walking mechanism, tagged Tiny Miss #42 outfit from 1955, original box with blue taffeta panties, blue socks, extra marked blue Ginny shoes, near mint, circa 1954 – 1956, $375.00. Courtesy McMasters Doll Auctions.

* at auction

7" brown hard plastic Hawaiian Ginny, brown sleep eyes, single stroke eyebrows, painted upper lashes, closed mouth, original wig, five-piece body, marked "Vogue//Doll" on back, dressed in original print top, grass skirt, panties, lei around neck, flower in hair, skirt slightly faded, hair mussed, pink cheeks, circa 1953 – 1954, $2,900.00. Courtesy McMasters Doll Auctions.

9" hard plastic Ginny, walker, marked "Ginny//Vogue Dolls//Inc.//Pat Pend.//Made in U.S.A.," blond braided wig, blue sleep eyes, painted lashes, closed mouth, rosy cheeks, wearing cowgirl outfit, white skirt and vest trimmed in silver, pink top, white hat, pink socks, silver boots, gun attached to dress with silver strap, circa 1954, $295.00. Courtesy Sharon Kolibaba.

With poodle cut wig

8"	$125.00	$400.00
Outfit only	$65.00 – $90.00+	

Ginny, 8", hard plastic walkers, 1950 – 1954

Transitional to walkers, sleep eyes, painted lashes, strung, dynel wigs, new mark on back torso: *"GINNY//VOGUE DOLLS//INC. //PAT PEND.// MADE IN U.S.A."* Coronation Queen, 1953, has elaborate braid on her costume, silver wrist tags.

Common dress	$95.00	$350.00
1950 Julie #8		$695.00*
1951 Glad, #42		$995.00*
1952 Beryl		$2,025.00*
1952 Carol Kindergarten		$925.00*
1953 Pamela #60		$510.00*

Straight leg walker, 1954, painted lash

	$85.00	$350.00

Black Ginny, 1953 – 1954

8"	$150.00	$600.00+
8"	$2,000.00* MIB	

Ginny, hard plastic, 1954 – 1956, seven-piece body, molded lash walkers, sleep eyes, Dynel or saran wigs. *Marked: "VOGUE" on head, "GINNY//VOGUE DOLLS//INC.//PAT. NO. 2687594//MADE IN U.S.A." on back of torso*

8"	$60.00	$225.00
Outfit only	$40.00+	

Davy Crockett, coonskin cap, brown jacket, pants, toy rifle, in box

8"	$935.00*

Crib Crowd, 1950

Baby with curved legs, sleep eyes, poodle cut (caracul) wig

8"	$175.00	$650.00+

Easter Bunny

8"	$350.00	$1,400.00

Ginny, hard plastic, 1957 – 1962

Bent-knee (jointed) walker, molded lashes, sleep eyes, dynel or saran wigs. *Marked "VOGUE" on head, "GINNY//VOGUE DOLLS//INC.// PAT.NO.2687594//MADE IN U.S.A."*

8"	$45.00	$175.00
Outfit only		$40.00+

Ginny, 1960, unmarked, big walker carried 8" doll dressed just like her

36"	$350.00*

Too few in database for reliable range.

9" hard plastic Ginny Bride, red Dynel wig, blue sleep eyes, painted lash, closed mouth, straight leg walker, tagged satin wedding gown with gold trim, net veil and underskirt, prayer book, wrist tag reads "A Vogue Doll," marked "GINNY//VOGUE DOLLS//INC.//PAT PEND.//MADE IN U.S.A.," circa 1953, $400.00. Courtesy Carol Van Verst-Rugg.

9" hard plastic Ginny, blue sleep eyes, plastic molded lashes, brunette saran wig, straight leg walker, pink skater outfit, matching pink hat with feather, white skates, circa 1955, $300.00. Courtesy Darlene Foote.

Ginny, 1963 – 1965

Soft vinyl head, hard plastic walker body, sleep eyes, molded lashes, rooted hair. *Marked: "GINNY," on head, "GINNY//VOGUE DOLLS, Inc.//PAT. NO.2687594//MADE IN U.S.A." on back*

8"	$13.00	$50.00

Ginny, 1965 – 1972

All-vinyl, straight legs, non-walker, rooted hair, sleep eyes, molded lashes. *Marked "Ginny" on head, "Ginny//VOGUE DOLLS, INC." on back*

8"	$12.00	$50.00

Ginny, 1972 – 1977

All-vinyl, non-walker, sleep eyes, molded lashes, rooted hair, some with painted lashes. *Marked "GINNY" on head, "VOGUE DOLLS©1972//MADE IN HONG KONG//3" on back, made in Hong Kong by Tonka*

8"	$12.00	$50.00

Ginny, 1977 – 1982

1977 – 1979, "Ginny From Far-Away Lands," made in Hong Kong by Lesney, all-vinyl, sleep eyes, jointed, non-walker, rooted hair, chubby body, same as Tonka doll overall. *Marked "GINNY" on head, "VOGUE DOLLS 1972//MADE IN HONG KONG//3";* painted eyes, 1980 – 1981. *Marked "VOGUE DOLLS//©GINNYTIM//1977" on head, "VOGUE DOLLS©1977//MADE IN HONG KONG" on back*

8"	$9.00	$35.00

Sasson Ginny, 1981 – 1982

Made in Hong Kong by Lesney, all-vinyl, fully jointed, bendable knees, rooted Dynel hair, sleep eyes in 1981, painted eyes in 1982, slimmer body. *Marked "GINNY" on head, "1978 VOGUE DOLLS INC//MOONACHIE N.J.//MADE IN HONG KONG" on back*

8"	$9.00	$35.00

Ginny, 1984 – 1986

Made by Meritus® in Hong Kong, vinyl, resembling Vogue's 1963 – 1971

10½" vinyl Li'l Imp, marked "R" and "B//44" on head, "R and B Doll Co." on back, advertised as Brickette's little sister, orange rooted synthetic hair, freckles, green sleep eyes, closed mouth, bent-knee walker, tagged "Nancy//red-headed//Li'l Imp," in green outfit with white net skirt, mint in box, circa 1959 – 1960, $300.00. Courtesy Sharon Kolibaba.

9" composition, Oriental Toddles, original blue print kimono with red flowers in her hair, crica 1937 – 1948, $425.00. Courtesy of Jackie Litchfield.

* at auction

Ginny. *Marked "GINNY®" on head, "VOGUE DOLLS// (a star logo)//M.I.I. 1984//Hong Kong" on back.* Porcelain marked: *"GW//SCD//5184" on head, "GINNNY //®VOGUE DOLLS//INC//(a star logo) MII 1984//MADE IN TAIWAN."*

8"	$15.00	$55.00

Ginny, 1986 – 1995

Vinyl, by Dakin, soft vinyl. *Marked "VOGUE®DOLLS//©1984 R. DAKIN INC.// MADE IN CHINA" on back;* hard vinyl, *marked "VOGUE//®// DOLLS//©1986 R. DAKIN and Co.//MADE IN CHINA"*

8"	$8.00	$25.00

Ginny Baby, 1959 – 1982

Vinyl, jointed, sleep eyes, rooted or molded hair, a drink and wet doll, some *marked "GINNY BBY//VOGUE DOLLS INC."*

12"	$10.00	$40.00+
18"	$13.00	$50.00

Ginnette, 1955 – 1969, 1985 – 1986

Vinyl, jointed, open mouth, 1955 – 1956 had painted eyes, 1956 – 1969 had sleep eyes. *Marked "VOGUE DOLLS INC"*

8"	$75.00	$250.00

1962 – 1963, rooted hair Ginnette

8"	$50.00	$175.00

Jan, 1958 – 1960, 1963 – 1964

Jill's friend, vinyl head, six-piece rigid vinyl body, straight leg, swivel waist, rooted hair, *marked "VOGUE,"* called Loveable Jan in 1963 and Sweetheart Jan in 1964

10½"	$40.00	$150.00

Jeff, 1958 – 1960

Vinyl head, five-piece rigid vinyl body, molded painted hair, *marked "VOGUE DOLLS"*

11"	$25.00	$100.00

Jill, 1957 – 1960, 1962 – 1963, 1965

Seven-piece hard plastic teenage body, bent-knee walker, high-heeled doll, big sister to Ginny (made in vinyl in 1965), extra wardrobe, *marked "JILL//VOGUE DOLLS//MADEI NU.S.A.//©1957"*

10½"	$65.00	$225.00 MIB
Street dress	$15.00	$25.00
Special outfits	$50.00	$175.00

Jimmy, 1958

Ginny's baby brother, all-vinyl, open mouth, painted eye Ginnette, *marked "VOGUE DOLLS/INC."*

8"	$15.00	$60.00

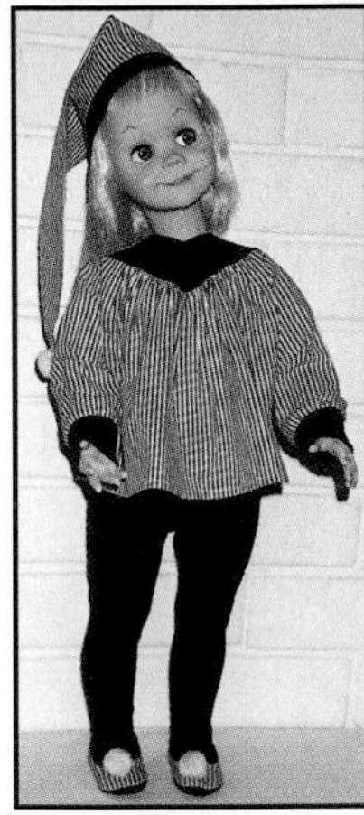

22" vinyl Brikette with orange hair, freckles, green flirty sleep eyes, closed smiling mouth, an impish character with rigid vinyl body and legs, ball-jointed swivel waist, original tagged outfit (cotton campus #8360), red and black pajamas and matching night cap, slippers with pompons, circa 1959 – 1961, $100.00. Courtesy Pat Graff.

Little Miss Ginny, 1965 – 1971

All-vinyl, promoted as a pre-teen, one-piece hard plastic body and legs, soft vinyl head and arms, sleep eyes; *head marked "VOGUE DOLL//19©67" or "©VOGUE DOLL//1968" and back, "VOGUE DOLL"*

12"	$10.00	$40.00

Miss Ginny, 1962 – 1965, 1967 – 1980

1962 – 1964, soft vinyl head could be tilted, jointed vinyl arms, two-piece hard plastic body, swivel waist, flat feet; 1965 – 1980, vinyl head and arms, one-piece plastic body

15 – 16"	$15.00	$45.00

GINNY EXCLUSIVES

Enchanted Doll House

1988, limited edition	$40.00	$160.00

GiGi Dolls

1987, GiGi's Favorite	$25.00	$95.00
1988, Sherry's Teddy Bear	$25.00	$95.00

Little Friends, Anchorage, AK

1990, Alaska Ginny	$22.00	$95.00

Meyer's Collectibles

1986, Fairy Godmother	$50.00	$210.00
1987, Cinderella and Prince Charming	$50.00	$210.00
1988, Clown	$25.00	$95.00
1989, American Cowgirl	$25.00	$95.00

11" all-composition Dora Lee, brown sleep eyes, closed mouth with rather sad wistful expression, reddish-blond mohair wig, red shirt with dog on front, green plaid shorts, missing hat, circa 1939, $375.00. Courtesy Peggy Millhouse.

Modern Doll Convention

1986, Rose Queen	$50.00	$200.00+
1987, Ginny at the Seashore	$18.00	$75.00+
1988, Ginny's Claim	$20.00	$80.00+
1989, Ginny in Nashville	$27.00	$110.00+
1990, Ginny in Orlando	$25.00	$95.00+
1991, Ginny in Las Vegas	$25.00	$95.00+
1992, Poodle Skirt Ginny	$18.00	$75.00

1993, World of Elegance		
	$15.00	$60.00+
Shirley's Doll House		
1986, Ginny Goes Country		
	$25.00	$95.00
1986, Ginny Goes to the Fair		
	$25.00	$95.00
1987, black Ginny in swimsuit		
	$25.00	$95.00
1987, Santa & Mrs. Claus		
	$25.00	$90.00+
1988, Sunday Best, boy or girl		
	$15.00	$60.00
1988, Ginny Babysits		
	$15.00	$60.00
Toy Village, Lansing, MI		
1989 Ashley Rose		
	$35.00	$130.00
Vogue Doll Club		
1990, Member Special		
	$25.00	$95.00
U.F.D.C. (United Federation of Doll Clubs)		
1987 Miss Unity		
	$45.00	$155.00
1988 Ginny Luncheon Souvenir		
	$35.00	$140.00
Vogue Review Luncheon		
1989, Ginny	$65.00	$250.00
1990	$30.00	$110.00
1991	$25.00	$95.00+
1993, Special Christmas	$18.00	$75.00
1994, Apple of My Eye	$18.00	$75.00
1995, Secret Garden	$18.00	$75.00
Ginny Accessories		
First price is played with; second price is mint-in-box or package.		
Book: *Ginny's First Secret*	$35.00	$125.00+
Furniture: chair, bed, dresser, wardrobe, rocking chair		
each	$18.00	$75.00
Ginny Gym	$120.00	$500.00
Ginny Name Pin	$12.00	$50.00
Ginny Pup, Steiff	$45.00	$175.00+
Ginny's House	$300.00	$1,200.00
Luggage set	$25.00	$100.00
Parasol	$4.00	$15.00
School bag	$20.00	$75.00
Shoes/shoe bag	$10.00	$40.00
COMPOSITION		
Dora Lee, sleep eyes, closed mouth		
11"	$100.00	$375.00

Jennie, 1940s, sleep eyes, open mouth, mohair wig, five-piece composition body

13" $80.00 $350.00

Cynthia, 1940s, sleep eyes, open mouth, mohair wig, five-piece composition body

13" $80.00 $350.00

HARD PLASTIC & VINYL

Baby Dear, 1959 – 1964

18" vinyl baby designed by Eloise Wilkin, vinyl limbs, cloth body, topknot or rooted hair, white tag on body *"Vogue Dolls, Inc.";* left leg stamped *"1960/E.Wilkins."* 12" size made in 1961.

18" $125.00 $325.00

18" $315.00*

Baby Dear One, 1962

A one-year-old toddler version of Baby Dear, sleep eyes, two teeth

Marked "C//1961//E.Wilkins//Vogue Dolls//Inc." on neck, tag on body, mark on right leg

25" $125.00 $250.00

Baby Dear Musical, 1962 – 1963

12" metal, 18" wooden shaft winds, plays tune, doll wiggles

12" $40.00 $150.00

18" $65.00 $250.00

Baby Too Dear, 1963 – 1965

Two-year-old toddler version of Baby Dear, all-vinyl, open mouth, two teeth

17" $65.00 $250.00

23" $85.00 $350.00

Brikette, 1959 – 1961; 1979 – 1980

Swivel waist joint, green flirty eyes in 22" size only, freckles, rooted straight orange hair, paper hang tag reads *"I'm //Brikette//the//red headed//imp" marked on head "VOGUE INC.//19©60"*

22" $75.00 $250.00 MIB

1960, sleep eyes only, platinum, brunette, or orange hair

16" $35.00 $125.00 MIB

1979, no swivel waist, curly blond hair, or straight blond or brunette

1980, no swivel waist, curly pink, red, purple, or blond hair

16" $15.00 $60.00

Li'l Imp, 1959 – 1960

Brickette's little sister, vinyl head, bent knee walker, green sleep eyes, orange hair, freckles, *marked "R and B//44" on head and "R and B Doll Co." on back*

10½" $20.00 $75.00

9" vinyl Ginnette, molded painted hair, painted blue eyes, open mouth for bottle, marked "VOGUE DOLLS INC.," in sleeper bag with bottle and rattle, circa 1955 – 1956, $410.00. Courtesy McMasters Doll Auctions.

9" hard plastic Oriental Poppy Ginny, from the Botanical Babies Collection, marked "Ginny's Signature TM//1988//The Vogue Doll Company//Made in China," brunette rooted hair, brown plastic sleep eyes, jointed hard plastic body, pink poppy petaled skirt with an underskirt of poppy stamen, black felt top and tights, circa 2001, $39.95. Courtesy Vogue Doll Company.

16" vinyl Love Me Linda, marked "Vogue Doll © 1965" on back of head, rooted blond hair, large painted brown eyes, molded lids and lashes, closed mouth, molded tear on cheek, five-piece jointed body, similar to Lonely Lisa by Royal, Love Me Linda has a slight smile, Lonely Lisa is sad, print dress, circa 1965, $55.00. *Courtesy Barbara Hull.*

Wee Imp, 1960

Hard plastic body, orange saran wig, green eyes, freckles, marked *"GINNY//VOGUE DOLS//INC.//PAT.No. 2687594//MADE IN U.S.A."*

8"	$100.00	$400.00

Littlest Angel, 1961 – 1963; 1967 – 1980

1961 – 1963, also called Saucy Littlest Angel, vinyl head, hard plastic bent knee walker, sleep eyes, same doll as Arranbee Littlest Angel, rooted hair, *marked "R & B"*

10½"	$85.00	$200.00

1967 – 1980, all-vinyl, jointed limbs, rooted red, blond, or brunette hair, looks older

11"	$25.00	$55.00
15"	$10.00	$40.00

Love Me Linda (Pretty as a Picture), 1965

Vinyl, large painted eyes, rooted long straight hair, came with portrait, advertised as "Pretty as a Picture" in Sears and Montgomery Ward catalogs, *marked "VOGUE DOLLS/©1965"*

15"	$25.00	$65.00

Welcome Home Baby, 1978 – 1980

Newborn, designed by Eloise Wilkin, vinyl head and arms, painted eyes, molded hair, cloth body, crier, *marked "Lesney"*

18"	$35.00	$65.00+

Welcome Home Baby Turns Two, 1980

Toddler, designed by Eloise Wilkin, vinyl head, arms, and legs, cloth body, sleep eyes, rooted hair, *marked "42260 Lesney Prod. Corp.//1979//Vogue Doll"*

22"	$75.00	$200.00

Robin Woods

Ca. 1980s+. Creative designer for various companies, including Le Petit Ami, Robin Woods Company, Madame Alexander (Alice Darling), Horsman, and Playtime Productions.

Price indicates mint complete doll; anything else would bring a lesser price.

Early Cloth Dolls

Price depends on how well painted and quality of clothing and construction. The quality varies greatly in these early cloth dolls.

Children, very rare

Betsy Bluebonnet	$250.00
Enchanted Baby	$300.00
Jane	$300.00
Jessica	$250.00
Laura	$250.00

Children, rare

Mollie	$225.00

Rachel		$200.00
Rueben		$200.00
Stevie		$200.00
Children, common		
City Child		$50.00
Elizabeth		$50.00
Mary Margaret		$50.00
How Do I Love Thee		$50.00
Clowns, very rare		
Aladdin		$300.00
Sinbad		$300.00
Wynter		$250.00
Yankee Doodle		$300.00
Clowns, rare		
Cinamette		$250.00
Happy Holiday, 1984 – 1986		$200.00
Kubla		$200.00
Clowns, common		
Bon Bon		$150.00
1986, Childhood Classics		
Larissa	14"	$45.00
1987		
Catherine	14"	$75.00+
Christmas dolls, Nicholas & Noel, pair	14"	$200.00+
1988		
Dickens	14"	$125.00
Kristina Kringle	14"	$125.00
Scarlett Sweetheart	14"	$75.00
1989		
Anne of Green Gables	14"	$75.00
Heidi, red, white, blue	14"	$150.00
Heidi, brown outfit	14"	$75.00
Hope	14"	$100.00
Lorna Doone	14"	$50.00
Mary of Secret Garden	14"	$100.00
Scarlett Christmas	14"	$125.00
William Noel	14"	$75.00
1990 Camelot Castle Collection		
Bobbi	16"	$50.00
Kyleigh Christmas	14"	$75.00
Lady Linet	14"	$35.00
Lady of the Lake	14"	$150.00
Marjorie	14"	$50.00
Meaghan (special)	14"	$150.00
Melanie, Phebe	14"	$50.00
Tessa at the Circus	14"	$75.00
Tess of the D'urbervilles	14"	$150.00

* at auction

1991 Shades of Day collection		
5,000 pieces each, Dawn, Glory, Stormy, Joy, Sunny, Veil, Serenity		
Each	14"	$50.00
Others		
Alice in Wonderland	24"	$75.00
Bette Jack	14"	$50.00
Bouquet, Lily	14"	$50.00
Delores	14"	$100.00
Eliza Doolittle	14"	$75.00
Mistress Mary	8"	$50.00
Miss Muffet	14"	$50.00
Princess & Pea	15"	$100.00
Rose, Violet	14"	$50.00
Rosemary	14"	$50.00
Sleeping Beauty Set	8"	$150.00
Tennison	14"	$50.00
Victoria	14"	$50.00

Robin Woods Limited Editions

Merri, 1991 Doll Convention Disney World, Christmas Tree doll, doll becomes the tree	14"	$150.00
Mindy, Made for Disney's Robin Wood's Day, limited to 300	14"	$125.00
Rainey, 1991 Robin Woods Club	14"	$60.00
J.C. Penney Limited Editions		
Angelina, 1990 Christmas angel	14"	$150.00
Noelle, Christmas angel	14"	$150.00
Julianna, 1991, little girl holiday shopper	14"	$125.00
Robin Woods Exclusives		
Gina, The Earthquake Doll, The Doll Place, Ann Parsons of Burlingame, CA	14"	$150.00

Bibliography

Anderton, Johana Gast. *Twentieth Century Dolls.* Wallace Homestead, 1971.

———. *More Twentieth Century Dolls.* Wallace Homestead, 1974.

———. *Cloth Dolls.* Wallace Homestead., 1984.

Axe, John. *Effanbee, A Collector's Encyclopedia 1949 – 1983.* Hobby House Press, 1983.

———. *The Encyclopedia of Celebrity Dolls.* Hobby House Press, 1983.

———. *Tammy and Her Family of Dolls.* Hobby House Press, 1995.

Blitman, Joe. *Francie and Her Mod, Mod, Mod, Mod World of Fashion.* Hobby House Press, 1996.

Casper, Peggy Wiedman. *Fashionable Terri Lee Dolls.* Hobby House Press, 1988.

Clark, Debra. *Troll Identification & Price Guide.* Collector Books, 1993.

Coleman, Dorothy S., Elizabeth Ann, and Evelyn Jane. *The Collector's Book of Dolls' Clothes.* Crown Publishers, 1975.

———. *The Collector's Encyclopedia of Dolls, Vol. I & II.* Crown Publishers, 1968, 1986.

Crowsey, Linda. *Madame Alexander, Collector's Dolls Price Guide #22.* Collector Books, 1997.

DeWein, Sibyl and Joan Ashabraner. *The Collector's Encyclopedia of Barbie Dolls and Collectibles*, Collector Books, 1977.

Garrison, Susan Ann. *The Raggedy Ann & Andy Family Album.* Schiffer Publishing, 1989.

Hedrick Susan, and Vilma Matchette. *World Colors, Dolls & Dress.* Hobby House Press, 1997.

Hoyer, Mary. *Mary Hoyer and Her Dolls.* Hobby House Press, 1982.

Izen, Judith. *A Collector's Guide to Ideal Dolls.* Collector Books, 1994, 1999.

Izen, Judith and Carol Stover. *Collector's Encyclopedia of Vogue Dolls.* Collector Books, 1997.

Jensen, Don. *Collector's Guide to Horsman Dolls, 1865 – 1950.* Collector Books, 2002.

Judd, Polly and Pam. *African and Asian Costumed Dolls.* Hobby House Press, 1995.

———. *Cloth Dolls, Identification and Price Guide.* Hobby House Press, 1990.

———. *Composition Dolls,Vol I & II.* Hobby House Press, 1991, 1994.

———. *European Costumed Dolls, Identification and Price Guide.* Hobby House Press, 1994.

———. *Hard Plastic Dolls, I & II.* Hobby House Press, 1987, 1994.

———. *Glamour Dolls of the 1950s & 1960s.* Hobby House Press, 1988.

———. *Santa Dolls & Figurines.* Hobby House Press, 1992.

Langford, Paris. *Liddle Kiddles.* Collector Books, 1996.

Lewis, Kathy and Don. *Chatty Cathy Dolls.* Collector Books, 1994.

Mandeville, A. Glenn. *Ginny, An American Toddler Doll.* Hobby House Press, 1994.

Mansell, Collette. *The Collector's Guide to British Dolls Since 1920.* Robert Hale, 1983.

Melille, Marcie. *The Ultimate Barbie Doll Book,* Krause Publication 1996.

Mertz, Ursula R. *The Collector's Encyclopedia of American Composition Dolls, 1900 – 1950.* Collector Books, 1999.

Morris, Thomas. *The Carnival Chalk Prize, I & II.* Prize Publishers, 1985, 1994.

Moyer, Patsy. *Doll Values.* Collector Books, 1997, 1998, 1999.

———. *Modern Collectible Dolls, Vols. I, II, III.* Collector Books, 1997, 1998, 1999.

Niswonger, Jeanne D. *That Doll Ginny.* Cody Publishing, 1978.

———. *The Ginny Doll Family.* 1996.

Olds, Patrick C. *The Barbie Doll Years.* Collector Books, 1996.

Outwater, Myra Yellin. *Advertising Dolls.* Schiffer, 1998.

Pardee, Elaine and Jackie Robertson. *Encylopedia of Bisque Nancy Ann Storybook Dolls, 1936 – 1947.* Collector Books, 2003.

Pardella, Edward R. *Shirley Temple Dolls and Fashions.* Schiffer Publishing, 1992.

Perkins, Myla. *Black Dolls.* Collector Books, 1993.

———. *Black Dolls Book II.* Collector Books, 1995.

Robison, Joleen Ashman and Kay Sellers. *Advertising Dolls.* Collector Books, 1992.

Schoonmaker, Patricia N. *Effanbee Dolls: The Formative Years, 1910 – 1929.* Hobby House Press, 1984.

———. *Patsy Doll Family Encyclopedia Vol. 1 & II.* Hobby House Press, 1992, 1998.

Smith, Patricia R. *Madame Alexander Collector Dolls.* Collector Books, 1978.

———. *Modern Collector's Dolls.* Series 1 – 8, Collector Books.

Tabbat, Andrew. *Raggedy Ann and Andy, Identification Guide.* Gold Horse Publishing, 1998.

Collectors' Network

It is recommended that when contacting the references below and requesting information that you enclose a SASE (self-addressed stamped envelope) if you wish to receive a reply.

Accessories
Best Dressed Doll
P.O. Box 12689
Salem, OR 97309
800-255-2313
Catalog $3.00
e-mail: tonilady@aol.com

Alexander Doll Company
The Review
PO Box 330
Mundelein, IL 60060-0330
847-949-9200
fax: 847-949-9201
website: http://www.madc.org
Official publication of the Madame Alexander Doll Club, quarterly, plus two "Shoppers," $20.00 per year.

American Character
Tressy
Debby Davis, Collector/Dealer
3905 N. 15th St.
Milwaukee, WI 53206

Antique Dolls
Matrix
PO Box 1410
New York, NY 10023
Can research your wants

Antique and Modern Dolls
Rosalie Whyel Museum of Doll Art
1116 108th Avenue N.E.
Bellevue, WA 98004
206-455-1116
fax: 206-455-4793

Auction Houses
Call or write for a list of upcoming auctions, or if you need information about selling a collection.

McMasters Doll Auctions
James and Shari McMasters
PO Box 1755
Cambridge, OH 43725
800-842-3526 or
740-432-4419
fax: 740-432-3191

Theriaults
PO Box 151
Annapolis, MD 21404
800-638-0422
www.theriaults.com

Barbie Dolls, Mattel
Miller's Fashion Doll
PO Box 8488
Spokane, WA 99203-0488
509-747-0139
fax: 509-455-6115
Credit card subscription
800-874-5201
Six issues, $29.95

Dream Dolls Galleries & More, Collector/Dealer
5700 Okeechobee Blvd. #20
West Palm Beach, FL 33417
888-839-3655
e-mail: dollnmore@aol.com

Jaci Jueden, Collector/Dealer
575 Galice Rd.
Merlin, OR 97532
e-mail: fudd@cdsnet.net

Steven Pim, Collector/Dealer
3535 17th St.
San Francisco, CA 94110

Betsy McCall
Betsy's Fan Club
Marci Van Ausdall, Editor
PO Box 946
Quincy, CA 95971
Quarterly, $15.50 per year

Celebrity Dolls
Celebrity Doll Journal
Loraine Burdick, Editor
413 10th Ave. Ct. NE
Puyallup, WA 98372
Quarterly, $10.00 per year

Chatty Cathy, Mattel
Chatty Cathy Collector's Club
Lisa Eisenstein, Editor
PO Box 140
Readington, NJ 08870-0140
Quarterly newsletter, $28.00
e-mail: Chatty@eclipse.net

Composition and Travel Dolls
Effanbee's Patsy Family
Patsy & Friends Newsletter
PO Box 311
Deming, NM 88031
e-mail:
Patsyandfriends@zianet.com
Bi-monthly, $20.00 per year

Contemporary Doll Collector
Scott Publications
30595 Eight Mile
Livonia, MI 48152-1798
Subscription: 800-458-8237

Costuming
Doll Costumer's Guild
Helen Boothe, Editor
7112 W. Grovers Ave
Glendale, AZ 85308
$16.00 per year, bimonthly

French Fashion Gazette
Adele Leurquin, Editor
1862 Sequoia SE
Port Orchard, WA 98366

Deluxe Reading
Penny Brite
Dealer/Collector
Carole Fisher
RD 2, Box 301
Palmyra, PA 17078-9738
e-mail: rcfisher@voicenet.com

Dionne Quintuplets
Quint News
Jimmy and Fay Rodolfos,
Editors
PO Box 2527
Woburn, MA 01888

Connie Lee Martin
Collector/Dealer
4018 East 17th St.
Tucson, AZ, 85711

Doll Artists
Jamie G. Anderson
10990 Greenlefe, P.O. Box 806
Rolla, MO 65402
573-364-7347
e-mail: jastudio@rollanet.org

Martha Armstrong-Hand
575 Worcester Drive
Cambria, CA 93428
805-927-3997
Betsy Baker
81 Hy-Vue Terrace
Cold Spring, NY 10516

Cynthia Barron
7796 W. Port Madison
Bainbridge Island, WA 98110
206-780-9003

Charles Batte
272 Divisadero St. #4
San Francisco, CA 94117
415-252-7440

Atelier Bets van Boxel
De Poppenstee
't Vaartje 14
5165 NB Waspik, Holland
website: www.poppenstee.nl
e-mail: bets@poppenstee.nl

Cheryl Bollenbach
P.O. Box 740922
Arvada, CO 80006-0922
303-216-2424
e-mail: cdboll@aol.com

Laura Clark
P.O. Box 596
Mesilla, NM 88046

Ankie Daanen Doll-Art
Anton Mauvestraat 1
2102 BA HEEMSTEDE NL
023-5477980
fax: 023-5477981

Jane Darin
5648 Camber Drive
San Diego, CA 92117
619-514-8145
e-mail: jdarin@san.rr.com
website: www.janedarin.com

Marleen Engeler
m'laine dolls
Noordeinde 67 1141 AH
Monnickendam
The Netherlands
31-299656814
e-mail: mlwent4.2@globalxs.nl

Judith & Lucia Friedericy
Friedericy Dolls
1260 Wesley Avenue
Pasadena, CA 91104
626-296-0065
e-mail: friedericy@aol.com

Originals by Goldie
8517 Edgeworth Drive
Capitol Heights, MD 20743
301-350-4119

Lillian Hopkins
2315 29th Street
Santa Monica, CA 90405
310-396-3266
e-mail: lilyart@compuserve.com

Marylynn Huston
101 Mountain View Drive
Pflugerville, TX 78660
512-252-1192

Joyce Patterson
FabricImages
P.O. Box 1599
Brazoria, TX 77422
409-798-9890
e-mail: clothdol@tgn.net

W. Harry Perzyk
2860 Chiplay St.
Sacramento, CA 95826

Daryl Poole
450 Pioneer Trail
Dripping Springs, TX 78620
512-858-7181
e-mail: eltummo@aol.com

The Enchantment Peddler
Kathryn Williams Klushman
Nellie Lamers
HC6 Box 0
Reeds Spring, MO 65737
417-272-3768
e-mail: theenchantmentpeddlers
@yahoo.com
website: www.inter-linc.net/The
EnchantmentPeddlers/

Peggy Ann Ridley
17 Ribon Road
Lisbon, ME 04250
207-353-8827

Anne Sanregret
22910 Estorial Drive, #6
Diamond Bar, CA 91765
909-860-8007

Sandy Simonds
334 Woodhurst Drive
Coppell, TX 75019
512-219-8759

Linda Lee Sutton Originals
P.O. Box 3725
Central Point, OR 97502
541-830-8384
e-mail: linda@lindaleesutton.com
website: lindaleesutton.com

Doll Manufacturers

Alexander Doll Company, Inc.
Herbert Brown
Chairman & CEO
615 West 131st STreet
New York, NY 10027
212-283-5900
fax: 212-283-6042

American Girl
8400 Fairway Place
P.O. Box 620190-0190
Middleton, WI 53562-0190
800-845-0005
website: www.americangirl.com

Collectible Concepts
Ivonne Heather, President
945 Hickory Run Land
Great Falls, VA 22066
703-821-0607
fax: 703-759-0408
e-mail: invonnehccc@aol.com

Effanbee Doll Company
19 Lexington Ave.
East Brunswick, NJ 08816
732-613-3852
fax: 732-613-8366

Susan Wakeen Doll Co., Inc.
P.O. Box 1321
Litchfield, CT 06759
860-567-0007
fax: 908-788-1955
e-mail: pkaverud@blast.net

Robert Tonner Doll Company
Robert Tonner, CEO/Designer
P.O. Box 1187
Kingston, NY 12402
914-339-9537
fax: 914-339-1259

Vogue Doll Company
P.O. Box 756
Oakdale, CA 95361-0756
209-848-0300
fax: 209-848-4423
website: www.voguedolls.com

Doll Reader

Cumberland Publishing, Ic.
6405 Flank Dr.
Harrisburg, PA 17112
Subscriptions: 800-829-3340
e-mail:
dollreader@palmcoastd.com

Doll Repairs

Doll Doc. Associates
1406 Sycamore Road
Montoursville, PA 17754
717-323-9604

Fresno Doll Hospital
1512 N. College
Fresno, CA 93728
209-266-1108

Kandyland Dolls
PO Box 146
Grande Ronde, OR 97347
503-879-5153

Life's Little Treasures
PO Box 585
Winston OR 97496
541-679-3472

Oleta's Doll Hospital
1413 Seville Way
Modesto, CA 95355
209-523-6669

Gene – Ashton Drake Galleries

9200 N. Maryland Ave.
Niles, IL 60714-9853
888-For-Gene

Ginny

Ginny Journal
Suzanne Smith, Editor
P.O. Box 338
Oakdale, CA 95361-0338
877-848-0300 (toll free)
website: www.voguedolls.com
$15.00 dues

Girl Scouts
Girl Scout Doll Collector's Patch
Pidd Miller
PO Box 631092
Houston, TX, 77263

Diane Miller, Collector
13151 Roberta Place
Garden Grove, CA 92643
Ann Sutton, Collector/Dealer
2555 Prine Road
Lakeland, FL 33810-5703
e-mail: Sydneys@aol.com

Hasbro — Jem Dolls
Linda E. Holton, Collector/Dealer
P.O. Box 6753
San Rafael, CA 94903

Hitty
Friends of Hitty Newsletter
Virginia Ann Heyerdahl, Editor
2704 Belleview Ave
Cheverly, MD 20785
Quarterly, $12.00 per year

Hitty Artists
Judy Brown
506 N. Brighton Ct.
Sterling, VA 20164
703-450-0206

Ruth Brown
1606 SW Heather Dr.
Grants Pass, OR 97526

DeAnn Cote
5555 – 22nd Avenue South
Seattle, WA 98108-2912
206-763-1871
e-mail: DRCDesigne@aol.com

Patti Hale
2301 Aazure Lane
Vista, CA 92083

JANCI
Nancy Elliott & Jill Sanders
2442 Hathaway Court
Muskegon, MI 49441
e-mail: janci@gte.net

Lotz Studio
Jean Lotz
P.O. Box 1308
Lacome, LA 70445
e-mail: lotz@gs.verio.net

Ideal
Ideal Collectors' Newsletter
Judith Izen, Editor
PO Box 623
Lexington, MA 02173
e-mail: Jizen@aol.com
Quarterly, $20.00 per year

Internet
Ebay auction site
website: www.ebay.com

About.com Doll Collecting
Denise Von Patten
website:
www.collectdolls.about.com
e-mail: denise@dollymaker.com

Internet Lists & Chat Rooms
AG Collector
For American Girl, Heidi Ott, and other 18" play dolls, no selling, just talk. e-mail: ag_collector-request@lists.best.com

Barbie chat
e-mail: Fashion@ga.unc.edu

Doll Chat List
Friendly collectors talk dolls, no flaming permitted, a great group. E-mail is forwarded to your address from host, no fees, to subscribe: DollChatRequest @nbi.com then type "subscribe" in body of message

Dolls n Stuff
e-mail: dollsnstuff
@home.ease.lsoft.com

Not Just Dollmakers
e-mail: carls@isrv.com
website: www.notjustdoll makers.com

Sasha
e-mail: sasha-1-Subscribe@ makelist.com

Shirley Temple
e-mail: shirleycollect-subscribe@makelist.com

Postal Rates
website: www.usps.gov

Preservation
Twin Pines
website: www.twinpines.com

Publications
Collectors United
711 S. 3rd Ave.
Chatsworth, GA 30705
706-695-8242
fax: 706-895-0770
e-mail: collun@Alltel.net

Contemporary Doll Collector
Scott Publications
30595 Eight Mile
Livonia, MI 48152-1798
800-458-8237

Dolls
170 Fifth Ave., 12th Fl.
New York, NY 1010
212-989-8700
fax: 212-645-8976
e-mail: snowy@lsol.net

Patsy & Friends Newsletter
P.O. Box 311
Deming, NM 88031
e-mail: sctrading@zianet.com

Klumpe Dolls
Sondra Gast, Collector/Dealer
PO Box 252
Spring Valley, CA 91976
fax: 619-444-4215
e-mail: klumpe@home.com

Lawton, Wendy
Lawton Collectors Guild
PO Box 969
Turlock, CA 95381

Toni Winder, Collector/Dealer
1484 N. Vagedes
Fresno CA 93728
e-mail: TTUK77B@prodigy.com

Liddle Kiddles
For a signed copy of her book, *Liddle Kiddles,* $22.95 post pd.
Write: *Paris Langford*
415 Dodge Ave
Jefferson, LA 70127
504-733-0676

Modern Doll Convention
Judith Whorton, Coordinator
17017 61st North
Wilsonville, AL 35186
205-669-6219

Museums
Arizona Doll & Toy Museum
(Stevens House in Heritage Square)
602 E. Adams St.
Phoenix, AZ 85004
602-253-9337
Tues. – Sun., adm. $2.50, closed Aug.

Enchanted World Doll Museum
"The castle across from the Corn Palace"
615 North Main
Mitchell, SD 57301
606-996-9896
fax: 606-996-0210

Land of Enchantment Doll Museum
5201 Constitution Ave.

Albuquerque, NM 87110-5813
505-821-8558
fax: 505-255-1259

Margaret Woodbury Strong Museum
1 Manhattan Square
Rochester, NY 14607
716-263-2700

Museum of American Architecture & Decorative Arts
7502 Fronden Rd
Houston, Texas 77074-3298
281-649-3811

Rosalie Whyel Museum of Doll Art
1116 108th Avenue N.E.
Bellevue, WA 98004
206-455-1116
fax: 206-455-4793
website: www.dollart.com

Nancy Ann Storybook
Elaine Pardee, Collector/Dealer
3613 Merano Way
Antelope, CA 95843
916-725-7227
fax: 916-725-7447
e-mail: epardee@jps.net

Oriental Dolls
Ninsyo Journal — Jade
Japanese American Dolls Enthusiasts
406 Koser Ave
Iowa City, IA 52246
e-mail:
Vickyd@jadejapandolls.com

Raggedy Ann
Rags Newsletter
Barbara Barth, Editor
PO Box 823
Atlanta, GA 30301
Quarterly $16.00

Robert Tonner Doll Club
Robert Tonner Doll Company
PO Box 1187
Kingston, NY 12402
fax: 914-339-1259
Credit card: 914-339-9537
Dues: $19.95

Roldan Dolls
Sondra Gast, Collector/Dealer
PO Box 252
Spring Valley, CA 91976
fax: 619-444-4215

Sandra Sue Dolls, Richwood Toys Inc.
Peggy Millhouse, Collector/Dealer
510 Green Hill Road
Conestoga, PA 17516
e-mail: peggyin717@aol.com

Sasha Dolls
Friends of Sasha
Quarterly Newsletter
Dorisanne Osborn, Editor
Box 187
Keuka Park, NY 14478

Shirley Temple
Australian Shirley Temple Collectors News
Quarterly Newsletter
Victoria Horne, Editor
39 How Ave.
North Dandenong
Victoria, 3175, Australia
$25.00 U.S.

Lollipop News
Shirley Temple Collectors by the Sea
PO Box 6203
Oxnard, CA 93031
Membership dues: $14.00 year

Shirley Temple Collectors News
Rita Dubas, Editor
881 Colonial Road
Brooklyn NY 11209
Quarterly, $20.00 year
website:
www.ritadubasdesign.com/shirley/
e-mail: bukowski@wazoo.com

Terri Lee
Daisy Chain Newsletter
Terry Bukowski, Editor
3010 Sunland Dr.
Alamogordo, NM 88310
$20.00 per year, quarterly

Ann Sutton, Collector/Dealer
2555 Prine Road
Lakeland, FL 33810-5703
e-mail: Sydneys@aol.com

Betty J. Woten, Collector
12 Big Bend Cut Off
Cloudcroft, NM 88317-9411

Videos
Leonard A. Swann, Jr.
SIROCCO Productions, Inc.
5660 E. Virgina Beach Blvd.,
Suite 105
Norfolk, VA 23502
757-461-8987
website: www.siroccovideo.com
e-mail: iswann@specialty
products.net

Vogue
Ginny Doll Club
PO Box 338
Oakdale, CA 95361-0338
800-554-1447

United Federation of Doll Clubs
10920 N. Ambassador Dr.,
Suite 130
Kansas City, MO 64153
816-891-7040
fax: 816-891-8360
website: http://www.ufdc.org/

Woods, Robin
Toni Winder, Collector/Dealer
1484 N. Vagedes
Fresno, CA 93728

Name Index